The Torah

The Torah

Theology and Social History of Old Testament Law

Frank Crüsemann

Translated by
Allan W. Mahnke

FORTRESS PRESS   MINNEAPOLIS

First English-language edition published 1996 by Fortress Press.

This book is a translation of *Die Tora: Theologie und Sozialgeschichte des alttestamentlichen Gesetzes*, by Frank Crüsemann. Published 1992 by Chr. Kaiser. German original copyright © 1992 by Chr. Kaiser Verlag.

Library of Congress Cataloging-in-Publication Data

Crüsemann, Frank.
    [Tora. English]
    The Torah : theology and social history of Old Testament law / Frank Crüsemann : translated by Allan W. Mahnke. — 1st English-language ed.
    p. cm.
    Includes bibliographical references and index.
    ISBN 0–8006–2856–X
    1. Law (Theology)—Biblical teaching.   2. Bible.   O.T. Pentateuch—Criticism, interpretation, etc.   3. Sociology, Biblical.   I. Title.
BS1225.6.L3C7813   1996
222'.106—dc20
    96–42165
    CIP

AF 1–2856

00	99	98	97	96	1	2	3	4	5	6	7	8	9	10

Typeset by Waverley Typesetters, Galashiels
Printed and bound in Great Britain by Biddles Ltd, Guildford

Contents

Abbreviations

AASF	Annales Academicae Scientiarum Fennicae
ABR	Australian Biblical Review
AfO	Archiv für Orientforschung
AGJu	Arbeiten zur Geschichte des antiken Judentums und des Urchristentums (Leiden, Cologne)
AION	Annali del' istituto Orientali di Napoli
AJBA	Australian Journal of Biblical Archaeology
AJBI	Annual of the Japanese Biblical Institute
AJSL	American Journal of Semitic Languages and Literature
AK	Archiv für Kulturgeschichte
ALGHL	Arbeiten zur Literatur und Geschichte des hellenistischen Judentums
AM	Annual of the Akademie der Wissenschaften und der Literatur in Mainz
An Bib	Analecta Biblica
AncB	Anchor Bible
ANET	Ancient Near Eastern Texts
ANRW	Aufstieg und Niedergang der römischen Welt (Berlin 1972)
Ant	Josephus, Antiquities of the Jews
AOAT	Altorientalische Textes zum AT
AOB	Altorientalische Bilder zum AT
APD	Archives de philosophie du droit
ArOr	Archiv orientálni
ARW	Archiv für Religionswissenschaft
ASTI	Annual of the Swedish Theological Institute, Jerusalem
ATA	Alttestamentliche Abhandlungen
ATD	Das Alte Testament Deutsch (Göttingen)
AThANT	Abhandlungen zur Theologie des Alten und Neuen Testaments, Zürich
AThD	Acta Theologica Danica
AzTh	Arbeiten zur Theologie
b	Babylonian Talmud
BA	Biblical Archaeologist
bAr	Babylonian Talmud, tractate 'Arakin

BBB	Bonner Biblische Beiträge
bBm	Babylonian Talmud, tractate Baba Mes'ia
bBQ	Babylonian Talmud, tractate Baba Qamma
BC	Biblischer Kommentar 1872 (Keil)
BeO	Biblica et Orientalia
BEThL	Bibliotheca Ephemeridum Theologicarum Lovaniensium
BEvTh	Beiträge zur evangelische Theologie
BGBE	Beiträge zur Geschichte der Biblische Exegese
BHF	Bonner historische Forschüngen
BHS	Biblia Hebraica Stuttgartensia
BHTh	Beiträge zur historische Theologie
Bib.	Biblica
BiBe	Biblische Beiträge
BiLi	Bibel und Liturgie
BK	Bibel und Kirche
BN	Biblische Notizen
BR	Biblical Research
BRL	Biblisches Reallexikon (Tübingen)
BS	Biblischen Studien
bSan	Babylonian Talmud, tractate Sanhedrin
BSHT	Breslauer Studien zur historischen Theologie
Bst	Biblische Studien (Neukirchen)
bSuk	Babylonian Talmud, tractate Sukka
BTB	Biblical Theology Bulletin
BWANT	Beiträge zur Wissenschaft vom Alten und Neuen Testament
bYom	Babylonian Talmud, tractate Yoma
BZ	Biblische Zeitschrift
BZ NF	Biblische Zeitschrift (New Series)
BZAW	Beihefte zur Zeitschrift für die Alttestamentliche Wissenschaft
CAT	Commentaire de l'Ancien Testament
CB	Cultura Biblica
CB OT	Coniectanea Biblica Old Testament
CBC	Cambridge Bible Commentary
CBQ	Catholic Biblical Quarterly
CHJ	Cambridge History of Judaism
CP	Classical Philology
CRAI	Comptes rendus de l'Académie des inscriptions et de belles lettres
CRB	Cahiers de la Revue biblique
CSSH	Comparative Studies in History and Society
CThM	Concordia Theological Monthly
DBAT	Dielhemier Blätter zum Alten Testament
DBS	Dictionnaire de la Bible Supplement
EdF	Erträge der Forschung
EeT (O)	Église et theologie. Ottawa
EHS.T	Europäische Hochscholschriften. Reihe 23, Theologie
EJ	Encyclopedia Judaica

EK	Evangelische kommentare
EKK	Evangelish-katholik Kommentar
EKL	Evangelischen Kirchenlexikon
ErJb	Eranos Jahrbuch
EstB	Estudios Biblicos
ET	Expository Times
EThL	Ephemerides Theologicae Lovanienses
EThST	Erfurter theologische Studien
EvTh	Evangelische Theologie
EWNT	Exegetisches Wörterbuch zum Neuen Testament (Stuttgart)
FolOr	Folia Orientalia
FRLANT	Forschungern zur Religion und Literatur des Alten und Neuen Testaments
FS	Festschrift
GAT	Grundrisse zum Alten
GK	Gesenius' Hebrew Grammar, ed. E. Kautzsch
GNT	Grundrisse zum Neuen Testament
GTA	Göttinger theologische Arbeiten
HAT	Handbuch zum Alten Testament, Tübingen
HG	Hammurabi's Gesetz
HK	Handkommentar zum Alten Testament (Göttingen)
HO	Handbuch der Orientalistik
HSAT	Die Heilige Schrift des AT (Kautzsch)
HSM	Harvard Semitic Monographs
HThR	Harvard Theological Review
HUCA	Hebrew Union College Annual
HZ	Historische Zeitschrift
ICC	International Critical Commentary
IDB	Interpreter's Dictionary of the Bible
IEJ	Israel Exploration Journal
j	Jerusalem Talmud
JAAR	Journal of the American Academy of Religion
JAOS	Journal of the American Oriental Society
JARG	Jahrbuch für Anthropologie und Religionsgeschiche
JBL	Journal of Biblical Literature
jBm	Jerusalem Talmud, tractate Baba Mesi'ah
jBer	Jerusalem Talmud, tractate Berakot
jShevu	Jerusalem Talmud, tractate Shevu'ot
jYom	Jerusalem Talmud, tractate Yoma
JBTh	Jahrbuch für biblische Theologie
JCS	Journal of Cuneiform Studies
JEOL	Jahrbericht Ex Oriente Lux
JESHO	Journal of the Economic and Social History of the Orient
JJS	Journal of Jewish Studies
JK	Junge Kirche
JNES	Journal of Near Eastern Studies
JNWSL	Journal of Northwest Semitic Linguistics
JQR	Jewish Quarterly Review

JRAS	Journal of the Royal Asiatic Society of Great Britan and Ireland
JRE	Journal of Religious Ethics
JSJ	Journal for the Study of Judaism
JSOT	Journal of the Society for Old Testament Studies
JSOTS	Journal of the Society for Old Testament Studies (Supplement)
JSS	Journal of Semitic Studies
JThS NS	Journal of Theological Studies (New Style)
KAI	Kanaanaische und aramaische Inschriften (H. Donner and W. Rollig, eds)
KAT	Kommentar zum Alten Testament (Leipzig, Gutersloh)
KBL	L. Koehler and W. Baumgarten, Lexicon in veteris testamenti libros
KEH	Kurzgefasstes exegetisch es Handbuch zum Alten Testament (Leipzig)
KHC	Kurzer Hand-Commentar zum Alten Testament (Freiburg i Br, Leipzig, Tübingen)
KT	Kleine Texte für theologische und philosophische Vorlesungen
KTU	Keilalphabetische Textes aus Ugarit
LM	Lutherische Monatshefle
LXX	Septuagint
m	Mishnah
MAR	Mythology of All Races
MBPF	Münchener Belträge zur Papyrus-Forschung und antiken Rechtsgeschichte
MHUC	Monographs of the Hebrew Union College
MIOF	Mitteilungen des Instituts für Orientforschung
mShevi	Mishna Tractate Sevi'it
mSan	Mishna Tractate Sanhedrin
mBQ	Mishna Tractate Baba Qamma
MT	Masoretic Text
MThSt	Münchener Theologische Studien
MUS	Mélanges de l'Université St Joseph
NBL	Neues Bibel-Lexikon
NCB	New Clarendon Bible
NCeB	New Century Bible
NEB	New English Bible
NF	New series
NRSV	New Revised Standard Version
NT	Novum Testamentum
NTA	Neutestamentliche Abhandlungen / New Testament Abstracts
OBO	Orbis Biblicus et Orientalis
OLA	Orientalia Lovaniensia analecta
OLoP	Orientalia Lovaniensia periodica
OTL	Old Testament Library
OTS	Oudtestamentische Studien
PEQ	Palestine Exploration Quarterly

PhB	Spinoza
PRE	Real-Encyclopadie für protestante Theologie und Kirche
QD	Quaestiones disputatae
RA	Revue d'Assyriologie et d'Archéologie Orientale
RB	Revue Biblique
RHDF	Revue Historique de droit français et étranger
RHPhR	Revue d'Historie et de Philosophie Religieuses
RHR	Revue de l'Histoire des Religions
RIDA	Revue Internationale des Droits de l'Antiquité
RivBib	Rivista Biblica
RSFen	Rivista di studi fenizi
RSLR	Rivista di Storiae Letteratura Religiosa (Turin)
RThPh	Revue de Théologie et de Philosophie
RV	Religionsgeschichte, Versuche und Vorarbeiten
RVV	Religionsgeschichtiches Versuche und Vorarbeiten
S	supplement
SBAB	Sitzungsberichte der Deutschen Akademie der Wissenschaften zu Berlin
SBB	Stuttgarter biblische Beiträge
SBL	Society of Biblical Literature
SBLDS	Society of Biblical Literature Dissertation Series
SBLMS	Society of Biblical Literature Monograph Series
SBS	Stuttgarter Bibelstudien
SBT	Studies in Biblical Theology
SbWGF	Sitzungsberichte der Wissenschaftlichen Gesellschaft . . . Frankfurt a.m.
SDGSTh	Studien zur Drgmengeschichte und Systematischen Theologie
SEC	Studies in Eastern Chant
SGKAO	Schriften zur Geschichte und Kultur des Allen Orients
SJLA	Studies in Judaism in Late Antiquity
SKG.G	Schriften der Konigsberger Gelehrten Gesellschaft
SNVAO	Skritter utgitt Det Norske Videnskaps-Akademie (Oslo)
SR	Sciences religieuses
SSAOI	Sacra scriptura antiquitatibus orientalibus illustrata
SSN	Studia Semitica Neerlandica
St Th	Studia Theologica
StANT	Studien zum Alten und Neuen Testament (Munich)
STAT	Suomalaisen Tiedeakatemian Toimitusia
StEv	Studia Evangelica
SThU	Schweizerische theologische Umschau
StOr	Studia Orientalia
StUNT	Studien zum Umwelt des Neuen Testament
t	Tosefta
tAZ	Tosefta, tractate 'Aboda Zara
tBQ	Tosefta, tractate Baba Qamma
tKet	Tosefta, tractate Ketubot
tYom	Tosefta, tractate 'Yoma

TA	Texte und Arbeiten
TAPhS	Transactions of the American Philosophical Society
tAZ	Tosefta, tractate 'Aboda Zara
TBC	Torch Bible Commentaries
tBQ	Tosefta, tractate Baba Qamma
Th Ph	Theologie und Philosophie
Th St	Theologische Studien
ThA	Theologische Arbeiten
THAT	Theologisches Handbuch zum Alten Testament
ThB	Theologische Blatter
THE	Theologische Existenz heute
ThGl	Theologie und Glaube
ThLZ	Theologische Literaturzeitung
ThQ	Theologische Quartal schrift
ThR	Theologische Rundschau
ThWAT	Theologisches Handwörterbuch zum Alten Testament
ThZ	Theologische Zeitschrift
TRE	Theologische Revue
TThZ	Trierer Theologische Zeitschrift
TUAT	Texte und Untersuchungen zur Geschichte der altchristen Literatur
UF	Ugarit Forschungen
UTB	Ugaritic Textbook (C. H. Gordon)
UUA	Uppsala Universitetsarsskrift
VT	Vetus Testamentum
VT.S	Supplements to Vetus Testamentum
VuF	Verkündigung und Forschung
WdF	Wege der Forschung
WMANT	Wissenschaftliche Monographien zum Alten und Neuen Testament
WO	Die Welt des Orients
WThJ	Westminster Theological Journal
WuD	Wort und Dienst
WUNT	Wissenschaftliche Untersuchungen zum Neuen Testament
ZA	Zeitschrift für Assyrologie
ZAW	Zeitschrift für die alttestamentliche Wissenschaft
ZBK	Zurcher Biblekommentare
ZDPV	Zeitschrift des Deutschen Palastina-Vereins
ZEE	Zeitschrift für evangelische Ethik
ZKG	Zeitschrfit für Kirchengeschichte
ZLThL	Zeitschrift für die (gesammte) lutherische Theologie und Kirche
ZNW	Zeitschrift für die neutestamentliche Wissenschaft
ZSRG	Zeitschrift der Savigny-Stiftung für Rechtsgeschichte
ZThK	Zeitschrift für Theologie und Kirche

Preface

I began writing this book during winter 1989–1990, completing it during the ensuing semester breaks. Events in world history, particularly German history, during this period occasionally made it difficult to stay at my desk, but problems that became evident during this time confirmed my feelings that a study of the foundations of biblical ethics was needed. I added a bit to the manuscript and completed the final version during the Christmas holiday 1991–1992. In earlier portions of the book, therefore, some recent literature has received insufficient attention.

When I began to study Old Testament legal texts more than a decade ago, it appeared I might be able to do justice to the topic by selecting a narrowly defined period of history. When, however, we combine social-historical perspectives with basic theological questions and place them against the background of a need to develop a new relationship with Judaism, and then add to this our current, pressing ethical concerns; we are forced to expand our horizons. Some of the bases upon which we constructed our study, while appearing adequate at the outset, had to be replaced. Furthermore, the trend in modern research toward greater specialization (this has been especially true in Old Testament legal studies), has proved to be a mixed blessing. It is sometimes even counterproductive.

There are important tasks that require attention from scholars in this field. At times we are compelled to make textbooks or popular summaries related to the legal history of biblical Israel. This means, of course, that important questions are not given priority.

It seems to be absolutely necessary that we view our subject as a whole, and that we try to write in such a way that those outside our discipline, but interested theologically, are not frightened off. This means that I have not been able to pursue all the implications in my discussions of details. I have tried to strike a balance by referring to the broader scholarly discussion.

Translator's Preface

Passages citing the Bible in English are largely based on the New Revised Standard Version, but adaptations conforming more closely to the German have been made. "YHWH" has been restored in passages where NRSV has LORD. Furthermore, sometimes strict adherence to this translation would have clouded or even completely obscured Crüsemann's point. Where this occurs the translation is a compromise between NRSV and the German. See, for example, the references to Deut 7:13; 28:4, 18, 51 on pp. 137f. [German p. 164] that mention Astarte and Sagar. NRSV uses circumlocutions in place of these deities.

Allan W. Mahnke

1

꽃

The Torah in the Pentateuch:
The Challenge and the
Framing of the Question

Torah: this Hebrew word is a central biblical concept, and it is an issue
Christian theology has only recently begun to address. It is my hope to
make a contribution to this work, so that the term becomes more generally possible and theologically necessary. I will offer an interpretation of
the most important Old Testament legal documents in their social-
historical context. This implies an attempt to redraw or reconstruct the
main lines of an Old Testament legal history from its very complicated
beginnings during the pre-state period up through the completion of the
Pentateuch. The study is concerned with Israel's path to the Torah. The
challenges in these documents – the most important questions that they
raise – need to be mentioned against the background of current research.[1]
The starting point, however, can and must be Torah itself.

The Torah and Christian Theology

Christians traditionally discuss Torah under the broader heading of
"law." Thus, it often contrasted with "gospel." Historically as well as
theologically, however, such opposition can only give us a distorted
picture of the biblical concept of Torah.

The word *Torah*[2] in the everyday speech of Old Testament times meant
instructions given by a mother (Prov 1:8, 6:20; cf 31:26) and a father (4:1f.)
to their children to instruct them in matters of living and to warn them
about mortally dangerous situations. In that early function as well as all
later uses, the word implies information, advice, instruction, the establishment of norms, demand as well as encouragement, the command but
also the benefits included. The concept of Torah became a technical term
for priestly instruction to the laity (Jer 18:18; Ez 7:26), but it also
designates speech of the wisdom teachers (Prov 7:2; 13:14) or the
prophets (Isa 8:16, 20; 30:9) to pupils. Finally, in Deuteronomy Torah
became the most important concept for the comprehensive written

---

1 There are overviews in Boecker, *Recht und Gesetz*; Patrick, *Law*; Crüsemann, *Recht
   und Theologie*. For the controverted issues, see Knierim, *Problem*.
2 See especially the article in Liedke/Petersen, "*Torah*" as well as the overview in
   Cazelles, *Torah et Loi*.

will of God (e.g. Deut 4:44f.; 30:10; 31:9).[3] Already here "Torah" contained narrative (especially Deut 1:5) and laws (see especially also Ps 78:1, 5, 10). This deuteronomic concept was a later designation for the Ezra law (e.g. Neh 8:1), the entire Pentateuch,[4] but also the prophetically proclaimed eschatological word of God (Isa 2:3 and its parallel Mi 4:2, and also Isa 42:4).

The concept of Torah includes both sides of the Word of God. What systematic theology divides into law and gospel, command and promise (and then often contrasts them) are all contained in Torah. The term identifies the unity of law and gospel and thus the unity of divine word and will. One of the most basic biblical categories is lost when the two are placed in conflict or potential tension, and made into a badge of theological identification or ecclesiastical confession.

We see this again in the context of the struggles of the German church.[5] The old, exclusively negative view of Old Testament law, which held sway for so long, was fundamentally challenged. Probably the most articulate representative of this earlier view was Julius Wellhausen.[6] He labeled the law as the calcified Jewish form of once lively Israelite faith. This attitude toward the law gave a historic locus to all negative protestant ideas about the law and Judaism (especially since the Enlightenment). Until recently, in spite of thorough criticism,[7] this view was widely accepted. Of the studies treating the inseparable connection between law and covenant (*bᵉrit*), Martin Noth's "Die Gesetze im Pentateuch" is especially important. He showed that the Old Testament legal corpus should not be understood as civil law, rather it must be interpreted in the context of God's covenant (for him it came from the early period of the nation). Noth, as he states in his introduction, said that this is inseparably connected with the contemporary significance of this text. "It is no accident that the 'the law' has become an especially important theological question again today. In fact, it is even more important . . . because contemporary (1940) discussions have raised the same topics again. It is important that we consider the same questions again with a fresh eye."[8] If biblical law is an integral part of the covenant, Noth's statement must still be valid, "theological ethics must make Old and New Testament law the basis of its task, if it would be more than a branch of philosophical ethics (which it indeed quite frequently has become)."[9]

Noth's exegetical assertions correspond to what the systematician Karl Barth said about "law and gospel," when he called law the necessary

---

3 See in addition to Preuss, *Deuteronomium* 195, especially Lindars, *Torah*; Braulik, *Ausdrücke*; also below pp. 204, 209f.

4 For the problems of the designation of Ezra law and Pentateuch, see below pp. 330ff.

5 For this Nicolaisen, *Auseinandersetzungen*; Kraus, *Geschichte der historisch-kritischen Erforschung* 452f.; Kraus, *Das alte Testament*; Kraus, *Tora und Volks nomos*; Crüsemann, *Tendenzen*.

6 Especially in *Prolegomena* 420ff.; for Wellhausen, see Perlitt, *Vatke*; the discussion in *Semeia* 25, 1982; Smend, *Deutsche Altestamentler* 99ff.

7 For analysis and criticism of Wellhausen's views, see e.g., Liebeschütz, *Judentum*; Hoheisel, *Judentum*.

8 Noth, *Gesetze* 10.

9 Noth, *Gesetze* 10.

form of the gospel.[10] The exegetical[11] as well as systematic[12] work done since that time has supported and disseminated these ideas. One view of the law, originally from Judaism but doubtless in agreement with the biblical texts, has taken root in protestantism.[13] It is based on "Torah as grace."[14] The need to reintegrate Torah into Christian theology[15] is an inescapable theological consequence.

Of course, most of these discussions take place on an extremely abstract level without connection to actual content of Torah. The debate in which F.-W. Marquardt raised the need for such a "re-integration" ends with the sentence: "We protestants are not so far yet that we are able to undertake an existential study of the 613 *mizwot*."[16] It is my hope that this study will help ask whether this is the correct formulation of the problem. We will only reach that goal if from the very beginning we remember the distance separating us from Torah. Christians have been eclectic and thoroughly contradictory in dealing with it. With respect to our own experience, we must confront two important areas determinative for the relationship of Torah and the Christian faith. They are not the same neither can one be reduced to the other. They are: The law of Israel and the will of the one God.

Torah is concerned with transmitting the one will of the one God, creator of all humanity, to a single people – his Israel. Torah begins with creation and early history. We find instructions for all people (especially Gen 9:1–7) throughout. Nevertheless, from the patriarchs onward, Torah is concerned with the one people with whom alone the covenant was made; Torah is at home only within this covenant. It was transmitted to Moses for Israel at Sinai. Laws make repeated reference to this history, especially the exodus.

Even if Torah is given only to and for Israel,[17] there is a place *within* it for God's instructions to all people. The covenant and commands of Gen 9 are directed to all people – post Noah. Judaism has made from this the canon of the seven commands of the children of

10 Barth, *Evangelium und Gesetz*.

11 See, e.g. von Rad, *Theologie I*, 203ff.; Zimmerli, *Gesetz*; Gese, *Gesetz*; Martin-Achard, *La Loi*; Siegwalt, *La Loi*; Brunner (ed.), *Gesetz und Gnade*; Gross, *Torah und Gnade*; Braulik, *Gesetz als Evangelium*; Rendtorff, *Bedeutung*; Köckert, *Das nahe Wort*; compare also Perlitt, "Evangelium"; Kraus, *Telos der Tora*.

12 We should mention as exemplary Kraus, *Systematische Theologie* 159ff.; Welker, *Erwartungssicherheit*; Welker, *Gesetz und Geist*. The term is indeed frequently separated from its Old Testament context (for an overview, see H.-M. Barth, article "Gesetz," especially 139f.). For Roman Catholic theology, see Pesch, *Begriff*; but also Soete, *Ethos*.

13 This played an important role in the recent synodical statements on relationships with Judaism, e.g. the synodical resolutions (Thesis V, see Rendtorff/Henrix, *Dokumente* 594f.) the theses of the Reformed union (Leitsatz V, see *Wir und die Juden* 32ff.).

14 See Werblowsky, *Tora als Gnade*; e.g. also Ehrlich, *Tora*. There is an overview of the Torah in Judaism in Maier, *Torah*.

15 Marquardt, *Reintegration*.

16 Marquardt, *Reintegration* 676.

17 Nevertheless, we must note the universal dimension of the Torah. For this, see e.g. Greidanus, *Universal Dimension*; Levenson, *Theologies of Commandment* 25ff.

Noah.[18] The early church overtly associated itself with these in the rules of the Apostolic Council (Acts 15:20, 29),[19] and connections with natural or human rights in general are presumed.[20] It is time these traditions were also taken seriously in Christian theology and reworked,[21] especially since the Christian connection to Torah risks divesting and disinheriting Israel.

New Testament association with Torah is in no way limited by these human ground rules. Rather it mirrors the contradiction that, on the one hand, every access to the God of Israel represents a connection to Torah that is inseparable from him, and on the other, Torah was formulated for Israel and only valid for her. It was not only Matthew who still believed Torah is the abiding will of God, from which not a "jot" might be lost (5:17ff.), which Jesus' disciples were to keep in its entirety (e.g. 23:2). Torah is also "holy and just and good" (Rom 7:12) for Paul,[22] and it does not contradict the gospel he proclaimed.[23] In the final analysis he supports Torah by what he teaches (Rom 3:31) and enables its fulfillment in love (Rom 13:10). On the other hand, belief in Israel's God does not turn gentiles into Jews, and circumcision, the path to incorporation into Judaism, would render the gospel ineffectual (Galatians).

In reality every Christian connection with Torah always was, and still is, eclectic. At times this is important, at times not. Some parts have always been adopted and some not, which is sometimes quite arbitrary. The same M. Noth who identified Torah as part of the covenant, regarded the postexilic wandering as a fall from the true faith,[24] thus contributing to the general anti-semitism of that period (1940!). Even had that been overcome,[25] it was not the real problem. There are classic attempts to distinguish *within* Torah, for example, between ceremonial and moral law.[26] Some have believed that natural law, the true law of God, is a gauge for the parts of Torah that apply and those that do not.[27] This is how Christians adopted and elevated the Decalog, the "first chapter" of Torah, above everything else. From the outset, this process was problematic for Judaism,[28] and it contributed to massive alienation from

---

18 Especially bSan 56 (administration of justice, commands against blasphemy, idol worship, fornication, the shedding of blood, the consumption of a part of the body of a living creature), see also tAZ 8.4 and elsewhere; for this Novak, *Image*; Millard, *Gebote* 8ff.; especially K. Müller, *Torah* 14ff., 80ff.

19 For this, Simon, *Apostolic Decree*; Flusser/Safrai, *Aposteldekret*; Pesch, *Apostelgeschichte II* 68ff. (Lit.).

20 Thus already Cohen, *Religion* 143.

21 Thus with emphasis K. Müller, *Torah*.

22 The following items from the abundant literature on this topic seem to me to be especially important: E. Stegmann, *Der eine Gott*; Stegmann, *Umgekehrte Tora*; Stegmann, *Heiligkeit der Tora*. For the New Testament in general, see the overview in Kertelge (ed.), *Gesetz*.

23 Thus especially v. d. Osten-Sacken, *Befreiung*.

24 *Gesetze* 140, compare 122: the law as "an absolute quantity in the late period."

25 See Kutsch, *Menschliche Weisung*; Köckert, *Das Nahe Wort* 503ff.

26 See the abundant material in Diestel, *Geschichte* 41ff.

27 For the corresponding view of Luther, see H. Bornkamm, *Luther* 104ff. For the current problem, see also Barr, *Biblical Law*.

28 For this, see Vermes, *Decalogue*; Stemberger, *Dekalog*; Weinfeld, *Decalogue*; as well as pp. 351f. below.

the ethical tradition of the Bible within the history of the Christian church and its theology.[29]

This arbitrary treatment of Torah is also amazing because it is controlled by self-interest. Love of neighbor (Lev 19:18) became a central issue in the New Testament (Mt 19:19 par.), but the love of strangers (Lev 19:34) was practically ignored. Prohibitions against theft and covetousness were applied to human affairs, but not within the context of business law (e.g. prohibitions against interest on loans). Christians have not used criminal law to reconcile opposing parties, nor have they employed biblical procedural rules to limit demands for the death penalty.

Above all, recent suppression of an established, fixed, extra-biblical natural law, against which even biblical truths can also be measured makes necessary a new and changed relation to Torah as foundation of every system of biblical ethics (or law). A rational, reasonable establishment of norms or a self-styled distillation of norms from the pure gospel are no substitute. If, on one hand, Torah is the foundation of the canon (thus New Testament ethics); and on the other, it is formulated particularly for Israel, not universally, we have isolated the historical-exegetical problem: How should we interpret these texts theologically?

Confusing Relevance and Historical Distance

The confusing relationship of Christianity to Torah is increasingly being replaced by another equally contradictory. Furthermore, it is also affected by it. The following two-fold experience applies to all Bible texts, but it applies especially to Torah:

1. Important contents of Torah are given in secular societal discourse, outside ecclesiastical and theological tradition, illustrating the confusing relevance of the Torah for contemporary problems. This reminds us of current national debates over whether to charge interest and/or remit the debts of third world countries buried by financial obligations; or whether to protect rights of asylum or to grant to refugees and foreigners rights all citizens have – all this in the face of increasing distinction between social classes, plus mounting hostility toward foreigners. Or, ought we to have a day off work shared by all alike, an issue over which we now have actual conflict? In view of decreasing opportunities for work and a reduction in the age of compulsory retirement, suggestions are even being made for a sabbatical year. We have the unresolved problem in both church and state that statutory law appears to become the ancient, divinely ordained authority figure. Last but not least, there is the obvious need to protect animals, plants and all of nature. First, we use law to grant them a place within our system of justice.

There are ready bases within Torah for an ethical system that is autonomous, not simply a short-winded, instinctive system but one founded in biblical ethics, and such deep-seated problems, which are indeed the products of the history of failure of the European church and its theology, simultaneously explode the old, apparently immovable

29 Crüsemann, *Tora*; Crüsemann, *Freiheit*.

fronts – like the contrast of ceremonial and moral law (in which political aspects of Torah are always first to go). We need only remember the need to protect life itself – as it is presented in the prohibition against the shedding of blood, a part of rules of the covenant with Noah, thus part of the rules of being human (Gen 9:4).

On the other hand, we should not overlook the fact that Torah is a document from a period quite distant from our own time. It came from an agrarian and pre-industrial society that our modern technical and industrial processes are rapidly making even more remote. In general, we are more conscious of this distance in the real situations that we have just discussed or those that have always given opportunity for critique – whether that might be cultic laws, which even Israel could not observe since the end of the Temple cult; or Israel's relationship to those who lived in the land before they did, where the distance appears and is handled within the Bible itself; or not least, in the area accepted into Christianity quite intact – family and sexual laws, together with the underlying patriarchal family structure and its rigid prohibitions against deviant sexual relationship.

Every interpretation must face this double experience. A Christian *halakha* cannot behave like fundamentalism.

A Christian *halakha* nevertheless appears to us as the one will of the one God of the Bible and literally necessary for life, and it is separated from Torah by an especially great gulf. This is why our attempt to complete Israel's path to Torah simultaneously raises the question of our path to her.

The One Torah and the Series of Law Books

Thus far, we have referred to Torah as a single thing, but all attempts to interpret it historically have thus far dissolved this unity and treated Torah as a series of law books and sources. The question of what it means to interpret Torah historically runs into a fundamental problem in modern exegesis and especially Pentateuch research: the relationship of sources to the final text, of a synchronous and diachronic view. Today there seems to be an alternative, and to follow it might mean to abandon the actual task of interpretation. Conversely, methodological and hermeneutical problems appear nowhere so massive as in exegesis of Torah. In any case, the starting point can only be that which is also the goal of every investigation – the available biblical evidence.

Here we need only remember the basic outline of biblical material. According to the Pentateuch, Torah was transmitted to Israel by God through Moses. There was, after the arrival of the people at the mountain of God, a kind of prelude in which the legal organization was founded (Ex 18). Then, in connection with a theophany (Ex 19), we have the delivery of the Decalog in direct, divine speech (Ex 20). In view of the people's reaction, they were unable to bear God's direct speech (Ex 20:18–21), the first block of laws were given to Moses (Ex 24:7), called the Book of the Covenant (Ex 20:22–23:33). After the solemn covenant ceremony (Ex 24), explicit instructions were given to Moses for the construction of a tent shrine (Ex 25–31). Before they could be carried out

(Ex 35–40), we have the narrative of the golden calf as an interlude. Next we have God's threat to destroy the people, ultimately prevented by Moses, the destruction and renewal of the stone tablets of the law and the giving of a new block of divine laws (Ex 32–34). From Lev 1 through the departure of the people from Sinai in Num 10, God issued a great number of additional instructions through Moses. After the long journey through the desert, forty years later, Moses gave the people a second law in the long address of Deuteronomy before crossing the Jordan river. He continued what he had received from God on Horeb (Deut 5:31).

As we know, historical-critical research began with the actual plan in mind of dismantling the Pentateuch and extracting older documents from it.[30] Sinai law was quickly included in this research. The unified gift of Torah, which remained valid during all pre-critical interpretation, was reduced to a series of self-contained, independent law books: the Book of the Covenant (Ex 20:22–23:33), the Deuteronomic Law (Deut 12–26), the mass of priestly/cultic regulations, from which came the so-called Holiness Code (Lev 17 or 18–26), shorter texts like the Decalog and the collection of cultic/religious commandments (Ex 34:11ff.) J. W. von Goethe regarded as the first contents of the Sinai tablets.[31]

An observation formulated by de Wette in 1805 has proven critical for dating of Old Testament materials.[32] According to de Wette, the book found in the Jerusalem Temple in 622 BCE by Josiah (2 Kg 22f.), which was transformed by him into a series of reform measures, was only Deuteronomy or its literary core, and it could not have been written much earlier. Thus, a central part of the Torah was shown not to have come from the period of Moses or Horeb, but was a product of the late royal period. The debate connected with this regarding the classification of the other legal texts was brought to a qualified conclusion by Wellhausen.[33] It was critical that many priestly laws were dated later than Deuteronomy, that they did not correspond to reality in the monarchic period because they were formulated during the exile or postexilic period. Furthermore, he regarded the older texts as a product of the royal period in the sequence formulated in Ex 34:10ff., Book of the Covenant, Decalog. Though there have been endless attempts to correct and improve it during the twentieth century, this nineteenth-century literary achievement has remained fundamentally unshaken, as we will see when we discuss the date and historical arrangement.

There has been a complete revision of literary-critical work on the Pentateuch.[34] It is amazing how quickly the persuasive power of classical source theory has disappeared, considering the fact that it has been thought nearly uncontestable for a century. There are new models

---

30 For the history of this research, besides the introduction in Kraus, *Geschichte*; Schmid, *Mose*; and especially de Pury/Römer, *Pentateuque*.
31 Goethe, *Biblische Fragen*, here: *Was stund auf den Tafeln des Bundes?*
32 *Dissertatio Critica*; for this especially Smend, de Wette; de Wette, *Deutsche Alttestamentler* 38ff.
33 Wellhausen, *Composition*; and *Prolegomena*.
34 For an overview, see de Pury/Römer, *Pentateuque*; Whybray, *Making*; de Pury (ed.), *Pentateuque*.

of interpretive theory, including many that reckon on additions and gradual growth around (a) central core(s).[35] Nevertheless, for the legal texts such an interpretation is still improbable or even impossible.[36] If we examine just the three great legal codices – the Book of the Covenant, the Deuteronomic Law and the Holiness Code, we see that they could not have been intended as simple expansions of their respective older forms; they could only be replacements. This is shown by their mainly parallel construction, with very different altar regulations at the beginning (Ex 20:24f.; Deut 12f.; Lev 17:3ff.) and the statements of blessing or cursing at the end (Ex 23:20ff.; Deut 27f.; Lev 26). It is also illustrated by many areas with very different regulations. Important points of the slave laws in the Book of the Covenant (Ex 21:2–11) are repeated in Deuteronomy, especially as they apply to female slaves (Deut 15:12–18). In the Holiness Code slaves are freed after forty-nine or fifty years, not in the seventh year (Lev 25:39f.). This is of great consequence for a slave. All three of the codes have cultic calendars (Ex 23:15ff.; Deut 16; Lev 23), regulations for sacrificing Ex 22:30, 23:18f.; Deut 15:19ff.; Lev 22), the prohibition against charging interest (22:25; Deut 23:20f., Lev 25:36f.), etc. There is no path leading us back behind the dissolution of the one law of Sinai into a series of temporally consecutive law books with significant contradictions.

It is perhaps best that we set out upon what is a half of a path. The reconstruction of pre-history cannot replace an understanding of what happened. Thus far, the questions of "how," "why" and "by what means" different law books were combined into one Torah, one Pentateuch and one canon have only been addressed with inadequate tools. The prohibition against viewing all things from their historical context is apparently so great here that it prevents our carrying out the actual historical task. This is not a matter of one question among many, but of *the* literary processes, those to which the Pentateuch owes its dignity as Torah, the process of canonic development.

The situation has grown more serious since the nineteenth century, when older biblical law books thought on principle to have formed a unity, now – because of ever improved techniques – display many facets themselves or at least they give us that impression.[37] Some of the findings appear themselves to break apart into a variety of pieces – into small and even tiny fragments. Along with basic skepticism about the appropriateness of methods of this kind, there is a certain research-historical *peripeteia* that was first identified by Halbe in his work on the Book of the Covenant, a work he demonstrated to have been a unified and planned composition.[38] This assessment of what is a demonstrable compositional structure must be supplemented with the legal-historically insoluble question about the intention of the law-giving

---

35 See especially the works of von Blum, *Komposition and Pentateuch*.
36 We ought to remind ourselves here that the legal documents were either not included at all or could only be included in an extremely hypothetical way in classical source theory. See Soggin, *Poetry*; as well as already Noth, *Pentateuch*.
37 See the discussion of the individual corpora, below pp. 112ff., 204ff., 280ff.
38 *Privilegrecht*. For a related discussion, see below pp. 113ff.

author during the codification processes.[39] Legal pronouncements have a clear meaning only in the context of the entire legal document of which they are part.[40] Blind use of purported literary-critical methods[41] is not appropriate. Rather, only the questions regarding the intra-literary and the legal-systematic structure of codified documents are in order. For this, in addition to the ancient Near Eastern documents, we must consult other ancient legal corpora for comparison.[42]

Still, the question regarding the transition from a series of law books from different historical situations to a single Torah cannot be treated in isolation. The very obvious parallels in redaction of earlier sources for individual legal texts are not enough for interpretation. We must find something else. The Pentateuch, the new entity, did not come into being as a law book simply by using older material, but rather by juxtaposing totally unbalanced, even contradictory documents from different epochs. As important as it might be, consideration of the literary composition does not really help us understand what has happened.

The first question this raises is that of exegesis. We must attempt to understand the path to the Torah preserved in Torah. We must try to reconstruct so that we grasp the historical process in the shift from "path" to the "sum of all previous paths," from combination to coordination of what was brought together, from variety to unity. Only when we have a clear understanding of the legal-historical problem, and ask what exactly a legal corpus (which is a combination of obviously disparate parts) might be, can we begin to understand such a text in a way connected with our own time, because the difference in periods is obviously a characteristic of Torah.

Ancient Near Eastern Legal Culture and Israelite Faith

Torah demonstrates an astonishing breadth of content. It comprises legal, moral, cultic, religious, theological and historical statements. We need not quibble over definitions here. Ancient as well as modern possibilities have been included in each case. Nor do we have to list aspects, dimensions or areas of ancient life not encountered within Torah.

A few biblical references should be sufficient. In the Decalog the prohibition against having foreign gods along with the prohibition against killing are basic norms with legal aspects. Coveting is not really acceptable in any society. The intent probably was to forbid legal misappropriation of property. The Book of the Covenant connects instructions for altar construction (Ex 20:24), many legal statements

39 For the problem and the difficulties connected with it, see Knierim, *Customs* 8ff. For the question of whether there was an actual law-giving, see below p. 11.
40 See especially Osumi, *Kompositionsgeschichte* 2ff.
41 The question of the pre-eminence and dominance of literary-critical or legal-historical investigation is methodologically a point of controversy in contemporary discussions. See e.g. Rofé, *Methodological Aspects* on the one side, and Westbrook, *Studies* on the other (to list two non-German speaking authors). In so doing, the – spoken or unspoken – hypothesis of a certain stylistic purity in the literary-critical principles and the results are interpreted. These questions require careful attention.
42 See below pp. 13ff.; examples, pp. 73ff., 175f.

functioning as laws (e.g. Ex 21:18f.) and some that we might at least raise a question about (like assistance for an enemy's animal – Ex 23:5) with the first commandment. Deuteronomy incorporates constitutional provisions with the monarchy (Deut 17:14ff.) or with the judicial organization (Deut 17:18ff.). The Holiness Code has regulations treating interpersonal relationships – hatred, bearing a grudge (Lev 19:17f.) and love of neighbors and aliens (Lev 19:18, 34) along with massive cultic regulations on sacrifice (Lev 22) and eating blood (Lev 17:10ff.). The legal formulae are diverse in language and content. Argumentation, narrative and reflection are all combined in the diverse regulations.

Since the end of the last century, our increasing knowledge of ancient Near Eastern legal documents[43] has shown this breadth is quite remarkable but not at all obvious.[44] We find close parallels in the very wording of Old Testament laws.[45] We see ever more clearly that there were especially close connections in basic legal thinking, legal system and the codification of laws.[46] The codes were, however, strictly secular;[47] they assume complete separation of legal, religious, and moral–ethical norms. Ancient Near Eastern legal corpora were not divine law,[48] nor do they contain moral–ethical norms as we find in collections of proverbs. They are associated with religious procedures, especially in connection with legal institutions like trial by ordeal, however, nowhere do we find provisions on things like altar construction, sacrifice, cultic taxes and priestly regulations. Naturally, they have no theological argumentation[49] or constitution-like provisions on the enthronement of kings or the limits of their authority.

43 The following description is concentrated corresponding to the overall state of the work. The rather more comprehensive investigation of the basic presuppositions, e.g. righteousness, must remain in the background (for this, see especially Weinfeld, *Justice*). In addition documents other than the Egyptian legal documents with their conceptions of Ma'at are especially important, see Hornung *Ma'at*, but especially Assmann, *Ma'at*. Finally, Helck, *Ma'at* has referred to the problem of the reference to reality.

44 Bibliography and German translation in Borger, "Akkadischer Rechtsbücher," TUAT I 17–125; see especially Driver/Miles, *Assyrian Laws* and *Babylonian Laws*; Yaron, *Eshnunna*; for a German translation, e.g. also Haase, *Rechtssammlungen*; there are overviews in Haase, *Einführing*; Korosec, *Keilschriftrecht*; Theodorides/ Zaccagnini/Cardascia/Archi, *La formazione*.

45 For comparison, see in overview Boecker, *Recht und Gesetz* (Lit); and now especially Malul, *Comparative Method*; for the theoretical and methodological problems, Jackson, *History*, for the history of the research in the relationship, Otto, *Körperverletzungen* 11ff. Otto's personal point of view, according to which, in spite of great similarity, "the individual Israelite legal pronouncements originated independently tradition-historically of cuneiform laws." In contrast, "the redaction of the collections of laws shares in the cuneiform legal culture" (*Körperverletzungen* 169f., cf pp. 170ff.) presupposes that the individual casuistic pronouncements behind the oldest identifiable compositions can be pursued back, and that they originated in a time when there were not yet institutions of legal scholarship in Israel that corresponded to those in the surrounding culture. In many respects this is methodologically and substantially improbable, see below pp. 149f., 165f. and elsewhere.

46 See e.g. Westbrook, *Studies*; Otto, *Rechtsgeschichteder Redaktionen*.

47 S. Paul, *Book of the Covenant* 8, "a strictly secular institution;" cf e.g. Sonsino, *Characteristics* 205ff.

48 See below p. 15.

49 See Gemser, *Importance*; Rücker, *Begründungen*; Sonsino, *Motive Clauses*.

For a long time, A. Alt *Die Ursprünge des Israelitischen Rechts* (1934) had profound affect on the study of Old Testament law. He employed form and tradition-historical methods developed since the turn of the century from ancient Near Eastern parallels on early legal documents in the Bible. His effort to get behind written codes and classify them in two categories was extremely important. He found "casuistic laws," which with "if, ... then" statements (e.g. Ex 21:18f., 20f.). They are closely related to ancient Near Eastern law in form and content, and ultimately come from there. They have their *Sitz im Leben* in normal judicial pronouncements at the village gate. Alt distinguished between this and the "apodictic laws," which include various kinds of utterance, for example, commands and prohibitions, cursings and participial laws. Ultimately, this law came from Israel's cult (thus, her religion). Alt regards it as the original Israelite law, "which had [its] home in the desert."[50] He thought it "humanly speaking – Israelite, and divinely speaking – Jahwist."[51] As articulated especially by M. Noth, it existed in the institutions of the amphictyonic central cult of the pre-state period.

Today, we must reject any attempt to find what is specifically Israelite in a single portion of the law books, especially to regard what is oldest as most original. Sources do not support what is here presumed about the early period of Israel. Neither the amphictyony nor the concepts of covenant and divine law connected with it are historically probable.[52] Most of the alleged evidence comes from texts that are quite late. The greater part of the apodictic law has no cultic-religious roots,[53] and the ages of the central commandments (first, second and possibly the sabbath) are highly controverted.[54] Methodologically, the supporting hypothesis that fixed forms of address come from an established *Sitz im Leben* is doubtful.[55]

This last criticism has shifted attention from hypothetical re-construction of oral pre-history to available literary documents and thus to a comparison of law books. The character of ancient Near Eastern legal codes played an important part in this study. If at first they were

---

50 Alt, *Ursprünge* 330.
51 Alt, *Ursprünge* 323.
52 For a discussion of the sources and the problems of the early period of Israel, see e.g. Donner, *Geschichte I*.
53 This has been demonstrated especially by Gerstenberger, *Wesen*.
54 For modern discussion of the age of Israel's so-called "monotheism" see the collected volumes: Keel (ed.), *Monotheismus*; Lang (ed.), *Der einzige Gott*; Haag (ed.), *Gott, der einzige*; in addition to Hutter, *Monotheismus*; Hossfeld, *Einheit*; W. H. Schmidt, *Jahweh*; de Moor, *Rise of Jahwism*; Niehr, *Der höchste Gott* and many others.
55 For review and reformulation of the form history, see especially, Hardmeier, *Texttheorie*. The very speculative and correspondingly radical, improbable char-acter of additional parts of tradition-historical hypotheses has grown increasingly clear from a wide variety of widely divergent corners. The altered view of the basic documents has played a part in this also with respect to their dating (important impetus from Rendtorff, *Pentateuch*; H. H. Schmid, *Jahwist*), the use of the final texts of the canon (especially Childs, *Old Testament*), the growing awareness of the inner structure of the legal documents (especially Halbe, *Privilegrecht*) and empirical investigations of transition from the oral to the written character of the tradition (e.g. Assmann/Hardmeier (ed.), *Schrift und Gedächtnis*).

instinctively interpreted, in analogy to later jurisprudence, as law books with judicially binding power, scholars have fundamentally revised this hypothesis[56] as representing only the surface meaning.[57] They are more like royal decrees[58] than statutory law. They offer something like academic-legal treatments, perhaps based on actual model legal decrees, but they are theoretical works. "The legal codes are descriptive and not prescriptive . . . They are essentially a record of ordinary laws."[59] Correspondingly, these materials from scribal schools are not actual legal documents, and are never cited in the documents.

The study of the origin and development of what is peculiarly Israelite – that which elevates above common ancient Near Eastern legal culture, has shifted to the exegesis of the oldest Old Testament law book – the Book of the Covenant, and an examination of the origin and relationship of its widely differing parts – roughly speaking, Alt's "casuistic" and "apodictic laws." In any case, the later legal documents, Deuteronomy and the Holiness Code, presuppose and represent the material peculiar to Israel, even if partially indebted to ancient Near Eastern legal culture. Westbrook, who is quite typical of the present debate, regards biblical law as "another kind of source" than the ancient Near Eastern law books, because "it contains the voice of dissent, just as strong – if not more – than that of the establishment"[60] thus, simultaneously suggests an interesting theory regarding the origin of the difference. Since we see what is special more clearly at the end, not the beginning, of Old Testament legal history, we should examine the circumstances and forces leading up to this and just how it ought to be understood.

The emergence of Israel's special faith in God, more than their God's role in legal history – a basic theme in modern Old Testament studies – is usually treated under the concept of "monotheism."[61] Scholars of the history of law who study the Book of the Covenant concern themselves with dating, and they evaluate its parts. At the moment the two are in opposition. For Westbrook, for example, the Book of the Covenant and it alone is the integral part of common ancient Near Eastern legal culture.[62] It is not distinct from it, and must be interpreted in that culture. He goes further to say that we may not draw any conclusions from the lack of other particular features of ancient Near Eastern law in Israel – like the amazing punishment, which we would explain as part of the Old Testament conception of humanity:[63] "Biblical law cannot be treated like an autocratic system."[64] For him even the Book of the Covenant is a textbook lacking binding power. It remains unclear for Westbrook how

---

56 See Petschow, *Beiträge* and "Die §§45 und 46"; Klima, *Perspective historique*; Demare, *La Valeur*. For review, see especially Westbrook, *Origins*.
57 Kraus, *Hammurabi*; Bottero, *Le "Code"*; Finkelstein, *Law Code*; Renfger, *Stele*; Krecher, *Rechtsleben*; Mauer, *Schreibübung*; Westbrook, *Origins*.
58 Texts in Kraus, *Verfügungen*; for their efficacy Olivier, *Effectiveness*; for a discussion Westbrook, *Origins*.
59 Westbrook, *Studies* 5.
60 Westbrook, *Studies* 134.
61 See above note 54.
62 *Studies* (in summary) 134f.
63 See especially Greenberg, *Postulates*.
64 Westbrook, *Studies* 134.

obviously religious features of the Book of the Covenant (e.g. its character as divine speech, the subject of altar construction coming at the beginning, the central position of the first commandment, etc.) relate to this. Schwienhorst-Schönberger regards all of these features of divine law as late and largely products of deuteronomistic redaction.[65]

Halbe represents the opposite view.[66] For him, Ex 34:10ff., the parallel to parts of the Book of the Covenant, is the beginning of the tangibly written legal history of Israel. It deals with so-called "right of privilege" which comes from belief in God and the cult, formulating it normatively. Everything else, especially parts most closely connected with ancient Near Eastern law, were integrated into this foundation later.

Thus we are compelled again to ask "when," "how," "why" and "under what circumstances" did what is peculiarly Israelite come about, especially the so-called "monotheism" expressed in a radical formulation of the first commandment? How did its relation to broad elements of common ancient Near Eastern culture look?

However we answer this question, it does not affect the question: "How did the process look in which what was special was better and better understood and formulated with increasing comprehensiveness and clarity?" Torah as a whole, with all its vast comprehensiveness and theological claim, is what is peculiar to Israel. We are dealing with the coherence of its development.

Legal History and Social History

Law is not only an indispensable source for ancient Israel's social history (as for any social history), it is itself a critical part of that history. When I began my investigation of Old Testament law I was interested primarily in social history, and this perspective, especially, sheds new light on our questions.

The relationship of law and reality, written law and societal reality, is quite complex and multi-faceted. We should not regard legal statements simply as descriptions of factual social orders – as is frequently done regarding ancient Israel because we lack other sources; nor may we simply contrast written law as an ideal with reality. What we say about each law gets more complicated when we add to our equation the character of ancient Near Eastern legal codes as products of scribal schools.[67] Could this be true of the divine law of ancient Israel? If so, to what degree? Were it not for the many extant examples of court cases, agreements, contracts as well as the contrasting situations of royal decrees with binding legal power, we would be unaware of this character in the world of that time.[68] There are virtually no such sources for ancient Israel, and we can only partially compensate for the lack, with a legal-historical analysis of Old Testament narrative material.[69] This is why it is

---

65 Schwienhorst-Schönberger, *Bundesbuch* 38ff. in summary 43.
66 Halbe, *Privilegrecht*.
67 See above pp. 11f.
68 See above note 58f.
69 See especially Daube, *Narratives and Rechtsgedanken*. In opposition, the theory of Carmichael (*Law*) according to which the written law of Israel might have originated in conjunction with the transmitted narrative material is hardly probable.

methodologically important to compare other law, especially Greek[70] –
similar to Israel in so many respects – or the great quantity of legal-
ethnological material, in order to understand.[71] The problem is clearest in
the Old Testament, where there is a lack of any kind of control group as a
reality check for sources.[72]

We must view the many studies specifically on Old Testament history
of law against this background. Within Jewish and English/German
traditions, scholars like Daube,[73] Falk,[74] Yaron,[75] Jackson[76] and Westbrook,[77] and others, have shed light on the structure of Old Testament
legal documents by comparing them with ancient Near Eastern as well as
later Jewish jurisprudence. Their studies have been accepted by German
biblical scholarship with a degree of hesitation,[78] which may be due to
the fundamentally different role of Torah in religious as opposed to
scientific study.[79]

All of these studies have, as a rule, been affected by aspects of
historical sociology.[80] There are occasionally differences of accent – and
some are significant. Do we, for example, investigate slave law according
to its legal construction and modification compared to ancient Near
Eastern traditions as well as the Old Testament; or – as nearly as we can
tell from the available sources – were existing laws consistent with the
social reality of slaves of the period, or, what was the intent and effect of
laws within their social context? In general, this study will attempt to
examine the latter.

There are, however, basic aspects for which legal historical perspectives in the narrower sense are not adequate. Again we begin with
an obvious fact of Torah. The laws were given by God to Moses on Sinai.
For his part, Moses gave them to Israel and wrote them down (Deut 31:9).
We find the direct act of God writing only in the tradition of the stone
tablets (Ex 32:16, 34:1; Deut 9:10 and elsewhere). We have divine laws
transmitted by a human figure in the distant past. This is not at all

---

70 See e.g. Gagarin, *Greek Law*. For comparison with Near Eastern and Israelite law,
    see Mühl, *Untersuchungen*. Comparisons with other legal areas are also important.
    For an overview, see Diamond, *Primitive Law*; for Roman law, see Cohen, *Jewish
    and Roman Law*.
71 See especially Roberts, *Ordnung*; Hoebel, *Recht*; Pospisil, *Anthropology* in addition
    to below pp. 65ff., 73ff.
72 The sociology of law (e.g. Dux, *Rechtssoziologie*; Luhmann, *Rechtssoziologie*) is of
    little assistance here.
73 *Studies; Witnesses* among others.
74 *Hebrew Law* among others.
75 *Biblical Law; Evolution* among others.
76 *Theft; Essays* among others.
77 *Studies; Law Codes* among others
78 The work of Otto represents somewhat of an exception (e.g. *Depositenrecht;
    Körperverletzungen*). Nevertheless, there is a central point of difference in the clear
    prearranged of literary- and tradition-historical reconstruction of the documents
    before their legal-historical interpretation (*Körperverletzungen* 188 and elsewhere;
    Rofé, *Methodological Aspects*). Since this is also valid for the ancient Near Eastern
    corpora, there is barely any legal-historically factual interpretation made of the
    transmitted documents.
79 Thus also Yaron, *Evolution* 95.
80 Here we refer especially to the work of Jackson on the semiotics of biblical law (e.g.
    Semiotic Questions; Ideas of Law; Legalism and Spirituality).

obvious. As historical criticism has demonstrated, the apparently simple image in the text is not only extremely complex, but it does something unusual.[81] Those ancient Near Eastern legal documents, so very similar to the Old Testament that they influenced, understand themselves so very differently that comparison makes the uniqueness of Israel's documents stand out clearly.

The prologs and epilogs of ancient Near Eastern legal documents indicate that they are from the king.[82] "(These are) righteous judicial maxims, which Hammurabi the mighty king established, (through which) he bestowed durable solid traditions and good leadership on our land." Thus begins the closing portion of the *Codex Hammurabi* (XLVII 2–8).[83] The king repeatedly calls the collection of laws "my stele" (XLVIII 6f., 10f., 15 and elsewhere). The gods assigned him the job of collecting the laws in written form: "When Marduk commissioned me to guide the people and to have moral laws established for the people, I placed justice and righteousness in the mouth of the land" (verses 14–22). Nevertheless, these concrete laws did not come to the king through divine revelation, but by decree. This is also true of individual formulations and is stated repeatedly with complete self-confidence. The "true order" expressed in the substance and form of these laws does not derive directly from the power of the gods nor is it subject to the power and arbitrariness of the gods. On the contrary, it is also binding on the gods. This is why all ancient Near Eastern laws are named for the kings who wrote them. Law is also a human construct in other ancient societies, for example, Greece[84] and Rome.[85] Concrete, written law as well as the act of writing the laws and proclamation all emanate from the person who was assigned the task.[86]

The basic notion that Israelite law is direct divine utterance is not at all common in the ancient world. The idea that a character from the distant past mediated the law is equally unusual. That laws are named for a king or law-giver, centuries after they were created, is quite different[87] from the idea that while written in the "present," they trace their origin and authority to the past. This needs explanation. We cannot ignore the fact that the provocation for this is still with us. As in the ancient Near East, our laws are a function of the state, but in Israel the function preceded the state and thus is above the state.

---

81 Against the frequently encountered assessments that divine or religious law occurs at the beginning of legal history, in early law this is almost never the case. See Daube, *Narratives* 1ff.; Diamond, *Primitive Law* 59; Ries, *Prolog und Epilog* 75ff.; Sonsino, *Characteristics* 202f.; Yaron, *Evolution* 89ff. Even more striking than that of Moses as a giver of divine law is that of Moses as a fictional figure of mediation from the distant past.

82 See e.g. Paul, *Book of the Covenant* 11ff.; Ries, *Prolog und Epilog* 75ff.

83 Translation after TUAT.

84 See the early establishment of laws by Zaleukos (see Mühl, *Gesetze*); Drakon (Ruschenbusch, ΦΟΝΟΣ; Gagarin, *Drakon*), Solon (Ruschenbusch, ΣΟΛΩΝΟΣ) and the laws of Gortyn (Willets, ed. *Gortyn*); for the whole, see Gagarin, *Greek Law*, for the result of the research, see Cohen, *Greek Law*.

85 Düll, *Zwölftafelgesetz*, see also Eder, *Political Significance*.

86 See e.g. Szegedy-Maszak, *Legends*.

87 This is where, e.g. we would classify Islamic law.

If we want to know "when" but especially "how" and "why" things developed, we must study the institutions which underlie the written law, and how they related to God (or to Moses). We are deeply indebted to form criticism for raising these questions. The institutions it named, the "legal gathering at the gate" and the "amphictyonic central cult," are not adequate answers, even if they are correct. M. Noth was rather vague about the survival of amphictyonic institutions during the royal period.[88] Still, there are completely unresolved problems for just the questions connected to the origin and background of deuteronomic law.

The close connections between Old Testament Law (or at least a large part of it) and ancient Near Eastern law makes answering the questions especially difficult, but also important. Were there schools for royal scribes and jurists behind the formulation of the codes? If so: Could corresponding circles perform similar functions? How could they act without the king's authority? Were connections to the king eliminated during the exilic or postexilic periods?[89] Might we even, following recent hypotheses, assume that the activity of such court schools occurred already *before* the establishment of the kingdom?[90] Do the unusual features and contents of Israelite law show us the real problems: Could the great religious traditions, cultic prescriptions and theological insights have been formulated by the same groups as those we label juridic in the narrow sense? What does it mean that the texts represent themselves as God's speech transmitted through Moses? How can law that claims this authority base itself in the distant past having come from Sinai, far from where they had been living for centuries?

This is the heart of the problem, simultaneously legal-historical and social-historical. This is why we will examine societal relationships in Israelite jurisprudence, the groups and institutions underlying the legal documents, their social intent and effects, the societal context of their theological bases and historical fictions. In this way we will try to clarify the problems of the origin and durability of Israel's unique characteristics, the juxtaposition of legal documents and their combination into one Torah, and the challenges that Israel's Torah places before Christian theology.

88　Noth, *Gesetze* 46ff.

89　Thus, e.g. Whitelam, *Just King* 218 and elsewhere.

90　Thus now Schwienhorst-Schönberger, *Bundesbuch* 206ff., 271ff. Similar questions are raised when Otto (*Körperverletzungen* 169ff.) tries to trace individual legal pronouncements – but not the collections of laws – to village judicial establishments.

2

✦

The Historical Context:
Prophetic Criticism of Written Law

The prophet's song is a rare thing,
what actually happens is doubly rare.

J. W. v. Goethe[1]

Where and when does the history of written Torah begin? God himself wrote the first commandments – the Decalogue or the instructions of Ex 34 – on stone tablets (Ex 32:16f.; Deut 9:10; 10:4) after the events at Sinai. Later, Moses wrote all of Torah in one book (Deut 31:9) before the people entered into west Jordan, and Joshua wrote the same thing on stones covered with plaster on Mount Ebal (Deut 27:4; Josh 8:32). These concepts are a central component of the historical orientation of Torah at the beginning of Israel's history. This is why scholarly reconstruction of the law is usually based on attempts to classify the individual parts – relatively then also absolutely. This has and still does include many well-known uncertainties.

There are texts of written law in Israel whose historical classification is uncontroverted, and we will begin with these texts. They alone can yield us a certain sure context for the genesis of Torah. These involve a few passages from the prophets of the eighth and seventh centuries (Hos 8:12; Isa 10:1f.; Jer 8:8). For the most part, these texts are interpreted in the light of current notions of the history of written law. It is, however, useful to do the reverse: to interpret the texts from the texts themselves, identifying what they tell us for certain or at least with very great probability.

Written Cultic Instructions from God
in the Northern Kingdom

The oldest reference to written, divinely given instructions are found in Hosea, thus in the Northern Kingdom of Israel in the eighth century BCE. Hosea 8:12 is part of the larger Hos 8:1–14.[2] This passage begins facing a threatening enemy with a trumpet call (8:1a) and announcement of an imminent return to Egypt when the divine punishment ends (8:13b). The

---

1 Prologue (1814) to the "Weissagungen des Bakis," 241.
2 For the arrangement and stratification, see especially Jeremias, *Hosea* 102ff. He regards verses 1b, 6a, and 14 as secondary (104; for verse 14, see especially Emmerson, *Hosea* 74ff.); see also Gnuse, *Calf*.

plaintive reaction of Israel (8:2) is "unmasked as deceitful."[3] The basic accusation – "Israel has spurned the good" (8:3) – is explained by reference to charges of instituting kings and a calf cult (8:4–6), wrong foreign policy (8:7–10) and improper cultic practice (8:11–13a). In the last section, between references to altars (8:11) and sacrifice (8:13a) we read:

> *Hos. 8:12 Though I write for him the multitude of my instructions, they are regarded as a strange thing.*

There are problems in the textual evidence, but scholars have resolved the important points nearly unanimously.[4] The masoretic text speaks of "my Torah" in the singular. Early translations, especially those done since the time of Aquila and Symmachus,[5] suggest the word originally was plural.[6] The current reading is a deuteronomic accommodation to 8:1b.[7] In any case, the preceding word[8] is intended to include a great number.[9] We probably should retain "(ten)thousand(fold)," which is the *lectio difficilior.*

Scholars do not contest the appropriateness of this verse to the ancient Hosea tradition. Hosea is clearly aware of written instructions from the hand of God himself. This idea, which probably does not *a priori* exclude human assistance, is quite remarkable. We may consider the instructions to be factual since condition contrary to fact can be excluded for grammatical reasons.[10] Hosea recognizes the instructions and acknowledges them without question, but they have been given in vain as all God's other benefits. Ephraim regarded God's instructions as something foreign (*zār*). The same word is used to describe foreigners in verse 7 who would swallow up Israel. They pay as little attention to God's written instructions as they do to those that come from the prophets.

We can answer some of the questions this verse raises, although not with the same confidence. Until the present time scholars have presumed Hosea is here referring to ancient divine law[11] and have assumed that the

3 Jeremias, *Hosea* 103.

4 See e.g. the commentaries by Robinson, Wolff, Rudolph, Mays, Deissler and Jeremias on this passage. See especially Nyberg, *Problem* 251ff. and *Studien* 65ff. Apart from Neef, *Heilstraditionen* 160 (see also note 6) only Andersen/Freedman, *Hosea* 509 take exception, nevertheless, the purely content reasons for their treatment of the text are insufficient.

5 Besides LXX, Vulg., Syr., see especially Aquila (*plēthynomenous nomos [mou]*) and Symmachus (*plēthē nomōn mou* or *plēthos nomōn mou* in Syh).

6 It is thus not, first of all, the plural verb in the final clause that requires a plural as Neef, *Heilstraditionen* 160, note 144 suggests.

7 It is thus not first of all the plural verb of the final clause, which demands a plural, as Neef, *Heilstraditionen* 160, note 144 suggests.

8 The Qere *rubbē* has a plural that appears only here, *rōb*, "multitude;" the ketib, in contrast, is *ribbō*, a noun that during the postexilic period meant "10,000" (Jonah 4:11; Neh 7:66, 70f. and others). Ps 68:18 can probably be interpreted in a more general manner. Thus there is not a great amount of difference between these meanings.

9 For that reason, it will not work to change the text. This might be an intentional exaggeration, but it might also be a conceivable report of many shrines (for this, see Mays, *Hosea* 122).

10 See GK §159b; Meyer, *Grammatik* §122.

11 Most recently, for example, Daniels, *Hosea* 113ff. Especially Jeremias, *Hosea* 111 is an exception. He speaks of "priestly instructions."

"law" includes the Decalogue as well as great figures like Moses or Sinai. For all of this nothing guarantees this, and it is highly unlikely the prophet would speak this way if he had actually known such a tradition. There is no connection to the many other historical traditions attested in Hosea. Verb forms used in the first and final clauses must first be interpreted in the sense of "basic rules," for which "the imperfect ... serves to express the conditions and consequences that are intended to be possible to *fulfil* in the present or the future, while the perfect represents the conditions that have already been fulfilled in the past and represents them as the existing consequences of completed facts"[12] in the conditional clause. While it is clearly established that Israel did not heed the instructions, God's act of writing is regarded as an opportunity for a potential present and future.[13] Hosea speaks of instructions that can be taken as God's word in the present.

What can we know about the contents? The *torot* regards "him" (Ephraim, 8:11) as the people as a whole. This eliminates the possibility that this "oldest direct evidence for written priestly instructions"[14] might have been associated with, for example, an internal professional awareness for the priests. The instructions were for the people and they were to follow them. *Tora* used in Hos 4:6 as a parallel to "knowledge" (*da'at*) is used by the priest and is associated, as frequently elsewhere in the Old Testament,[15] to instructions that were especially given by the priests. This designation already makes it improbable that we are to think especially of the classic Decalogue. That was never described as *tora* and certainly not *torot*, and the purported allusions to it in Hos 4:2 suggest rather that Hosea was not even aware of it.[16] Furthermore, if Hosea, like other eighth-century prophets, shows he is aware of legal and ethical traditions, this does not necessarily refer to written law.[17] The immediate context is also reminiscent of decidedly priestly material. There are cultic themes in the narrower sense – of altars and sacrifice – in the verses before and after. We should not read a contrast of cult and ethics into Hosea. The written *torot* apparently contain that which the priests, according to Hos 6:4, have forgotten, and to which Hosea knows himself to be obligated. These instructions, however, are something foreign (*zār*) in Israel. Hosea himself refers to illegitimate children this way in 5:7, and the priestly texts of the Pentateuch designate illegitimate cults – thus dangerous – as *zār*.[18] In view of the cult practised in Israel (8:11, 13 see also 8:4b, 5) the true instructions of God could only appear cultically illegitimate. Thus it is probable the contents of *torot*, insofar as they can be identified, were associated with the activities of the cult.

12 GK §159b.
13 Thus far also traditional Jewish interpretation. See Wünsche, *Hosea* 361f.
14 Jeremias, *Hosea* 111.
15 For the priestly Torah, see Liedke/Petersen, article on *tora* 1035ff. and many others.
16 Crüsemann, *Freiheit*; Jeremias, *Hosea* 62, especially note 4. The reasons presented in Neef, *Heilstraditionen* 193ff. are not convincing, he is himself only able to speak of a "precursor to the decalog."
17 See e.g. Zimmerli, *Gottesrecht* 220ff.; Klopfenstein, *Gesetz* 287ff.; also Neef, *Heilstraditionen* 175ff.
18 See especially Snijders, article on *zûr* 560f.

Thus, on the basis of Hos 8:12, we are able to establish the following theses regarding the history of written law in Israel:

- During the last period of the Northern Kingdom there were written instructions presented as the words written by God to Israel, and Hosea acknowledged them as the Word of God.
- Their contents probably dealt with cultic themes such as altars, sacrifice, possibly images, etc.
- It is unlikely that this material represents ancient tradition, coming from the early period and connecting itself with Moses and Sinai/Horeb.

The only evidence that God himself wrote his instructions occurs here and in the tradition of the stone tablets. This is a coincidence that we will discuss more fully later.[19]

Laws against the Weaker Elements in Eighth-Century Judah (Isa 10:1ff.)

The lament in Isa 10:1–4 is not over divine but human ordinances. It ends in 10:4b with the same transitional verse as in Isa 5:25. Nevertheless, it is usually assumed that its position at the end of this text directed against the Northern Kingdom is due to a complicated redaction-historical process in Isa 5:1–10:4.[20] This does not mean this passage is concerned with activities in the Northern Kingdom,[21] but as elsewhere in Isaiah's social criticism it deals entirely with Judah and Jerusalem. Frequently 10:1–4a is placed as a seventh word, the original beginning or end of 5:8–24.[22] Here, however, we must – and can – take it by itself.

> *Isa 10:1f. Ah, you who make iniquitous decrees*
> *who write oppressive statutes,*
> *2 to turn aside the needy from justice*
> *and to rob the poor of my people of their right,*
> *that widows may be your spoil*
> *and that you make the orphans your prey.[23]*

The cry (*hōy*) of the ritual lament over a corpse is sounded here before a people who give rise to harmful legal proceedings by their written laws.[24] Verse 2 lists the intents, or at least the inescapable consequences of such proceedings. In contrast, verse 3 and probably also (often

---

19 See below pp. 53ff., 141f.
20 See e.g. Wildberger, *Jesaja* 186f.; Barth, *Jesajaworte* 109ff.; Kaiser, *Jesaja* 102ff., 211ff.; Vereylen, *Isaie* 169ff.; L'Heureux, *Redaction*.
21 Especially, Duhm, *Jesaja* 95f. on the basis of the context. However, in spite of similar assessments, see e.g. Proksch, *Jesaja* 107 in 9:20 the transition to the speech about Judah. We must especially take note the varying remarks about orphans and widows (9:20, 10:2).
22 See above, note 20.
23 MT is quite understandable, significant manipulation of the text (e.g. Wildberger, *Jesaja*) is unnecessary.
24 For an interpretation of the lament and for a critique of the translation common since LXX, "Woe, to you . . . ," see Hardmeier, *Texttheorie* 174ff.; 375f.; Vermeylen, *Isaie* 79f.

isolated) verse 4a,[25] describes the calamity God will cause. We may take 8:1–4a as a self-contained word of prophetic judgment. Only those who do not accept[26] the existence of any Isaianic tradition, or regard its continued existence as limited, dispute the connection to the long-term existence of the eighth-century prophetic word.[27] Without going into greater detail,[28] we can show that there are no specific reasons (for example, deuteronomic language) for a late dating. It is quite unusual that the national catastrophe of 587 should be traced to anti-social human ordinance instead of the usual disobedience toward divinely given commandments, as usually happens. Thus, we must assume that 10:1–4a deals with part of Isaiah's social critique; the text addresses events in Judah or Jerusalem of the eighth century BCE.

It is clear that Isaiah is attacking people – in the plural – who are responsible for legal procedures that are written. "Writing" (*ktb*, pi) in verse 1, means writing in an iterative sense, "the usual records."[29] Still, we should note that the usual word, or official title "scribe" (*sōfēr*) is not used. The people referred to belong to the propertied class – note "wealth" (*kābōd*) in verse 3 – and they profit from the activities in verse 2. The widows become "their spoil" (*šᵉlālām*), and they "make the orphans their prey." Generally it is assumed that this passage is about royal officials acting on the king's behalf,[30] but this is never said explicitly, and there are none of the usual titles for officials given. Isaiah, who seems to know the Judean government quite well (see, for example, Isa 1:10, 23; 3:2f., 14), does not regard the king as responsible. Legal-historically, we should note here that apparently a group of Judean élite is setting up independent laws.

What exactly does this mean? Scholars give three different interpretations. The passage might refer to the establishment of laws, to decisions rendered by the courts, or to contractual arrangements. To choose from among them we must examine the terminology used. Despite – or even because of – the fact that we do not find the usual legal language, we can still be sure about our interpretation. The root (*ḥqq*) found at the beginning (and used twice) – thus affecting what follows – has as a basic meaning "to carve into." Elsewhere, it usually describes written records and is always connected with an authoritative arrangement, decision or directive.[31] This hardly agrees with Porath's recent interpretation.[32] He accepts mutual written agreements which, as described in verse 2a, are outside the usual legal avenues, but the word "set, arrange" (*ḥqq*) is never used for contracts of this type. And since, in any case, such things technically cannot occur in the form of a one-sided arrangement, this must involve a disqualifying term, which again would

25 For the argumentation, see Hardmeier, *Texttheorie* 272, note 25.
26 Thus especially Kaiser, *Jesaja* 104.
27 See now Kilian, *Jesaja* 79f.
28 See for the topic in general, Ringgren, *Israelite Prophecy*; for the problem of the underlying methodology, Hardmeier, *Jesajaforschung* 13–19.
29 See Jenni, *Pi'el* 160f.
30 Thus, e.g. Wildberger, *Jesaja* 198 and many others.
31 See Hentschke, *Satzung*; Liedke, *Gestalt* 154ff. and his article *ḥqq*; Ringgren, article *ḥqq*.
32 Porath, *Sozialkritik* 160ff.

have been recognizable in context by a contemporary reader. In addition, however, pronouncements of judgment in the Old Testament never use the word *ḥqq*. Job 23:14 is often cited in this connection.[33] Nevertheless, the text belongs to a much later period and the noun (*ḥoq*) used does not mean "judgment," but rather "that which is measured." Furthermore, there is no evidence of written judgments in Israel, but what is special about a judgment is never its written character. At most, judgments could have been intended for their precedent-setting effect. Thus, David's decree in 1 Sam 30 was made a statute and ordinance (*leḥōq uleṃispat*) (verse 25). This, furthermore, is only about the side issue of how permanent laws come about in detail.

Thus, we are not far from the old interpretation,[34] that the meaning is something like *legislation*. The wording causes no problems for this interpretation, it just conflicts with usual notions of an ancient, written divine law. If we presume this sort of thing is the basis for all law in Israel, we can say "that it is conceivable that those whom Isaiah attacked, were responsible for these changes in law."[35] Because nothing can exist that is not permitted to, this understanding is immediately seriously challenged by exegetes who deal with legislation. Dietrich,[36] for example, suggests that this must be the "implementation of regulations," which for all practical purposes reversed basic rights without formally abrogating them. This means we are not speaking about "laws," but rather of "statutes and ordinances"[37] or of "decree(s) and orders."[38] We should not try to transfer our modern abstract classification to the ancient Near East. We should avoid interpreting rich Old Testament legal terminology in the sense of hierarchical arrangement (basic rights – laws – ordinances and decrees). Instead, let us simply assume Isa 10:1 refers to issuing written laws – in other words: legislation.

For Isaiah this kind of law has harmful effects (*'āwen*)[39] (cf Isa 31:2; Mi 2:1 and elsewhere), there is only hardship and torment (*'āmāl*).[40] These words, not part of legal vocabulary, are expanded in verse 2. The word "for, so that" (*le*) lets us see the writer's intent. Those who are weak in society (*dallīm*)[41] are steered away from legal recourse (*din*), or they have their legal claim stolen (*gzl*) or forced away (*nṭh*, hiph.)[42] from them, and consequently are robbed of their rights or legal claim (*miṣpāt*).[43] Isaiah uses legal vocabulary to indict harmful laws. The written (thus in a sense

---

33 Thus, especially, Kaiser, *Jesaja* 217; first Falk, *Terms* 352; for a critique already Liedke, *Gestalt* 167 note 5.

34 Thus already Knobel, *Jesaja* 78.

35 Porath, *Sozialkritik* 164f.

36 Dietrich, *Jesaja* 40, see also Jacob *Isaïe* 146, who speaks of adaptation of older laws to meet new political and economic circumstances.

37 Dietrich, *Jesaja* 40.

38 Dietrich, *Jesaja* 46.

39 See Knierim, article on *'āwen*; Bernhardt, article on *'āwen*.

40 See Otzen, article on *'āmāl*; Schwertner, article on *'āmāl*.

41 For the word and the issue, see Schwantes, *Recht* 20ff.; Fabry, article on *dal*.

42 For *nṭh*, hiph. with *min* see especially Job 24:4; Isa 30:11; for *din* see Hamp, article on *din*; Liedke, article on *din*.

43 For the term, see Liedke, *Gestalt* 62ff.; Liedke, article on *ṣpṭ*; Johnson, article on *miṣpāt*; Niehr, *Herrschen*.

"statutory") laws steal justice from the poor and weak. Verse 2b speaks of widows who become the plunder (it is probably the author's intent that we think of enslavement here) and theft from orphans by those who write the laws.[44] Is the fate of the widows and the orphans a further consequence of the law or – indirectly – a result of the theft of the rights of the weak?

Most scholarly attempts to understand what is meant here are rather vague. They suggest that these are decrees dealing with debt law or basic rights, through which normal social interdependences (for example, routes to freedom from debt-slavery) are expedited and become more effective.[45] Others have suggested that it refers to effects of taxes and tribute.[46] Nevertheless, as Schwantes points out, we cannot dilute the precise sense of verse 2a in this way. New laws functioned in such a way that weaker people no longer had the right to sue for the redress of their claims and grievances: "They were excluded entirely from the legal community."[47] Legal avenues previously available to them had been stolen (*gzl*).

On the basis of Isa 10:1f. we can say the following about the history of Israel's written law:

- In the eighth century a group of the wealthy Judean élite increased their societal influence at the expense of weaker members of the community by means of special, written legal activities.

- This probably involved proper legislation, i.e. it established written law.

- This meant the weak and poor had the possibility of legal recourse taken from them. It even went so far that widows and orphans were victims of the greatest exploitation.

We will discuss at a later time the remarkable coincidence of Isaiah's charge – the theft of all legal recourse from the poor by the rich – with the basic content of the laws in all preexilic collections in which this possibility is available only to free landowners.[48]

YHWH's Torah and the Seventh-Century Scribes (Jer 8:8)

Jer 8:8 has been called "one of the most important,"[49] but also the most difficult[50] passages in Jeremiah. Together with the report on the Book of the Law of 1 Kg 22f.,[51] this text is undisputed evidence for the existence of a written version of Torah in late preexilic Jerusalem.

> *Jer 8:8 How can you say, "We are wise*
> *and the law of YHWH is with us,"*

44 With Schwantes, *Recht* 106.
45 Thus, e.g. Wildberger, *Jesaja* 198; Liedke, *Gestalt* 179f.; Dietrich, *Jesaja* 40.
46 Thus, e.g. Hogenhaven, *Gott und Volk* 176.
47 Schwantes, *Recht* 104.
48 See below pp. 166ff.
49 Duhm, *Jeremia* 88.
50 Especially Nicholson, *Jeremiah* 86.
51 See below pp. 208f., 211, 270ff.

> *when, in fact, the false pen of the scribes*
> *has made it a lie?*
> 9 *The wise shall be put to shame*
> *they shall be dismayed and taken;*
> *since they have rejected the word of YHWH,*
> *what wisdom is in them?*

An unnecessary and unwarranted manipulation in verse 8 has quite profoundly influenced the interpretation of this passage: An object has been attached to "he makes" (i.e. "effects") (*'śh*) by re-pointing. Thus the meaning becomes, "He makes it" (i.e. the Torah) "into a lie." What underlies this manipulation (especially in conjunction with equating Torah and Deuteronomy) affects our discussion of the passage. Formerly scholars referred to grammatical possibilities,[52] but no longer. It is offered today practically without support, in fact, it is almost regarded as obvious.[53] Nevertheless, that Torah could be transformed into lies and deception is an unusual and serious charge, especially since its origin in protestant law-criticism, without actual support in the text, is apparent.[54] There is no such support.[55] The Hebrew text is quite clear, even if it is possible to translate it in several different ways; and no other version allows us to identify a Hebrew text fundamentally different from the masoretic text.[56]

Only when someone regards his or her own idea about a particular text as absolutely true, is it possible for that person to regard the ancient translations as falsifications.[57] It is important to note that the older Jewish translations were only attempts to interpret the masoretic text.[58] The simplest and thus the preferred interpretation is the one above taking the absolute *'śh* in the sense of "work, effect" (cf Gen 30:30; Hag 2:4; Prov 21:25, 31:13, and others).[59]

"All terms are clear, having no difficult or obscure words, but what does the poem mean?"[60] We can immediately see what is most important: the one YHWH. There is clear attestation here of the written version of the concept of the one will of God understood as a totality,[61] perhaps already present in Hosea. While the matter may otherwise be unresolved, the text has an important function for the history of Torah.

---

52 Duhm, *Jeremia* 88: GK §91e; Cornill, *Jeremia* 117: GK §58g.
53 Thus Rudolph, *Jeremia* 60; Weiser, *Jeremia* 70; Nicholson, *Jeremiah* 84; Carroll, *Jeremiah* 228; McKane, *Jeremiah* 185f. For the effect on translations, see especially the *Züricher Bibel, Einheitsübersetzung* and others. See also *Lutherrevision* 1964.
54 Cf the similar sentiments in Duhm, *Jeremia* 88f.; Cornill, *Jeremia* 116f.; also Weiser, *Jeremia* 72 and others.
55 See the entire body of older exegesis. For this, see Keil 129; Volz, *Jeremia* 116f.; also Weiser, *Jeremia* 72 and others.
56 The LXX and Vulgate formulations are in the passive, and for Targum Jonathan, "scribe" is the subject of the deception.
57 E.g. Cornill, *Jeremia* 116; Rudolph, *Jeremia* 61.
58 Aquila reads *eis adikon epoiēsen grapheion adikia grammateōn* ("the unrighteousness of the scribes make the scripture into something unrighteous").
59 See Vollmer, article on *'śh*.
60 Carroll, *Jeremiah* 229.
61 Especially Hos 4:6, see Jeremias, *Hosea* 66, "a summary of the many means of life support from God."

The relation of the text to Jeremiah and its dating is, of course, especially important. The solution is dependent upon complex questions of the origin of the Book of Jeremiah. In Jer 8:4–9:26 there is an essentially poetic text, thus from the classic vantage of source A.[62] This means it was thought "genuine"[63] and part of the "original scroll."[64]

Jer 8:8f. is often thought to be a text by itself; close examination, however, shows that it is tightly embedded in its context. Reference to the possession of Torah in verse 8 is an answer to the accusation that they do not know the ordinance (*mišpāṭ*) of God (8:7).

Verses 10f. connects reference quite neatly with 8:8f. The careless reference to a non-existent peace (verse 11) is simply an expansion of that idea, which might underlie the refractory reference to Torah on thoughts of security. This is more than a superficial collection of catch phrases. This is a thoroughly reasoned composition. If there were older individual texts, they could not have been more clearly combined. As in other prophetic writings, we have to wonder whether there is something behind this composition.

At best new discussion of the Book of Jeremiah's poetic texts is only just beginning. Carroll is probably correct when he suggests that sayings of uncertain origin might underlie this composition.[65] It is, however, very important that this would involve undeuteronomistic and pre-deuteronomistic language and modes of thinking in the redactional process.[66] This is clear in the way the term Torah is used. Deuteronomistic passages speak of this authority completely differently.[67] Our poetic passage presupposes deuteronomistic redaction and composition. If we question the older strata of Jer 8:8 as Levin does without a rationale, the text would be "puzzling."[68] Any solution of the conflicts and events occurring during the final, preexilic decades could only make our text more difficult. The later we date the passage, the more "puzzling" it becomes. This suggests that Jer 8:8 must include material from preexilic Jerusalem.

From the text, unfortunately, we cannot be sure about answers to many questions. Who call themselves wise because they possess Torah? Are they more or less the same as the scribes?[69] Or do the people as a whole describe themselves in this way on the basis of Torah?[70] We can no more answer these with certainty than the central question: whether the "word" (*dābār*) in verse 9 is used in contrast to Torah or whether it is another designation for the same thing.[71] Nearly everyone contrasts law

---

62 Mowinckel, *Komposition* 20.
63 Rudolph, *Jeremia* 20.
64 E.g. Holladay, *Architecture* 97ff., 171ff.; and Holladay, *Jeremiah* 277.
65 Carroll, *Jeremiah* 47f.
66 Especially, Thiel, *Jeremia I* 235ff.
67 In a similar section, especially Jer 9:12; besides Jer 16:11; 26:4; 32:23; 44:10, 23. See Thiel, *Redaktion* 101, 137f. Nowhere within the deuteronomic area is it conceivable that the Torah is so problematic as in 8:8f.
68 Levin, *Verheissung* 259 note 11.
69 See especially McKane, *Prophets* 102ff.
70 Thus with emphasis, Whybray, *Intellectual Tradition* 32ff.; Gilbert, *Jérémie en conflit* 111f.
71 Especially Gilbert, *Jérémie en conflit* 111f.

with prophecy; speech written and dead with living and oral.[72] These do not come from the text itself. We do not know what exactly the scribes had to do with Torah. There is no support in the text for speculation whether this referred to Deuteronomy itself or just its cultic portions, or whether it referred to amplifications or commentary and application. The material is too general for us to be specific.

We can, however, tell what is most important: The activities of the scribes produced lies and deception. The word *šéqer*[73] is a central concept for Jeremiah, meaning the deceptions and self-delusions characteristic of Judah and Jerusalem.[74] Verse 8 cannot be weakened to "in vain."[75] Even "holding fast to deceit" contradicts the use of this word in context. "All" have been drawn into the deception, says verse 10: priests, prophets, great and small, even the scribes themselves. Groups that worked with Torah are no exception, and for that reason Torah brings no salvation. Some things suggest that the reference to possession of Torah is simultaneously an expectation of salvation and security, for example, reliance upon the Temple (7:4) and earlier promises of salvation (especially 4:10). Read in this way, there is no reason to see Jeremiah as an antithesis to Torah, he is not fundamentally in conflict with Temple or YHWH's desire for the salvation of his people, but for Jeremiah everything, even Torah, is involved in profound deception about their situation, it even contributes to it.

Jer 8:8 suggests the following about the history of Torah:

– In the late preexilic period in Jerusalem, there was a written form of the will of Yahweh, and it went under the name of Torah.

– Groups of scribes (and possibly also the wise men) worked on Torah.

– It was interpreted as that which guaranteed wisdom and probably also security.

We will examine the much discussed relationship between the text and the prophet Jeremiah to Deuteronomy and the Josian reform[76] in another place.[77]

---

72 See most recently, e.g. Carroll, *Jeremiah* 229f.
73 See Klopfenstein, article on *šqr*.
74 See especially Overholt, *Falsehood*.
75 Thus, e.g. Weinfeld, *Deuteronomy* 160 with reference to 1 Sam 25:21, the translations of LXX as well as Kimhi.
76 See especially Hyatt, *Jeremiah and Deuteronomy*; Rowley, *Jeremiah*; Scharbert, *Jeremia*; Cazelles, *Jeremiah and Deuteronomy* and others.
77 See below p. 211 and elsewhere.

3

༺ༀ༊༻

The Mountain of God and Divine Law:
The Way of Torah at Sinai

The trumpet's place deep in the
glowing empty text.

P. Celan[1]

According to the Pentateuch, Torah was given to Israel on the mountain of God Sinai/Horeb with Moses as mediator. This place is a very special part of the mystery of Torah. The fact that Israel understood its own legal system as more than just an arrangement of God is part of the uniqueness of their legal and religious history. More precisely, it was an arrangement connected with a special moment in Israel's early history. The significance of this idea becomes immediately apparent when we examine other alternatives. The law was not issued by a king or a state. It was not, as in Greece, the work of a law-giver to whom responsibility was given, nor was it conceived in temples or by priests. The fact that, for Israel, God's will and his righteousness are pre-eminent over all institutions of this kind is connected with the special site associated with their God.

Nevertheless, historical criticism has long agreed that these laws connected with Sinai belong to a much later period. Even the oldest of the laws presuppose that Israel was an agrarian society, already a settled community. Prophetic passages cited here from the royal period speak at least in part of divine instructions – Hos 8:12 even presupposes that God himself wrote them, but there is no mention made of Moses or Sinai. Clearly the prophets are speaking about activities of their own time. If the laws were already understood to be a part of the ancient past, that was unimportant for the disputes they addressed. The real quarrel was not over this. How did this historical orientation come about; what role did it play in the origin of Torah? Were there old traditions that suggested the occasion, the possibility, or even the necessity for such an arrangement? Were the legal corpora, from the very beginning connected with Moses and Sinai, or was this association only attached later?

The Literary Problem of the Sinai Pericope

Thus far, scholars have only tried to answer these questions by analyzing the Sinai pericope. Thus in this chapter the question of Torah's place is wrapped up with complex literary-critical problems.

1 *Zeitgehöft* 42.

The narrative of Israel's stay at Sinai is, as a whole, structured in a completely logical, clear manner. After their arrival at the mountain and the momentous theophany (Ex 19) came the Decalogue. It is in the form of direct speech from God (Ex 20). Additional legal formulations were first given just to Moses (Ex 21–23). The covenant was concluded (Ex 24) based on these events, and preparations for the construction of the shrine were attached to it (Ex 25–31). The turning point came when Israel's astounding revolt resulted in worship of the calf image (Ex 32). It was only through Moses' lengthy negotiations that the people were forgiven (Ex 32–34). Nevertheless, the break affected everything that was to follow – sin and forgiveness were a continuing possibility during the construction of the shrine and appurtenances of the cult. As clear as the broad lines and theological intent may be, the extent of the gaps and contradictions in the Sinai pericope in both larger outline and details, is unparaleled elsewhere in the Pentateuch. For example, Israel is at the mountain of God in Ex 18, but they arrive again in 19:1. We nearly miss the central question: What was on the stone tablets? Was it the Decalogue, as it says in chapter 20, or cultic instructions (34:11ff.)? Just try to follow Moses' "up" and "down" from/to the place from which God speaks, or the instructions who may and who may not come near him, and you will find obvious contradictions. The canonic concluding text of these chapters shows quite clearly the lack of consistency we find elsewhere. There are obvious (intentional?) contradictions in the final product. If literary criticism is useful anywhere, it is here.

Over the last century scholars have given much assistance especially regarding the literary and historical place of the law – but the answers are hardly convincing. The location of the priestly texts is clear. They are in two large blocks, Ex 25–31 and 35–40 and beginning Lev 1. Scholars agree regarding the inclusion of Ex 19:1(2a) and 24:15b–17(18). In contrast, the non-priestly material in Ex 19–24 and 32–34 is generally regarded as pre-priestly and we look for much earlier traditions there. This is not new, scholars also find the great Pentateuch sources – Yahwist and Elohist – here. Two non-priestly strata did not extend into this portion at all, and ascriptions were so different and so interchangeable that they have proven to be without foundation.[2] There are serious problems for source criticism here, particularly for analysis of the law texts into particular strata. The closer we look, the more apparent it becomes that the law texts are very loosely located, we might almost call it disconnected. It is surprising to find the Decalogue in 20:1ff. without any transition from 19:24f. Even the continuation in 20:18ff. does not presume that the Decalogue came immediately before. Indeed, the Book of the Covenant (20:22–23:33) does connect relatively well with 20:21, but not to 24:1. Thus the old observation remains valid – it is arbitrary to assign these laws to individual strata, whether or not we use the classic labels.[3]

This is why connecting the law documents with earlier literary strata has grown increasingly problematic in recent discussions. It is for this reason Perlitt revived the old Wellhausen interpretation in his study of

---

2 See already Noth, *Pentateuch* 6; see especially Perlit, *Bundestheologie* 181f.
3 Thus already Noth, *Exodus* 124, 140; most recently especially Soggin, *Ancient Israelite Poetry*.

covenant theology. "The ancient, real significance of Sinai is entirely independent of the giving of the law. This was the place of God, the holy mountain."[4] He only found an ancient, pre-deuteronomic nucleus in the theophany of chapter 19, and "a view of God and the festive banquet" in 24:1f., 9–11.[5] Only in deuteronomic/deuteronomistic strata have covenant and obligation been introduced, with which we should also classify Ex 19:4ff. and 32:34 with the cultic commands in addition to 24:3–8.[6] In addition to Perlitt, Zenger's analysis has also influenced recent discussions.[7] According to Zenger, the text is broken into small, even miniscule, fragments called "entities," which he then rearranges to form new documents.[8] In this way, he believes he can analyze meager bits of the ancient Yahwist and Elohist sources.[9] According to Zenger, the Yahwist had already referred to "covenant" or "obligation," which, however, are limited to the miracle promised in 24:10. He believes that the first introduction of law texts, which deal with ancient right of privilege in 34:11ff., goes back to the Yahwists at the end of the eighth century, but we lack solid evidence for this.[10] More or less deuteronomistic strata with the Decalogue and the Book of the Covenant were added after the Yahwist.

A relatively large number of recent studies refer to Zenger and Perlitt.[11] For some of them Zenger provides a rather dogmatic foundation. We don't have to[12] nor should we discuss them in detail here. In general, they show that deuteronomistic theology had a large hand in shaping the Sinai pericope, associating the introduction of the law texts with it. This could not have been before the late monarchic period, but the exilic period is thought especially influential. We will see that these views can be supported – and even become more radical – by a different methodological route.

Literary-critical methodology has dominated recent studies, dissolving the document into many strata. The analysis, let alone the reconstructions of as many as ten or more strata, demonstrate uncertainty and even arbitrariness. Often the reasons given are inadequate or they are developed after the fact.[13] When we cut puzzle pieces as we think

---

4 Wellhausen, *Prolegomena* 342.

5 Perlitt, *Bundestheologie* 181ff., 90ff.

6 Perlitt, *Bundestheologie* 167ff., 203ff.

7 Zenger, *Sinaitheophanie*, see also his *Israel am Sinai*.

8 Zenger, *Sinaitheophanie*, for conclusion, see pp. 100ff.

9 Zenger, *Sinaitheophanie*, 119ff.; see especially the summary in the synopsis 164ff.

10 Even in his more recent *Israel am Sinai* 155 he is brief and theoretical about JE. His analyses recognize the J proto-form.

11 Mittmann, *Deuteronomium* 145ff.; Phillips, *Fresh Look*; Levin, *Dekalog*; critical of it, Homan, *Dekalogexegese*; Johnstone, *Decalogue*; Vermeylen, *Sections Narratives*; Weimar, *Das goldene Kalb*; Renaud, *La théophanie* and others.

12 Hossfeld, *Dekalog* especially 163ff.; Dohmen, *Tafeln*; and in part Dohmen, *Bilderverbot*.

13 This is true of a large number of the conclusions that have been offered. Unwittingly, an investigation is conducted into the entire text, regarding references and problems, studying the text word for word, sentence for sentence, down to the slightest "tensions" and immediately these are given a literary-critical evaluation. In my opinion, two points demonstrate quickly the absurdity of this endeavour: First, regarding the results (in other words, the texts reconstructed as unified) – the

they ought to be, no two pictures will ever be alike. This process needs to be examined more carefully.

Of course, no one would deny that this technique can be helpful. We should note, however, that in many recent studies scholars exceed the bounds of literary-critical methodology. When literary analysis breaks the texts into rubble,[14] it is time to switch methodology. No one disputes the need for and potential of literary criticism, but, the literary-critical tools at our disposal procedure have clearly not helped the complex problems of the Sinai documents. Increasingly, literary criticism leads to the destruction of the structure of the text rather than understanding.

For similar reasons, E. Blum has tried other avenues.[15] He has chosen to work strictly with clearly recognizable larger compositions. At most, he makes occasional reference to the older proto-forms underlying these compositions. Frequently, he sees no possibility of extricating these from their literary context. Blum identifies a deuteronomistic stratum at Sinai as elsewhere in the Pentateuch. This is the D composition and it was enlarged and corrected with the priestly texts, which produced the "P composition." Nevertheless, extraction and interpretation of the root "D composition" of the Sinai pericope fails to answer the same basic questions that have hindered literary-critical scholars. Blum regards the essential parts of Ex 19–24 and 32–34 as part of this deuteronomic textual relationship. As careful and circumspect as he is, he can only explain the massive contradictions by equally massive cuts. Perhaps the two largest contradictions, the mountain of God pericope before Sinai in Ex 18[16] and the disagreement between the Decalogue and Ex 34:11 over the content of the stone tablets[17] meant he had to consider post-priestly additions, and thus disturb the overall composition of the final version. Any detailed analysis of both texts, not just the more recent, suggests there are more very old pieces completely woven into the fabric.[18] Thus, it may not be the textual evidence as such, but the basic hypothesis of an essentially

---

same criteria that were applied for a literary-critical division can be used again. For the most part, they can be used even more aggressively, since we are dealing with fragments that barely hang together. If we add the expressions that are commonly used, like "possibly," "maybe," "perhaps," and so on – if, in other words, we take the author at his own word – the improbability of the whole affair becomes apparent. Should not scholarship try to establish a secure foundation and avoid a whole series of mere possibilities? Furthermore, if we were to examine, e.g. documents that have been discovered through archaeology, Hebrew ostraka, for example, they would be immediately torn to shreds.

14 Thus Levin, *Dekalog* 185, in part regarding Ex 19. Not because we are dealing with "Holy Scriptures," for which we ought to have special respect. Because any attempt to understand so remote an epoch is led into total absurdity, we do it to counteract the complete cynicism and presumptuousness of the modern commentator ("again he [the restorer] makes a mess of the whole scene," 179).

15 Blum, *Pentateuch*.

16 See Blum, *Pentateuch* 153.

17 Blum, *Pentateuch* 67.

18 Thus also Blum, *Pentateuch* 155f. considers a proto-deuteronomic tradition, contained in Ex 3f. and Ex 18, nevertheless, only partially picked up by his K[D]. Furthermore, in comparison with Deut 1:9ff., Ex 18 represents an essentially older tradition. For the problem of particulars, see below pp. 45f., pp. 84ff. The discussion of Ex 34:11ff. will have to be taken up elsewhere, see below p. 115ff. For Blum's view, see *Pentateuch* 369ff.

unified and (at least regarding important questions) contradiction-free D composition that led Blum to such an insufficiently supported analysis of such an important text.

The main problem for analysis of the Sinai pericope is that because of the obvious complexity of the documents, the respective premises and methodological and content "prejudices" affect the results more profoundly than would otherwise be the case. Simple analysis and dating of the strata obviously do not answer questions about the origin of the texts. This is why we will examine the origins and background of the linking of Torah and Sinai. This is all we will try to do. We will set out upon a different path by looking for a starting point outside the old tried and true paths around which we can organize analysis of the literary evidence.

The Mountain of Salvation: The Older Sinai Tradition

1. We must begin with the negative evidence in order to find a secure starting point to understand the Sinai tradition and the Sinai pericope. We have known this for a long time, but not paid it proper attention. We are dealing with the text of the so-called historical credo of Israel, in which G. v. Rad is thought to have discovered the outline of the Hexateuch with its Yahwist foundation in 1938.[19] All of these texts, whether Deut 26:5b–9, 6:20–24; Josh 24:2b–13 or the historical Ps 78, 105, 106, 135, 136, or Ex 15 mention the patriarchs and they address the oppression of the people, their being led out of Egypt and the gift of the land. As we know, these texts omit Sinai completely. G. v. Rad regards the construction of the Sinai pericope as one of the Yahwist's most important achievements.[20] He explains the omission by referring to the transmission of the material during the pre-literary phase where he assumes a different *Sitz im Leben*. He does not even ask how a historical picture including neither Sinai or Torah could last into the postexilic period, centuries after the Yahwist.

Nevertheless, we must begin with the question, "How could the very heart of the Pentateuch have been omitted in clearly postexilic psalms like 105 and 136?" Why only the golden calf in Ps 106:19ff.? In Neh 9:13ff. Sinai appears in an apparently anachronistic passage that "undoubtedly should be regarded as one of the most recent parts of the Old Testament."[21] It is amazing that even though additional research into the so-called credo texts has made us much more aware,[22] it resists a convincing solution. This increase came about especially because Rost proved[23] that Deut 26 is not very early, but rather it bears the strong imprint of the deuteronomist. He regards only 26:5b, 10 as an ancient harvest prayer. Other studies have designated the historical arrangement of most of the texts as a product of deuteronomic theology.[24] Long after

19 G. v. Rad, *Hexateuch*.
20 G. v. Rad, *Hexateuch* 60ff.
21 See Kreuzer, *Frühgeschichte*.
22 Gunneweg, *Nehemia* 129.
23 Rost, *Credo*.
24 In summary, Kreuzer, *Frühgeschichte* 63ff. In contrast Daniels, *Creed* opts for the proto-deuteronomic foundation, out of a provenance in the pre-state period.

the traditional date to which the Yahwist has been assigned, and to which a Sinai pericope has been ascribed until recently, a historical portrait developed in late preexilic times containing no reference to the mountain of God or the commandments given there. No one would date Josh 24 much before the deuteronomic movement, and recent studies even suggest the exilic period or later.[25] In view of the trend in scholarship toward later dating of quite a few texts, in general, we can say the following: The later we date texts like Josh 24 or even Deut 6 and 26 in the exilic or postexilic periods, the more remarkable the absence of Sinai grows and the more it is in need of an explanation. There is no convincing interpretation of the evidence for the credo texts. Even Kreuzer, who most recently has re-investigated them, re-adopts the solution of G. v. Rad – that the material might even have been tied more strongly to Sinai in a different *Sitz im Leben* than the Exodus stories connected with the cult.[26] Nevertheless, this is an unsatisfactory argument from the moment of literary shaping on. Furthermore, Kreuzer presumes there were literary proto-forms of the present version of the Pentateuch. He feels we cannot conclude "that the writer did not know the Sinai tradition" from Deut 6:20–24, where the question of the meaning of the divine command is supposed to be answered.[27] This notion is, nevertheless, unsupported. In fact, the giving of the commandments appears here also, as it must, and it is supposed to answer the question posed by the children in verse 20. Nevertheless, the commandments are connected to the exodus and the gift of the land. This is theologically and temporally important – but nothing is said about Sinai or Horeb.

We can only conclude from this that from the giving of the law until the postexilic period, Sinai was not a part of the historical portrait whose dominant influence was the deuteronomist. Still, we would need very good reasons to stay with an ancient or only a pre-deuteronomic Sinai tradition with elements of covenant and law – indeed better than we get from the problematic analysis of the Sinai pericope.

2. We would throw the baby out with the bath water if we concluded from this that "We can no longer speak of an ancient, Israelite 'Sinai tradition!'"[28] In this context the age and importance of Judg 5:4f.; Deut 33:2; Ps 68:8f. are often mentioned.[29] We would have to reject any historical understanding and put this formulation into the heads of "late hymn writer(s)" merely for the sake of the consistency of a hypothesis.[30] Even the most critical consider the Song of Deborah (Judg 5)

---

25 See Perlitt, *Bundestheologie* 239ff.; Blum *Vätergeschichte* 51ff.; Seters, *Joshua* 24. Even Mölle, *Landtag* makes claim for only very small portions for his pre-state stratum. In general, see Kreuzer, *Frühgeschichte* 183ff. For the history of the research, see Koopmans, *Joshua* 24. His own view of the text as pre-deuteronomic "poetic narrative" similar to the linguistic-statistic comparison by Sperling, *Joshua* 24 is less convincing.

26 Kreuzer, *Frühgeschichte* 254f.

27 Kreuzer, *Frühgeschichte* 146.

28 Levin, *Dekalog* 189.

29 See already G. v. Rad, *Hexateuch* 27; Perlitt, *Bundestheologie* 234; Jeremias, *Theophanie* 11.

30 Levin, *Dekalog* 190.

preexilic.[31] Furthermore, everything suggests a much earlier origin for verse 5.[32]

> *Judg 5:4 YHWH, when you went out from Seir,*
> *when you marched from the region of Edom,*
> *the earth trembled, and the heavens poured,*
> *the clouds indeed poured water.*
> *5. The mountains quaked before YHWH, the One of Sinai,*
> *before YHWH, the God of Israel.*

Without emendation,[33] we can understand the text entirely in the present tense.[34] However, it refers to the saving event, which is sung throughout the Song of Deborah. As customary in descriptions of theophanies,[35] the coming of God is pictured as affecting nature: the earth and heaven, mountains and clouds. This God comes, as it says in the adjoining verses, from the mountain of Seir.[36] Seir is traditionally associated with the family of Edom/Esau (e.g. Num 24:18). In addition to Seir, there is mention of Paran (Deut 33:2) and Teman (e.g. Hab 3:3) in related texts.[37] The coming is like the one which brings the salvation proclaimed in the song.

YHWH is called "the one (from) Sinai" (*zēh sīnay*) in verse 5. This sounds just like a divine name: YHWH is "the one (from) Sinai." He is thus connected with the authority of Sinai more closely than with other regions named as his place of origin – he may even be called "Sinai." It has been debated whether the Hebrew usage *zēh sīnay* can be interpreted as "the one from Sinai" in the sense of "YHWH of Sinai" as in other semitic languages.[38] It must have been a gloss referring to the Sinai tradition or theophany. In any case, this would be a possibility only for Judg 5. The use of the idiomatic expression in Ps 68:9 is firmly embedded in composition and paralelism. Just the fact that a potential gloss could thus have become a designation for God, and that both texts were handed down and continued to be interpreted in this fashion, shows that philological objections are lacking in substance.

31 Especially Garbini, *Il Cantico*; Soggin, *Deboralied*, especially 635f.; Bechmann, *Deboralied* 212f. proposes an origin between the collapse of the Northern Kingdom and that of Judah.

32 Soggin, *Deboralied* 636 regards 5:2–5, 9–11, 13 (23) as a theological reworking of the older "Lay source" (636) text in the Josian period. Nevertheless, the arguments he suggests are not solid or they rather prove the contrary point (see also Axelsson, *The Lord Came* 52). There can really especially not be anything like an "orthodox theology" in the above verses. The complete paralelism, even interweaving the treatment of human and divine activity in the introduction (verses 2ff.), but also the statement regarding God's righteousness (*ṣeḏāqā*) in verse 11 is something completely different from something, e.g. of a deuteronomic nature (thus Soggin, *Deboralied* 636). It is hardly conceivable that it be post-prophetic at all, and it is, in any case, without parallel.

33 See only Jeremias, *Theophanie* 7ff.; Lipínski, *Juges*; Globe, *Judges*; Axelsson, *The Lord Rose* 51f.

34 Lipínski, *Juges*; Soggin, *Deboralied* 628.

35 See especially Jeremias, *Theophanie*.

36 For the identification, most recently Görg, *Seir-Länder* (Lit.).

37 See Axelsson, *The Lord Rose*; Weinfeld, *Tribal League*.

38 Especially Birkeland, *Hebrew ze*; see also Allegro, *Uses*; for a discussion, Jeremias, *Theophanie* 8f. and especially the material in McDaniel, *Deborah* 173.

God also comes in Ps 68:7,[39] but the bringing of rain is the important activity here (verse 10):

> Ps 68:7 O God,[40] *when you went out before your people,*
> *when you marched through the wilderness,*
> 8 *the earth quaked, the heavens poured down rain*
> *at the presence of "YHWH," the "YHWH" of Sinai.*

If there is an ancient epithet for God in Judg 5 and Ps 68, in Deut 33 there is a clear reference to a place name:

> Deut 33:2 *YHWH came from Sinai,*
> *and dawned from Seir upon us;*
> *he shone forth from Mount Paran . . .*[41]

The psalm that frames Moses' benediction (Deut 33:2–5, 26–29), including the addendum in verse 4, is extremely old.[42] Jeremias, for example, regards it as "the oldest text in the Old Testament that speaks of the kingdom of Yahweh."[43] Clearly, this again is the coming of God to his people from his desert region. As difficult as many details of the verses that follow are, the most important consequence of the coming is clear: It guarantees their security in the face of their enemies, the great powers (33:27–29).

"The constituting element in the Sinai tradition is the coming of God," says G. v. Rad[44] on the basis of his study of our texts. Only God does not go to Sinai; he rather comes from there. And this coming effects the salvation of his people. How far should we carry this idea when we interpret other very old texts?

3. There is an important preexilic Mountain of God tradition in 1 Kg 19. Here, the prophet Elijah flees in despair to the Mountain of God and there laments his persecution and the backsliding of the people. The narrative amounts to a three-fold commissioning of Elijah. His assignment was to go and anoint Hazael, Jehu and Elisha as executioners of God's judgment, however, he also received a promise that there would be 7000 left alive in Israel who had not bowed down before Baal (19:15–18).

Only Würthwein disputes that most of this chapter is pre-deuteronomic.[45] He finds only an old fragment of a Mountain of God narrative in verses 8*, 9abβ, 11aα*, 13*. This is a fragment in which there is nothing of importance. Nevertheless, Würthwein's reasons are not at all convincing. It is simply not true that verses 15–18 do not fit with the lament in verse 14.[46] We could hardly find evidence of the deuteronomist

39 For Ps 68, see Jeremias, *Königtum Gottes* 69ff.
40 Perhaps this was originally a YHWH in the Elohist psalter. See especially Jeremias, *Königtum Gottes* 83.
41 We need not discuss the difficult continuation of this text in this place. See most recently Jeremias, *Königtum Gottes* 83.
42 See especially Seeligmann, *A Psalm*.
43 Jeremias, *Königtum Gottes* 82.
44 G. v. Rad, *Hexateuch* 27.
45 Würthwein, *Könige II* 223ff.
46 Thus Würthwein, *Könige II* 226. The other inconsistencies that he lists here are also not convincing.

within God's answer in verses 15–18, because, in the remaining portions of the books of the Kings none of the tasks was completed in the manner described. For example, Elisha as a "tool of God's judgment" is a totally foreign concept, especially in the deuteronomic passages of the Elisha chapter. We should most likely find a deuteronomic reworking of the material in verses 9b, 10.[47] The most convincing solution for the duplication in verse 14, which disturbs the whole flow, is the simplest.[48] Thus we only need deal with a few additions in 19:3b–18 (verses 1–3a should be regarded as a redactional connection to chapter 17f. and verses 19–21 should be seen as independent Elisha narrative). The mention of a covenant (*bᵉrīt*) in verse 14,[49] and possibly also the name of Mount Horeb can be included.[50] Frequently, verses 15b–17 is regarded as a redaction stratum,[51] but this is unlikely. There is hardly a connection here with the composition of a pre-deuteronomic Elijah collection. They are ill-suited to compare with the texts that are most like them in contents: 1 Kg 19:19–21; 2 Kg 8:7–15; 9:1–6; 10–13. Furthermore, the alleged counterpart to verse 18 is not there.[52] On the contrary, verses 15–17 as well as 18 are an inadequate answer for the lament over the backsliding and persecution. Thus 1 Kg 19 demonstrates itself to represent, at root, a pre-deuteronomic tradition, which, as verses 15ff. shows, at least knows the period of Jehu and the Aramean war – thus, it originated at earliest, the end of the ninth century,[53] but probably before 722 BCE.[54]

It has long been thought of critical importance to compare the Sinai pericope with the Horeb narrative.[55] 1 Kg 19 has generally been regarded an imitation of the older story.[56] The similarities are apparent. Nevertheless, Steck already, who even draws a comparison to Ex 32–34 himself, but with reservations, points out the main problem: the shape of the Sinai tradition is unknown to us.[57] Since, in fact, it is not at all certain, whether there were only portions of Ex 19ff. already in existence, perhaps in oral form. We should avoid making comparisons. It is of much more value to interpret this chapter decisively against the background of the only tangible Sinai tradition. In so doing, the structure and the theological content of 1 Kg 19 reveal themselves convincingly.

The prophet flees from a threatening situation to a place where YHWH is in residence, to the mountain from which God saves his people. The situation is quite different from the time of Deborah. Israel's need arises not so much from outside threats, it revolves around Israel's own apostasy. This was the subject of Elijah's lament (verse 14). More

---

47 Smend, *Wort Jahwes* 138f. in conjunction with Wellhausen, *Composition* 280 note 1.
48 Schmoldt, *Begegnung*, would see verses 9–14 as an insertion.
49 Thus, e.g. Steck, *Elia-Erzählungen* 22 note 3, on the basis of the omission in LXX.
50 E.g. Würthwein, *Könige II* 224.
51 Especially, Hentschel, *Eliaerzählungen* 56ff.
52 Thus Hentschel, *Eliaerzählungen* 58f.
53 See Steck, *Elia-Erzählungen* 95; Smend, *Wort Jahwes* 152f.
54 See e.g. Seebass, article on *Elia* 498.
55 Gunkel, *Elia* 23.
56 In addition to the literature listed thus far, see the special studies: Stamm, *Elia*; Carlson, *Elia*; Seybold, *Elia*; Nordheim, *Prophet*; Sekine, *Elias Verzweiflung*; Coote, *Yahweh Recalls* among others.
57 Steck, *Elia-Erzählungen* 112ff.

precisely: If the narrator of 1 Kg 19 had in mind the problems of the Aramean war, the external enemy – like YHWH's intervention – would have been interpreted quite differently. Things follow in sequence: God does not come, Elijah must go to him. Even God's answer to Elijah's lament is not the announcement of a theophany, but rather an assignment for the prophet. God's activity is mediated entirely through human emissaries, especially the prophet Elijah. Elijah does things that previously would have been accomplished by a direct theophany. We might infer that the opposite of the "voice of hovering silence"[58] in verse 12 is part of the traditional manifestation of a divine theophany. In any case, we need not be immediately reminded of Ex 19; the comparison with Judg 5:4f.; Ps 29 as well as the corresponding Baal traditions are sufficient.[59]

If the God from the Mount of God here acted very differently than in the past, the intent is the same. Elijah wanted to save himself and his people with his lament in verse 14. Precisely the same thing happens in Elijah's commissioning. The coming of God into a situation of apostasy can mean only one thing: judgment. This is the first goal of Elijah's assignment, but this judgment brings, at the same time, salvation, as promised in verse 18: There would be a remnant in Israel who did not bow down before Baal, and the people would not fall before the horrible tool of God's judgment. It was spoken in the context of the Aramean war, for comfort for those to whom it was said: YHWH would spare the faithful from his wrath.

We don't need to belabor that 1 Kg 19 is unaware of a connection linking the Mountain of God with justice and law. The apostasy was described without any reference back, it would have been quite obvious. Even if the discussion of covenant in verse 14 belonged to the ancient text, it doesn't mean that God was, as it were, imprisoned on top of the mountain. What the text knows and actualizes in a new time and situation – and to which it gives new significance – is YHWH's connection with this mountain and the certainty that even in great, self-inflicted danger, salvation comes from here.

4. Finally, we can hardly overestimate the importance of the Mountain of God tradition in Ex 3f. Here, Moses, a shepherd for his father-in-law in Midian, accidentally set foot on the Mount of God, and God spoke to him out of the burning bush. He was assigned the task of leading the oppressed people out of Egypt and was honoured by a revelation of the divine name.

We need not go into the complex of questions regarding the literary strata and the tradition-historical provenance of this passage here. For our purpose, it makes no great difference whether we accept the classical division into Yahwist and Elohist versions, with supplementary material and amplifications[60] or the convincing reasons for the idea that the great insertion of Ex 3:1–4 represents an entity anticipating

---

58 Translation after Buber.
59 See e.g. Macholz, *Psalm* 29.
60 See most recently especially Weimar, *Berufung* (for a critique of this Müller, *Puppe*); Kohata, *Yahwist* 15ff.; W. H. Schmidt, *Exodus* 106ff.

4:13–16.[61] It is clear we are dealing with an essentially pre-deuteronomic tradition to which we must always ascribe the combination of Midian, the Mount of God, the Exodus commissioning and the revelation of the divine name.[62] The text as we have it exists clearly in a deuteronomic form and redaction.[63]

In this chapter we raise again G. v. Rad's question: "Why didn't the event in Ex 3 evoke greater amazement? It tells us – as every child knows – that Israel only reached Sinai after considerable wandering, and there – as every reader can sense – they learned something very new."[64] He states correctly that Ex 3f. is "completely self-contained" and is thus in no way open to Ex 19ff.[65] This is why Rad speaks of "two traditions originally completely independent of each other, and representing two very different Sinai traditions in their contents,"[66] only one of which dealt with covenant and law. The separate, peaceful co-existence that scholars accept even today, with only a few exceptions,[67] is itself questionable. In any case, we first must read Ex 3f. in the light of the earliest Sinai tradition, exactly as we read 1 Kg 19. The Mountain of God, somewhere in the desert of Midian, is connected with this God, YHWH, and for that reason, it is the place from which salvation comes. The important assignment to lead the people out of Egypt came after Moses accidentally stumbled upon God and the mountain. The foundational event of the exodus is set in motion from that mountain. The structure is similar to Judg 5. As we know, the Song of Deborah has exact information about other ancient traditions but not the pre-eminent role of the exodus. Instead, the song speaks about the same divine experience – salvation from real threats by very powerful enemies.

Any comparison made between Sinai and Exodus traditions on the basis of Ex 3 is problematic. At the same time clearly both events are not of equal importance. The Mount of God is the starting point for the saving God (or the one whom he has commissioned); it is not simply a stopping place along Israel's route (see from verse 12).[68]

This is how the role of Sinai/Horeb appears, from the activity of Deborah up to the security of which Deut 33 sings, from the commissioning of Moses up to the Aramean war. Sinai is the mountain of salvation in all clearly preexilic traditions because it was the place of the God who saves. *If Torah is attached to Sinai, it is therefore understood to be an act of salvation.* The event on Sinai therefore cannot be regarded as an alternative to the exodus, nor only as a consequence or an aspect of the act of liberation: it gives them their shape. This classification is by no means, indeed, an obvious and simple path.

---

61 For the re-adoption of Wellhausen's thesis (*Composition* 71) see especially Blum, *Pentateuch* 22ff.; Fischer, *Jahwe unser Gott*.
62 Thus, in spite of all reservation, Blum, *Pentateuch* 42.
63 Following H. H. Schmid, *Yahwist* 19–43, we have, e.g. W. H. Schmidt, *Exodus* 137ff.; Blum, *Pentateuch* 26ff.
64 G. v. Rad, *Moseerzählung* 194.
65 G. v. Rad, *Moseerzählung* 194.
66 G. v. Rad, *Moseerzählung* 197.
67 See especially Levin, *Dekalog*.
68 See below p. 45.

Between Marah and Shechem: Deuteronomic Statements about the Giving of Torah

If we examine the path of Torah on Mount Sinai, we find a whole series of texts addressing (divine) legislation, but they are not associated with Sinai/Horeb. On the contrary, they are associated with very different locations. If we look more closely, there is an astonishing array of statements, according to which Israel received law and instruction at various times and places. There are even different people who take part in the action. Because we have read these texts out of the obvious presupposition of a dominant, ancient Sinai tradition, it has only been since the work of Booij that their significance has been recognized.[69] The breadth of these concepts is especially amazing, because they all belong within the sphere of deuteronomism, and most of them cannot be assigned to the preexilic period. There is always a linking of exodus and law in their contents.

1. The theme is sounded already in the first episode after the people were saved at the Red Sea, thus at the very beginning of the period in the desert. After three days of wandering in the desert, Israel encountered, as it is told in Ex 15:22–27, the bitter waters of Mara. When the people complained, God "showed" (*yrh*, hiph.) a piece of wood that would make the water potable (verse 25a). Thereafter, we find another statement astonishingly and incongruously added: "There YHWH made for them a statute and an ordinance (*hōq ūmišpāṭ*) and there he put them to the test" (verse 25). Verse 26, which follows, connects obedience to the voice and observance of the commandments of YHWH with protection from the diseases of Egypt in a conditional promise of blessing. Apparently there are several changes of subject in verse 25. While the "methods" of the wood and the testing probably come from God, we would probably have to identify Moses with the "throwing" and the establishing of the law.[70]

There are two widely held ideas, first, that verses 25, 26 represent an insertion into an older narrative, and second, that this insertion shows deuteronomic language and theology.[71] While that is clear for the phrasing of verse 26, the expression of verse 25b only appears yet in Josh 24:25; Ez 7:10 and 1 Sam 30:25.[72] Though we sometimes think early deuteronomistic groups were responsible for this,[73] Lohfink's detailed study led him to regard the passage as post-priestly, thus representing very late deuteronomism.[74] Following this, Blum now regards verses 25, 26 as one of the latest post-priestly additions to the Pentateuch in conjunction with similar post-priestly additions in Ex 16:4f., 28f.[75]

---

69 We refer especially to Booij, *Mountain*.
70 See Lohfink, *Jahwe, dein Arzt* 19f., especially there, note 21.
71 E.g. Noth, *Exodus* 101; Fritz, *Israel* 7f. (for older literature); Lohfink, *Jahwe, dein Arzt* 29ff.; Blum, *Pentateuch* 154f. On the other hand Margiolot, *Mara* and Robinson, *Symbolism* regard the text as a single unit.
72 See also Ps 81:5. The difference from the normal formulation of the expression in the plural is noteworthy and important. See the overview in Liedke, *Rechtssätze* 13ff.
73 Especially Gese, *Sinaitradition* 32 note 10.
74 Lohfink, *Jahwe, dein Arzt* 32ff.
75 Blum, *Pentateuch* 144. For Ex 16, see especially, Rupprecht, *Mannawunder*.

We can be very sure that the place of a text in the larger compositional context is very important for its interpretation. Already at the very beginning of the way through the wilderness, directly after the miracle at the sea, Moses set up laws and statutes. God's testing and the potential for sickness and health, life and infirmity, are connected to these commandments. How should we interpret this giving of the law before Sinai? It may already be correct to say here,

> Each individual pericope always stands for the whole and expresses the whole. The whole, however is the outline for Israel's order of life; the Pentateuch is "Torah." Then each pericope, if necessary – even before the events on Sinai – can be made transparent on the whole.[76]

Lohfink refers to glosses in the Abraham story (e.g. Gen 26:5) and the priestly laws after Gen 9 for this. Nevertheless, from the priestly perspective, Sinai is combined with the origin of shrine and cult, even though the concern was previously something completely different. If the sense of the deuteronomistic reference to Torah before Sinai ought to be so intended, as Lohfink formulates, they contain an astonishing relativization of the role of the Mountain of God. For this point of view, Sinai has no monopoly on the giving of the law, and this would be even more emphatic, if we compare Ex 15:25b, 26 with other deuteronomistic statements.

Let us compare the last of those mentioned with the first in the narratives narrative context. In the terms that they employ, they are nearly identical. This passage refers to the giving of statute and ordinance ($h\bar{o}q$ $\bar{u}mi\check{s}p\bar{a}t$), but curiously, not through Moses but Joshua. They are not in the desert, but in Shechem, however, it occurs only after the conclusion of the conquest of the land. In Josh 24:25f. "Joshua made a covenant with the people that day, and made statutes and ordinances ($h\bar{o}q$ $\bar{u}mi\check{s}p\bar{a}t$) for them at Shechem. Joshua wrote these words in the book of the Torah of God ($s\bar{e}fer$ $t\bar{o}rat$ '$^el\bar{o}h\bar{i}m$)." Covenant, law and book of Torah – all are connected here as they are with Moses. Sinai has even less of a monopoly here than in Ex 15. As we know, there is no reference to such a mountain in the long list of historical acts in Josh 24. Note the unabashedness with which activities elsewhere ascribed to Moses are here attributed to Joshua at Shechem. He even wrote everything in the book of the Torah of God (verse 26). The wording suggests that this is not to be identified first and foremost as the law mentioned in the verse immediately preceding[77] rather that which preceded it.[78] Some have even tried to identify a "Hexateuch" here.[79] Ex 15 and Josh 24 might form a kind of temporal bracket that frames a period during which law was transmitted.

---

76 Lohfink, *Jahwe, dein Arzt* 70f; similar Diebner, *Exodus* 15; Blum, *Pentateuch* 144f. note 184 ("if we would like, Horeb/Sinai as a place of the transmission of the law, could annex all of the preceding stations in the desert into our final form.'")
77 And the idea that there had at one time been a law book before verse 26 (e.g. Schmitt, *Landtag* 13ff.) is exuberantly speculative.
78 Blum, *Vätergeschichte* 60.
79 Blum, *Vätergeschichte* 60f.

We need not go into discussions of the location and age of Josh 24 here, but we could say that it came from within the deuteronomistic movement and in nowhere else.[80] The obvious difference between an early and a late deuteronomic dating (between pre-Josian and post-priestly) is very great. The later in this period we try to fix the statements in verse 25, the more amazing it is that covenant and law, indeed – even the completion of a written book of Torah – cannot at all be limited to Moses and Sinai.

2. In the temporal and geographical framework of Ex 15:25f. to Josh 24:25 – between Mara and Shechem, the conclusion of the deliverance from Egypt and the conquest of Canaan – there are a whole series of statements with deuteronomistic character. They all connect the transmission of divine wisdom (often concentrating upon the first commandment) with the exodus.

There are first, a few passages from the Book of Jeremiah that speak of the "day" of deliverance and the divine claim that it entailed.

> *Jer 7:22 For in the day that I brought your ancestors out of the land of Egypt, I did not speak to them or command them concerning burnt offering and sacrifices. 23 But this command I gave them, "Obey my voice, and I will be your God, and you shall be my people ...*
> *25 From the day that your ancestors came out of the land of Egypt until this day, I have persistently sent all my servants the prophets to them.*
> *Jer 11:3 You shall say to them, Thus says YHWH, the God of Israel: Cursed be anyone who does not heed the words of this covenant, 4 which I commanded your ancestors when I brought them out of the land of Egypt, from the iron-smelter, saying, Listen to my voice, and do all that I command you. So shall you be my people, and I will be your God.*
> *7 For I solemnly warned your ancestors when I brought them up out of the land of Egypt, warning them persistently, even to this day, saying, Obey my voice.*

Regarding the old covenant, which it contrasts with the new one with Torah inscribed in the heart:

> *Jer 31:32 It will not be like the covenant that I made with their ancestors when I took them by the hand to bring them out of the land of Egypt ...*

Finally, in conjunction with the manumission of the slaves under Zedekiah, a reminder is made of corresponding instructions:

> *Jer 34:13 Thus says YHWH, the God of Israel: I myself made a covenant with your ancestors when I brought them out of the land of Egypt, out of the house of slavery, saying:*
> *14 Every seventh year each of you must set free any Hebrews who have been sold to you and have served you six years ...*

---

80 See above, note 25.

The many shared items are obvious. They all belong to the D stratum of the Book of Jeremiah. In each the proclamation of the divine claim is connected with the "day" of deliverance from Egypt.[81] In the process we see the inter-relationship or even the interchangeability of covenant and Torah. Regarding contents, Jer 7 and 11 speak about the basic commandments: heeding the voice of the saving God is that – this is the point – which what is called the interrelationship of God and people in the covenant formula enables. In contrast, Jer 34 speaks of a single law and in the version we find in Deuteronomy (Deut 15:12ff.). In Jer 31 we find presented a concept of a written Torah that is moreover to be replaced by one written in the heart, in place of one merely written in a book.

Interpretations generally presume there was a tradition regarding the events at Sinai abbreviated by Jeremiah.[82] Nevertheless, this is by no means certain, and in Jer 34 the author would have to have meant Deuteronomy together with its transmission in Moab.[83] The wording of the "day" of deliverance sounds rather more as if it were completely independent of the knowledge of the concluding of a covenant, shaped on a particular day that was itself many days distant from the exodus. The entire content depends on the interrelatedness of Exodus and claim. The act of freeing and commanding belong inseparably, even temporally, together. It is especially clear in Jer 7 and 11 that the announcement of YHWH's claim did not remain tied to this "day." It followed in unbroken continuity from that time until "today" (*'ad hayyōm hazzē*; 7:25; 11:7), from the fathers up to the present and even through the prophets. Simultaneously, all texts proclaim that Israel has not followed, has not listened – and broke the covenant.

Closely related in their basic characteristics, there are two texts with a deuteronomistic[84] character, from the Book of Judges:

In Judg 2:1ff. the emissary of YHWH (*mal'ak-yhwh*) in Bochim says:

> I brought[85] you out of the land of Egypt, and brought you into the land that I had promised to your ancestors. I said, 'I will never break my covenant with you. For your part, do not make a covenant with the inhabitants of this land; tear down their altars.' But you have not obeyed my command . . .

The prohibition against making a covenant with the inhabitants of the land, as we know, has close parallels with passages in Ex 23:34 and

---

81 Individual references to older literature in Thiel, *Jeremia I* 121ff., 143ff.; *Jeremia II* 25ff., 39ff. For the interrelation of these texts Thiel, *Jeremia I* 148ff. as well as – with rather wild literary criticism and far-reaching consequences – Levin, *Verheissung* 75ff.

82 Levin, *Verheissung* is an exception. For him Jer 7:22f. is the beginning of a covenant theology directed against the deuteronomist and concentrating on the first commandment.

83 See e.g. the complex deliberations in Thiel, *Jeremia I* 146ff.

84 For Judg 2:1–5, see the details in Veijola, *Verheissung* 185 note 25; for Judg 6:7–10, see especially Richter, *Bearbeitungen* 97ff. Finally, see Becker, *Richterzeit* 49ff., 144f.

85 The remarkable PK form is more normally connected, as in GK 107b, to the long duration of the event. Would not a penetration of the historical garb in which it is wrapped in a direct address seem more likely (see below, pp. 42f. for Ps 81)?

Deut 7.[86] Nevertheless what is formulated in these texts as occurring at Sinai or in Moab, is, according to the tradition of Judg 2, based on Exodus and demanded by God *after* the conquest of Canaan. "The passage speaks . . . in this way, as if the prohibition had not been given on Sinai, but only after Israel's entry into the land,"[87] thus similar to the way Josh 24 does.

There is an insertion in the Gideon narrative that is closely related. In Judg 6:7–10, God sends a prophet ('*iš nābī*) in response to the people's crying because of Midian. The prophet says:

> *Judg 6:8bff. Thus says YHWH, the God of Israel: I led you out of the house of slavery; 9 and I delivered you from the hand of the Egyptians, and from the hand of all who oppressed you, and drove them out before you and gave you their land; 10 and I said to you, 'I am YHWH your God; you shall not pay reverence to the gods of the Amorites, in whose land you live.' But you have not given heed to my voice.*

Again the speech in substance follows the foundation of Exodus and the giving of the land. The theological juxtaposition is also expressed in the lapse of time: the unusual variation of the first commandment only occurs within Canaan. The rejection follows immediately.

Similarly, God's word in Ps 81 should be located within deuteronomistic language and theology:[88]

> *Ps 81:6 "I relieved your shoulder of the burden;*
>   *your hands were freed from the basket.*
> *7 In distress you called, and I rescued you;*
>   *I answered you in the secret place of thunder;*
>   *I tested you at the waters of Meribah.*
> *8 Hear, O my people, while I admonish you;*
>   *O Israel, if you would but listen to me!*
> *9 There shall be no strange god among you;*
>   *you shall not bow down to a foreign god.*
> *10 I am YHWH your God*
>   *who brought you out of the land of Egypt.*
>   *Open your mouth wide and I will fill it.*
> *11 But my people did not listen to my voice;*
>   *Israel would not submit to me.*
> *12 So I gave them over to their stubborn hearts,*
>   *to follow their own counsels.*

The divine claim (verses 9f.) concentrated in the first commandment is associated with release from Egypt (verses 7, 11). Unfortunately, the text does not permit us to recognize any narrative flow, this is especially true of verse 8. Is the answer from the cloud an allusion to the Sinai tradition or does it connect itself directly to the testing at Meribah (Ex 17:2–7)? Then it would present a close parallel to Ex 15:25b, 26, and the publishing

---

86 See in detail Schmitt, *Frieden*; Otto, *Mazzofest* 203ff.; Halbe, *Privilegrecht*; Becker, *Richterzeit* 51ff.; Achenbach, *Israel* 239ff. see below pp. 124f., 128ff.

87 Schmitt, *Frieden* 39.

88 See Kraus, *Psalms II* 727ff.; Jeremias, *Kultprophetie* 126f. See a comparison with the previously mentioned texts already in Beyerlin, *Rahmen* 28f.; Booij, *Background*.

of the claim would connect with the events at the station in the desert, Meribah.[89]

The combination of historical report and "contemporary" speech is clearer here than the previous texts. The cultic *Sitz im Leben* and the inclusion of divine speech in verse 5b ("I hear a voice I had not known") make it especially clear that everything is designed for a contemporary audience. The emphasis on Israel's apostasy, which characterizes all the deuteronomistic passages mentioned, is simultaneously stimulus and demand for changed behavior. The historic orientation toward the exodus, the wandering in the desert and the conquest of the land, blend together in an indistinguishable unity with contemporary address during the exilic period or later.

Finally, we should also refer here to Ezek 20. The series of events portrayed in this chapter differs markedly from the Pentateuch, but also from deuteronomism.[90] God's foundation-laying speech and the command to put other gods away (verse 7) were already proclaimed in Egypt, and it was there the people rebelled (verses 8f.). Then God made the laws and the statutes known to the people in the desert (verse 11). The sabbath received special mention (verse 12). After the people's disobedience (verse 13), another address was made to the next generation (verses 18ff.). Finally came the speech regarding the giving of the "statutes that were not good and ordinances by which they could not live" (verse 25). Again, the foundational claim of YHWH and the giving of his commandments are connected in time and substance with the sojourn in Egypt, the exodus and the wandering in the desert. Nevertheless, this is not regarded as a one-time act, there is frequent mention of the proclaiming of divine commandments. It is clear that the exilic Ezekiel tradition here still does not presuppose the canonic image of the Pentateuch.[91]

In summary we can say that the deuteronomistic tradition, like that of Ezekiel, did not recognize a connection between Sinai and Torah until into the exilic, perhaps even the postexilic period, but it probably did associate Torah with the exodus and the conquest of the land. When places are named, they span the distance from Egypt to the end of the conquest of the land in Shechem. It is clear that above all, the connection between the exodus and the law is primary. This, however, does not fix it to a specific time and locale. It is more likely that there was wide variation.

3. Deuteronomy remains the most important text here. We cannot overestimate its contribution to the connection of Torah and the Mountain of God but it seems to me that scholars have thus far ignored its importance.

Deuteronomy is promulgated as Moses' speech in Moab across the Jordan, across from Jericho (1:1–5 and elsewhere). We see this in the

---

89 Booij, *Mountain* 14f. and Booij, *Background*.

90 For the similarity and difference from deuteronomism, see Liwak, *Probleme* 155ff.; Pons, *Vocabulaire*; and in general Krüger, *Geschichtskonzepte* 199–281; Sedlmeier, *Studien* 212ff.

91 What the usual interpretation does (Zimmerli, *Ezechiel*; Greenberg, *Ezekiel I* for this passage) is to make Ezek 20 into a kind of parody of earlier concepts (Lust, *Parodie*).

introduction (1:1ff.) and it is presumed throughout the book.[92] While chapters 1–3 are a retrospective of the period since the departure from Horeb, Deut 4f. and 9f. tell of the events at Horeb. There, only the Decalogue, as it appears in Deut 5, was given in the form of direct address from God. It was written by God on stone tablets. At the request of the people (5:28ff.), all of the other instructions were given just to Moses. He was to teach them to Israel (5:31) and make them known before they entered the land.

This picture of events at the mountain of God represents a complete departure from what is depicted in Exodus through Numbers. Not only are the many priestly laws absent, but also absent are the Book of the Covenant and everything else reported in Ex 24. We need, however, to go one step farther. There is no doubt any more that there is a later stratum in Deut 4:5 and 9:7–10:11. These are not part of Deuteronomy's oldest strata.[93] The older Deuteronomy would understand itself simply as the report to the people of the laws given to the people by God in Moab through Moses, before they conquered the land. While the view back toward the exodus is fundamental and constitutive for deuteronomic theology, this is not true of Horeb. They appear only in a small number of later texts.

Thus, the older Deuteronomy understands itself as the decisive report of God's laws – indeed the first and only report. If something similar happened on Horeb, it is either unknown or it is consciously ignored (or corrected). For the following reasons this is conceivably not true of Deuteronomy's older strata. If those who were responsible for locating the address in the land east of the Jordan were acquainted with a correlation of the legal tradition and Sinai or Horeb, why did they settle so far from there? If the speech was delivered on the traditional mountain from which God came or where he was present, a work like Deuteronomy could not be placed anywhere else. Any connection of Horeb with the covenant or the law must make Deuteronomy into what its name suggests: the second law, something secondary and subordinate. Still, he obviously intends it to be regarded as the one Torah of God (4:44 and elsewhere).

We can conclude there was no real tradition connecting the Mount of God with covenant and law known to Deuteronomy's authors because they locate Moses' speech east of the Jordan. Deut 5 and 9:7–10:11 are clearly a later arrangement. The Decalogue is placed there and the remainder of Deuteronomy is made subordinate to it. We cannot say more clearly than the statement in 5:22, that God did not continue to speak ($w^e l\bar{o}$ ' $y\bar{a}s\bar{a}f$), that this is a reaction to other ideas and is intended to correct them. That is a critique of another notion. It clearly argues against the idea that something else might claim to have been given by God on Horeb. The theological weight of Deuteronomy also hinges upon it. There is no other law directly transmitted by God casting a shadow over it.

92 Thus with Lohfink, *Kerygmata* 90.
93 See the summary of previous discussion in Preuss, *Deuteronomium* 48ff. For Deut 4, see most recently Knapp, *Deuteronomium* 4; for Deut 5, see Brekelmans, *Deuteronomy* 5; for Deut 9f., see Hossfeld, *Dekalog* 147ff.; in general see also Achenbach, *Israel*.

The breadth of the variations in the laws in the deuteronomic texts between Marah and Shechem (from the miracle at the sea to the conquest of the land) suggests that Moses' speech in Deuteronomy positions itself about in the middle. The speech was delivered after the desert and the first part of the actual conquest and before crossing the river. For deuteronomism this orientation did not imply a final fixing that excluded other possibilities. When did this orientation of Deuteronomy take place? This is not dependent upon the dating of Deuteronomy, but rather – especially – on whether we accept an original Josian law that as yet had not been historicized in this way.[94] If we can accept the historical vesture of Deuteronomy in Moses' speech, mainly in conjunction with its incorporation into a deuteronomic history, what we said above applies. We would then probably have to date it in the exilic period.

Theses on the Development of the Sinai Pericope

We will attempt to sketch the origin of the Sinai pericope beginning with traditions of the Mount of God and traditions of the place where divine commandments were given. Such clear, tradition-historical evidence as is offered here represents a more secure basis for relative ascription and absolute classification of the many strata and fragments of the Sinai text than the usual linguistic observations. Thus far, linguistic observations have given us few generally convincing solutions. Nevertheless, what follows is in no way a new literary analysis. The following four theses only list the most important steps and phases of the connection of the Mountain of God and God's law.

1. *Do not expect an old, pre-deuteronomistic and pre-prophetic narrative of Israel's stay at the Mount of God to accompany a report of divine instructions.*

This is nothing at all new. It simply restates the work of many scholars.[95] It may have started with a narrative of those who had been saved staying at the mountain, perhaps associated with Ex 3:12. It is doubtful whether anything apart from Ex 18 can be extracted from the confusion of strata in Ex 19. Nor should we expect to find communion with God on his mountain as in the unusual 24:9–11, often regarded the centerpoint of an ancient Sinai pericope.[96] This supports what recent scholars have demonstrated regarding Ex 24: The closest parallels, linguistically as well as substantively, are in the exilic Ezekiel texts.[97]

Let us look briefly at a text that is surely pre-deuteronomic, Ex 18. We will discuss its legal-historical significance later.[98] The first half of the chapter has frequently been regarded a narrative resolution of the promise in 3:12.[99] It is precisely this chapter, in addition to Deuteronomy,

94 Thus e.g. Lofink, *Kerygmata* 90–92; Levin, *Verheissung* 85f., see also below p. 209, note 43.
95 See above pp. 28ff.
96 Especially, Perlitt, *Bundestheologie* 181ff.
97 See especially, Rupprecht, *Ex 24*; see also Welten, *Vernichten* 137ff. For an understanding of Ex 24:10 we refer especially to Ez 1:26ff.; 8:2f.; 10:1.
98 See below pp. 82ff.
99 Kessler, *Querverweise* 188f., 229; Childs, *Exodus* 327; for a discussion, see Blum, *Pentateuch* 155ff.

however, which is the strongest argument against an earlier tradition of a divine transmission of law on the Mount of God. Indeed, 18:13–26 is completely devoted to Moses' legal activities. Here, Moses inquired of God and then announced God's laws to the people (*'et ḥuqqē hā'ᵉlōhīm we wᵉ 'et-tōrōtāw*, verse 16). The text, however, revolves around the problem of Moses' overburdening and the consequent need for an entirely new legal system. This problem is not resolved by Moses or God himself in the context of the inquiries (18:15,19). It was the advice of a non-Israelite, Midianite priest who wanted redress. If there had been an ancient, traditional connection between the Mount of God and God's law, if the Mount of God was associated with legal instruction, this would have been senseless and incomprehensible. There is an awareness of Moses' role within the legal system, and inquiry of God in legal matters is part of this. There is, however, no fundamental dependence upon the Mount of God where the story takes place. As many texts show, the mountain and the Midianites are what belong together.[100] Ex 18 must be from a time when the extensive legal system in Israel (and nothing less)[101] could only find its legitimation where it would later be disqualified, a heathen priest.

References to the lack of any "ancient" connection between divine law and the Mount of God are intensified in Ex 18. At the same time and for the same reasons, this chapter should be regarded as the heart and beginning of such a connection. Both are fundamental and diametrical opposites of the whole Sinai pericope, but they are connected: An important, new legal organization came into being at the Mount of God. Together with Moses' authority to make legal decisions, and the practice of asking God for legal decisions, we have a starting point that we will discuss later.

2. We cannot assume the connection of the Mount of God and divine law came into existence within deuteronomistic theology or that it was merely shaped by it.

This attacks one of the fundamental assumptions dominating modern thinking. The general study of pre-deuteronomic strata in Ex 19–24, 32–34 is nearly synonymous with the idea that what is important here comes from deuteronomistic theology and language. In their evaluation, investigation and method, various studies are otherwise in general agreement on this point.[102] Analysis shows many deuteronomistic strata in the Book of the Covenant and the Sinai pericope especially clearly. Even though texts discussed thus far cannot refute such ideas, the basic significance of Deuteronomy, the ease with which legislation is discussed before and after Sinai, and especially, the disputation of a continued divine address at the Mount of God in Deut 5:22 suggest caution and perhaps also encourage new study of the Sinai pericope.

100 Already, Gunneweg, *Midian* in summary. W. H. Schmidt, *Exodus, Sinai und Moses* 110ff.
101 Knierim, *Exodus 18*; see also below pp. 85f.
102 Perlitt, *Bundestheologie*; Zenger, *Sinaitheophanie*; Hossfeld, *Dekalog*; Mittmann, *Deuteronomium*; Levin, *Dekalog*; Vermelen, *Sections*; Renaud, *La Théophanie* and others.

No one disputes the importance for the Sinai pericope of the deuteronomistic texts. 19:3ff., just like the central act concluding a covenant in 24:3–8, is thoroughly shaped by deuteronomism. 24:3 presupposes a relation to the Book of the Covenant which comes before. We should also note the basic similarity of the Decalogue and the Book of the Covenant to deuteronomic/deuteronomistic language and theology. We do not quarrel with the existence and the importance of such passages, but the tradition-historical evidence – in my opinion – gives occasion to discuss again the assumed *sequence* of the strata.

3. *Deuteronomistic shaping of the Sinai pericope should most probably be interpreted as a reaction to the priestly influence that preceded it.*

The rarely examined starting point for nearly all analyses of the Sinai pericope is the idea that non-priestly portions of Ex 19–24, 32–34 might themselves be pre-priestly or in any case, at least independent of the priestly portions.[103] Priestly writings had already discovered most of these portions or at least the majority of their texts and consequently amplified or corrected them. This, however, can no longer be simply assumed. There are enough places where deuteronomistic formulations rely upon and extend priestly work. This is the case in Ex 16 (verses 4f., 28).[104] Ex 15:25b also presupposes priestly language.[105] Precisely in the Sinai pericope, the idea of a closed pre-priestly D composition leads to difficulties and unconvincing literary-critical cuts.[106] Since for both textual areas we must reckon on a long-term, many-faceted growth, a decidedly joint, simultaneous, reciprocal relationship of deuteronomistic and priestly theology from the period of the exile until the phase of the completion of the Pentateuch is a possibility. Overt discrepancies in the chapters Ex 19 and 24 indicate conflicts of the kind we encounter elsewhere with brutal clarity (especially Num 16), and they seem to stem from differences within the groups that together produced Torah during the postexilic period.[107] They are the differences between the deuteronomistic and priestly circles together with their respective theologies.

It is not my intention to go into a detailed analysis of the Sinai texts here, and it is unlikely whether we could extract ourselves from the morass of arbitrary assumptions. I will mention a few ideas evoked by the tradition-historical evidence, supported by the literary structures, and not in fundamental contradiction to them. With respect to the literary structure we notice two things, which permit us to infer a "precursor" to the priestly texts before the essentially deuteronomistic passages in

---

103 It is remarkable how the idea of very clearly differentiated strata in *dtr* as well as in the passages with a priestly character is regarded as a basic sequence of the two types of strata.
104 See Rupprecht, *Mannawunder.*
105 Thus Lohfink, *Jahwe, dein Arzt*; and above pp. 38f.
106 Thus Blum, *Pentateuch*, who must throw out from his D composition many texts that seem relatively old and refer to the very latest of the post-priestly reactions (e.g. Ex 18, 34:10ff., the malak texts, further in Ex 33, etc.). It is problematic that the greatest interruption and contradiction is transferred to the last redactional stratum and a remote analogy to the inclination of source models to shift out everything that is not in two or three parallel levels, disposing of them in redactional strata that cannot be explained.
107 Most recently Blum, *Pentateuch* 333f. See also below pp. 357ff.

chapters 19–24. The one is the datum in 19:1f., a priestly formulation creating a basic demarcation from the pre-deuteronomistic tradition of chapter 18. Only in this way is it possible to have completely different scenes in chapters 18 and 19ff.[108] The other is the ring composition in Ex 32–34 of the priestly shrine texts. Do not the instructions to Moses in Ex 25–31 to build a shrine presume that their carrying out in Ex 35ff. is separated from them by the remarkable events in 32–34?[109] We cannot really imagine a text in which instructions and their fulfillment simply follow each other without some kind of break. The discussion referred repeatedly to clear, if also antithetical, references to 32–34:[110] While Moses was on the mountain learning all about the divinely ordained cultic place, the people, with Aaron, were constructing their own. This is reminiscent of the Aaronic priests of Ex 29 and the Levites of Ex 32 who built very different tent shrines – the priestly and the one in Ex 33, both of them nevertheless bearing the same name ('ōhel mō'ēd).

The cultic instructions in Ex 34:11ff. show that, as a whole, chapters 32–34 are concerned with correct worship, and the adjoining priestly texts could connect positively or negatively. It is nevertheless doubtful whether we should interpret the priestly conception, in which all the emphasis is laid upon the establishment of true worship, as an extrapolation and interpretation of a legal document which preceded it.[111] It is more likely that in Ex 32–34 the redactor had an older, preexilic tradition in which there was already a concern for the matter of the correct YHWH cult. The priestly document had to set everything in the presence of the holy God. This would have suggested the idea of going back to the mountain from which God had at one time come. From there he could move to the shrine (Ex 40:34). Much evidence can be convincingly explained in this way.

This also applies to the lack of a conception of covenant in the priestly texts, which has always been surprising.[112] Such a concept would only have come overtly into the Sinai pericope in Ex 19 and 24 late, post-

---

108 Zenger, *Sinaitheophanie* 55ff. shows that 19:1, 2a are to be taken as a unity. And thus both mentions of Sinai belong to P. The sentence [they] "camped in the wilderness" that disputes P, does not present evidence; the arguments are not convincing. Already in verse 3b, however, there is the start of the passage that is clearly affected by *dtr*. We would really need to keep in front of our eyes – by not questioning anything – the conception of a source model in order to be able to construct the hypothesis of a pre-priestly and pre-deuteronomic Sinai pericope on the slender fragment in 19:2b, 3a (whereby a separation from 3a and 3b is indeed possible but not very compelling, see Zenger, *Sinaitheophanie* 57). And then, with what does it connect? With Ex 18? Hardly. If that were true the arrival at an especially important mountain would not have been described again. In short, the new scene, which separates itself from chapter 18, is opened with the P text 19:1, 2a. And even Deuteronomy presumes this opening, nothing else is available.

109 We refrain completely here from attempting a discussion of the complex questions of the development of the P texts, the frequently discussed older stratum of 25–31, etc. (see Fritz, *Tempel* 113ff.; Utzschneider, *Heiligtum* and most recently Steins, *Struktur*).

110 Most recently Utzschneider, *Heiligtum* 82f., 86f.; especially Blum, *Pentateuch* 359, 333f.

111 Thus especially Utzschneider, *Heiligtum* 278 and elsewhere. For P, see below pp. 277ff.

112 N.B. – Zimmerli, *Sinaibund*.

priestly. Conversely, the remarkable absence of a framework in non-priestly texts[113] could perhaps best be explained by the fact that in general they presuppose them. In my judgment, there is no substantive reason from tradition-historical evidence capable of countering the theory – in conjunction with the observably older tradition in Ex 32–34 – that it was the priestly document that made Sinai what it is today: the place where cult and law were established. It is then no wonder that it is not the deuteronomic texts but the priestly that present the great number of Sinai laws contained from Ex 35 to Num 10. If, however, we presume the priority of portions of the priestly document in this way,[114] how do we explain the shaping of the idea of the Mount of God through divine law by the deuteronomist?

4. *The shift of emphasis from cult to law is connected with development during the Persian period and the shaping of the Pentateuch to the legal basis of Persian-period Judaism.*

In the first postexilic period all emphasis was on rebuilding of the temple and its cult (Hag; Zech; Ez 1–6), and the priestly shrine texts are inseparable from these.[115] The concept of a cult commanded and ordained by God rather than inaugurated by a king, with temple worship carried on by the people and priests, became the foundation of postexilic Judaism. If social and legal questions could be regarded as a part of the cultic duties, anticipating a position similar to that of Trito-Isaiah, the accent would nevertheless shift noticeably during the Ezra-Nehemiah period. Here concern is for the political and legal autonomy of Judaism (or the province of Judah) in the framework of the Persian empire.[116]

It is to be expected that such an important thematic shift would be reflected in the texts. The connection of Deuteronomy with the Tetrateuch-becoming-the-Pentateuch is an especially important factor. Such an entity is not yet presupposed in Deut 1–3, 4, 5, 9f. At latest, when it came into existence, it had become absolutely essential that both conceptions were harmonized with each other at least roughly. At latest, now the Decalogue stood at the head of all laws, as Deuteronomy presupposes. Its very loose insertion into Ex 20 suggests a very late redaction.[117] The insertion should most probably be understood in a similar temporal and material context. Placed before the priestly material, it functions as a kind of place marker for the Deuteronomy bound to Moab. It could serve as a foundation for the act of obedience in Ex 24:3ff. Only with this late development could Sinai become the centre of the deuteronomic as well as the priestly Pentateuch. Only from that moment on was the event formulated here, which had to appear in the

---

113 Most recently, see Blum, *Pentateuch* 137.
114 The model that is at the basis of these theses presumes that there was a long period during which there was a simultaneous, mutual coexistence of D and P statements and accents in a larger text. In the meanwhile, the generally accepted phenomena of the P texts affecting the D as well as P reacting to D could be explained in this manner. This agrees especially with the historical situation that is generally accepted for the postexilic period.
115 See Utzschneider, *Heiligtum*; Blum, *Pentateuch*.
116 See Crüsemann, *Perserzeit*, as well as below pp. 277ff.
117 See below pp. 351ff.

chain of the canonic *Heilsgeschichte*, as Neh 9 attests. The omission of Sinai as late as the postexilic credo was the starting point of our analysis. What else could really explain the application represented here?

Words on a Tablet instead of the Calf Image: The Origin of Sinai Law

Since Goethe, the question, "What was on the stone tablets?" has been an important topic for the study of events on Sinai and the origin of the law.[118] The question is still of great importance today. Of course, the discussion has changed from what it was in his day. For a long time Ex 32 and its image of the golden calf seemed an oddity in the Pentateuch narrative,[119] because it was clearly associated with Northern Kingdom shrines beginning at the time of Jereboam I – a source, like the Yahwist, but dated much earlier. This reference made the heart of this chapter an Archimedean point in the Sinai debates. Discussions have caused Ex 32–34 to emerge as a pre-priestly core around which everything else developed. We now need to support this in detail, especially in view of the question about the stone tablets and their contents.

1. Like nothing else, the insertion of verses 7–14 demonstrates clearly that Ex 32 is essentially pre-deuteronomic.[120] Moses discovers again for himself (verses 19ff.) what God tells him at the beginning of the chapter. If otherwise the chapter is about punishment of the guilty in regard to the apostasy with the calf image (verse 33) and with a plague upon the people, but especially continued relations with God, apparently verses 7–14 are concerned with the possibility of total annihilation (verses 10, 12).

The indissoluble narrative unity of chapters 32 and 34 is extremely important. Recent studies have again dealt with the old separation of 32 and 34, based on the ascription of chapter 34 to the Yahwist.[121] Nevertheless, Perlitt's[122] reasons for the unity of chapters 32 and 34 need not be rehearsed here. There has since been detailed evidence showing a literary seam in the critical spot, between 34:8 and 9.[123] Furthermore, the generally concise coherence of the entire complex of Ex 32–34 has already been described in detail many times.[124] Since our focus is the investigation of the (at first literary) place of 34:11ff., it is important that 32 and 34 form an indissoluble unity dealing with sin and forgiveness. We can allow to

118 Goethe, *Was stand*; for this, see e.g. Galling, *Goethe*; Eissfeldt, *Goethes Beurteilung*; Schottroff, *Goethe*.
119 Noth, *Pentateuch* 160.
120 Noth, *Pentateuch* 33 note 113 and many others. For Ex 32:7–14, see Aurelius, *Fürbitter* 41ff. For Vermeylen's thesis that that earliest stratum was deuteronomic (exactly like three other strata), see Blum, *Pentateuch* 73f. note 127.
121 Zenger, *Sinaitheophanie* 227f.; Wilms, *Bundesbuch* 146ff.; Valentin, *Aaron* 214 (note however the careful-unsure demarcation that most people don't bother to discuss); Dohmen, *Bilderverbot*, 66ff.; Weimar, *Kalb*; Aurelius, *Fürbitter* 58ff.
122 Perlitt, *Bundetheologie* 203ff.
123 Walkenhorst, *Mose*.
124 Coats, *Loyal Opposition*; Davies, *Rebellion*; Moberly, *At the Mountain*; in addition to Blum, *Pentateuch* 54ff.

remain unresolved here, how much of chapter 33 we must regard as part of a pre-deuteronomistic narrative and consequently how long the conversation between God and Moses was between the first plea for forgiveness in 32:32 and the repetition in 34:9 as this appeared in the original narrative.[125]

Discussions of 34:11ff. and the tablet motif are rather important. For that reason it might be not too convincing to separate chapter 32 from 34. The problem of sin and forgiveness in 32:34 is not at all resolved.[126] If there is a resumption, narrative logic says we should expect that the tablet motif, which first ended in 32:19 with the destruction of the first tablets, has been taken up again. This then also happened in 34:1ff. If the destruction of the first tablets was an expression of wrath, it also meant the end of God's benefit as symbolized by the tablets, then there could be no forgiveness without renewal of the tablets.

The questions of what was on the second tablets, and whether they are connected with the commandments given in 32:11–26, are answered in a wide variety of ways. In my opinion, we ought to begin with the clear context in verses 26–28. There is no reason in the text to suspect a literary seam. The command is given to write down all the things that God just said, and Moses does this. The many attempts suggesting divisions come from the larger context, especially the parallel in Deuteronomy, and two problems in the text will have to be ignored entirely here. One is the disagreement between 34:1, where God himself would write, as he had on the first tablets (32:15f.), and 34:27f. where Moses wrote. The other is in 34:28, that this was "the ten words" ("$\check{a}\check{s}\acute{e}ret\ hadd^e$-$b\bar{a}r\hat{i}m$"). Verses 1 and 28 are a clear compromise with the description in Deuteronomy or the reference to the Decalogue in Ex 20. All we need is a change of single verb form in 34:1 ($w^e k\bar{a}tabt\bar{a}$ instead of $w^e k\bar{a}tabt\hat{i}$). Furthermore, verse 28 is an obvious emendation pointing back. From Goethe, who looked for a Decalogue in 34:11–26 because of verse 28, to Blum, who in working on his D composition found reference to Ex 20 and thus lifted out 34:12–26 declaring it post-deuteronomist,[127] the problems are in these two statements, plus the fact that scholars have had some success reconciling Ex 34 with Deuteronomy and the Decalogue.

Apart from these two theories of textual alteration in Ex 34:1, 28, in the context of Pentateuch redaction nothing else is necessary; because a report of what first God, then later Moses, wrote on the tablets is in the narrative context of 32–34 logical and necessary. Chapters 32–34 do not presuppose previous communication to the people of, for example, commandments. First there is reference back to previous revelation, and

---

125 See especially, Blum, *Pentateuch* 59. He sets up a working hypothesis in the context of the reconstruction of the D composition for Ex 32–34 that "diachronically our main text of Ex 32–34 owes its shape in chapter 32 to an editorial extension, in contrast in chapter 33f. to a (more or less free) reorganization and/or radical re-shaping (of the tradition)" (75).

126 Aurelius, *Fürbitter* 60 regards Ex 32:34 as the full closure of a narrative. Nevertheless, the destruction of the tablets is so potent an argument that it must be taken up again narratively in the context of the forgiveness. If we wanted to construct a stratum of Ex 32 without the tablets, the motive for the absence of Moses is also missing.

127 Blum, *Pentateuch* 67ff.

only as an addendum to 32:8. If the text on the tablets had already been given, and thus already known to the people, the destruction of the tablets would only have been of marginal importance. Even without them the people would have known God's will. The destruction of the tablets raises the fundamental question of God's accessibility to Israel. That is why 32:34, leading the people from the mountain, does not resolve the problem. As long as the people do not know God's will, they are unable to restrain him and escape future catastrophe. The narrative unity of 32–34 requires disclosure of the contents of the tablets as well as the renewal of the destroyed tablets, and there are no literary-critical reasons that could justify the dissolution of this clear structure.

When did this narrative originate? We must begin with the association of the calf image and the shrines of Jeroboam I, the state shrines of the Northern Kingdom. This is evidence for the identification of Ex 32:4 with 1 Kg 12:28. We are dealing with these sins and their forgiveness. Inevitably we arrive at the situation after 722 BCE, the end of the Northern Kingdom and the destruction of the cultic sites. There was, of course, criticism of the images from at least the time of Hosea (Hos 8:4ff., 10:5f., 13:2), but before 722 it could be a theology which regarded this state cult as an expression of Israel's sin. It was only concerned with ending the calf cult or its consequences, not our problem here: Was there to be a future with YHWH and what shape would it take? If this narrative were about sin and the future of the former Northern Kingdom, there must be good reason to date it in the time of Josiah a whole century later.[128] The insertion of 32:7–14 shows that chapter 32 is pre-deuteronomistic, and like chapter 34, it is also un-deuteronomistic. Later we will discuss in greater detail the fact that 34:11–26, in language as well as content, contains a completely pre-deuteronomistic version of the command-ments.[129] There are otherwise only a few terms or phrases typical of deuteronomistic speech,[130] which establishes neither form nor content. This could have happened in the context of a late redaction.[131] We must pay particular attention to the completely un-deuteronomistic character of 34:11–26. There is no reason to isolate the narrative from its historical context and the place where it seems to belong. Since the question of Israel's future with its God must have been raised shortly after 722, this must be a narrative from the last decades of the eighth century.[132]

This is the only way we can decipher the details of this text. While Moses is on the mountain to receive the tablets with God's instructions – the beginning of the narrative is missing and perhaps is inserted in 24:12ff., 31:18 – Aaron and the people complete construction of the calf image. This sin describes the state cult of the Northern Kingdom as practiced by priests and people. God punished the people for their action,

---

128 Thus Perlitt, *Bundestheologie* 211f. and elsewhere.
129 See below pp. 115ff.
130 Thus, for example, the usage "stiff-necked people" (34:9 and already 32:9, 33:3).
131 Thus Blum, *Pentateuch* 75.
132 This fixing is in very close proximity to that of a Yahwistic redaction at the end of the eighth century, to which Zenger, *Sinaitheophanie* 164f. traces back the first addition of a legal text, namely that of the right of privilege in 34:11ff., in the Sinai pericope. See also Weimar, *Kalb* 147f. and elsewhere. Nevertheless, the method-ological presuppositions as well as the literary demarcations are different.

according to 32:25, a verse that oversteps the bounds of narrative fiction. The people must drink the bitter water of their action (32:20), in other words their consequences. Against this backdrop, the concern between God and Moses is now whether God would continue his relation with his people and how he would do it.

The forgiveness consists of two acts each called "covenant" (*b*ᵉ*rīt*). God obligates himself to miraculous deeds, the like of which had never been seen before. In its historical context this could only refer to a hoped-for political-military resumption of conditions before 722. The "people among whom you live" (verse 10) reveals the fiction and can only be understood in a situation where Israel is among a foreign people, hardly before 722. In the second, Israel is obligated to observe what is written on the tablets (verse 27).

The contrast, like the connection of calf image and stone tablets, arises especially from the contents, because in 34:11 the central concern is with worship and cult, as in the "cultic Decalogue." The alternative is not between calf-cult and ethics, calf-cult and law, but rather a cult that is wrong or right, that which is divinely commanded or that which is self-conceived. Forgiveness expresses itself in the renewal of the tablets on which the cult desired by God was proclaimed, giving Israel a possible future with this God. The cult-commandments give the stipulations for the possible presence of God in Israel.

This narrative is the first connecting the Mount of God with the proclamation of divine instructions. What was the reason and occasion for this? Why did a narrative dealing substantively with the question of Israel's future with YHWH at the end of the eighth century take place in the early period and at this mountain? It could hardly have been the calf image that led to this: the calf cult was already associated with the exodus in 1 Kg 12:28, and it is perhaps an adequate description of the state cult in the Northern Kingdom, but the images were not there connected with Moses and certainly not with Sinai. There is no evidence that they were historicized in this way. From the earlier Mount of God tradition this deals more with the central problem which led to the Mount of God: Israel's salvation. In spite of the guilt that led to the catastrophe, they might survive Assyrian rule. In short, as with Deborah (Judg 5) or Elijah (1 Kg 19), this is the salvation, traditionally coming from this mountain. Instead of sending a prophet to the mountain, there is a description of Israel's stay at the mountain. There may have been other points of inducement, for example, a previous association of Moses with the tablet motif or even the calf image, or something similar. There is, however, no mention of this. It is very important that saving forgiveness takes the form of the renewal of the tablets and the possibility to revere this God according to his will. The words on the tablets are the form in which God's salvation appeared after the end of the Northern Kingdom.

2. Modern scholars are in fundamental agreement that there were no stone tablets from Sinai, especially not those of Ex 34. Contemporary explanations[133] of the tablets range from understanding them as

---

133 See the collection in Dohmen, *Tafeln* 10ff. note 6 and already Zenger, *Ps 87*.

geological peculiarities[134] through suggestions that they are royal contracts,[135] coronation oracles,[136] citizenship lists,[137] or purely theoretical constructions.[138] Recently Dohmen suggested that they were a public certification of activities on Sinai.[139] Now any study of historical reality must begin with the narrative location in which it appears. This is the case with the story in Ex 32–34 and the alternative of stone tablets or calf image.

The next question, "What historically was behind the motif of the stone tablets?" must consider two things: the unlikelihood that neither narrator nor listeners could answer the simplest question: "Where were they?" The calf cult was a reality in Israel and there were things connecting back to Moses, like the ark or the bronze snake (Num 21; 2 Kg 18:3) during the monarchic period. According to Deuteronomy, the tablets were put into the ark, but that did not mean that they were simply gone, at least, not as long as there was still an ark or the memory of it. This is demonstrably true until the first postexilic period (Hag 2:3). With the dominance of overt etiological thinking, for which there is much attestation during the Old Testament period, this could not be something purely symbolic. We must deal with the questions that are raised, particularly if we are inclined toward an exilic origin of the narrative. Ex 34:11 is not a description of miraculous activity, as in Deut 9. The second tablets are inscribed by Moses (Ex 34:28) and are thus entirely capable of being recorded, but where are they? The other presumption is the high probability that in Ex 34:11ff. the writer is quoting another independent, much older document. The text was not formulated for this document. For this reason it includes, even in the first half, a prohibition of covenants with those who lived in the land, not even the narrative world of Ex 32–34. Everything suggests a document produced for the narrative or only slightly altered.[140]

There is an additional, basically incomprehensible element: the two-part form of the tablets. Why are there two tablets and not one or three? The enduring attempt to divide the Decalogue into two halves and the

---

134 Lehming, *Versuch* 37.
135 Maier, *Urim* 22ff.
136 Nielsen, *Gebote* 33 note 3.
137 Zenger, *Ps* 87.
138 Thus Perlitt, *Bundestheologie* 210f.; Loretz, *Gesetztafeln*.
139 Dohmen, *Bilderverbot* 132ff. and *Tafeln* 19ff. He refers to Assyrian (sales!) documents that are called *ṭuppu dannutu*. Correspondingly, the expression used in 24:12, 31:18 "tablets of stone" (*lūḥōt ében*) may refer to a certain form of publication of a legal document. Setting aside the questionable literary foundation, the thesis does not stand because *ṭuppu dannutu* means a legitimate, in others words – binding – document (CAD III 94f. see dannu: binding document, valid declaration). Dohmen would conclude, on the one hand, on the basis of a comparison of such documents with stone border markers (*Bilderverbot* 135f.), and on the other hand, on the basis of an analogy between the stone documents with stoney hearts and the like (*Bilderverbot* 136 note 211) that there is something that corresponds to this in Hebrew – tablets of stone (*lūḥōt ében*). Neither works. Furthermore, the notion of tablets without text is very questionable. In short, for that which has much archaeological attestation for the royal period, namely writing on relatively small, portable stones is evaded with great pomp and problematic conclusions. Why indeed!
140 See below pp. 115ff.

clear lack of success in so doing only support the idea that this was not originally part of the Decalogue. Both complete Deuteronomy or certain strata of it primarily and secondarily, but it would be remarkable to think that the number two came from an anonymous copyist's error.[141]

The story is of two portable stone tablets, on which is written the will of God regarding correct worship as it was to be carried out in the place of the state calf cult shortly after the end of the Northern Kingdom. Historically, the medium is no problem. There are analogies from the Gezer Calendar all the way to the Moabite Stone.[142] Legal documents were published similarly, as well as calendars, as the Gezer Calendar shows. Remains of such stone inscriptions have been found in Samaria and Jerusalem.[143] Thus, there is no real reason to doubt that such tablets actually existed in the Northern Kingdom, and that their contents were basic rules for worship.

The story has a convincing narrative profile first, because of the belief that there such tablets really existed in the Northern Kingdom. It is not vital whether or not there was *one* text on two tablets, or whether the two tablets were, for example, in Bethel and Dan or Bethel and Samaria. The contrast in narrative form of calf cult and written, divine, cultic instructions corresponds exactly with what Hosea shows us about the last days of the Northern Kingdom (especially Hosea 8:12).[144] The narratively described act of forgiveness by God, which opened a new future for Israel (Ex 34:10) was why these instructions continued to be of value.

We can only make a good guess that tablets of this kind existed until the end of the Northern Kingdom, and that they are behind the *torot* of Hos 8:12 like the tablets of Sinai, and that the text of Ex 34:12ff. or a variation thereof was written on them. Only archaeology will be able to tell us the answers.

Summary: How and Why Torah Came to Sinai

1. To summarize: we note the following steps from Torah to Sinai:

  – In the earliest documents, Sinai is the mountain from which God comes to save his people (Judg 5:4f.). It was from here that the exodus was initiated (Ex 3) and punishment as well as rescue were promulgated until into the period of the Aramean war (1 Kg 19).

  – Ancient narratives about Israel's sojourn at this mountain cannot be reconstructed on the basis of Ex 19ff. The worship of God proclaimed

---

141 Dohmen, *Tafeln* proposes that originally there was a "plurality of form" (*Bilderverbot* 137f.), from which an early Deuteronomistic redactor made a numeric plural in Deut 9 (*lūḥōt ha-ʾᵃbanim*), which then led to the number two in a later Deuteronomist stratum in Deut 9. Apart from the questionable literary criticism, transforming the origin of potent motifs into a series of mis-understandings by extremely stupid redactors (and thus, e.g. renouncing the power of tradition) is hardly convincing.

142 For the Gezer Calendar, see the illustrations in AOB 609; *Inscriptions Reveal* No. 8. For the Moabite Stone, see AOB 120.

143 For stone inscriptions from Samaria, see *Inscriptions Reveal* No. 43 + Samaria III. 33f.; for Jerusalem, see Naveh, *Fragment*.

144 See above pp. 17ff.

on this mountain corresponds most probably to Ex 18. In this chapter is presented the earliest connection of the Mount of God and a legal problem. Nevertheless, the legitimization of an Israelite legal institution here goes back to the advice of a Midianite and is thereby in conflict with all later conceptions of divine law.

– We should begin with Ex 32–34* to connect the Mount of God with divine law. The cult, ordained by God himself and formulated on the stone tablets, was opposed to the official calf cult of the Northern Kingdom, which led to its downfall. Forgiveness came in the narrative form of cultic renewal, opening for Israel a future with YHWH.

– Priestly shrine texts clustered around this centre at earliest, during the exilic period. The instructions (Ex 25–31) and finally the construction (Ex 35ff.) of the tabernacle of encounter and the establishment of the cult based on the presence ratified the rescue on which the priestly theology was centered.[145] The non-royal cult continued the ideas of Ex 32–34, connecting and contrasting, and became the foundation of the postexilic temple.

– There is a line with a theologically different emphasis in the various deuteronomic-deuteronomistic texts. Concern is always with the exodus, the giving of the land and the divine commandment. Torah is the other side of the exodus, the need for preservation of freedom and ownership of the land. There is great latitude for narrative realization and historic orientation of the theological connection: from the "day" of deliverance (or even before that, as is Ex 20) up to the conclusion of the acquiring of the land. The most important example, by far, is the placement of the delivery of Deuteronomy in Moab in the midst of taking the land. The late emendation of Deuteronomy in Deut 5 and 9f. is a corrective reaction to Ex 32–34 and perhaps already to its connection to the priestly texts. Here the Decalogue replaces Ex 34:11ff. and is thus connected with the stone tablets and the Mount of God. At the same time Moses' speech in Moab is traced back to a revelation at Horeb and featured as the only legitimate resumption of God's speech from that place.

– The Sinai pericope found its ultimate shape in the deuteronomistic strata of Ex 19–24. With the aid of the allegedly older documents of the Book of the Covenant and the Decalogue, this chapter was placed before the various priestly laws as a marker and counter-balance to make a legal basis for Persian-period Judaism, probably first in conjunction with the association of Tetrateuch and Deuteronomy. A late formation might help explain the omission of the law giving at Sinai in late postexilic texts of the "Credo."

2. What happens theologically in this step-wise association of the Mount of God and divine law must be understood against the background of ancient Near Eastern culture. Law that is not custom or tradition comes from the king. The divine dignity of a state underlies its law, and the same is true of its cult.

---

145 For the concept of rescue in this context, see also Utzschneider, *Heiligtum* 80.

Sinai is, however, a utopian place. It is temporally and physically outside state authority. The association of divine law with this place is completed by steps, which the catastrophe of Israel both enabled and compelled. Sinai became the fulcrum of a legal system not connected with the power of a state and therefore not a mere expression of tradition and custom.

The end of the Northern Kingdom as the first powerful impetus, the deuteronomic movement that reacted to it, the theological challenge of the exile and finally the possibilities of the authorization of the Persian empire – these are the historically essential stations underlying the way from Torah to Sinai. A place was created for an alternative to royal law and cult parallel to the development of the text itself, but not identical with it. Torah itself became the important form of rescue as cult and law were anchored at this place from which God had already been rescuing. The very real survival of Israel, in spite of the kind of conquest that had destroyed other nations, depends on a fictional place in an invented past. They escaped every earthly power and therefore are put ahead of those kingdoms.

4

❧

Moses as Institution?
The Organizational Form of Israelite Law

Judaism is humanity standing on the threshold
of a morality without institutions.

E. Lévinas[1]

The Question of Moses as a Question
about the Legal System

God gave Torah to Moses on Sinai, and apart from the Decalogue it only reached Israel through his mediation. That Torah can be called YHWH's Torah (1 Chr 16:40; Neh 9:3, cf Josh 24:26 and elsewhere) and Moses' Torah (2 Chr 23:18, cf 35:12; Josh 8:31, 23:6 and elsewhere) clarifies the significance of this statement. The question "Who is, or who was this Moses?" was an impetus for historical-critical research, and it will probably never be answered. Usually the question refers exclusively to the historical Moses. As with Jesus, everyone has their own solution to who he was,[2] but historical-critical research has especially shriveled the figure of Moses. He becomes a barely recognizable dwarf very different from the giant whose name is on the Pentateuch and all events, from the oppression in Egypt through the beginning of the conquest of the land. Even if we are doubtful of much of the excessive skepticism, according to which at first there was only a tradition about an (unknown!) grave,[3] little remains that is historically tangible. The Egyptian name is certain,[4] but that gives us little solid information.

In studying the historical Moses we are unavoidably led to wonder about the other shadowy figure. How did the things, about which we know so very little, which the Bible connects with Moses, actually come about? If this is the first time we have wondered about this, we are amazed how rarely this question has been asked at all. In fact, it is only just now being discussed seriously. Naturally, much of Pentateuchal research is useful for the continuing story of the figure of Moses, but the study of the historical processes through which everything came about has taken second place to the problems of reconstruction and historical

---

1 E. Lévinas, *Namenlos* 105.
2 For Moses research, see Smend, *Mosebild*; Osswald, *Bild des Mose*; H. Schmid, *Gestalt des Mose*.
3 Thus Noth, *Pentateuch* 189f.
4 See W. H. Schmidt, *Exodus* 73f.; Donner, *Geschichte I* 107ff.

classification of the sources, their respective intent and theology. Why were all the laws associated with the name of Moses? What is the significance of that assignment? Most likely Moses did not write any of the Israelite legal corpora, or the connection was established after the fact. This is probably also true of the Decalogue (even central theological concepts, like the first and second commandments, or the sabbath).[5] How was all of this ascribed to Moses, so that he grew into a giant, bigger than anything else in the history of Israel?

Along with the study of the connection of divine law and the Mount of God, this question leads to a sense of authority which belongs to the distant past. Nevertheless, with Moses the question poses itself differently, more grandly. The law is basically concerned with power and authority. If a legal system is associated with an authority figure who no longer is alive – who represents this law now, and to whom does it apply? In any case, Moses' special position appears to be especially important.

Who actually could have dared to speak and write in his name? There is no question that someone did. Matt 23:3 says "The scribes and the Pharisees sit on Moses' seat." According to Jewish self-understanding, the Sanhedrin was entirely capable of speaking with Moses' authority,[6] but the problem was naturally different in the post-canonical period than at the origin of the biblical texts. Who would have dared to write Deuteronomy as the words of Moses, and how did they understand their role? The question: "Who is Moses?" includes, "Who represented this authority at a later time?" Even formulating the problem properly is difficult, because the question itself always contains part of the answer.

All authorities from Israel's past have had recognizable representatives and are identified as such. Genealogically, according to the patrilineal manner of thinking, these representatives are called sons.[7] All humanity is the sons of Adam, the Israelites are the sons of Jacob – they are Israel as a nation. Each tribe had a father to whom it traced itself back, whom they represented.

This is also true of social authorities who are not constituted by kinship: the sons of the prophets are their pupils (1 Kg 20:35 and elsewhere);[8] the sons of David, his dynastic successors; the singing group called itself "the sons of Korah" (Ps 42:1 and elsewhere); and the handicraft guilds (Neh 3:8). According to this dominant mode of thinking in Israel representation and lineage belong together. Through it identity and distance are expressed simultaneously. This is also true for those around Moses – the Israelite priests trace their lineage back as the sons of Aaron, Moses' brother (Lev 1:5 and elsewhere).

Only Moses, the greatest and most important figure, has no such "sons." No social-historical authority in Israel bears Moses' name and represents him. It is true there are a few places where sons of Moses are mentioned (Ex 2:22; 4:20; 18:2–6), and there was probably a priesthood

---

5 See above pp. 11f.
6 See below pp. 106f.
7 For genealogical reflection, see especially Blum, *Vätergeschichte* 285.
8 Evidence in detail, e.g. in Haag, article on *ben* 675.

whose membership was traced back to Gershom, Moses' firstborn son (Judg 18:30).[9] Nevertheless both are marginal references.

In Judg 18 "Moses" is associated with "Manasseh." It is also true that one of the principal lines of the Levites carries the name of Moses' son Gershom/n, and conversely, there is a "Mushi" line among the Levite groups descended from Merari. A link with Moses has been proposed.[10] Moses is not just a Levite, he perhaps had a greater role as the ancestor of a particular line of Levitic or priestly groups.

It is equally significant that a few vestiges remain which are rather difficult to evaluate. If we take them as old tradition, coming from a time before the destruction of the shrine at Dan (see Judg 18:30), it is all the more certain that Moses' rise as the central mediation figure in the Pentateuch is not the foundation upon which this is built, it caps the narrative.

It is different than with Aaron.[11] Moses' "rise" was not coupled with a certain group or institution. Moses was of course a Levite, but Levites did not represent Moses. This is even less true of other groups like priests, prophets, lawyers, or wise men. Moses did not at first refer to a group in Israel, nor did he, like Abraham or Jacob, represent all Israel.

There have been a few attempts to study institutional authorities associated with the name of Moses. Thus, H.-J. Kraus speaks of an office "endowed with the highest authority . . . a sacral institution," in short, a "prophetic and covenant-mediating office," the juridical and law giving functions in the central cult during the early period, practiced in the name of Moses.[12]

Kraus' theory has found little acceptance, even for the period during which all sorts of amphictyonic offices were in fashion, and it has disappeared along with so many formerly popular theories about the early period. Furthermore, Kraus' pointed question – "What was actually behind the many speeches by Moses in the Pentateuch?" – and his suggestion that the widely held opinion is hardly adequate as an answer, "This or writer set out their schemes 'under the authority of Moses,'"[13] – nevertheless probably has more weight than is usually given it. Kraus' own answer, however, remains rather vague, even apart from the historical uncertainty.

The same thing is true, for example, for Childs's theory, who speaks of a "Mosaic office," connecting it with the proverbial covenant mediator and charismatic character.[14] The explanations by Knierim for Ex 18:[15] are of significantly more weight. He finds an aetiology for the Mosaic office in the juridical organizations established in this chapter. Nevertheless, he

---

9 According to the usually emendation of the MT on the basis of the old translation. MT reads (*mᵉnaššēh*) with a nun-suspensum.
10 See especially Schulz, *Leviten* 45ff.; for the relation of Moses and the Levites, see also W. H. Schmidt, *Exodus* 65ff.
11 See e.g. Gunneweg, *Leviten* 81ff.; Valentin, *Aaron*.
12 Kraus, *Worship in Israel* 109f.; and Kraus, *Prophetische Verkündigung*. Kraus refers here to Noth, *Amt*.
13 Kraus, *Worship in Israel* 109.
14 Childs, *Exodus passim*, especially 351ff.
15 Knierim, *Exodus* 18.

draws no conclusions for the Moses tradition. His observations will need to be taken up again later.[16]

Not least the post-canonical tradition, already mentioned, shows that from the very beginning, the question of the Mosaic institution as broadly understood[17] is not inappropriate. We remember that, for example, the Mishna tractate Abot includes "institutions" as well as the prophets and the "great gathering" in the successors of Moses, in addition to individual people (1:1).

The examination of a Mosaic institution,[18] studying the powers and processes that spoke in the name of Moses and lifted his figure high above human standards of measurement, comes up against nearly insoluble problems of sources. We could accomplish much were we able to examine each particular period and aspect. Of course, this question connects directly and necessarily with another, with which we may be more secure.

When studying a legal system that supports itself with an authority from the distant past and derives everything exclusively from that authority, the question of the representation of this figure in the present is also the study of the judicial system as a whole. Part of the problem is not only who is able to establish law in the name of Moses and remains able to do so, but also who rendered justice. Who applied, interpreted and translated "Moses" in everyday legal documents? This is not ultimately about the specter of "theocracy." Furthermore, we cannot avoid such a study in view of modern terrorist states whose legal pronouncements support themselves with ancient divine law.[19]

Theocracy is the name Hellenistic authors gave the more or less stateless community of Jews and their peculiar legal language.[20] The label was accurate in that only divine law was valid in Israel. Of course, from the very beginning, the term was tinged with "priestly rule." God did not rule directly and did not declare laws himself, but it is important how and by whom he was represented.

Study of the judicial system is a necessary part of the study of the meaning of the figure of Moses as the origin of all law. In the closely connected problems of judicial function and legislation in Israel under

16 See below pp. 83ff.
17 For the concept of institutions, see especially Utzschneider, *Hosea*. He would also begin with a similarly broad interpretation.
18 Here is how the following discussion is arranged. The question when and why Moses became a "law-giver" and when and how the transmission of legal texts was ascribed to him (see e.g. Nielsen, *Moses*; Timpe, *Gesetzgeber*) are discussed in the context of the individual corpora (see below pp. 199f., 237ff. and elsewhere).
19 See Weiler, *Theocracy*. Written in view of the problems of the modern state of Israel, the book is a "case study in political theory" (IX) that severely criticizes the concept and the religious politics that in certain ways are expressed by it. Weiler regards that which was completed by Ezra and Nehemiah after the exile as "depoliticization" in the process of which Israel was transformed "from a political nation to a holy community" (114). In so doing he adopts much of his terminology and interpretation from Max Weber. For the problems concerning the historical questions of the Persian period, thus the time during which the Torah originated, see Crüsemann, *Perserzeit*.
20 First by Josephus, *Contra Apionem* 2.165f.; see e.g. Michaelis, article on *kratos* 909f. In detail, Weiler, *Theocracy* 3ff.

the name of Moses, we are dealing with the correlation of historical ascription and contemporary practice.

"Justice without a Gate": The Origins in the Pre-state Period

A critique of current research

Current ideas of law during the pre-state period of Israel rest on three pillars, none of which can survive critical review.

Since Ludwig Köhler first described the "Hebrew legal community" in 1931,[21] it has been regarded entirely as something inherited from the pre-state period.[22] Widely held theories include: "The nomadic familial or tribal jurisdiction developed itself into a local jurisdiction by the ever more firmly established cultural occupants of the land. The famous 'Hebrew legal community' came into existence."[23]

The picture is of a judicial gathering made up of free, landowning males "at the gate" of a village,[24] coming together as needed. The elders of the group render the actual decisions. The evidence collected since Köhler is a mosaic with bits of information from different books and periods.

Ruth 4 is a kind of framework, with prophetic and narrative material from the Book of the Covenant through Job filling in the details. Today, no single text is thought to come from the pre-state period. The most important evidence (especially prophetic) for the theory of a Hebrew legal gathering comes from the monarchic period. With the juxtaposition of royal and temple jurisdictions, which are unclear when taken separately, we are able to reckon on such an institution.[25]

The obliviousness with which such legal procedure is projected back into the early period before the state is amazing. This is why there is no single text that can be used. Never, for example, is there report of legal action by the elders.[26] Niehr indeed believes that he has found "evidence" of this,[27] but outside the Book of the Covenant, which is surely to be dated later,[28] he employs only Gen 31. Laban is supposed to make an appeal to a "legal community," which Niehr immediately calls a "court,"[29] but this passage refers to "my kinsfolk and your kinsfolk" (verse 37), the respective opposing parties.[30] Niehr does not introduce other evidence for a "legal community" during the pre-state period.[31] The confidence with

---

21 Köhler, *Rechtsgemeinde*.
22 Niehr, *Geschichte* has described the history of the research.
23 Boecker, *Recht und Gesetz* 23.
24 The formulations of Horst, *Recht und Religion* 262f. have become especially influential. Further, see McKenzie, *Juridical Procedure*; Machholz, *Gerichtsverfassung* 158f.; Thiel, *Entwicklung* 104; Kaiser, *Einleitung* 68 and many others.
25 For the current picture, see Niehr, *Rechtsprechung* 58ff.; in addition, see below pp. 76ff.
26 Thus e.g. Wilson, *Enforcing* 61, 64; Niehr, *Rechtsprechung* 42, 50; Thiel, *Entwickung*.
27 Niehr, *Rechtsprechung* 50.
28 See below pp. 111f., 197 and elsewhere.
29 Niehr, *Rechtsprechung* 51.
30 See below pp. 67f.
31 For the Book of Ruth, see below p. 66.

which an institution is projected back into the early period, an institution that is not clearly attested until the monarchic period, is not at all based in Old Testament texts. Apparently it comes only from the untested conviction that a legal institution based on the authority of the elders of "kinsfolk," which was in competition with the king's judges during the monarchic period, must have had an earlier origin. There is a presumed tension in the legal organization during the monarchic period that leads some to think one of the two sides is older.

There is a small, but important indication of the problem in this projection backward: early iron age settlements in Israel have no fortifications and consequently, no gates.[32] This is why there could not have been the proverbial "justice at the gate."

The second approach to pre-state law is connected with the biblical conception of this period, the time of the "judges." We have long known that the concept of "judging" (*špṭ*) is not just associated with "legal affairs," it especially means to "rule."[33] If the so-called great judges, with the exception of Deborah, had something to do with such judging in the deuteronomistic milieu, when we examine the "lesser judges" on the list in Judg 10:1–5, 12:8–15 we find only the verb. Consequently, we can only hypothetically conclude some kind of concrete activity.[34]

There remain only the references to Deborah (Judg 4:4f.) and Samuel or his sons (1 Sam 7:15f., 8:1–3). It is, however, debatable whether the statements here do not represent a later[35] perception of how "judges" succeeded to the office. Furthermore, if it had been otherwise, there would have been nothing but the pure concept of "judging" (*špṭ*), whereas we see these people engaging in other activities.

Samuel and his sons exercise functions at particular shrines, and Deborah is called a prophetess in Judg 4. If this judging deals with judicial activities, which is rather doubtful, there is nothing about contents, procedures, jurisdictions, etc. This is especially true for the idea that law was practiced here "through instances of private arbitration."[36] However, Judg 4:4f. gives no indication of private arbitration,[37] and we

---

32 See Fritz, *Einführung* 142; H. Weippert, *Palästina* 403; especially Finkelstein, *Archeology* 261ff. The ring-shaped arrangement of the houses in Beersheba VII with two buildings that have been interpreted by the excavators as gate structures. See Herzog, *Beer-Sheba II* 25ff., 75ff., there Fig. 34f. Herzog dates the stratum 1025–1000 BCE (ibid. 66–68), thus already in the period of the establishment of the state. Previously, there was a wall only in Giloh, see Mazar, *Giloh*.

33 Especially Richter, *Richter*; most recently Niehr, *Herrschen*.

34 For a discussion of the judges, see Soggin, *Judges* 1ff. The reflections by Mommer, *Samuel* 1ff. are very general and practically nowhere rely upon the sources.

35 See Becker, *Richterzeit* 138ff.; Neef, *Sieg Deboras* 40f. Veijola, *Königtum* 53f. Even with another evaluation of the literary tradition (e.g. Crüsemann, *Widerstand* 60ff.; now also Mommer, *Samuel* 18ff.) there is no direct historical source for the pre-state period. Furthermore, according to the text's understanding of itself, it is dealing with the immediate predecessor of the monarchy.

36 Thus Schäfer-Lichtenberger, *Eidgenossenschaft* 344.

37 For Judg 4:4f. see especially Niehr, *Herrschen* 102f., who shows that the statement "she judged Israel" (*šōpṭāh ʿet-yiśrāʾēl*) in verse 4b is an insertion (together with Noth, *Studien* 51; Halbe, *Privilegrecht* 473 note 64 among others). The concept *mišpāṭ* (court) in verse 5b is then to be interpreted in conjunction with the prophetic activity of Deborah. It deals with an oracle or non-legal decisions (Niehr, *Herrschen*

could hardly conclude it from the segmented character of the society alone.[38]

There is no longer any need to justify the elimination of the law books themselves,[39] the third traditional source for early law in Israel. Texts, long regarded as old, such as the Decalogue, Ex 34:11ff. and the Book of the Covenant are products of the monarchic period, some would even regard them as more recent still.[40] Even the rather naive, but commonly held notion that divine law is typical of early cultures has been proven to be legal-historically and ethnologically wrong.[41] In spite of this, even a critical author like H. Donner would retain the notion of an early divine law, ". . . it is remarkable that the entire Old Testament, no matter what periods and parts, always proceeds from the basic conviction that all law stems from Yahweh, that it is given by him. This consequently makes the idea probable that its roots extend back into pre-state times."[42] He must, of course, add – and this shows the weakness of his theory – "Unfortunately, we have no exact knowledge about the contents of the early Yahweh-law."[43]

Sources and Methods

According to current Old Testament thinking, there are no direct sources for pre-state law in Israel. The few poetic texts that we can discuss at all as originating at least partially in this period on the basis of their wording contain no pertinent information. The only remaining path is inference from texts formulated or shaped at a later time.

As so much critique of tradition-historic hypotheses has demonstrated, such inference from ancient traditions is extremely problematic. Without independent sources, which enable us to have a control, all we can do is make unsubstantiated suppositions. This is why it is understandable that research relies increasingly upon ethnological material to shed light upon Israelite relationships.[44]

Acephalic societies, recognizing no ruler or leader,[45] similar to Israel in so many ways, offer rich material in the area of legal ethnology and have been studied frequently.[46] We may be assured that the basic features of

---

180). Niehr mentions Judg 13:12 in the context of a birth oracle (like KTU 1.124) as an analogy, as well as, especially Prov 16:33, 16:10.

38 See below, p. 66.

39 Thus e.g. Thiel, *Entwicklunglung* 152, 160 and *passim* supports his picture of the social shape of pre-state Israel to an astonishing degree with the Book of the Covenant; similar for law Niehr, *Rechtsprechung* 43ff.

40 See below p. 352, note 132; pp. 115ff.

41 Already Daube, *Biblical Law* 1ff.

42 Donner, *Geschichte I* 148.

43 Donner, *Geschichte I* 148.

44 Thus Schäfer-Lichtenberger, *Eidgenossenschaft* 342ff., Wilson, *Enforcing*; Bellefontaine, *Customary Law*; Niehr, *Rechtsprechung*; Neu, *Anarchie* 320.

45 Instead of listing much evidence here, we mention only Sigrist/Neu, *Ethnologische Texte I*, especially 23ff. (for law ibid. 193ff.).

46 From the great amount of literature, the most important might be the following theoretically argued works, which treat rather in summary: Abel, *Theories*; Barkum, *Law*; Gluckmann, *Politics*; Gluckmann, *Reasonableness*; Hoebel, *Recht*; Poposil, *Anthropologie*; Roberts, *Ordnung*; Spitteler, *Konfliktregelung*.

the "Hebrew legal community" were valid in principle, and have been supported or concretized by ethnological parallels.[47]

Thus, for example, Neu speaks of "empiric-ethnological evidence for such a gathering" in Tiv,[48] but this parallel to an "assembly of neighbors and kinsmen who decide disputes"[49] is not at all usual, nor is it the only model of the judicial decision-making process. Rather more frequently, "the traditional methods of conflict resolution in societies without a state are extremely diverse."[50] For this reason we must remember the entire gamut of law in decentralized societies. This extends from cases where there were little more than "mediators" who limit themselves to the delivery of messages, taking no initiative themselves, all the way to real mediators who function in situations as arbitrators.[51]

This is why it is so important that ethnological parallels are not conclusive for Israel. Their power lies in their heuristic value: in other words, they can give us the meaning and context of situations and processes in very unusual societies, but they can never completely replace sources. It is much more important that we remain attentive for Old Testament approaches to pre-state law.

There are, of course, no direct historical sources. We should, nevertheless, emphasize that – apart from the legal texts sometimes used by scholars but transposed back into the early period – not only do our sources not come from the period of the judges, they have nothing to say about that period. In my opinion, all the evidence used to supporting "Hebrew legal community" is about procedure from the monarchic period, if not later.[52]

Ruth 4 seems to be the only exception. It is, nevertheless, unlikely that Ruth is from the monarchic period. The ten men function only as *witnesses* not as arbitrators or even as those who render judgment.[53]

There is, however, another group of Old Testament texts that give – by design – information about legal procedures during the pre-state period: narratives of legal conflicts from the pre-monarchic period. Thus far texts have been employed, legal-historically, under the influence of the dominant theory of the "legal community," and they have been

47 See the works listed above in note 44.
48 Neu, *Anarchie* 38f. with reference to Bohanan, *Justice* 161.
49 Bohanan, *Justice* 161.
50 Roberts, *Ordnung* 121.
51 See e.g. the instructive summary in Roberts, *Ordnung* 120ff. with examples from Jale, Maring, Nuer, Ndendeuli, Arusha and others.
52 Even if the Book of Job, from which an astonishing amount of evidence is elicited (Köhler, *Rechtsgemeinde* 153ff.) were located before the monarchy, we are unable to place any confidence in its historical memory.
53 If we do not, as is usually done, presuppose that the Hebrew legal community is uncontroverted, it is by no means obvious that a "sitting of the court of elders" is what is being described in Ruth 4, as Zenger, *Ruth* 80, in agreement with nearly all expositions of this text, states (see Gerleman, *Ruth*; Rudolph, *Ruth*; Würthwein, *Ruth* in part). In any case, the text is about the discussion carried on "before them." thus, that took place in their presence (verse 4), and they are expressedly called "witnesses" ('*ēdīm*) in verse 9, and they say it of themselves in verse 11. See especially Ringgren, article on '*wd* 1116. See also Campbell, *Ruth* 154ff. who refers to the archaeologically proven gates (from the period of the monarchy.) For witnesses, see Daube, *Witnesses*; Schenker, *Zeuge*. The elders here have no mediating, arbitrating, or even judicial function.

classified as, e.g. "pre- or extra-judicial."[54] Nevertheless, this is method-ologically doubtful.

I will use four or five such narratives as illustrations in the paragraphs that follow. There is no doubt they must be regarded as from the monarchic period. I will give the respective consensus view or the most important reasons why they should not be dated even later. These texts contain the image of the legal processes of the preceding period that Israel constructed for itself. It is extremely important, in my opinion, that this gives us a surprisingly unified picture. It contradicts all previous ideas, but is completely consistent with the framework of what we know about segmented societies and only achieves a precise meaning when we employ ethnological parallels.

Gen 31: Apart from a few later verses, the narrative contains un-disputedly preexilic material. Traditionally the material is thought to come from Yahwist and Elohist sources.[55] Westermann finds a unified basic stratum (J) as well as a series of later emendations,[56] but Blum's analysis is more convincing, apart from verses 3, 17f., 21*, 33a (D or P stratum); the chapter fits in the compositional stratum of the Jacob story, which he dates to the time of Jeroboam I. An edited Jacob–Laban narrative, redacted here (especially verses 19–23, 25–29a, 30–37) and a separate tradition (verses 46*, 51–55) are even older.[57]

The narrative is concerned with intra-familial legal conflict. The outcome of events is that Jacob and his family are recognized as independent by a treaty.[58] Jacob's secret flight, taking along his wife, Laban's daughter, and all of his possessions, created a problem. It was complicated because Rachel took Laban's teraphim (verse 19).[59] When Laban was told about the flight (verse 22), he took "his kinsfolk" (*'eḥāw*) and pursued Jacob. The groups set up their tents in two separate camps, facing each other (verse 25). A dispute arose in which Laban accused Jacob of stealing his "heart" (verse 26, cf verse 20), consequently causing a malicious split in his family (verses 26–30a). There was also the theft of his goods (verse 30b). As a result, Jacob invited Laban to search for the stolen items among his possessions – of course "before our kinsfolk" (*néged 'aḥēnū*, verse 32). In so doing, as *pater familias* Jacob issued a death

---

54 Thus Niehr, *Rechtsprechung* 40f. It is important that Boecker, *Redeformen* repeatedly selects his evidence for pre-judicial discussions from this kind of narrative, which takes place in the pre-state period (pp. 34ff: Josh 22; Gen 13; Judg 20; Gen 31 among others) which is not valid for the "forms of address before the gathered legal forum."

55 Thus e.g. Gunkel, *Genesis* 340ff.; v. Rad, *Genesis* 247ff.; finally again Scharbert, *Genesis* 210ff.

56 Westermann, *Genesis II* 481ff. He finds later emendations in verses 3, 5b, 9f., 12a, 20, 24, 29, 45, 46b, 47, 53a plus other smaller additions.

57 Blum, *Vätergeschichte* 117–140. For the Jacob narrative, in summary, 149ff.; for the K stratum, 175ff.

58 For this basic outline, see especially Mabee, *Jacob and Laban*. For the narrative technique, see Sherwood, *Examination* 257ff.

59 See Greenberg, *Rachel's Theft*. The suggestions in Fuchs, *Way of Women* are helpful for a few problems in the narrative. She opines that many necessary narrative features are simply missing, like e.g. the motivation for the theft or the consequences of the action. The fact that this incompleteness only affects women arises from a lack of interest in women.

sentence upon the potential thief. When Laban found nothing, Jacob made counter-charges (verses 36–42). He asked Laban to present evidence of theft and to put it "before my kinsfolk and your kinsfolk" (*néged 'aḥay wᵉ aḥēkā*, verse 37). This was to show what is just "between us" (*ykḥ*, hiph. with *bēn*).

The verse is important, not only for the meaning of the verb (*ykḥ*, hiph.), but also for the thesis of the existence of councils of arbitration in early Israel.[60] Boecker suggests that "Gen 31:37 deals with a situation in which the 'kinsfolk' are to render a legal decision between two parties in contract, in other words – concretely – that they are to establish which of the two is right and which is wrong."[61] While the expression (*ykḥ*, hiph. with *bēn*) is used in one parallel, Job 9:33 (where it deals with two contracting persons), we cannot assume that it means the same thing in Gen 31. No neutral forum is offered.

The people mentioned are expressly "my kinsfolk and your kinsfolk" (verse 37). Laban took along "his kinsfolk" to pursue Jacob (verse 23), and they are the force by which he was able to obtain justice, as he asserted with threats (verse 29). Only God's timely intervention (verse 24, cf verse 29) prevented this from happening. Even then, God had already determined what was right (*ykḥ*, hiph. in verse 42). The identity of Jacob's "kinsfolk" is somewhat less clear to us (verse 37, 46). Nevertheless, as in the context of the Jacob narrative, it is presumed that others were present besides his sons (e.g. slaves and servants).

The group that was to render judgment is in no sense a forum or court of mediation. It is rather a group that came into existence at the bidding of one side or the other. We also cannot exclude the possibility that the legal decision was reached in battle, Furthermore, Jacob's offer is more or less only rhetorical, since he already knew what the outcome of the investigation would be (verses 33–35).

Jacob's great reproach of Laban for accusing him of theft does not suggest that Jacob's flight with the assistance of his wives was not punished, nor that God's intervention did not balance the obvious superiority of Laban. Everything was resolved with a pact and the establishment of a peaceful border in the concluding section.

Gen 34: Literally speaking, the question at issue is whether this chapter contains one or two strands. Westermann adopted the old theory that it presents a combination of two sources.[62] Nevertheless, he sees an "independent author" rather than a redactor in the final version.[63] Tensions in the text are far more convincingly explained by a unified underlying narrative, which underwent extensive reworking.

---

60 Especially Niehr, *Rechtsprechung* 50f.
61 Boecker, *Redeformen* 45; with reference to Liedke, article on *ykḥ*; Mayer, article on *ykḥ*.
62 Of course, J and E. Thus first Wellhausen, *Composition* 45ff.; 314ff.; cfs e.g. also Gunkel, *Genesis* 369ff. Procksch, *Genesis* 199ff., 542ff., for example, thinks it was J and P, nevertheless with a noticeably different estimate for P. The stratification that Lehming, *Genesis 34* has worked out is extremely complex. For the historical question, which we will sidestep completely, see most recently Kevers, *Les Fils.*
63 Westermann, *Genesis II* 535ff.

Following a series of older studies,[64] Blum[65] recently isolated the underlying narrative in verses 1–3, 5, 7, 11–14 (15–17*?), 20–23, while the redaction-stratum appears in verses 4, 6, 8–10 (15–17*?), 20–23 with which the insertion of "Hamor" in verses 13, 18, 24, 26 as well as a pair of glosses are included. It is important that the more recent stratum strengthens the essential ideas of the earlier.[66]

The question "when did it originate?" is more significant for our investigation. Westermann has proposed an exilic or postexilic date for the entire narrative, especially because of the similarity of verse 9 to Deut 7, and he maintained that there is a kinship with Gen 14 and to the Priestly documents.[67] Of course. only verse 9 allows us to establish a clear relationship to Deut 7. The entire narrative can best be summarized as a critique of this kind of claim and its outgrowth. There is, however, no impetus for it to be since there is no reference to a divine norm for Simeon and Levi's action.

This narrative deals with a rape and its consequences, it is not fundamentally a problem of intercourse with Canaanites or even Samaritans.[68] This shows quite clearly that the rejection of inter-marriage and consequent planning of the revenge murder in verse 13 is designated as deception (*mirmāh*).

Blum has correctly emphasized the aetiological intent of this narrative, through which the special existence of the tribes of Simeon and Levi is supposed to be explained.[69] They react out of all proportion to what Shechem did. Furthermore, Shechem made a completely respectable offer, conforming precisely to Israelite law. For this reason, it is convincing to regard the chapter as preexilic. Apart from a later deuteronomic stratum in verse 30, Blum regards it as a part of a late monarchic period Judean expansion of the Jacob narrative.[70]

The story begins with the rape of Dinah by Shechem (verses 1f.). After the rape he remains with her, wanting to marry her. He offers an especially high bride price (verses 11f.) This is precisely in accord with the claims of Israelite law as they are known to us (Ex 22:15f.; Deut 22:28f.) and this is what they demand. This is what Tamar demanded in 2 Sam 13:16 after having been raped. As a reaction to this act of shame (*nᵉbālāh*), to this thing that "ought not to be done," Jacob at first waits (verse 5). Only when his sons return from the fields (verses 5, 7) does he gather the sizeable force. They have a conference (verse 7). There is a large-scale offer from the offending side (verses 8–12) with which, insofar as possible, reparation might be made for the action. The sons of Jacob respond with additional demands (verses 14–17). These become the basis

64 Noth, *Pentateuch* 31 note 99; Eising, *Jakobserzählung* 295ff., Nielsen, *Schechem* 242ff., Kevers, *Genèse XXXIV*; Otto, *Jakob* 172ff.
65 Blum, *Vätergeschichte* 213ff.
66 Blum, *Vätergeschichte* 216.
67 Westermann, *Genesis II* 6535ff. He would date the document to the period of the patriarchs or the conquest of the land.
68 Against Diebner, *Genesis 34*. He does not list specific reasons, which go beyond the facts, that all texts in later times could be and could have have been interpreted in a natural way.
69 Blum, *Vätergeschichte* especially 217ff.
70 Blum, *Vätergeschichte* especially 228ff.

of an agreement. Of course, the settlement is followed by deception (*mirmāh*, verse 13) by the sons of Jacob. When the weakening of the residents was accomplished by circumcision, Simeon and Levi break the agreement. They attack the city, plunder it, commit mass murder on the male residents and sell the women and children into slavery (verses 25, 28f.).

Judg 17ff. and *19–21* are held together by the framework formulae (17:6; 21:26 as well as 18:1; 19:1), however, from other points of view they form a unity.[71] Veijhola's attempt to explain the framework formula as deuteronomistic[72] is unfortunate.[73] We should note that separate analyses of the texts have repeatedly demonstrated their age, and it does not seem necessary to discuss here the few possibly later emendations.[74]

Most recently, Niemann has offered a literary-critical analysis.[75] He thinks the basic, preexilic narrative was edited twice. Only a few verses (especially 18:27a, b) are late and deuteronomistic.[76] Trible[77] and Jüngling have impressively shown the inner unity of Judg 19. Jüngling accepts an early monarchic origin.[78] Earlier, as well as more recent observations support this.[79] There is no reason to think, regarding Judg 20f., the narrative substance (or with Judg 19) is late. The narrative is monarchic.[80]

Judg 17ff. begins with the theft of a considerable amount of silver. Only the mother can curse the at first unknown thief (verse 2). More important is the rather violent theft of sacral paraphernalia by the wandering Danites together and the caretaker Levite priest (18:17ff.). When the owners discover the theft, "the men who were in the houses near Micah's house called out" (verse 22), that is, they were gathered by Micah's call for assistance and they hurried in pursuit of the Danites.

Immediately after the theft, the Danites prepare themselves to defend against attack. They put children and exposed possessions in front so that they can arrange their warrior/troops in the rear (verse 21). When the pursuers reach them, a dispute breaks out (verses 23ff.). Micah demands his possessions back (verse 24), but he is mockingly repulsed with undisguised threats against his own and the lives of those with him

---

71 Cf Crüsemann, *Widerstand* 162ff.

72 Veijola, *Königtum* 15f. See also Dumbrell, *In Those Days*.

73 See especially Jüngling, *Richter 19* 68–73. The formula identified by Veijola as deuteronomistic: each acted "according to [his own] desires" (see e.g. Deut 12:8) has parallels in pre-deuteronomistic literature (see e.g. Judg 14:3, 7; 1 Sam 18:20, 26 among others).

74 Veijola, *Königtum* 17–27 regards 17:5, 7b, 13; 18:1b, 19*, 30; 20:4*–27b–28a as deuteronomistic redaction.

75 Niemann, *Daniten* 61–147, summary 129ff.

76 The placenames of Zora and Esthaol 18:2, 8, 11 as well as 18:12, 13*, 27*, 28*, 29* are supposed to belong here (summary Niemann, *Daniten* 134) in addition to a few other verses "of indeterminate age" (137).

77 Trible, *Mein Gott* 99ff.

78 Jüngling, *Richter 19*, summary 294.

79 Discussions with older literature in Crüsemann, *Widerstand* 155ff.; now also Soggin, *Judges*. Most recently Amit, *Hidden Polemic*.

80 In contrast, Becker, *Richterzeit* has explained the chapter as late deuteronomistic (thus also for Judg 17f.*) even, perhaps, post-deuteronomistic (thus for 19–21*), whereby 19–21 belongs in the context of P or of the Pentateuch redactor (298). Here a detailed discussion is necessary, but cannot take place within this study. I find neither the method nor the individual observations convincing.

(verse 25). When Micah sees that they are stronger than he (*ḥᵃzāqîm hēmmāh miménnū*, verse 26), he returns home with empty hands.

Judg 19–21 deals with the rape and murder of a Levite's concubine (*pilégeš*) while in Gibeah. During the night, men of the city surround the house, into which the Levite and his concubine had been welcomed (19:22) and the men of the city demand the surrender of the guest. The master of the house refused: "No, my brothers, do not act so wickedly . . . do not do this vile thing" (*nᵉbālāh*) (verse 23). In order to save his guest, the master offers his daughter as a replacement. The Levite instead brings his concubine out to the men.

The next morning the woman is found dead in the doorway (verses 27f.), and the Levite loads her body on his donkey and takes her home. Once there, he cuts her into pieces and sends them into all the territory of Israel. Because of the uniqueness of this horrible deed (verse 30), there was an uproar through all of Israel. All the people from the cities gathered, and the Levite described everything that happened (20:1–7). He called what happened a "vile outrage" (*zimmāh ūnᵉ bālāh*, verse 6), a judgment accepted by Israel (verse 10).

Israel demanded the tribe of Benjamin, to which those who committed the crime belonged, hand them over (verse 13) in order to root out the evil in Israel, but the tribe stood by the offenders. The situation resulted in military conflict, which nearly caused the death of the whole tribe. In chapter 21, in an epilogue, hundreds of women were forcibly taken from Jabesh-Gilead for the remaining Benjamites.

2 Sam 14: This narrative is part of the history of the royal succession of David. Since E. Meyer[81] and L. Rost[82] the text has been viewed as a shining example of early monarchic period Israelite historical narrative.[83] Recently, V. Seters has suggested that it might be a "post-deuteronomic emendation of the history of David from the postexilic period."[84] His overall view stems from a comparison (problematic in detail) to Greek history, which in any case is not compelling.

Recently, in a critique of V. Seters, O. Kaiser, who has consistently championed a late date, dated the work to the monarchic period, "the time between Hezekiah and Jehoachim."[85] Nevertheless, it is conceivable that a deuteronomistic or post-deuteronomistic origin is unlikely. Würthwein especially rejected 2 Sam 14 for the history of the royal succession.[86] It might be a wisdom insertion from a later redaction. Bickert has taken up this thesis, which relies upon the fact that David, after 13:19 might have decided to bring Absalom back. According to Bickert, a proverbial anecdote in chapter 14 was deuteronomistically reworked twice.[87] In my opinion, neither the theory nor the literary criticism that he employs works, nor is it convincing. Indeed, if we follow this line, the essential characteristics must be preexilic.

81 Meyer, *Geschichte* II/2 285.
82 Rost, *Thronnachfolge.*
83 See Crüsemann, *Widerstand* 180ff.
84 V. Seters, *Historiography* 290.
85 Kaiser, *Thronnachfolgeerzählung* 20.
86 Würthwein, *Thronfolge* 46f.
87 Bickert, *List.*

Since 2 Sam 14 deals with the operation of the newly established monarchy in a court case, of course, it does not belong among these texts,[88] but that is also why it lets us see the old as well as the new material especially clearly.

In order to bring about a reconciliation between David and Absalom, who was guilty of fratricide, Joab sent a wise woman to David to describe an imaginary legal case (verses 5–7).[89] She was to represent herself as a widow whose one son has killed her other son. The incident happened on an open field where "there was no one to part them" (verse 6). A legal decision could not be reached on the basis of the available facts.

Everything seems to favour the idea that here, as elsewhere, the "one who was to part them (*maṣṣil*) is always a term reserved for YHWH."[90] [Crüsemann here uses the word *Retter* (= saviour, deliverer, redeemer) since this corresponds to the Old Testament usage of *maṣṣil*.] The frequent usage "but there was no one" (*wᵉᵉn maṣṣil*) is made more precise here by the addition of the unique "between them" (*bēnēhēm*). Thereupon, as the mother reports, the entire clan (*kol hammišpāḥāh*) arose (*qāmāh*) against her and demanded to be given the killer in order to fulfill the vendetta (verse 7). They must be from the family of her deceased husband who had claim to the inheritance, since there was neither "name nor remnant" (*šēm ūšᵉ 'ērit*, verse 7) for his land. What happens next, which we will examine more closely[91] was left up to the king.

Self-Reliance and Negotiation

In all their variety, the texts cited thus far give us an astonishingly consistent picture of reaction to egregious breaches of law. Reactions can be characterized by the terms: self-reliance and negotiation.

The conflicts discussed here occur: within very close relationships (Gen 31; 2 Sam 14); between groups or tribes in Israel (Judg 18, 19f.); and even between Israelites and non-Israelites (Gen 34). Offenses range from infractions of simple rules of etiquette or conflict over familial possessions (Gen 31), through theft including images of gods (Gen 31, Judg 18), all the way to rape culminating in death (Judg 19f.) and murder or deadly force (2 Sam 14).

When overt violation of law occurs, people automatically divide themselves into parties. Groups organize themselves along familial lines, even in the closest relationships: brothers of both sides who oppose each other (Gen 31), the family of the deceased husband are against the mother of his children (2 Sam 14). Clearer for us are the confrontations in which neighbors fight with traveling strangers (Judg 18), or all of Israel against a single tribe (Judg 19f.) or the Israelites against the non-Israelites (Gen 34). When in the midst of "legal action" the return of the person who committed the crime is demanded, as with the mother in 2 Sam 14 and the tribe of Benjamin in Judg 20, obviously, relatives protect and hide criminals.

---

88 See Bellefontaine, *Customary Law*.
89 For the concluding conversation, see especially Hoftijzer, *David*.
90 Hossfeld/Kalthoff, article on *nsl* 574.
91 See below pp. 76f.

In nearly all cases, the initial reaction of the injured party is to organize their own group, making use of the powers designated for this purpose. The purpose is to display strength and then to use it. Laban gathered his "kinsfolk" for pursuit in Gen 31; Jacob waited until his sons came back from the fields before undertaking his first actions (Gen 34); Micah gathered the neighbors together (Judg 18); and in 2 Sam 14 it is even the "whole family" that rose up against the widow. The Levite from Judg 19f. even suggests that he would have to gather all of Israel against the perpetrator.

Against this background, the negotiations involve more or less extensive debate. Demands are made and offers given. They are discussed and decided, even if often with a negative outcome. In accord with the facts the injured party demands an acceptable agreement through which injustice is rectified, insofar as it is possible. The perpetrator is punished, the injured receives justice and peace is restored. In this way appropriate norms and values were brought into play.[92] We should note that there are also reports of legal procedures, in which negotiations ultimately collapse because parties reject any settlement (Judg 18) or they stage a boycott (Gen 34), and a final decision is only reached by means of force. The resulting settlements span a broad continuum: sometimes there is the negotiation of a new agreement regulating a broken relationship (Gen 31), or the losing party occasionally withdraws (Judg 18), or there is military conflict (Judg 20f.). A final settlement is always possible when force resolves the conflict (Gen 34).

It is remarkable that the texts lack a mediation figure. They never mention the possibility of neutral settlement or intervention by a third party. The parties can expand their base, if it seems necessary. Thus the Levite in Judg 19f. is able to call out all of Israel, for example, instead of just his own tribe. The entire tribe of Benjamin was in solidarity with the town of Gibeah. However, there were only two sides: the victim and the perpetrator. At most, a group is summoned comprising members of the two sides to reach a decision (Gen 31), but even when it seems most plausible, no one assembles a public forum including the elders of the participating communities. The thought should at least have arisen in a city like Gibeah. In 2 Sam 14, there is no suggestion of anything like a council of elders, if such a thing could have existed.

We can establish the following theses about legal procedures described in the above narratives or presumed by them: *In pre-state Israel there were legal cases that were not within the province of the pater familias, which were resolved in some way, without the use of a mediating authority, but only through direct negotiation between the participating groups.* These were formed along family lines. Even the procedures themselves were affected by the physical strength of the parties, and consequently, as a first reaction, the respective groups were gathered and visibly brought into the action. This is especially true in the case of negotiations that failed; physical force decided the issue.

The picture presented by the texts can be expanded on two sides. On the one, we should note the obvious fact that these are special rather than

92 Similarly, see below, pp. 74f.

ordinary cases. They are dramatic not everyday conflicts. They are always concerned with certain aspects and personalities, events occurring over a long period of time, not legal procedures as such. Thus, we should not regard negative events and dominance of power as typical. We must also remember we began with only a few narratives. In my opinion, they describe the most important, egregious violations of law in the early period and their consequences. Naturally, events must be tested against the texts that might apply. A preliminary overview of all of the texts under consideration shows there are no other basic features.

Once again, this is how Israel's legal procedures of the monarchic period looked. It was not the legal community at the gate. The texts are not direct historical sources, nevertheless, they are probably all that we have. No wonder that students of these narratives have not thus far regarded them as an expression of a real legal system.

The significant role of power, the lack of any mediating authority, as well as the uniqueness of the norms employed, suggest that we see the narratives not as actual legal procedures but rather as pre-judicial disputes or conflicts described in military terms. This is exactly where ethnological material is needed, because the picture of pre-state law in Israel sketched here is unlimited regarding the possibilities of acephalic societies.[93]

Self-reliance and negotiation are two concepts this kind of society uses for justice,[94] when, as in Israel, there are no mediators.[95] The old argument, whether rules of conflict are law in such decentralized societies, need not be discussed here. It is a matter of definition. Ethnologically, there is no doubt about the material.[96] A legal system where there is no objective, neutral authority demonstrates that the substance of any law, even modern, is an expression and critique of existing power relationships.[97]

Evidence from Norms instead of Divine Law

With the rape of Dinah, Shechem committed "an outrage in Israel" (*nᵉbālāh*), an act of which it is said, it "ought not to be done" (Gen 34:7). The rather formulaic character of the phrase shows clearly that at the time of which the narrative speaks there was not yet an "Israel," nor was Shechem part of it. Closely related statements appear frequently. In Judg 19:23ff. the egregious violation of the rule of hospitality is also labeled an outrage (*nᵉbālāh*), cf also Judg 20:6, 10. In 2 Sam 13:12, Tamar defends herself from impending rape with the same words, "Such a thing is not done in Israel: do not do anything so vile (*nᵉbālāh*)."

Similar language is used elsewhere. In Gen 29:26 Laban supports his breach of agreement with Jacob, having switched Leah for the previously agreed Rachel, with the words, "This is not done in our country – giving the younger [in marriage] before the firstborn."

93 For literature, see p. 65 above.
94 See especially Spittler, *Konfliktaustragung* from whom I have borrowed the German terminology.
95 Examples included especially in Roberts, *Ordnung*.
96 There is an overview of the pertinent debates, e.g. in Roberts, *Ordnung* 17ff., 196ff.
97 This is a combination of the central points of Geiger, *Vorstudien* 350 and Noll, *Diktate* 23.

Elsewhere, the singularity of a crime is described with historical references, "Has such a thing happened since the day that the Israelites came up from the land of Egypt until this day?" (Judg 19:30).

The statements in our texts contain the established formulations of norms. They are reminiscent of norms and appeal to their undisputed applicability. There is no commandment quoted, no legal statement cited verbatim, there is no written legal corpus in Israel. Most interesting of all is the lack of any authority underlying these standards. Who would dispute that people should not steal, rape, kill or violate rules of hospitality?

The formulations presuppose their validity. The central concept of an "outrage" (*n^e bālāh*)[98] is occasionally used even later. Then, however, it loses its quality of referring to something self-evident and certainly the aspect of rebuke that it has in these early narratives.[99] The formula "for such a thing is not done in Israel" (Gen 34:7; 2 Sam 13:12; cf Gen 20:9, 29:26) is not found later.

This evidence, yet again, expressly supports what we have seen often in the general history of law[100] as well as Israelite legal history:[101] at first there were no divine instructions. The ethical and legal norms in force in Israel were developed gradually and were established under the authority of God.

This, however, does not mean that such norms did not exist. They were always present. The obviously valid character of their origin, their indubitable power, they are in force together with marriage law, inheritance, also commandments against theft, murder and rape. All of this combines with their unimpeachable evidence. Their validity is not dependent upon their formulation.

As in the case of procedures for conflict resolution, we can only understand the full sense of this kind of formulation of norms when we clarify the problem in its ethnological context. Decentralized societies have, on the one hand, norms that cannot be called into question. Nevertheless, one of their most important characteristics is that these norms are not formulated in a fixed way, nor are they unbending.

> Where no one has authority to make a binding decision and execute it, the social norms of the affected group cannot determine the outcome of a proceeding simply and clearly, theoretically possible where there is a judge and a circumstance where normative power is in effect. So long as the solution is achieved through bilateral negotiation or with the assistance of an intermediary, norms must be capable of being flexible. Otherwise, the latitude required to bring parties together would be lacking ... Norms in acephalic societies should be understood as guidelines.[102]

98 See Phillips, *NEBALAH*; Marböck, article on *nābāl*: "a grave dislocation of the community in important areas" (183).
99 See Deut 22:21, Jer 29:33; in addition to Josh 7:15. These are three of a total of nine appearances of the formula (Marböck, article on *nābāl* 181).
100 Daube, *Biblical Law* 1ff.
101 E.g. Gerstenberger, *Wesen und Herkunft* 110 and throughout.
102 Roberts, *Ordnung* 143.

Our texts contradict Donner's theory, that all parts of the Old Testament presuppose that God is the exclusive source of law.[103] Early law was not divine law.

The Ambivalence of the Legal System of the Monarchic Period

The Problem: The State of Research

At first the distance between this reconstructed, pre-state law and Mosaic law seems extraordinarily great. On one side we have flexible, less explicit norms and on the other the detailed formulations of written Torah. Personal initiative and legal action without the aid of central mediating figures contrasts with, in many respects, a completely ordered system of levels of jurisdiction. Nevertheless, there is astonishing continuity within the flexibility. We need only remember Israel's participation in and responsibility for law, or the fact that many legal formulations are not directed toward the administration of justice but rather a legal contract.[104] With some alteration, pre-state law probably became the basis of Torah.

First, it is useful to grasp the confrontation of pre-state law with the recently established monarchy, and thus the state alteration and re-formation of the law. We assume that a state, having a monopoly on power, would control law.

In spite of the existence of courts of elders and the similar structures, this is also true of nearly all of Israel's ancient Near Eastern neighbors[105] and for much of the rest of the history of law. We should also note that the third pillar of their legal system, the temple cultic-priestly court, like the temple itself, was subject to royal influence.[106]

2 Sam 14 shows especially clearly the nature of the demands the monarchy must have made upon pre-state law.[107] The invented case of a widow whose one son had killed her other son was presented to the main participants, including the king himself. In a legal dispute, nothing is more decisive than an underdog turning to a stronger party and asking for (legal) help.[108]

If law, affected by the power relationships of the parties, is more public in a pre-state society than would otherwise be the case, the new central authority is legal-historically significant because of its superiority. "From a judicial perspective, the case being considered consists of an appeal of a member of a 'clan'/village community to a third party above the group with both the authority to override customary law and local authority and the means to enforce compliance."[109]

103 Donner, *Geschichte I* 148.
104 See especially Jackson, *Ideas of Law* 197ff. ("self-executing law").
105 For the ancient Near Eastern legal system, see e.g. Haase, *Einführung* 119ff.; Krecher, *Rechtsleben*; Soden, *Einführung* 134ff.; Boecker, *Recht und Gesetz* 15ff.; see also below p. 81.
106 See e.g. Lipínski, ed., *State and Temple*; Heltzer, *Internal Organization*.
107 See above pp. 71f.
108 See also Ben-Barak, *Appeal*.
109 Bellefontaine, *Customary Law* 60.

"The usurpation of the power by the local community over this particular case is total and final."[110] We must evaluate the relationship of law and power, or our interpretation will be wrong. Thus, in ancient law it was not simply a situation of unresolvable cases (thus setting a precedent) being brought before the king.[111] Furthermore, it is reasonable to say the king, "was sought for his assistance not because of his legal authority, but his physical power"[112] – as though the two could be separated.

We see the king's dilemma quite clearly; perhaps this is why the narrator allows David to equivocate for so long (verses 8–11).[113] The decision that David is called upon to make is very difficult in any case. Should a brother who has killed his brother really be allowed to go unpunished if or because there are no other brothers?

To be sure, this is at first only a case without context. This is not a precedent for all future cases, like 1 Sam 30:25. But could not this be cited as an example of royal decision? It shows quite clearly that the establishment of a central authority in acephalous societies automatically affects the existing system of jurisprudence. This accords with the remarkable evidence from many texts dealing with legal problems in the early monarchy. It is always the king himself who makes the decision and pronounces judgment.

This hardly ever happens in later periods.[114] It is well-known that problems encountered in the beginnings of state authority in Israel are mirrored here. Right from the very beginning we see the basic problem of the institutionalization of state power in law.

For scholars, the question deals with the legal system of the monarchic period, especially the relation of royal decree to pronouncements made by the elders at the gate.[115] On one hand, we have Machholz's theory that the monarchy did not "interfere with the jurisdiction of the local authorities."[116] Furthermore, it established itself as responsible for new societal groups and problems, e.g. for justice in the army.

It also took on cases that "could not be resolved with the instruments of traditional law because legal norms came into collision."[117] The concern is for new, precedent-setting cases and especially, the further development of law. Along with this commonly held view of essentially peaceful coexistence between lay legal jurisdiction and the newly

110 Bellefontaine, *Customary Law* 61.
111 Thus Macholz, *Stellung des Königs* 166ff.
112 Neu, *Anarchie* 317.
113 See Machholz, *Stellung des Königs* 166ff.
114 Thus, of the twenty cases of royal jurisdiction in Machholz, *Stellung des Königs* 160–175, sixteen are from the period of Saul to Solomon, and only four (1 Kg 20:38ff.; 2 Kg 6:24ff.; 8:1ff.; 1 Kg 21) are from the entire remaining monarchic period. See also Whitelam, *Just King* (chapters 4–8), who constructs his entire system of the royal administration of justice entirely on cases from the early monarchic period. Similarly also Mabee, *Problem of Setting*; Ben-Barak, *Appeal.*
115 Buchholz, *Älteste* 55ff. especially 83ff., has indeed disputed this kind of linking for the preexilic period. He regards the elders alone as responsible in legal matters.
116 Machholz, *Stellung des Königs* 181.
117 Machholz, *Stellung des Königs* 177.

established royal prerogative, other scholars believe the state supplanted pre-state institutions from the very beginning or gradually.

Thus, for example, Whitelam states in his study of "Monarchical Judicial Authority": "It appears that the monarchy had influence over local jurisdiction from an early date."[118] Josian reforms especially brought about a system "in which local and priestly judicial authority was made subordinate to that of the king."[119] According to Neu, this kind of centralization of the legal establishment found its expression in the re-shaping of the legal authority which the social-critical prophets of the eighth century criticized so harshly.[120] Now "the rulers who collect rent and taxes . . . [control] the court" (e.g. Am 5:11),[121] where a "contrast between the sovereign gate-justice of earlier times and the new centralized legal system" ought to be recognizable.[122]

It is very important that all previous theories begin with the idea that the monarchy encountered a well-developed system of justice based on courts of elders. If this is incorrect since we find no evidence of such a judicial form, making the theory improbable, we must re-examine the legal system of the monarchic period.

The Court of Elders at the Gate: An Instance of State Law

Scholars often note "there is no recognizable case in which tradition jurisdiction and the judicial function of the king appear in competition."[123] This would indeed be remarkable if we meant a superior, newer system replacing an older one.

Especially 2 Sam 14 shows the opposite to have been the case. Here we have conflict in which the new authority is summoned against the old, but the old authority is not the court of elders at the gate. If there were no circle of elders that dominated the legal system before the monarchy, the theory that this judicial form came about then as an expression of the state legal system of the monarchic period seems convincing and necessary. Decisions by elders and free men at the gates of the communities came into existence with and through the monarchy, and it was the most important form of jurisprudence in Israel.

A brief review of the relevant texts of the monarchic period illustrating on one hand the character of law at the gate, and on the other the role of the elders, shows that the basic assumption of replacement of one form by the other is not attested in the texts. Rather, the texts show coexistence of organs of state power and elders (or lay) judiciary.

First is the narrative of the judicial murder of Naboth in 1 Kg 21, concerning which, even the severest critics regard verses 1–16 as an "ancient, northern Israelite self-contained novella."[124] The elimination of a man who refuses to turn his vineyard over to the king is accomplished by royal letters, instigated by Jezebel, "to the elders and the nobles" (verse 8).

---

118 Whitelam, *Just King* 220.
119 Whitelam, *Just King* 220.
120 Neu, *Anarchie* 324ff.
121 Neu, *Anarchie* 325.
122 Neu, *Anarchie* 328.
123 Niehr, *Rechtsprechung* 84.
124 Thus Würthwein, *Könige* 247.

From these written instructions, "the elder and the nobles … did as Jezebel had sent word to them" (verse 11). Naboth was condemned and stoned outside the city (verse 13) because of the testimony of two false witnesses (*'el-hazzᵉqēnim we 'el haḥōrīm*) of his city. Traditional theories of legal history suggest that this narrative is about the influence royal power had on the court of elders, but the evidence does not support this theory.

The narrative does not raise the question, "Why did the elders obey?" They do so as a matter of course. Likewise, the queen presumes the obedience of her royal subjects (*mᵉlūkāh*, verse 7). The narrative deals with the conflict between the king and an Israelite farmer,[125] it is not between the king (or Naboth) and the elders.

In order to get the coveted piece of land, the king must, with the elders, employ false witnesses to render an unsupported death sentence. It is not mentioned that the elders must play along and follow his instructions. Where, if at all, we might expect conflict between the court of elders and the power of the king, nothing is stated. The same is also true for the continuation of the narrative in verses 17ff. (often regarded as later) which describes interference with God (or his prophets). The ultimate punish-ment applied only to the king and his family.

The king's letter to those with legal responsibility was not addressed just to the elders. It was also written to the "nobles" (*ḥōrim*). There is no literary-critical reason to isolate this group.[126] In addition to the kin designated as leaders, there are also those who have power and influence in the city, and who can affect court decisions. They were allied with the king and obedient to him.

If we read 1 Kg 21 without assuming there was an ancient, pre-monarchic legal structure, we see a coherent picture of a legal structure in the Northern Kingdom. The local courts of elders and the powerful members of the community are representatives of the king in the judiciary, and they support the king's instructions – usually at least. Complicity in a judicial murder is not a particular stumbling block for the narrator of 1 Kg 21. Censure is directed only at the royal house.

Descriptions of the judiciary in the eighth-century Northern Kingdom are generally in agreement. For Hosea 5:1, the entire "house of Israel" (*bēt yiśrāᵉēl*) is qualified for the judiciary (*mišpāṭ*).[127] All together have fallen

---

125 For the questions dealing with the transfer of the property, see e.g. Timm, *Omri* 123ff.

126 Buchholz, *Älteste* 76 regards the mention of the *ḥorīm* as a deuteronomic insertion through which "the accusation that was originally leveled only against the elders of the city of Jezreel was generalized to the entire elite of the city". Nevertheless, the term *ḥorim* was used frequently during the postexilic period (Neh 2:16; 4:8, 13; 5:7; 6:7; 7:5; 13:17; Koh 10:17; as well as Isa 34:12) in addition to only two references in the Book of Jeremiah (Jer 27:20' 39:6). Even if we were to consider these two appearances to be part of the Jeremiah D stratum (thus e.g. Thiel, *Jeremia II* 8ff., 54ff.), *ḥorim* is not a typical deuteronomic expression. It occurs in Deut G only in 1 Kg 21, but is omitted in the parallel passage in 2 Kg 25. It is absent in the passage often regarded as deuteronomic 1 Kg 21:17ff. We cannot support the theory of a deuteronomic redaction with this evidence. Tensions in the text that might allow us to conclude that there was an insertion (or something similar) in the text do not appear. An exclusion is supported by nothing more than the already presumed picture of the development.

127 See e.g. Jeremias, *Hosea* 74.

short and stand under the prophetic judgment (verse 2). For Hosea the
three usual forms of judiciary in the ancient Near East[128] (and monarchic
Israel) form an inner unity.

It is no different for Amos. The societal injustice and exploitation at
the root of his judicial pronouncement happens at the gate. Where justice
and righteousness flow like a river (Am 5:24) and justice is established
(5:15), the one who would bring justice is hated (5:10) and the needy are
"pushed aside" (5:12 cf 2:7). The powerful who exploit the poor set
themselves in the gate as the place of justice. What happens in the palaces
of the capitol (3:10; 6:1ff.) and thus also at the king's court is thereby
inseparably connected. The élite whom Amos attacked, who had the poor
in their power, dominated the legal proceedings at the gate. There was
no perceptible contrast between them and the state institutions, but they
were apparently closely connected (see especially 5:10f.).[129]

The prophets in Judah present a similar picture. For Micah the "heads
of Jacob" (rōšē ya'ᵃqōb) and the rulers of the house of Israel (qᵉṣīnē bēt
yiśrā'ēl) were responsible for justice (3:1 cf 3:9). These two groups built
Jerusalem with blood and made judicial decisions based on bribes. They
gave preference to money and influence. The terms used by Micah
here hardly allow us to interpret in any other way than to assume that
he "heads" functioned within familial circles, and the "rulers" functioned
in the state.[130] For the prophets the two categories are not at all unrelated.

We see this even more clearly in Isaiah. On one hand he is aware of
"judges" (šōpᵉṭīm) and "officials" (śārīm) responsible for law and justice.
This is especially clear in Isa 1:21–26. The "officials" (śārīm), however,
love bribes and seek gifts (verse 23). After the court of purification,
Jerusalem was again to have had "judges" (šōpᵉṭīm) and "counsellors"
(jo'es, verse 26), as "at the beginning" or "in former times" (kᵉbārišōnāh/
kᵉbatᵉḥillāh). They always existed in the city but now they were spoiled.

On the other hand, Isaiah mentions the elders in a list with warriors,
judges, prophets, soothsayers, advisors and magicians in 3:2f.. They are
all the staff and stay of the system of injustice that God wanted to destroy.
The elders and the officials (śārīm) ought to be grouped together in the
same way. Both have "devoured the vineyard" (verse 14) – thus, the
people – and what they have stolen from the poor can be found in their
homes.

This eighth-century prophecy is, in spite of some difference in terminology and evaluation, directed against the upper classes as a group.
They rob the poor and the weak. They consist of the elders, the heads of
the leading families and royal officials, judges, warriors and most of the
religious establishment.

Justice at the gate is one of the tools used to plunder the poor. There is
no evidence in the sources to suggest that the elders and the judicial

---

128 For an overview, see Niehr, Rechtsprechung.
129 The unusual terms used in 5:11 (bšs and mś') were normally employed with state
    levies (see, e.g. Wolff, Amos 268, 290) giving evidence of a close connection
    between the legal proceedings at the gate and state taxes.
130 See especially Wolff, Micha 67f.; for rōš see Bartlett, Use; for qāṣin Schäfer-
    Lichtenberger, Eidgenossenschaft 303ff.

organization established by the state were being played off against each other. We would never be able to regard them as clearly differentiated institutions. Historically, we cannot verify a separation into an "official administration and judiciary working together in a complex combination"[131] nor, as in a recent study, is it possible historically to imagine a separation of administration and judiciary.

We find precisely this same situation in later texts, for example, Jer 26.[132] This same constellation is clearly apparent in Deuteronomy. The elders had jurisdiction in specific cases.[133] Judges are also frequently discussed.[134]

Evidence throughout the monarchic period suggests there is no problem conceiving such a coexistence. Instead, we should expect it. Both groups have legal jurisdiction. However, a demand to establish judges throughout the country is new and specifically deuteronomistic (Deut 16:18).[135]

The image of peaceful, untroubled coexistence between elders and royal officials in the judicial establishment during the monarchic period corresponds exactly with elsewhere in the ancient Near East.[136] One view of the legal establishment's relationships during Ur-III has it: "We don't know precisely how, but trials were held before an 'assembly' of the 'citizens of the city', which did not exclude participation by judges or the designation of the decision as the 'judgment of the king'."[137] Similarly, we also note that a mayor could preside as a functionary of the palace over a court of elders.[138]

Canaanite culture offers the same picture.[139] There was a gate, the seat of royal and state legal function. According to the Ugaritic Aqht epic, King Daniel sat at the gate and rendered justice for widows and orphans.[140] "The gate (or a place or building near the gate) was often mentioned as the place for a court" elsewhere in the Near East.[141]

It follows then that the elders' role in the gate-court of a particular locality was a monarchic period institution and because it was the most widely disseminated form of state law in Israel, it was probably the most important institution. The elders functioned very simply together with other influential officials.

---

131 Thus Buchholz, *Älteste* 99, and *passim.*
132 The cooperation of priests, prophets and people here is remarkable. The *śārîm* apparently played the critical part. For Jer 26, see especially Hardmeier, *Propheten* 174ff.
133 Deut 19:1ff.; 21:1ff., 18ff.; 22:13ff.; 25:5; see Preuss *Deuteronomium* 122 and now Buchholz, *Älteste* 60ff.
134 Deut 16:18ff.; 17:8ff.; 25:1ff.; see Buchholz, *Älteste* 88ff. Buchholz regards Deut 16:18 as a late Deuteronomistic text, the intent of which is to generalize the activity of the so-called minor judges, but this does not reflect preexilic reality. For the problem of the stratification in Deuteronomy, see pp. 203ff.
135 See below pp. 237ff.
136 For the following, especially Weinfeld, *Judge and Officer* 81ff.
137 Krecher, *Rechtsleben* 341 cited by Dijk, *Gerichtsurkunden* 76.
138 Walther, *Gerichtswesen* 8, 56ff.; Krückmann, *Beamter* 445; in summary Niehr, *Rechtsprechung* 28f.
139 Liverani, *Communautés* and *Royauté*; cf Niehr, *Rechtsprechung* 33ff.
140 KTU 1, 17, V6ff.; translation ANET 151; Aistleitner, *Texte* 70.
141 Thus Soden, *Einführung* 134.

We cannot isolate a precise division of labor; such a thing would have been highly unlikely. We should also note that officials, like military leaders, were recruited from the most important families of the country.[142] From the point of view of critical prophets (also 1 Kg 21), the élite of the society are represented as a single group in judicial power. Elders, officials and the king formed a single entity.

Important facts are implied about the structure and function of the state which we will not discuss here.[143] After initial conflicts, the Israelite as well as the Judean state, relied upon leading families and elders to support themselves. They became an important part of the state apparatus. What they might have lost in political power[144] and only achieved again during the exile,[145] they won in judicial significance.

Finally, it is important where the court functioned: the gate of the city. That even small cities were surrounded by a wall with a gate was an achievement of the monarchic period.[146] Like no other urban structure, cost and size alone suggest these must be state institutions. We can see this, especially since they are generally similar in appearance, rooted in a common, basic plan.[147] If only because the court functioned on behalf of the military security of the city and thereby represented the state military presence, it should be regarded as a state institution.

We should also note the ambivalent character of a court functioning in this way. It is immediately apparent when we read relevant judicial pronouncements in preexilic law books. The Book of the Covenant and Deuteronomy not only place legal decisions in the collective hands of the people who render them, they also have information about the legal procedures themselves. Ex 23:1ff. is directed at conduct in this court. Deut 16:18, 17:14ff. and elsewhere make Israel responsible even for the establishment of judges. Since individual clans could be drawn into the state judicial process by means of the elders, all Israelites could be made responsible for the judicial system.

We should note that a circle of elders is attested elsewhere as a principal judicial jurisdiction in pre-state societies,[148] but the basic sources do not support this sort of organization in Israel. An important innovation in state law was that any kind of public legal venue at all existed: a forum, before which legal disputes could be brought, able to hear witnesses, render judgments, apply legal principles ensuring a balance of power in the legal relationships. The function of the king as a judge, especially important during the first monarchic period, was granted to the elders of clans who functioned along with the king's

---

142 See e.g. Rüterswörden, *Beamte* 138 note 57; especially, however, Kessler, *Staat und Gesellschaft* 192ff.
143 See Kessler, *Staat und Gesellschaft*.
144 For the position of the elders in the pre-state period, see especially Schäfer-Lichternberger, *Eidgenossenschaft* 290f. For the elders in the Old Testament, see Bornkamm, article on presbys; Ploeg, *Les anciens*; McKenzie, *Elders*; Roeroe, *Ältestenamt*; Conrad article on *zāqen*; Reviv, *Elders*.
145 For the special significance of the elders in the exilic period, see Buchholz, *Älteste* in summary 381ff.
146 See especially H. Weippert, *Palästina* 426ff.
147 H. Weippert, *Palästina* 427; see also e.g. Shilo, *Town Planning*.
148 See above p. 34.

officials. If leading clans and their representatives were attracted into governmental structure, they also had potential power within and even over the state. While to eighth-century prophets elders (just like judges) were part of the corrupt social élite, later in Judah there was a reform movement originating within the groups.[149] In any case, the characteristic of Mosaic law that made all Israel responsible for justice and law, thus wresting law away for the state and the people, had the Hebrew legal community that originated in the monarchic period as its social basis.

Ex 18 and the Mosaic Institution

The picture of the preexilic legal system is utterly dependent upon a Mosaic institution, as the traditions regarding a Jerusalem central court are criticized in 2 Chr 19 and Deut 17:8. Does this show the monarchic period's essential legal-historical innovation, the critical step toward nationalization of law,[150] or is it a completely unhistorical, exilic or post-exilic projection backward – or even a simple utopian view?[151]

The matter of a central court is connected with whether there was a Mosaic institution, or at least one legitimized by Moses, because of the close relationship of these texts with those that speak of the establishment of judges by Moses (Ex 18; Deut 1) or of Moses' giving of the spirit to the elders (Num 11). Knierim's theory of a Mosaic institution in monarchic Jerusalem uses Ex 18:13ff. as a point of departure.[152]

According to Ex 18:13, Moses sat to judge from morning until evening (verse 13). When questioned by his Midianite father-in-law (verse 14), Moses explained this judging (*špṭ*) further (verses 15f.) as (1) inquiring of God (*drš*), (2) judging (*špṭ*) in the sense of deciding or arbitrating between two parties (*bēn 'iš ûbēn rēʿēhū*), (3) declaring (*jdʿ* hiph.) the statutes and instructions of God (*ḥuqqē ha 'elōhim wᵉ 'et tōrōtāw*). The Midianite suggested he share his responsibilities with qualified men, to be placed as officials or officers (*śārim*) over thousands, hundreds, fifties and tens of the people (verse 21); they "judge" (*špṭ*, verse 22).

What duties remained for Moses? He judged cases which were too "important" (verse 22) or too "hard" (verse 26). Other judges took small cases. Further, according to the suggestion of verses 19f., Moses continued to bring people's cases before God and teach the people "the commandments and instructions and make known to them the way they are to go and the things they are to do" (verse 20). This meant that of the three assignments, Moses retained two entirely for himself, and of the third – resolving disputes – he kept only the most difficult cases. He was relieved of all of the smaller, simpler ones.

In general, scholars now agree that this text deals with legitimation of a judicial organization. By tracing their history back to Moses, judges are etiologically supported and legitimized. The dating of the text and the judicial order behind it as well as the literary entity (of concern for Moses' activity and the judges' jurisdiction) is controversial.

149 See below pp. 212ff.
150 Thus with Albright, *Judicial Reform*; Knierim, *Exodus* 18; especially Maccholz, *Justizorganisation*; Whitelam, *Just King*; Wilson, *Judicial System*.
151 Thus with Wellhausen, *Prolegomena* 186; e.g. Niehr, *Rechtsprechung* 114f., 121f.
152 Knierim, *Exodus* 18.

Regarding the literary criticism of Exodus 18, Schäfer-Lichtenberger recently offered an analysis, summarizing and focusing previous studies.[153] He believes there is a basic narrative supplemented with three groups of additions: verses 15b, 20b; verses 16b, 20a; as well as verses 21b, 25b. The last group concerns the assignment of the judges following the quadripartite military hierarchy, from tens through thousands.

There is much evidence for the old idea that it is a literary emendation.[154] It is not quite clear what precisely the contents intend. Is it indeed a four-fold hierarchical division from tens through thousands corresponding to the military organization?

In my opinion, it is methodologically more significant that 21a does not connect easily with 21b. Following the word order, the verse says first that the officers were set over previously selected men, "set over them officers of a thousand . . ." There is no real need to repeat an object, which all translations do ("set such men over them . . ."),[155] but the context and especially verse 25 suggest this must have been intended.

The designation of the judges as "able men" = "men of the army" (ʾanšē ḥayil) in verses 21 and 25[156] fits with their simultaneous roles as officers in the usual military groupings, and is suggested by normal governmental structure[157] and ancient Near Eastern parallels.[158] Still, the basic narrative has shifted accent here.

Whether there are also additions in verses 15b, 16b, 20 is of greater importance and requires a different methodology. All aspects of Mosaic activity relating to asking God and then transmitting the divine instructions are part of later strata. This is supported exclusively from the contents. Moses' procedure would be different in 15b, 16b, 20 than in 13f.[159] This kind of inquiring of God (drš) is especially an activity of prophets,[160] but they, on the other hand, did not keep regular "office hours."

Alleged tensions in the text that have led to this literary criticism come from exclusively modern interpretations of what is happening in the text. It is true the activities appearing together here are reported separately elsewhere; this is not sufficient reason to divide them completely everywhere; it fails to explain how or why they are together here.

Further: Schäfer-Lichtenberger draws attention to texts like Lev 24:11ff.; Num 9:6ff., 15:32ff., 36:1ff.[161] These are individual cases brought before Moses where a divine decision was given.[162] This meant that

---

153 Schäfer-Lichtenberger, *Exodus* 18.
154 Junge, *Wiederaufbau* 57f.; Knierim, *Exodus 18* 155, 167f.
155 See e.g. Noth, *Exodus* 114.
156 For the term, see Schäefer-Lichtenberger, Stadt 316f., where he attempts to distinguish between gibbōr-ḥayil and ben-ḥayil.
157 See Rütersworden, *Beamte*.
158 See Weinfeld, *Judge and Officer*, with much material from the ancient Near East and Israel.
159 Schäfer-Lichtenberger, *Exodus 18* 64ff.
160 For drš see especially Westermann, *Fragen und Suchen*.
161 Schäfer-Lichtenberger, *Exodus 18* 67f., see below pp. 98ff.
162 The term drš is never used here, nevertheless the significance of inquiring of God is clear (see prš in Lev 24:12, Num 15:34; qrb hiph. Num 27:5, as well as šmʿ Num 9:8).

general, binding rules were made of the decisions. These were precedent-setting cases in which Moses acted precisely as described in Ex 18, and in which all three of the Mosaic activities are connected in a manner that renders them substantively and organically inseparable.

Methodologically, however, it would be inadmissible and a pure *petitio principii* to attempt to separate this from Ex 18 by literary criticism, as long as we are unable to find linguistic reasons for stratification within the text, and indeed there are none. Moses' office combines duties often separated and practiced by other people, but which do appear elsewhere performed by Moses, and in a certain sense they comprise what is specifically Mosaic.

We already find such a picture in Ex 18. The entire structure of Old Testament law demonstrates that the activities combined here (the prophetic or priestly inquiry of God, judicial decision and instruction in law) are not combined by accident. The primary intent of the text emphasizes that in Ex 18 all of these things are combined in the activity of Moses.

Dating of Ex 18:13 is somewhere between the time of David and the Persian period. The reasons for such extreme positions are less convincing and they raise issues that are at best marginal. 1 Sam 8:10ff. is cited as a parallel for a dating as early as the Davidic period.[163] However, the officers there do not have any juridic function.

Furthermore, general considerations about the early need for a state legal system are raised[164] which can be refuted from concrete reports of the early monarchic period. In fact, it is central for Ex 18 and unique within the Old Testament that the critical impulse came from a foreigner,[165] but this doesn't force us to date in the Persian or Babylonian periods[166] during which there may have been outside impulses for an intra-Israelite legal system. Everything we know suggests this was not the case. Rather, the Persian political structure enabled an autonomous legal organization, oriented toward its own traditions.[167]

Dating of Ex 18 is difficult. The text is isolated in its context, having been surrounded by priestly passages,[168] and the traditional ascription to

163 See especially, Reviv, *Traditions* 568ff.
164 Schäfer-Lichtenberger, *Exodus 18* criticizes the connection drawn by Knierim, among others, with 2 Chr 19 and thus Jehoshaphat's reform (79ff.). Discussing 2 Chr 19, she mentions three levels of appeal. In addition to the court of appeal, the king should also function as an appellate judge (which the intent of the text apparently contradicts) and the differentiation of easy and hard cases is dropped in 2 Chr 19. All of this points to a "greater societal complexity" (82) and for that reason, the event that is mirrored in Ex 18 must be dated earlier. In addition, she cites (83) a few of David's legal decisions (1 Sam 30:21ff.; 2 Sam 12:5f. as well as 14:1ff.). But texts of this very kind show clearly that the tradition does not recognize a level of appeal alongside or below the king that had been authorized by him.
165 For a more recent interpretation of the unusual tradition, see Baskin, *Pharaoh's Counsellors.*
166 Thus Buchholz, *Älteste* 97f.
167 See above pp. 49f. and below pp. 334ff.
168 For both, see Blum, *Pentateuch* 153ff. On the one hand, Blum himself regards Ex 18 as standing outside the D composition and consequently a late addition to the Pentateuch. On the other hand, he accespts ancient, pre-deuteronomistic

the Elohist is no longer assumed. Indeed, everything argues compellingly for a preexilic and pre-deuteronomistic date. It contains nothing referring to later language or theology. It must come from a time or group, for whom it would not have been wrong to have a "heathen" impetus for a basic judicial organization in Israel and the awareness of divine participation in legal decisions. Even the relation to Ex 18:1–12 does not suggest a late monarchic date.[169] We could only say more because of the close relationship with 2 Chr 19 and the dating of the legal organization attested there.[170]

Ex 18 also attests the establishment of judges within the context of a fixed judicial organization in the monarchic period, giving them legitimacy by tracing their lineage back to Moses. The description of criteria for selection in verse 21 suggests we are dealing with officials who are related to the militia. The difficulty, however, lies in the judicial organization.

In my opinion, the other question is far more important for the legal history of Israel: *Who was this Moses?* Of the three activities ascribed to him, two remain his entirely, and he retains the difficult cases of the third. Moses represents an institution having jurisdiction in especially difficult cases, these are cases that are inseparably connected to previous law – precedent-setting decisions.

At the same time, Moses asks direction from God, as a prophet or a priest would do. This correlates with the establishment of precedents, but is hardly limited to it. Asking God for a decision and judgments from God play a large role in Israelite law just as they do in the rest of the ancient Near East, and these activities are associated with the cultic site.[171] Furthermore, the people are given instruction on the divine teachings in Ex 18. There is no reason to make a content or literary-critical distinction in these activities, for in order to understand Moses, we must (even apart from Ex 18) investigate *that* place connected with all these activities. Laws of the Old Testament tracing themselves back to Moses already contain laws and cultic instructions and are within themselves instruction in law. Whom did this Moses represent during the period of the Israelite monarchy?

At least during the early monarchic period, the *king* handled especially difficult cases, and there are Near Eastern traditions where equally difficult cases are shifted from lower courts to the king.[172] Indeed, the inquiring of God and the instructional report to the people of divine legal decisions are not otherwise attested for the king, but the king was also priest and administrator of the large state shrines. It is consistent with the

---

connections between Ex 3f. and 18. Thus, only the sequence remains that an older Moses tradition "partially taken up by K^D (Ex 3f.) elsewhere, however, only appended in a later version (Ex 18)" (122). This construction is really hardly probable, having been dictated by the needs of a unified D composition.

169 For a possible postexilic sense connection, see Blum, Pentateuch 161f. Nevertheless, according to Blum this does not argue for an origin at this time, the differences are clear enough.

170 See below pp. 91ff.

171 See Boecker, *Recht* 19, 27f.

172 E.g. especially from the Hittites, see Weinfeld, *Judge and Officer* 75f.

sacral monarchy that God is close to it and gives his decisions to the king.[173]

We might also want to find other royal features in the person of Moses.[174] We might guess Jeroboam I was similar to the figure of Moses.[175] It is, however, unlikely that the Israelite king at any time performed the duties in person or was even able to lay claim to things here associated with the name of Moses. There are duties of the king as supreme judge and there are duties of a cultic court at the shrine. Moses' name brings together things that are elsewhere ascribed to different characters, things that might be described as central characteristics of Israelite law. If, according to Ex 18, an official judge is given legitimacy by association with Moses, this presumes there had not previously been such a Mosaic institution. Before we go any farther correlating with the establishment of a central court, we should look at two other texts that support the preexilic dating of Ex 18, because they are later and independent of it.

First, we have the variant in Deut 1:9–18,[176] which is a part of the introduction to the Book of Deuteronomy in Deut 1–3 in which we see the foreword to the deuteronomistic historical account.[177] It stands here at the pinnacle of the retrospective of events since the sojourn at Mount Horeb.[178] The most startling feature of Ex 18 is missing: the initiative of a Midianite. Furthermore, the narrative does not take place at the beginning of the sojourn at the mountain of God, as in Exodus, but at the end.

In Deut 1, the starting point is the size of the population. The number of people, described by comparison with the stars of heavens (verse 10),[179] makes it impossible for Moses to bear the "heavy burden of your disputes" alone (verse 12). On his own initiative, he makes a proposal to lighten his load, and the people agree (verses 13f.).

Instructions for criteria for selection, organization and function of the men assisting Moses, are of such that they are frequent subjects of literary-critical analysis. In fact, it is more likely there is literary stratification here than in Ex 18.

---

173 We might refer here to the self-awareness as it is expressed in the royal psalms 2, 72, 110 and others.

174 Porter, *Moses*.

175 For the close relation of 1 Kg 12 and Ex 5 see, for the moment, Crüsemann, *Widerstand* 176. Furthermore, there is so great a similarity in the careers of the two men: the fulfilment of duties under compulsory service, assault or murder, flight from the country, return as a free person, that we can exclude coincidence. But is Moses modeled after Jeroboam or Jeroboam after Moses? The former seems much more probable.

176 For the closeness, see not least , the compensating combination in the Samaritan Pentateuch. For this, see Tigay, *Empirical Basis*. Rose, *Deuteronomist* 226ff. contains a detailed comparison of both texts as well as Num 11. See also, Perlitt, *Deuteronomium*.

177 First, Noth, *Studien* 12ff. For Deut 1–3, see Radjawane, *Israel*; McKenzie, *Prologue*; also Perlitt, *Deuteronomium*.

178 For the text, see especially Cazelles, *Institutiones*; Rad, *Deuteronomy*; Radjawane, *Israel* 118ff. The thesis in Lohfink, *Darstellungskunst* that Deut 1:9–18 disturbs the context and is therefore a later insertion, is not taken up, e.g. by Braulik, *Deuteronomium*.

179 For the deuteronomistic character of the evidence, see Köckert, *Vätergott* 218ff.

Verse 15 "I took the leaders ... and installed them as leaders ..."
seems especially excessive.[180] We should again refer to the methodological problem, that this kind of manipulation presumes a previous
knowledge of it, which ought to be intended here. From where would
this knowledge have come? We must try to get a real understanding of
the words before us[181] in order to answer the question whether there
really are contradictions here or perhaps we are simply imagining them.
Furthermore, we should always try first to understand the intent of the
emendations and what they produce.

If we choose to remain with the text as we have it, the following
would probably be what was intended: Moses urged the people to
select wise and insightful men, by tribes (*lᵉšibṭēkem*). He wanted to
establish these men as leaders of the people (verse 13). The people
selected them by tribes and according to the level of their wisdom. Moses
then installed them without regard to his own criteria, as for example
in Ex 18 where he presided over the selection. After the people agreed
with this procedure (verse 14), it was occasionally said that Moses
chose the heads of the tribes and established wise, insightful men
as leaders of the people (verse 15). Verse 15b then closes the statement with asyndeton: "commanders of thousands, commanders of
hundreds ..."

When we try to interpret these statements, it appears there were
already men at the head of the tribes who were wise and insightful. They
were then re-established by Moses as the leaders. In other words, they
were attested in the function that they already had: They received Mosaic
legitimacy. Seen in this way, the situation is not at all unreasonable or
self-contradictory. It is expressed in an obviously complex manner, and
dependence upon the older tradition of Ex 18 is evident. However, the
procedure has its own inner plausibility, especially when we see (as we
would expect from the introduction to the deuteronomistic history in
Deut 1–3) problems and events of the exilic period mirrored within it.
The leaders of Israel, together with their traditional structures, then
assumed the Mosaic assignments. It is curious that the judges referred to
in verse 16, cannot be immediately recognized. Furthermore, Moses'
description of the problem in verse 15 mentions legal problems with only
one of the three terms used (*rîb*).

Administration of justice, as it is presented in Ex 18, is at best only a
part of the job. Judges might have participated in Mosaic legitimation
since others did.

Finally, we also see a change over against Ex 18 in the linguistic style
and manner in which Moses' remaining duties are described. Only verse
17, one single sentence, remains. That sentence only appears after the
important sentence in the description of the duties of judges in 17a, "for
the judgment (*mišpāṭ*) is God's." Thus, Moses is rendered unnecessary in
human relations with God in legal matters. All that remains for Moses is

---

180 See Bertholet, *Deuteronomium* 4; Steuernagel, *Deuteronomium* 51f. Much more
comprehensive manipulation in Mittmann, *Deuteronomium* 24ff. Nevertheless, see
Perlitt, *Deuteronomium* 55f., 69f. a "very early ... addendum" (70).
181 The analyses of Christensen, *Prose and Poetry*; Schedl, *Prosa und Dichtung* require
no literary-critical manipulation.

to hear cases which are too difficult. Bring the problem to him, "and I will hear it" (verse 17).

Is it an accident that we read more of "hearing" – in other words: listening to case pleading, and not of judging and rendering a decision? Rabbinic tradition, in any case, reprimanded Moses because he wanted to hear such cases alone, without the assistance of God.[182] In many respects, the difference between this and Ex 18 is clear, even though it is certainly a variation of the same tradition. Tribal leaders, wise men, warriors and judges all have the same assignment as Moses, and they were all selected by the people themselves and no one else, and they share Mosaic authority. They also share in direct negotiations with God. Thus, there is hardly anything left for Moses to do.

Perhaps Num 11:4–35 represents yet one other, more significantly altered variant of this text. We should regard the text as an entity, even though tradition-historically we can isolate an older quail narrative (at most verses 4–6, 10, 13, 18–23, 31–35) and its interpretation in a narrative of the elders (verses 11f., 14–17, 24f.). Nevertheless, both stories "blend together in a unity which is no longer divisible."[183]

There is much to suggest that we regard this then as Deut 1 and as a part of a deuteronomistic compositional stratum.[184] As in Deut 1, Moses is unable to bear the burden of the people. He gives the child with whom God was pregnant and then bore, as it were, back to him (verse 12). The magnitude of the crisis appears especially clearly in verse 15: Moses asks to be allowed to die. This is about nothing less than the death of the people and of Moses.

A solution to the crisis is achieved in which YHWH "took some of the spirit that was on him and put it on the seventy elders (šotᵉrīm)[185] of the people" (verse 16) who then prophesied. A widely accepted interpretation speaks of "ecstatic prophecy," which in this way was given legitimation by Moses,[186] but how were these ecstatics to help resolve the problems of Moses or the people? And why were elders chosen to become this kind of prophet?

The verb employed here (nbʾ, hithp.) can in fact indicate rapture (1 Sam 10:5f., 10; 19:20ff.), but it can also refer to a prophetic speech (1 Kg 18:8, 18; Jer 14:14; Ez 37:10) or activity (Jer 26:20) and this predominates in later passages.[187] The specifically ecstatic element is given little stress in Num 11. There is much more concern with the fact that the elders,

---

182 Sifre Deut §17, see Weinfeld, *Judge and Officer* 65, note 3.
183 Noth, *Pentateuch* 34, note 119, and *Numeri* 74ff.; similar Fritz, *Israel* 16ff. and especially Aurelius, *Fürbitter* 177f.
184 Traditionally the quail narrative has been regarded as part of J (otherwise especially Seebass, *Num XI*; see also Heinen, *Last*). Nevertheless, H. H. Schmid, *Jahwist* 72ff. has pointed out the similarity to Jeremian and deuteronomistic texts. For the compositional cohesion of the chapter, see Blum, *Pentateuch* 76ff. The reasons for placing Num 11 after Deut 1 are given in (among others) Rose, *Deuteronomist* 241ff.; see also Perlitt, *Deuteronomium* 59. For the analysis of Jobling, *Sense*; as well as Fisch, *Eldad*, see (critical) Blum, *Pentateuch* 79f., note 151. For interpretation, see also Heinen, *Last*; Gunneweg, *Gesetz*.
185 There is certainly a gloss here already apparent from the sentence structure.
186 Noth, *Numeri* 79; Rad, *Theology I* 303; Perlitt, *Mose* 601f.
187 Jeremias, article on *nābiʾ* 17; Müller, article on *nābiʾ* 156.

typical representatives of a traditional order, became prophets and thereby charismatics.[188] As in Ex. 24:1, 9, for example, the seventy elders are representatives of the people as a whole. If the text is speaking out of the context of the exile or the period thereafter, it is making a clear and important statement. Elders must become prophets who are filled with the spirit in order to prevent the death of the people and of Moses.[189] They maintain the spirit of Moses and he "rests" on them as otherwise the spirit of Elijah or Elisha (2 Kg 2:15) or of God rests on the future king (Isa 11:2).

It is rather significant for our interpretation that the spirit of Moses even reached two people who were not present at this event (verses 26ff.). They did not have to be present at the shrine and all attempts by the people to resist them were rejected by Moses (verses 28f.). Whether we think of the diaspora or another group remote from the shrine, the statements are clear.

Narratively, the statement is unprepared, but probably can be explained from practices of the exilic/postexilic periods that both men belonged among the registered (verse 26).[190] The purpose – even beyond the representative function of the 70 – becomes clear in Moses' answer in verse 29, "Would that all the Lord's people were prophets." There are perhaps comparable things in a comparable time, but otherwise only in eschatological expectation as in Joel 3:1; Ez 39:29.[191]

In summary: While the goal of the preexilic Ex 18 is the legitimation of the establishment of official judges, it is also clear that there is an authority identified with Moses behind the event that identifies the judicial function of the king with the important shrines and their priests or prophets. There is a difference in the exilic or postexilic variants of this tradition in Deut 1 and Num 11. Here there is a much stronger emphasis upon the groups established by Moses or supplied with his spirit.

Unlike Ex 18, both of these are dealing with traditional authorities – elders and tribal leaders. They represent and lead the people, and for their duties they have Moses' spirit and legitimation from him. Moses gives his authority through the intent if not in the narrative details of the story. In this way they represent him as he legitimizes them.

The traditional leadership of the people, possibly even the entire people (Num 11:29), must become "Moses" in order to surmount the crisis and guarantee a future. The question, whether we can identify the authority behind the Moses of Ex 18 more clearly remains unresolved.

The Jerusalem High Court and its Significance

The study of Moses in the monarchic period is especially an investigation of legislative jurisdiction in this period. In the ancient Near Eastern world this function would suggest the role of the king, but Israel's laws are

---

188 We find the, especially here, obvious terminology of Max Weber already in Noth, *Numeri* 78.
189 For such an interpretation, see also Weisman, *Personal Spirit*.
190 See e.g. Ezra 2:62 and for this Gunneweg, *Esra* 65.
191 See Gamberoni, ". . . *wenn doch* . . ." and especially Blum, *Pentateuch* 79f., 194f.

decidedly not royal, and it would be pure conjecture to think that such an awareness is due solely to later revision.[192] This notion is too deeply rooted in the basic structure. Whatever role a king may have, Moses has in Israel.

To whom do we owe the preexilic laws? So that we can avoid having to answer a question before we raise it, we have but one option in dealing with this matter: We must bring into the discussion the only institution mentioned in this text alongside the king: the high court in Jerusalem. According to 2 Chr 19:5ff., the court was established by King Jehoshaphat in the ninth century, and according to Deut 17:8 it became a fundamental component of Israel's order in the land.

Wherever a high court exists, it plays a significant role in the judicial life of the country, even in matters such as drafting laws, gathering cases, etc. For that reason, it is necessary to study questions of existence, structure and styles of operation of this institution and to inquire after possible connections with the laws of preexilic Israel.

Even the problem of the very existence of the high court is a subject of great controversy. This is especially true for the theories that 2 Chr 19:5ff. represents a reliable tradition. To regard this text as a "historical report" is to commit the "fundamental error(s) of research into judicial organization in Israel."[193] Even today the discussion is dominated by Wellhausen's assertion that the justice reforms described in 2 Chr 19 are a fiction spun from the name of the king who was responsible – Jehoshaphat = "YHWH judges."[194] Ever since the time of Wellhausen this controversy has continued to rage.[195]

We might find an avenue for resolution of this dilemma in the fact that even the most critical studies of Chronicles regard at least a small part of their material as representing a historically reliable tradition. This is the case, for example, for 2 Chr 11:5ff., 26:6a, 32:30a.[196] Since generalizations are inappropriate, we will have to make decisions on a case by case basis.[197] Adequate reasons[198] supporting the tradition represented in Chronicles have been offered and they are increasing. This suggests that we might be able to come to a fairly solid conclusion.

At the outset, we can say that the topic of judicial organization and the administration of justice are not otherwise important for Chronicles.[199] They cannot be regarded as a *topos* for these historical documents, and 2 Chr 19:5ff. contains more and different material for the purpose of

---

192 Thus e.g. Whitelam, *Just King* 218 and elsewhere.
193 Niehr, *Rechtsprechung* 121.
194 Wellhausen, *Prolegomena* 186; for a review, see especially Machholz, *Justizorganisation* 320, note 10a.
195 Rather critical: Ackroyd, *Chronicles*; Coggins, *Chronicles*; Becker, *2. Chronik*; Mosis, *Theologie* especially 177 note 22; Welten, *Geschichte* 184f. Rather positive: Kittel, *Chronik*; Galling, *Chronik*; Rudolph, *Chronikbücher*; Michaéli, *Chroniques*; Myers, *Chronicles*.
196 See especially Welten, *Geschichte* 191ff. For the history of the research into the fundamental question, see Japhet, *Historical Reliability*.
197 Thus especially Machholz, *Justizorganisation* 319ff.
198 Especially Machholz, *Justizorganisation* 319ff. and Williamson, *Chronicles*, 287ff.
199 Machholz, *Justizorganisation* 319f.

popular instruction.[200] Torah is as a rule valid for Chronicles, but its own validity must be achieved.[201]

But this is exactly what does not happen in 19:5ff. Rather, there is a great deal of conflict between Torah and other legal traditions (*miṣwāh*, *huqqîm* and *mišpaṭîm*, verse 10). The events in verses 5ff. are in clear disagreement with those contained in verse 4. This already argues strongly in favour of the fact that verse 5 illustrates a different tradition.[202]

Within verse 5 the central terms in the context are not those of the chronicler because they never appear elsewhere. This is also true of the "instruction" (*zhr*, hiph., cf Ex 18:20) as well as "incur guilt" (*'šm*) in verse 10. The division of priestly and secular duties in verse 10 is hardly consistent with the chronicler's theology. And the "officer" (*nāgîd*) of the house of Judah is an interesting term. Would we not expect here the otherwise so important "officers of the house of God" (*nāgîd bet hā'elohîm*; see 2 Chr 28:7, 31:13 and elsewhere).[203]

Finally, the observation that we have a theme comparable to 19:5ff appearing only one other time in Chronicles – in conjunction with the same king – is of special importance. According to 2 Chr 17:7–9, Jehoshaphat assigns a group of officials (*'sārîm*), Levites and priests to teach in Judah (*lmd*, pi.) from the "book of the Torah of YHWH." This is what should be expected from the chronicler. 2 Chr 17 could only be regarded as an account typical of the chronicler of what is described in 19:5ff.

There is a precisely parallel situation in 2 Chr 32. There we have the historically reliable narrative in verse 3 and the same material presented in the chronicler's language in verse 30a (which had already been described in verse 3).[204]

In view of all of these reasons, we *must* consider the possibility that 2 Chr 19:5ff. represents an older tradition.[205] The text is indeed parenetically structured (especially verses 6f., 9b, 10b, 11b) and at this time we need not go into whether the conflict is more that of the chronicler[206] or deuteronomistic.[207]

The question remains, however, whether the ascription of the judicial organization to Jehoshaphat is correct. The alternative would probably be to associate it with Josiah, especially because of the similarity with Deut 17:8.[208] This text already presumes such an institution and is not

---

200 Welten's construction of a *topos* of popular instruction in Chronicles (*Geschichte* 184f.) is rendered highly unlikely by his own thinking in note 19.

201 See Willi, *Thora*; Shaver, *Thora*; Kellerman, *Anmerkungen*.

202 Thus especially Williamson, *Chronicles* 287.

203 See Hasel, article on *nāgîd* 216f.

204 See Noth, *Studien* 139f.; Welten, *Geschichte* 39.

205 The opposing reasons listed in the literature are extremely general up to Wellhausen. See above, note 200. This is especially true of Niehr, *Rechtsprechung* 121f. who in his discussion dispenses with the reasons advanced by Machholz and Williamson.

206 Thus Machholz, *Justizorganisation* 221, with an attempt to determine the Chronicler's share.

207 Thus Williamson, *Chronicles* 287f. who regards especially from 4 on as a piece that has been taken over. It is influenced by the deuteronomist, but in 5.8.11a there is a core of pre-deuteronomistic material.

208 Galling, *Chronik* 124 and Junge, *Wiederaufbau* 81ff. have considered a dating under Josiah.

interested in establishing it,[209] but rather, like all other sections of Deut 16–18, to reform it. A different value attaches to the assertion, related to material other than 2 Chr 19, that the fragments of tradition in Chronicles "are used in close association with the names of the respective kings." They have "come from annal-like sources."[210]

According to 2 Chr 19:5 Jehoshaphat placed judges in all of the fortified cities of Judah (*bᵉkol ʿārē yehūdāh habbᵉṣūrōt*). This information could not have come from Deut 17. Furthermore, according to Deuteronomy, judges were supposed to be set up in all localities (16:18). 2 Chr 19:5 sheds a special light upon the relationship, also known from Ex 18, of the military and judicial system. What exactly is meant here? We may deduce that we have here a group of fortified cities that played a special role for the military establishment.[211] For this reason, Machholz thinks that this text is dealing with an expansion of the royal judiciary into a militia.[212] We know from archaeological evidence, however, that the cities of the monarchic period were thoroughly fortified.[213] An unfortified city was a village not a city.[214]

The great expense that the construction of the city wall and gate entailed,[215] which first appeared to be in correlation with and as a consequence of the formation of the state, now appears to have been an element of state construction. 2 Chr 19:5 states that judges were placed in the cities of Judah by the king. Here we have what otherwise is referred to as "judgment at the gate" being established. The gate that we are talking about is that which is the constitutive and prominent element of the fortification.

The court and the gate that come together in the gate of a particular locality, as our verse tells us, were authorized by the king. They functioned in his name. This is precisely what we would expect on the basis of all of the other sources from the monarchic period treating legal matters. It supports the observations made above.[216]

The establishment of a public court in the city gate as the place of convergence of city development and state military security presence is attested in 2 Chr 19:5. According to the sources, there was not such a thing during the Davidic and Solomonic periods. But by the time of Amos these were taken for granted. The period of Jehoshaphat's rule is right in the middle of the two. It is approximately parallel to the first evidence of elders present in the courts of the northern kingdom in 1 Kg 21.[217] Unfortunately, 2 Chr 19:5 says nothing about the origin of the judges. According to everything else we know, they were the officials of the royal administration and army as well as the elders of the larger families.

209 Machholz, *Justizorganisation* 335, and below pp. 96ff.
210 Welten, *Geschichte* 193f.
211 Thus especially Machholz, *Justizorganisation* 324ff.; see also Phillips, *Criminal Law* 18f. and many others.
212 Machholz, *Justizorganisation* 324ff.
213 See H. Weippert, *Palästina* 427ff., 440.
214 We are reminded here of the system of daughter cities in Josh 15f.
215 See the material in Herzog, *Stadttor* 85ff.
216 See above pp. 78ff.
217 See above pp. 79f.

Then from verse 8 on, we are dealing with a structure in the capital. A court was set up there to which, according to verse 10, certain men from Judean cities were assigned particular legal cases. These were, for one, "between blood and blood" (*bēn dām lᵉdām*) and then also "between Torah and commandment, statutes and ordinances" (*bēn tōrāh lᵉmiṣwāh lᵉḥuqqīm ūlᵉmišpaṭīm*).

The first group dealt with the shedding of blood. These might be either capital offenses or only murders.[218] The wording "between blood and blood" points rather in the direction of the latter. Thus, we have here cases where blood stands against blood (cf Gen 9:6). Basically, this would mean that all murder cases were assigned to the Jerusalem high court. Now, the act as in the blood revenge of a clan as it is first attested in the Book of the Covenant Ex 21:13f. is very serious.[219] It is obvious that such cases would not be decided by the court at the gate of a particular city in which the clan and its elders played essential roles.

The second group include the cases in which, to echo the formulation here, norm opposes norm. They are cases that involve a "collision of norms"[220] and thus automatically involve something like precedents. Where the former legal tradition had contradictory ways, the high court was supposed to "instruct" (*zhr*)[221] the brothers so that they might not incur guilt (verse 10) upon themselves. This is a correlation clearly reminiscent of the Moses of Ex 18. Decisions in problematic cases (in other words, important or difficult cases) should have inducement for judicial instruction. It is important for our understanding of this formulation that we note that the markedly deuteronomic concept of Torah is not present here. To be sure, *tōrāh* has already been supersede by other legal terms and stands in contrast to them, but it does not include them.

Such a court, functioning in the capital and assuming all cases of revenge of blood and norm collision (thus precedent-setting cases) will become a place where we might most likely surmise the recording of such decisions, the systematic collecting and possible codification in law. We will discuss this further at a later time.[222]

At the same time we clearly note the ambivalent character. On the one hand, it does not argue against, rather it is in favor of seeing this institution against the backdrop of the problems discussed in Isa 10:1f.[223] If anywhere, this court is the place where the anonymous powers of the Jerusalem élite attacked by Isaiah were able to advance their own interests by means of written legislation. On the other hand, however, there are completely different possibilities.

Let us now examine the inner structure of the court as we see it in 2 Chr 19. According to verse 8, the institution consists of Levites (whose presence is unusual in Chronicles),[224] priests and the heads of families

218 With Machholz, *Justizorganisation* 327, he allows either option.
219 See below pp. 174ff.
220 With Machholz, *Justizorganisation* 327.
221 For *zhr*, see Machholz, *Justizorganisation* 328f.; Görg, article on *zāhar*.
222 See below pp. 165f., 195f.
223 See above pp. 20ff.
224 See Williamson, *Chronicles* 288.

(*rōšē hā'ābōt*). Thus, laity and cultic personnel functioned together. According to verse 11 the duties were divided in such a way that the highest priest (*kōhēn hārōš*) was responsible for "all matters of YHWH" (*l*ᵉ*kol d*ᵉ*bar-yhwh*); the "governor of the house of Judah" (*nāgîd l*ᵉ*bēt yēhūdāh*)[225] had "all the king's matters" (*l*ᵉ*kol d*ᵉ*bār hamélek*).

At the outset we should emphasize that we neither can, nor may we separate this double structure by means of literary criticism. It is supported by Deut 17 and corresponds exactly with the different aspects of Moses' activities in Ex 18. Such a structure is quite similar in the assignment of duties as well as the shape and design of the legal system elsewhere during this period. It is especially important that this makes the basic characteristics of Israelite law comprehensible. We would have to postulate them, if they were not already clearly attested.

The roles of the priests (and Levites) and the high priests present no special problems. The significance of cultic decisions, of divine judgment and oath, is well attested.[226] There is much attestation that the shrine in the capital had an important function even before the centralization of the cult, and this is also likely for a variety of reasons.

There may also have been something like difficult cases in the application of cultic law. In any case, we are concerned here with "matters of YHWH." The priests functioned, for example, in procedures involving divine judgment: they rendered the decision.

Furthermore, regarding the duties of instruction, we must consider whether the main job of the priests in earlier times was not to inquire of God by means of the tools of an oracle and then to transmit God's answer to the people.[227] We must remember that the actual priestly Torah applies not only in the narrow area of cultic activity, but also – because of Hosea's accusation – it extends far beyond the narrow confines of the cult (Hos 4:4ff.; 5:1). Even the teaching function of the court may correlate with the activity of the priests.

The special role of the king is of importance. On the one hand, he embodies the entire institution. On the other, there are within the institution "matters of the king" and they represent only half of his duties. According to 19:11, there is the "governor (*hannāgîd*) of the house of Judah" who is responsible for these "matters."

Correctly, we are reminded of something like the elders of Judah[228] except that they could not make absolute decisions. However, this person had a representative function for both Judah and the king (which again corresponds to the state role of the elders within the court). If he is responsible for royal matters, this probably means that the king himself had decided in these affairs previously, and still did in others.

Neither the king nor his representative was responsible for the "matters of YHWH." God himself rendered the decision through the

---

225 For the translation, see Hasel, article on *nāgîd*.
226 For the cultic court, see especially Rost, *Gerichtshoheit*; Horst, *Eid*; Press, *Ordal*. See also the so-called prayers of the accused in the Psalter. For these, see H. Schmidt, *Gebet*; Beyerlin, *Rettung*.
227 For the duties of the priest, see e.g. Cody, *Priesthood*; Budd, *Instruction*; Huffman, *Divination*; Sklba, *Teaching Function*; de Ward, *Superstition* among others.
228 See e.g. Rudolph, *Chronikbücher* 257.

mediation of cult personnel. Thus, even though the king initiated and founded the entire institution in the same way as he constructed and watched over the state shrines, he was not directly responsible for this law. He did not stand in God's stead or in that of the high priest. We see here a central judicial institution initiated by the state, which like the temple and cult – in spite of their proximity to the king – can be regarded simply as functions of the monarchy. God and priests, but also the general population of Judah fulfilled roles that we ought not to underestimate.

The court whose consultation is recommended in Deut 17:8–13 is closely related to this institution; however, it illustrates the characteristic difference. Here again a brief review of the literary-critical questions is not absolutely necessary. The clause is part of a block of institutional laws in Deut 16:18–18:22. It has, as a whole, been regarded as an exilic or deuteronomistic emendation.[229] Nevertheless, this interpretation may be regarded as disproven.[230] Furthermore, we will take it up again later.[231]

Within Deut 17:8–13, the juxtaposition of Levite priests and the judge in verse 9 has provided impetus for scholars to employ literary criticism. It has been emphasized in the literature that each party makes sense by itself, but to juxtapose in rendering a decision implies that both are necessary.[232] Nevertheless, both are not necessary, and furthermore, above all, it is methodologically inadmissible to have both. We find the same simultaneity in verse 12, so we must assume it is consciously intended. We also find something similar in evidence in 2 Chr 19 and in a sense also in Ex 18. This means that we must have an explanation. Methodologically, in operations of this kind there is always a procedural judgment regarding the institution involved that has been made which is unknown to us and which can only be revealed to us through the text. It is a pure and arbitrary point of view that one must have been functioning before the other.

The only thing remaining for literary criticism to accomplish is to investigate the origins of verse 11.[233] There is nothing essential involved because verses 12f. has similar material. This duplication, however, does not imply that we should consider stratification; there are no contradictions in the material.

In Deut 17:8, we see a "procedural rule for local courts" that presumes the existence of a central court" which had not been only recently established.[234] Verse 8 sets up an arrangement for cases that require consultation with the high court, mentioning the people to be addressed. The cases that are to be decided in the gate (*biš͏ᵉ ʿārēkā*) but seem too "difficult" (*plʿ*) for the lower court, or too "heavy," to use the vocabulary of Ex 18, are the ones that should be brought here.

---

229 Especially Lohfink, Sicherung; cf Preuss, *Deuteronomium* 53f.
230 Especially Rüterswörden, *Gemeinschaft*.
231 See below, pp. 208ff., and elsewhere.
232 Already Hempel, *Schichten* 213ff. Complex, but hardly convincing literary criticism can be found in Merendino, *Gesetz* 175ff.; Seitz, *Studien* 200ff.; and most recently Foresti, *Storia* 76ff.
233 Thus, Rüterswörden, *Gemeinschaft*.
234 Machholz, *Justizorganisation* 335.

We find a three-part description of the cases in verse 8. In each of them, we are faced (exactly as in 2 Chr 19) with problems between two parties or claims (*bēn . . . lᵉ*). First, there are again the cases "between blood and blood," to which the third group relates, where we are obviously dealing with physical injury: "between one kind of assault and another" (*bēn néga' lānéga'*). Between these two formulations, we have: "between one kind of legal right and another" (*bēn dīn lᵉdīn*).

Unfortunately, this all-encompassing and obviously important usage is quite puzzling for us. We may surmise that it corresponds substantively with the expression "between *tōrā* and . . ." from 2 Chr 19:10. Apparently, the intent is to suggest "law against law." It is possible that *din* was selected as a more comprehensive expression that meant more than just "the substance of legal traditions, " including with it procedures which are involved. Thus, for example, these might be cases where statement opposes statement (or put another way, legal claim opposes legal claim). This is the classic situation for cultic jurisprudence (Ex 22:8).

The central court that dealt with these cases consisted of priests (Levites, of course), and a supreme judge, and it convened in the central cultic site. These people were to investigate the matter, or settle it by means of inquiry (*drš*). The same term used in Ex 18:5 reappears here in an extremely interesting place. It was their duty to announce the facts of the case (*ngd*, hiph.) or instruct (*jrh*, hiph. Deut 17:10). And in this manner the local jurisdiction kept *tora* in the community (verse 11). And the legal process reverted back to the lower level.[235]

The decision rendered is of special significance. The people are not to depart from it, either to the left or the right (verse 11), and in this way evil will be purged[236] from Israel, and "all the people will hear and be afraid and will not act presumptuously again" (verse 13). The same thing held true regarding the observance of the words of God or Moses elsewhere (Deut 13:6; 17:7; 19:19; 21:21; 22:21; 24:7).

The conclusion we must draw from this is absolutely clear: The decisions of the court have the same significance and the same rank as the things that Moses himself said – which means Deuteronomy itself. The Jerusalem high court rendered decisions with the authority of Moses and it had his jurisdiction. It spoke in the name of Moses and extrapolated forward the will of YHWH.

It has already been noted that Ex 18; Deut 17 and 2 Chr 19 belong together. Two of the three texts speak of a central courtyard (Deut 17; 2 Chr 19). The decision in difficult cases, where there is a concern for precedent, is connected with the function of the cultic court and its inquiry of God, and both of these were correlated with the duty to instruct in the law. The dual function corresponds with the combining of priests and laity. The institution was indeed inaugurated by a king but the court was no more subordinate to the king than the Jerusalem cult and its God were. Simultaneously, it is probable that a representative of the Judean people assumed the authority previously exercised by the king.

235 With proper emphasis, Machholz, *Justizorganisation* 337f.
236 For the so-called *bi 'arta* laws, see Preuss, *Deuteronomium* 119f. (Lit.); also Dion, "Tu feras . . ."

It was not the king but Moses who transmitted the Israelite law originating ultimately from God. If we were to ask whom it was that this "Moses" represented during the monarchic period, and who could speak in Moses' name, the only authority would be the Mosaically legitimized high court in Jerusalem that spoke in the name of Moses. In each case, this court played an important part in the history of Judean jurisprudence.

It remains to be seen to what degree we might be able or we must associate the Old Testament legal texts (Torah) with him. The composition and function of the court correspond so closely with the composition of Israelite law, unique in the ancient Near East, that we would have to conjecture or invent such an institution were it not already so well attested in the sources.

Tradition and Autonomy: The Postexilic Legal System

Traces of a "Mosaic" judicial jurisdiction

Martin Noth described this problem precisely! In his exposition of Lev 24:10ff., where Moses resolved an unusual legal problem by inquiring of God, Noth writes that since this text obviously comes from a later time, the question must be asked: "Who in this latter day could represent the archetypal Moses?" He goes on to speak of "charismatic conflict resolution."[237]

But is this kind of charismatic power really conceivable in exilic/postexilic times? The question, "who represented Moses in this and a whole series of other incidents?" arises even though the documents render a decision impossible. We must begin with an analysis of the five comparable texts.

The first text is Lev 24:10–23, a text from the Holiness Code.[238] It fairly leaps from the context in which it is set, as we see from the series of repeated structural formulae. The context is a collection of admonitions from God to Moses.[239] The location, on Mount Sinai (which is always presumed) is named immediately after our narrative in 25:1. In contrast, 24:10ff. treats a legal matter in the Israelite camp. The son of an Israelite woman and an Egyptian blasphemed the name of God in a quarrel with another Israelite.[240] As the following legal decision shows, the problem probably lies in the juncture of the themes. The regulation handed down regarding blasphemy settled the case (verses 15, 16a). Simultaneously, however, it is asserted that the same law applies to both Israelites and foreigners alike (verses 16, 22).

This was what happened: first they brought the criminal to Moses (verse 11); then, since Moses was unable to make an immediate decision,

---

237 Noth, *Leviticus* 156.
238 For all of the associated questions, see below pp. 277ff.
239 Lev 11:1; 12:1; 13:1; 14:1; 15:1; 16:1; 17:1; 18:1; 19:1; 20:1; 21:1, 16; 22:1, 17; 23:1, 9, 23, 26, 33; 24:1.
240 For the question of exactly in what did the sin lie, whether in the pronouncement of the already taboo tetragram or in a curse involving God or a combination of both, see Weingreen, *Blasphemer*; Gabel/Wheeler, *Blasphemy Pericope*; Livingston, *The Crime*.

the man was put into "custody" (*mišmār*),[241] until they received a decision (*pr̄s̆*) from God (verse 12). Finally, God spoke to Moses (verses 13–22), and Moses made known the information from God (verse 23). The decision as we have it wraps the judgment in the concrete facts of the case (verse 14), and the consequent death sentence was carried out immediately (verse 23).

But the decision involved much more: in particular, the fundamental principles governing situations like this case. These are questions that were apparently previously unresolved in law (verses 15f., 22). Furthermore, they were listed in the midst of regulations (verses 17–21) that had nothing to do with the resolution of this particular case. We might, therefore, conjecture that older, already formulated laws were amplified, later becoming a framework for this narrative example.[242] This would, however, take only one of the paragraphs into consideration.

Still, the text as it stands should probably be read in another way. Above all, the inclusion of the statements dealing with the same law in verses 16 and 22 tells us that all of the material in the middle is to be associated with this theme. It is thus intended that these decrees on murder and physical assault "were intended to be used not just for the people of the community, but also for foreigners."[243] Thus, the narrative described here gives occasion for far-reaching basic legislation regarding equality under disparate areas of law.

In the second case, we are dealing with a purely cultic problem. In Num 9:6–14, in conjunction with the announcement by God of the date of the Passover festival (verses 2–5), we are told that men who were rendered unclean from touching corpses and who therefore could not participate in the Passover celebration came to Moses and Aaron (verse 6). They did not want to be "kept from" (*gr̄ʿ*, niph., verse 7) the blessings(?) of the festival. Even though it is expressly stated that they came also to Aaron as the high priest, only Moses responds.

While they stand waiting (*ʿmd*), Moses wanted to listen to (*šmʿ*) what command God would give (verse 8). The divine answer (verses 9–14) begins with an injunction to instruct the people of God regarding the divine command. The resolution of the problem lay in the possibility of a post-celebration one month later. This regulation has an axiomatic character. In addition to the case presented here, there is an intention to handle cases like, for example, the possibility of a delay because of travel (verse 10). Above all, it is asserted that there may be excuses beyond those listed here to postpone the festival (verse 13). The participation of foreigners is also regulated here (verse 14). These are cultic questions, but nevertheless, the answer comes through Moses, not Aaron.

The third case of this kind is in Num 15:32–36. Unlike the first two, which took place during Israel's sojourn at Sinai, this narrative takes place while traveling in the desert. A man who had gathered wood on

---

241 For the language and the reality of such prisons, see Blumenfeld, *Imprisonment*.
242 Thus e.g. Elliger, *Leviticus* 330ff.
243 Noth, *Leviticus* 157. Hoffmann, *Leviticus II* 314 refers to the juxtaposition of assault and curse, which appears in Ex 21:15, 17.

the sabbath[244] was brought by those who had "found" (*mṣ'*) him to Moses (verse 33). This time, however, Aaron and the entire congregation (*ēdāh*) stand alongside Moses. Again, the criminal must be held in custody (*mišmār*) "because it was not clear (*prš*, pu.) what should be done to him" (verse 34). Then YHWH told Moses what he had decided (verse 35a). This only affected the concrete case this time, so it appears to be a pure judgment. Nevertheless, we are able to deduce that it had an axiomatic character and set precedent for similar cases. The complex procedure, and especially the initial inability to reach a decision, shows that there was not a legal norm to apply in such cases, but one had to be invented.

The last two cases are in Num 27 and 36; they treat the right of women to inherit.[245] In Num 27 the daughters of Zelophehad bring their problem before Moses, but simultaneously also before the priest Eleazar, the disciple of Aaron; before the leaders (*nᵉśī'im*), and before all the congregation (*ēdāh*, verse 2). Their father had died without sons, and they wanted to inherit his "possession" (*'ªḥuzzāh*) in the company of his brothers (verses 3f.) Moses then brought this problem (*mišpaṭ*) before YHWH (verse 5). The first part of the divine answer affected this particular case (verse 7). In conjunction with this – along with an expressed injunction to teach the law (verse 8a) – we encounter a fundamental regulation. It reaches far beyond this single occurrence, regulating the entire procedure for inheritance. The sequence of heirs was established: sons, daughters, brothers, father's brothers, next of kin. In so doing, all options were covered. The postscript in verse 11b states expressedly that this command of God to Moses should become a "statute and ordinance" (*huqqat mišpāṭ*) for Israel.

In Num 36 we are dealing with another legal question under the same circumstance: a supplement to the law regarding daughter as heirs.[246] The male members of the clan want to be assured that their daughters/heirs may not marry members of another tribe. This would permit the land of one tribe to pass into the ownership of another. According to verse 1, they bring this problem before Moses and the leaders (*nᵉśī'im*), the heads of the ancestral houses of Israel (*rāšē ha'ābōt*). These two groups are apparently equal to each other The answer is given in verse 5 as a command (*ṣwh*, pi.) from Moses to Israel on the basis of a word of God (*'al pī yhwh*). Again, it consists of two parts, a decision for the particular case (verses 5b–7) and an axiomatic regulation (verses 8f.). In conclusion, verse 10 speaks again of a command of God to Moses.

These narratives are extraordinarily important for an understanding of the development of law in Israel. There are always problems that have not been foreseen in previous systems of laws and norms, which remain

244 For the controversial question, what exactly this new and ignored problem was, according to texts like Ex 31:14; 35:2, see (besides the commentaries) Weingreen, *Woodgatherer*; Philips, *Wood-gatherer*; Robinson, *Strange Fire*.

245 In addition to the commentaries, see Snaith, *Daughters* who regards the problem not to be one of family inheritance, but of a tribe's possession of land, especially that of Manasseh in West Jordan, for which, however, the text supplies no support. See also Weingreen, *Daughters* who gives the basic legal-historical significance of as well as other cases from relevant legal decisions.

246 For the placement of both texts in the composition of the Book of Numbers, see below pp. 362ff.

unregulated. This is shown quite clearly by the fact that a decision cannot be rendered immediately, but the people must await an answer from God. These are precedent-setting cases, decided by a judgment that can be described.

It is, however, even more important that other related legal problems can be decided by the case. Analogous, related cases are associated with it. Further consequences are considered. Additional regulations are formulated to take care of these that correspond to the substance and linguistic form of other Old Testament laws. If we had not the case narratives and concrete examples of particular cases, other parts of Torah would present an incomprehensible piece of law. A precedent case becomes an occasion for fundamental changes that go far beyond the particular case.

The legal questions that the case raises are of great importance. This is true, for example, for basic issues regarding women's rights to inheritance (Num 27, 36), as well as legislation regarding foreigners or mixed people who commit crimes such as blasphemy, murder, assault (Lev 24). Besides the secular questions like inheritance, there is the great cultic problem of the possibilities and boundaries of a postponed cultic celebration (Num 9). Naturally, we should not underestimate the importance of questions regarding the death penalty for breach of sabbath (Num 15).

Aspects that otherwise appear to remain unconnected and basically separate are brought together in a case: judgment with legislation on one hand and secular law with inquiry of God on the other. The cases correspond precisely with the duties Ex 18 reserves for Moses: the great or difficult cases, resolution through inquiring of God, and instruction of the people about these things. These are the same duties that the regulations in Deut 17 and 2 Chr 19 assigned to the Jerusalem high court. We are able to go a good distance in understanding the origin of new law, and thereby the processes that must lie behind the composition of law books.

All five of the case narratives discussed belong to late strata of the Pentateuch. There is nothing to suggest moving their composition back into the preexilic period, everything points much more in a postexilic direction. Especially the texts in Num 27 and 36, the question of the rights of women to inherit, must be considered among the very latest texts and dated in the final redaction of the Pentateuch.[247]

We need to go one step farther. At least in the last three texts, Num 15, 27 and 36, the events are no longer situated during the sojourn at Sinai. They take place while traveling in the desert.[248] Thus they contain problems that cannot be resolved at Sinai, problems that were not contained in the comprehensive regulations given.

The basic problem of new law, of amplification and extension of the Sinai law is treated in narrative form. This is nothing less than the question of how Israel, living on this side of Sinai – and Moses – was to resolve legal problems that would arise, solutions that would be regarded as equal to

247 See Noth, *Numeri* 11f., 101, and see below pp. 362ff.
248 For the relation to the context, see Olson, *Death*.

Sinai law.[249] This illustrates yet again that the question of who represented this Moses had become very important.

The similarity in the structure of the narratives with the directives regarding the central court in Jerusalem may give reason to ascribe both of these texts to this same period. But neither are the reasons given for a preexilic origin of the institution annulled, nor the fact that many basic questions regarding the origin of law from (royal) precedent-setting judgments are also true for ancient Near Eastern law and are not peculiar to Israel.[250]

Above all, with all the similarities there are also differences, not least in the roles played by the participants. While in Ex 18 Moses set up judges who were to take care of smaller cases in his name, in Deut 17 and 2 Chr 19 the court consisted of priests and lay judges. In four of the five cases, the difficult cases were not judged by Moses alone, but they were simultaneously judged by Aaron or the entire congregation and its leaders.

What is noteworthy here is that the questions were presented to them, but they did not participate with Moses in the rendering of judgment or the inquiring of God; Moses did it all alone, nor did he function *like* Aaron or the priests. It is no accident that we find no indication of a cultic role for Moses in the texts. The texts are in the context of the priestly writings. According to priestly texts, there is always a tent of meeting in the camp where they are staying and with it the entire cultic apparatus.[251] Nothing could, for example, be more evident than to connect the conversation between Moses and God with this tent and then with the temple. But this never happens. Moses does not function like Aaron, nor as a priest. He is as different from Aaron as he is from the congregation and its leaders. It is not by chance that the two groups are placed beside Moses.

Moses in Postexilic Law

The two groups standing beside Moses in the narrative examples, who actually rarely have something to do with the actual legal procedure, are the two decisive ingredients in the postexilic legal system. This is true first and especially for pronouncing judgment.

On one side we have the entire congregation (*kol hā'ēdāh*) and their representatives. Perhaps one of the most important changes made over against the preexilic period is that all of the males of Israel make up the legal community. We only need to mention the fact,[252] we will discuss the legal-historical reasons later.[253] The whole congregation was not consulted along with Moses in the narratives mentioned. They play a part in rendering the decision in texts such as Num 35 (especially verse 24) and Josh 20:6.[254]

249 For this, see Olson, *Death* 176f., see also below pp. 361ff.
250 For this aspect of ancient Near Eastern law, see above pp. 11f., 86. as well as (especially) Locher, *Ehre* 85ff.
251 We think especially of the role of the majesty of YHWH (*k°bōd yhwh*) in texts such as Num 14, 16, 17, 20. For this, see especially Westermann, *Herrlichkei, Gottes* 128ff.
252 See Niehr, *Rechtsprechung* 106ff.
253 See below pp. 286ff., 308ff.
254 See Niehr, *Rechtsprechung* 107f.; for these texts and the asylum regulations, see below pp. 177. Niehr also refers to texts such as Ps 1:5; Num 32 as well as those "that speak of *qāhāl* in parallel to *'edāh*" (Prov 5:14; 26:26; Sir 7:7; Ez 23:36ff.; Ruth 4).

When the issue of mixed marriages arose, Ezra assembled the entire population (Ezra 10:7ff.). After the charges were made, the people authorized a legal organization to function on their behalf.[255] the officials (*śārîm*) were supposed to act on behalf of the whole congregation (*'mdl'*), and the litigants with the elders and judges of particular localities convened before them (verse 14).

Thus, the entire congregation is responsible for the organization of justice, as it is for other questions, as a final human resort. It is the fundamental potential that expresses itself here and even penetrates the judicial organization, but also the necessity for a stateless people to organize themselves autonomously. The last resort is the assembly of the congregation.[256] Other circumstances permit their representatives, who are variously designated and probably also recruited in a variety of ways, to function on their behalf.

We must remember here to see the people's representatives and especially the elders as we find them in the exilic/postexilic variants of the story from Ex 18 in Deut 1 and Num 11 as functioning in the line of Moses, as established and imbued with his spirit.[257] The pronouncement and interpretation (or application) of law made by them is thus a part of a comprehensively interpreted Mosaic office. When, in Matt 23:2, the Pharisees and the Scribes sit on the seat of Moses, this goes far beyond the question of the existence of a seat of Moses in the synagogue – an actual piece of furniture[258] – and it refers to the same phenomenon.

Nevertheless, in three of the five example narratives Aaron stands beside Moses. In Num 9 (in a cultic event) he is alone, in Num 15 and 27 he is with the people and their leaders. But even the chief priest does not exercise his office. There had always been a cultic court along with the other varieties.[259] The most important, if not the only duties, were oath and divine judgment.

According to a series of texts, the priests retained much broader juridical functions in the exilic/postexilic period. According to Deut 33:9b, 10, a later emendation of the older Levite passage in the Mosaic benediction,[260] the Levites have the duty to instruct (*yrh*, hiph.) the people

---

255 Gunneweg, *Esra* 183 correctly surmises that "an institurion that actually existed at the time of the chronicler" was legitimized "by lineage from the time of Ezra" and thus also the "early synagogal jurisdiction in cases of divorce."

256 For the concept of congregation and its problems, see Crüsemann, *Perserzeit* 208ff. The opinion that the *'edāh* might be an "ancient institution" that "certainly dates from before the monarchic period and perhaps even before the conquest of the land" (Levy/Milgrom, article on *'eḏāh* 1082) is dependent upon an early dating of the P texts, see Ringgren, *op. cit.* 1092 as well as Rost, *Vorstufen.* The definition of congregation in Num 1:2f. is, however, important. It gathers together the men of the clan and larger families who are capable of battle (*l'mišp'ḥotām l'bēt 'ebotām*; see Levy/Milgrom 1081).

257 See above pp. 87ff.

258 Since Sukenik, *synagogues*, people have in this connection referred to archaeologically attested things in the ancient synagogues. See, e.g. Hüttenmeister/Reeg, *Synagogen*, as well as Renov, *Seat of Moses* (Lit.).

259 See above p. 76.

260 They protrude from the context because of the plural verb forms and are remarkable because of the marked theological understanding. See already, Steuernagel, *Deuteronomium* 176f., who would, however, retain 9b by textual emendation; as well as Schulz, *Leviten* 15. On the other hand, Cross/Freedman, *Blessing* 194, 203f., regard verses 8–10 as amplification.

in the laws and teachings of God. The priestly definition of priestly duties in Lev 10:11 includes instruction in matters of law. They were supposed to teach (*yrh*, hiph.) the decrees given to them by Moses.

There are two additional texts, clear additions to older texts, that go an important step further. They assign responsibility for *every* legal dispute to priests. This is formulated in the Pentateuch especially in Deut 21:5, a supplement to the purification ritual occasioned by the discovery of a body of a person unknown (Deut 21:1–9).[261] While there was no discussion of priests in the preceding context, surprisingly, there is in verse 5, ". . . and by their decision all cases of dispute and assault shall be settled."

This goes far beyond the usual demands of a judicial organization in Deuteronomy, especially regarding the law regarding the high court in 17:8ff. In no way were all of the cases of assault to be decided by this court, only the disputed ones (*bēn néga' lᵉnéga'*, Deut 17:8). And the judges who were appointed throughout the country, according to Deut 16:18 were not priests or Levites. Conversely, in discussing the duties of the priests in Deut 18:1ff., law is not mentioned. For that reason, we could hardly regard Deut 21:5 as Deuteronomistic.[262] In principle, we find the same thing in Ez 44:24, "In a controversy they shall act as judges, and they shall decide it according to my judgments."[263]

Thus, we have here a fundamental claim of the priests, that they be consulted in *all* legal matters. This far exceeds preexilic relationships.[264] This is probably connected with an advance in priestly interests and, for example, the fact that a priest stood at the apex of the community.[265] This priestly duty was apparently not understood as legitimized to the same degree by Moses as the representatives of the people. To be sure, Deut 21:5 is part of the address of Moses in Deuteronomy, and in 33:8ff. we might think it is the "loyal one" (*ḥésed*) who is spoken of here, and so according to the common view Moses could be intended.[266] We do not find, however, a direct claim to the succession of Moses through commission, transfer of spirit or anything similar.

The five example narratives treat far more than normal judicial declaration. These are problems without precedents, whose solutions contain important innovations or extensions of law. And they cannot be assigned to either one group or the other that dominated postexilic jurisprudence. Nor do they belong where one of the groups stand alongside Moses. Moses alone acts, and only through him does God proclaim his law.

What authority did this Moses represent in postexilic Israel or Judah? The answer can only be that we do not know of an institution that in reality corresponded to the narrative role of Moses. Furthermore, it is

261 In addition to the commentaries, see Zevit, *The 'Egla-Ritual*; Dion, *Deutéronome 21*; Wright, *Deuteronomy 21*. There are barely differences regarding verse 5.
262 For the usual, rather vague interpretation, see e.g. Preuss, *Deuteronomium* 55.
263 See Zimmerli, *Ezechiel* 1135f.
264 Thus Niehr, *Rechtsprechung* 112ff.
265 As this is now supported by the discovery of a coin. See Mildenburg, *Yehud-Münze* 724f.; Barag, *Silver Coin*.
266 For a discussion, see Gunneweg, *Leviten* 38f.; Schulz, *Leviten*.

methodologically inadmissible to try to postulate such an institution on the basis of of these narratives. It is not so easy to transpose reality into narrative fiction.

There is no clear answer to the question of who corresponded to this Moses and his function in postexilic Israel. And probably, there simply cannot be one. Nevertheless, the investigation leads us to a few important aspects for elucidation:

- The assembly of the people or the congregation and their representatives are not only placed in a lively coexistence with the priests and their head, the high priest, in the texts discussed. They are together with them or otherwise they are the representatives of all the people. In important decisions both are involved. Thus, the Jews of Elephantine direct their request for the rebuilding of their temple first to the governor of Judah, and then "to the high priest Yahohanan and his colleagues, the priests in Jerusalem, and to 'Ostana, the brother of 'Anani and the leaders of the Jews."[267]

In Neh 5, both authorities determine the course of the important social reform which the rebuilding of the wall enabled. Here as elsewhere, however, there is no common unifying or overarching authority or institution. Both groups determine the critical theological and legal documents of the period, the Pentateuch, which can only be regarded as the common product of heavily priestly and rather deuteronomistic (in other words: oriented toward lay representation) groups with partially open disagreement.[268]

What connected them was really "Moses," that is, the Pentateuch as the book and work of Moses. But the cases that appear in our example narratives apparently stand out, not least because of the importance of their contents. They do not permit themselves to be reduced to being interpretations of older traditions, but they contribute something decidedly new. What "Moses" means here is then at least the possibility and reality of mutual recognition and reception between two groups with their divergent interests. Moses is more than the legal decisions of one of the two groups could possibly be.

- Now there is one figure who was already designated in the biblical texts as a Moses or a second Moses: Ezra (especially Ezra 7).[269] The later tradition related him quite closely to Moses,[270] which means, for example, also that he is greater than Aaron.[271] Ezra conveys the authorized law of God, already widely known. He introduces it in power and establishes judges for its operation, etc.[272] Now the figure of Ezra, despite its closeness to Moses, is fundamentally different. He does not receive the law directly from God, but from Moses. The law of Ezra, which always includes this,[273] has its authority as the old

267 Cowley, Aramaic Papyri 112 (no. 30, 1.18f.)
268 A reference to Blum, *Pentateuch* 333ff. may suffice. See further below pp. 340ff.
269 See Gunneweg, *Esra* 138.
270 4 Esra 14:21ff.; bSan 21b; bSuk 20a; see Munk, *Esra* especially 187ff.
271 QohR I, see Munk, *Esra* 188.
272 See below pp. 334ff.
273 See below pp. 337ff.

law of Israel and Moses. Still, the proximity to Moses is remarkable and it shows, not least that Ezra combines the two functions: he is priest and companion of Aaron (Ezr 7:1–5) and he is scribe and legal interpreter (Ezr 7:6). Ezra's law was not read and given power in the temple, but in the square in front of the Water Gate (Neh 8:1). Ezra is an outstanding figure in the process of development of the Pentateuch and so, as he begins his exposition, he plays a central role in the establishment of the Mosaic law and its Mosaic (Mt 23:2) interpretation.

– While we are not aware of a central jurisdiction during the period of the developing Pentateuch, a jurisdiction that functions in the succession and with the authority of Moses, the situation is different later. In the Sanhedrin and probably its predecessor, the Gerusia of the Hellenistic period as well, Judaism possessed an agency for its own guidance that, in addition to political, had legal jurisdiction[274] over the people. It comprised priests and laity together. It handled especially disputed cases, and thus also extensions of existing law.[275]

This Sanhedrin regarded itself as being in the succession of the judges established by Moses. Num 11, with its tradition of the seventy elders, who received the spirit of Moses,[276] as well as Deut 17 with the regulation of a central court,[277] but also the establishment of the judges in Ex 18[278] and Deut 1:9ff. are the bases for legitimation of the Sanhedrin.

We do not know whether this is the way it was from the very beginning. Nevertheless, its composition of seventy or seventy-one members, which correlates with references to a representative council in Num 11 and elsewhere in the Bible, points toward the fact that it regarded itself as being in the succession of Moses from very early on.

In part, today, it has been accepted that the Gerusia[279] (earliest attestation 197 BCE) had roots extending back before the Hellenistic period.[280] It is true that there are no more reasons for it than its aristocratic name, which we see as being in tension with the rather democratic institutions of hellenism. Nevertheless, there are other traditions.[281] It may be due to the times that this took the form of a central council to which the most powerful representatives of the priests as well as circles of laity belonged, from which the Persian governor of Judah as well as the others ceased participation and the high priest became the head of the community. Unfortunately there are no documents dealing with all of this, and even the tradition of the Mishnah, according to which the "great assembly" (kᵉnéśet haggᵉdōlāh) and the scribes who led the assembly

---

274 For the state of the discussion, see especially, Safrai, *Self-Government* 379ff.; Schürer/Vermes, *History* 199ff.; as well as Lohse, article *synedrion*; Hengel, *Judentum* 48ff.; from earlier literature, Mantel, *Sanhedrin*; Zucker, *Selbstverwaltung*.
275 See Safrai, *Self-Government* 394ff.; Schürer/Vermes, *History* 218ff.
276 Especially mSan 1.6.
277 Already Josephus *Antiquities* IV.218, see Sifre Deut 152f..
278 Mechilta to Ex 18.
279 In a decree of Antiochus III; Josephus *Antiquities* XII 138ff.
280 See e.g. Lohse, article *synedrion* 860; Schürer/Vermes *History* 202.
281 Thus especially Hengel, *Judentum* 49f, with reference, e.g. to Sparta.

played an important part in the chain of tradition[282] from Moses until the Sanhedrin cannot replace such sources.

It is not least because the Moses of the late narratives about important divine legal decisions belongs to Sinai and the distant past, long before the existence of their own state and long before the dominance by any foreign power, that he does not correlate with any historical figure. He can only play the role that he played because he is a figure of the tradition and not of the present.

There probably was a Mosaically legitimized institution during the monarchic period that made a decisive contribution to the establishment of a legal system independent of the state and royalty. Nevertheless, it was a transitional institution.

In the postexilic period Moses was just an image, but an extremely effective one for the correlation of tradition and autonomy. He stood for the possibility and necessity to bring together the interests and traditions of divergent groups, especially between priests and laity. He is thus not an identifiable authority figure, but neither does he stand for the whole, like Abraham. Moses is finally not an institution, he does not merge those who convoke themselves in his name. He is more the need for the possibility that his Torah might survive all institutions and thereby be preserved. Moses stands for the legal intention of God and its realization in the shaping of autonomy. He is the tradition of the renewal of tradition and as such the "actually existing one," but the highly effective basis for freedom.

---

282 See especially mAbot 1.1ff.; see especially Mantel, *Great Synagogue*; Finkelstein, *Great Synagogue*.

5

꿈꾼

The Book of the Covenant:
The Supporting Foundation

With it began the slave revolt
in morality.

Friedrich Nietzsche[1]

Introduction: The State of the Discussion

Every study of the so-called Book of the Covenant in Ex 20:22–23:33 can and must begin with the following assertions, which are recognized today as indisputable facts:

– The Book of the Covenant is older than Deuteronomy and so is the oldest law book in the Old Testament. This shows itself in the character of the whole as well as each detail. Deuteronomy shows itself to be a more recent development all over. This temporal sequence remains valid for the essential portions even when, as is occasionally suggested, a few passages of the Book of the Covenant (e.g. the parenetic bases for law) are said to be deuteronomistic, and hence dependent upon Deuteronomy.[2]

– The Book of the Covenant demonstrates all of those characteristics that distinguish biblical law (Torah as a whole as well as the older legal corpora preserved within it) so profoundly from all the other ancient Near Eastern legal documents. Along with the actual judicial pronouncements, there are cultic and religious, ethical and social demands together with their theological and historical foundations. The entire composition is dominated by the first and second commandments (20:23; 22:19; 23:13, 24, 32f.), and they appear as the words of God which were given to Israel through the mediation of Moses at Sinai.

– The Book of the Covenant is in every respect, an extremely colourful portrait. Its assembled character is almost tangible. This is especially

---

1 Nietszche, *Jenseits von Gut und Böse* 653. The sentence and the reversal of values described in it are of the Jewish people.
2 Since Wellhausen (*Composition* 89f.) at most a part of the statements formulated in the second person plural have been regarded as secondary and deuteronomistic (especially 20:22f.; 22:20b, 21, 23, 24b, 30; 23:9b, 13 among others). Most recently, e.g. Otto, *Rechtsbegründungen* 4ff.; Schwienhorst-Schönberger, *Bundesbuch* 284ff.; otherwise: Lohfink, *Bearbeitung*. See below pp. 114, 197ff.

109

shown by – in addition to the breadth of the contents – the varied forms of the laws:[3] casuistic decrees (e.g. 21:18ff.) stand alongside prohibitions (e.g. 20:23; 22:21, 27f.) and commandments (e.g. 22:28b, 30a; 23:10, 14), decrees including conditional statements (e.g. 20:25a; 21:14, 23; 22:24f.) along with participial formulations (21:12, 15–17), or the unique talion formula (21:24f.). The words of God (20:22ff.) dominate, but major portions are speech about God (e.g. 21:6; 22:7f.). Most frequently "you" (sing.) is used, but occasionally it is exchanged for the plural.[4] The superscription in 21:1 is not at the beginning, nor is the subscription in 23:13 at the conclusion. All of these things are also the product of a history covering a long period of origin.

From these three points we see that the history of the development of the Book of the Covenant is simultaneously the story of its genesis. It is what makes up the essence and character of Old Testament law and what then from Deuteronomy on is given the name Torah. When and why, under what circumstances and for what purpose, for what groups and from what institutions the birth of the Torah ensued must be gleaned from its composition with its gaps and tensions.

Of course, it is precisely on this point that minds and methods separate. The Book of the Covenant, its place in the history of Israel as well as its pre-history will receive diverse assessments. Thus, the context is made clear by means of some basic questions of current Old Testament research – like, for example, the origin of the radical worship of YHWH alone, which is so clearly attested within the Book of the Covenant. Everything is dependent upon the methodology by which we proceed and the care of the investigation and observation. At first we will only try (out of the multiplicity of the attempts) to filter out the observations and evaluations upon which we may build. All particulars must be discussed at a later time. I will limit myself to the two main points: the dating of the origin and the literary stratification.

The Historical Place

The Book of the Covenant presumes an agricultural society, which presupposes the conquest of the land, and it is older than Deuteronomy. Those are the extremes in dates and are undisputed. All attempts at dating operate within this wide expanse of time,[5] if we disregard the possibility of even later (in other words – the post-deuteronomistic strata and additions).[6]

---

3 There is a complete list of the forms that appear in the Book of the Covenant most recently in Osumi, *Kompositionsgeschichte* 21f.

4 See above, note 2.

5 Cazelles, *Études* and *L'Auteur* who regards Moses as a possible direct source, is an exception.

6 Pfeiffer, *Transmission* theorizes that the ritual Decalogue originated in the time of the conquest of the land, the humanitarian laws were around 650 BCE shortly before Deuteronomy. The text might then have been edited deuteronomically around 550 BCE and then finally expanded around 450 BCE with the addition of the Mishpatim.

Until well into our own century a date from older research in the Israelite monarchic period was popular and well supported. In addition to the most important reason for this, proximity and kinship with the conflicts and judgments of the great prophetic movement,[7] a possible connection with the state[8] (with figures like Jehoshaphat,[9] Jehu,[10] or Manasseh)[11] played a special role, but also its similarity to as well as difference from Deuteronomy.

In the twentieth century, scholarship has been compelled to relinquish important bases of this older research. The reason that this happened was that much older, but in many respects unmistakably similar, ancient Near Eastern law books were discovered. If this made it seem that an earlier date was appropriate, other considerations were also adduced. Very typical argu-ments ran: "There are no positive indications of the monarchic period. There is no king listed. There is no fixed organization. Regular taxes are still unknown. All of these things would have had to find some kind of expression in a later date of origin."[12]

Is this indeed the case? The reasons suggested for an early date are generally arguments from silence and are not well founded. Further-more, all dates that place great emphasis upon individual passages or isolated concepts are quite problematic. We would refer to the mention of "ruler" (*nāśî*') in 22:28. Apart from the fact that this term is attested exclusively in late texts, such isolated occurrences could always represent later amplification or emendation.

It follows from all of this that we can only derive a sure dating from such terms and themes when they are a part of the structure of the whole or are firmly anchored in important parts of it and appear frequently. If we follow this, it clearly supports the older theses. We can especially exclude the themes of slave law[13] and laws regarding foreigners (*gērîm*),[14] central to and frequently occurring in the Book of the Covenant, for the pre-state period on the basis of clear literary evidence. Since the reasons that Halbe, for example, has given for a date early in the monarchic period are inadequate – the starting point having been the appropriateness to certain literary sources and an ostensible criticism of the state of the early monarchic period[15] – estimates that would place the Book of the Covenant out of the period between the

---

7 Especially Baentsch, *Bundesbuch*. He places the Mishpatim between David and the ninth century – the "demands of morality" in the eighth century. As a whole, he regards the book to be the product of the prophetic age (122).

8 E.g. Weber, *Judentum* 71; Nowack, *Bundesbuch* 140; Beer, *Exodus* 125 place the origin in the first centuries of the monarchic period.

9 Thus e.g. Reuss, *Geschichte* 235f.

10 Thus Menes, *Gesetze Israels*.

11 Thus Stade, *Biblische Theologie* 246ff.

12 Jepson, *Bundesbuch* 99. Very similarly: Paul, *Studies* 44; in addition to Noth, *Exodus* 141, Childs, *Exodus* 456f.; Boecker, *Recht* 121ff. and many others, most recently Schwienhorst-Schönberger, *Bundesbuch*, especially 268ff., who misses the mention of a city ('*ir*) or something similar.

13 See below pp. 151ff.

14 See below pp. 183ff.

15 Halbe, *Privilegrecht* 459ff.; see also Wanke, article on Bundesbuch; Zenger, *Israel am Sinai* 154; for the mishpatim see also Phillips, *Criminal Law* 158ff., who regards them as (pro)monarchic.

secured monarchy and Deuteronomy are supported.[16] In the following
we will attempt to be more precise.[17]

Composition and Literary Stratification

An acquaintance with the well-known disunity of the book is more
important, in fact, it is decisive for the question of dating. For the various
phases of research and under the dominance of various methods, the
Book of the Covenant has always been the starting point for the study of
the earlier forms of Israelite law. Consequently, it has been frankly
cannibalized.

This is true first for the form-critical work influenced by A. Alt. Alt
believed that within the Book of the Covenant we find the coming
together of the two legal forms typical of the "original Israelite law" – the
apodictic and the casuistic.[18] He was only interested in the presumed oral
pre-history, especially that of the "humanly associated Israelite and
divinely associated Yahwistic" apodictic law.[19]

Even if we ignore the many hypotheses from such an approach that
are no longer accepted as valid,[20] our goal would be in error from the
outset because the Torah structure of the Book of the Covenant (that is:
the unity of disparate things, which are divided by Alt) is typically
Israelite and it could not be given up. On the basis of this form- and
tradition-historical research, the Book of the Covenant already appears
to be a late form and even more so, a more or less accidental, confused
collection of varying traditions and legal forms.[21]

Even where form-critical observations directly encourage literary
stratification, the situation does not appear much different. With all of
this, under form-critical methods only those things are advanced which
earlier literary criticism has shaped: the sources of the Book of the
Covenant are divided in the various types of law and then the reassembly
is examined as something from which the original purity and clarity are
lost.[22] Jepson, for whom the connection of law and cult in the Book of the
Covenant is a "Canaanization of the Mosaic religion"[23] is an example of
this.

The methodological problem involved with an investigation below the
surface of the Book of the Covenant can be described as follows: for legal
texts (just like, for example, but in another way, narratives) we must first
lift out the inner structure of the whole, then describe and understand it

---

16 According to rather isolated statements in this direction (e.g. Fohrer, *Einleitung*
   149f.; Cardelini, *"Sklaven"-Gesetze* 365, he considers the pre-deuteronomic period
   from the "last quarter of the eighth century to the first half of the seventh century")
   there is increasing agreement with this view: Otto, *Rechtsbegründingen* for example
   40ff.; Osumi, *Kompositionsgeschichte* 156ff.; Schenker, *Versöhnung* 22; Schwienhorst-
   Schönberger, *Bundesbuch* 271f., 312 and elsewhere (for his proto-deut. "divine law
   redaction").
17 See below pp. 183, 197f.
18 Alt, *Ursprünge*. See also above pp. 10f.
19 Alt, *Ursprünge* 323.
20 See above pp. 11f.
21 See e.g. Noth, *Exodus*, 140f.; most recently and similarly Scharbert, *Exodus*.
22 For this trend in the research, see e.g. Otto, *Rechtsbegründungen* 54, but his inclusion
   of Halbe in this classification (*op. cit.* for note 191) is incorrect.
23 Jepsen, *Bundesbuch*.

as law. Only then, on the basis of such a foundation, we can investigate the older sources within the text.

We cannot, however, leap over the inner systematic unity of a law book and collect individual observations that might give opportunity for literary criticism.[24] If we precede a concise legal-historical exegesis with an attempt at literary criticism, we doom any chance for a legal-historical interpretation at the outset. We can make this clear with a modern example: The fact that a contemporary law book might contain formulations and traditions from perhaps hundreds of years ago cannot invalidate its interpretation in the literary (or extra-literary) context of a self-contained law book of the second half of the twentieth century. The legal-historical examination of an individual part can neither replace nor dominate the analysis of such laws in their context.

Halbe first made possible an interpretation of the Book of the Covenant as a compositional unity that by design is subdivided.[25] He demonstrated that the overall structure of the text as we have it could be a ring composition. Halbe designated as the center 22:20 with its singular and very remarkable formulation: "Whoever sacrifices to any god, other than the Lord alone, shall be devoted to destruction." Around this center we have as the inner ring 21:12–22:19 and 22:21–23:9. Both blocks are held together with similar framing pieces. In the first block are laws with the death penalty attached 21:12–17 and 22:17–19. In the second we find the theme of the rights of foreigners in 22:20 and 23:9. 21; 2–11 forms a second medial ring with slave law and 23:10–12 with the sabbath and the sabbath year. These pieces have in common the respective sequence of from six to seven years (or days). Finally, the outer ring is formed by the cultically influenced regulations of 20:22–26 and 23:13–19 – altar and sacrifice commandments.

This structure is clear and convincing and it has to be the starting point for all further analysis. We may not, nor can we deny that formerly certain parts of the Book of the Covenant were eliminated by literary criticism[26] because they made any investigation of the composition as planned fundamentally impossible. The structural outline by Halbe supports itself in the details where other, deviating observations can be made or different conclusions can be drawn.[27]

In addition to this structure, the most important result of Halbe's work is his observation that Ex 34:11ff. is a text older than its parallels in the Book of the Covenant. Thus, it should be regarded as one of the sources

---

24 Certainly not in such a way that overlapping legal-historical theses produce the literary criticism, as generally occurs in Otto, *Rechtsbegründungen*. For Otto, see below pp. 144ff. among others, especially 150.
25 Halbe, *Privilegrecht* 413ff. and especially his sketch 421.
26 Thus Otto, *Rechtsbegründungen* 58 (especially note 205) with a reference to Otto, *Mazzotfest* 262ff. Otto's theory of a second originally independent collection (Ex 21:2–22:26/22:28–23:12) does not justify this, for a critique, see Schwienhorst-Schönberger, *Bundesbuch* summary p. 37.
27 This is true, e.g. for Schwienhorst-Schönberger, *Bundesbuch*. His table on p. 23 (see Schwienhorst-Schönberger, *Rechtsvorschriften* 121) in spite of a few differences, shows precisely the same basic structure as Halbe. See also Osumi, *Kompositionsgeschichte* 24ff.

or models for the Book of the Covenant.[28] Many of the differences, especially the structure of the calendar of festivals, can only be explained in this way, not by a theory of assuming the dependence of Ex 34 upon the Book of the Covenant.[29]

If this is correct, then the various contents viewed by Alt as a tradition-historical unity of apodictic law, namely the religious and ethical commandments, first came together in the process of the establishment of the Book of the Covenant. While the cultic-religious demands of Ex 34 are classified as socio-ethical ordinances, especially for the protection of the weak in society, something theological happened that was extremely important. Halbe designated that as "structural enlargement step #1"[30] in contrast to the settled ring composition, which he labeled "structural enlargement step #2." The block of actual casuistic legal formulation (21:1–22:16) that Halbe did not investigate further is included in the latter group.

The only study to continue along Halbe's line without immediately falling back into literary-critical shortcuts, is that of Osumi.[31] He examined the gaps and blind spots left by Halbe: the block of casuistic laws[32] not thoroughly studied by Halbe, the various types of legal pronouncement only occasionally studied and taken into account regarding their significance for the inner structure,[33] and Halbe's inadequate explanation of the super- and subscripts in 21:1; 23:13 and similar. In so doing, Osumi refines Halbe's rather unfinished description of the inner compositional structure. The following are the most important benefits for our investigation:[34]

- In the block of casuistic laws, defined by Osumi as 21:1, 12–22:18(19), we find a second, more ancient source for the Book of the Covenant. This is important because this allows us to identify a noticeable difference between whether divine law precedes secular or vice versa.[35] This is a false alternative..

- The two ancient sources (Ex 34:11ff. and the mishpatim-book) were combined with a few additions into the main composition of the

---

28 Halbe, *Privilegrecht* 449f.
29 See below pp. 115ff.
30 Halbe, *Privilegrecht* 451f.
31 Osumi, *Kompositionsgeschichte.*
32 Halbe, *Privilegrecht* 460ff. with the barely supported thesis that the casuistic portion might be "as a whole intended as part of the right of privilege in the Book of the Covenant" (460).
33 Especially the change from second person singular to plural, unnoted or explained by Halbe.
34 See the summary Osumi, *Kopmpositionsgeschichte* 219f.
35 Thus, most recently Schwienhorst-Schönberger, *Bundesbuch* 1, where this alternative, which affects the entire study is posed (as if there were no other possibilities). His own underlying thesis, however, is only achieved because the "casuistic law book" (chapter 4) is then regarded as the basis for several operations (chapter 5). He did not investigate the fact that material and formulations from Ex 34:10ff. are frequently used in the "divine law redaction" (405). The most important difference in accent and point of view that we find in Osumi is that here the shape ultimately so influential for the Old Testament first appeared. Furthermore, there is much happily on which they agree.

Book of the Covenant by a single hand. In every respect, this is one well-thought and shaped composition and not a product of an accident. We see the decisive phenomenon in legal and theological history in this book.

– Outside of a few verses, in the so-called appendix,[36] there was only one additional redactional stratum added to the text as now presented of the main composition: the verses in the second person plural. They are likewise pre-deuteronomistic[37] and have a connection with the Jerusalem cult. This probably indicates that the work was incorporated in a cultic proclamation of law.

In the following paragraphs we will first examine both of the more ancient texts in the Book of the Covenant – thus the beginnings of written law in Israel. Against this background we can examine the process of the composition of the Book of the Covenant itself.

The Sources: The Double Beginning of Written Law

The Practice of Exclusive Veneration (Ex 34:11–26)

a. STRUCTURE AND STRATIFICATION

11 *Observe what I command you today. See I will drive out before you the Amorites, the Canaanites, the Hittites, the Perizzites, the Hivites, and the Jebusites.*

12 *Take care not to make a covenant with the inhabitants of the land to which you are going, or it will become a snare among you.*

13 *You shall tear down their altars, break their pillars, and cut down their sacred poles*

14 *(for you shall worship no other god, because YHWH whose name is Jealous, is a jealous God).*

15 *You shall not make a covenant with the inhabitants of the land, for when they prostitute themselves to their gods and sacrifice to their gods, someone among them will invite you, and you will eat of the sacrifice.*

16 *And you will take wives from among their daughters for your sons, and their daughters who prostitute themselves to their gods will make your sons also prostitute themselves to their gods.*

17 *You shall not make cast idols.*

18 *You shall keep the festival of unleavened bread. Seven days you shall eat unleavened bread, as I commanded you, at the time appointed in the month of Abib; for in the month of Abib you came out from Egypt.*

19 *All that first opens the womb is mine, all your male livestock, the firstborn of cow and sheep.*

20 *The firstborn of a donkey you shall redeem with a lamb, or if you will not redeem it you shall break its neck. All the firstborn of your sons you shall redeem.*

36 Ex 23:25aβ, b, 26, 27, 31bβ, 33a.
37 See Lohfink, *Bearbeitung*.

21 Six days you shall work, but on the seventh day you shall rest; even
    in plowing time and in harvest time you shall rest.
22 You shall observe the festival of weeks, the firstfruits of wheat
    harvest, and the festival of ingathering at the turn of the year.
23 Three times in the year all your males shall appear before the Lord
    God, the God of Israel.
24 For I will cast out nations before you, and enlarge your borders: no
    one shall covet your land when you go up to appear before the Lord
    your God three times in the year.
25 You shall not offer the blood of my sacrifice with leaven, and the
    sacrifice of the festival of the passover shall not be left until the
    morning.
26 The best of the firstfruits of your ground you shall bring to the
    house of the Lord your God.
    You shall not boil a kid in its mother's milk.

This text assumes a special position in Old Testament law. It is the
only one containing exclusively cultic-religious instructions. It is the only
one that is not affected by Torah structure with its connection of cult and
law, religion and ethics. That, together with the facts that first, it places
the narrative context in competition with the classic Decalogue of Ex 20
and second, that most of its regulations are repeated either word-for-
word or with slight variation, shows its key position for any understanding of Old Testament law. This, however, is what makes the argument
over its historical and theological place so unusually heated.[38] One group[39]
places it or a proto-form of it at the beginning of the history of Israel, in
the early period of their life in the land. They regard it as the original text
of the covenant, the Yahwist Sinai text, the "Privilege Law" (Ger.
Privilegrecht)[40] of this God, which from the very beginning constitutes the
basic relationship to YHWH. Their entire legal history can be described
as an unfolding and extension of this. On the other hand, some regard it
as a late product, an excerpt from other texts. Scholars either view it
entirely as deuteronomistic[41] or as a post-deuteronomistic[42] amplification.
    As with any text, the key to understanding this, which thus far no one
seems to have found, lies in its structure, its overall form. The text,
however, seems rather confusing. There are on the one hand numerous
stylistic breaks. Part appears to have God speaking (verses 11, 18, 19, 20,
24a, 25). Other passages speak of God in the third person (verses 14, 23,
24b, 26a). It speaks in the second person singular, but in verse 13 in
second plural. The inhabitants of the land are spoken of in the singular
(verses 12, 15a, 16) and then in the plural (verse 15b).
    There is on the other hand the remarkable structure of the calendar of
festivals in verses 18–22. Unlike all the other descriptions of Israel's

38 For the history of the research, see Wilms, Bundesbuch 18ff.; Halbe, Privilegrecht
    13ff.
39 See especially Halbe, Privilegrecht; Otto, Mazzotfest and many others.
40 This term comes originally from European feudal law and was introduced into
    Old Testament scholarship by Horst (Privilegrecht) and frequently adopted by
    others (especially Halbe, Privilegrecht 227f.).
41 Thus, especially Perlitt, Bundestheologie 216ff.
42 Thus, Blum, Pentateuch 68ff., 369ff.

seasonal festivals, different even than the parallels in Ex 23:15f., the festivals of unleavened bread, weeks and harvest are not listed in immediate succession, they are separated by long regulations regarding firstborn (verses 19f.) and sabbath (verse 21). We cannot have a real grasp of this text without a convincing explanation of this ordering. In view of this textual evidence, we can reject a whole series of interpretations rendered thus far; they do not consider the overall form of the text nor the function of the individual statements adequately (or perhaps even at all.)

This is true first for the many earlier attempts to find a decalogue or commandments in a multiple of ten, which we might surmise on the basis of the context, especially Ex 34:28. The many attempts, from Goethe to Noth,[43] have been abandoned, but not without having some effect on exegesis. Which texts were retained, which were eliminated, was ultimately determined arbitrarily. We hope that the days of such attempts are over.

Other interpreters begin on the basis of the alleged or actual deuteronomistic formulations contained in it. Indeed, the many thorough investigations of the text[44] have shown beyond a doubt that a great number of its expressions and turns of phrase are not deuteronomistic. Others are similar to deuteronomistic language, but different in detail.

We do not need to review all this material here. It is important that most of the concrete instructions in the text can be clearly differentiated from deuteronomic/deuteronomistic parallels, they are definitely older. Individual exegesis will support this. But all attempts to use the alleged deuteronomism directly as a literary-critical instrument are problematic.

This is what Cazelles especially has done. He regards the expressions "YHWH your God" (verses 24b, 26), "jealous God" (*'ēl qannā'* verse 14b), "house of YHWH" (verse 26), the "exodus from Egypt" (verse 18), "take care" (verse 12), the verb "cast out" (*grš*, verse 24), as well as the destruction of the monoliths (verse 13) as deuteronomistic.[45] Since they appear with very undeuteronomistic phrases and concepts, they are assigned to a later stratum. This is true of verses 12, 13a; for "[he] is a jealous God" in verse 14b; verse 15b, 18b, 24, 26a as well as parts of 19.[46]

This, of course, raises the question to what extent is it legitimate to use literary criticism on phrases and expressions like "take care that ..." simply because they are found only or predominantly in Deuteronomy or in deuteronomistic texts. This eliminates the possibility that this might be, for example, an early deuteronomistic text. What justification is there to regard phrases such as "jealous God" (*'ēl qannā'*) which appears next to the unique "jealous YHWH" (*yhwh qannā'*) in verse 14 as only an

---

43 See e.g. the overview in Wilms, *Bundesbuch* 200ff.; as well as e.g. Otto, *Mazzotfest* 272f.

44 See, in addition to Wilms, *Bundesbuch*, and Halbe, *Privilegrecht, passim*, especially Langlamet, *Israel*; Otto, *Mazzotfest* 28f. On this, however, see the questions in Blum, *Pentateuch* 370ff.

45 Cazelles, *L'Alliance* 178f.

46 See the synopsis in Cazelles, *L'Alliance* 180f.

addition, because it is otherwise found only in Deuteronomy and the Decalogue? The stylistically impressive doubling in verse 14 is then destroyed. By what right do we exclude as deuteronomistic the formula already found in Hosea, "your God;" or the designation, though not word-for-word at least present in substance in pre-deuteronomistic material, of another temple besides Jerusalem as "house of God?"[47]

It is also worth noting that Cazelles is aware that he cannot achieve a convincing, self-contained text by his use of literary criticism. His reconstructed reading demonstrates the same basic stylistic breaks as the biblical *textus receptus*. This is also true of the remarkable sequence of the calendar of festivals. The only statement that is, because of its subject-matter, certainly deuteronomistic – verse 25b, where the family festival of Passover is called a pilgrimage festival (*ḥag*), which can only be explained by a deuteronomistic central cultic place – finds no objection.

The most recent attempt to explain the text is by Blum. On the basis of his reconstruction of a D composition in the Pentateuch, especially in the Sinai pericope, the Decalogue of Ex 20 plays a central role.[48] Blum regards Ex 34:11ff. as a late addition. He would explain the text as a kind of summary of the preceding instructions (from Ex 12f.) from the broader context: "34:11–26 stands ... for the totality of the previous divine revelation."[49] Apart from the beginning,[50] the fact that most of the regulations of Ex 34 have already appeared in Exodus would be very important for this view. We refer to verses 11–16 (= Ex 23:20–23), verses 21–26 (= Ex 23:12, 16–19) and verse 17 (= 20:23).[51]

In so doing, numerous aspects of the text are ignored, but even more important, the preceding context. We remember unique formulations that are no more explainable by their context than by deuteronomistic theology, such as "jealous YHWH" (verse 14), or the invitation to sacrificial banquets (verse 15), the peculiar sabbath formulations in verse 21b, etc. that so late a text would reproduce the pre-deuteronomic separation of unleavened bread and passover, that it avoids the term "sabbath," that it uses the term "cast out" (*grš*, qal) in a unique way (verse 11b).

All this and more remains unexplained by this thesis. It makes no sense. First, why does the most important part of the previous material, the Decalogue of Ex 20 (with the exception of the sabbath, which is

---

47 For the temple in Shiloh in 1 Sam 1:7, see also with "God" (*ᵉlōhīm*) Judg 17:5, 18:31, besides Am 7:13. "House of X" is not once but regularly used as the temple of other gods (1 Sam 5:2; 31:10; Judg 9:4, 46 and elsewhere).

48 See above p.30 and elsewhere.

49 Blum, *Pentateuch* 70.

50 Blum, *Pentateuch* 69f. The abrupt transition from the speech about the people (verses 9f.) to the one to the people (ameliorated by the end of verse 10 is disturbing. If verses 11ff. are not about an ostensible bit of tradition regarding the narrative, which was already valid for the first table; then the situation regarding this point is not fundamentally different than it is with the theory of a later addition. The message to Moses of the will of God for the people is an expression of God's forgiveness. Only the lack of a formula common (later?) "Thus shall you say to the Israelites" (Ex 20:22 and elsewhere), is noteworthy.

51 See also Toeg, *Lawgiving* 70.

however formulated in a characteristically different way), play no role in this repetition. Second, why are all of the social commandments not mentioned? The special problems of the sequence of verses 18–22 remain unexplained.[52] Ex 34 cannot be explained as just a summary of the commandments from the larger context.

We have always known this about the narrower context of Ex 32–34. Attempts to discover a second – or even the original – Decalogue itself have made sense, at least because the text of 34:11 could not have been written just against the backdrop of the mountain of God. In fact, we are compelled to regard essential portions and passages of the narrative of the calf image as older.

Nevertheless, there are also parts that can only be understood if taken out of their context. There is first the "as I commanded you" (*[a]šer ṣiwwītīkā*) in 34:18. The same formulation is found in Ex 23:15. In fact, a command to observe the feast of unleavened bread, given anachronistically, is included in Ex 13.[53] It is not because the command was not given in the month of Abib, causing the relative clause to disturb the flow slightly, that scholars are compelled to regard this as an amplification necessitated by the context to which the historicizing information in verse 18b belongs.

The same is true of the relative clause in verse 12. It is said here concerning the land, "to which you are going." In each case, the speech presumes a great distance and differentiation between Israel and its land from the "inhabitants of the land" (a phrase that did not yet include Israel; verses 12, 15). Nevertheless the relative clause breaks the connection to the "that" (*pen*)-clause in 12b. Its participial formulation can actually only be interpreted as a statement of the future, presupposing an historicizing placement of the text as a speech before the conquest of the land. At the same time, the text, with all its distancing from the "inhabitants of the land," presumes concrete, neighborly relationships (verse 15) with those same inhabitants.

Halbe[54] is the only one to make an attempt to grasp the inner structure of the text (apart from those who propose to find a Decalogue). He differentiates first, an introduction (verses 10a[1]–11a) to the obligations (verses 11b–26; there are two parts here: the main commandment [verses 11b–15] and the individual regulations [verses 18–26]). He regards verses 15b, 16, 17, 24a as well as 19b, 25b[1] as later amplifications.

His attempt to describe the inner structure of the statements is especially important. He describes the main commandment as chiastic around verses 13, 14a.[55] He regards the earliest stratum of the individual regulations as the disposition of a festival (unleavened bread – seven

---

52 Blum, *Pentateuch* 375, thinks that he can conclude on the basis of Ex 34 that "the priestly composition already [presupposes] the recapitulation of the commandments of 34:11–26." Were it otherwise, the sequence of Ex 12f. (feast of unleavened bread and firstborn), 16 (sabbath) and 22f. would be a real analog for the remarkable sequence in 34:18–22. Nevertheless, so late a date would only strengthen the characteristics of the text that deviate from the context.

53 See Kessler, *Querverweise* 290.

54 Halbe, *Privilegrecht* summarizing 210ff., 223ff.

55 Halbe, *Privilegrecht* 97.

days) followed by obligations for cultic levies. After the festival of unleavened bread are rules regarding firstborn and the demand that they should not appear with empty hands (verse 20b[1]); after the day of rest we find laws regulating sacrifice (verses 25b, 26b).[56]

Halbe believes this earlier composition to have been amplified and over-layered by a so-called "pilgrimage stratum." It is already aware of all three annual festivals and adds the festival of weeks and that of ingathering in verse 22, as well as statements regarding the three times per year pilgrimage festival (verses 23f., 26).[57]

Now we must follow Halbe through his two-part division of the text. The basic structure is: (verses 11–16) the relation to the inhabitants of the land (verses 18–26) festivals and cultic levies. Essentially, both parts are about exclusive veneration of YHWH in a social climate characterized by polytheistic religion.[58] The two sides of this coin are: relation with the neighbors, the veneration of other gods on one side; and basic regulations about the YHWH cult which exclude worship of other gods on the obverse.

Between the two halves, thus right in the middle, we find the prohibition against images (verse 17), "You shall not make cast idols."[59] The subject is not part of either of the two blocks of text,[60] but as a single verse it is closely connected with the narrative context in Ex 32–34. It is, in fact, inconceivable that the words of God on the tablets (which were broken in reaction to the calf cult and then renewed as an expression of divine forgiveness) would be unconnected with the sins that this material is all about. This is precisely the function that verse 17 has, also with the related formulation in 32:4, 8.

The phrasing of the prohibition of images in verse 17 has been taken as deuteronomistic.[61] Doubtless, the next formulation in Lev 19:4 (thus in the Holiness Code) in addition to Deut 9:12 are all comparable Nevertheless, the conclusion that this is deuteronomistic language is not convincing.

We already find the same term "cast images" (*massekāh*) in Hos 13:2 and it is used by Hosea in his critique of the calf cult of the northern kingdom. As we know, Hosea was the first person in the northern kingdom to attack the calf cult that is at the center of Ex 32–34. There is no reason to propose a later redaction or something similar in Hos 13.[62] This

---

56 Halbe, *Privilegrecht* 210.
57 In summary – Halbe, *Privilegrecht* 210
58 See Halbe, *Privilegrecht* 225ff. Not least because of the wide ranging historical dating, we must deal with noticeably different accents in the general overlapping material. See below pp. 123ff. and especially p. 126.
59 For *massekāh*, see Dohmen, *Schmiedeterminus* and his article on *massekāh* in addition to Schroer, *Bilder* 310ff.
60 For this reason already Halbe, *Privilegrecht* 122ff., especially 215ff. regarded it as a later emendation.
61 Dohmen, *Bilderverbot* 182ff., and already Hossfeld, *Dekalog* 209f.
62 Otherwise, Dohmen, *Bilderverbot* 148ff., note 243 who sees a deuteronomistic redaction here. Methodologically it is doubtful that ownership of the term *massekāh* by deuteronomism (Deut 9:12; 2 Kg 17:16) is a decisive argument. It argues in a circle. The other reasons given by Dohmen, e.g. the stylistic difference between Hos 13:1–3 and the context and the statement "he died" (verse 1) are hardly adequate for literary-critical activity. See the Hosea commentary.

means, however, that Ex 34:17 is an addition to this narrative (which is otherwise an older document) required by the context in Ex 32–34. On the basis of the parallel to Hos 13:2, it may be connected with the cult of the northern kingdom. It does not stand in the way of our interpretation of the overall unity of Ex 32–34 as a reaction to the collapse of the northern kingdom.[63]

Otherwise, Halbe's stratum and structural analysis is less convincing. The main reason is that it simply does not achieve its goal: to explain this unusual textual evidence. The thesis of an expansion of an earlier text that only discussed the feast of unleavened bread by the addition of a "pilgrimage stratum" in which, as in all of the other Old Testament festival calendars, the three annual feasts were listed in immediate proximity, sidesteps the evidence presented in the text.

Why was verse 22 not placed immediately after verse 18? What was the intent behind the order as we have it? Furthermore, the structure of the oldest stratum as Halbe has worked it out is not at all convincing. If we accept a placement of the feast of unleavened bread together with the firstborn in verses 18–20a, the very general injunction not to appear before God with empty hands does not seem of equal significance. And the juxtaposition of resting on the seventh day (verse 21) with animal sacrifice (verses 25*, 26b) dispenses with any kind of inner unity.

Halbe just does not demonstrate a correlation of the subject-matter of this text. He is even less successful regarding the formal and stylistic structure. The remarkable, but unexplained stylistic breaks in the text are still with us in the strata as Halbe constructs them.[64] They remain unexplained and misunderstood.

It is quite remarkable that in the research there is no analysis of this text that makes use of its formal characteristics and inner tensions as would be expected in literary criticism. The search for a hidden Decalogue, and the determination of alleged deuteronomistic portions and analysis based on context and not the characteristics of the text have dominated scholarly investigation. We need not adhere to the questionable theory of original stylistic purity to bring together the difficulties of the text with its stylistic breaks.

First, verses 13 and 15bα are outside the usual language of the text. While elsewhere the inhabitants are referred to in the singular (verses 12; 15a, bβ; 16), here it is plural. Furthermore, only in verse 13 are the persons addressed plural. The structure of verses 12–15 as described by Halbe is only partially affected by the removal of verse 13. The omission of the statements of verse 13 in the parallel passages in the Book of the Covenant is thus more or less understandable.[65] There is also an essential doubling of the more concrete statements of verses 15bα, 16.

---

63 See above pp. 49ff., 52.
64 Thus, Halbe's base stratum changes from the first person address of God (verses 11b, 19f., 25) to speech referring to God in the third person (verse 14). Israel is most often referred to as "you," but in verse 13 it is "Thou." The pilgrimage stratum is divine address in verse 18aβ (relative clause), but speech about God in verses 23, 24b.
65 For this in detail Osumi, *Kompositionsgeschichte* 73ff.

Certainly, most remarkable of all is the change between divine speech and speech about God. The beginning of verse 11 suggests that the whole will be speech by YHWH. But the "I" first appears in the relative clause of verse 18 and then in verses 19f. In contrast, the important formulations of verse 14 speak of God in the third person. In the concluding part there is a sudden change. While verses 23, 24b, 26a talk about God, verses 24a, 25a are divine speech.

If we want to attempt an analysis of the strata on the basis of these observations, we must deal with two questions: Which of the two styles of address is older? And how are those passages to be classified, which do not mention God at all?

Regarding the first question, the narrative context, as also the important beginning in verses 10f., both probably presuppose divine speech. For this reason, it is surprising and unexpected that in central and in theologically important phrases (verses 14, 23) God is spoken of in the third person. Furthermore, the reception of Ex 34:11ff. into the Book of the Covenant clearly smooths everything so as to suggest divine speech.[66] All of this suggests that the earlier stratum spoke of God in the third person and that this then was changed to divine speech by later additions.

The important question is, however, whether there are criteria for the classification of statements that do not mention God at all. In my opinion, we must take note of the fact that no single law regulating animal sacrifice mentions God in the third person. If we begin with these observations, the structure of an older base stratum is permitted to emerge, and we may describe the development of the text in the following manner.[67]

In verses 18–26, the older stratum spoke of the feast of unleavened bread (verse 18a without the relative clause), a weekly day of rest (verse 21), festivals of weeks and harvest (verse 22), pilgrimages three times each year (verse 23) and the protection of the land during these pilgrimages (verse 24b) as well as the offerings of firstfruits connected with these pilgrimages (verse 26a).

The warning against a covenant with the inhabitants of the land because God is jealous (verse 12 without the relative clause in 12aβ; 14; 15a, bβ; 16) groups itself with the first part. Both parts are introduced with the same term "observe" (šmr, qal/hiph.). By a later redaction this became words of YHWH.

Therefore, verse 11 is important. In this verse there is a new introduction before the two parts, each beginning with the same word "observe" (šmr), this time in divine speech, as well as the removal of the inhabitants. In the second part, the demands in "I" language are supplemented with material related to the firstborn (verse 19f.) and animal sacrifice. We find later emendations and amplifications, in part connected with the narrower and broader narrative context, in verses 12a1, 13, 15ba; "as I have commanded you" in verse 18a, 18b as well as the addition of passover in verse 25b.

66 Thus, Ex 23:18b unlike the version in 34:25b speaks of "my festival." Ex 34:24b and especially verse 14, with all their statements about God, are missing entirely.
67 See the translations and detailed exegesis below pp. 123ff.

b. THE PROHIBITION AGAINST COVENANTS

b1. Separation from Neighbors

The first half of the reconstructed older base stratum reads:

12 *Take care*
   not to make a covenant with the inhabitant of the land,[68]
   or it will become a snare among you,[69]
14   *for you shall worship no other god*
       because YHWH, whose name is Zealous, is a zealous God,
   15 *that you shall not make a covenant with the inhabitant of the land,*[70]
       and he will invite you and you will eat of his sacrifice,
16   *and you will take wives from among his daughters for your*
       sons,
           and his daughters prostitute themselves to their gods,
   ●   *and make your sons prostitute themselves to their gods.*

The text is structured by the double appearance of the clause "that you shall not make a covenant . . ." in verses 12, 15. In both cases this must correlate with the introduction, "Take care." The covenant is prohibited because "the inhabitants of the land" can be a danger, even a mortal "snare."

Unfortunately, we do not know what exactly such a "snare" (*mōqēš*) is. They were apparently used for bird hunting (Ps 124:7; Am 3:5 and elsewhere), but also for the hippopotamus (Job 40:24). It might perhaps have been a net or a piece of thrown wood, a kind of boomerang.[71] The danger from the other inhabitants in the land threatens "in the midst" (*bᵉqirbekā*) of Israel (verse 12). The text presumes that Israel was living in close proximity with their neighbors.

We must regard the possible consequences of such a covenant described in verses 15f. as a concrete example of what is intended by a "snare."[72] It begins with the invitation from the inhabitants to participate in a sacrifice-banquet. Added to this are marriage links with the inhabitants, whereby, in accord with the patrilocal family structure, only the women who are marrying into the society are mentioned. These women bring along their gods.

We might at least conjecture in greater detail the context this refers to. If the sacrificial cult to which the Israelite is invited had orgiastic/sexual aspects, the marriage relationships are produced from it, in that the daughters who prostitute themselves after their gods seduce the Israelite young men into doing the same thing. Sacrifice, cultic banquet, sexual-religious seduction and marriage links are all closely related. The prohibition against covenants with the inhabitants prevents all this from the outset. It demands a separation in bed and board from the "inhabitant" of the land.

68 For the secondary character of the relative clause, see above p. 119.
69 Verse 13 is an addendum in the sense of Deut 7, see above pp. 121f. and below p. 126.
70 An addendum correlating with verse 13, see above pp. 121f.
71 See Ringgren, article on *yāqaš* (Lit.).
72 With Blum, *Pentateuch* 371f. who correctly criticizes Halbe's interpretation (*Privilegrecht* 130) that this is concerned with the prevention of threatening superior power among the inhabitants.

The two clauses in verse 14 beginning with "because" (*kī*) give the reason. Participation in all of this would include and signify "falling down" before a strange god. It could be that there was such a "falling down" during the course of the sacrifice. This is not possible in the relationship to YHWH without placing this relationship in question.

The second "because" gives the reason for the prohibition against such "falling down." It is because YHWH is "zealous." This is a term used for people who are associated with enviousness or jealousy. In every case it includes emotional and passionate activity.[73] The reference to this characteristic of God – although not however as something like a concrete threat – is the last reason given here, and it is sufficient. It is this characteristic of the God of Israel, rendering links to other gods impossible without invalidating the relationship to YHWH.

The text of the base stratum shows itself to be a stringent creation that formulates the consequences of the jealousy of this God. Neighborly links with the inhabitants of the land and venerating other deities are forbidden insofar as they include communal, cultic meals and marriage relationships.

Certainly, the text has an important role in reconstructing the religious history of Israel. This is demonstrated by the oft studied[74] connection to the closely related texts in Ex 23; Deut 7 and others. The scholarly debate is still, as it is for Ex 34:11, whether to date early or late. Are these formulations an expression of the will of YHWH as given from the beginning, or are they what makes up the special relationship of Israel and its God? Or did they originate in deuteronomistic or post-deuteronomistic theology?

We must both ascertain and note proximity as well as distance from deuteronomistic language.[75] If one thing suggests that it is exclusively in the circle of deuteronomic/deuteronomistic theology that the "jealous God" ('*ēl qannā*') is otherwise referred to; another suggests that the companion phrase "Jealous YHWH" has no parallel there. The same thing is true of the formula "another god," which is deuteronomistic in the plural, but not singular.

The marriage prohibition is certainly deuteronomic/deuteronomistically important (Deut 7:3; Judg 3:5f.), but elsewhere it is never limited to the importation of foreign wives or coupled with sacrifice invitations. The "prostituting . . . to" (*zānah 'aḥᵃrē*) is attested as deuteronomistic (and priestly),[76] but elsewhere it refers only to Israel and its apostasy from YHWH. Here, however, it refers to the daughters of the inhabitants of the land and the cult with which they are associated.[77] Furthermore, Hosea had also already used the concept of prostitution as a religious image.

73 See Brongers, *Eifer*; Renaud, *Dieu jaloux*; Sauer, article on *qin'ā*; Reuter article on *qn'*; Dohmen, "*Eifersüchtiger ist sein Name*."

74 See Schmitt, *Friede*; Lohfink, *Hauptgott Gebot* 172ff.; Seitz, *Studien* 77ff.; Halbe, *Privilegrecht* especially 108ff.; Otto, *Mazzotfest* 203ff.; Blum, *Pentateuch*, especially 365ff.; Achenbach, *Israel* 249ff.

75 See the collection of linguistic parallels in Langlamet, *Israel*; Otto, *Mazzotfest*; Halbe, *Privilegrecht*.

76 Deut 31:16; Judg 2:17; 8:27, 33; Lev 17:7; 20:5f. and elsewhere.

77 Thus Halbe, *Privilegrecht* 153ff.; Blum refers to places like Jer 3:17; 12:14–17; 18:7–10 as examples that even late intra-Israelite evaluations were used for the worship of other people (*Pentateuch* 374). Nevertheless, the special note of Ex 34 is absent.

It is certainly correct that the differences from usual deuteronomistic style lie rather in linguistic detail. This does not suggest that because of those differences we should separate them by several centuries from deuteronomistic parallels that are related in so many respects.[78] But to ignore the difference and simply ascribe it to the deuteronomistic school is likewise questionable. We do not find such a concrete picture of the dangers presented by neighboring peoples in deuteronomistic material.

The only real parallel at all is in Num 25:1–5.[79] The desertion to Baal of Peor discussed there follows the same model. There are Moabite women who invite to sacrifice to their gods (verse 2a). The people fall down before the gods of these women at the banquets (verse 2). They are all referred to as "whores" (*znh*) together with these women (verse 1), and the wrath of YHWH is called down (verse 5). We can neither regard Num 25:1ff. as deuteronomistic,[80] nor is it simply a model for Ex 34:12ff. But it apparently mentions comparable events and experiences. We should especially note that Hosea already presumes this tradition. In spite of the concise formulation in Hos 9:10, we can recognize that Hosea is concerned about an apostasy to foreign deities and that simultaneously, this can be described as intercourse with lovers (*'oh°bām*).[81]

If we set about to place our text in its historical context, proceeding with care, we have to consider the period before Hosea, especially the ninth century. The threads that lead us in that direction are slender but clearly present. The prohibition against worshiping foreign gods is more restricted, more concrete and therefore tradition-historically older than the version of the first commandment in the Decalogue.[82]

"Zealous for the Lord" is first referred to in the traditions about Elijah (1 Kg 19:10, 14)[83] and Elisha or Jehu and the ancestors of the Rechabites in 2 Kg 10:16. Unless we forced the text, we would hardly be able to argue against the idea that the phrase, used here in connection with YHWH's demand, is rooted in pre-deuteronomistic texts.[84]

The same thing is true of the concept of the prostitute as a designation for a relationship between foreign women and their gods. 2 Kg 9:22 speaks of the "whoredom" (*z°nūnim*) of Jezebel, which apparently refers

78 See especially Blum, *Pentateuch* 370ff.

79 See Halbe, *Privilegrecht* 157ff.; Otto, *Mazzotfest* 211; Blum, *Pentateuch* 374.

80 Traditionally, Num 25 is considered part of J; see e.g. Noth, *Numeri* 170ff. Also Blum, for whom it is part of his comprehensive D composition, asserts that there is not a "specific classification to the deuteronomistic tradition" (*Pentateuch* 115f.).

81 See Vollmer, *Rückblicke* 76ff.; Jeremias, *Hosea* 121f.; Neef, *Heilstraditionen* 60ff.

82 See W. H. Schmidt, *Erwägungen* 204f.

83 For 1 Kg 19, see above pp. 34ff.

84 For convincing reasons, 2 Kg 10:16 (just like 9:22) is considered by most to be the older, pre-deuteronomic Jehu narrative. From the more recent literature, see Gray, *Kings*; Schmitt, *Elisa* 228ff.; Timm, *Omri* 136ff.; Trebolle-Barrera, *Jehú* 199f.; Hentschel, *2 Könige* 39ff.; Cogan/Tadmor, *II Kings* 117ff. Considering deuteronomic or even post-deuteronomic emendations here are Würthwein, *Könige* 326ff. and Minokami, *Jehu* 37ff. The literary criticism used here is rather questionable since it shreds the text into the tiniest fragments before making judgments regarding construction and style. These are reassembled into suspect strata again with the help of questionable linguistic statistics and uncritical associations.

to her religious activities. In spite of all of the uncertainty in the analysis of the text and its stratification, we must regard 2 Kg 9f. as pre-deuteronomic.[85]

In general, this is not ultimately about the question whether we are dealing with predecessors in the theology and language of Hosea (apart from their specifically prophetic predictions) or whether Hosea shaped the language himself. What is specific to Hosea is, for example, his complaint that Israel, not the other people, is whoring after foreign gods ... that Israel's priests are engaging in sexual practices (Hos 4:7f.), probably in cultic contexts. In much of this, however, he obviously makes use of older language.[86]

While Hosea and the later parallels in Ex 34:12–16 are concerned with problems in Israel itself, our text speaks of conflicts between two population groups and their religions. This is quite reasonable for the ninth century. Especially the Jehu rebellion,[87] together with its presuppositions and consequences, shows that it is a conflict between identifiable population groups and their respective religions. If our text, as considerations of style and construction have led us to think, did not understand itself as placing itself – historicizing – before the conquest of the land, but as speaking directly for a real, present situation, it would presuppose a context in which the worshipers of other gods and the worshipers of YHWH lived as closely together as neighbors, but remaining clearly separate. It was already true for Hosea and extremely important for the period after him that such a situation no longer existed. The reason for this state of affairs lies not least with the bloody conflict proclaimed in the Jehu rebellion.

In short: It is neither an early nor a late dating that permits us to understand the text, rather the slender, but clearly recognizable threads that connect it with the theological and historical decisions of the ninth century. It is entirely probable that the YHWH faith of the period of Elijah, Elisha, Jezebel and Jehu would have attempted to formulate the basic demands of the "jealous YHWH." Everything argues in favor of the notion that we have here an early formulation of YHWH's claim to exclusive veneration.

b2. YHWH and the Canaanite People

The reconstructed older stratum has been emended in several places in such a way that new and radical accents were introduced in the relationships with the original inhabitants. We might need to combine the destruction demanded in verse 13 of the altars, pillars and Asherah with the shift in accent from the concrete danger represented by the daughters to the general activities of the inhabitants themselves discernible in verse 15bα. Especially the similar stylistic formulation in the third person argue in favor of this.

85 In addition to the literature mentioned note 84 above, see Olyan, *Hāšālôm*; Steck, *Elia-Erzählungen* 35, note 1.
86 See e.g. Jeremias, *Hosea* 28, note 4. The borrowing that Hosea allegedly makes of Ex 34:4 is not at all so obvious as Reuter, article on *qn'* 59 suggests. See Dohmen, *"Eifersüchtiger ist sein Name"* 269f. The language points in another direction.
87 See e.g. Donner, *Geschichte II* 274ff.

The instruction in verse 13 does not correlate with anything in the Book of the Covenant, where 23:25 is only talking about the feast of unleavened bread. On the other hand, it presents a very close parallel to Deut 7:5. We might conclude from this that there is (with other references to the broader context – verses 12aβ, 18b) a related emendation in verse 13, 15bα which itself is most likely to be viewed in connection with a larger deuteronomistically influenced composition.[88]

Verse 11b, placed before the whole as an introduction, makes an important, and as we shall shortly see, non-deuteronomistic accent. With "See ... I," God proclaims direct and imminent activity against the inhabitants. It is critical for a proper understanding that the word translated here "cast out" (*grš*, qal) is not used in this form in any of the otherwise so similar parallels. Thus even in Ex 23:29–31 as always in the related passages "cast out" (*grš*, pi.).[89]

In the qal the verb is used almost exclusively[90] as a designation for a divorced woman (passive participle *gᵉrūšāh* in Lev 21:7, 14; 22:13; Num 30:10; Ez 44:22). For this reason we need to understand the sense of Ex 34:11b on the basis of this analogy and should not read in the much sharper sense of the piel.

YHWH announces that he will cast out the Canaanite people, in other words, from an already presupposed union with him. This does not imply a direct act of force to drive them out. Certainly, such a woman having been thrown out of her husband's home will probably return to her father. However, the accent is placed upon the announcement regarding the relationship, not the physical act of driving out.

God's action here stands as a kind of introduction to the behavior which is demanded of Israel in verses 12ff. As Israel was supposed to separate itself from the other inhabitants with respect to the cultic and marital relationships, so also YHWH separated himself from them.

Both are formulated in the language of family law. As a husband separates himself from his – for example, unfaithful – wife, thus YHWH separates himself from the inhabitants. There is an analogy to this concept in the older, so-called Yahwistic primal history.[91] If it might be said here without restriction that in the earliest times people called upon the name of YHWH, this means that all the people he created worshiped him as God, and that this changed with the misdeed of Ham, the "father of Canaan" in Gen 9:21ff. Noah's curse in 9:25f. makes the Canaanites servants and designates YHWH as the God of Shem.

In the table of the nations, which is the part of the pre-priestly primal history in Gen 10:15f., we see five of the six nations listed in Ex 34:11, including Canaan with his sons.[92] The list of the nations in Ex

---

88 See Osumi, *Bundesbuch* 24ff.
89 The appearance of the word on the Moabite Stone (KAI 181.19) is probably to be read as piel (thus Donner/Röllig, KAI II 177).
90 Whether the verb is the same (see Gesenius 18th ed.) as in Isa 57:20, where it talks about mud being brought up by the water of the sea (as possibly also in Ez 36:5), or it is a different root (Blau, *Wurzeln* 245f.; KBL 3rd ed.) is disputed. See Ringgren, article on *gāraš*.
91 For the following, see Crüsemann, *Urgeschichte* 24ff.
92 Only the Perizzites are missing, they are represented by the Girgashites.

34:11b[93] has numerous parallels, especially in deuteronomistic contexts. Nevertheless, the sequence, like the selection, is unique,[94] and most of the national names also appear in older contexts, many even with the expressed addition of "the inhabitant" (*yōšēb hā'āreṣ*),[95] so that a compelling conclusion regarding a late deuteronomistic formulation is not possible.

As Israel is supposed to separate itself from its Canaanite neighbors who worship other gods, so God himself does the same thing as it says in the important introductory formulation of God's "I" speech.

Overview: Radicalization, Historicization, Marginalization

What begins in Ex 34:11–16 already has a long history in Old Testament legal texts, which we will examine briefly.[96] We can only discuss a small part of the legal text that is so important for the complexity of the commandment to expel and annihilate the previous population, which is so important for our picture of the Old Testament. Furthermore, there are no newer, convincing analyses of the many-faceted questions of the origin and shaping of the traditions regarding the conquest of the land. What begins in the earlier stratum of Ex 34 with the separation from the Canaanites who were living as their closest neighbors can be described in the more recent parallels by the terms radicalization, historicization and marginalization.

First, there is certainly an observable *radicalization* and intensification of understanding from the older to the more recent texts. Ex 34 deals with separation from the Canaanites. Furthermore, if we add the later statements of verse 13 – suggesting that we are talking about a power functioning only "against things" – then already in Ex 23:20ff. this is a matter also of a force against the Canaanites themselves. This happens only through God. It is said about him that he causes the people to disappear. This is how the verb used in 23:23 (*kḥd*, hiph) is best understood.

He will send his "terror" (*'ēmāh*, verse 27) and the numinous powers, the *ṣir'āh* (verse 28) which can mean either hornet or wasp or something like "dread, suppression,"[97] or he will cast them out (*grš*, pi.). If we follow the most convincing analysis of the (in every case) extremely complicated sequence of strata in Ex 23:20–33,[98] the earliest stratum deals with using force against the pillars (verse 24) and in regard to the people, there is only a general word of protection for Israel (verse 22). In the later

---

93 See especially Ishida, *Pre-Israelite Nations*; and most recently Na'aman, *Canaanites*.
94 See especially Halbe, *Privilegrecht* 142ff.
95 See Gen 13:7 (Canaanites and Perizzites); 50:11 (Canaanites); Josh 24:8 (Amorites); Judg 1:17 (Canaanites); 1:21 (Jebusites); 2 Sam 5:6 (Jebusites); cf also Num 13:29.
96 See Weinfeld, *Ban*. Most recently Achenbach, *Israel* 249ff. would demonstrate that Deut 7 ought to be placed at the beginning of this series (287). Thus Ex 23:20ff.; 34:11ff. would be late, postexilic developments of the tradition. We can only pursue a discussion of its presuppositions and methods indirectly here.
97 See KBL 3rd ed. 989 (Lit.).
98 For each, see Osumi, *Bundesbuch* 631ff.; 187ff. as well as the table with the finding on 216. According to it verses 20–21a, 21bβ, 22–23a, 24, 32, 33bβ belong to the oldest stratum. Three later additions were made to this: (a) verse 23b, 28–31a; (b) 21ba, 25aα, 31ba; (c)–25aβ, 25b, 26, 27, 31bβ, 33a, ba. The first two are pre-deuteronomic, and the third correlates with Deut 7.

stratum, God drives the inhabitants out (verses 23b, 28–31a), the next says that they are already given into Israel's hand (verse 31b), and the latest stratum finally states expressly that Israel itself is supposed to undertake the task of expulsion (verse 31bβ). This stratum stands, just as the more recent stratum in Ex 34, in close proximity to Deut 7, without taking on the special gravity of this text.

In Deut 7 entirely new and even more radical terms are used. We see there first and foremost the proscription (*ḥrm*), described, for example, as a total annihilation of enemy cities, by people and plague.[99] It is applied to relations with the previous inhabitants.[100] What is meant by this is explained by terms like "devour" (*'ākal*, verse 16) and "destroy" (*šmd*, verses 23f.). It is an annihilation and slaughter of all living things (verse 20). Especially the frequent and apparently necessary statements that there will be no mercy or compassion (verses 2, 16) make the radicality clear. The avoidance of neighborly association has turned into total annihilation.

In order to understand what has happened here, we must take note of the parallel process of *historicization*. Neither strata of the older document used in Ex 34 is aware yet of historicization. This means that it functions as instruction and, in the later redaction, as God's word to the Israelites in the present. It does not understand itself as being placed back before the conquest of the land looking forward.

Ex 23 is already preparatory for what has been achieved in Ex 34, first – in the context of its inclusion in the narrative of Ex 32–34, and then the insertion of this into the narrative context of the Pentateuch. At least in the later strata of chapter 23 the topic is: being led into the land together with consequent activity (verses 20, 23). In connection with this entry into the land, we have the expulsion of the previous residents.

This is even clearer in Deut 7. Framing Deuteronomy in a speech by Moses before the conquest of the land makes its intent clear. The text foresees the coming activities and commands the deeds of annihilation.

If we would understand these texts, we cannot ignore their actual historical context. It is uncontroverted among scholars that the location before the conquest is fictional, it really takes place later (or at the end of the monarchic period). It is misleading to introduce categories from the contemporary historical reconstruction of the Israelite early period and to make that a vehicle for our own understanding. But this is what happens when we formulate thus, "the free and egalitarian tribal society of Israel could not coexist with the exploitive Canaanite city-states."[101] According to everything we know, the free and egalitarian tribal society never exhibited this kind of fantasies of annihilation. The question is: why did Israel, increasingly oppressed and itself already nearly completely annihilated but threatened with even further destruction, raise increasingly more radical demands for a past already centuries behind them?

99 See especially Num 21:1–3 and quite similarly in the Moabite Stone (KAI 181.17).
100 See e.g. Lohfink, article on *ḥāram*, and *Gewalt* especially 69ff.; Welten, article on Bann I.
101 Braulik, *Deuteronomium* 62.

Thus, the concrete context of life among the worshipers of other gods, so clearly identifiable in Ex 34, recedes into the background. There is no longer discussion, for example, of invitations to sacrificial celebrations; the sympathy for seductive, orgiastic cults disappears. The "snares" that are still being talked about (Ex 23:33; Deut 7:16) are described along with great threats for deviant behavior, but never as enticements with great allure.

Furthermore, Hosea already speaks only of Israel's lapse into the cults of Baal, but never of the encouragement in that direction from other population groups. We would probably have to classify the discussion of the seven nations as part of this. They are powers existing in the present, of an (invented) past, in which the texts were supposed to have been written and function, but where they did not exist. Their appearance in the military law in Deut 20 shows this quite clearly.[102] After the regulations for war and besieging of cities, including the killing of the male population, but not all life, there is an abrupt shift after verse 15. We have an order for the complete destruction of the cities of the seven nations but delivered before the conquest of the land in Moses' speech.

The clear instruction in Ex 34, focused on the present, is thus gradually and then especially in Deut 7 associated with a fictional situation in the distant past, but simultaneously also with something much more terrible. We see here extreme radicalization and obvious historicization coming together hand in glove. At the same time, we see something that was still present at the time of the authors of these texts and their readers: the danger emanating from the gods of these people. This is the problem.

The great prohibition in Ex 23:24 applied to the gods of the people among whom they were to live. This is quite independent of whether the promise of annihilation at the end of verse 23 is original or not. Israel should not turn to the ways of these people. The negative side, the danger of deviant behavior, completely lacking in Ex 34, is still unclear in formulations like those of verse 21.

It is different in Deut 7. Already verse 4 mentions the wrath of God toward Israel. This discussion of his anger increases until the climax in verse 25f. Those who bring the images of these gods into their houses are like the person "set apart for destruction." The ban applies to Israel itself. This is the real threat. Now the historical background becomes clear: It is the actual possibility of annihilation occasioned by the arrival of the Assyrians. This was obvious to everyone after the end of the northern kingdom.

It is against this background that the radicalization is completed. The Israelites will be struck – if, when and because they behave like Canaanites. This is the lesson learned from the prophets. The radicalization of the tradition of separation from the Canaanites, from the way it appears at the beginning of Ex 34 all the way to the order for destruction, is part of the task of preventing Israel's own impending destruction.

Finally, we must examine the process of *marginalization* in order to see the whole picture. In Ex 34 the covenant commandment is the important

---

102 See below pp. 243ff.

first part of the basic regulations regarding the exclusive veneration of God. In Ex 23 the complex is already shifted to the end of the Book of the Covenant and turned into a kind of appendix. In Deut 7 the theme is then moved entirely away from the Torah regulations in Deut 12–26 and made a part of the foreword. In short, it is no longer an integral part of the laws themselves. But it is not less important; the theological importance, for example, of Deut 7 would prevent that. But in the overall construction of the book, it is clearly moved away from the laws formulated for the present and turned into a kind of historical reflection or sermon.

The first commandment itself and the prohibition against having anything to do with other gods was already formulated differently in the Book of the Covenant and separated from the question of relations with the previous inhabitants of the land (Ex 20:23; 22:20; 23:13). As we know, along with the *šma‘ yiśrā’ēl* (Deut 6:4ff.), this finds its most important expression in the command in Deut 7 to unify.

Already in the Book of the Covenant and even in the book of Deuteronomy, there are, in addition to historicizing instructions regarding relations with the previous inhabitants,[103] strictly limited by name, important directions for the protection of foreigners who were living in Israel. These regulations would exclude any unthinking application of a command to annihilate worshipers of other gods who happened to be living in Israel.

The horrible image of the expulsion and slaughter of the Canaanite people by Israel and their God emerged out of the instruction to maintain distance from the worshipers of other gods in Ex 34. It came with the step by step anchoring of Torah in the distant past. In an age of power, in which the Assyrian people subjugated nations and totally annihilated many, and in which Israel itself was threatened with a similar fate, an analogous but contrasting picture is outlined. In this sketch the little, threatened nation (see Deut 7:17!) is represented as devouring superpower.

The power fantasy was clearly and strictly tied to a certain, long-distant period and it is expressly limited to the no longer extant nations listed. Simultaneously, there were commandments to protect foreigners and against the murder, for example, of those who did not recognize YHWH in Israel of the monarchic and exilic periods.

c. YHWH CULT AND AGRICULTURE

c1. The structure of time and firstfruits

The second half of the reconstructed older stratum of Ex 34 reads as follows:

18 *You shall keep the festival of unleavened bread.*
Seven days shall you eat unleavened bread[104]
at the festival in the month of ears of grain.[105]
21 *Six days you shall work,*
but on the seventh day you shall rest
even in plowing time and in harvest shall you rest.

103 See below pp. 181ff
104 For the puzzling relative clause, see above pp. 119, 121f.
105 For the reference to the exodus, see above pp. 119, 121f.; for the insertion of verse 19f. see above pp. 121f. and below pp. 137.

22　And you shall observe the festival of weeks,
　　　the firstfruits of the wheat harvest,
　　　　and the festival of ingathering at the turn of the year.
23　Three times in the year
　　　shall all your males appear
　　　　before YHWH, the God of Israel.[106]
24　No one shall covet your land
　　　when you go up to appear before YHWH your God
　　　　three times in the year.[107]
26　The best of the firstfruits of your ground
　　　you shall bring to the house of YHWH your God.

The text is a two part unit. The first part (verses 18*, 21f.) begins and ends with the names of the three – each time using the term "festival" or "pilgrimage festival" (*ḥag*) – great, annual celebrations. The second part is structured by the double use of the phrase "three times in the year" (verses 23, 24), which refers to the three festivals mentioned in the first part.

The second part summarizes what is supposed to happen during the festivals: there is an appearance before God (verse 23) and the offering of the firstfruits (verse 26). In the middle there is the promise that the land that has been deserted during the festival will not be threatened by anyone. The key word, "firstfruits" (*bikkūrīm*), connects the first with the second part. It is placed explicitly at the end of the first (verse 22) as well as the second part (verse 26). But both of the other two festivals are also related to harvest and are associated with the gift of firstfruits.

Stylistically, the first part is held together by the repeated use of the number seven. They are to eat unleavened bread for seven days. Then, the six/seven days rhythm of the week is attached (verse 21). This connects with the festival of weeks in its "sevenness" (*šābū'ōt*). The second part is characterized by the number three.

What appears by its construction and keywords to be a well-structured unity is, in fact, first revealed by its contents. The text begins with the admonition in verse 18 to celebrate and observe (*šmr*) the festival of unleavened bread. Thus, of course, it is already assumed. Matzah is bread baked from unleavened dough.[108] The term especially includes barley loaves. The word might have been connected with a Greek equivalent, *māza*, which means barley cake.[109]

The time of the festival is determined by the expression "in festival of the month of ears of grain." The terms "established time," "festival" or "time of the gathering" (*mō'ēd*)[110] refers to a fixed, known time in the early month of the year, March/April. In discussions the new moon has been considered[111] – thus the beginning of the month – because the word for month (*ḥōdeš*) is also the word for new moon. But the vernal equinox is also possible.[112]

106　For verse 24a, see pp. 121f.
107　For verses 25, 26b, see above pp. 121f. and below pp. 138ff..
108　See Kellermann, article on *maṣṣāh* 1076.
109　A semitic derivation is not possible, see Kellermann article on *maṣṣāh* 1075.
110　See especially Koch, article on *mô'ed*.
111　Especially Auerbach, *Feste* 7, see also Otto, article on *Feste* 97.
112　Thus especially Koch, article on *mô'ed*.

Later, after it was combined with passover, which we are not able to consider here, it began on the fifteenth of Nisan (= Abib). Thus, it began after the first full moon of the early year. To be sure, the exact time of the celebration of the feast of unleavened bread in this earliest festival calendar of the Old Testament remains unknown to us, but it is clear that it is connected with a fixed, astronomically determined time, independent of the condition of the grain crop.

The festival is set in the month of "the ears of grain."[113] "Abib" refers to the half-ripe ears that are still tender.[114] Since barley harvest takes place in April only on the plains, in the mountainous areas it is in May,[115] the festival is celebrated before the actual harvest, but at a time when the half-ripe grain can still be roasted and eaten. This is the first time the harvest can be sampled. At that time matzoth were to be eaten for seven days. This was a festival called a *ḥag*, during which people from a wide area came together at a shrine.[116] In this way the entire harvest season was opened with a YHWH festival.

Between the festival of unleavened bread and the next celebration, the festival of the firstfruits of wheat, we have the instruction to observe a weekly day of rest (verse 21). On the basis of content and logic, this is in the necessary spot, because the seven-day weekly cycle of the festival of unleavened bread is continued to the festival of weeks. Because of its name, it is often called the "festival of sevenness" *šābū'ōt*. Thus, we cannot even think about it apart from the rhythm of the week around which it is structured.[117] This does not tell us how many seven-day units are supposed to separate the two festivals. Already in Deuteronomy we find the number seven, thus seven times seven days (Deut 16:9f.) and perhaps that was even assumed here.

Attempts have been made to correlate the festivals of the agricultural year as well as the weekly day of rest with borrowed Canaanite customs.[118] The similarity cannot be disputed, but it is precisely in that similarity that we are able to see the difference. Due to the absence of sources, we cannot tell whether there was a Canaanite festival corresponding in character and date of celebration to the festival of unleavened bread, but it is possible.[119] According to everything that we know the monthly (or moon) rhythm was determinative.

Sacrifices on the day of the new moon and then again fourteen or fifteen days later (in other words, the day of the full moon) are mentioned repeatedly in Ugaritic cultic texts.[120] A fixed seven-day

---

113 For the old Hebrew names of the months, see especially Koffmahn, *Monatsbezeichnungen*.
114 Dalman, *Arbeit und Sitte* II 305, see also ibid. 245, for this, see also Borowski, *Agriculture* 88.
115 Dalman, *Arbeit und Sitte* I/2 415.
116 See Kedar-Kopfstein, article on *ḥag*.
117 Other interpretations that correlate the festival with the Pleiades (Pentecost) or abstractly as the festival of plenty (Laach, *Wochenfest* 177) are not convincing.
118 A reference here to Kraus, *Gottesdienst* 50ff., 104ff. may suffice.
119 For the various theories regarding the origin of the festival of unleavened bread, see e.g. Laaf, *Passa-Feier* 122ff.; Halbe, *Erwägungen*; Wambacq, *Maṣṣôt* and others.
120 See e.g. KTU 1.41, 1.109, 1.112. For the Ugaritic cultic calendar, see especially Tarragon, *Culte*.

rhythm,[121] independent of all phases of the moon, however, quickly and unavoidably runs into other festival dates and thus to separation from all non-Yahwistic rhythms. This is obviously the decisive point that connects the two halves of the text in Ex 34 – the prohibition of covenants and the festival calendar. The second, annual festival is connected to the first by an interval of weeks.

The ordered day of rest, to be observed every seven days, does not yet have the name "sabbath." Since this word in the texts that are certainly preexilic (Isa 1:13; Am 8:5) often stands second alongside the new moon, it is likely that "sabbath" designated a full moon day, but was not interchangeable with the day of rest. If these theories are correct,[122] then what is specifically Israelite is not the name (it was transferred to this regular day of rest at a later time), but in the weekly rhythm and especially in the abstention from work. Regarding which, our text clearly states that it applies to the important seasons for agricultural work.[123]

The day of rest within the weekly cycle is first connected to the festival of unleavened bread and affects the time until the festival of weeks.[124] This and the period after is the time of the harvest (*qāṣir*), or more precisely, the time of the cutting of grain. The formulation in verse 21b refers to the "plowing" (*ḥāris̆*), which takes place after the harvest festival, especially happening during the months of November and December.[125] The regular cycle of cessation of work every seven days is a central part of the connecting of the YHWH faith with agricultural conditions in Palestine.

This is first expressed in the matter of firstfruits, that is, the offering of the best (*rēs̆it*) of the first things harvested. It is a part of the symbolic character of this activity[126] that they are given to the deity to whom people are grateful for the growth of the crop. The assignment of firstfruits to YHWH is necessarily connected with the question: to whom should people be thankful for the fertility of the land? A claim to exclusive veneration is always immediately resolved with this question.

Our text places all of the emphasis on the fact that the firstfruits are given only to the "God of Israel" (verse 26) or "YHWH your God." On

---

121 In spite of the significance of the six/seven patterns in Ugaritic texts (see especially Loewenstamm, *Seven-Day-Unit*) as already previously in Mesopotamia (see Hehn, *Siebenzahl*) there is no parallel to a weekly rhythm independent of the moon (see e.g. Hallo, *New Moons*).

122 See especially, Robinson, *Sabbath* (summary 167). The theory ultimately goes back to Meinhold, *Sabbath*; furthermore, see Lemaire, *Sabbat*; Bartelmus, *Arbeitsruhegebot*; Veijola, *Propheten*, and others. For (less convincing) critique, see Kutsch, *Sabbat*; Hasel, *"New Moon and Sabbath"*.

123 Robinson, *Sabbat* 130ff. shows in what way and the fact that the regular day of rest grew out of a new understanding of these seasons and agricultural work in general.

124 For this connection, see Kraus, *Worship in Israel* 55f.; Robinson, *Sabbat* 130ff.

125 For the agricultural calendar, see especially the Gezer calendar (KAI 182) for this see especially Borowski, *Agriculture* 32ff. Furthermore, see Dalman, *Arbeit und Sitte* I/1 164ff., 261ff. For plowing and sowing, see especially also Borowski, *Agriculture* 47ff.

126 The custom is widely attested in the history of religion (see e.g. Asmussen/Lessø ed., *Handbuch* I 269, II 58, III 169f.; Widengren, *Religionsphänomenologie* 283f.) also for Egypt (te Velde, article on Erntezeremonie; Giglula, *First Fruits*) and Canaan (KTU 1.6 II 30ff. for this, Gray, *Legacy* 56ff.; Gese, *Altsyriaen* 73f.). For the Old Testament, see Eissfeldt, *Erstlinge*; Murray, *Firstfruits*; Tsevat, article on *bᵉkôr*.

the three dates given, these things are to be presented to him within the context of the annual festivals at one of his shrines. The combining of festivals arising out of the agricultural rhythm with the completely independent, weekly rhythm inevitably separated the festivals of Canaanite gods from those of YHWH. To this is added the physical separation that the order entailed – to bring the firstfruits to the house of YHWH (verse 26) and to celebrate the three annual festivals only in that place.

At the same time this separated the three great festivals from familiar, local shrines and activities. If verses 18, 21f. and 23–26 belong together, this can only mean that the festivals together with the offering of firstfruits were associated with regional shrines. Verse 24 makes something clear that is already part of the concept of "festival" (*ḥag*) and "gathering" (*mōʿēd*), that every farmer did not have his own private altar where he offered his gifts. The intention is to use larger cultic sites. Since, however, the festival of unleavened bread occurs before the grain harvest and the festival of weeks before the actual wheat harvest, it is simultaneously clear, what dangers threatened the crop still on the stalk and thus, what was behind the coveting referred to in verse 24. Additionally, life in close proximity with worshipers of other gods, as assumed in the first part, and with whom they lived in at least partial conflict, must have caused anxieties that were to be accounted for by the promises in verse 24.

Our verse contains regulations for an exclusive veneration of YHWH precisely in that area where the universe of Canaanite deities was strongest. We are dealing with the seasonal rhythm of nature, the fertility of the land, rain and harvest, in other words, the one who is to be thanked for barley and wheat, wine and fruit.

The answer given here by YHWH faith lies in an independent restructuring of the seasonal rhythm of life. The week with its day of rest plays a decisive role because it separates this calendar from all the festivals that are bound to the moon calendar. The necessary and desired consequence must have been a temporal disjunction of the Canaanite and Israelite festival calendars. There was added another structure made of a brief unit of time by means of the weekly day of rest. The land and its natural, annual rhythm was not separated from YHWH and relinquished to others, but it was divided in a new and different way in the calendar of weeks and years.

It is clear that the establishment of this calendar with a weekly day of rest at its heart was a central event for the history of theology and religion. Our text is probably not the record of its founding, but it may be very close to the origin. The unique placement of the day of rest between the annual festivals is closely connected with the inner logic of the process of establishment.

The fears represented in verse 24 are just as concrete and unique as the invitations from Canaanites to participate in the sacrificial banquets in verse 15. We might want to correlate this text with the process of conquering the land.[127] But the close resemblance to deuteronomistic theology[128] – we can hardly tell the difference – makes this early dating

127 See above p. 116.
128 See above p. 117 and elsewhere.

rather unlikely. We find no trace of it in the texts that are clearly older. Again, I see a few references that are rather slender but undeniably present. These point to an origin in the fundamental conflicts of the ninth century BCE.

First, there is the group in Israel that did not participate in the basic decision underlying our text: the Rechabites,[129] who, as we know, are mentioned for the first time in conjunction with Jehu's rebellion (2 Kg 10:15ff.), but we know more about them from Jer 35. These did not build houses, plant vineyards, and most important, they did not plant. In other words, they did not grow bread grain (Jer 35:7).

We can only understand their role in the Jehu revolution if they had played an important part in the preceding religious disagreements. Their agenda implied that they regarded any wine or grain production as a (potential) lapse from YHWH. The establishment of such a "sect" would most likely have come through the same conflict situation that underlies our text. It is just that their decision went in the opposite direction.

A short narrative in 2 Kg 4:24–44, dealing with Elisha, is important for the role of the firstfruits.[130] In it a man brings twenty loaves of firstfruit barley to the man of God.[131] If YHWH lays claim to the gifts of the firstfruits, they could apparently be given to the man of God, Elisha, as the representative of this God. Elisha, by feeding these loaves to one hundred people, causes them to be satisfied.

The narrative shows clearly that the question of giving firstfruits played a part during the religious conflicts in the Omri dynasty (or in the later prophetic narratives that dealt with it). We would have to consider the possibility that the alternative between YHWH and Baal that developed during this period was resolved in the area of regular agricultural offerings, where every notion regarding the guarantee of the fertility of the land found direct expression.[132]

c2. Firstborn and Animal Sacrifice

If the base stratum centers around the annual festivals related to the harvest and God's claim upon the firstfruits, the more recent layer brings

---

129 In addition to the descriptions in the histories of Israel, see Abramsky, *House of Rechab*; Frick, *Rechabites*. For the problems of 2 Kg 9f., see above pp. 125f.

130 Even Würthwein, *Könige* II 296, regards the text as pre-deuteronomistic, apart from the additions in verses 43bβ, 44b, which supplementarily introduce divine speech. Schmitt, *Elisa* 99ff. regards the text as a (pre-deuteronomistic) product of the "man of God redaction."

131 For the incomprehensible word b^eṣiqlōnō in verse 42, see most recently Dietrich/Loretz, ug. b^eṣq ʿrgz.

132 First , against the background of these relationships, we need to mention other correlations that by themselves do not have great significance. E.g. the fact that the shrine of Gilgal, where according to Josh 5:10ff. the Israelites celebrated the first festival of passover-unleavened bread. Compare, under completely different literary and historical presuppositions, Otto, *Mazzotfest*. 2 Kg 2:1 and 4:38 play important roles in the Elijah and Elisha traditions. The prehistory and roots of the ideas transmitted in in the ninth century and then in the deuteronomic/deuteronomistic context regarding the early history of Israel, particularly regarding the conquest of the land and the relationship to the previous inhabitants probably lies in the conflicts of the ninth century and the underlying, radical YHWH groups. This urgently needs closer scrutiny (thus far Noth, *Joshua* 9ff. remains important, in spite of very different presuppositions).

the second dimension of agricultural work and existence: animal husbandry and consequent animal sacrifice. Especially after the introduction in verse 11, we find the phrasing that turns the entirety into divine address. First of all, in verses 19f. the concern is with regulations regarding firstborn:

> 19 All that first opens the womb is mine.
>> And all your possession >shall you remember<,
>>> the firstborn of cow and sheep.
> 20 The firstborn of a donkey you shall redeem with a lamb,
>> or if you will not redeem it you shall break its neck.
>> All the firstborn of your sons you shall redeem.
> No one shall appear before me empty-handed.

The passage begins with the general formulation in verse 19. Unlike all later regulations regarding the firstborn of animals, there is no limitation in the law. It even includes female firstborn. Even the parallel in the Book of the Covenant begins unmistakably with the injunction, "The firstborn of your sons . . ." (Ex 22:29).

Most often, the puzzling "she will/you will remember" (*zkr*, niph) in 34:19b is conjectured to be "the male" (*hazzākār*) in the old translations.[133] But this leads to a contradiction in the wording "all your possession, the male . . ." Furthermore, the emphasized "all" (*kol*) would be incomprehensible if we read in this way. Traditionally, Jewish exegesis has tried to find something like a "masculine" (*zākār*) related verb here – "give birth to a male,"[134] but finally, even the sentence structure opposes this.

The passive niphal form,[135] as we have it, of course does not make much sense with the "you" being addressed and does not correlate with the "possession" (*miqnēh*, fem.). It is most likely that we should read "you shall remember" (*tizkōr*). The person addressed is supposed to remember to offer the firstborn of all he possesses and surrender all firstborn of cattle and sheep. It might be that in situations with great, scattered numbers of cattle,[136] whole herds were left unattended. This would even be true when the more valuable, young, female animals were enclosed, and also if we might possibly consider still other deities who were provided for (but secretly!?).

The claim to all firstborn without exception emphatically reclaims the sole jurisdiction of YHWH over everything connected with the fertility of animals – and of people. The form of speech preserved yet in Deuteronomy shows quite forcibly that this was not altogether obvious in the late monarchic period. Cattle and sheep are called by the names of two Canaanite goddesses, "Sagar of your cattle" and "Astarte of your sheep" (Heb., Deut 7:13; 28:4, 18, 51).[137] The new offspring in these

---

133 E.g. Baentsch, Beer, Holzinger, Noth, Childs, Scharbert, Willi-Plein among others.
134 Thus Orlinski, *Notes* 199.
135 For other examples, see Eisring, article on *zakar* 581.
136 We need only think, e.g. of Laban's flocks in the Jacob narrative or those of Nabal in 1 Sam 25.
137 See Delcor, *Astarté*; Perlman, *Ashera* 102ff. and especially Müller, article on *'štrt* 461.

"linguistic icons"[138] are regarded as direct expressions of the power, even so far as to call these the embodiment of the goddesses themselves. This is the background against which the formulation of 34:19 is to be heard: all firstborn belong to YHWH because all birth, each Sagar and Astarte, is received thanks to him. Everything capable of being sacrificed to him ought to be sacrificed. The remainder should be ransomed or not used.

The last sentence of verse 20 includes the command not to appear before the face of God empty-handed. The context shows that this is a regulation concerning the offering of firstborn as part of the three pilgrimages to the shrine each year. This does not say "at some time" or "at some place," but at these three occasions should the firstborn animals be offered. This also enables the placement to make sense in which verses 19f. was added to the older context of the festival of unleavened bread and the day of rest.

If verse 18 deals with the great festival in the early part of the year, at which people gathered for an entire week, then in order to make sense, the addition of the offering of firstborn must occur before the reference to the day of rest, which structures the period of time after the festival. The firstborn are to be offered at the festival of unleavened bread as at the other festivals. Since the principal period for lambing occurs in the early months, before the "month of the ears of grain,"[139] there exists a temporally as well as factually well-thought correlation.

While God's claim upon the firstborn underscores and develops the intentions of the older texts, we are unable to see it to the same degree for all three of the sacrifice regulations in verses 25f. Their intent, especially the original intent, is burdened with all sorts of problems. This is true, first of all, for both sentences of verse 25:

> 25 You shall not offer the blood of my sacrifice with leaven,
>   and the sacrifice of the festival (of passover) shall not be left
>   until morning.

It is especially noteworthy that suddenly passover is being discussed. This festival is first connected with the festival of unleavened bread in Deuteronomy and then only loosely (Deut 16:1–8).[140] By its very nature it was not a pilgrimage festival (*ḥag*), but it was celebrated within the family and at home.[141] Furthermore, the regulation in verse 25b, not to leave meat for sacrifice until morning, is otherwise only recorded regarding passover (Ex 12:10; Deut 16:4). Is verse 25b altogether a later emendation?[142] On the other hand, there is a parallel in the Book of the Covenant (Ex 23:18), which speaks of just the fat of a sacrifice.[143]

138 Knauf, *Herkunft* 158.
139 Dalman, *Arbeit und Sitte* I, 421.
140 See especially R. Schmitt, *Exodus* 64ff.
141 For passover, see Kraus, *Gottesdienst* 61ff.; Laaf, *Pascha-Feier*; Haag, *Pascha*; Otto, article on *pāsaḥ* (Lit.).
142 Thus e.g. Haag, *Pascha* 29f.
143 For a discussion of this passage, see e.g. Cassuto, *Exodus* 305 and especially Childs, *Exodus* 485. Childs correctly denies an original connection to the festival of passover. Otherwise, for the traditional Jewish interpretation, see e.g. Snaith, *Ex 23:18* and Haran, *Temples* 327ff.

The connection to passover can only be traced back to a later emendation,[144] while at root it presents a sacrifice regulation no longer regarded as being in force. The sense of this rule is no longer clear to us. This is also true for the regulation presented in verse 25a.[145] Although, it is asserted in later priestly texts that people ought not to offer leavened bread to YHWH.[146] Thus, leavened bread should not have been eaten with sacrifice-meat.

Unfortunately the original sense of the regulation formulated in verse 26b (cf 23:19b, Deut 14:21b) (from which, as we know, one of the basic dietary rules of Judaism developed) is not clear:

> Ex 34:26b *You shall not boil a kid in its mother's milk.*

This made Israel an exception to the extremely widespread dietary custom in the Near East (from that time until the present) of cooking meat in milk.[147] The old discussion of the original intent of this prohibition has been raised again in an entirely new way by O. Keel.[148] He refers to a widely attested pictorial motif in which the unity of mother animal and the suckling young is represented and which gives evidence of great religious significance. This motif has been frequently attested on seal amulets from the tenth through eighth centuries found in Israelite locations,[149] but it is also widely attested in the ancient Near East and Canaan. For a long time the thesis was regarded as correct that Israel was here rejecting a Canaanite custom[150] that appears to be attested by Ugaritic text (KTU 1.23.14).[151] Nevertheless, this interpretation is regarded today as disproven,[152] in any case there is no attestation for cooking a young animal in its own mother's milk as a Canaanite custom.

Whether we might conclude that the Israelites adopted the respect for the divine life-force manifest in the unity of mother and young, as it is already attested in the ancient Near East,[153] remains open to question.[154] As long as it is not settled absolutely that the birth of every animal reflects the power of a particular goddess, and that this goddess is venerated by the observance of a particular dietary custom or prohibition, the religious-historical context as well as the precise intent of the Old Testament prohibition against cooking a young animal in its mother's milk must remain open for discussion.[155]

---

144 With Halbe, *Privilegrecht* 195ff.; see there also the discussion of earlier proposals.
145 This also is frequently connected with passover (Snaith, *Ex 23:18*; Haran, *Temples* 327ff. and others). For the remarkable use of *šḥṭ* in this place, see e.g. Snaith, *Verbs*.
146 For this regulation and other exceptions (Am 4:5!), see Kellermann, article on *ḥms* 1063f.
147 See Gen 18:8 and especially Sinuhe B 87ff.; for this, Knauf, *Herkunft* 163ff.
148 Keel, *Böcklein* 13–40. See the discussion of earlier interpretations.
149 See Abb. 89–94 as well as 120 in Keel, *Böcklein*. Haran, *Böcklein* 142f. refers to an additional amulet from Tell Michal.
150 For earlier interpretations of this kind and their problems, see Keel, *Böcklein* 28ff.
151 First Ginsburg, *Notes* 72.
152 See especially Ratner, *A Kid*; in addition to Keel, *Böcklein* 37f.; Milgrom, *Kid* 50.
153 Thus, especially Keel, *Böcklein* in summary 142ff.
154 For a critique (in part!) of Keel, see Haran, *Böcklein* 147ff. and Milgrom, *Kid* 54f.
155 The observations of Haran, *Böcklein* 152 ("an expression of human tenderness . . . proceeding out of an inclination toward sensitivity") and Milgrom, *Kid* 54 ("according to Philo, the root rationale behind the kid prohibition is its opposition to commingling life and death;" see also Carmichael, *Separating*) are rather vague.

Independent of this, however, we might consider that this prohibition is connected with the widely attested religious emphasis upon the unity of a mother animal and her young, and that this was reshaped into a divine command in a manner that is not otherwise attested. In the same way that we might say the YHWH faith in the whole context of Ex 34:18ff. is formulated in the narrower and specialized sphere of activity of Canaanite gods and goddesses and there demonstrates its own unique characteristics, the same thing is true here. He is justified in representing the fertility of animals with the divine powers of that time in the same or even a better way. Perhaps we can come closer to the original intent if we consider that the regulation might not have been connected with the YHWH pilgrimages[156] and the offering of the firstborn simply by accident. If this originally were a regulation connected with the offering of firstborn, then we must note that the *first* production of milk occurs because of this birth. In each case, however, it is evidence of a close interconnectedness between the animals.[157]

This concluding sentence in verse 26b is a part of the theme that is central to verses 18ff. The YHWH faith that is formulated here describes what it means to venerate this God exclusively, and it is expressed in the context of Iron Age agriculture in Palestine. It expresses what it means to belong to this God in terms of the annual festivals with their connection to harvest, as it relates to the fertility of plants and animals, to the day of rest during the main seasons of agricultural work. All these customs and regulations are very closely related to Canaanite usage. Nevertheless, in all of the really important features there is an agricultural faith, unique and independent in calendar and rhythm. The offering of the firstfruits and firstborn, the celebration of harvest and the weekly rhythm (instead of the moon) and perhaps also the sacrificial rites, express that people must worship YHWH alone, and it is to him alone that they must express their gratitude for the land and its fertility.

c3. Overview: The Temporal Structure of Biblical Faith[158]

The temporal structure first found in Ex 34 becomes a sign of the biblical God. It is evident in the calendar of festivals[159] as well as the weekly rhythm[160] of the later laws. The blended elements in Ex 34 are separated out already in the Book of the Covenant, and the themes that are still interwoven here are placed side by side. The festival calendar with its three annual celebrations (Ex 23:14ff.), the weekly day of rest (23:10–12) which was enlarged into the sabbath year, and the offering of the firstborn (22:28f.), are placed next to each other. The individual variations in sequence of the dates and consequently in the history of the festivals

156 Thus also Milgrom, *Kid* 55.
157 The next step in the history finds the regulation in Deut 14:21 in conjunction with other dietary laws. The steps that lead to the fundamental prohibition of a milk-meat combination cannot be reconstructed with certainty. See Sigal, *Judentum* 264.
158 For the cultic offerings, see below pp. 215ff., 222; for the food rituals and the approach to animals, see below pp. 261ff., 291ff.
159 Ex 23:14ff.; Deut 16; Lev 23; Num 28f. For this, see Morgan, *So-Called Cultic Calendars*.
160 Ex 23:10ff.; Lev 23:3 and elsewhere. Deuteronomic law is the great exception. There in Deut 5 the day of rest is added to the Decalogue in the more recent stratum. For this, see below p. 203.

which can be followed by the changes need not be discussed in detail here.[161]

The combining of the festival of unleavened bread with passover in Deuteronomy is, for example, especially important. In the priestly texts the autumn harvest festival appears along with the day of atonement. The basic temporal structure, however, remains intact and is preserved throughout. Each of the law books has its calendar of festivals as well as its sacrificial code. This is an essential part of Torah.

This is about the temporal structure of the biblical faith, the putting of exclusive veneration of God into a rhythm that is just as closely connected with the rhythm of the year and of nature as it is separated from those of the other gods.

The weekly day of rest had the name "sabbát"[162] from, at latest, the exilic period – especially in the Decalogue – probably referring to the full moon day during the preexilic period. If it appears in context with mention of the fertility of the land and agricultural labor, already in the Book of the Covenant (Ex 23:12) and especially in later contexts (Deut 5:12ff.) its social aspects are emphasized in that slaves and animals are included in the rest. The Sabbath conflicts of the exilic/postexilic period (Jer 17:9ff.; Neh 13:5ff.) allow us to see that the extension of the sabbath, from agricultural production – "plowing and sowing" – in Ex 34:21 outward to distribution, supply, transportation, etc. was a slow and always disputed process.[163]

d. HISTORICAL PLACE AND SOCIAL CONTEXT

There is nothing against – in fact there is much in favor of – the idea that the divine commandments handed down in Ex 34:11ff. and God's written instructions[164] attested in the eighth century by Hos 8:12 are not far apart. If Hosea was aware of and acknowledged God's written commandments, and there are, on the other hand, a collection of basic cultic regulations from YHWH believers rooted in the religious conflicts of the ninth century, we would need a special reason not to connect the two together. Nevertheless, even the context in which Ex 34:11ff. occurs points to the same correlation.

The conflict, about which Ex 32–34 writes in a narrative fashion, revolves around calf images, thus the official state cult of the northern kingdom.[165] The stone tablets could only go back to a tradition of the northern kingdom. One of the oldest inscriptions that we have from the monarchic period is a calendar giving the most important agricultural duties during the course of a year. This Gezer calendar[166] is a small, "stone tablet" from the ninth or tenth century. In Hosea's view, the catastrophe occurred because Israel did not follow the will of God as they knew it formulated in the Torot, but rather they supported the calf cult and things connected with it. The catastrophe ensued, according to the

---

161 See Kraus, *Worship in Israel*, Chapter 2; De Vaux, *Lebesordnungen* 322ff.
162 See especially Robinson, *Sabbat*.
163 For the Jewish sabbath, see e.g. Spier, *Sabbat*; Heschel, *Sabbat*.
164 See above pp. 17ff.
165 See above p. 52.
166 KAI 182. See Talmon, *Gezerkalendar*; Borowski, *Agriculture* 32ff.

historically remote Ex 32ff. because Israel gave its allegiance to the calf cult. The breaking of the tablets is an expression of this break, and their renewal is a sign of the forgiveness that opens a future for them.

Ex 34:11ff. is a document of the religious separation from other gods and the people who worship them. It marks the decisive point in their separation. The alternatives YHWH or Baal, occur, so far as we are aware, for the first time in the conflicts of prophetic figures like Elijah and the circles associated with him during the time of Omri.[167] We have almost exclusively epic, prophetic narratives that certainly bear traces of a long historical tradition. Nevertheless, the Jehu rebellion and the energy supporting it, his explosiveness and ferocity, demonstrate for us some of the radicality of the religious conflicts. There are not many, but there are clearly a few threads connecting the document in Ex 34 with the central themes and concepts of this period.[168]

Whether we want to identify the prophetic group as those at work directly behind the commandments of Ex 34, and the critical religious separation from the worshipers of the other gods reflected in those commandments, and regarding this as a school-like organization at particular shrines, especially Gilgal; or rather see in them in connection with permanent groups[169] of YHWH priests, who, according to Hosea, are actually supposed to have a knowledge (da'at) of YHWH and his commandments;[170] these may be alternatives between which we could hardly choose, given the sources that we have available to us. Furthermore, both functioned at shrines.

Fundamentally, both have an authority to which we can credit the "neutral" style of the older stratum as well as the decidedly "YHWH speech" style of the more recent stratum. If we want to judge on the basis of later characteristics, there is much to argue in favor of priestly circles.[171]

If we ask, who is the "you" being addressed, the formulation of verse 23 ("all your males" kol-z^{e}kūr^{e}ka) is especially noteworthy. The person being addressed is responsible for a great number of men and must, for example, decide which of them were to participate in the pilgrimage. This person is not simply the head of a family or property owner, but at least the head of an extended family, probably a clan (mišpāḥāh). The persons addressed are landowners (verse 24), but are themselves completely involved in agricultural duties (verse 21).

The formulation of verse 22 is especially interesting: "you shall observe the festival." The subject of the cultic action is being addressed. He, himself "observe[s]" ('śh) the festival, in other words, he determines the "what" and "when" and then carries it out. It is he, himself, not the king, as would be added immediately. Thus, the persons addressed are

---

167 See, e.g. Donner, *Geschichte* II 270f.; Lang, *Jahwe-allein-Bewegung* 58ff.; Albertz, *Religionsgeschichte* 330ff.
168 See above pp. 125f., 135f.
169 See e.g. Schmitt, *Elisa* in summary 189.
170 See especially Hosea 4; 6 where "knowledge" and "Torah" are parallel to each other. See Jeremias, *Hosea* 65f. as well as Wolff, *Wissen um Gott*; ibid., *Hoseas geistige Heimat*.
171 The lack of any reference to obeying the commandments (see below p. 144.) or the great interest in animal or crop sacrifice at the shrine are probably of priestly provenance.

the heads of clans in an agricultural region. They live in a situation where their neighbors are clearly worshipers of other gods (verse 15) and they have a tradition of good relations (or at least they are not enemies) with these neighbors. In principal, the basic tenor of all preexilic laws that apply to free, landowning males is already assumed.

In contrast to all later legal documents – if we follow the literary reconstruction attempted here – this text does not speak out of a fictive historical situation. Even in the later stratum, God speaks in the present for the here and now. Only in the narrative context of Ex 32–34 is there a historicization that shows itself in the additions to the text itself.[172] Nevertheless, the historical dress on the discussion of the collapse of the northern kingdom might have originated in a reference to Sinai at the time of Moses and Aaron through the unmistakable and overwhelming association of the northern kingdom calf images with the exodus theme (especially 1 Kg 12:28), rather than that historicization would have come about because of association with the already independent record of the commandments.

It is interesting to note that two important things are not even mentioned in this text: the basic relation to God, from which the commandments and the instructions proceed, as well as the positive and negative consequences of Israel's actions. These are two aspects embedded in the commandments that are considered obvious and constitutive for all of the later Torah texts. Their omission can only mean that the divine instructions come out of a relationship that is regarded as taken completely for granted, and that this relationship is so certain and so unbroken that its validity remains firm without any reference to possible consequences. All of this is pre-prophetic and before the all-encompassing catastrophe – even before it was conceivable.

The Jerusalem Code: The Mishpatim (Ex 21f.)

The collection of casuistic legislation in Ex 21:1–22:16 (or 19) is clearly set apart from its context as a separate entity. It is unmistakably different in both language and character, and in form and content there is no analog in other Old Testament legal documents. The text, however, is similar to other ancient Near Eastern legal literature. They are so similar that there have been suggestions made of extra-Israelite provenance for this text.[173]

The interpretation of this law book has thus far been generally based on the fact that it is imbedded in the Book of the Covenant. Thus, for example, with respect to both intent and effect the slave law of the Mishpatim has been interpreted on the basis of its contextual correlation with other social and "humanitarian" passages, even all of Torah.[174] For a reconstruction of the history of Israelite law, however, it is important first to work through the statements (and with them the function of the complexes) independent of context.

---

172 See above pp. 121ff.
173 Especially Jensen, *Bundesbuch* 57ff., 73ff.; e.g. also Waterman, *Pre-Israelite Laws*; Lemche, *Hebrew Slave* 143.
174 Thus, the widely held interpretation of slave law as regulation for protection, e.g. in Noth, *Exodus* 143; Paul, *Studies* 47; and most recently especially Otto, *Wandel* 35ff.

Correspondingly, there is at the heart of what follows an interpretation of the legal provisions in their social context. Only against this background can we describe the entirety of the Book of the Covenant in a historically, legally, and theologically appropriate manner. In addition, we must first describe its inner structure, boundaries, divisions and literary stratification.

a. CONSTRUCTION AND STRATIFICATION

At its core the Mishpatim consist of a series of casuistic laws, beginning with their characteristic "When" (*ki*) or "And when" (*w^eki*). Contrary or ancillary conditions are introduced with "if" (*'im* or *w^e'im*).[175] This objective, juridic style, originating in ancient Near Eastern legal language, is subdivided by a series of statements in a different style. Thus, already the first paragraph begins in 21:2 with a remarkable "You." We find the same thing again in Ex 21:13f. and especially 21:23 at the beginning of the *lex talionis* in addition to 22:17.

Laws carrying death penalties in 21:12–17 and 22:17–19 depart from the casuistic style. Likewise, talion formulations in 21:(23), 24 and the legal principal in 22:8 are unmistakably different. There is an apparent confusion (or at least an interlinking) of material from two different legal questions in 21:37–22:3, in which 22:1, 2a has frequently been regarded as an insertion.[176]

In the past scholars have often turned the objective casuistic style into a literary-critical principle. The consequence has been that all elements of another style have been regarded as secondary additions.[177] Ex 21:2ff. is a notable exception, where this at most has led to attempts to reconstruct an older wording to approximate other casuistic statements.[178] If we presume an original stylistic purity, with V. Wagner[179] we will find a total of sixteen paragraphs that treat consecutively themes of slave law (21:2–11), bodily injury (21:18–32), liabilities in farm work or manufacturing (21:33–22:14) as well as a case from family law (22:15f.). The construction and inner divisions of such a law book would generally correspond to those of ancient Near Eastern legal codes.[180]

From the outset the application of stylistic form-critical observations to literary-critical hypotheses is methodologically problematic. A series of relatively recent studies,[181] especially that of Osumi[182] have gone far beyond and added more precise observations regarding the

---

175 For an analysis of the laws, see Liedke, *Gestalt und Bezeichnung* 101ff.; Osumi, *Kompositionsgeschichte* 93ff.

176 E.g. Noth, *Exodus* 148.

177 E.g. Jepsen, *Bundesbuch* 1ff. and especially 54; Wagner *Systematik*.

178 E.g. Jepsen, *Bundesbuch* 1; Alt, *Urspringe* 291 note 2; Otto, *Wandel* 35.

179 Wagner, *Systematik* 176ff.

180 See Petschow, Codex *Hammurabi*, upon which Wagner, *Systematik* relies. See also Petschow, *Eshnunna* and most recently especially Sauren, *Aufbau und Anordnung*. For a discussion of the arrangement and structure of ancient Near Eastern law, see Otto, *Rechtsgeschichte* 9ff. The "attraction" of themes and key words that are purposely used is especially important.

181 Otto, *Wandel*; ibid. *Rechtsgeschichte*; see also Crüsemann, *Bundesbuch*; Jackson, *Literary Features* 240.

182 Osumi, *Kompositionsgeschichte* 87ff.

linguistic as well as juristic-logical construction, which cause the very close inter-weaving of the individual parts as well as the essential inner features to emerge. Even his reference to the copula at the beginning of the laws, which had been previously inexcusably neglected, shows that especially the complex of 21:12–36 was consciously shaped as a linguistic unity,[183] the only exception being the talion law in verses 24f.

It is also important that central words and themes continue to repeat thus permitting the unity of sections to emerge.[184] The frequent verbs for "strike" (*nkh*, hiph., *ngf*, *ngḥ*) appear grouped from 21:12 on and then especially in verses 18ff. Similarly, the term "replace" (*šlm*, pi) characterizes the entire passage 21:33–22:14. Alternating negation and intensification to *figura etymologica* by means of infinitive absolute, causes the intended shape – in content as well as style – of the entire textual block to emerge.[185]

As regards contents, especially the axiomatic regulation in 21:12, "Whoever strikes a person mortally shall be put to death," is clearly presumed to be an overarching principle in the decrees of 21:18ff.[186] The reality and limits of the principle in 21:12 are established in detail in 21:18–36. The section cannot be considered apart from 21:12. Similarly, the axiomatic regulation in 22:8 does not at all contradict its context, but rather formulates a principle necessary for the interpretation of the passage.[187]

All of this illustrates that the purity of the casuistic style may not be made into a principle for literary-critical partition. This is also true of the manner of address in the second person singular in 21:1, 13, 23. In all these cases it is of course not, as in other apodictic portions of the Book of the Covenant, a person affected by the court case (the plaintiff or defendant) who is being addressed, but rather the authority who administers justice.[188]

Thus, we see this is a composition thoroughly formed in every detail.[189] Its characteristics emerge especially clearly if we attempt at subdivision and study the inner structure. It is then that we are able to distinguish the

---

183 Osumi, *Kompositionsgeschichte* 93ff.
184 Otto, *Wandel* 12ff., 24ff.; Osumi, *Kompositionsgeschichte* 110.
185 Especially Otto, *Wandel* 12ff.
186 See Osumi, *Kompositionsgeschichte* 110.
187 Osumi, *Kompositionsgeschichte* 123–127; somewhat differently, Otto, *Wandel* 17.
188 Thus correctly, Osumi, *Kompositionsgeschichte* 22f. and elsewhere.
189 Schwienhorst-Schönberger (*Bundesbuch*) has proposed a new, three-layer model. See the table 234 (in the deuteronomistic verse Ex 21:25 there are even four layers). There is a base stratum (Ex 21:12, 18f.; 22aα, bα, 28f., 32, 33aβ*-b, 34aα, 37; 22:3.9f.*, 13abβ) which was first expanded by 21:31, 33aαβ*, 34aβb, 36; 22:4f., 6–8, 11f.13bα, 14. In conjunction with the divine law redaction (to which, e.g. 21:2–11, 22:20ff.* also belong), there are the amplifications – 21:13–17, 20f., 22aβbβ, 23f., 26f., 30; 22:1f., 9f.*, 15f. We cannot pursue a detailed analysis here. A different model is presented, among others, in the many detailed observations in Osumi, *Kompositionsgeschichte* 87–134. With a few exceptions it shows the inner unity of the Mishpatim. For the question of talion law, see below pp. 147ff. For the question whether slave law fits with the social protections of 22:20ff., see below pp. 151ff., especially pp. 156f. It is not easy to accept that the divine law redaction in the Mishpatim is partly classic casuistic but otherwise something completely different. Schwienhorst-Schönberger criticizes my methodology in conjunction with a discussion of talion law, suggesting that I have not exhausted all of the possibilities to understand the text as a unity (103). This prinicple certainly does

two great themes of life (21:12–36) and property (21:37–22:16). They are not simply placed side by side, but dovetailed.[190] The crime of murder appears yet again in 22:1, 2a in the midst of the section on theft 21:37–22:8. But we also find crimes against property within 21:33–36.

The dovetailing of the two halves of the section on property appears structurally quite similar. There 21:37–22:8 is about theft, which then appears once more in 22:12. The juridical question of "safe-keeping" is treated in 22:9–14, but the theme had already appeared once in 22:6–8. The axiomatic principle in 22:8, valid for both complexes, holds the two together. This compositional and redactional technique is to be regarded as especially typical for the Mishpatim.

Only the combination of stylistic, structural as well as juridical-content aspects permits us to answer the recently controverted questions regarding the beginning as well as the end of the independent existence of the legal document of the Mishpatim appropriately. Concerning the beginning, Osumi would designate the section on slave law (22:20–26*) as a later addendum, which came about only because of the inclusion of the Mishpatim in the larger Book of the Covenant.[191] Conversely, Otto regards the section 22:20–26* as a part of the independent legal document 21:1–22:26.[192] For the first thesis, the singular "you" of 21:2 is likewise introduced as well as the correspondence of the six/seven rhythm (so important for the entire Book of the Covenant) in 21:2ff. and 23:10ff. which may not belong to different strata. The structural correspondence of 21:2–11 and 22:20–26* is the only substantiation in the chiastic structure of 21:2–22:26 as Otto described it.[193]

Thus, the slave law (21:2–11) and the provisions for protection of foreigners, widows, orphans and the poor (22:20–26) in both theses can be traced back to a single hand.[194] But the tension between slave law and the provisions for protection makes single authorship doubtful. If we interpret slave law on its own,[195] it has a completely different social intent than 22:20ff., and it cannot be described simply as "provision for protection;"[196] thus we must be quite hesitant.

The fact that slaves are also mentioned in the section on bodily injury (and elsewhere as well) argues authoritatively in favor of the appropriateness of the slave laws to the remainder of the Mishpatim. We also

---

not underlie his own work. Apart from the individual disagreements, the fight is over how much one can use relatively chance observations for literary criticism – especially before grasping the inner literary-critical structure, but especially before understanding the juristical shape.

190 For what follows, see Osumi, *Kompositionsgeschichte* 133ff.
191 Osumi, *Kompositionsgeschichte* 107ff., 146ff.; similarly Schwienhorst-Schönberger, *Bundesbuch* 30 and elsewhere.
192 Otto, *Wandel* 9, 38ff. He regards the statements formulated in the second person plural in 20aβ, b, 21, 23, 24b as deuteronomistic (see below p. 198f.).
193 Otto, *Wandel* 9f.
194 Thus also Schwienhorst-Schönberger, *Bundesbuch* in summary 287, and elsewhere. He would also ascribe the provisions for slaves Ex 21:20f., 26f. to the later divine law stratum, along with 22:20ff.* and others (234, 284).
195 See below pp. 151ff.
196 Thus Otto, *Wandel* 9f.; Schwienhorst-Schönberger, *Bundesbuch* 236 and elsewhere, emphasizes its "humanitarian character."

find there discussions of the killing of slaves (21:20), serious bodily injury (verses 26f.) as well as goring by an ox (verse 32). This kind of resumption and continuation of themes from a previous section is quite similar to other thematic crossovers.[197]

Since the Mishpatim contain other axiomatic regulations (e.g. 22:8), and since the establishment of the duration of debt slavery (like all other legal statements in the Mishpatim) brings together the interests of two legal parties, there is no fundamental difference between the slave law and other legal provisions. Everything argues in favor of slave law being a part of this legal document.

The placement of 21:1 after the superscription would otherwise be difficult to explain, as long as we regard the superscription as a relevant, literary-critical signal. Only the surprising nature of the address in 21:2 remains.[198] It is, however, difficult to say whether we could now theorize a later reshaping, or whether the "you," under certain circumstances, might represent the same collective authority as in 21:13.

The thesis that 22:20–26* belongs with the preceding legal document is not well supported. Apart from the great tensions with slave law already mentioned, there is above all a completely different linguistic style that stands in opposition. It is not just the fact that the casuistic style is not continued that makes the difference, but already the characteristic language of this style. "If" (kī) and "when" ('im) are used completely differently. The important regulations are introduced by "when" ('im) (22:22, 23, 24, 26), but "if" (kī) is reserved for axiomatic principles (22:20, 22, 26a, b). The dominant "I" style of the divine address (22:22, 23, 24, 26), which could only be eliminated by literary-critically questionable means,[199] does not combine with the basic flow of the language in 21:2ff. Thus, it is apparent that the end of the Mishpatim is in 22:16 or 19.

The talion law of 21:(23), 24f. together with its position in the context presents a most interesting problem of literary stratification within the Mishpatim. While critical exegesis has long regarded the law to be an insertion, actually disagreeing only whether verse 23 (or a part of it) also belonged with it,[200] a few more recent studies have proposed the traditional Jewish interpretation in the sense of proper restitution[201] as

---

197 The texts from 21:12ff. related to slavery can easily be added to the table in Osumi, *Kompositionsgeschichte* 134.

198 The compositional analogy of the six/seven rhythm in 21:2ff. and 23:10ff. cannot be decisive. The composition of the Book of the Covenant could be working here as elsewhere with previously existing material. In no case can we trace the varying applications of cultic unity of time (individual in slave law, collective in the sabbath year) back to the same source; see also Lemche, *Manumission* 45.

199 According to Otto, *Wandel* 38f. the introduction of the YHWH address is to be traced back to the redactor. This apparently refers to the same person who also collected other older material into a single block 21:2–22:26. But then why is a continuous theological approach absent?

200 Thus Wagner, *Rechtssätze* 3f., and Alt, *Talionsformel* 303f. propose that the addition already begins with verse 3. Otherwise, e.g. Jackson, *The Problem* 94; Jüngling, *Auge für Auge*; see Crüsemann, *Auge um Auge* 413ff.

201 See especially mBQ 8.1; bBQ 83b–84a; Mekhilta Ex 21:23f. and eleswhere. See Mikliszanski, *Law of Retaliation*. For the traditional Jewish interpretation, see further Amram, *Retaliation*; Horovitz, *Auge um Auge*; Norden, *Auge um Auge*; see also Crüsemann, *Auge um Auge* 413ff.

the approach already for the Old Testament period and the original interpretation for the Book of the Covenant.[202]

In view of the wide attestation in the ancient Near East for a talion principal,[203] formulated literally, and in view of the already very difficult case of injury to a pregnant woman (verses 22f.),[204] which is somewhat surprisingly associated with this formula, there is a whole tangle of problems.[205] For the moment, we will only deal with the literary problems.[206] If we take literally the formulations in verses 24f. – "eye for eye, tooth for tooth . . ." – they very clearly contradict the basic principles of the Book of the Covenant, according to which bodily harm may be compensated by payment of restitution and not necessarily physical retribution against the offender (21:18f., 22, 29). There is, furthermore, a different penalty depending whether the victim is slave or free (verses 20f., 26f.). For that reason, if we accept the literary unity of Torah or at least the immediate context, it is obvious the formula can only be understood as a compensatory payment. This is, indeed, how Judaism has interpreted it.

Nevertheless, it is quite unlikely that it would have been formulated this way if, from the outset, it were supposed to express such a settlement. Even the variants of the formula in 1 Kg 20:39,[207] 10:24 as well as Deut 19:21 (cf verse 19)[208] and Lev 24:17ff.[209] suggest a literal

202 See Otto, *Wandel* 25ff., who regards the talion formula as a means of integration and the basis for the entire section on bodily injury in 21:18–21; see ibid, *Geschichte der Talion*. The context basically excludes a retributive punishment (*Geschichte* 118) and effectively annuls its ancient Near Eastern sense (128) even in the earliest literary stratum. Schwienhorst-Schönberger, *Bundesbuch* 99ff. (see ibid, *Auge um Auge*) regards verse 22aβ, bβ, 23f. as a consistent interpretation of the older law in verse 22aα, bα (verse 25 might be deuteronomisitic). The fact that the formulation "you shall give life for life" in verse 23 is not to be interpreted in the sense of a death penalty is already decisive for him (see below note 210). There is information on recent studies in Martin-Achard, *Recent travaux*.

203 See especially Cardascia, *Place du Talion*; Jüngling, *Auge um Auge* 5ff.; Frymer-Kenski, *Tit for Tat*; Otto, *Geschichte der Talion* 107ff. CH §§195ff. are especially clear. We find an explicit exclusion to this compensatory payment in a very close Greek parallel, "If anyone strikes out an eye, he ought to suffer the loss of his own eye, and there should be no possibility for substitute material compensation" (Zaleukos according to Demosthenes, Or. 24 §140; see Mühl, *Gesetze des Zaleukos*), for a comparison with Israel, see Crüsemann, *Auge um Auge* 417ff.

204 See e.g. Jackson, *The Problem*; Isser, *Two Traditions*.

205 In addition to the literature mentioned, see Daube, *Lex Talionis*; Doron, *New Look*; Loewenstamm, *Exodus xxi*; Kugelmass, *Lex Talionis*; Weinfeld, *Concepts*. The interpretation of Westbrook, *Lex Talionis* is based, among others on the interpretation of the word *'āsōn* as a designation for an unknown and therefore not possible to arrest criminal, which is hardly consistent with the other appearances of this word.

206 For the content, see below pp. 162f.

207 This makes the explicit alternative, "or else you shall pay a talent of silver" quite clear.

208 Deuteronomy draws a boundary for the talion formula at the reprisal for false testimony. The phrase "Show no pity" underscores the harshness of the required sanction. The interpretation of Otto, *Geschichte der Talion* 121ff. in a circular fashion presupposes the Book of the Covenant.

209 See especially Jüngling, *Auge für Auge* 34.

interpretation. According to style, language and content, 21:24f. contradicts both the narrower and the wider context.[210]

We *must* presume this is an insertion with which we would expect disagreement over its context and legal consequences.[211] It follows a passage where we find a similar phrase, "life for life" in verse 23, expanding it to include all physical harm. Simultaneously, there is a close relationship to verses 26f., where the concern is with consequences of physical injury to slaves, with special examples given regarding eye and tooth (in other words, the first two body parts listed in verses 24f.).

Osumi takes this as a continuous insertion, including verses 24–27.[212] His main reason is that the entire section 21:12–36 is not about physical injury, but – unlike the usual interpretation – only the problem of whether or not to hold in detention a person accused of murder.

The limits of the principle formulated in 21:12 are being debated. When are they to be applied and when not? Verses 26f. does not fit here, since in that verse it is clear that the discussion is about physical injury that does not present mortal danger.

In my opinion, such a view regarding the theme is only partially correct for verses 18ff. Without a doubt, verses 18f. treats a situation (and its consequences) in which no one has died. In such a case blood feud does not apply, rather compensatory payment is negotiated or determined. We find here battery against a pregnant woman which results in "simple" miscarriage or the death of the mother.[213] Ex 21:18ff. is about cases of serious bodily injury that are regulated by compensatory payments, as well as the delineation of difference between these and cases of mortal injury. For this reason, everything in verses 26f. argues that serious, but not mortal injury should be handled just like the killing of slaves (verses 20f.) or death caused by an ox (verse 32).

210 The abrupt transition from a special case of a pregnant woman to something that has nothing substantive to do with it and the general valid formula in verses 24f. is important. The writers of the Mishpatim, skilled in law, never write in so confused a manner elsewhere. The aspects mentioned by Schwienhorst-Schönberger, *Bundesbuch* 99ff. do not apply against this central argument. He correctly refers to the problem that the phrase "you shall give . . ." in verse 23 creates, and the differences between it and other formulations of the death penalty in the Book of the Covenant. Nevertheless, what is always suggested is that it cannot be about the same thing as in verse 22 where there is no *'āsōn*. If verse 22 deals with a monetary fine, this is something different. There is only an alternative to the possible death penalty for someone who commits an unintentional murder according to the provisions of 21:13f. (102) because Schwienhorst-Schönberger considers both to be part of the same stratum, which is debatable.

211 It is remarkable that authors such as Otto and Schwienhorst-Schönberger, who otherwise are none too careful about literary criticism, and use a scissor for many other less strong contradictions and alleged tensions, refuse to recognize a classic case of literary stratification. Does that have to do with the consequences of their understanding of the Mishpatim which necessarily results when 21:24f. is supposed to be formulated against the laws of the Mishpatim?

212 Osumi, *Kompositionsgeschichte* 119ff., 152ff.

213 Other ancient Near Eastern parallels demonstrate that this is about an alternative to verses 22f. The parallels never deal with the problem of an induced premature birth. Thus also the rabbinic interpretation. See Loewenstamm, *Exodus 21:22–25* (352ff.); Jüngling, *Auge für Auge* 27ff.

Besides 21:24f., the only other literary insertion to the Mishpatim is in 21:13f. The regulation regarding asylum for unintentional murder interrupts the clear, well-structured design of the section on crimes deserving of capital punishment (21:12, 15, 16, 17).[214] These are not on the same plane with the regulations in 21:18, 21, 22.[215] Here again the subject is not purposeful, planned murder. We would have to regard 21:13f. as an insertion.[216]

Thus, in 21:1–22:16(19)[217] the Mishpatim shows themselves as a closed and tightly constructed composition in which we need only reckon 21:13f. and 21:24f. as later additions which determine accent. Three subject areas, "slaves" (21:2–11), "striking" (21:12–36) and "property" (21:37–22:16), are treated in succession, emphasizing the inner subdivision. Seen this way, the overlapping of the boundaries of the sections becomes evident and the compositional principles become especially clear.

Does this very closed composition reflect its own history? Or put another way, does it allow us to recognize traces of earlier pre-forms? In one place the answer is surely "yes." While 21:12 represents the presumption of and the point of connection for setting apart 21:18–32, the other *mōt-yūmāt* statements in 21:15–17 are not taken up again in the remainder of the document. Since, on the other hand, 21:12, 15–17 represents a very precisely constructed unity, we would have to theorize that this is one of the ostensible authorities for the Mishpatim. It could have been a written collection, but we cannot exclude the possibility of an oral tradition.

Apart from this passage there are no other places in the Mishpatim that suggest older pre-forms. This above all rejects the viewpoint of E. Otto. He allegedly sees blocks in 21:2–22:16 that have a longer history.[218] Slave law (21:2–11) and capital offenses (21:12–17; 22:17–19c), physical injury (21:18–32) and the regulation of compensatory payment (21:33–22:14) were each supposed to have formed small collections.[219] Each of the collections permits us to recognize several stages in its development. Each is supposed to reflect the basic legal-historical process of development from an internal law of restitution to a more general right of sanction.[220]

This proposal is insufficiently supported in many respects and methodologically suspect.[221] Convincing reasons must be apparent in order to divide a unified work, as Otto does it, into older pre-forms. In no place are there contradictions in content. Nowhere is it apparent that individual thematic blocks were literally independent.

We are unable to identify small, thematically discrete unities of this kind either by form criticism or literary criticism; they remain pure con-

214 See especially Otto, *Wandel* 31f.
215 See Osumi, *Kompositionsgeschichte* 122.
216 See Schwienhorst-Schönberger, *Bundesbuch* 39f. See also below pp. 160., 174ff.
217 Ex 22:17–19 might likewise most probably be regarded as a supplement or conclusion to the Mishpatim, even though we lack compelling arguments.
218 Otto, *Wandel* 12–44.
219 Added to this are the provisions for protection in 22:20–26*.
220 Otto, *Wandel* 61ff. see also ibid, *Aspekte*; ibid, *Interdependenzen*.
221 For what follows, see Osumi *Kompoisitionsgeschichte* 11ff., 149f.

jecture. Above all, Otto's guiding principle to separate older from more recent elements, is his preliminary conviction that there were no sanctions in early Israelite law and that all the remaining compensatory regulations might be remnants of older law.

Apart from the inner inconsistencies and things that are not clear in these theses – even if they were legal-historically universal and clear – we may not simply turn them into a standard for literary-historical or tradition-historical hypotheses. Israel adopted at least in part, for example, a very long legal history from the ancient Near East as its own heritage. Thus, it need not repeat all of the steps taken elsewhere for the previous thousand years in exactly the same way. What we have before us in the Mishpatim is a well thought out and balanced juxtaposition of provisions for restitution and sanction. Furthermore, the document before us does not suggest that we regard one of the two sets of provisions as older and the other more recent, and certainly not to treat the individual provisions in this way.

Thus, we have in the Mishpatim, along with the formulations in Ex 34, the oldest known written law in Israel. It is a corpus that is closer to ancient Near Eastern law, as much as we know of it, than any other known parts of Israelite law, but in many respects it is clearly different from it. We will examine its historical place as well as its institutional provenance in the following pages, first in relation to the social-historical interpretation of the individual sections.

b. LEGAL STRUCTURE AND SOCIAL EFFECT

b1. "His money" (Ex 21:21) – Slave law

At the climax of the Mishpatim, in 21:2–11, we find slave law with the fundamental regulations regarding the duration of slavery and the opportunity to regain freedom. The theme of slavery runs through the entire section 21:12–32. In 12:16 kidnapping is discussed as a possible source of slaves, and in 21:18ff. we find a three-part sequence of crimes against free persons, in each case followed by analogous cases for slaves.

First, Ex 21:18f. treats an offense of physical injury committed against a free person without direct mortal consequence. The matter concludes in 21:20f. with a discussion of an assault committed against a slave with immediate or delayed mortal consequence.

Second, the matter of battery against a pregnant woman (verse 22) is connected with treatment of serious bodily injury committed against a slave without mortal consequence (verses 26f.). The connection is interrupted by an insertion of the talion law (verses 24f.). Third, we have the case (begun in verse 28) of death caused by an ox to which is attached the death of a slave in verse 32.

This central placement of slave law enables us, first of all, to make a rather reliable approximate dating for the Mishpatim. At the time of its establishment, there must have been a real need for legal regulation of slavery.[222] Slaves must have been a social presence worth mentioning,

---

222 For slavery in the ancient Near East as well as Israel, we still refer to Mendelssohn, *Slavery*; in addition, now, to Cardellini, *"Sklaven"-Gesetze*. For Israel, see Heinisch, *Sklavenrecht*; Häusler, *Sklaven*; de Vaux, *Lebensordnungen* I 132ff.; v.d. Ploeg, *Slavery*; Fontala, *Esclavitud*; Jackson, *Laws of Slavery*.

but at the same time they were a completely unresolved, controversial problem.

It can now be compellingly demonstrated that during the period before the monarchy there was not much slavery of the kind described in the Mishpatim.[223] If we study the linguistic usage from the books of Joshua to 2 Samuel, the word "slave" (*'ébed*) is used increasingly. It is used, how-ever, almost exclusively as a courtly self-designation expressing the speaker's reliance upon the king.

Only in a few places during the early phase of the establishment of the monarchy is the word used to describe real slaves. We have, for example, the listing of the rights of a king in 1 Sam 8:16 and the slaves of Gideon in Judg 6:27 or of Ziba in 2 Sam 9:10f. Otherwise, the "servants" of that period are known by a different word, *n^e'ārim*. These are "free persons who are in a volunteer and dependent relationship to their king."[224]

We see a transition in linguistic usage from the pre-state to the state period in 1 Sam 25. Nabal's attendants are called "servants" (*n^e'ārim*),[225] likewise David's attendants, nevertheless a few times they are also referred to as "slaves" (*'ābādim*).[226] On the other hand, we must associate Nabal's observation in verse 10 – "There are many servants today who are breaking away from their masters" – to the relationship of David to Saul.

Thus, according to Old Testament texts, there were no "slaves" as the Book of the Covenant uses that term in the period before the monarchy. Perhaps there were some in the case of foreigners (1 Sam 30:13) or of prisoners of war, but they were certainly not an ordinary part of pre-state society and they were not at all an important societal problem.[227]

This is even true for the early monarchic period and the conflicts occurring then. Thus, "slaves" (*'ābādim*) of the Israelites are mentioned (verse 16) in the rights of the king in 1 Sam 8. That is not the problem in the text, rather the fact that free Israelites are supposed to be "slaves" (*'ābādim*) of the king – in other words, his subjects (verse 17). The conflicts of the early monarchic period exist between the king and his people, not between slave and free people.

Slavery only gained currency and significance under the monarchy. This is reflected in a narrative like the one in 1 Kg 4:1–7 in which Elijah used a miracle to prevent an incidence of debt slavery. We see this especially in the prophecies of Amos (Am 2:6; 8:6). The evidence gained from a concordance search is fully supported by everything that we know about pre-state Israel as well as other related, decentralized tribal societies.

Agricultural production did not rely upon dependent labor.[228] Furthermore, there was apparently enough land at their disposal. Texts

---

223 See Schäfer-Lichtenberger, *Eidgenossenschaft* 310ff.
224 Stähli, *Knabe* 179.
225 Verses 8, 14, 19.
226 *n^e'ārim* in verses 5, 8, 9, 12, 25, 27; *'ābādim* in verses 10, 39, 40, 41 in addition to being a polite self-designation in verse 8.
227 According to Thiel, *Soziale Entwicklung* 156ff. the existence of slavery in pre-monarchic Israel has been deduced almost exclusively from the relevant texts in the Book of the Covenant.
228 See Judg 6:11; 1 Sam 11:5.

like Judg 9:4; 11:3; 1 Sam 22:2 permit us to see that it was escape, not slavery, that was the usual, expected consequence of economic need and indebtedness.

It is only during the monarchy that we find all the requirements for the widespread appearance of slavery.[229] Judging from other Old Testament literature, the problems must only have become really serious only during the period of written prophecy.[230]

The interests that came into collision and must have been the reason for the existence of each particular regulation, show themselves quite explicitly and openly in the laws against the murder or physical injury of slaves:

> Ex 21:20 *When a slaveowner strikes a male or female slave with a rod and the slave dies immediately, the owner shall be punished.*
> 21 *But if the slave survives a day or two, there is no punishment; for the slave is the owner's property.*

The first sentence first correlates with the basic principle of Ex 21:12. There also the concern is with battery with mortal consequences, but against a free person (*'īš*).[231] What is expressly formulated in verse 20, that the perpetrator should be killed in a blood feud (*nqm*),[232] is presumed to be the normal state of affairs in verse 12. This is still the case in the postexilic law of Num 35 (verse 19).[233]

Nevertheless, the phrase in verse 12, "... shall be put to death" (*mōt yūmāt*), is no accident. In the case of a free person the death sentence for the offender is absolute, in other words independent of whether there is an avenger and whether he is in the camp. Revenge must be taken. For slaves the resolution of the matter is also expressly named. Slaves, however, who are foreigners or even who were only purchased in foreign territory, in short, all who are separated from their families, are a special category. In that case it is doubtful whether someone would appear who might exact vengeance.

The more important difference is hidden in the phrase "under his hand" (verse 20), and it becomes even more clear in the next sentence in verse 21. If the slave can stand on his or her own two legs for a day or two, there is no vendetta,[234] "for he is his property." The death of the

---

229 For the general factors that encouraged the existence of slavery, see Domar, *Causes*. It is quite amazing to me how Gottwald, *Tribes* who dates the traditions of the Book of the Covenant to the pre-state period (58), spends so little time on these problems. Slavery on a larger scale together with related laws, had to have disturbed the conception of an egalitarian society noticeably.

230 To be sure, the prophets practically never used the term "slave," but they speak of the righteous (*ṣaddīq*), the poor (*'ebyōn*) or the young woman (*na'ʰrāh*). Quite obviously, this had to do with their intention or their view of reality. It is all the more important that, e.g. the speeches about "buying" and "selling" and the terms they used amazingly correspond exactly with each other. Compare especially Am 2:6; 8:6 with Ex 21:2, 7. See Lipínski, *Sale*; ibid., article on *mkr*.

231 For *'īš* see below p. 167.

232 See Lipínski, article on *nāqam* 605ff.

233 For blood feud, see below pp. 161., 174ff.

234 Schwienhorst-Schönberger, *Bundesbuch* 78 regards such an interpretation as "absurd." See in detail pp. 63ff. The master would much much more likely be defended "from an unjustified charge by the family of his debt slave of having

slave was to the detriment of the slaveholder. He lost the money that he had invested in the slave, therefore the vendetta was prohibited.

Probably the vendetta was also traditionally followed in cases of serious bodily injury; in such cases the Mishpatim established compensatory payments.

Ex 21:18f., where an early death is not precluded, shows this especially clearly.[235] This is an analog, even a consequence, of compensatory payments in cases of bodily injury, that slaves thus receive their freedom (21:26f.) and the slaveholder sustain the financial loss.

The financial regulations of 21:21 and 21:26f. are in complete conformity with the rest of the legal thinking of the Mishpatim. We need not regard this as later addition in the sense of talion law.[236] Thus, two principles of legal thought in the Mishpatim run headlong into each other: the killing of people is to be avenged by vendetta, but slaves are the property of their owners. The compromise is apparent: if the slave dies only after a few days, only the loss of money is affected. Here the right of the slaveholder is protected over against the body of the slave even in cases of serious or most serious mistreatment.

The protection of a slave is limited to the particular situation in which there is immediate death. This special case might be an exception to the rule for slaves. Murder or manslaughter, in the usual sense, is rarely an issue in relations between masters and slaves. The widespread use of beating is more likely to be encountered as a problem. Prov 29:19 states, "By mere words servants are not disciplined."[237] The Mishpatim presume the physical mistreatment of slaves, and it is not prohibited. Only when slaves sustain permanent, serious physical handicap do they go free, causing the owner to sustain a loss. Even when a slave sustains a mortal injury, it is only when he or she dies immediately thereafter that a vendetta may be carried out. When death happens after a few days, which is the more normal consequence of a mortal beating, there was to be no other consequence than the owner's own financial loss. In theory the law here protects the interests of both sides, the slave and the slaveholder, conflicting though the interests may be. In practice, however, there was virtually no concern or ability to prevent even the harshest mistreatment.

The same is true of the basic regulations dealing with the duration of slavery.

> Ex 21: 2 *When you buy a male Hebrew slave, he shall serve six years, but in the seventh he shall go out a free person.*

---

caused the death from natural causes of a debt slave" (analogous to CH §115f.). This would overlook the analogy to 21:18f. (see Jackson, *Laws of Slavery* 95), from which we may not literary-critically separate verses 20f. It is the wording, not the (alleged) intent that is decisive: If the slave can hobble around for another day yet (verse 19!), no sanction may take place, no matter what the cause of death might have been. The tendency to deny the harshness of verse 21 is even stronger in Schenker, *Versöhnung* 57ff.

235 See below pp. 159ff.
236 Osumi, *Kompositionsgeschichte* 116f., 153f.
237 For the role of physical abuse, see below pp. 162f.

3 *If he comes in single, he shall go out single; if he comes in married then his wife shall go out with him.*
4 *If his master gives him a wife and she bears him sons or daughters, the wife and her children shall be the master's and he shall go out alone.*
5 *But if the slave declares, "I love my master, my wife and my children; I will not go out a free person,"*
6 *Then his master shall bring him before God. He shall be brought to the door or the doorpost; and his master shall pierce his ear with an awl; and he shall serve him for life.*

At the outset[238] we have the basic principle that a purchased, Hebrew debt slave[239] should be set free in the seventh year. Unfortunately, we do not know whether this regulation was new in Israel or whether it changed or fixed an older custom.[240] The Code of Hammurabi describes a period of service for only three years (§117) for similar debt servitude. If this length of time were also customary in Israel or Canaan, the change to seven years, even if it were based in a sacral temporal rhythm, would have been a significant step backward for the slaves. As always, however, the law of manumission limited the rights of the one who purchased slaves. He must release his property "without compensation" (ḥin-nām) without harm or receiving payment. However much or little the slave owed, the debt that led to the person being sold was considered to be paid off. It could be the sandals in Am 2:6 or the unpayable five cows of the thief in Ex 21:37.

238 The law is quite precisely constructed, see Osumi, *Kompositionsgeschichte* 104ff. The far-reaching stratigraphic analysis by, e.g. Cardellini, *"Sklaven"-Gesetze* 247ff., is conceivably improbable; see also Otto, *Wandel* 36f.
239 We are unable to discuss the significant, hidden problems within the concept of the "Hebrew slave" (*ébed 'ibri*). We would not be able to make the interpretation of the law exclusively or even primarily dependent upon this difficult problem. Whether the Hebrew concept is still used in the same sense as the other ancient Near Eastern texts of the second millenium BCE primarily sociologically (e.g. Lemche, *Hebrew Slave*) or already nationally, as later, (see e.g. Lipínski, *L'esclave hebreux*) is especially controverted. For more recent discussions, see Loretz *Hebräer*; Cardellini, *"Sklaven"-Gesetze* 148ff. Freedman/Willoughby, article on *'ibri* (respective literature). For the period of the formulation of the Book of the Covenant, in my opinion, we ought to consider the Old Testament usage of the Hebrew term, which includes a wider circle of peoples related to or neighbors of Israel (see e.g. Koch, *Hebräer*). However, independent of this decision is the fact that, in my opinion, it is clear that a debt slave is intended here (see also Jackson, *Laws of Slavery* 92f.; Schwienhorst-Schönberger, *Bundesbuch* 303ff.). This is demonstrated, not least, by the prophetic texts and the parallel of the female slave, but also the emphasis which is placed on "gratis," in other words without compensation for injury. Debt slavery was widespread in the ancient world (see e.g. Finley, *Schuldknechtschaft*; Knippenberg, *Typik* 39ff.), and even in the ancient Near East the corresponding regulations for manumission (see Cardellini, *"Sklaven"-Gesetze* 246 note 25), so that Cardellini's thesis, which supports his interpretation of Ex 21:2ff., seems nearly incomprehensible to me: "No one would buy a slave if he knew that after a period of time he had to set the slave free without receiving compensation" (*"Sklaven"-Gesetze* 245). Deut 15:18 shows that one might have gained more income or cheaper labor from a debt slave than from a paid laborer (which, furthermore, may not yet have existed). A workforce for six years for a pair of sandals (Am 2:6; 8:6), what is so difficult about that?
240 We might think, e.g. of Gen 29:18, 27.

Exegesis has frequently placed all the emphasis on the requirement that a slave be manumitted, interpreting this as a provision for the protection of slaves.[241] The greater portion of the law, however, does not discuss manumission, it rather treats the modalities that facilitated a transition into permanent slavery. If the slave declares before the deity (*hāʿlōhîm*), "I love my master," placing him in first place – what cynicism! – "my wife and my children," then he becomes a permanent (*lᵉ ʾōlām*) slave and receives a permanent mark cut into his ear.[242]

We must assume that it was in the interest of the slave owner to facilitate this transition. The problems raised by marriage are expressly mentioned in the text. If the slave received a wife from his master, she remained in slavery. This corresponds with the regulation on female slaves in 21:7ff. It means, however, that in practice any marriage between slaves led automatically, not by law but by social dynamics, to permanent slavery.[243]

Male slaves at first were in most cases children or youths (e.g. 2 Kg 4:1ff.; Neh 5:2, 5). If they were about 8–12 years old, they still had only to serve six years, and there is much to suggest that many married during these years. It was not expected that an adult male remain unmarried during such a period of time. Thus, only in the first case mentioned, in which a married slave entered service together with his wife (who, it seems, was not a slave herself), would he be released at the end of his service without problem. Otherwise, familial ties would hold him fast. Indeed, he had few prospects afterward, for example, to procure the usual dowry. This is quite apart from the problems of being able to get along on his own. Everything depended upon the family whose resources he should have been able to use previously but was unable to do so. Furthermore, there were practically no jobs at that time from which he might earn money.

When we read a law like this one against the backdrop of the social realities of the time as we know them, Ex 21:2–6 is not a provision for protection, but a regulation that in the majority of cases must have forced male slaves into permanent slavery. To outward appearances the law is intended to equalize the interests of both parties, and it may be that in former unregulated situations it might have secured the rights of slaves. Nevertheless, it quite certainly guaranteed the establishment of permanent servitude and thus for all time cut off access to justice for the slaves. Ex 21:2–6 could be one of the laws attacked in Isa 10:1f.

The situation in the case of female slaves is even more egregious.[244]

---

241 See above, note 174 in addition especially to Phillips, *Laws of Slavery* 62.

242 Here we should most likely think of the household deities and residential door posts. See e.g. Paul, *Studies* 50. For ancient Near Eastern parallels and for a discussion, see Draffkorn, *Ilani*; Falk, *Exodus 21:6*; Fensham, *New Light*; ibid., *Role of the Lord*; Vannoy, *Use*; Loretz, *Ex 21:6*; Russell, *Sabbat* 133, 337ff.; Otto, *Wandel* 36 and others.

243 Jackson, *Literary Features* 236; ibid., *Laws of Slavery* 93f. correctly refers to the fact that thus male slaves were also used for sexual purposes, "effectively, to breed permanent slaves for his master" (*Features* 236).

244 For interpretation, in addition to the commentaries, see Mendelsohn, *Conditional Sale*; de Boer, *Remarks*; Cardellini, *"Sklaven"-Gesetze* 251ff. (Lit.); Schenker, *Affranchissement*.

> Ex 21:7 *When a man sells his daughter as a slave, she shall not go out*
> *as the male slaves do.*
>
> 8 *If she does not please her master, who has not yet made a decision*
> *regarding her,*[245] *then he shall let her be redeemed; he shall have no*
> *right to sell her to a foreign people, since he dealt unfairly with her.*
> 9 *If he designates her for his son, he shall deal with her as a daughter.*
> 10 *If he takes another wife to himself, he shall not diminish the food,*
> *clothing or housing*[246] *of the first wife.*
> 11 *And if he does not do these three things for her, she shall go out*
> *without debt, without payment of money.*

While for male slaves the question of the reason and occasion for being sold is not discussed, the situation has changed here: We are dealing here with the sale of daughters. Family structure in a culture in which land ownership (and therefore independence) is connected with sons is such that daughters are usually the first to be sold when situations of need arise.[247] Their work capabilities as well as their sexual possibilities also would have been attractive to slaveholders. Daughters, subject to the authority of their fathers, legally speaking, were in a situation more secure than that of widows.[248] "That widows may be your spoil" (Isa 10:2) could refer to such negotiations.

Female slaves, unlike their male counterparts, were not freed in the seventh year of their servitude. Their fate was usually sealed. The only exception recognized by law, according to Ex 21:10f., was made if the basic necessities of life – food, clothing, housing – were denied them. The meaning of the last item on this list, "housing," is not completely clear,[249] the Hebrew word (*'onāh*) is usually connected with sexual intercourse, which may not be denied the female slave. However, this would have no parallels either in the Old Testament or in the rest of the ancient Near East.

It is also improbable because this law speaks in rather broad terms, meaning, for example, that it would also apply to older women. The woman remained in permanent slavery, not least because she was compelled into a marriage-like sexual relationship. The law places primary stress upon this, and it is precisely here that we find the law's ambivalence.

Am 2:7 criticizes the practise that "father and son go in to the same girl." It is most likely that Amos is referring to a dependent woman (*na*
ʿărāh), probably a slave who has been turned into a sort of "family

---

245 Thus the Ketib of the MT, see below pp. 158f.
246 The usual interpretation of '*onāh* as sexual intercourse (KBL³; cf NRSV "marital rights;" see also Cazelles, *Études* 49; Noth, *Flesh*; Boecker, *Recht* 138f. and elsewhere) is doubtful; even for purely moral reasons the· master could not be compelled to do this. Soden's interpretation (*Wörterbuch* 198f.) is more convincing than Paul's "oil" (*Studies* 57ff.). He would understand the word as "residence;" see also Stenbach, article on '*ānāh* I 246.
247 See especially Neh 5:5. For the familial structure that underlies this, see Crüsemann, *Mann und Frau* 42ff.
248 The opinion that this deals exclusively with young girls who were still virgin (thus e.g. Lemche, *Hebrew Slave* 143), is not supported by the wording. Why e.g. should young widows be excluded?
249 See above note 246.

whore."[250] The law in Ex 21:7ff. was intended to prevent precisely this practice. The female slave should be brought into a single, permanent sexual relationship.

The text speaks of assigning the woman to the slaveholder himself or to his son. The regulation of verse 9, stating that the slave is entitled to rights of daughterhood, thus the same dowry that a daughter should receive, did not ensure that this happened on a regular basis. Before the master assigned her to a man, according to verse 8, his dissatisfaction could permit him to allow her to be "redeemed."

Scholars often suggest, by altering the Hebrew consonantal text, that the master had first assigned her to himself,[251] and later she no longer pleased him. But this would be in conflict with verses 10f., where in spite of the master's preference for a different woman, this slave should nevertheless receive a secure livelihood. Under any circumstance, she should not then be sold, but should be given her freedom, without compensatory payment.

Thus, we must remain with the *ketib* of the Hebrew text.[252] This would mean then that verse 8 deals with a "first opinion" occurring *before* any assignment to a man This opinion would help determine what her future would be after the sale. Most probably, in case of dissatisfaction (in other words, situations in which it was decided that she was not to belong to the master or the son), the master was to offer to sell her back to her own family. Her family might, however, also not be able to purchase her. The need that had compelled them to sell her would not easily go away. There is disagreement over whether he might then offer her for sale again, probably to other Israelites, but he certainly could not sell her to foreigners where there would not have been any guarantee of rights.[253]

Probably – even frequently – however, it happened that she would be assigned to another male slave, as 21:4 presumes. This would always have been the case when a rich person obtained many slaves, both male and female. We should also bear in mind that in addition to the rather insecure position of the female slave, the regulations regarding corporal punishment, including serious physical injury (21:20f., 26f.) also applied to females.

The slave laws of the Mishpatim mediated between the interests of the ones who purchased or owned the slave and those of the slaves and their families. They placed boundaries on both sides of the law. The slave laws were certainly intended to secure at least a minimal degree of justice for the enslaved, including for example, the right of freedom in the seventh

---

250 Fendler, *Sozialkritik* 43; for an analysis, see Reimer, *Recht* 39ff.
251 For discussion and literature, see Cardellini, *"Sklaven"-Gesetze* 253 note 53; Schenker, *Affranchissement* 548.
252 For the reasoning, see Osumi, *Kompositionsgeschichte* 106f.
253 On the basis of the wording "foreign people" (*'am nokri*) a foreign family might be meant; thus e.g. Jepsen, *Bundesbuch* 28 note 2; Paul, *Studies* 54 note 6; otherwise, e.g. Noth, *Exodus* 136, 144; Boecker, *Recht* 138f.; Cf Hoftijzer, *Ex xxi:8*; Cardellini, *"Sklaven"-Gesetze* 254. On the basis of the general attitude of the Mishpatim (and especially the slave law within it), we must regard it as quite improbable that it might not be entirely out of the question that a sale was made within Israel *before* a sexual assignment had been completed (there was also no free choice for female debt slaves).

year for men, the prevention of regular, excessive sexual abuse or total neglect in the case of women.

At the same time, however, we cannot deny that it is the rights of the slave owner himself that predominate. The slaves are "his property." The right that is fixed here presumes the social reality. The slave laws could only legitimate, for example, serious physical injury. In a cynical way, they force a slave into permanent servitude when "before God" he had to confess his "love" for his owner. And in practice the presence of female slaves facilitated the transition to permanent slavery for the males. Isaiah's (10:1f.) upbraiding of the laws would have fit these regulations, if the laws were generally practiced.

Overview: The inclusion of the Mishpatim in the whole of the Book of the Covenant affected slave law in a two-fold way. While Ex 22:24 opposed the economic pressures that led to the establishment of slavery, by its prohibition of personal loans and interest,[254] the talion law of Ex 21:24f. attacked physical injury to slaves in a massive way. It gave value even to their teeth and eyes, "eye for eye, tooth for tooth." There is an interesting, but thus far unprovable theory, that the "burn" wound of the talion law in 21:25 refers especially to the branding iron applied to slaves (both male and female).[255]

The alterations in the slave law in Deut 15:12ff. illustrate that this harsh interpretation of the law is justified.[256] According to it, when a slave is set free, "Provide liberally out of your flock, your threshing floor, and your wine press" (verse 14) so that he might have an opportunity for a fresh start. The transition into permanent slavery is no longer compelled for the woman whom it is not possible to release – she too is freed – rather she becomes a permanent slave only "because he loves you" (verse 16). This would mean that only good treatment could lead to permanent slavery.

Everything that was true for male slaves was also true for females. Since the right of asylum was extended to all slaves in Israel (Deut 23:16f.), Deuteronomy's criticism of the slave laws of the Mishpatim is quite obvious.[257] There is no longer any discussion of special laws with regard to slaves who have been killed or serious cases of physical harm. The Holiness Code only orders the manumission of slaves during the year of jubilee (Lev 25:39f.), but at the same time, as we will see,[258] it was not slavery in the actual sense of the term.[259]

b2. *"The assailant shall be free of liability" (21:19): Murder and Injury*

While Ex 21:12 asserts absolutely, "Whoever strikes a person mortally shall be put to death," the Mishpatim attempt to regulate crimes of

---

254 See below pp. 185ff.
255 Osumi, *Kompositionsgeschichte* 117.
256 For a comparison, see Chamberlain, *Exodus 21–23* 110ff.; Phillips, *Laws of Slavery* 55ff.; Japhet, *Relationship*.
257 See below p. 232.
258 See below p. 285.
259 For the post-canonical development and interpretation, see, for example, Stern, *Society* 6224ff.; Urbach, *Laws Regarding Slavery*.

murder and personal injury related to this overarching principle in the
section 21:18–32.[260] In so doing, we find two cases treated in verses 18f.
and 22f. immediately recognizable as having been derived from actual
cases. At the same time, however, their selection and placement covers a
number of cases in a judicially very skilful manner:

> Ex 21:18 *When individuals quarrel and one strikes another with a stone*
> *or fist so that the injured party, though not dead, is confined to bed,*
> 19 *but recovers and walks around outside with the help of a staff,*
> *then the assailant shall be free of liability, except to pay for the loss*
> *of time, and to arrange for a full recovery.*
> 22 *When people who are fighting injure a pregnant woman so that*
> *her children come out, and yet no (further) harm follows, the one*
> *responsible shall be fined what the woman's husband demands,*
> *paying as much as the judges allow.*
> 23 *If any harm follows, then you shall give life for life.*

We can see that both provisions originated in independent, real cases.
In the first, for example, there was an injury that resulted in one party
hobbling around on a cane. Thus, he was not harmed in his head or torso.
In the second we are struck by the use of the plural "children" (there is no
reason to pass over this), thus it was a multiple birth, and we see the
traces of a real situation.[261] Nevertheless, this is not simply a collection of
especially controversial cases. The placement covers a whole series of
basic problems, especially when we keep in view the rights of slaves and
the killing by an ox in verses 28ff.

The question "Why?" is a problem that obviously underlies the whole
paragraph. We cannot find such a clear solution as we see found in the
addendum in 21:13,[262] which is in agreement with provisions in ancient
Near Eastern law.[263] In verse 18 we find a motive given with the word
"quarrel" (*rīb*).[264] Thus, there is a conflict between two parties, and pure
chance is excluded. Physical injuries are intentionally inflicted, even if
only with "a stone or fist," i.e. without a weapon.

On the other hand, in verse 22 a brawl leads to the injury of an innocent
bystander, thus planning and intent are excluded. According to verse 18,

---

260 For the question of principles of this kind in Israelite criminal law, see the
    controversy between Greenberg, *Criminal Law*; ibid., *More Reflections*; Jackson,
    Criminal Law. McKeating, *Development* gives an overview of the history of the
    crime of murder; see also Phillips, *Another Look at Murder*; Haas, *Structure of*
    Homicide.
261 Schwienhorst-Schönberger, *Bundesbuch* 96ff. considers the possibility of a
    collective plural (GK 124a; Joüon, *Grammaire* §136), which includes the difference
    between "child" and embryo/fetus. Nevertheless, the form is not explanable by
    the usual construct of the abstract plural (See GK 124; also Michel, *Syntax* 88f.).
    We have no parallels exactly in this legal language, but texts like 21:18f., Deut
    24:1ff. likewise give evidence of single precedent cases. I regard it as a mis-
    interpretation of this kind of law that more frequent, normal cases are not phrased
    alike (Schwienhorst-Schönberger 97).
262 See below pp. 174ff.
263 See especially Sick, *Tötung*. Closest are the Hittite laws, for these, see Sick, *Tötung*
    94ff.
264 See Liedke, article on *rīb*. The word also designates a quarrel outside of the courts,
    but nevertheless always one that leads or at least could lead to the courts.

even a serious, intentional physical injury should only be compensated for by a financial payment reimbursing loss of work and medical costs. The formulation does not exclude the possibility that the disabled party might also die later as a consequence of injuries received.[265] The only requirement is that he be able to return to some kind of mobility.

Also in the case of the pregnant woman, when there is no mortal injury (*'āsōn*)[266] – thus *only* a miscarriage – the only penalty is financial. We are probably to understand verse 22 as meaning "only when the mother dies."[267] Only then should there be paid "life for life."

The principle in 21:12 came into play in cases of unplanned and unintentional death. In verses 28–32 we find the killing by an ox is treated,[268] and from verses 29f. especially describes situations in which this killing is a consequence of the owner's negligence. Still, in these cases, probably in contrast to other cases like verse 23, there is the possibility of financial payment as expiation (*kōfer*) for the ransom of his life (*pidyōn nafšō*).

The section 21:18–32 proves to be a juridically well-reasoned and self-contained treatment of the most important questions relating to 21:12 regarding murder and serious bodily injury. To be sure, it does not include every conceivable example, but many of the important and typical problems of physical confrontation either between free people or between free and slave are regulated. The matter of personal responsibility is of special concern,[269] as we note by the absence of other directions regarding the degree of punishment.[270]

It is clear that in the case of intentional as well as unintentional physical injury, and even killing through negligence, the usual practice was restitution by compensatory payment.[271] The formulations we find in a few places allow us to see that this dealt with limiting, permitting or

---

265 Thus tBQ IX.7 and in connection with this, Schmitt, *Ex. 21:18f.*

266 The unusual word appears several times in the Joseph story (Gen 42:4, 38; 44:29) and there it can only mean a serious accident with mortal consequences. Less convincing is Westbrook's attempt (*Lex talionis*) to interpret this as a term for the problem of an unknown and therefore not apprehendable offender is less convincing.

267 The evidence in ancient Near Eastern law, where simple premature birth is never mentioned, argues in favor of this. As a rule, the alternative is just the death of the fetus or also of the mother (Kodex Lipit. Eschtar III.2–4; Sumer. Laws §1f.; CH §209–214; MAR §21. 0–52; HG §17f.). Thus also Loewenstamm, *Ex 21* (otherwise, e.g. Kline, *Lex Talionis*) as well as the traditional rabbinic interpretation (see Rubin, *Nasciturus*). For that reason the killing of the unborn is not the same as killing a child who has been born. On the other hand, the traditional Christian concern about killing the unborn is based upon the LXX version of Ex 21:22f. There we find an alternative in the degree of development of the fetus (*mē exeikonismenon – ean de exeikonismenon*) from which Augustine derived the distinction between *formatus-informatus* regarding the embryo. The death penalty applied, "life for life" in the case of the developed fetus. For the whole, see Feldman, *Birth Control*.

268 See Selms, *Goring Ox*; Jackson, *Goring Ox*; Yaron, *Goring Ox*; Finkelstein, *Ox*.

269 See Fensham, *Nicht-Haftbar-Sein*.

270 With Osumi, *Kompositionsgeschichte* 135ff.

271 There is here a developed and apparently thoroughly differentiated terminology. Thus financial restitution is mentioned several times in 21:19, 22, 30. For post-canonical Jewish law, see Kahana, among others, *Bodily Damages*. For a comparison with ancient Near Eastern law, see Otto, *Körperverletzungen*.

denying the practice of the vendetta:[272] The slave who is killed outright may be avenged (21:20); on the other hand if the victim of the assault is able to stand up again, there is no punishment (21:19). In the case of 21:29f. the resolution is reserved for the families of the victim and the offender to determine what will happen.

The talion formula, which with its "eye for eye" all the way to "bump for bump" stands at the center of this text, obviously in contrast with everything else. It protests not only against the class justice with its distinction between slave and free but also against the financial regulation of physical harm. The juridical regulation of battery and physical injury, as presented here, also has a social dimension. We must investigate the social side if we want to understand the effect of the regulations of the Mishpatim and the intention of the talion formula.

We encounter direct physical force not only in relationships of masters and slaves (Prov 29:19), but also in other social conflicts that are part of the world of the Old Testament. Thus Job, the patient sufferer, swears in order to show his innocence, " . . . if I had raised my hand against the *innocent*[273] because I had supporters at the gate . . ." (31:21). Thus, someone who would have had sufficient "supporters" at the gate, the place of trials, could have been able to inflict physical abuse on innocent people.

The same Job who complains that people strike him on the cheeks (16:10) pats himself on the back, saying – in addition to many good deeds done for those who were socially weak – "I broke the fangs of the unrighteous" (29:17). Yet again the phrases in Proverbs – "To flog the noble (n^edībīm) for their integrity" (17:26), "Blows that wound cleanse away evil; beatings make clean the innermost parts" (20:30) – are of comparable force. Thus, bumps and bruises, the last two items in the talion formula from Ex 21:25, were generally employed against "evil" (ra' see further Prov 17:10, 19:25). Furthermore, there is an awareness in the Book of Proverbs of the possibility of absolving offense by payment of money, "Wealth (kōfer) is a ransom for a person's life" (Prov 13:8).[274]

We can point to these texts as evidence from the wisdom literature regarding the role of "striking" or physical injury that shows an awareness of the prophet's complaints. Especially in the eighth century, the suppression of the weak by those who were stronger is described in terms of direct physical aggression. Many of the following prophetic texts may be literal descriptions, but for the most part they are, of course, only metaphors:

> Am 2:7a *They who trample the head of the poor and helpless . . .*
> Isa 3:15 *What do you mean by crushing my people, by grinding the face of the poor?*

272 See Merz, *Blutrache*; Tullock, *Blood Vengeance*; Lemaire, *Vengeance*.
273 Instead of 'al-yātōm I read (along with many commentators) as more likely '^alē-tām because the orphans have already been mentioned in verse 17.
274 See further, Jer 20:2; 37:15; Isa 58:4. Even the psalmists frequently request – corresponding, e.g. to Job 29:17 – that God would knock their enemies' teeth out (Ps 3:8, 58:7). It is unlikely that there was a legal "ritual" behind this, thus, Hacklett/Huehenergard, *Teeth*.

Mi 3:2b . . . who tear the skin off my people
and the flesh off their bones,
3 who eat the flesh of my people
[flay their skin off them]
break their bones in pieces,
and chop them up [like meat] in a kettle,
like flesh in a cauldron.[275]

The prophets lay special emphasis upon the fact that justice can be bought. Bribery is a key word in prophetic criticism. Wasn't this the reason the rich were able to get around many things with a law like the Mishpatim – because they were able to afford the necessary monetary penalties? Quite interestingly, exactly the opposite is more frequently attested: money was extracted from the poor and weak because of indebtedness that in fact did not exist. As a result they were driven farther into actual debt:

> Am 2:8 They drink wine bought with fines they imposed (ʿᵃnūšῑm).
> Am 5:12 You . . . who take a bribe (kṓfer), and push aside the needy in the gate.

Thus, the prophets of the eighth century regarded the judicial establishment as an opportunity to make money and cut the poor off from access to justice.[276] Physical attacks as well as a system of laws that was oriented toward money played a role, as we see in the Mishpatim. This is the social context from which we must interpret the talion formula as a law based on completely different principles.

b3. "But if unable to do so [make restitution]" Ex. 22:1

Ex 21:37–22:16 treats offenses against property. The central term, which recurs repeatedly, means "pay, get a replacement" (šlm, pi). The word helps structure the entire section.[277] This successively includes theft (21:37–22:3), damage to another's fields or vineyards caused by cattle or fire (22:4f.), loss incurred to another's goods that were entrusted for safe keeping (22:6f., 9–12), loaning or renting of animals (22:13f.) as well as – to be classified here on the basis of the overall structure[278] – detracting from the paternal claim for a bride price for his daughter (22:16). Ex 22:7, 8, 10 again shows the important role of oath and ordeal in this area of jurisprudence.[279] Traditional regulation by the help of relatives and neighbors was apparently no longer adequate to control conflicts in this area of society.

275 Text after Wolff, Micha 59.
276 See also Isa 1:23 "Everyone loves a bribe and runs after gifts." The gifts (šalōmōnîm) are to be understood on the basis of the Akkadian parallel "gift of greeting" for bribable officials, thus Janowski, Vorgeschichte 242 note 73; Kümmel, Bestechung 61ff. From the concept as well as the related root, a connection with the central legal concept of the Book of the Covenant (šlm, pi.) "get a replacement, make reparation" is plausible.
277 See especially Otto, Wandel 12ff.; Osumi, Kompositionsgeschichte 122ff.
278 According to Osumi, Kompositionsgeschichte 132f., most of the provisions regarding one's own family must be regarded as part of the personal property regulations.
279 For the ancient Near Eastern material, see Frymer-Kenski, Judicial Ordeal.

This section, like the preceding, is completely within the tradition of ancient Near Eastern juridical language. It is very consciously and consistently constructed and is intended to take care of all of the problems that occur, especially in the area of personal responsibility. The basic principle expressed in 22:8 shows that we are dealing not so much with individual cases here as fundamental principles that apply to many analogous cases. Juridical particulars and refinements are not discussed at all.[280] They are one thing, their effect in social reality is another. In only a few cases do they allow themselves to be reasonably evaluated.

We find an important key to a social-historical understanding in 22:1, "The thief shall make restitution, but if unable to do so, shall be sold for the theft." The context is dealing with the theft of cattle (21:37ff.).[281] Replacement for stolen goods is to be made at a rate four or five times the original amount. This already shows to what degree the ownership of cattle was protected here. The sanctions are harsher than for many other offenses.

The problem of the killing of a thief caught in the act, which is connected as an addendum to this section by attraction, shows how significant this theft was (22:1, 2a). In each case the thief, according to 22:1b is supposed to pay the replacement (*šallem yešallem*), even in multiple. Even if the stolen animals are found still in his possession, so that the goods could be returned, nevertheless, two-fold replacement is demanded (verse 1).

In this context, the problem arises of what to do if the thief has nothing and cannot pay the compensation. In that case he is to be sold into slavery. *Someone who steals because of poverty is threatened with slavery.* This regulation may have been an important source for slavery.[282] The strong protection of property must be seen against the background of the increasing poverty in society. The man with one sheep in Nathan's parable (2 Sam 12:3) would have had to be sold into slavery, had he acted as his rich neighbor had. Furthermore, when Amos speaks of the fact that righteous people (*ṣaddīqīm*) are sold (2:6), the term could be a reference to the fact that he would not call them captured thieves here.

In Ex 22:6, the broad questions, rich in detail, of contracts dealing with safe keeping and rent may be still more relevant for the everyday problems of the poor. There is much to suggest that impoverished people had to loan themselves or hire themselves out as shepherds or even work with their animals for other people.

We find one of the few examples that we know from narratives in 2 Kg 6:1ff. One of Elisha's disciples had borrowed an ax and lost it when it fell

---

280 See in detail Otto, *Depositenrecht*.

281 Ex 21:37–22:3 is frequently divided up by literary criticism, see the overview in Schwienhorst-Schönberger, *Bundesbuch* 162ff. (he regards 22:1f. as an insertion in 21:37–22:3). Nevertheless, there is nothing significant to suggest the use of literary criticism if we consider the possibility of attraction, see Osumi, *Kompositionsgeschichte* 127f.

282 See also Jackson, *Laws of Slavery* 97, who correctly refers to the fact that the verb (*mkr*) can also be connected with assignment to the injured party.

into water. He was threatened with catastrophe, for it was beyond the realm of possibility for a poor man to earn enough to repay the owner for such a valuable possession. The prophetic miracle saved a family member from being sold into slavery.

When herding cattle for another (22:9–12), a laborer had to pay for losses due to theft (verse 12). If, for example, a poor shepherd boy could not prove that a lost sheep was "mangled by beasts" or that the injury or death of the animal was not his fault, as he was required to state in an oath (verses 10f.), he had to pay compensation. The regulation is juridically obvious; this was why the animal would need to be guarded. Nevertheless, when we examine the social context, we note that the law was written down and rigidly formulated, therefore it was unavoidable. It made it difficult or even impossible to make local agreements intended for special situations.

The sociological problem of borrowing animals, which is regulated in verses 14f., is quite clear. The juridical distinction in the injury or death of a borrowed animal, treated here, lies in whether the owner was present or not. If the owner of the borrowed animal were present, obviously he could have prevented the incident. In this case, compensation would not be required (verse 15a).

It certainly must have happened that a poor man borrowed an animal from a rich neighbor, perhaps for plowing. The owner of the animal, however, would hardly have been present himself. Exactly the opposite is more likely. When a poor man placed himself and his animal at the disposal of a rich neighbor for hire, the poor man would have been present, working with the animal. If his animal were then injured, he would have no claim to compensation because he was present. Possibly the (unfortunately very ambiguous)[283] regulation in verse 15b – "if he were a hired worker, only the hiring fee is due" – suggests that harm to the animal was included in the wage agreed upon.

Unfortunately, in this case, as in most of the situations treated here, we lack material to study to gauge precisely the social dimension of the effects and consequences of these laws. Nevertheless, the formulation in 22:2b casts a very clear light on the whole complex of these laws and should not be overlooked. For the poor who have nothing (or must function with their own possession) situations could develop quickly and easily in which misfortune might strike, causing irreparable harm, forcing them, for example, into debts that exceed their capabilities, and thus into slavery. That is a fate that loomed over anyone who might steal because of hunger and need.

C. PLACE, MEANING AND CHARACTER

We may summarize the subject-matter of the Mishpatim as follows:

– *The Mishpatim formed a legal document of the monarchic period.*

---

283 Among other things, it is unclear whether a wage laborer or an animal is being referred to, or what the relation to verse 15a might be. Is this a detail of the last case to have been discussed or a completely different problem? See the various possibilities in Cazelles, *Études* 73; Paul, *Studies* 95f.; Noth, *Exodus* 150 among others.

The great significance of slave law in the first half of the monarchic period makes this clear beyond a shadow of a doubt.[284] Slavery first appeared in Israel during the monarchic period, and the regulations in Ex 21 were a reaction to it.

There are other characteristics that support this hypothesis. The Mishpatim presume a developed monetary economy. Many legal problems are resolved by the payment of silver (Ex 21:11, 21, 32, 34, 35; 22:6, 16), other situations are similar, or at least they do not preclude the possibility (21:19, 22, 30; 20:14).

The close kinship with other ancient Near Eastern laws encourages us to think along the same lines. The Mishpatim originated in the royal court with its schools of scribes and jurists.[285] Furthermore, all of the independence of Israelite legal development, which is also illustrated in the Mishpatim,[286] shows us that this quite certainly was not taken over from elsewhere as a finished legal document. It used material from this heritage and could only have originated in a very similar milieu.

– *The Mishpatim constitute the legal code of the Jerusalem Court.*

We know of no other institution of the monarchic period that fulfills all of the requirements proposed for the development of the Mishpatim quite so well as the court mentioned in 2 Chr 19 and Deut 17.[287] Furthermore, if there were such an institution as has been proposed to have existed from the time of Jehoshaphat, like no other, it must have been the place where a knowledge of the juridical traditions of the surrounding nations was gathered, and where the people were similarly well trained. The precise juridical language and the logical structure of the Mishpatim could only have come from a trained juridical establishment.

Furthermore, we can be certain that such a court would, at a time in which the ability to read and write would be increasingly observable in every region, have disseminated collections of its legal decisions and the laws it had codified. On one hand, we are able to recognize quite clearly the origin of the Mishpatim in precedent cases and judgments (21:18f., 22f.). On the other hand, it does not offer a collection of sample decisions, rather, they are in part now far-reaching completely formed regulations dealing with particular areas. Decisions based on newly arising axiomatic questions, together with the legislation and legal instruction based upon them – as might be expected from such a court – determined the juridical structure of the Mishpatim.[288]

The responsibility of the Jerusalem court for the structure of the Mishpatim is especially clear in one point. In Ex 21:12–17 and 22:17–19

---

284 See above pp. 151ff. Schwienhorst-Schönberger, *Bundesbuch* 270f.311f. is only able to avoid this by literary critical separation of the entire slave law from its "home." His early dating, for which he is only able to give a vague rationale, leads directly to the hypothesis of the existence of scribe schools in pre-state Israel – otherwise always monarchical! – (especially 280f.).

285 See Klima, *L'apport*; Krecher, *Rechtsleben*; Westbrook, *Law Codes* among others.

286 For the degree of systematization, see Otto, *Depositenrecht* 27; ibid., *Wandel* 66ff.

287 See above pp. 91ff.

288 See above pp. 94., 97 and elsewhere.

there is a collection of offenses for which the death penalty is prescribed. Scholars have demonstrated correctly that these come from very different legal contexts.[289] Thus, the assault (21:15) and cursing of parents (21:17) is in the context of purely intra-familial conflict. Sorcery (22:17) and sacrifice to another god (22:20) deal with sacral-legal blasphemy. We also have the sexual-legal problem of sodomy (22:19). Kidnapping (21:16) and especially murder (21:12) overlap and are related to offenses within clans and families.

Whatever theories we would propose regarding the pre-history and proto-forms, the written collection of various kinds of death penalty offenses included in the Mishpatim is what matters. At the time of the development of the Mishpatim, it makes no difference who it was that had traditional jurisdiction over such offenses (either declaring or carrying out a death sentence), whether cultic or local gathering, head of family or avenger; it is only the document of laws (collected, arranged and written down), which indicates the existence of the institution that is speaking in the Mishpatim and which has claim to final legitimacy in matters of the death penalty.

According to Deut 17 and 2 Chr 19 this is precisely what we should expect of the Jerusalem court. All cases between "blood and blood" (*bēn dām lᵉdām*) are assigned to it. We can establish here a consistency with the Mishpatim and its claim more clearly than in any of the other formulations of the duties of this court.

– *The Mishpatim and the legislation attacked in Isa 10:1–4 are probably identical.*

The Mishpatim is the only legal document known to us that could have some connection with the laws attacked in Isa 10,[290] and which might have produced a social effect suggesting this identification.

We are dealing with laws that, for example, make debt slavery an undisputed starting point for its legal pronouncements. The foundations of slave law include the facts that Israelites sold themselves or they were purchased by others, and that fathers sold their daughters. Marriage laws included in the Mishpatim would have required many people to pass over into permanent slavery with its consequent loss of individual rights.

Other laws must also have had the sociological effect of suppressing the legal rights of the weak. The laws of the Mishpatim are generally class law in which the "free man" (*'īš*) is clearly distinguished from the slave and the free man's rights are legally secure. The "man" stands at the center of Mishpatim law;[291] all rights are granted to him.

We would not dispute that the Mishpatim generally administer a law formally impartial to the competing parties, at least as well as could be expected for the time. There are laws for conflicts between masters and slaves, between those who assault and the ones who are assaulted, between people who possess and thieves, between cattle owners and shepherds, etc.

289 Most recently, Otto, *Wandel*, 31ff.; see already Schulz, *Todesrecht*.
290 See above pp. 20ff.
291 Thus in Ex 21:7, 12, 14, 16, 18, 20, 22, 26, 28, 29, 33, 35, 37; 22:4, 6, 9, 13, 15.

Nor would we dispute that the laws for both sides, even the socially weak, led to a fixing of their rights and an important degree of reliability and security. Nevertheless, this illustrates what a sociological approach to the law has always been aware of, "that the legal order ... is nothing other than the legitimation of the intercursive power relationships that exist between the various groups within the legal community."[292] Here as elsewhere, "the legal state of a society [is] ... a function of its actual structure."[293]

Isaiah decried societal conditions, and no one could doubt that this also implied an attack upon the related laws which prescribed these conditions. Of course, we probably cannot prove that the Mishpatim are the law criticized in Isa 10:1ff., and for that reason we can only raise the question. We probably only know a small portion of the law and legal procedure of that period. All of their laws may not have been included in the Book of the Covenant.

Nevertheless, the Mishpatim, if we understand them correctly – do not contain just any laws, but the authoritative code of the Jerusalem court, which was focused at and systematically attacked fundamental conflicts of society, such as slavery, but also acts of physical violence, and the property crimes of a society that was extremely divided socially. To the prophets of doom it was a law that only treated the formal regulation of legal questions; it was a part of the approaching, all-encompassing, catastrophic disaster.

– The abiding significance of the Mishpatim lies above all in their model of a perpetrator–victim settlement

The Mishpatim are the part of the Book of the Covenant (and consequently of all of Torah) which most broadly corresponds to the laws of Israel's ancient Near Eastern neighbors and thus probably to law as it was actually practiced in preexilic Israel. When we do not attempt to interpret the Mishpatim in the light of the criticism it gets because of their inclusion in the Book of the Covenant, but attempt first to understand the Mishpatim on their own terms, we see that they do not contain ideal law, but rather a law, which we would probably call the "statutory law" of its time (with all due reservation about that modern term).

This clearly reflects the societal power relationships from which it developed. It gives us a picture of a law that, like almost any law, was pervertable. It was used one-sidedly, and thus was misused. It may be that Isa 10 voices the concerns. It was reconciled in Torah with strong principles of interpretation and direct corrective measures.[294]

The Mishpatim gained entrance to Torah and even became part of its foundation. This is an extremely relevant theological fact. This happened, first, because of the basic legal principle of balancing perpetrator and victim. The Mishpatim are oriented entirely in this direction. We can ascertain on one hand the boundaries of responsibility, and on the other basic principles for reparation or restitution to the injured party for both

292 Geiger, *Vorstudien* 350.
293 Geiger, *Vorstudien* 350.
294 See above pp. 147ff. and below pp. 169ff.

of the larger legal areas (physical injury and property offenses). Apart from cases requiring the death penalty, the penalty was a compensatory or punitive damage[295] paid to the injured party. This main feature, which has reconciliation as a goal,[296] stands firm for the clarification of all individual questions beyond all scholarly dispute. In no place do we find prison terms, fines imposed solely to punish or any kind of payment to the state instead of the victim. They are unknown and inconceivable.[297]

It should be noted here that in the discussions of criminal law that have taken place in recent decades, in view of modern criminal law, attempts have been made to point this distinction between biblical and modern thinking in order to make a new approach to this area fruitful.[298] While we might find much that is exegetically questionable in these studies,[299] there is, in fact, a great potential contribution Torah could make for a view of criminal law that is theologically based, and it would find its heart in the Mishpatim as a part of Torah.

In its widely received 1990 study, the German Evangelical Church made a study, in which they spoke of the need "for criminal law to overcome the habit of thinking in terms of retribution, rather to consider the possibility of peace-making through conflict resolution."[300] As far as I can tell, this is done without any connection to biblical foundations.[301]

God's Law: The Conception of Torah in the Book of the Covenant

Basic Outlines and Principal Emphases

There are two very different texts at the beginning of the history of written law in Israel, which were adopted and integrated into the Book of the Covenant. Both of them are rooted in conflicts produced by the development of the state in the ninth century BCE. One contains the demands of the religious opposition in the northern kingdom, and presupposes exclusive veneration of YHWH. The other is a piece of state legislation in the ancient Near Eastern tradition, which the societal élite of Judah used in reaction to the immense problems of the developing society for the introduction of slavery and a monetary economy.

---

295 Restitution and sanction are placed side by side. This juxtaposition was systematically reasoned and may not be turned into a literary-critical principle. For Otto's relevant attempts, see above pp. 150f. While we generally view the development legal-historically (this can remain completely unresolved here), it is important that both were exclusively for the benefit of the victim or the victim's family.
296 See e.g. Schenker, *Versöhnung*.
297 For the complex process of legal change, suffice it to make an eclectic reference to Hentig, *Strafe* II 159ff.; Bianchi, *Tsedeka-Modell*; Foucault, *Überwachen und Strafen*.
298 See e.g. Bianchi, *Tsedeka-Modell*; ibid., *Alternativen zur Strafjustiz*; Wiesnet, *Die Verratene Versöhnung*; Koch, *Jenseits der Strafe*.
299 Referring to Stolz, *Exegetische Anmerkungen*, there would be much to regard critically that can remain implicit here.
300 *Strafe: Tor zur Versöhnung?*, 57ff.
301 The unresolvable dilemmas referred to in the study (especially 66ff.) which indeed can hardly be conquered in and of themselves, are prime examples of theological helplessness which inevitably occurs when the relevant biblical foundations are abandoned.

The Book of the Covenant[302] combined both of these texts and demanded social justice as the most important of its own accents. The protection of foreigners (Ex 22:20f.; 23:9) and the poor (Ex 22:24f.) as well as the correction of the slave law (Ex 21:24f.) are main accents in the contents,[303] the formulation of principles for judicial practice (Ex 23:1–8) is a central judicial tool. The exclusive veneration of Israel's God is identified here with a relationship aimed at justice for the socially and legally impoverished as well as the old calendar and sacrificial regulations.

The Mishpatim were taken over as a block in this form, generally unaltered and simply corrected in two places. These two corrections (Ex 21:13f., 24f.) clearly establish different accents and bracket the composition within the Mishpatim. On the other hand, the Torot, compared with the version in Ex 34:11ff., have been generally reshaped.[304] They were newly arranged, in part newly formulated and expanded with new provisions (altar law 20:24ff., prohibition of cursing 22:27, sabbath year 23:10ff.).[305] Beyond this, however, they are most closely tied to the commandments for righteousness. Halbe has described this process essentially as literary at first; only later was theological significance recognized.[306]

Especially the altar law (Ex 20:24–26), standing at the forefront, provides stimulus to regard the entirety as divine speech, an emphasis which is continued and maintained in 22:20ff. Only the Mishpatim (apart from the emendation in 21:13ff.) do not seem to follow this practice.

This special position of the Mishpatim, which can be explained by literary-criticism and tradition-history, is also of theological significance: This "statutory" law is an integral part of the total composition. Without it, God's law as we see it here for the first time in the Book of the Covenant, would be inconceivable.

Simultaneously, however, it is given new accents (especially 21:24ff.) and confronted with a demand for justice for the weakest members of society. Furthermore, it is not direct divine speech in quite the same way as its context, but it is taken up as a part of that speech.

In order that we might grasp this theological and legal conception of the Book of the Covenant upon which the rest of the Torah history is based, let us examine the formulations that include the most important of the new accents. We cannot understand what they mean if we study them in isolation, out of context. We must understand the meaning and function of the context to be able to interpret the earlier sources. Only then will we be able to understand the contours of this newly developed whole. The most important texts are not just those that include new accents, but especially the elements that stand out in the literary composition of the work.

302 The entire book is meant here, except for the slight redactional stratum which is formulated in the second person plural. See below pp. 197ff.
303 See in detail below pp. 182ff.
304 Particulars in Halbe, *Privilegrecht* 440ff.; Osumi, *Kompositionsgeschichte* 70ff.
305 We will go into this in conjunction with Deuteronomy, see below pp. 226ff.
306 Halbe, *Privilegrecht* 423ff., 451ff.

God's "Place": The Book of the Covenant as Divine Speech

a. THE "PLACE" OF GOD AS A COMPOSITIONAL ELEMENT

Three places in the Book of the Covenant speak of a "place" (māqōm) marked by the special activity of God, and thus having an important connection with the speaking God, which is important for the whole. Even the distribution of these places illustrates their significance for the overall composition: They are at the climax (20:24) and the end (23:20ff.) as well as the middle of the older block of the Mishpatim (21:13f.).

In Ex 20:24b, in the middle of the altar law which opens the Book of the Covenant, we find the promise by God that in "every" place where he causes his name to be called upon, he will himself come and bless. God's promise, that he would prepare a "place" to which anyone who has committed involuntary manslaughter might escape, is formulated in Ex 21:13f., in a supplemental provision to the murder law in 21:12. Finally, at the beginning of the concluding part of the Book of the Covenant (23:20), we find the promise that God would send a messenger to bring the person being addressed safely to the place that God had prepared.

In all three passages the "place" is founded or constituted by God's initiative. He causes his name to be proclaimed there, he determines and prepares it. In the first two passages the place is most closely connected with the altar of God, and in the first and the third the place is referred to in conjunction with the "name" (šēm) of God. Furthermore, this name is discussed in the central passage of the Book of the Covenant (Ex 23:13).

If I am correct, scholars have thus far taken too little cognizance of the correlation of the three passages.[307] In any case, it cannot be doubted that they belong together. They relate to each other and must be studied and interpreted together. Since they are in places that affect the entire composition a special way, there is a key within them without which it would not be possible to gain a proper understanding of the God speaking in the book or especially how and in what way his presence and power functions.

b. PRESENCE (Ex 20:24–26)

In the Old Testament the altar signified "the nearness to people of the majesty of God, which attracts those who approach it as only God can do"[308] (see especially Ps 43:4). If the original Book of the Covenant began with altar law, the presence of the God who speaks in the Book of the Covenant and proclaims his law is no longer an unquestioned matter of course. Because the altar law is so significantly placed first, it is immediately clear that much depends upon proper access to God for a proper understanding of the Book of the Covenant.

---

307 Halbe, *Privilegrecht* 369ff. discusses the relationship of the first and the third, Schwienhorst-Schönberger, *Bundesbuch* 41f., 296f. discusses the first two (however, see 410).

308 Görg, *Altar* 291.

> Ex 20:24 *You need make for me only an altar of earth and sacrifice on*
> *it your burnt offerings and your offerings of well-being, your sheep*
> *and your oxen; in every place[309] where I cause my name to be*
> *remembered I will come to you and bless you.*

This law is, in the first place, concerned with the external form of the
altar of burnt offering. "Altar of earth" (*ªdāmāh*) refers largely to a construction with unfired, air-dried, clay bricks of the kind we find
archaeologically attested.[310]

In verses 25f. we have descriptions of other altars, at least insofar as
they are made of stone and have no steps. The formulation includes,
for example, the design of the altar at the shrine of Arad.[311] It was built
of small, uncut field-stones, which were held together by mortar and
clay.[312] Verse 25 eliminates widely produced altars of the kind with built-
in basins (the depressions and grooves suggest blood rituals)[313] but
which are probably also erected with cut stone blocks,[314] as we find in
Beersheba.[315] There is much, however, that argues that simple altars that
were traditional in Israel are being contrasted with new forms that were
associated with foreign deities.[316]

It is not, however, simply the construction of a proper altar that
constitutes a legitimate cult site. The formulation in verse 24 shows this
clearly. There is the description of every place at which God causes his
name to be remembered (*zkr*, hiph.): "place" (*māqōm*) – first and foremost,
this is a frequent designation for the elevated holy place.[317] We must
begin with the ancient presumption that a cultic place is not constituted
by the construction of an altar. The actual procedure is quite the reverse:
Altars were erected where a divine revelation demonstrated that the
place is holy. Holy places were not placed at the discretion of human
beings, they were established by tradition, and their cultic legends traced
their history back to an act of discovery or revelation that demonstrated
the special character of the place.[318]

Thus, the altar law of the Book of the Covenant deals exclusively with
the fact that the altar and the cult at the YHWH shrines corresponds to
the God who is venerated in this book, and not the establishment of new

---

309 It is not necessary to alter the text (Jepsen, *Bundesbuch* 12; Cazelles, *Études* 42;
     Schottroff, *Gedenken* 247), even MT can mean "in any place" (Conrad, *Altargesetz* 6
     with examples).
310 Conrad, *Altargesetz* 26ff.; see also Stenbach, *Altarformen* 186f.; Reichert, article on
     Altar.
311 Conrad, *Altargesetz* 41.
312 See e.g. Fritz, *Temple* 47ff.
313 Conrad, *Altargesetz* 45ff..
314 Conrad, *Altargesetz* 44f. excludes such an interpretation, since the term *gāzīt* in
     verse 25 could also refer to "square stone." (AM 5:11; Isa 9:9), but as such they did
     not exist in the early period from which the altar law is supposed to have come.
     However, we should operate with the date of the *writing down* of the Book of the
     Covenant, and then there would be a connection with *cut* square-stone altars.
315 See Aharoni, *Altar*.
316 Thus especially Conrad, *Altargesetz* 138f.; see also Görg, *Altar*; and especially
     Dohmen, *Bilderverbot* 172ff., who sees nomadic traditions and a critique of urban
     customs behind this.
317 See Gamberoni, article on *māqōm* especially 1118ff.
318 See Lindblom, *Theophanies*; W. H. Schmidt, *Glaube* 31ff.

cult sites or the arbitrary construction of altars. The blessing expected during the visit to the shrine depends upon this, and it is to the God who is present here that sacrifice is made, in the correct manner (the altar law is to insure against incorrect performance of the sacrifice).

Verse 24 adds the critical limitation, however, over against a traditional understanding of shrines. It is not the place as such, or the proper altar and cult that guarantees the divine presence, but only the fact that God causes his name to be remembered there, in other words, to be proclaimed and called out.[319] What Israel should not do by the names of other gods is what is intended here (Ex 23:13). Nevertheless it is only in 20:24b that God uses this verb (*zkr*, hiph.) referring to himself.

What precisely did he mean? We have referred to the necessity that this place be marked by YHWH-related shrine legends (we think, for example, of Gen 28:10 for Bethel). "It is through the proclamation of the name in the shrine's legend that it is legitimized as a YHWH cult site."[320] But such a limitation is hardly sufficient. It must deal with a proclamation in the present, "a self-identifying proclamation, YHWH himself is speaking."[321] The divine presence is exclusively dependent upon the bringing-to-speech of the divine name by God himself.

In our discussion of the understanding of this verse, we have always had the connection to the deuteronomic centralization and its root expressions of causing the name to proclaim or to dwell before one's eyes.[322] Of course, there it was about just one place, but here clearly it is a number of sites. Is this, perhaps, a polemic against the trend toward centralization?

The truth is much closer at hand. First, look at the fact that with this provision there is clearly a *selection* effected of those holy places under discussion. The formulation contains an immense *critique of every purely cultic definition of a shrine*. He does not promise his presence and blessing at even all sites with associated (ancient) traditions, but only on those where his name is still proclaimed. This is not a critique of the deuteronomic understanding, but rather an – incomplete – parallel to it.[323] If we draw a correlation using the fact that the divine *name* is what constitutes a true shrine, then we are justified in speaking of a pre- or early form of the deuteronomic demand for centralization together with its underlying theology.[324]

This formulation reveals its intent, if we interpret it in the temporal context of the period to which evidence compels us to date the Book of the Covenant:[325] in the monarchic period after the collapse of the northern kingdom. It is obvious what the theological reaction would be from the prophetic cult-critique as well as the Assyrian occupation, together with

---

319 For *zkr*, hiph., see Schotroff, *Gedenken* 244ff.; Eising, article on *zākar* 582ff.
320 Schottroff, *Gedenken* 248; already Stamm, *Altargesetz* 306; Cazelles, *Études* 43; for a critique see Halbe, *Privilegrecht* 377ff.
321 Halbe, *Privilegrecht* 371.
322 For a discussion, see Conrad, *Altargesetz* 11ff.; Halbe, *Privilegrecht* 374ff.
323 See below pp. 222ff.
324 See Halbe, *Privilegrecht* 377; Lohfink, *Zentralisationsformel* 168f., 173; Osumi, *Kompositionsgeschichte* 161.
325 See below pp. 183f., 197.

settlement of those deported: not all of the traditional YHWH shrines would be regarded for this reason alone as places of his presence. Foreign deities were venerated at many of them, either exclusively or along with YHWH. Many succumbed to foreign influence. While we can see a linkage between groups involved with the cult of YHWH and hyper-regional shrines underlying Ex 34:11ff.,[326] we are now dealing with a few of these.

It is not the holy place and not even the proper altar with its cult that reveals the presence of God. In spite of, or because of the foreign powers and super-powers in action here, the formulation of verse 24b establishes that it depends upon the wishes of YHWH himself where he will cause his name to be remembered, so that he can appear. It is he alone, not the Assyrians, the new settlers or the accommodating groups in Judah or Israel who can determine where this will happen.

At the beginning of the Book of the Covenant, thus in the altar law, reference is made to the presence of God at the holy place. At its conclusion we read that God's presence is not limited to this place, rather it takes place as his messengers accompany people during travel and while they are at home.[327] Thus, the presence of God frames the book.

In both passages this presence is not without that Word through which God's name is proclaimed. What happened when the basic principles of exclusive veneration were turned into divine address,[328] is now significantly expanded: God's self-revelation now determines his presence. It causes the traditional holy place to become what he had always claimed it to be: the place of his presence, and the text at whose climax this occurs shows the content of this self-revelation. It gains its final form in the Book of the Covenant itself, which is conceived in the form of the words of God himself.

C. ASYLUM (Ex 21:13f.)

Ex 21:13 also discusses the "place" (*māqōm*) and the appropriate altar. The text even stands out stylistically from its context in the Mishpatim and also contrasts with similar formulations and the structure of the contents in the capital offense laws in Ex 21:12, 15–17. We read in conjunction with the basic regulations in 21:12, which are formulated comprehensively and without exceptions, and according to which anyone who kills a person will find death (*mōt yūmāt*):

> 21:13 *If it was not premeditated, but came about by an act of God, then will I appoint for you a place to which the killer may flee.*
> 14 *But if someone willfully attacks and kills another by treachery, you shall take the killer from the altar for execution.*

While the borderline issues in the principle presented in 21:12 (in matters of injury without mortal consequence, offenses against pregnant women and slaves and all those for whom the question of intent is unclear)[329] are resolved in 21:18 entirely as ancient Near Eastern law

---

326 See below pp. 134f.
327 See above pp. 178ff.
328 See above pp. 121ff.
329 See above pp. 160ff.

would handle them, there is a clear distinction made in verses 13f. between intentional and unintentional murder. Asylum is granted in one case, but not in the other.

The formulations used here are circumstantial and quite obviously tentative. "Involuntary" manslaughter[330] is covered by the omission of a pursuit of the perpetrator[331] but especially by the phrase that "it came about by an act of God."[332] All of the later redactions of this juridical material leave God out of the activity. Is God the one who "committed the murder?"

More recent exegesis has recognized the theological danger in the formulation as it is used and – by silence – limited. Stylistically, it is remarkable that here God (*hā 'elōhīm*) is spoken of in the third person in contrast to the addition in verse 13 with its first person divinity. Since we need not deal with a literary-critical classification, this might be a turn of phrase in which there is a simultaneous attempt made to distinguish between the person speaking – "I" – and an unknown power relating to God. In later texts, dependent upon this passage, the point is paraphrased with an illustration (for example, the ax head that slips from the handle, Deut 19:5). Here, there is a contrast between ambush (thus planning) and "arrogance,"[333] thus addressing ethically reprehensible behavior.

What happens with this distinction is a process of great legal-historical significance. Ancient Near Eastern law had never articulated such a difference, and at best had only made rudimentary efforts.[334] In contrast, there is a useful parallel among the Greeks, where "Draco considers the intention of the offender first when deciding between voluntary or involuntary manslaughter."[335] "The entire legislation of Draco ... consists of protection for offenders from the vendettas by next of kin of the murder victim; he permitted them to escape into the protection of foreigners."[336] Draco's reform is dated to the end of the seventh century BCE.[337] The formulation of the Book of the Covenant must be placed at least a century before this.[338] The great significance ascribed to Draco as the first Athenian law-giver,[339] should be borne in mind as we evaluate the Book of the Covenant.

With the YHWH shrine in Israel we have a parallel to the legitimate, safe flight to a foreign land, which was possible in Athens. Behind this opportunity for escape, in both cultures there is a wide-ranging process of public procedure for self-help. The control of avengers and their vendettas by public councils is necessarily and inseparably connected with the distinction between intentional and unintentional murder. This

---

330 Such a formulation for the Greek counterpart in Latte, article on *Mord* 281.
331 For *ṣdh*, see 1 Sam 24:12; Thr 4:18.
332 For the interpretation of the phrase and its role in Jewish tradition, see Daube, *Causation* 246ff., for comparison, see especially Sir 15:13.
333 For *zid*, see Scharbert, article on **zûd* 551f.
334 See Sick, *Tötung* there also 94ff. for the attempts in Hittite law.
335 Ruschenbusch, *Recht Drakons* 142; for Dracon, see also Stroud, *Drakon's Law*; Gagarin, *Drakon*.
336 Ruschenbusch, *Recht Drakons* 142f.
337 See Gagarin, *Drakon* 1.
338 See below pp. 184., 197.
339 See Ruschenbusch, *Recht Drakons* 154; Schlesinger, *Asylie*.

distinction can only be effective if all homicides are subject to thorough public investigation of a claim.[340] This is independent of who, for example, carries out the punishment. Furthermore, the distinction between intentional and unintentional had the purpose and function of determining who was guilty and what the nature of the guilt was.

In Ex 21:13f. the authority upon whom jurisdiction devolves (a judge, the local community or any free Israelite who is able to participate in such a procedure) is addressed as "you." God will prepare ($\acute{sim}$) for this person a "place" ($m\bar{a}q\bar{o}m$), to which the perpetrator may flee. This takes place before a third person, who is presumed here, but in later parallel texts he is explicitly mentioned (e.g. Num 35:12; Deut 19:6; Josh 20:3). He is the avenger ($g\bar{o}'\bar{e}l\ hadd\bar{a}m$). Thus, we have an informative interplay of cultic and legal authorities.

The shrine (or the altar in it) guaranteed asylum as it probably already had done according to previous tradition and widely held religio-historical practise,[341] but a judicial authority had the right and duty to take the perpetrator away from the shrine if it were determined by the court that his claim to asylum had been unjust. It was apparently not the shrine and its authorities that made the decision whether or not the claim to asylum was just.

In any case, the discussion is not about oath and divine judgment in conjunction with homicide as it is, for example, in matters of personal property (Ex 22:8).[342] There is a juridically well-thought interplay between the institutions of blood revenge, the shrine and the judiciary. Furthermore, the authority behind the formulation of Ex 21:13f. apparently had the right and the opportunity to supervise this interplay in a binding way in the name of God.

In this passage as elsewhere, the authors of the Book of the Covenant speak in the name and on behalf of God to whom the saving altar belongs ($mizb^e\hbar\bar{i}$ 21:14). Thus, according to the claim, all of the YHWH shrines in the land are under their jurisdiction. These provisions encroach significantly upon the right of asylum maintained by the individual holy places.[343] These are not places of refuge for thieves, murderers, adulterers or perjurers. It is not a "den of thieves" as Jer 7:11 puts it. The traditional right of asylum is thus extremely limited, and even in cases of homicide it is subject to the judicial authorities.

340 "The presumption of this regulation is judicial restraint, in other words, the exercise of blood feud had been made dependent upon a judicial decree. This was a phase which German law only achieved with the treaty of 1234" Ruschenbusch, *Recht Drakons* 152).

341 In Israel, see 1 Kg 1:50ff. For religious-historical dissemination, see e.g. Hellwig, *Asylrecht*; Schlesinger, *Griechische Asylie*; Woess, *Asylwesen Ägyptens*; Compare Schottroff, *Unantastabarer Raum*; Wissmann, article on *Asylrecht* I; de Vaux, article on Refuge; the ancient Near Eastern temple may have been an important exception.

342 It is doubtful whether we can identify this person with the so-called defendant of the Psalms, studies (especially Beyerlin, *Rettung*) remain rather vague here.

343 Milgrom, *Sancta Contagion* 309 note 84 refers to the radicality of this turning point. On the right of asylum in general, and the disputed question of the dating of the asylum cities, see Löhr, *Asylwesen*; Nicolsky, *Asylrecht*; Greenberg, *Asylum*; deVaux, article on Refuge; as well as below, note 345.

Ex 21:13f. speaks in the name of a God who is not limited to the shrine and its district or to the place of his presence (20:24). Even the non-cultic judiciary is subject to him, which parallels the literary result achieved when the Mishpatim were imbedded in the first person address of the Book of the Covenant. One of the great turning points in the history of law is accomplished in the formulation of the Book of the Covenant, and 21:13f. is inseparably connected with the way it begins (20:24) and the way it ends (23:20). Indeed, as far as we know this was perhaps the first time in history that such a thing had happened. Legal expertise and jurisdiction must go hand in hand with the possibility of speaking in the name of God. For this reason the formulation of Ex 21:13f. is of special importance for the investigation of the groups and institutions underlying the Book of the Covenant.[344] Theological, cultic and legal jurisdictions come together and cannot be reduced to any one of the three.

Overview: We find later and more detailed texts dealing with possibilities for asylum in cases of unintentional homicide in Deut 19; Josh 20 and Num 35. All the passages are about the establishment of so-called cities of asylum together with appropriate regulations. The texts are concerned with the three (or six) cities set aside for this purpose rather than shrines and altars. We need not discuss here the numerous problems this raises. Recent studies[345] have reinforced the old thesis that these cities are a substitute for possibilities for asylum lost in the deuteronomic cult centralization. Problems caused by a flight over a great distance, as referred to in Deut 19:6, suggest this.

More recent texts give a more detailed description of the interplay of these jurisdictions, which we see only indirectly revealed in Ex 21:13f. Thus, Josh 20:4 speaks of a kind of pre-investigation that takes place at the gate of the intended asylum city, but Deut 19:12 assigns the duty to demand the offender be handed over to the elders of the place where the crime was committed. They indeed presided over the proceedings. In addition to the asylum cities, we must conjecture that only the shrine at Jerusalem offered opportunity for asylum, and in reality it was probably more important than they were.

According to Josh 20 and Num 35, the period of asylum might last until the death of the high priest who was in office. After his death, the killer was able to return home again, free. This adjusts a legal dilemma produced by basic principle formulated in Num 35:31, according to which no ransom may be paid in the cases of homicide, not even unintentional (35:32).[346] We are probably indebted to some of these asylum seekers for a whole series of some of the best known and most beautiful of the psalms. They were sung in thanks to those who prepared a table for them before the face of their enemies. (Ps 23:5).[347]

344 See below pp. 195f.
345 For what follows especially Rofé, *Cities of Refuge*; in addition to ibid., *Joshua 20*; Auld, *Cities of Refuge*, as well as the literature mentioned above in note 343.
346 See especially Greenberg, *Postulates*.
347 For the interpretation of Ps 23 against this background, see especially Schottroff, *Psalm 23*. We might at least mention the theory that much of the psalter might be indebted to this institution (Delekat, *Asylie*) though it is not widely accepted.

d. ACCOMPANIMENT (Ex 23:20ff.)

At the beginning of the concluding portion of the Book of the Covenant the "place" (*māqōm*) prepared by God is discussed for the third time. Ex 23:20–33[348] demonstrates a series of stylistic and substantive breaks, the majority of which permit us to see sharply contrasting redactions. If we attend to the stylistic gaps,[349] the oldest stratum is probably the following:

> Ex 23:20 See, I am going to send an angel in front of you, to guard
> you on the way and to bring you to the place that I have prepared.
> 21 Be attentive to him and listen to his voice; do not rebel against
> him,[350] for my name is in him.
> 22 But if you listen attentively to his voice and do all that I say,
> then I will be an enemy to your enemies and a foe to your foes.
> 23 When my messenger goes in front of you and brings you to the
> Amorites, the Hittites, the Perizzites, the Canaanites, the Hivites,
> the Jebusites.[351]
> 24 You shall not bow down to their gods, or worship them, or
> follow their practices, but you shall demolish them and break their
> pillars in pieces.[352]
> 32 You shall make no covenant with them and their gods,
> 33 [353]for it would be a snare for you.

The text begins with a promise from God to send a messenger accompanying the person to whom God is speaking. The messenger (*mal'āk*) of God[354] in Old Testament texts is either human[355] or a kind of angel. It is

---

348 For the overall structure of the text, see Osumi, *Kompositionsgeschichte* 213. See an overview of previous literary-critical theses in Blum, *Pentateuch* 375f. note 61.

349 We note the following: a change from second person singular to second person plural; the inhabitants of the land are indicated in singular and plural; there is a repeat of the list of people, a parallel usage of messenger and '*ēmā* among others. For an analysis see Osumi, *Kompositionsgeschichte* 63ff., 204ff., 212–216. The result (see Tabelle 217) finds a base stratum in verses 20–21a, 21bβ, 22–23a, 24, 32, 33bβ, and a three-fold expansion by verses 23b, 28–31a/21bα, 25aα, 31bα/25aα, b–26, 27, 31bβ, 33a, bα. It is generally accepted that there is an addition in verses 28–31a . The most important reasons are given below in note 352 and repeated again below in note 457 without all of the arguments. It is methodologically important that the literary-critical stylistic observations and those from the meaning of the phrase *heqin māqōm* as well as the correlation of 23:20 with 20:24, 21:13 originate completely independent of each other, but nevertheless supplement each other.

350 The formulation in second person plural contradicts the context and belongs to a redactional stratum throughout the Book of the Covenant.

351 In verse 23b, as in verses 28–31a , the inhabitants of the land are referred to in the singular, but in verse 24 they are plural.

352 Verses 25–31 is an addendum (which in itself is stratified). Its beginning is marked by the change to second person plural as well as substantive parallels to other parts.

353 The verb in verse 33bβ, plural in the older versions, could hardly refer to the previously mentioned gods, but most probably to the covenant (*bᵉrit*) in verse 32 (see Ex 34:12). In contents verse 33abα resembles Deut 7.

354 Important special studies: Stier, *Engel*; Baumgartner, *Jahweengel*; Hirth, *Gottes Boten*; Röttger, *Ma'lak Jahwe*; Jacob, *Variations*; Guggisberg, *Ma'lak Jahwe*; compare Freedman/Willoughby, article on *ma'lāk*.

355 Thus in Hag 1:13; Ez 30:9; Isa 44:26; 2 Chr 36:15f. a prophet; and in Mal 2:6f.; Koh 4:17ff. a priest.

typical of a whole series of texts that the messenger has an obvious and astonishing similarity to God himself.[356] We read, for example, in verse 22 that his voice, to which attention is to be paid, is equivalent to God's voice. The messenger is to accompany and guarantee protection to the person with whom he is speaking (verse 20). The messenger offers to accompany the person (a function similar here to many other texts), "in situations of permanent danger, uncertain expectation and varieties of threatening situations . . . on a path characterized by chronic unpredictability and constant peril."[357]

What is absolutely certain in Ex 23:20–33 – that the sending of the messenger and his protection has to do with Israel's journey into the land and among the people who live there (verse 23) – is also obvious from the literary context (the proclaiming of the Book of the Covenant at Sinai), and it has also always been the unquestioned starting point for scholars. Independent of any decision regarding literary stratification or the form of the original Book of the Covenant, the difficulty of this interpretation lies in the language used in verse 20.

The path that the angel leads goes to the "place" (*māqōm*) which God has "prepared." The land to which Israel was led was never described in these terms. To be sure, it is called the "place" of the Canaanites, Hittites, etc. (Ex 3:8), nevertheless, that is not normal.[358] Furthermore, *qūn* hiph ("prepare," "found") when used of a place, is always in a clear context: It is always the place of the "ark,"[359] the "altar,"[360] the "house of God,"[361] in short, the Jerusalem temple. All evidence for the phrase (*hēqin māqōm*) has this connection.

From early to more recent examples, there are many parallel expressions, that combine this verb (*qūn*, hiph.) with the "preparation of sacrifices, cultic sites, holy persons and celebrations,"[362] saying the same thing about YHWH himself.[363] And all of the Old Testament parallels for

---

356 Especially Gen 21:11ff.; Judg 6:17ff.; cf Gen 22:11; 31:11ff.; Ex 3:2ff. For this, see especially Rad, *Theologie* I 298.

357 Welker, *Engel* 203.

358 Gamberoni, article on *māqōm* 1118, for a meaning as "land," refers, besides Ex 23:20, to Ez 21:30; Ex 3:8, 17; Gen 13:3, 4, 14–17; nevertheless, in Gen 13:3, 4 it is the holy places (which are introduced in chap.12) that are intended. Clearly, in Gen 13:14 a fixed place is intended from which one can look in every direction. The *māqōm* of verse 14 is just not identical with the land, even though it lies within it. Also in Ez 21:30 the parallel of the "place where you were created" and the land of origin are without problem. Thus, only Ex 3:8 remains to support the meaning "land." It is here that the *māqōm* of the Canaanites, Hittites, etc. are mentioned. The passage does, in fact, have similarities to Ex 23:20. Nevertheless, it does not mean that *māqōm* can simply be defined as "land." KBL³ places "the land as the place of the Canaanites" together with Num 32:1 "a place for cattle" and Judg 18:10 for the meaning "area, region"; in other words the special role of *māqōm* in Ex 23:20 is exclusively dependent upon a context that seems to refer to the taking of the land.

359 1 Chr 15:1, 3.

360 2 Chr 33:19.

361 2 Chr 3:1; 35:20.

362 Koch, article on *kûn* 101.

363 Compare Deut 19:3; 1 Kg 5:32, 6:19; Ez 4:3; Isa 14:21, 40:20; Zeph 1:7; there are about 110 hiph. citations here, including 30 in 1/2 Chr alone (Koch article on *kûn* 102).

the phrase "prepare a place" (*hēqin māqōm*) are found exclusively in Chronicles.[364] The few examples we find do not permit us to conclude convincingly that this is necessarily a later usage; there are similar phrasings used already much earlier, even in the Book of the Covenant. Furthermore, there are significant problems if such a late chronistic addendum cannot be associated with the land as the context demands. If we compare 23:20 with the clearly parallel texts discussed above (Ex 20:24 and 21:13), the reason to associate the "place" of 23:20 with a shrine (or a temple) is so overwhelming, that a new look at the context and the traces of its growth would prove rewarding.

If we presume a literary stratification derived apart from this interpretation of the "place," the following interpretation seems plausible. Ex 23:20 speaks of a path to *the* shrine, which was also discussed in 20:24 and 21:13 to the cult site determined by right proclamation as well as right cult. The messenger takes care of protection along the way.

The almost identical formulation in 23:23 says that the messenger leads along the path to the nations whose names are listed.[365] Here the tradition of Ex 34 is adopted and varied. They should not venerate the gods of these nations, but along with the "pillars," they should destroy them (verse 24), and no covenants should be struck with either gods or people (verses 32f.).

If we may not associate 23:20 with the facts of the conquest of the land, these formulations cannot be associated with them either, or those of Ex 34. The older text does not speak from the distant past or about a fictive place outside the land. It deals with people and nations with whom the people were living. If 23:20 mentions the procession to the shrine, together with the protection along the way (it is thus comparable to the protection of neglected fields in Ex 34:24), then Ex 23:23 refers to the same trip but the other direction. It talks about accompaniment on the way back from the shrine at which the presence of God is promised. The people who are addressed live, in any case potentially and fundamentally, together with people who worship other gods. God's messenger accompanies the people on the way to these people.

If we interpret Ex 23:20 in conjunction with the parallels in 20:4 and 21:13f. and we stick to the wording as given, 23:20 is about God's accompaniment outside of the "place" (*māqōm*) in which he is present in a special way. The angel is the form in which God comes and guarantees his protection.[366] God's presence in the messenger is not the same as his coming to the shrine (20:24), but it is very close.

The name of God that is proclaimed in the shrine (20:24) is in the angel (23:21). To listen to the messenger means to listen to that which God himself has spoken (23:22), and the blessing mediated at the shrine (20:24) finds its shape in the protection from enemies and

---

364 See above note 359–361.
365 For the chiastic structure of 23:20–23, see Osumi, *Kompositionsgeschichte* 64.
366 It is especially the unmistakable duty of the messenger to be a protector that argues against regarding him to be a human being, "a cultic dispenser of oracles" as Schmitt, *Frieden* 15; Halbe, *Privilegrecht* 369ff. have attempted. In its narrower as well as broader (see Ex 33) contexts, 23:20ff. is concerned with God's long-term accompaniment – even outside of the holy place.

oppressors that God guarantees to be present in the listening to the messenger.

If the text were formulated at a time[367] in which these enemies were overwhelmingly present in the form of the Assyrians, and the path to and from the shrine was threatened by them, the act of heeding the commandments of this God (as they received them in so exemplary a fashion as the Book of the Covenant) would be combined with protection and survival. We see how the prophets' criticism of the lack of social justice and the reference to the catastrophe, which arises from this lack, is here transposed into an act of God.

The first commandment, the demand for the exclusive veneration of YHWH, was formulated frequently and emphatically already before this closing section in the Book of the Covenant, as we can see by the placement in the center of its respective context (Ex 22:19; 23:13). The mention of the nations living in the land of Israel and their gods has a supplemental character to the basic commandment of exclusive veneration. The problem is obviously no longer the enticement to relations with the neighbors, as in Ex 34. The nations and their dangers are now already tradition and have been adopted from the older text, then marginalized and combined with the promise of protection that God's accompaniment guarantees. The Amorites, Hittites and whatever they were called might still have existed in the northern kingdom in the ninth century, but by the end of the eighth century in Judah, this at most could only be said of their gods.

The path to the inhabitants (who were enumerated in verse 23) became a gate to the historicization of the text in the later strata of verses 20–33. The occupation which had already taken place and consequently turned the Book of the Covenant, which seeks to be paid attention to in the present, into a document from the past that now (supporting itself with authority from the past in order to empower those in peril in the present) is mirrored in the formulation of the so-called addendum. This change affected the Book of the Covenant in ways which require further study.[368]

"I am compassionate" (Ex 22:27): The Right of Mercy
In the overall construction of the Book of the Covenant, the block Ex 22:20–23:12 is a parallel and a counterbalance to the Mishpatim

---

367 The placement of the text in the total structure of the Book of the Covenant is so clear that this small-scale composition must have preferential treatment over the larger-scale observations regarding relationships, which Blum, *Pentateuch* 365ff. places outside his Mal'ak stratum. He points to the correlation between Ex 14:19a; 23:20ff.; 33:2f.; 34:11ff. and Judg 2:1–5 and considers here a late, supplementary stratum, dated after the D composition. The dating does not ultimately rest upon the already thoroughly studied and well-known deuteronomism of this text, which is supposed to be near the end of the Pentateuch redaction. Nevertheless, the overarching observations cannot emphasize the close relationships and the small-scale structure. And furthermore, they presuppose a closed D composition which in other places has led to the exclusion of older, more cumbersome texts (see above pp. 30., 118 and elsewhere).

368 See below pp. 199f.

(21:1–22:19).[369] The six/seven rhythms of the slave law are in a chiastic relationship with those of the sabbath or sabbath year, (21:2–11/23:10–12). The parts thus framed illustrate again their own framework. This happens through the capital offense laws (21:2–17/22:17–19) and the laws regarding aliens (22:20/23:9). The obvious structural design is focused on the contents.

Justice and the formal law of the Mishpatim compete like two opponents in a court case. Justice favors those who are legally and socially most vulnerable (22:20–26), and thus affects the course of events (23:1–8). Above all, the two great themes of the Book of the Covenant are expressed here, and the relationship of formal law to mercy must be worked out.

In the paragraphs that follow, we will first discuss the two primary social problems; the alien and the poor; the central portion will deal with the judiciary. Only then will we be able to study the character of these legal provisions for mercy. Are we talking about law or "just" ethics?

a. ALIENS – THE LITERARY FRAMEWORK AND THE MEASURE OF THE CONTENTS

The entire section of social provisions in the Book of the Covenant is framed by the theme of aliens:

> 22:21a You shall not wrong or oppress a resident alien, (for you were aliens in the land of Egypt . . .)[370]
> 23 If you abuse them, when they cry out to me, I will surely hear their cry.
> 23:9 You shall not oppress a resident alien: (for you were aliens in the land of Egypt).[371]

The placement of the theme within this framework permits us to see its significance. The theme appears with the provisions regarding the capital offense (21:12–17; 22:17–19). What death penalty offenses are to the Mishpatim, the alien theme is to the mercy law: These are provisions on the margin of the law, by which a person is given meaning and measure. In the alien law, once again, all of the social problems discussed between 22:20 and 23:9 are at issue in a special way.[372]

People who live for a long time in a place where they did not originally reside, where they have neither relatives nor property are called foreigners (*gēr*).[373] This term is the exact opposite of ethnic-national

369 See Halbe, *Privilegrecht* 421; see especially Osumi, *Kompositionsgeschichte* in summary 151.
370 The change to plural points to the more recent supplementary stratum; see above pp. 109., 115 and below pp. 197ff. Verse 22 also belongs to this theme.
371 See note 2.
372 For the following, Crüsemann, *Fremdenliebe* (Lit.); in addition to the older standard work, Bertholet, *Stellung* see especially K. L. Schmidt, *Israels Stellung*; Ruppert, *Umgang*; Stamm, *Fremde*; Schwienhorst-Schönberger, ". . . *denn Fremde* . . ."; Albertz, *Fremde*. For the surrounding world, see Cardascia, *Le Statut*; Glassner, *L'hospitalité*; Pirenne, *Le Statut*; Helck, *Die Ägypter*.
373 See Martin-Achard, article on *gūr*, Kellermann, *gûr*, for etymology, see also Görg, "*Der Fremde*". Critical for an understanding of the term *gēr* is a distinction from related words like *zār*, "one who stands outside, an outsider," by which foreigners (especially Isa 1:7) are designated, but also laity as over against priests (Ex 25:33;

powers. In addition to those who were from other nations and religions (e.g. Isa 14:1), members of the Israelite nation who were living with another tribe (e.g. Judg 17:7) might also be aliens.

A person became such an alien for two reasons especially – famine[374] and war[375] which had driven people from their homes. The theological importance of this subject is demonstrated, not least, by the fact that all of Israel's patriarchs were called "aliens." Collectively, even Israel itself, because of its sojourn in Egypt, was an alien.[376] Ex 22:21b and 23:9b support this.

Aliens were not only socially poor and weak, they especially were without rights. They were unable to have their own voice in a trial at the gate. Like women, children and slaves, they were unable to express their rights there and enforce them. The alien theme deals with gaining rights for those who have none. Other social groups included in Ex 22:20 and 23:9, the poor (22:24ff.), widows and orphans (22:21, 23), were likewise legally handicapped. Nevertheless, what was a problem for them was magnified in the case of foreigners, because there were also women and children among the foreigners. Justice for those who had none was to be given at the place of justice. We find the measure of the judiciary in how it deals with those who were neither permitted to appear before judges nor were they provided for.

The great significance of the foreigner in the Book of the Covenant allows us to see where the main redaction of the Book of the Covenant took place.[377] We can tell quite accurately when aliens became a problem in Israel, and required legal assistance of this kind. They are barely mentioned in texts dealing with the pre-state period in Israel.[378]

The noun "alien" (*gēr*) occurs four times[379] in the books from Joshua to 2 Samuel, two of these are in texts that are incontrovertibly deuteronomistic.[380] The verb *gūr* appears eight times,[381] but never is the existence of foreigners regarded as a social problem. Thus, for example, the conflict in Judg 19 did not come about because there were resident foreigners present in Gibea (Judg 19:6), but because of the short-term stay of some foreign travelers.

30:33 and others). (Cf Snijders, *Meaning*; ibid. article on *zûr*) See especially *nokrī* "foreigner, one who is unknown" which can mean: different from one's self (Prov 27:2) or one's own family (Gen 31:15) or often also the foreigner (1 Kg 8:41; especially *ben nekār* Gen 17:12 and elsewhere); see Lang, article on *nkr*; Martin-Achard, article on *nēkār*. For the relationship with travelers remaining for a short-term, see Schreiner, *Gastfreundschaft*.

374 For the patriarchs of Israel, see Gen 12:10; 26:3; 47:4; also Ruth 1:1; 2 Kg 8:1.

375 See 2 Sam 4:3; Isa 16:4.

376 See Spina, *Israelites*.

377 For what follows, see Crüsemann, *Bundesbuch* 33f.

378 Schäfer-Lichtenberger, *Eidgenossenschaft* 311f.; the other view, e.g. of Thiel, *Entwicklung* 154f., relies almost exclusively on the fact that the texts of Genesis are regarded as evidence for pre-state relationships. For methodological reasons this is quite problematic.

379 Josh 8:33, 35; 20:9; 2 Sam 1:3.

380 For Josh 8:33, 35, see Noth, *Joshua* 51ff.; for Josh 20:9 we note the correlation with Num 35 (verse15!); for this Rofé, *Joshua* 20:131ff.; ibid., *History* especially 231.

381 Josh 20:9; Judg 5:17; 17:7, 8, 9; 19:1, 16; 2 Sam 4:3.

Even among the eighth-century prophets, "aliens" are not among those regarded as oppressed and at whose side the prophets stand. This only changes with Jeremiah[382] and Ezekiel,[383] in other words, the seventh and six centuries. Literary and archaeological sources show that when the Assyrians captured the northern kingdom, this especially caused a broad stream of refugees to be unleashed.[384] The metropolitan area of Jerusalem expanded rapidly, there was an explosion of new suburbs.[385] We can draw only one conclusion from all of this: that the main preoccupation of the Book of the Covenant, with its social law concerned for aliens, could not be dated before the end of Samaria in 722 BCE. The Book of the Covenant was compiled in the last decades of the eighth or the beginning of the seventh century.

In view of this historical background, we should point out that the category of the "alien" (*gēr*) was not restricted to those with ethnic relationship to Israel. Of course, the majority of aliens may have been Israelites from the north, but the advance of the Assyrian army with its concomitant horrors would have affected other peoples as well and driven them into Judah, which had as yet remained relatively untouched. In the history of Torah, there developed a strong counterbalance to the tradition adopted from Ex 34:11ff., not to make ties with the nations of the land and the radicalization of this tradition – to proscribe the people, drive them out and eradicate them.[386]

The protection of aliens, without respect to their ethnic and religious background, is among the most important commands of the same God who demanded that he alone be worshiped. And this command to protect foreigners could not be ignored. We are only able to evaluate the hatred of nations of the former inhabitants of the land when we see it in tension with the rights of aliens. Hatred of aliens had become less and less important for Israel and it was historicized.

Prospect: The protection of aliens was increasingly emphasized and more comprehensively formulated in later legal documents. Theologically, this theme is of primary importance, second to none. It is equivalent to exclusive veneration of God or observance of sabbath. In Deuteronomy, social legislation is fully inclusive of aliens, placing them with widows, orphans and Levites (for example Deut 16:11, 14; 24:17, 19, 21; 27:19).[387] They received economic security through the third-year-tithe[388] (14:28f.; 26:12f.). Key theological principles are found in Deut 10:17ff.

Here the unique phrase, "who loves the strangers (*gēr*) providing them with food and clothing," grows out of a divine epithet, "God of gods and Lord of lords . . .," as well as the hymnic, participial expression, "who executes justice for the orphan and the widow," for which there are

382 Jer 7:6; 14:8; 22:3.
383 Ez 14:7; 22:7, 29; 47:22f.; and many others.
384 See J. Maier, *Fremdlinge*.
385 See Broshi, *Expansion*; Otto, *Jerusalem* 67f.; Avigad, *Jerusalem* 54ff.; for evaluation of the population figures, see Broshi, *Population*.
386 See above pp. 126ff.
387 See below pp. 233f.
388 See below pp. 216ff.

parallels in other hymns of the ancient Near East. This hymnic, divine epithet is then the basis for the ethical demand: "You shall also love the stranger (*gēr*), for you were strangers (*gērîm*) in the land of Egypt" (verse 19). The demand to love the aliens and to treat them in the same way that God treats them (and as he also treats Israel!) is based in the love of God as well as their own past.

The most wide-ranging legal demands are found in Old Testament texts with priestly character. Thus, in the Holiness Code, love of one's neighbors (Lev 19:18)[389] is amplified with love of aliens (19:33f.). The illustrative narrative in Lev 24:10ff.[390] orders the same law for aliens as for Israelites (verse 22). The same thing is stated, for example, in Num 15:14ff., ". . . there shall be for both you and the resident alien (*gēr*) a single statute (*ḥuqqāh*) . . . (16) you and the alien (*gēr*) who resides with you (*gūr*) shall have the same law (*tōrāh*) and the same ordinance (*mišpāt*)."

Unlike Deuteronomy, where aliens are not subject to the same dietary laws as Israel (14:21), priestly texts apply cultic legislation to strangers as well as Israelites.[391] Laws regarding sexual relations (Lev 18:26) and sacrifice (Lev 17:8; 22:18) are also valid for them and they participate in passover celebrations.

Later Jewish interpretation generally regards strangers (*gērîm*) as proselytes,[392] in other words, people who have joined fully with Israel.[393] In a diaspora, where small groups live scattered among heathen nations, the social problem of strangers could no longer exist. Anyone who joined with Israel there was a proselyte, and thus we must adjust our interpretation accordingly, but under no circumstances may we transpose this interpretation back into the original meaning of the priestly texts, as is often done.[394] In the same way that we are unable to find proselytes in the conflicts of the Persian period,[395] they also cannot be found in the priestly writings.

b. THE POOR – THE BEGINNING OF BUSINESS LAW

If, as in the case of widows and orphans,[396] aliens are people who are in a very real sense without rights, dependence upon others is a critical factor in making someone poor (*'ānî*):

> Ex 22:25 *If you lend money to my people, to the poor among you, you shall not deal with them as a creditor; (you shall not take interest from them.)*[397]

389 See below pp. 322ff.
390 See above pp. 98ff.
391 For the theological background, see below p. 309.
392 First in the LXX.. See Simon, *Les débuts*; Safrai, *Das jüdische Volk* 25ff. For a discussion of the late Old Testament texts under this aspect in Cohen, *Le "Ger"*.
393 For proselytism, see e.g. Bialoblocki, *Beziehungen*; Goldstein, *Conversion*; Zeitlin, *Proselytes*; Rosenblom, *Conversion*.
394 E.g. Kellermann, article on *gûr* 988.
395 See Crüsemann, *Perserzeit*; see also below p. 309.
396 See especially Fensham, *Widow*; Patterson, *The Widow*; Weiler, *Schicksal*; Schottroff, *Witwen*.
397 Verse 25b belongs to the plural supplemental stratum. See above, p. 109 and below p. 199.

*26 If you take your neighbor's cloak in pawn, you shall restore it before
the sun goes down;*
*27 for it may be your neighbor's only clothing to use as a cover; in
what else shall that person sleep? And if your neighbor cries out to me,
I will listen, for I am compassionate.*

Thus reads the oldest business law in the Bible. It applies to the same
point as the later – the heart of social dependence: indebtedness.[398] "The
borrower is the slave of the lender" says the proverb (Prov 22:7).
Relationships of economic dependence and exploitation, as in every
agrarian society, pivot-point in this place.[399] Unfortunately, we have no
lending contracts from Old Testament Israel, but many references show
that in general the same laws applied as in the rest of the ancient Near
East and later, for example, in the Jewish Elephantine colony.[400] Anyone
who borrowed so that they would not go hungry or could buy seed grain,
had to pay a high rate of interest, and above all, either immediately or
after a certain period of time, owed a deposit as security for the debt.

People were ranked with articles of value. A story like the one
presented in 2 Kg 4:1ff. makes the procedure quite clear. After the death
of the father of the family, who probably had made a guarantee regarding
repayment of his loan, the children were taken as slaves and as security.
The loss of land and personal freedom, things of which the prophets
speak so frequently, were dependent upon the legality of indebtedness.[401]

How can God's law attack the laws of business with their economic
mechanisms? The Book of the Covenant begins with the procedure for
making a pledge. Unfortunately, the full Hebrew terminology for debts
and borrowing is only approximately reproduced in this text. In Ex
22:25a two different terms for borrowing are used.[402] One simply means
"lend" (*lwh*) and it has a positive connotation.[403] The other word (*nšʾ/nšh*)
has a very negative tone. It suggests "loan" with all the negative consequences. As 2 Kg 4:1f. shows, this is especially involved with the
problem of personal pledges.

The double terminology illustrates the contradiction that this
procedure entails:[404] For the poor and needy, borrowing was a necessity
of existence in order to secure survival and freedom. But it can lead to
increased legal and social dependency, making the situation permanent.
Appropriate to the situation, Ex 22:24 demands a renunciation of
personal pledges in cases of loans made to the poor. The example in
verses 25f. deals with the seizure of the necessities of life, thereby giving
us an opportunity to view the realities of life for the people. They have
but one suit of clothes, the one that they are wearing; the nakedness of
the poor, so frequently mentioned,[405] is no metaphor.

398 For the following, see especially Kessler, *Schuldwesen.*
399 See Finley, *Schuldknechtschaft.*
400 Examples in Pap. Cowley No. 10, 11 and others. See e.g. Kippenberg, *Religion* 58f.
401 For this understanding of the prophetic social critique, see especially Kessler,
     Staat.
402 See Kessler, *Schuldenwesen* 183.
403 E.g. Ps 37:26; 112:5; Prov 19:17.
404 See Kessler, *Schuldenwesen* 183.
405 See Isa 58:7; Job 22:6; 24:7, 10; Ez 18:7, 16 and many others.

Who are these poor? A closer examination of the text shows quite clearly that these are people who are technically still free and legally qualified. They are impoverished and indebted small farmers.[406] The terms that are used for them have vivid meanings:[407] "one who cowers" (*'ānī*), "one who is gaunt, emaciated" (*dal*), the "socially impoverished" (*'ebyon*). They are people who make their way in servitude, loss of land and enslavement, but who are still capable of engaging in a trial (*rīb*) (Ex 23:3, 6). The dependency required by loans involving interest and pledges of payment, makes the technical equality under law held by the poor into a farce. Every trial at the gate involving these people is always affected, if not decided, by their sociological dependency and the complications that spring from it. For all that, precisely this central point must not be allowed for in a formal law like the Mishpatim.

The intervention into the economic and traditional forms of business here is the beginning of biblical business law. God's law runs contrary to economic law in those places where the latter leads to exploitation and dependence. The prohibition against interest (22:25b) was added to the renunciation of pledges of payment (25a) in the more recent stratum. Both are repeated and developed in later Old Testament law.[408]

The theological importance of this activity against business law clearly arises from the formulations of verse 27. God promises to hear the cry raised by the poor for their last clothing. This is a fundamental benefit from the God of the Book of the Covenant for the poor and disenfranchized. It is the goodness of God, his grace, that determines this attitude. Because God is gracious, because he hears the cry of the poor, the right of the poor to have loans without pledge or interest is a basic right of Torah. A gloss in verse 25 illustrates what this implies theologically. "My people" becomes a clarification for the expression, "the poor."[409] These poor are his people in a special way.

C. ADMINISTERING JUSTICE AND HAVING MERCY (Ex 23:1–8)

How a policy, that lives up to the goodness of God, oriented toward the impoverished and disenfranchised, should function over against questions treated in the Mishpatim regarding juridical responsibility and contractory legal claims must find expression in the law courts as the place of justice. This is what Ex 23:1–8 addresses. It is a critical passage for the self-understanding of the Book of the Covenant.

> 1 *You shall not spread a false report.*
> *You shall not join hands with the wicked*
> *to act as a malicious witness.*
> 2 *You shall not follow a majority in wrongdoing;*
> *when bearing witness in a lawsuit,*
> *you shall not side with the majority so as to pervert justice.*
> 3 *nor shall you be partial to the poor in a lawsuit.*

406 Thus especially Schwantes, *Recht* 98f., 201ff.
407 For the term see especially Schwantes, *Recht* 16ff.
408 See Deut 23:20ff.; 24:6, 10f., 17f.; Lev 25:36f. See below p. 199.
409 We may place them around deutero-Isaiah (Isa 49:13) and the postexilic psalm theology. For an overview, see Lohfink, *Gott auf der Seite der Armen.*

4 *When you come upon your enemy's ox or donkey going astray*
   you shall bring it back.
5 *When you see the donkey of one who hates you lying under its*
   burden
   and you would hold back from setting it free,
   (you must help to set it free).[410]
6 *You shall not pervert the justice due to your poor in their lawsuits.*
7 *Keep from a false charge*
   and do not kill the innocent and those in the right
   for I will not acquit the guilty.
8 *You shall take no bribe,*
   for a bribe blinds the officials,
   and subverts the cause of those who are in the right.

The text clearly illustrates a chiastic structure. At the center, we find
the two sentences introduced with "when" (*kī*), talking about the treatment of animals of an enemy. Outside of those are the two phrases about
those who are unimportant (*dal*) or poor (*'ebyōn*) and their lawsuits (*ribbō*)
in verses 3 and 6. And on the outside, verses 1 and 7 clearly correlate with
each other. The concern here is with basic questions of behavior in a
lawsuit before a court – the guilty (*rš'*) and the innocent (*ṣaddīq, nāqī*),
matters of majority and bribery. The overall structure is made clearer by
a whole series of additional references.[411] Thus, we have in verses 1 and 7
a command or prohibition of fundamental character followed by a rather
specific prohibition (vetitive).

This structure argues decisively against seeing a later development in
verses 4f., as frequently is done.[412] The same reasons that led to *the*

---

410 Cooper, *Plain Sense*, forcefully points out the problem in the formulation of this
     verse. He shows beautifully that from the time of the prescription of Deut
     22:4 and the LXX translation, the entire Jewish and Christian interpretation of
     this verse up to modern times, without exception, has understood it as a parallel
     to verse 4, thus in the sense of assistance for the animal, which the wording of the
     MT actually does not do. Because '*zb* means "let, leave" but never "help" or
     something similar. A '*zb* II (still KBL[3]; Stähli, article on '*zb* leave) cannot be
     adopted (especially Williamson, *Reconsideration*; for the Ugaritic, see especially
     Dietrich/Loretz, '*DB*; see Gerstenberger, article on '*āzaḇ*). Cooper suggests that
     the "plain sense" leads to the reverse: one should not touch the animal of an
     enemy. Of course, there are problems here which make such an interpretation
     improbable. Cooper has to presume that the owner of the animal is present (but
     why indeed?), or that the animal had not collapsed under the load (with Hoffmon,
     Comparative Study; one must still presume that the animal is unable to stand up on
     its own); and that the sentence beginning *wᵉhādaltā* in verse 4aβ ought to be
     translated "and you would refrain to leave it" (15), but above all, that "with him"
     (*'immō*) in verse 5b might simply be over done (cf 15 note 69, "an intractable
     problem.") For this reason the "plain sense" is not *so* clear that the great weight of
     tradition can simply be ignored. Obviously, there is still between verse 5aβ and
     5β the difference between '*zb* and '*zb* '*immō*, and especially in the latter we do not
     recognize the linguistic usage. A change of object (and for that reason probably
     the suggestion of an original gloss for verse 5b) is probably the simplest theory.
     Verse 5a, in any case seems to me to require that it be understood as a credible
     parallel to verse 4 (just as verse 6 is to verse 3 and verse 7 is to verse 1).
411 See Osumi, *Kompositionsgeschichte* 56ff.
412 So many since Wellhausen, *Composition* 90 (for the history of the interpreta-
     tion, see Cooper, *Plain Sense* 2 note 5); auch McKay, *Exodus XXIII*; Otto,
     Rechtsbegründungen 47, 53; Schwienhorst-Schönberger, *Bundesbuch* 379ff. believes

objection in verses 4f. also apply to verses 3, 6. Here, even more so, the theme is treated that we inevitably find throughout the entire composition of the Book of the Covenant: how the judicial provisions of the Mishpatim are to relate to the provisions which stand side by side with them for the protection of the poor and the alien. The court with which we are concerned here is the critical place where this tension is played out.

At the beginning – verses 1f., as at the end, verse 7 – the formulation is concerned with the basic issues of justice: how the guilty receive condemnation and the innocent are freed, and how, for this reason, everything should be avoided that hinders this. Verses 3 and 6 deal with the next question: how the poor receive justice. The fact that the central verses, framed by these two (4f.) have nothing directly to do with legal procedure, but deal with assistance for suffering animals and at the same time, behavior toward one's enemies, is certainly an intensification of the theme.

The intermediate position of verses 3 and 6 between the two problem areas of, on the one hand, judicial proceedings (verses 1f., 7f.) and pity for animals on the other (verses 4f.) shows what the overall composition is aiming at: the relation of these two attitudes and thus the correlation of the two great themes of the Book of the Covenant. How else could that, which is formally apparent in structure and design, be made comprehensible on the level of contents?

Like no other texts, the instructions regarding behavior in a trial, which we find in verses 1f., 7f., give us a picture of legal procedure during the monarchic period. The prospects and dangers become clear. The "you" being addressed here is the "subject" of the court case. The person identified as "you" is not just someone who is involved in a case as a defendant or witness, this is a "judge," in other words, someone who renders a decision. It depends upon "you" – any free Israelite – whether justice will be perverted or not (verse 2); in other words it is a matter of life and death for the person brought before the court (verse 7). "You" will decide whether or not rumors determine the direction of the court proceeding (verse 1). And above all, "you" are responsible for whether the most dangerous form of power, the majority, would be permitted the only say (verse 2).

The free individual being addressed in the Book of the Covenant is responsible for everything. It is the duty of this person and this person alone to see that justice, as it is formulated in the Book of the Covenant, is meted out. No king, no state, no professional judge or jurist comes before him.

In the Israelite court of the monarchic period, the great opportunity implied by the absence of formalized responsibility and power and the concomitant potential inclusion of any free male, is at the same time its greatest danger. The discussion of the "many" (*rabbīm*) in verse 2, which ultimately is powerful because it is a majority, is certainly a key

---

it is possible to identify four strata. His editing is a model of what can happen if the text itself is given no chance before beginning literary-critical structural analysis.

to this understanding. There must be criteria independent of the majority (after all, who can or should ultimately be trusted?) precisely where majority justice is perverted, to give a place from which justice can establish its perspective. The pressure that arises from the mixing together of rumors (verse 1), majorities (verse 2), power (verse 1), money (verse 8), etc. becomes apparent in these verses. Nevertheless, according to the Book of the Covenant, the court at the gate of monarchic period cities (thus, the state judiciary) is the only place where matters of life or death, good or evil, and guilt or innocence are to be handled.

The word of God formulated in verse 7b, which is of primary concern, is that both the guilty and the innocent should receive justice. As God is gracious to the poor and oppressed (22:26), he does not acquit the guilty. It is the intention of this text as well as the entire Book of the Covenant to hinder the activities of the guilty. For the sake of the victim and that person's rights, there can be no rule of justice that exists on the basis of the reverse of 27b and evades the truth formulated here.

Still, even with all these rules governing the practise of the Mishpatim, only one half has been said. For how do these people receive justice, the ones who are deprived of their rights in the mishmash of power and divine law – the poor, the dependent, the inferior? Furthermore, we can never simply presume that they are the righteous and the innocent. It is equally difficult just to employ the categories of guilt and innocence in the formal sense with them. This problem is approached in the composition's mutually contradictory instructions.

In verses 3 and 6 we are first dealing with the poor in their "lawsuit" (*ribbō*). Verse 6 formulates the central point: justice (*mišpāt*) for the poor should not be perverted. This is precisely what the prophets said over and over again.[413] Nevertheless, verse 3 first addresses a different problem with an unusual formulation. The people should not "be partial to (*hdr*) the weak (*dal*) in a lawsuit." Frequently, the mention of the "insignificant" or "weak" (*dal*) is altered to "great" (*gādōl*),[414] for which Hebrew only requires the addition of a single letter, and then it correlates with the parallel passages (especially Lev 19:15). Nevertheless, there is no support for this conjecture in the history of the text. Such a change is purely arbitrary and runs contrary to the apparent intention of the text.

But neither should a person who is socially oppressed count on partiality. The verb *hdr* is used elsewhere in the Old Testament above all for the reverence offered to an older person.[415] We may not conclude from the parallel passage, Lev 19:15, that this is about a legal terminus. For that reason the usual translation "prefer, show preference for" is problematic. Justice for the poor should not be perverted, but on the other hand, a poor person should not be treated with special respect as a king or an older person would be.

---

413 E.g. Am 2:7; 5:10; Isa 1:23; 10:1 and many others.
414 E.g. Baentsch, Holzinger, Noth, commentaries – in part; otherwise Childs, Scharbert, Willi-Plein, commentaries – in part.
415 Lev 19:32; Thr 5:12 (niph.); and with the nouns in Prov 20:29. The latter is involved with various kinds of splendor, especially God and the king. See Warmuth, article on *hādār*.

Independent of all legal problems, rules for mercy are formulated in verses 23:4f., the center of this unified passage. If the "framing" verses are about justice and guilt, here we find the stray animal and beasts lying down under their load. These are suffering domestic animals that are the property of one's personal enemies and opponents.[416] Behavior toward these animals should not be determined by relationships with their owners and possible lawsuits.

We are dealing with a clear graduation: one's legal opponents (verses 1f., 6f.) – those who are legally and socially weak (verses 3, 6) – those who suffer and are without justice (verses 4f.) The facts that, according to Prov 12:10, a righteous person knows the "soul" of his animals, and according to Ps 36:7, God saves animals as well as people, point to the correlation with which we are dealing here. Those who are weak and suffering ought to be helped, whether they are people or animals, friends or enemies. On the other hand, the guilty are to be condemned, even where they are powerful and try to assert their rights.

Nevertheless, those who are poor are not permitted to enjoy a "distinction" that allows them to evade the categories of guilt and innocence. The formulations show quite clearly where the real dangers lie: that sympathy stops because of animosity, that justice is denied to the poor, that the majority exerts pressure, and that money and power dominate justice. We encounter all of these in this early reflection on the relationship of justice and mercy.

d. JUSTICE OR ETHICS? THE LEGAL CHARACTER OF SOCIAL COMMANDMENTS

The Book of the Covenant is shaped by the thoughts that the rights of aliens, the poor and other exploited people are demands of God to his people that have the same importance as the basic religious principles of the exclusive veneration of God (together with the regulations regarding sacrifice and celebrations). The literary development of this connection is the birthplace of Torah, and it is a central event for biblical theological history and its conception of God. This was already occuring in the prophets of the eighth century, but only in a negative way. Thus, Isaiah confronted the dominant statutory law that held the poor in check by means of a concept of law that robbed and withheld from the poor and by which they were pushed aside.[417] What really collapsed in eighth-century Jerusalem (and actually was a reality only in an idealized past),[418] was expressed in the Book of the Covenant in the form of a legal document.

With increasing clarity, scholarship has grasped and described this process.[419] There is, however, much less consensus on the matter of what actually happened in relation to the instructions and commandments concerned. They appear, unlike the Mishpatim or other ancient Near Eastern law, as commandments from God and they rely expressly on the action of God as their standard and foundation (especially Ex 22:26; 23:7).

416 See Barbiero, *L'asino*.
417 Especially Isa 1:23, 21, 26; 10:1f.; also 5:7 and others. See e.g. Kessler, *Staat* 46ff. and elsewhere.
418 Especially Isa 1:21, 26.
419 First Halbe, *Privilegrecht*.

Are these demands "law?" Are they to be regarded as legislation in the same sense as the Mishpatim or other "statutes" – always thought of separately?[420] Earlier research regarded this as "apodictic law," and Alt even believed that the specifically Israelite law was based in the wilderness.[421] Nevertheless, in my opinion, the investigation of the juridical function of such formulations, in the strictest sense, and their function in a mixed corpus, like the Book of the Covenant, has never been precisely formulated.

Today, E. Otto especially has maintained and thoroughly supported their differentiation from real law.[422] It is worthwhile to study his theses since they formulate the claim in the context of contemporary sociology and legal scholarship. Otto speaks of a "separating out of ancient Israelite ethos from law." He finds that there is an omission of "a provision for sanction in cases where laws are not followed" for the slave law of Ex 21:2–11, the provisions for social protection of Ex 22:20–26* and for Ex 23:4f.[423] It should follow from this that "the suitability of the case for the legal process is given up in favor of ethical exhortation ... whereby the legal sphere might be abandoned."[424] A statement like the following is particularly instructive: "Lacking this further development of provisions for social protection and sanction from law to ethos (and thus the power of the judicial institution to carry them out), norms that have the intention of potential preference for the economically disadvantaged over those who have more point all the more toward voluntary compliance and thus insight."[425] The "broken line" of "cracked Israelite society" would be thus the starting point for the development of an ethos independent of the law.[426] According to Otto a new correlation of societal foundations, which would be able to transcend what exists in the disorder of society, is found in the concept of God, not in law.

Our goal here is to establish, on the one hand, a rather ordinary description of what happened in Old Testament legal history (e.g. in the structure of the Book of the Covenant and in the increasing theologization of law, as provisions for social protection were integrated into the Torah). Otto describes this process as a "refining out" of ethos from law and thus he makes use of an exegetical and legal-historical understanding that in my opinion is theologically rather oblique. In the following points I will summarize my critique and offer an alternative point of view.

– There is no way that we can define the nature of law by examining the characteristics of sanctions alone. The thesis that "provisions for indemnification and sanction (are) characteristics of laws, thus

---

420 For the problem of the legal status of ancient Near Eastern legal corpora, see Kraus, *Problem*; Preiser, *Nature*; Renger, *Hammurabis Stele*; Krecher, *Rechtsleben*; Westbrook, *Lawcodes*; also Klima, *gegebenheiten*; Roth, *Scholastic Tradition*. See also above pp. 10ff.
421 Alt, *Urspringe*, especially 330f.
422 Especially Otto, *Ausdifferenzierung*.
423 Otto, *Ausdifferenzierung* 145.
424 Otto, *Ausdifferenzierung* 145.
425 Otto, *Ausdifferenzierung* 145f.
426 Otto, *Ausdifferenzierung* 149.

evaluations of the legal consequences of an act",[427] is decidedly too narrow. Definitions and apodictic formulations are also a part of law, whether it be of the ancient Near East, the Mishpatim, or of our own time.

Provisions for consequences in laws are not the only criterion for legislation, especially not in the external form of certain types of law. Otto himself considers certain commands and prohibitions to be a part of law, for example Ex 23:1–3, 6–8, even though there are no sanctions attached.[428] If someone did not free a slave in accord with the provisions of Ex 21:2ff., how would he be distinguished, in principle, from someone who did not pay a fine that had been imposed?

Cultic laws and other religious legislation only very infrequently have direct sanctions attached. According to Ex 22:24ff., a society can sanction inappropriately harsh requirements for pledges to obtain credit either informally or formally as failure to measure up to other norms. This means, however, that the legal character of individual provisions does not depend upon either the pure form of the law itself or above all, it is independent of the presence of provisions for legal consequences alone.

- The introduction of the authority of God does not directly affect the character of the provisions as law. Furthermore, the long history of divine law in its various forms should not cause us to doubt our evaluation.[429] We need refer only to the fact that the legal character of provisions of this kind is ultimately dependent upon whom they satisfy and to what degree. Thus, the question of how serious the legal consequences were for the person who exploited aliens (especially within the Israelite legal system), depends upon who might win a legal proceeding at the gate. The thesis that the religious authority behind legislation affected its legal character only makes sense if we ignore the question of force or power in legal matters, or – and this is more likely – if we have a vague idea of an objectively present, but non-religious authority that carries out the law. Are we presupposing like a religiously neutral modern state with its apparatus of power[430] in this?

- For this reason we should not speak of a "refining out of ethics from law," because this only makes sense under the presumption that the older law contained norms, from which written laws like the Book of the Covenant developed. Literarily – and this deals with the substance itself, not just external process – exactly the opposite is the case: various themes from which the individual norms came were

---

427 Otto, *Ausdifferenzierung* 143f.
428 Otto, *Ausdifferenzierung* 147f.; ibid., *Rechtsbegründingen.*
429 See Dreier, *Göttliches Recht* 369ff.
430 The formulation, "Without this further development of formulations for sanction in provisions for social protection (and thus the power of the judicial institution to carry them out) from law to ethos" (Otto, *Ausdifferenzierung* 145) shows that legislation ought to be concluded on the basis of power relationships. Nevertheless, it could hardly be this simple. The question whether codification is able to compel or otherwise prevail upon a judicial institution to observe its laws cannot be reduced to study of the laws.

gathered into a *single* legal document. This is what is new, and in the history of law, what is also surprising. This is not the usual, frequently attested juxtaposition of legal provisions on the one hand, and on the other, of ethics presented, for example, in proverbs.

The process of the development of the basic structure of the Torah is not a "distilling," to use Otto's phrase. If we wanted to use his term, we must relate it to the procedure in such a way that even a code like the Mishpatim with provisions for sanction and social protection are not "distilled" from the flexible and not completely formulated norms of the pre-state society shaped by solidarity and "amity."[431] We can probably say that the law in legal documents and ethics, for example, of earlier wisdom is refined out of the early norm tradition, but not classified as ethics or law.

How are we to understand the arrangement together in one corpus of overlapping, somewhat "ethical" sounding demands (e.g. the "apodictic" provisions for social protection) with other legal traditions? It will be helpful for us to examine modern analogies closely. The reduction of law to factual, practicable and in a sense "statutory law," excludes important aspects, not just in view of the ethical but also the juridical. In the debate regarding the modern, positivist conception of law, it has been convincingly argued

> . . . that the judge is also legally bound in the area of so-called "discretion" [In other words, not just ethically], and in a way that restores a necessary connection between law and morality. The basis of this thesis is the structural difference between rules and principles . . . Rules are norms that consist of the facts of the case and the legal consequences in such a way that the legal consequences always take effect when the facts apply. In contrast to this, principles are . . . tenders of optimization that can be fulfilled in a variety of ways – in other words, norms enjoining that something (a goal or a value) be realized to the highest possible degree.[432]

Thus, legally valid principles here make "the approximative realization of a moral ideal into a legal obligation." We can also say by right it is "required . . . as much as possible in the case of vagueness and collision of norms, for law 'as it is' to approach law 'as it should be.'"[433] In modern times such principles or "tenders of optimization" are especially to be found in provisions for fundamental rights as well as catalogs of human rights and determiners of national goals. "These claim validity as 'value-setting fundamental rights' for all areas of law and obligate all three powers of the state as much as possible to strive for dignity, freedom and equality in fact and in law."[434]

431 See e.g. Fleischer, *Von Menschenverkäufern* 302ff., in summary 344f.
432 Dreier, *Begriff des Rechts* 104. In this work, Dreier summarizes broad juridical discussions of the concept of law, especially the problem of the positivist conception of law. Of special importance is Dworkin, *Bürgerrechte*; see also Alexy, *Grundrechte*; for a discussion see Sieckmann, *Regelmodelle*; for the actual position, see Dreier, *Begriff des Rechts* 117ff.
433 Dreier, *Begriff des Rechts* 105.
434 Dreier, *Begriff des Rechts* 105 in conjunction with the formulations of the federal constitutional court.

In view of the wide juridical debate over these problems, which theology has approached, at least in the area of human rights,[435] it would be improper to separate law and ethics in the way that Otto has done. Of course, we must take care not to transfer modern structures and concepts back into ancient Israelite law, but in this distillation (and here the term is proper), they can show that it is not simply a matter of either/or with the imbedding of law into the more comprehensive question of the validity of ethical norms of various kinds.

This is true above all where both are consciously (unlike both the ancient Near Eastern and its own earlier tradition) combined into a single legal corpus. When the earlier "statutory" law of the Mishpatim was brought into the Book of the Covenant and was amended to include sweeping and corrective provisions for the protection of the weak, for behavior in court or for equality under the law (talion law), something extremely important for law was taking place.

The same thing Isaiah did in Isa 10:1f. when he criticized the written, "statutory law," holding it up to a larger standard of justice, happens in the Book of the Covenant in this transformation into a new law. Of course, the Mishpatim were still valid, but were amplified and corrected by the regulations for protection of aliens, the poor, widows and orphans as well as animals.

These regulations are extremely important for a proper understanding of the Mishpatim, and their exposition and use is even more so. We must probably understand the intent of the Mishpatim to be oriented and gauged by these laws. We might put it somewhat crudely that the provisions for social protection function in the Mishpatim in the same way that human rights operate in statutory law in our own day: They are meta-norms and critical authority. The tension between law and justice is taken up here within the law itself – and by no means as part of an ethic that does not affect the law – and it becomes an important principle of Torah. It is part of its very structure that "regulations" are always accompanied by "principles." This tension within Torah came about with the development of the Book of the Covenant.[436]

Pondering a Catastrophe: The Development of the Book of the Covenant

The Procedure of Codification

The Book of the Covenant is the oldest legal document of the Old Testament, and with it was developed the basic structure of Torah. The

---

435 Huber/Tödt, *Menschenrechte* especially Chapter II.
436 The question pursued here regarding the legal status of the provisions for social protection is not the same as the the the one debated between Greenberg (*Postulates; More Reflections*) and Jackson (*Reflections*), whether recognizable principles are at the root of biblical legislation. Nevertheless, there are correlations, because the question (whether we must interpret the "apodictic" provisions for protection as principles, which must be classified as correction for the regulations and their use) is possibly the explicitness of the principles, which Jackson missed. The principles are not always at the root but are associated with each other as correction in the literary process.

following can be said about the process itself and the circumstances under which it happened:

– As sources the two oldest sources that can be reconstructed are the Mishpatim, the law book of the Jerusalem high court which closely parallels other ancient Near Eastern legal corpora, and a collection of basic regulations regarding the exclusive veneration of YHWH, which were formulated in the northern kingdom as an alternative to the state cult of calf images.

– The Book of the Covenant combined both in a compact form through the promise of God's presence on the journey. The most important new accents were provisions for protection of aliens and the poor as well as instructions for justice in the courts. The ethical standard by which the prophets of the southern kingdom criticized the social developments and their causes were written down here as divine law.

– In the Book of the Covenant the individual, free, property-owning male is addressed in the second person. What began in the sources was continued, so that this became a decisive legal subject through the word of God.

Outside of these clearly recognizable characteristics, all other circumstances of the codification are unknown to us. At best we can only make hypotheses. Nevertheless, if we are careful, we can still make the following observations:

The Book of the Covenant is formulated as the word of God and thus lays claim to divine authority. On the other hand, we cannot tell from its wording that it was given in the distant past, perhaps even at Sinai, or that it required the mediation of a figure like Moses.[437] It is only in the later supplementary strata that historicization enters the picture. The main composition must be interpreted as the direct Word of God in the present.

For an understanding of the process of codification it is, of course, important which human authorities were such that they could and did speak in the name of God. It is also important to note that not only the collection of the Mishpatim, but also the main composition itself, must derive from juridically versed groups. Especially the introduction of the institution of sanctuary asylum for a perpetrator who had committed unintentional homicide (Ex 21:13f.) is a legal-historical act of the greatest significance.[438]

Earlier ancient Near Eastern and Israelite provisions are developed parallel to the Draconian law of Greece, but at an earlier time. It was not only necessary that there be a juridically trained author behind this (also to a degree behind the corrective insertion of the talion formula, 21:24f., and the inclusion of the "apodictic" provisions for social protection), there must also have been an institution of unquestionable juridical

437 For Ex 23:20ff., see above pp. 178ff. as well as the observations in Osumi, *Kompositionsgeschichte* 187, 220.
438 See above pp. 174ff.

authority. For this reason we may theorize that the Jerusalem high court, to which we may trace back the collecting of the Mishpatim,[439] also had something to do with the codification completed in the Book of the Covenant.

Since this institution included both priests and laity, which corresponds exactly with the breadth of subjects contained within the Book of the Covenant, we would not be able *a priori* to dispute that it had the authority to formulate something as God's Word. Nevertheless, there are problems here, as the supplementary stratum and the totality of further Israelite legal history demonstrate.

The extremely important theme of the aliens directs us compellingly to the period after the fall of Samaria. Not least because of its relationship to Deuteronomy, we would not be permitted to separate the development of the Book of the Covenant too far from the events of 722 BCE. It might have originated at the end of the eighth or the beginning of the seventh centuries. Thus, the Book of the Covenant is the most important theological work to come out of the catastrophe of the northern kingdom.

The prominent theological heritage of the northern kingdom combined regulations for the exclusive veneration of Israel's God with a juridical Jerusalem law book in the tradition of ancient Near Eastern law. To this there was added an important new accent from the social-critical prophecy of the southern kingdom in order to avoid the same judgment which had been announced for the southern kingdom. Something new came about through this combining of different elements that was more than the sum of its parts: the basic structure of the Torah. It proved to be a productive new structure of rather disparate parts of the tradition. Revelation happens here as a creative association of elements of the tradition.

Dating the development to the period after the end of the northern kingdom, above all, prompts us to regard the Book of the Covenant as a law book of King Hezekiah, corresponding to the connection of Josiah and deuteronomic law.[440] Nevertheless, the evidence rather argues against this. Hezekiah's reforms mentioned in 2 Kg 18:4ff., apart from their historical problems,[441] basically have nothing to do with the demands of the Book of the Covenant. There is no attestation for social reforms like those that had to come at the very first from the Book of the Covenant. Furthermore, the Isaiah texts from the years 705–701 (especially Isa 28ff.) do not portray Hezekiah in any way as a social reformer. Thus nothing is known about a direct, immediate effect of the Book of the Covenant.

Cultic Historicization: Later Interpretation

The Book of the Covenant presents a clearly recognizable redaction stratum, clearly different from its context.[442] Passages with address in the

439 See above pp. 166f.
440 Albertz, *Religionsgeschichte* 341ff. For a critique, see also Osumi, *Kompositionsgeschichte* 177ff.
441 For the question whether there might be an identifiable historical process behind the deuteronomistic formulations, see the controversial interpretations of Donner, *Geschichte II* 331f.; Speickermann, *Juda* 170ff., Hutter, *Hiskija*; Conrad, *Miszellen*; Cogan/Tadmor, *2 Kings* 281ff.
442 See especially Osumi, *Kompositionsgeschichte* 50ff., 183ff.

second person plural, which especially characterize the beginning and the supplement, are different than the juridically very precise, second person singular, because of their character, and in a few cases they distort clearly older correlations. Scholarship has known this for a long time, but for the most part labeled these deuteronomistic and then resisted working out the details.[443] As close as they are to deuteronomistic language, they are not typical and they illustrate important differences in style and content.[444]

The allowances made for aliens (22:20; 23:9) and the poor (22:24ff.) are amplified by the mention of widows and orphans as additional social-problem groups. Nevertheless we note the omission of any of the groups of four with the Levites, typical of Deuteronomy.[445] The protection of aliens from oppression is supported and strengthened significantly by a reference to Israel's own status as slaves in Egypt as Deuteronomy knows it.[446] This theme can be applied in many and varied contexts as support, but in the Book of the Covenant it remains limited to the theme of the alien. Furthermore, the final form of the Book of the Covenant is pre-deuteronomic.

The clearest new content accent of the redaction stratum makes a double connection to money (or gold and silver). At the beginning of the corpus we find the admonition:

> Ex 20:23 *You shall not make "me,"*[447] *nor shall you make for yourselves gods of gold or silver.*

This prohibition[448] against images[449] certainly incorporates the criticism of calf images in the northern kingdom that we hear frequently in

443 See the overview of older positions in Otto, *Rechtsbegründungen* 4. Similarly, see Schwienhorst-Schönberger, *Bundesbuch* in summary p. 286.
444 For what follows in detail Beyerlin, *Paränese*; especially Osumi, *Kompositionsgeschichte*; Lohfink, *Bearbeitung*.
445 Lohfink, *Bearbeitung* 96ff.
446 Lohfink, *Bearbeitung* 100ff.
447 Verse 23a in MT contains an incomprehensible anacolouthon ("You shall not make with/alongside me") and for that reason is either freely amplified (for example, Baentsch, Dillman, Holzinger and other commentaries); or contrary to the verse division, it is attached to verse 23b (e.g. Zenger, *Sinaitheophanie* 68 note 56; Hossfeld, *Dekalog* 180), or simply declared secondary (Dohmen, *Bilderverbot* 157). The problem is in the preposition "with/alongside" ('*itti*), which in this context is singular and hardly understandable. If we operate from the consonant text, we might consider the accusative particle ('*ōti*). There is attestation in verse 23b and many other parallels (Ex 34:17; Lev 19:4; 26:1 and others) that gods might be manufactured '*śh* '*elōhim*; see Dohmen, *Bilderverbot* 176ff. It is self-evident that such a text (the prohibition of the manufacture of a YHWH image by God in first person) would later become objectionable and be read in a different way.
448 There are many attempts to divide the beginning of the Book of the Covenant (20:22b, 23) into several literary strata and classify these with theological schools; see e.g. Hossfeld, *Dekalog* 176; Dohmen, *Bilderverbot* 155ff.; Schwienhorst-Schönberger 278ff.; for a discussion and critique, see Osumi, *Kompositionsgeschichte* 187ff. I follow his thesis that the introduction to the Book of the Covenant might not have been designed for its present context (192). Taken on its own it presents no ground for literary stratification.
449 For the prohibition against images, see Dohmen, *Bilderverbot*; for the wording of the decalogue see Crüsemann 47ff.; most recently especially Kennedy, *Social Background*; Tsevat, *Prohibition*; Hossfeld, *Funktion*; Hendel, *Images*.

Isaiah.[450] In this combination of God and gold/silver we should not forget the fact that the same stratum continues and amplifies the loan regulations of Ex 22:23aα by inserting the prohibition against usury[451] (24aβ). The protection of the poor is thus appreciably strengthened (cf Deut 23:20ff.; Lev 25:36f.).

So that we might analyze this supplementary stratum more precisely, let us note the following. As we know, the prohibition against usury appears, independent of the law books, in cultic texts from the Jerusalem shrine.[452] According to Ps 15:5, the taking of interest led to cultic disqualification and prevented access to the shrine.[453] We draw the same conclusion from cultic formularies prepared by the priest-prophet Ezekiel (18:8; 22:12 and elsewhere). The concern is with social aspects of cultic impurity. Ex 22:31: "You shall be people consecrated to me" [literally "You ought to be men of the shrine . . ."] . . . "and avoid eating mangled meat," both have similar implications. The concern is with access to the vicinity of the holy place.

The new introduction to the whole shows that the supplementary stratum brings the Book of the Covenant into a close relationship with the Jerusalem temple and cult.[454] Even before the prohibition of gold and silver images of God (20:23), we find the sentence: "You have seen for yourselves that I spoke with you from heaven" (20:22b).

In the present context of the Sinai pericope, it is almost inconceivable that there is no reference to the Decalogue, possibly even to the divine speech in Ex 19. However, neither of these speeches is spoken downward from heaven. This sentence cannot be explained on the basis of the literary context.[455] The people being addressed are reminded of an experience during which they had "seen" the voice of God.[456] If we want parallels, we will find them in the Jerusalem cult Psalms. Ps 76:9 speaks downward from God's court in heaven, and this does not contradict his presence on Zion (verse 3).

The historic-fictional vesting of this address was an especially important step which began in the later strata of the Book of the Covenant. There is clear reference to a fictional point before the conquest of the land in formulations like 23:28f. The authority speaking here is lodged in the past. This is how the process of historicization, so extremely important for the history of law, happens in this supplementary stratum.

450 Especially Isa 2:7f.; cf 2:20, 31:7.
451 For the biblical prohibition against usury, see especially Klingenberg, *Zinsverbot*; see also Hejcl, *Zinsverbot*; Neufeld, *Prohibition*; Cohen, *Backgrounds*; Gamoran, *Biblical Law*; for a legal comparison, see also Maloney, *Usury and Restriction*; ibid., *Usury*; for the terminology employed (*néek* in Lev 25:35f. and elsewhere, parallel *tarbit*) Loewenstamm, *nšk*; Lipínski, *Nešek*; for post-biblical Jewish law Salomon, *Le prêt à l'intérêt*; Gamoran, *Talmudic Usury*; ibid., *Talmudic Law*; Weingort-Boczko, *L'interdiction*; ibid., *Le prêt à l'intérêt*; for recent reception of the biblical tradition, for example, Nelson, *Biblical Idea*.
452 See Otto, *Kultus und Ethos*.
453 For this and for a comparison with the Ezekiel parallels, see Beyerlin, *Heilsordnung* 47ff.
454 With Osumi, *Kompositionsgeschichte* 210f.
455 See Osumi, *Kompositionsgeschichte* 185f.
456 Or "see" The AK forms could generally be present tense meaning, "You see that I am speaking with you from heaven."

Within the supplementary stratum the people gathered for the cult are addressed in the second person plural. The legally precise second person singular, referring to each of the Israelites, is amplified and and above all, framed by a homiletical device (20:22b; 23/23:31b). Cult psalms like Ps 50, 81, 95 shed light on the background against which this historicization took place. There is divine address in these psalms, which of course is supposed to refer to the later monarchic or exilic periods in Israel, but which has been incorporated into a particular moment of the salvation history.

The historical chasm that the emphatic "today" of Deuteronomy must bridge again seems nonexistent. The edited Book of the Covenant seems to think of itself as a "sermon," and thus is probably (part of) that proclamation of the divine name which alone can guarantee his presence (Ex 20:24). The transition from a law book to a cultic speech that is completed in the supplementary stratum is connected with the step toward historicization.

Another aspect points to the historical background of the process. Can we really separate the tremendous conflict with extremely powerful enemy nations, as they are reflected in the appendix,[457] from the incorporation of Judah in the Assyrian annexation? There is good reason that this might have occurred somewhat after 701 BCE, under Manasseh, when temple and king were obligated to loyalty against Assyria, in order to bring the divine law of the Book of the Covenant to strengthened significance based on a new invulnerable authority, to which the past of the salvation history referred. Still, framing this as a speech by an authority figure who was distant and long-gone (but nevertheless applicable to the Israel of the present) is a marginal phenomenon, which is only really developed as the Book of the Covenant is integrated into the Sinai pericope. It is, however, in Deuteronomy that we see what historicization was capable of achieving.

---

457 Especially 23:28–31a repeats the beginning 23:20ff. in a much more aggressive
    form. These passages, like verse 23, are to be regarded, together with the plural
    stratum (23:21b, 25a, 31ba), as older than Deut 7. See Osumi, *Kompositions-*
    geschichte 204ff., 212ff.

6

꧁꧂

Deuteronomy:
The Formational Development

> *No Democracy without Socialism, no*
> *Socialism without Democracy.*
>
> Ernst Bloch[1]

Continuity and Reassessment: The Historical Locale

With deuteronomic law (Deut 12–26)[2] Israel again attempted to formulate the will of her God in a law book. Normally, laws are extrapolated, changed and supplemented as the circumstances change. This is what we found in the Book of the Covenant. The sources employed for this work had already shown the effects of previous amplification and adaptation,[3] finally a supplementary stratum was added to the whole.[4] We will see this to an even greater degree in Deuteronomy itself, which shows many traces of alteration to make it more relevant. Contrasting with this continued manipulation of older material, there was an entirely new codification, which represented a radical change. It was connected with profoundly significant stimuli and notably altered circumstances – we are reminded, for example, of the constitutional law newly established after the Second World War and the Third Reich, which survived even the annexation of the GDR without a new constitution. Why did such a situation arise in Israel? Why were the opportunities for amplification and extrapolation no longer adequate? These questions will serve as a guide in the discussions that follow.

Extrapolation, Expansion, Conceptualization: The Relationship to the Book of the Covenant

The relationship of deuteronomic law to the older Book of the Covenant, viewed as a whole, compels us to regard the more recent document as a

---

1 *Naturrecht and Menschliche Würde* 232. Bloch defined the term is this way for Rosa Luxemburg (especially *Revolution* 133ff.).
2 The following portrayal concentrates upon the problems of deuteronomic law (Deut 12–26). The other portions of the Book of Deuteronomy including the many problems being discussed by scholars will only be addressed to the degree that it is necessary for an appropriate understanding of the law. For the state of the discussions of Deuteronomy, see Preuss, *Deuteronomium*; McBride, article on Deuteronomium; Lohfink, article on Deuteronomium; Clements, *Deuteronomy*.
3 See above pp. 114ff., 144ff.
4 See above pp. 197ff.

replacement for the older one. The decisive features, which made the Book of the Covenant different from other ancient Near Eastern law codes, were adopted by Deuteronomy and expanded. Thus, the whole appears as the command of Israel's God, even if at the same time it appears through the authority of Moses in a new way, having at its center the first commandment, the exclusive veneration of YHWH. The people being addressed are free, propertied Israelites. Just as in the Book of the Covenant, widely disparate traditions of theology, cult, law and ethos are held together in a single law book.

There are even similarities in the overall structure: at the center (Deut 12) there is an altar law with regulations for legitimate sacrifice and divine presence, and at the end provisions for blessing and cursing (Deut 27f.), which correlate in a special way with themes of the appendix of the Book of the Covenant (Ex 23:20ff.). Above all, a whole series of individual laws from the Book of the Covenant are repeated with alteration.[5] Thus, we find an adapted slave law (Deut 15:12ff.), a calendar of festivals with the same principle feasts (16). There are rules for behavior in court (16:19f.) and for the treatment of other people's animals (22:1f.) which obviously repeat the corresponding passages in the Book of the Covenant with variation.

These compel us to interpret deuteronomic law not as an amplification of the Book of the Covenant, but rather as a replacement for it. It seems that the intent was to be a new version containing the basic decisions as well as a large part of material law. It was only in the development of the entire Pentateuch that both of these law books were integrated into a single literary entity.

Indeed, changes from the Book of the Covenant are significant. The most significant new content accents are the character of Deuteronomy as the speech of Moses rather than God, thus shifting the speech from the present into the distant past. In the logic of centralizing the entire cult to a single, legitimate shrine (Deut 12), there is a radicalization of the concentration (which occurred in the Book of the Covenant) of cultic activity to the several shrines at which God causes his name to be proclaimed (Ex 20:24ff.).

Important parts of the Book of the Covenant were shortened significantly. This is true of the provisions regarding homicide and physical injury as well as property crimes.[6] On the other hand, the provisions for protection of the socially and legally impoverished,[7] established above as "principles," were significantly expanded. In addition, there are detailed regulations regarding family and sexual law – for example, virginity (Deut 22:13ff.), the remarriage of divorced persons (24:1ff.) – of which there was only a single example in the context of property law (Ex

---

5 For a comparison with the Book of the Covenant, see Preuss, *Deuteronomium* 104ff.; especially Chamberlain, *Study*.

6 The omission of the sabbath here (see below p. 203) might incline us to think that this was an intentional alteration. In fact, this has indeed been the course of the history of Jewish law. Still, there are so many reasons that argue that this was not the author of Deuteronomy's intention from the outset, that we should initially attempt to solve the problem differently, in other words, from the conception of Deuteronomy itself.

7 See above pp. 191ff.

22:15f.). There are the broad regulations in the middle section (Deut 16:18–20:20), where institutions like the monarchy, law, priesthood, prophecy and war are addressed, thus a wide sphere of activity that was omitted in the Book of the Covenant and other ancient Near Eastern law. Basically, it is only in modern constitutions that we find parallels to these regulations.

One problem shows with particular clarity how difficult it is to determine the relationship of the two legal corpora. The weekly day of rest, which already had played a central role in Ex 34:21, and which together with the sabbath year formed a central pillar of the compositional structure, is completely absent in Deuteronomy. It appears as merely one of the commandments of the Decalogue in Deut 5:12ff. In so doing, however, this use of the divine address proclaimed on Horeb could hardly have been the literary heart of this legal code.[8] Why is it missing? The great significance of the sabbath in deuteronomic texts should be borne in mind. The fact that we still do not have a real explanation for this shows how imperfectly Deuteronomy and its the relation to the Book of the Covenant has thus far been understood.

There is another area that must be mentioned, which opens another, completely new world, that of *theological reflections upon the law,* which analyze its meaning and the significance of this gift from God to his people. They are found in Deut 6–11 and 30f. and have no counterpart in the Book of the Covenant. There is a new theological language shaped here, determinative for every biblically oriented theology since.[9] This linguistic phenomenon is why we call Deuteronomy the *form that shapes* in Torah.

A few texts should suffice. There is Deut 6:20ff., where the children's question about the meaning of the command and customs is answered with reference to exodus, liberation and the gift of the land. Thus, its meaning is oriented both in the freedom story of God with his people and the stated present. There is, of course, Deut 7:6ff. which is the *locus classicus* for the concept of election (*bhr*).[10] It is only because of God's boundless love (7:8) that little Israel was chosen from all the nations (7:7). This love made itself concrete when God realized his promises to the patriarchs: in the liberating act of the exodus, in the gift of the land, and the love is also expressed in the commandments which guarantee the continued presence of this God among his people. We should also mention concepts like covenant (*berit*)[11] and Torah,[12] the *name* of God, and certainly not least the Shma 'Yisrael (6:4ff.), illustrating a conceptually sharp grasp of the unity and uniqueness of this God, which outstrips and radicalizes the older versions of the first commandment, approaching the

8 See Brekelmans, *Deuteronomy* 5. For the overwhelmingly complex topic of stratification, see the model overviews in the strata tables of Preuss, *Deuteronomium* 46ff. as well as Braulik, *Deuteronomium* 9ff.
9 For the significance of the theological terminology of Deuteronomy, see e.g. Herrmann, *Restauration*; Smend, *Theologie*; Braulik, *Evangelium* and others.
10 See especially Rendtorff, *Erwählung*.
11 See Perlitt, *Bundestheologie* 54ff.; Kutsch, *Verheissung*.
12 See Braulik, *Ausdrücke*; Lindars, *Torah*.

very threshold of monotheism.[13] Deuteronomic law taken as a whole is about the unity of God and the totality of the love for him, which is required of Israel, "with all your heart, with all your soul and with all your strength," throughout all activities of life, which are briefly summarized here.

We should not, however, analyze away the gift of Torah, God's love comprehended in commandments for life: it is the center, the shape of the connection between God and his people, the gift with which alone the liberating relationship can be established and verified. The fact that Christians believe they can cling to this theological reflection of an experience of God, which here became word, without the contents around which all of this speech revolves, without Torah, the deuteronomic law in Deut 12–26, means that they have a problem. This cuts out the heart and life of the theology and can only end in deadly formality.

Since this all deals with extrapolation – expansive, substantive amplification and a new kind of theological reflection – in which there are only a very few cases of substantive correction, most of these steps could be regarded as literary adaptation of the Book of the Covenant. Even a comparison of contents cannot answer the question about the reason for this new codification; the real reason could not be in the contents.

Basic Features of Stratification and Composition

We are now ready to ask, in view of the Book of the Covenant, why there is a new legal-historical document in Deuteronomy and what caused it, especially given the many traces and hints of theological emendation within the book.

Of course, several generations worked on Deuteronomy. Today it is no longer disputed that we have the book in a deuteronomistic, in other words, a later exilic form.[14] There is general acknowledgement that, for example, Deut 1–3 correlates with the deuteronomistic history from Josh through 2 Kg and with the embedding of Deuteronomy into this history. We can probably make a similar assignment for Deut 4, together with the related passages in Deut 29f.[15] Deut 4 demonstrates a great similarity to exilic/postexilic theology, especially that of deutero-Isaiah. Nevertheless, today large parts of Deut 5–11 or 12–26 are considered to be late supplementary material.[16] For whole chapters such as 5:9f. or the constitutional provisions in 16:18–18:22[17] this is maintained *en bloc*; for

---

13 From the wealth of literature, we would mention Nielsen, *Ein Jawe*; Suzuki, *Perspectives*; Höffken, *Bemerkung*; Janzen, *Most important word*; Moberly, *Yahweh is one*; for the proximity to "monotheism," see Crüsemann, *5. Mose* 6; also Braulik, *Geburt*; critical, Heller, *Sjemaʿ*.
14 See the overview of the discussion in Preuss, *Deuteronomium*.
15 See Knapp, *Deuteronomium 4*; for this see Lohfink, critique of Knapp.
16 In addition to the commentaries, we would refer to Hempel, *Schichten*; Plöger, *Untersuchungen*; Seitz, *Studien*; Merendino, *Gesetz*; finally, e.g. Suzuki in Walkenhorst, *Neueste Deuteronomismusforschung*. For chapters 1–5, see e.g. Lopez, *Analyse*; Peckham, *Composition*; Achenbach, *Israel*. The discussion is continued in studies of individual texts and text groups.
17 Especially Lohfink, *Sicherung*; for this, see below pp. 210ff.

other chapters it is thought that there are multiple additions. One look at a table of strata, for example, Preuss's (which is relatively conservative), and this is obvious.

Completely independent of the question of respective dating, it is precisely because traces of redaction are indisputable in virtually every text that we must again raise the issues of "how" and "why" a new codification occurred. There is no doubt that the Book of the Covenant was available to the authors and was known by them, because of the numerous references. It is not acceptable to analyze this work into a great mass of additions to additions, the theory of a "hundred hands in a hundred years."[18] The pace and present state of research makes it doubtful whether additional literary-critical study *alone* can give us consistency and a unified structure. We then, as elsewhere, will need to correct and supplement literary-critical study with other perspectives.

It is, of course for that reason rather difficult to uncover the inner organization and the structural principles of Deuteronomy, since at best this was only preliminarily successful in the past. What for the Book of the Covenant was completed gradually since Halbe's work,[19] is just beginning here.

Above all, Braulik's theses have been important. Beginning with a few earlier studies,[20] he regards the final form of deuteronomic law to be constructed analogous to the Decalogue.[21] Braulik has undoubtedly presented a number of convincing observations regarding the arrangement of the laws, especially regarding the overlapping of individual thematic blocks through the principle of attraction.[22]

The structural principles in ancient Near Eastern law and the Book of the Covenant are also found here. There is none of the often suggested arbitrariness here, rather there is a precise, well-reasoned order, if also possibly diachronically superimposed. We have indeed barely uncovered the overall design of 12–26, and in any case it is not simply structured analogous to the ten commandments.

18 This kind of formulation in Levin, *Verheissung* 65; for a systematic critique, see especially Hardmeier, *Jeremia* 29; see Seebass, *Vorschlag* for a "simplification" of current analyses.
19 Halbe, *Privilegrecht*, see above pp. 113ff.
20 Schultz, *Deuteronomium* III, 13; Guilding, *Notes* 43, especially Kaufman, *Structure*. For the history of the research, see Braulik, *Gesetze* 14ff., 19f. also a critique of the other assessments of Rofé, *Arrangement*.
21 Braulik, *Abfolge*; ibid., *Weitere Beobachtungen*; ibid., *Deuteronomium* 12f.; now newly summarized in ibid., *Gesetze*. According to this, there are broad correlations (*Gesetze* 22):

First commandment	–	Deut 12:2–13:9
Second commandment	–	14:1–21
Third commandment	–	14:22–16:7
Fourth commandment	–	16:18–18:22
Fifth commandment	–	19:1–21:23
Sixth commandment	–	22:13–23:15
Seventh commandment	–	23:16–24:7
Eighth commandment	–	24:8–25:4
Ninth commandment	–	25:5–12
Tenth commandment	–	25:13–16

22 See Petschow, *Systematik*; ibid., *Gesetzestechnik*; Otto, *Rechtsgeschichte*; Braulik, *Gesetze* 18f.

In relation to the first four commandments, Braulik himself sees "somewhat general parallels, which are to varying degrees clear."[23] Even if we can, for example, associate Deut 12f. with the first commandment (disregarding the prohibition against images), and Deut 14:22–16:7 with the sabbath commandment, a connection between 14:1–21 and the prohibition against misusing the divine name, with "only a few digressions"[24] is hardly convincing. In order to connect the commandment to honor parents with the official regulations (16:6–18:22), we must interpret it along the lines of Luther, which is done already in Philo. Braulik himself, however, thinks this is "problematic" and at best, it is only a "possible" correlation.[25]

Unlike Braulik, I find no connections to the other commandments. To be sure, there are substantive parallels between the prohibition against killing and Deut 19:1–21:23 ("preserve life")[26] or between the prohibition against adultery and 22:13–23:15 ("protect the honor of man and woman"), but to try to connect Deut 23:16–24:7 with the prohibition against theft by putting them under the heading "placing human needs and relationships above property" shows that, apart from 24:7, there is no real connection. The corresponding passages in the Book of the Covenant, which are a concretization of the prohibition against theft (Ex 21:37–22:14), are not continued in Deuteronomy.

It is even less precise and rather arbitrary to regard 24:8–25:4 ("denying the poor, the socially weak and debtors their rights") as corresponding with the prohibition against bearing false witness, or in 25:5–12 ("not hindering the begetting of descendants") as corresponding to the first half of the prohibition against coveting, and 25:13–16 to the second half. It is not possible to demonstrate more than a very weak connection from the first to the second table.

Interpreting deuteronomic law on the basis of the overall structure of Deuteronomy and the role of the Decalogue within it, as a kind of commentary on the Decalogue or provisions for its implementation[27] is here made into a literary structural principle to which the texts do not yield. We must raise questions, such as why the provisions regarding false evidence are in 19:15ff. rather than in connection with the eighth commandment, or why the section on parents does not contain the provision regarding the "obstinate son" in 21:18ff., etc.

My main argument, however, is that this thesis leaves recognizable structural principles of Deuteronomic law unattended. Above all, there is the obvious framework, which surrounds the greater part of the law. The first of the deuteronomic social laws in 14:22ff. treats the tithe, and this theme is taken up again at the conclusion of the work in 26:12ff. Both sections end with the theme of blessing (14:29; 26:15). Everything bracketed within has a relationship to the theme of the frame, in the same

23 Braulik, *Gesetze* 22.
24 Braulik, *Gesetze* 35.
25 Braulik, *Gesetze* 60f. with a reference to Philo, *De Decalogo* XXX. 165 (*Werke* I 406).
26 Headings of the individual sections according to Braulik, *Gesetze* 22 (for the following, see 62, 79, 94, 108, 111).
27 In summary Braulik, *Gesetze* 11–13.

way, for example, as we learned to expect from Ex 22:20 and 23:9 (the alien), a parallel to this bracket function.[28]

In fact, the theme of the tithe proves to be the key for the inner design of deuteronomic law.[29] We have the subject of religion, in the narrow sense, in 12:2–14:2 before the block Deut 14:22–26. There is a relationship between them similar to the one traditionally suggested between the first and second tables of the Decalogue. It is here, rather than the beginning, that we find the focal point: the unity of the cultic site (12), the guarding of exclusive veneration (13) and the guarding of the holiness of the people (14:1–21).

Besides the rules listed by Braulik, there is especially clear chiasmus and "framework" in the arrangement of the block Deut 14:22–26. Thus, 15:1–16:17, in a continuation of the theme of tithing, is concerned with the social consequences of sacral time. We find laws for the protection of the weakest in society again in the last portion, 23:16–25:19.

There are clear connections in contents here: both begin with regulations regarding slavery (15:1ff.; 23:16f.). There are also correlations between the blocks arranged more toward the center. The passages in 21:10–23:15, directed toward "private" institutions of family (and sexuality), are opposite the text in 16:18–18:22 on public institutions and offices. This section is framed by the regulations regarding war (21:10ff.; 23:10ff.). Thus the block 19:1–21:9, framed three times, stands in the center. This block deals with the protection of life.[30] This rough division seems more appropriate to the material than the other forced connection to the Decalogue. Still, this is just a first step; in details we would adopt many of Braulik's observations.

Finally, two seemingly contradictory facts are of special importance. On the one hand, we find clear signs of redaction, innovation and amplification in nearly every single section of the law. Scholars, if not in total agreement, recognize growth, extension, alteration in numerous passages. Many examples will be addressed.

On the other hand, the regulations fit together in a compact, nearly contradiction-free whole. In spite of the many indications of editorial work, the whole appears to have been conceived as a whole and is juridically well conceived. The theory of accidental, simultaneously developing additions, of redactions from widely differing historical epochs or divergent groups, can hardly be justified by this evidence.[31]

A Plea for a Preexilic Dating

When and under what circumstances have we come to such a comprehensive, legal-historically new assessment? The question of the dating of deuteronomic law in its constituent parts gives modern research two basic positions. Against the classic, and currently the dominant thesis of a late preexilic dating, part of the general trend

---

28 See above pp. 181ff.
29 See below pp. 215ff.
30 In conjunction with Braulik, *Gesetze* 62ff.
31 The observations of numerous groups of seven supports this, see Braulik, *Siebenergruppierungen*.

toward later dating, the notion is gaining ground that this might be a product of the exilic period, or even later .

This view might become quite plausible in conjunction with a determined search for the rationale and impetus for a new codification, because the exile doubtless represented a deep, legal-historical discontinuity in which a new codification might be possible or even likely. For this reason we should first test the arguments for such an assessment. We should state at the outset that thus far this theory has been supported in a rather general way, by assertion, and only for segments, but never in detail.

Gustav Hölscher, who first proposed an exilic dating in 1922, and to whom we still make reference, concluded his dating exclusively on the basis of the *utopian character* of many of the deuteronomic laws. In the king-laws (Deut 17:14–20), the war-laws (20) and many others, we find "ideal requirements," that are not attainable and could never have been fulfilled.[32] Deuteronomy could never have been a "genuinely valid law,"[33] and for that reason could never have been identified with the law book of King Josiah in 2 Kg 22f., rather, it can only be explained from the situation of the exilic/postexilic period.

Such an argument is nevertheless, not admissible. We can neither make a standard of modern notions of the current possibilities for applicability, nor can we say that preexilic laws could not have contained such "ideal" requirements. Examples here might include the seventh day rest from labor and the seventh year, but also the exclusive veneration of God or the prohibition against images. Furthermore, we should remember the character of ancient Near Eastern legal corpora as products of scholarship, at least portions of which were theoretical.

Nevertheless, this argument is still somewhat congenial, if less for the whole corpus than for the constitutional portion in Deut 16:18–18:22. For this very reason, the idea of utopianism (that is – for plans for the future restoration) is widely held today.[34] Furthermore, these regulations could hardly have been conceived for King Josiah.[35] Procedurally, the same weaknesses remain, and historically, other ideas are more likely.

Other arguments for an exilic dating are equally weak. Since 1805[36] the most important possibility for a dating of deuteronomic law is found in the correlation of its contents with the report of the discovery of a law book in the Jerusalem temple and a reform carried out by Josiah on the basis of the book (2 Kg 22f.). It cannot be doubted that this narrative is completely within exilic deuteronomic history and that it was written at a certain distance.[37] But this does not exclude the possibility of the use of other sources or traditions.

---

32 Hölscher, *Konposition* 227; for research-historical discussions, see Loersch, *Deuteronomium* 55ff.; Preuss, *Deuteronomium* 31.
33 Hölscher, *Konposition* 228.
34 Especially Lohfink, *Sicherung*; Preuss, *Deuteronomium* in summary 53ff.
35 Thus Lohfink in response to the preexilic dating of laws regarding officials by Rütersworden, *Gemeinschaft*; in Lohfink (review) Rütersworden. The rejected alternative for Lohfink is that the law might have been commissioned by Josiah (427).
36 De Wette, *Dissertatio critica*.
37 See an overview of the history of the research in Lohfink, *Discussion* and especially Paul, *Archimedisch punt*. Since then: Lohfink, *Cult Reform*; Minette de Tillesse, *A reforma*; Tagliacarne, *Untersuchungen*; Visticki, *Reform*; Conroy, *Reflections*; Paul,

The connection with the book of Deuteronomy is dependent upon the report of the reform in 2 Kg 23:4ff. The king's abolition of shrines outside of Jerusalem can, in fact, be only be explained with concepts of Deuteronomy (*if* indeed, this is a historical tradition). However, even this is disputed, above all because of a whole series of noteworthy Hebrew verb forms. Their appearance could be explained simply because of an Aramaic influence, having parallels only in late postexilic texts. The complex state of the discussions need not be rehearsed here.[38] It need no longer be disputed that fundamentally such forms do appear in preexilic texts and that they are not of themselves a compelling argument for a late date.[39]

The linguistic usage in Deuteronomy is somewhat different. We might mention the references – before the fact! – to Israel's occupation of the land as they appear in the so-called historicizing introductions to the commandments (e.g. 12:29; 17:14; 18:9; 19:1; 26:1).[40] Lohfink, especially has referred frequently to the fact that this deals with deuteronomic formulations, which belong to rather late strata,[41] and furthermore presuppose a literary connection to a narrative of the conquest of the land.[42] There are, however, no convincing reasons for the latter:[43] a fictional placement of a Mosaic law-giver, before the occupation of the land, who refers to the coming event, would presume a general knowledge of the course of history (which was never recorded within the text). The numerous references to law giving between the exodus and the events of Josh 24 attest to this.[44]

Lohfink also would ascribe these commandment introductions, including the pertinent land occupation narrative, to the late preexilic period.[45] Here, as elsewhere, the arguments for a *relatively* late dating of individual strata within the deuteronomic/deuteronomistic text corpus are by no means equivalent to an absolute late dating of the respective texts.

King Josiah's Renewal. Still of special importance are Würthwein, *Reform*; Hoffmann, *Reform* 169ff.; Spieckermann, *Juda* 30ff. See also below pp. 211., 270ff.

38 See Spieckermann, *Juda* 120ff. (Lit.).

39 See especially Spieckermann, *Juda* 125ff. The ostrakon of ṃeṣad Ḥashavyahu (KAI 200) still plays an important role. For this see most recently Weippert, *Petition*.

40 Further 6:10; 7:1; 8:7; 11:29, 31; 27:2. For this, see the excursus in Rüterswörden, *Gemeinschaft* 54ff., in discussion with Lohfink, *Kerygmata* who would demonstrate the possibility of a preexilic origin. Critical, Lohfink (review) *Rüterswörden*.

41 This is especially concerned with the *yrš* formulae. See Lohfink, article on *yāraš*; ibid., *Bedeutungen*.

42 Thus Lohfink, *Kerygmata* 90f. cf ibid. (review) *Bedeutungen*.

43 This is even less true for the thesis that in the history of the text of Deuteronomy there was an "phase . . . , in which the laws were not yet 'historicized'" (Lohfink, *Kerygma* 90). Furthermore, Moses was nevertheless already regarded as the author (loc. cit. 91); cf ibid., *Jahwegesetz oder Mosegesetz?.* Whether the few observations introduced for this, for example the places at which divine address peeks through the words of Moses, can be proof is more than debatable. If we proceed in this direction, that only divine speech dominates historically in the Book of the Covenant as well as later in the priestly laws, what is specific to Deuteronomy is its character as the speech of Moses. The process of historicization is at the root of Deuteronomy and cannot be eliminated.

44 See above pp. 38ff.

45 Most recently, Lohfink, article on Deuteronomium; ibid., review Rüterswörden.

Thus, the use of the term "Torah" as a designation for deuteronomic law certainly belongs to the later rather than the earlier strata.[46] Nevertheless, the appearance of this term in Jer 8:8 shows compellingly that this linguistic usage is attested in preexilic times.[47] Thus, relative dating cannot be employed directly for an absolute temporal classification.

The so-called historical introductions to the commandments, which Lohfink regards as evidence for a late dating, are clear references to a preexilic origin. The beginning of the king-law in Deut 17:14f. reads "When you have come into the land that the Lord your God has given you, and have taken possession of it, and you say, 'I will set a king over me, like all the nations that are around me,' you may indeed set over you a king ..."

The dating of the institutional portion of deuteronomic law is not ultimately dependent upon this formulation.[48] Certainly, it allows us to see correlations with deuteronomistic texts. If we interpret them through the exile, this would be a utopian plan for a possible restoration of their own monarchy, which would not succumb to the mistakes of the former. However, linguistically, everything argues that even the expression of the desire for a king is included within the conditional "if" protasis.[49] It is only with the beginning of verse 15 that the apodosis begins.

Does the possibility that Israel might not want a king make sense in plans for the new beginning after the catastrophe of the exile? Nevertheless, it would be necessary to draw clear inferences from previous experiences for such a utopia, as other exilic texts do.[50] Nevertheless, freedom of choice, the possibility of rejecting a king, does not argue for a utopian plan and can more easily be explained in another way.[51]

Things are even clearer at the outset of the prophet-laws. "When you come into the land that YHWH your God is giving you, you must not learn to imitate the abhorrent practices of those nations. No one shall found among you who makes a son or daughter pass through the fire ..." (18:9f.). There follows a long list of possibilities for foretelling the future (verses 10–14). The approved prophet will oppose all of these. The connection of the basic prohibition against divination with the future accession of the land cannot be understood in the context of the exile. Could it then be intended that all such things were permitted for Israel so long as they were not in possession of the land?

Deut 12:29f. is quite similar. Here the theme of service to idols is connected with the promised occupation of the land. This could only mean that at the time of the formulation there was undisputed possession of the land. Anything else would permit idol worship up until a specific time.

This is still the surest indication of a preexilic origin for the most important parts of deuteronomic law and of its predominant language,

---

46 Thus, Deut 4:44 as opposed to 4:45 might in fact represent the more recent form of the heading, with e.g. Preuss, *Deuteronomium*.
47 See above pp. 23ff.
48 See the discussion between Rütersworden, *Gemeinschaft* 52ff. and Lohfink (review) Rütersworden.
49 See Rütersworden, *Gemeinschaft* 52f.
50 We think of texts such as Isa 55; Jer 22:4 and Ez 40ff.
51 See below pp. 234ff.

including its theological implications: Deuteronomy presupposes Israel's secure possession of the land as well as its freedom. Exodus and the possession of the land as they are realized in the position of the free landowner are *presuppositions* of the validity of YHWH's commandments, both theologically and factually. Later, we will speak of this in greater detail.[52] Deuteronomic law had *not* worked through the legal-historical problems that came with the exile. It does not react to them or deal with all their aspects. Texts that do this appear quite different.[53]

Deuteronomy is only comprehensible as a preexilic text. Lohfink underscores this.[54] In Deut 12:1 we read that Israel is supposed to keep the statutes and ordinances (*ḥuqqîm umišpāṭîm*), "all the days that you live on the land." The significance of the law that follows is connected to the period of possession of the land. Lohfink regards this as an exilic redaction, which became necessary when many of the things demanded in Deut 12–26 were no longer immediately practicable under the conditions of the exile. Undoubtedly, this is correct. According to Lohfink, the addition at the beginning of chapter 12 is intended to remove the ensuing texts, for example, the *shma'* '*Israel* (6:4ff.) or the Decalogue (5), from such limitation, making their validity independent of all social and political circumstances. Such an arrangement presupposes the preexilic origin of that which is being commented upon.

At this point in the discussion, we must regard the old connection of Deuteronomy with the law of Josiah as essentially still valid, in fact, the most likely assumption. The question cannot be, whether, but only to *what degree* the Deuteronomy known to us coincides with this event. We could hardly doubt that the deuteronomistic narrator of the text of 2 Kg 22f. was talking about anything but Deuteronomy. Into 2 Kg 22f. there was probably already redacted an older historical "short story," which, following Lohfink, included, for example, 2 Kg 22:3–20; 23:1–3, 21–23.[55] The report of the reform in 2 Kg 23:4ff. is completely dovetailed into the overall structure of the deuteronomistic books of Kings,[56] and if we view it first on this level, it contains other points that hardly permit us to think of the report as a very late fiction. In spite of many differences in individual matters, this evidence makes it possible to understand why most recent studies presume a correlation of deuteronomic law or its core with the law book of Josiah and his reform. The existence of a Torah book in preexilic Jerusalem mentioned by Jeremiah (8:8) is most easily explained in this way.

The question of when Deuteronomy was written is not answered by this connection with the law book of Josiah. Even less is the question of the reason and impetus for the legal–historically new document resolved. The narrative of the "discovery" of a law book in the temple, allows the age of the book to remain unanswered. Narratively, it reconciles the Mosaic origin with the Josian reality. There have been many different attempts to explain the age and provenance of the Josian

---

52 See below pp. 219ff.
53 See below pp. 286ff.
54 Lohfink, *Ḥuqqîm ûmišpāṭîm* especially 22ff.; ibid., *Verständnis*.
55 Lohfink, *Cult Reform*; ibid., *Gattung*.
56 For this, see especially Hoffmann, *Reform* 169ff.

document.[57] They range from a theory of an old text originating in pre-state Israel or the early monarchic period, or an origin in the northern kingdom[58] or from the time of Hezekiah, all the way to the thesis that it was conceived shortly before or even for the reform.[59] Still, we need not repeat that the old observations make it necessary that the central ideas of Deuteronomy were as unknown among the eighth-century prophets as they were in the periods before – even considering the greater age of the Book of the Covenant.

If we still must presume a correlation between deuteronomic law and the reform measures of Josiah, the connection of these events with the geopolitical changes underlies the collapse of the Assyrian empire.[60] At the death of Assurbanipal 630 BCE, and probably even before, Assyria began a sudden and massive collapse. Unfortunately there are no clear reports about when the changes began to take place in Palestine, when the Assyrian troops and occupational government began to be withdrawn. Nevertheless, insurrections that began to take place in 626 BCE (in conjunction with which Nabopolassar made himself an independent king in Babylon) may have played a part. In any case, the commitment to the new law book in 622 BCE should be understood as a publicly proclaimed and executed covenant with Israel's God, which took the place of the covenant with the king of Assyria.[61]

All of this is a clear expression of the new constellation. Was deuteronomic law first conceived especially for this moment in history? Many scholars have, without much reflection, presumed this very thing. Still, it would have to have been developed especially for this – great – King Josiah and at his behest. On the basis of the contents of Deuteronomy, even that, however, is unlikely.

The Reign of the Judean 'am hā'āreṣ as the Reason for the New Codification

We will now advance and support in detail the thesis that the development of deuteronomic law was connected with circumstances at the beginning of the reign of Josiah, and that the many recognizable marks of its literary growth can and must be traced back to the historical development before the exile, and not the exile itself.

After the death of Manasseh, who for decades was a vassal of Assur, his son Amon became king in 642/1 BCE. In 2 Kg 21:23 we read the succinct statement, "The servants of Amon conspired against him and killed the king in his house." This was a coup carried out by the "servants" of the new king ('abdē 'āmōn), which means that it began with court functionaries who were specially for the king and his family. These "servants" are to be distinguished from the officials (śārim) who

---

57 Overview in Preuss, *Deuteronomium* 26ff.
58 Still useful, Alt, *Heimat*; most recently Lubszyk, *Bundesurkunde*.
59 Or one might see several of these periods at work, as Braulik and Lohfink.
60 For this, see Donner, *Geschichte* II, 339ff.
61 We can only refer to the much discussed connection of Deuteronomy with the Assyrian vassal agreements, thus a "primary conceptual and ritual structure of the dominant culture" (Lohfink, article on *Deuteronomium* 417) which gave this relationship an especially explosive effect.

functioned outside the palace.[62] The coup probably happened shortly after Amon acceded to the throne because, as we know, the two years of his rule required only a few months to contain within them a change of year, thus suggesting "two years" on the throne. There is no reason given for the coup.

On the basis of the sources, the supposition that Amon, in contrast to his father, wanted to pursue an anti-Assyrian policy following other insurrections of the time,[63] remains speculation. Because verse 24 states that "the people of the land killed all those who had conspired against King Amon, and the people of the land made his son Josiah king in his place," it is possible that groups involved in the coup wanted to force a change in dynasty

As in other cases (especially 2 Kg 11:14, 18) the Judean '*am hā'āreṣ* (probably referring to free, property owners of Judah)[64] ensured the security of the house of David, with which they had close political connections. These authorities took action and assured the security of the traditional dynasty.

Josiah, who had come to power in this way was, however, still a child of eight (2 Kg 22:1). For years all power would be in the hands of the '*am hā'āreṣ* or their representatives. Over thirty years later, when Josiah was unexpectedly killed on the battlefield at Megiddo, the same Judean '*am hā'āreṣ* still (or again) had power. According to 2 Kg 23:30, they alone determined Josiah's successor when they made Jehoahaz king.

Jehoahaz was not Josiah's eldest son, and so was not first in order of succession. Jehoiakim was two years older (see 2 Kg 23:31 and 36) and was passed over for clearly political reasons. When he later was made king by Pharaoh Neco, he pursued a policy that departed significantly from that of his father. Jeremiah, for example, criticized him for compelling forced labor to construct luxurious buildings (Jer 22:13ff.) and contrasted him explicitly with his father Josiah (22:15). Jehoiakim imposed the necessary tribute payments to Neco upon the '*am hā'āreṣ* causing them a heavy burden, instead of following the usual practice of paying Neco out of the state or temple treasury. Jehoiakim's political program becomes clear through this conflict. It was not an accident that the people of Judah chose his brother over him.

All of this comes from reports from the concise peripheral observation in the Books of Kings, which scholars agree came from the annals of the Jerusalem court. Thus, we have reliable sources. According to these sources the people of Judah held control at the time of Josiah's accession to the throne as well as at the time of his death. There is no reason to suspect that they gave up power for a period of thirty years. Josiah, as far as we know, did not pursue policies against the will and interests of the group that had brought him to power and trained him.

---

62 See Kessler, *Staat und Gesellschaft* 169ff.
63 Malamat, *Historical Background*.
64 See especially Würthwein, '*am hā'āreṣ*, as well as Kessler, *Staat und Gesellschaft* 204ff.; in addition to McKenzie, *People of the Land*; de Vaux, *Le sens*; Talmon, '*am hā'āreṣ*, Nicholson, *Meaning*; Ischida, *People of the Land*; Gunneweg, *Revolution*: for their role in the Books of Kings and deuteronomic theology, see especially Würthwein as well as Soggin, '*amhā'āreṣ*.

When the people of Judah placed a child on the throne, they themselves ruled for a rather long period of time. The traditional courtiers were abolished, as 2 Kg 21:24 reports, and thus their influence on public policy was eliminated. The '*am hā'āreṣ* had no political power over themselves, but the state was entirely in their hands. At latest, in this situation of need, a program had to be developed which was effective and according to which they might act. Such a thing would not be proposed in the form of a political "constitution."

Still, Deuteronomy, which was later connected with the cult reform of Josiah, had features that can be better explained by no other conceivable situation than the circumstances historically attested here. To what degree these essential characteristics of deuteronomic law down to the details of formulation are understandable from just this situation, will be discussed in the following chapters.

For the typical idea of cultic unity as powerfully expressed in deuteronomic law (Deut 12), which is quite remarkable and not yet attested anywhere in the eighth century, we must refer to another historical constellation. In 701 BCE, Judah was reduced to the small area around Jerusalem (in general we think of the city-state itself) by Sennacherib as a consequence of rebellion and the occupation of Jerusalem itself.[65]

Sennacherib wrote: "I separated its cities, which I have plundered, from the land and gave them to Miniti, the king of Ashdod; Padi, the king of Ekron; and Silbel, the king of Gaza, and thus reduced its territory."[66] For the shrines that had remained in these areas, this political arrangement was not without religio-political problems. Places like Mamre/ Hebron, Beersheba, Arad, among others, were in areas influenced by hostile neighbors with differing beliefs. If the interpretation of the altar law of the Book of the Covenant, as developed above, is correct – that the traditional YHWH shrines (the shrines "where YHWH causes his name to be proclaimed")[67] were distinguished by that altar book, and only they offered legitimate sacrifice – then a situation developed after 701 BCE which forced the radicalization of this view: to an even greater extent the God of Israel caused his name to reside or be proclaimed in only one single place. Tying Judeans who were living under direct foreign domination, even the Assyrians, to the city of Jerusalem must have had new importance. The remarkable fact that cultic unity is presupposed, rather than introduced, even in the earlier strata of Deut 12, may be connected with this situation.

Historically, it is not known when the portions of Judah separated in 701 BCE came again under the domination of Jerusalem.[68] Generally, scholars propose restitution under Manasseh.[69] Nevertheless, it is possible that it

65 In conjunction with Alt, *Bedeutung*; cf Donner, *Geschichte* II 321ff.
66 Report of the third campaign of Sennacherib, Luckenbill, *Annals* 33.172.
67 See above pp. 172ff.
68 The significance of 701 as a turning point is probably generally under-valued. If the high numbers of those deported are not completely "plucked out of thin air" (but see Sauren, *Sennachérib*), we need to consider a real exile (thus with emphasis, Stohlmann, "Exile"). Furthermore, the overwhelming experiences of foreign domination for most regions of Judah should not be under-valued.
69 E.g. Alt, *Bedeutung*; Evans, *Foreign Policy* 168 considers a correlation with the events of 671 BCE.

might have happened in conjunction with the weakening of Assur and the parallel expansion of Josiah. The enlargement of the region (Deut 12:20) and the Josian reform measures are not far apart in time.

According to the thesis that we will develop, deuteronomic law achieved its shape against the background of a situation in which the Judean 'am hā'āreṣ themselves seized power. The law gave form and legitimation to this genuine popular rule. The collapse of Assyrian domination brought additional possibilities for the application of new political ideas. If this seems plausible, we will need special documentation and support to be able to assign portions of the text to the exilic period after 586 BCE.

The beginning of what is traditionally called the exile was only one of many pivotal changes in the political constellation. The reduction of Judah to the area around the city of Jerusalem, the concomitant exile of portions of the population and temporary foreign domination (701), as well as the unknown duration of the disorder, the beginning of Josian rule (639), the withdrawal of Assyrian rule from Palestine (from c.626), the death of Josiah (609), the rule of Jehoakim, or Egypt (from 609), the transition to the new Babylonians (605), the first rebellion and its miscarriage (598), the period of Zedekiah and finally the second rebellion (586), the period of Gedaliah and then period of exile – these many, rapid changes in basic political conditions must be borne in mind, not simply making a dichotomy preexilic–exilic. Statements about a possible territorial expansion with its problems (12:20; 19:8) could make sense sometime after 701, or in conjunction with an expansion under Josiah, or they could offer hope during a period of exile. Viewed as a whole, the outcome can be anticipated in the actual corpus of deuteronomic law (Deut 12–26) without considering comprehensive, significant exilic strata.

Freedom and Solidarity: The Theological Logic

The Tithe and Its Key Role

The main part of deuteronomic law is framed by regulation on the offering of the tithe (Deut 14:22–29; 26:12–15). This is by no means an accident. The tithing regulation shows itself to be a key text from which we can deduce the theological and juridical thinking behind deuteronomic law. It illuminates the inner relationships of various parts of deuteronomic law.[70]

> Deut 14:22 Set apart a tithe of all the yield of your seed that is brought in yearly from the field. 23 In the presence of YHWH your God, in the place that he will choose as a dwelling for his name, you shall eat the tithe of your grain, your wine and your oil, as well as the firstlings of your herd and flock, so that you may learn to fear YHWH your God always. . . .
>
> 27 As for the Levites resident in your towns, do not neglect them because they have no allotment or inheritance with you. 28 Every third year you shall bring out the tithe of your produce for that year,

70 For what follows, see Crüsemann, *Produktionsverhältnisse* 86ff.

> and store it within your towns; 29 the Levites, because they have no
> allotment or inheritance with you, as well as the resident aliens, the
> orphans, and the widows in your towns, may come and eat their fill so
> that YHWH your God may bless you in all the work that you undertake.

The law begins in verse 22 in the way we might expect from a regulation regarding the payment of taxes. A tithe, thus about 10 percent, was
to be separated from all of the agricultural produce.[71] This included grain
(verse 23), must (or wine)[72] and olive oil as the three hallmarks of the
agricultural year. In addition to these items, the firstborn of animals are
included to be treated in the same way. All of these were to be brought
to the central cult site. It was, however, permissible to replace these
with money, as we read in verses 24–26. The tithe was then to be eaten by
Israelites there at the shrine. No other recipient is mentioned, neither
temple nor king, priest or God.

It follows immediately in verses 28f. that in every third year the tithe is
not to be taken to the central shrine, but it is to be taken to the various
towns for the Levites and others who owned no land, aliens, orphans and
widows. The distribution is to take place at the gate of these localities.
The firstlings are not mentioned, the previous rule about them remains
in effect (see Deut 15:19ff.). This presentation of the tithe to those who are
socially disadvantaged every third year is discussed again in the last
section of the deuteronomic law. According to 26:12ff., they are to swear
a solemn oath that they have really given the tithe to the intended
recipients. It is significant that 26:12 calls this year "the year of the tithe."
It was only in that year that there was an actual transfer of goods to
outsiders.

It is only when we examine what we know about the tithe from other
sources that we can begin to understand what happens in these
peripheral regulations of deuteronomic law.[73] The tithe existed in a few
other contemporary cultures. In those places it was to be paid[74] to the
king or to a specific temple[75] village by village (in other words, collectively).[76] The tithe is referred to especially in the so-called king-law of
1 Sam 8 (verses 15, 17).[77] It was one of the great burdens that a king could
lay upon his subjects.

---

71 Baumgarten, *Non-Literal Use*, correctly points out that the term "tithe" does not
   necessarily always mean exactly 10 percent, but it can also be used in a formulary
   way. Still, he gives, in contrast to other tax language, a ranking of size which also
   in later times must be taken with a pinch of salt.
72 *tirōš* refers especially to the grape in a cluster (Isa 65:8) or the wine-press (Hos 9:2).
   In the typical payment of tribute, wine was included with grain and oil (see KBL³
   1592).
73 See the details in Crüsemann, *Der Zehnte*; see also Kessler, *Juda* 148ff.; on this
   subject, in addition to Eissfeldt, *Erstlinge*; Weinfeld, *Aspects*; ibid., article on Tithes;
   Jagersma, *Tithes*; Milgrom, *Cult*; an overview also in Oden, *Taxation*.
74 For an overview of other systems of taxation, see Crüsemann, *Der Zehnte* (Lit.).
75 Thus in Sumerian city-states as well as, in part, in old Babylonian and especially
   new Babylonian periods; see Salonen, *Über den Zehnten*; Dandamayev, *Tempelzehnt*;
   also already Eissfeldt, *Zum Zehnten*.
76 Thus in Ugarit (that is, Bronze Age Canaan), see Heltzer, *Rural Community* 7ff.;
   ibid., *Tithe*; for other forms of payment, see ibid., *Internal Organization*.
77 For an analysis, see Crüsemann, *Widerstand* 66ff.; ibid. *Der Zehnte* 34f.

Because of this and other texts, which mention a state tax (though not called the tithe),[78] we would surmise that both Israelite states collected a tax or tithe since the beginning of the monarchy. Clear attestation is, of course, hard to come by. A tithe is only referred to obliquely in the Israelite ostraka.[79] The only clear places[80] are connected with the northern kingdom. Am 4:4 mentions a tithe which was brought to the shrine at Bethel together with other cultic gifts, and Amos criticizes the practice. Also corresponding to this procedure is Jacob's promise after his dream, in which the dignity of the place was revealed to him (Gen 28:22).[81] Thus, in the northern kingdom we can be certain that a tithe was to be paid at Bethel.

This is, of course, one of the most important state shrines (Am 7:13; 1 Kg 12:26). As elsewhere, the tithe here was a tax connected with the legal claim of the kingdom. It was given to the sacral monarchy, whether it went to the state temple or the sacral state, in each case it belonged to God and the king together. It is true that thus far we lack any clear evidence for Judah and Jerusalem. Nevertheless, we could hardly think it was not until Deuteronomy that the tithe was instituted for this region, rather, it presumes the existence of the tithe by eliminating it. Such a tax came also to Judah at latest while they were dependent upon Assur and had to make regular, high tribute payments.

The omission of reference to or legitimation of the tithe is important for a correct understanding of Torah tradition. From Ex 34:11ff. on, the texts seem only to know of other payments (firstborn and firstfruits); the tithe is never mentioned.[82] Only in Deuteronomy does the tithe appear, indeed by abolishing it. In two of the three years, it is supposed to be used by the person who offers it at the central shrine.

In order to understand this we need to make comparison with other passages. According to texts like Deut 12:6f., 11f., 17f.; 16:10f., 14 clients of every kind, slaves (male and female), Levites and aliens, widows and orphans, all who lived in the various localities along side the land-owning families – especially the problem groups – and not just the family, were to participate in the great seasonal festivals at the central shrine. If we add firstborn animals to the tithe and the food from the sacrifice-banquets, there would have been a considerable amount of meat and other food for everyone at the great pilgrimage festivals. Deut 14:23 makes this an object lesson: "so that you may learn to fear YHWH your God always."

In every third year the tithe was to be paid directly to the socially underprivileged groups (that is, those without land). This took place at

---

78 See especially 1 Kg 4:7ff.; 1 Kg 12:4ff. and elsewhere.
79 Neither the mention in one of the Ophel ostraka (Lemaire, *Ostraca* 159f.) nor the reconstruction of an Arad ostrakon (Aharoni, *Inscriptions* No. 5, p. 20.) are entirely certain. Still, a detailed system of taxation for Judah has been deduced from a series of ostraka.
80 On the contrary, the dating of Gen 14:20 is unclear (as the whole text of Gen 14). Most likely we ought to presume that the verse is from the postexilic period (Crüsemann, *Der Zehnte* 38f.).
81 For an analysis and dating, see Blum, *Vätergeschichte* 7ff., 88ff. Verse 22 probably still presupposes the existence of the northern kingdom.
82 See above pp. 131ff.

the gate, the place of public gathering and where court was held. It was done this way to gain a measure of public control. The activity could be supervised, but it was unbureaucratic, no state or temple intervened. We might call this the beginning of real social legislation; it represents *the first known tax for a social program.* With it, those who were landless and socially weak received a sure support which was guaranteed by law and public oath to bring agricultural produce (26:12ff.).

This was the way Deuteronomy abolished the traditional state tax, partially changing it into a direct contribution to social program and determining the remainder for the financing of the – probably new for many – connection to the central shrine. This handling of the payment of taxes, disputed and embattled since the beginning of the monarchy in Israel, can be connected with no other situation since the beginning of the monarchy so precisely as with the reign of the child-king Josiah. It is plausible that a landowning population, who had themselves seized power, and exercizing real authority, freed themselves of their greatest burden by means of regular, religiously legitimized payments, or at least formulated this in proposed legislation connected with the movement.

A formulation of the tithe law in Deut 12:17, and thus theoretically in the oldest stratum of the centralization law[83] at the high point of this collection of laws, allows us to surmise something else even more concrete about the situation. It states: "You may not eat within your gates the tithe of your grain, your wine and your oil . . ." (12:17). Something is forbidden here which seems incongruous in a requirement to tithe: it is forbidden for the donor to eat the tithe in the gate (thus, not at the shrine). In other words, this prohibition presumes that in reality the tithe had already been abolished.

There is no other way in which this phrasing makes sense. The Israelites were accustomed simply to take the tithe home and use it themselves. The authorities who were able to demand a tithe were apparently no longer present, or at least no longer had the power to enforce the demand. Such a practice of simply holding the tithe back was countered by the deuteronomic tithe laws. Deut 12:17 can only be understood as having come out of a situation in which there was no longer a monarchy to demand a tithe, nor was there another authority desirous of assuming this prerogative. The deuteronomic solution is that the offering be consumed by the people at the shrine and giving preference to the landless.

The significance of the frame-position of this law is apparent when we note how tightly it is dovetailed with all the central themes of Deuteronomy. The liberating act of God in the exodus, toward which Deuteronomy repeatedly points, is given substance here, likewise the cultic understanding in which central location, joyful celebration, de-sacralization (made possible by the sale of the offering) and social ties were connected and brought together with the concept of state which

83 For this, see Preuss, *Deuteronomium* 133, according to which 12:13–19, in the generally accepted view, is the oldest part of the chapter. Otherwise, Seebass, *Vorschlag* 96f.; however, verse 17 also belongs to the legal "foundation" of the chapter.

came about due to the weakened monarchy. This key role of the tithe for the inner correlation of deuteronomic law will be discussed shortly.

Deuteronomy as the Law of Free Landowners

Deuteronomy addresses free landowners, presuming that they are completely free and functioning.[84] One of the ways this happens is the historic fiction of an address by Moses after the liberation from slavery in Egypt, but all of the laws systematically and explicitly presume this to be the situation.

This is especially clear in Deut 6:20ff., a text that, in connection with the foundational *šᵉmaʿ Yiśrāʾel* (6:4), with its emphasis on the unity of God to which all mortal powers are related. There is much to suggest that both of these were conceived together as the beginning of the oldest version of the law.

> *6:20 When your children ask you in time to come, "What is the meaning of the decrees and statutes and the ordinances that the LORD our God has commanded you?" 21 Then shall you say to your children, "We were Pharaoh's slaves in Egypt, but the LORD brought us out of Egypt with a mighty hand . . . 24 Then the LORD commanded us to observe all these statutes, to fear the LORD our God, for our lasting good, so as to keep us alive, as is now the case."*

The child asks, why "our God" has commanded "you" to follow "such commandments."[85] A relationship to God precedes understanding of the law theologically, as well as socialization of the child. The basic question of the sense and purpose is answered by the correlation of law and exodus. Liberation from slave-status is presumed, indeed the really effective act of freeing which can be experienced. Keeping the commandments leads to fearing YHWH, and it protects property and preserves life.

Throughout Deuteronomy it is stated that deuteronomic commandments apply to those who have been freed. If the Book of the Covenant raised the issue of being aliens in Egypt (Ex 22:20; 23:9),[86] Deuteronomy deals freedom from slavery. It is because of this concern that the laws regarding slavery (Deut 15:15) or the protection of aliens and the weak are established (24:18, 22).[87] There is a clear connection with Passover (16:1, 3, 6), but there is also correlation with the festival of weeks (16:12). Reliance on God during war is also based on the exodus (20:1). Israel is reminded whenever they are in danger of falling away from the God of the exodus (13:6, 11).

The exodus, however, is only one half of the story, the other is possession of the land. The answer to the children's question lists the gift of the promised land as the goal and purpose of the trip out of slavery (6:23). The annual payment of firstfruits reminds the people of this connection (26:1ff.). In the historicizing introductions, possession of the land is explicitly mentioned as the binding presupposition of the validity

84 For the question of women, see below pp. 249ff.
85 See Preuss, *Deuteronomium* 100f.
86 See Perlitt, *Ermutigung*.
87 See above p. 198.

of the law (12:29; 17:14; 18:9; 19:1; 26:1).[88] This correlation is especially forcefully reflected in Deut 7: the possession of the land should lead to the destruction of the people of the land. The exclusive connection to the one God comes out of God's act of selection of these people (verse 6). The connection is founded in his love and completed in the event of the exodus (verse 8).

We need to know for whom Deuteronomy was written during the late monarchic period in order to understand the great legal-historical significance of the exodus and the possession of the land. Who is the "you" (singular or plural) constantly being addressed, and to whom everything that has been said or written applies? If we make a list of those with whom the people being addressed are contrasted, it becomes apparent rather quickly, at least who is not meant: other people, slave (male and female – 15:12ff.), aliens, widows and orphans, but also sons and daughters (e.g. 12:12; 16:11, 14), Levites and priests (18:1ff.), the king (17:14ff.) and officials (16:18). It is even clearer here than in the Book of the Covenant[89] or the Decalogue[90] that landowning, free, adult, Israelite males[91] are the people to whom the words are spoken.

On the basis of this evidence, we must say that the widely held notion that Deuteronomy applied to "Israel"[92] is rather imprecise. To be sure, "you" in 6:4f. could refer to all Israel, "Hear, O Israel . . . you shall . . ." Since it is given great theological emphasis here, we should take note. "Israel" is never used as a designation for this authority addressed as "you" within the actual laws. At first 20:3 appears to be an exception, but this is a quotation from the speech that priests are to give to the assembled army in case of war. There is also no juridically exact linguistic usage even here. Elsewhere in Deut 12–26, however, "Israel" always refers to a party *for whom* the people being addressed are to act. They are, for example, to purge the evil from Israel.[93] Those who are being addressed in the law are responsible for Israel and act on behalf of the people, but they are not simply identical with them.

The Levites or Levitic priests, of course, are an indisputable part of Israel. Nevertheless, they are distinguished clearly and in part explicitly from the people being addressed. They own no property (*ḥéleq, naḥālā*; e.g. 14:27; 18:1 and elsewhere). Deuteronomy contains no regulations for priests. Matters are somewhat more complicated for women.[94]

The boundaries, which are established with the deuteronomic "you," become quite apparent by the concept of the brother. Like no other, this concept is especially well suited to bridge the gap between Israel as a nation and the people being addressed.[95] The appearance of the term in the slave law illustrates this quite clearly. "If your brother, whether a

88 For the significance for the dating of Deuteronomy, see above pp. 209ff.
89 See above pp. 195ff.
90 See Crüsemann, *Dekalog* 28ff.
91 For the role of women, see below pp. 249ff.
92 See e.g. Preuss, *Deuteronomium* 182ff.
93 Thus in Deut 17:12, compare 19:13; 21:21; 21:2. Otherwise Israel is mentioned in 13:12; 17:2; 18:16; 21:8; 25:6, 7, 10; 26:15.
94 See below pp. 249ff.
95 See Perlitt, *Brüder*.

Hebrew man or Hebrew woman, is sold to you ..." (15:12) is how it begins. A brother or a sister become a slave, but they remain brother or sister. The commandment to release them after six years is ultimately grounded in this relationship. Even the persons addressed were themselves at one time slaves in Egypt, as their brother is now, and they should treat him accordingly (verse 15).

Nevertheless, during the period of their slavery, these brothers and sisters are not included in the "you" addressed in the law. It is possible that they be treated justly and they should be, however they are no longer subjects of law, only objects. They ought to be able to participate, but they cannot act on their own behalf. The situation is similar for the day laborer (24:15f.). In view of the precise legal language in which the validity of the law presupposes the exodus and the gift of the land, the reference to sibling relationship remains on the secondary level of motivation.

The connection to the exodus and the gift of the land precisely indicates the group, theologically as well as legally, for whom the laws apply. Moses addresses those who have been liberated through the exodus and gives them laws for the period after the time in the future when they will have occupied the land; the law, at the time of its origin, is only applicable to those who are qualified by personal freedom and present ownership of the land (thus, the great gifts of God).

Both are indeed in jeopardy. Freedom and ownership of land can be lost by social dependencies, by failure to observe the commandments, but also by the power of one's own king (17:16). The ownership of land and freedom of an individual and/or of the whole people are tightly interconnected.

The tithe law is part of the core of this deuteronomic freedom theology. It ensures that the Israelite farmers be obligated to no one for some kind of payment of tribute, except to the liberating God himself and to those who do not share in the blessings of freedom and ownership of land.

A look at Greece will clarify what we mean.[96] There, only those who were not free had to pay a general tribute, and then only in states ruled by tyrants. Freedom from tribute is a central expression of real freedom. The biblical variation regards the traditional tithe as the most important state tax, which is first contributed at a regular festival, and then donated to the poor. The priests, according to Deut 18:1ff., could retain only a limited portion of the sacrifice. Except for the Levite priests of the various localities who were also to eat, they did not share in the offering of the tithe. Thus, the law is a direct expression of deuteronomic freedom theology.

Overview: The further history of the tithe in Israel was shaped by the combination of deuteronomic and priestly concepts. Regarding the latter group, according to Num 18:8–32, a tithe was to be paid to the Levites who were in turn to hand over a portion of that to the priests. Furthermore, Lev 27:32f. gives evidence of a tithe of cattle. In any case,

96 See e.g. Andreades, *Geschichte* 109ff., 134ff.; Heichelheim, *Wirtschaftsgeschichte* 404ff.; Finley, *Wirtschaft* 95ff.

the tithe is here theoretically entirely separated from its connection to the state; it became a purely cultic tax.

Documents of the Persian period attest that such a tithe was always a controversial, but generally recognized presence (Neh 10:38; 12:44, 47; 13:(5), 12; Mal 3:8, 10), and it existed independently along with the Persian state tax[97] (Neh 5:4). As elsewhere, further development was shaped by it, so that the various texts in the Pentateuch were placed along side each other. As a consequence, first in Tob 1:6–8 and Jub 32:9ff., there is attestation that the Levitical tithe was mentioned first and the deuteronomic second (thus first in LXX of Deut 26:12) and the tithe for the poor in the third year is incidentally third. This system is attested frequently in ancient Judaism.[98] It is interesting to note that the correlation of the tithe with the sacral royalty always comes through. Thus, the Hasmonean kings repeatedly claim the tithe for themselves.[99] The early church later laid claim to the tithe,[100] and through the Carolingians it finally became the state-guaranteed material foundation for the Western Church and remained a part of the church through significant changes[101] all the way to its replacement by the modern European church tax system.[102]

The Powerless Center

The demand for a unified cult site is at the high point of deuteronomic law (Deut 12). All sacrifices and cultic payments were to be brought to the single shrine selected by YHWH. The particulars were established in a whole series of laws.[103] This was certainly one of the most significant turning points in Israelite cultic history, and it had tremendous consequences. The decontrol of secular slaughter, the separation of cult and religion, and finally the shape of Judaism and Christianity begin here.

Cult centralization is the shape which Deuteronomy gives to the first commandment. To be sure, cult unity is never based in the unity of God. Nevertheless, we cannot doubt that there is a correlation. The only question is *how* we should think about it. The formula of Deut 6:4 "YHWH – our God – one" in its ambiguity in grammar and substance, among other things, should be understood as a weapon against poly-YHWHism,[104] of the kind we find attested in phrases like "YHWH of Dan,"[105] "YHWH of Teman" and "YHWH of Samaria."[106] The one YHWH is to be associated with a single shrine.

We do not know what happened to bring about this earthshaking idea, and its application remains veiled. The eighth-century prophets, in spite

---

97 For this, see Dandameyev, *Geschichte* 43ff.; Stern, *Persian Palestine* 113.
98 See Oppenheimer, '*Am Ha-aretz* 34ff.
99 Oppenheimer, '*Am Ha-aretz* 34ff.
100 See Vischer, *Zehntforderung*.
101 E.g. Zimmermann, *Zehntenfrage*.
102 See Liermann, article on *Abgaben*; and the relevant material in Lienemann (ed.), *Finanzen*.
103 For the centralization laws, see Preuss, *Deuteronomium* 116.
104 For this, see e.g. Höffken, *Bemerkung*; further lit. above p. 204, n. 13.
105 Thus Am 8:14.
106 Thus attested in Kuntilet 'Ajrud (Meshel, *Kuntillet*), see also Smelik, *Dokumente* 144.

of all of their criticism of the shrines, seem to be unaware of such an idea, nevertheless, they were involved with its roots. Even the altar law of the Book of the Covenant recognizes a variety of places at which YHWH causes his name to be proclaimed (Ex 20:24).[107]

Prophetic criticism of cult, like altar laws, made distinctions. Not every shrine with an old tradition is a legitimate site; there was a reduction in number through critical selection. Nevertheless, the step toward the deuteronomic concept was a powerful one, and the situation after 701 BCE could have been an impetus for this.[108] The encroachment of the Assyrian King Sennacherib reduced Jerusalem to a small district, possibly only the area of the former city-state, and the remainder of Judah was divided among the Philistine states. As long as this situation may have lasted, we should probably reckon that there was great shock. The fate of the northern kingdom was readily apparent. Great old shrines like Hebron, Mamre, Beersheba and others known through the Bible or archaeology had all come under foreign control. What was the nature of the connection of the Judean population to the old capital with its religious significance? What else happened? All we have are questions, there are no answers! It is possible that there is a correlation with the notion of the uniqueness of the cult of the legitimate site. The regulations in Deut 12, especially those in verses 13–19 which we would have to regard as being the oldest,[109] already presume this unity and deal with how this unity is to be practiced.

The centralization of all cults must have led to a tremendous growth in the significance of Jerusalem and its temple. Decidedly greater portions of the wealth of the society flowed here than previously. Jerusalem now received what had previously been going to regional and local shrines. There was, of course, a significant decrease in the amount of sacrifice because of the spread of secular slaughtering, especially in the form of a general reduction in contributions to state and cult. Nevertheless, the economic effect of strengthening the position of the capital city should not be doubted. This was, of course, known and intentional. For this reason scholars have interpreted deuteronomic cult centralization as an attempt to direct a larger part of the resources to the capital rather than raising taxes. This could also be seen as a significant strengthening of the central power of the monarchy.[110]

Here, as in the system of social security, the deuteronomic concept can only be interpreted as a comprehensive movement, which worked on two levels. To be sure, greater wealth did flow toward the capital, and the weakening or abolition of other competing sites and shrines must have strengthened the role of the Jerusalem shrine. At the same time, however, those who were traditional leaders in society must have been considerably weakened.

No king, state, shrine or priesthood had control over the new revenues. Of course, the Jerusalem traders and the farmers of the area

---

107 See above pp. 171ff.
108 For the historical situation, see Donner, *Geschichte* II 322ff. and above pp. 214f.
109 With Preuss, *Deuteronomium* 133.
110 Especially Claburn, *Fiscal Basis*; see also Smith, *Parties* 51; Gottwald, *Tribes* 727 note 94; cf Oden, *Taxation* 170f.

could have profited when the offerings were changed to money (Deut 14:24–26), but Deuteronomy accomplished the general weakening of the king, the officials, the priests and it called to account the entire upper stratum of society. The priests of the central shrine, for example, received neither the tithe nor as many portions of sacrifices as formerly, or as had been granted in the priestly laws. Tithes and firstfruits no longer contributed to their livelihood; the number of sacrifices in general were noticeably reduced by the decontrol of secular slaughtering. Sacrifices were essentially brought only for special reasons.

The Deuteronomic cultic program meant that in general the Judean landowner was relieved of the burden of state taxes and cultic offerings. The abolition of the large number of shrines where people lived from cultic offerings is in some respects similar to certain aspects of the German reformation. We must remember what Deuteronomy does not mention, but we can deduce on the basis of its general assessment.

Included in this, above all, is the abolition of compulsory labor, which had existed in Israel since the early monarchic period, and which the discovery of a seal attests for the late monarchy.[111] The central position of the exodus makes a compulsory obligation of this kind to a king impossible. This would be rather like a king leading his people back into Egypt (Deut 17:16). The king was for all intents and purposes thrown back on the income from his own resources, if we are to take Deuteronomy at its word. This weakening of the state authorities, even economically, makes it clear what cult centralization was intended to do.

The Social Safety Net : Toward Social Legislation

a. SOLIDARITY AND BLESSING

The provisions of deuteronomic social law are often described as "laws of humanity."[112] The sympathetic character indicated in this way might be typical of ancient legislation for the poor, but the label doesn't really express the radicality of the law nor its theological role in deuteronomic thinking.

The significance of the social legislation arises first from its position within the structure of the corpus of laws and its connection with other religious and cultic themes. We first find the laws in the block of text between, on the one side, the basic provisions dealing with the subjects of cult unity (12), protection of the exclusive veneration of God (13) and cultic purity (14); and the so-called constitutional provisions beginning in 16:8 on the other.

It is shaped by the theme of cultic unity of time. The annual offering of the tithe and the tithe for the poor in the third year (14:22–29), the seven-year rhythm of the year of release (15:1–11) and the individual manumission of slaves (15:12–18), the three principle festivals of the year (16) – these are the cultic rhythms that regulate the most important social

111 See 2 Sam 20:24; 1 Kg 4:6; 5:28; 12:4ff.; Mi 3:10; Jer 22:13ff.; Hab 2:12; Avigad, *Chief*; also Smelik, *Dokumente* 127.; in summary now Kessler, *Staat und Gesellschaft* 154ff.
112 Weinfeld, *Deuteronomy* 282ff., ibid., *Origin*; Preuss, *Deuteronomium* 86f. and elsewhere; already Dillmann, *Komm.* 125.

provisions. It is not only the families and their house slaves that participate in the annual festivals, all the needy people of the various localities are included.[113]

Provisions for the forgiveness of debt and manumission of slaves in chapter 15 are framed by the provisions regarding the tithe (14:22–29) and the firstborn (15:19–22). Both bring significant relief from traditional burdens for farmers and tie them to the central shrine. This relief from burdens brings them into solidarity with the socially weak, and coordinates with the third year tithe, forgiveness of debt and manumission of slaves. Thus, the social laws are part of the religious calendar and are woven into the fabric of its seven-year rhythms.

The religious significance of the social laws is additionally underscored by a series of remarkable formulations found with all the important social regulations.[114] In conjunction with the third year tax for the poor, which created a secure livelihood for those who were socially weakest, Deut 14:29 says that Levites, aliens, orphans, widows were to eat their fill, "so that (*lᵉmaʿan*) the LORD your God may bless you in all the work that you undertake."

In conjunction with the establishment of a remission of debts every seven year, we read: "for on this account (*biglal hadābār hazzē*) YHWH your God will bless you in all your work and in all (*mišlāḥ*) that you undertake" (15:10). The same or similar formulations appear with the law about the manumission of debt slaves (male and female): "YHWH your God will bless you in all that you do" (15:18); with the inclusion of those who are socially weakest in the annual pilgrimage festivals: "for YHWH your God will bless you in all your produce and in all your undertakings, and you shall surely celebrate" (16:15); where charging interest is prohibited: "so that YHWH your God may bless you in all your undertakings in the land" (23:20); and finally, with the order to leave a portion of the harvest in the field: "so that YHWH your God may bless you in all your undertakings" (24:19).

These indications of purpose, clearly connected to each other, are included with the most important social laws, binding them, and only them, together. In this way a unified (not just for our categories, but also for deuteronomic thinking) block of provisions has been established. Security for social problem groups[115] (i.e. the traditional categories of needy persons, those without justice or land, aliens, widows and orphans, but also slaves, those deeply in debt, Levites without land or work, and the hungry) rests on the work of those free, landowners to whom the words are being spoken. Divine blessing for their work is explicitly connected to these needy people, so ensuring that a portion of the produce goes to benefit the weakest in society. Inclusion of the weak in the riches of the harvest guarantees blessing for the labor that makes these riches possible. The formulae are connected with the laws. They are new formulations of older cultic traditions, especially those of holy seasons. In Deuteronomy, blessing, which was probably

---

113 See especially Braulik, *Freude.*
114 For what follows, see Crüsemann, *Produktionsverhältnisse* 87ff.
115 For this, now, see also Lohfink, *Entwurf einer Gesellschaft* with a somewhat different assessment.

always expected to come from adapting to sacral temporal rhythms, is connected with the observance of social laws.

There is reference to blessing-as-consequence with a few other laws, but that we see the same formula as in the texts above, see 24:13 with the return of the pledge (see also 14:24; 15:4–6, 14; 16:10). The subject of blessing also shapes the beginning and conclusion of deuteronomic law.

In 12:7 there is a description of celebration at the one shrine. People were supposed to eat there and rejoice because of "all the undertakings in which YHWH your God has blessed you." At the end of the entire law section, we find the following petition as a conclusion to the oath in which payment of the third year tithe is pledged to marginal groups, "Look down from your holy habitation, from heaven, and bless your people Israel and the ground that you have given us, as you swore to our ancestors – a land flowing with milk and honey" (26:15).

Connecting blessing almost exclusively with the social laws gives at the same time special meaning to the blessing (and cursing) formulae in the closing chapters, particularly in Deut 28.

All of this shows how closely attached deuteronomic law remained to iron age agricultural reality and in a certain sense defined that reality. The wealth of agricultural production is a result of experience with Israel's God. The exodus and the gift of land, appear as constitutive experiences for a relationship to God, in the legal, political and social freedom of the Israelite farmers. No one has the right to place a burden on the backs of those who have been freed, except the God who liberated them, and the burden he lays is nothing more than a joyful pilgrimage festival. Everyone is to participate in this celebration, even those without power because they lack land or justice. This transmission of blessing guarantees future blessing.[116]

b. THE FORGIVENESS OF DEBTS IN THE SABBATH YEAR

The most important economic law in the Bible is the regular forgiveness of debts in Deut 15:1ff.:[117]

> 15:1 *Every seventh year you shall grant a remission of debts. 2 And this is the manner of the remission: every creditor shall give up from his hand what he has loaned to his neighbor. He ought not to harass his neighbor and his brother, because a remission for YHWH has been proclaimed. 3 You may harass a foreigner, but you must let go from your hand of whatever you loaned your brother.*

The wording of the whole law, especially verse 9, as later Jewish interpretation and tradition makes clear, deals with the remission of debts and cancellation of outstanding obligations. Unfortunately, there are significant problems in the wording of the critical formulation of verse 2. Most scholars amplify or emend the text.[118] The translation above

---

116 In conjuction with this we also note the blessing of the poor in 24:13 (cf 15:9; 24:15). For this, see now Kessler, *Rolle des Armes*.
117 For what follows, in detail, Crüsemann, *Schulden und Schuld*.
118 There is hardly a single interpretation without insertions in the received text. In the masoretic text *baʿal maššē yādō* forms a single unity; the relative clause would then be the object. But what exactly does that mean? Horst, *Privilegrecht* 82ff. regards this *baʿal* to be the lord who has loaned. If that is supposed to be the sense

assumes that verse 2 can and must be understood as parallel to verse 3. Since verse 1 uses (*šmṭ*) "letting go" as a kind of heading for the whole, and verse 3 uses the concept again, referring to the faithful person ("you shall release from your hand"), we should interpret verse 2 in the same way. This is not a pledge with the hand or something similar, but a letting go of the hand.

Whatever we decide, the meaning is clear: every seventh year all debts should be stricken from the record. This is not simply a rejection of harsh measures to force payment, but it goes to the heart of the agreements that underlie loans. It is ultimately stated clearly and unmistakably in verses 7ff. that personal pledges, especially those in which people are bound over, are rejected.[119]

At the same time, it treats the problem of who will still lend to a neighbor as a seventh year approaches. Furthermore, it is here that the entire weight of religious tradition is laid. The cry of those who can get nothing more at that time will reach God and cause him to intervene. Ultimately, the blessing of the land is dependent upon this remission of debts (verse 10b).

We have already discussed the fact that the existence of debt – the process of lending together with all of its consequences – had a fundamental significance for an agrarian society.[120] Deut 15:1ff. is an attempt to remove the power from the societal mechanisms at work there. This power is why debt is significant. If we examine the text against the background of the preceding ancient Near Eastern and Israelite tradition, we will see what a regularly required remission of debts every seven years might mean.[121]

In the states of the Mesopotamian region, there were so-called *mesarum* decrees quite early (from *ca.*2500 BCE – thus not long after the development of an entity resembling what we would call a state). These were remissions from debt occurring at irregular intervals.[122]

The ancient Babylonian kings used this device to declare a general forgiveness of debts, usually at the beginning of their reign. Perhaps this happened at a time of massive debts and interest, which had a paralyzing effect upon the entire economic life of the society. By this means economic misery and stagnation could be controlled.[123]

---

of the hiph. of *nšh* II, the hiph., in the relative clause does not agree and must be changed. Frequently today scholars propose the elimination of *maššē ʾet* before *maššē* (BHS; Mayes, commentary – in part; Merendino, *Gesetz* 108f.; Cavaletti, *Significato*; Hossfeld/Reuter, article on *nāšāʾ* 660). The alternative to this textual alteration is, in my opinion, to apply the expression of Neh 10:32 (*maššāʾ yad*) or that of Deut 15:3 (*šmṭ yad* with Pers. suff.) here. The latter already in Raschi, Luzzato and others according to Hoffmann, *Deuteronomium* 225 (there 221–234 a thorough discussion of the text and the rabbinic tradition). Finally, Weinfeld, *Sabbatical Year* 50 who would regard the relative clause as the subject of "not oppress."

119 Thus, correctly, Horst, *Privilegrecht* 83ff.
120 See above pp. 185ff.
121 A detailed comparison in Weinfeld, *Sabbatical Year*.
122 The material has been gathered and commented upon in Kraus, *Verfügungen*.
123 Especially Olivier, *Effectiveness*.

The best preserved of these decrees come from Ammi-Saduqa (*ca.*1646–1626 BCE) the fourth successor to Hammurabi.

§1, For the settlement of outstanding debts of the fiefs: farmers, shepherds, animal skinners, those occupied in the summer pasture and bringers of produce of the palace so that they grow strong and in order to treat them equitably: they are forgiven; the enforcer may not use violence to compel the family of the produce bringer.

§2 is addressed to the "merchants of Babylon."

§3 Whoever loans barley or silver to an Accadian or Ammuraian for interest or for a return . . . and has executed a document: because the king has restored justice to the land, his document is invalid. He cannot exact barley or silver in accord with the wording of the document.[124]

As further paragraphs of the decree show, exact provisions are made to apply respectively to precisely designated groups of the population. These vary with different kings and the measures that they take.

The lifting of or cancellation without some replacement of even "private" debts are a part of a so-called "just order," which the king (and therefore the state) imposes. Their irregularity of timing and un-predictability are typical.[125] The effectiveness of the decrees is demon-strable, unlike the situation with ancient Near Eastern legal corpora.[126]

Unfortunately, such decrees are only attested until *ca.*1600 BCE, and we do not know how later states operated, especially those who had direct dealings with Israel.[127] For this reason we also cannot tell whether deuteronomic law givers were aware of traditions of this kind and took them over in a varied form; or whether they freely invented the legal instrument themselves. The observation that Israel was not alone in its attempts at economic law is important for our evaluation of the biblical law. These are measures that were necessary for the maintenance of essential order and economic productivity, as modern debt crises show, even today. Methodologically, this means that we are not permitted to regard laws of this, from the outset, as utopian.

Like the ancient Near Eastern practice, we also know earlier Old Testament tradition in this situation. The Book of the Covenant is aware of a sabbath year alongside the weekly day of rest. According to Ex 23:10f., people were supposed to set free or let go (*šmṭ*) what they had produced every seventh year, using the standard term from Deut 15:1ff. "And what they leave, the wild animals may eat" (Ex 23:11).

What applies to the fields, as it says in a note, should also be practiced in the vineyards and olive groves. The formulations state quite clearly that, exactly like the weekly day of rest, the social purpose is not primary; it was an important consequence. We find in the sabbath year a

124 Translation after Kraus, *Verfügungen*.
125 For this, especially, Olivier, *Periodicity*.
126 For this, see especially Westbrook, *Law Codes*.
127 Olivier, *Periodicity* 228, mentions that "some of its features remained prevalent in the later practices of *kidinnūtū* and of the Neo-Assyrian royal decrees of *andurārum*". For the former, see Leemans, *Kidinnūtū*; and for the latter, see Lemche, *Andurārum*.

combination of religious, economic and ecological motives which parallel the weekly day of rest. According to this law, the surplus gained is not to be set aside for a contribution, nor is it to be converted into money; the field is to be left fallow. In the third and latest version in Lev 25:1ff., the rule is intensified and is treated by itself: the seventh year (unlike that of seven times seven, the year of jubilee) is for the land (or for God).[128]

Deuteronomy turns the Book of the Covenant's fallow fields and "the letting go" of a year's produce into a "letting go" of all debts. Instead of not planting and not harvesting for an entire year, using the produce of the other six years in such a way that they cover the seventh, Deuteronomy requires – using the same concept of "letting go" (*šmṭ*) – the remission of all outstanding debts and the social dependencies that they entail. We should not assume on the basis of the text, that Deuteronomy is aware of yet another sabbath year corresponding to the one in the Book of the Covenant. It rather develops the concept and substitutes a cancellation of outstanding debts and the possibilities that they include for the renunciation of harvested goods.

Excepting the notion that legislative powers in Israel were utopian, we believe the law in Deut 15:1ff. should be read on the basis of its economic intentions. How does a person make forgiveness of debts regular and thus fundamentally accountable? Apparently this was more important to the authors than the problem of who would continue to lend, against which they were reacting in verses 9ff. This is about *why* and *to what purpose* loans are made. Anyone making a loan with the intention, hidden or overt, of producing dependency, to get people and land into his own hands – which may have been the rule! – would lose his support by this law. The only person who has a chance to get his money back is someone who lends generously, so that there is an effective change of situation for needy people until the next sabbath year.

Overview: The Holiness Code in Lev 25 reduces the seventh year to a purely agrarian, fallow year for the benefit of the land, having no social consequences (verses 2–7). In contrast, liberation from debts is only discussed for the year of jubilee, the seventh sabbath year (verses 8ff.). The forgiveness of debts becomes a total return to the original state of affairs. We will discuss the theological and historical background later.[129] In any case, unlike the sabbath year, there is no demonstrable evidence of this year of jubilee in the further history of Israel.

According to the rabbis, it is connected with the presence of the whole people in the land, as it says in verse 1. This situation, however, no longer existed after the exile of the tribes east of the Jordan (733 BCE)[130] or the end of the northern kingdom. On the other hand, the traceable history of this institution begins with the obligation to the sabbath year *and* forgiveness of debts in Neh 10:32. Already in this verse there is an addition of the provisions of the Book of the Covenant with those of Deuteronomy.[131] The sabbath year was observed in Judaism, as a series of occasional

128 See below p. 283.
129 See below pp. 283ff.
130 See *bAr* 32b; *sifra behar* 2.2.
131 See below p. 341.

references in historic books and ostraka demonstrates.[132] It was an integral part of Torah.

This did not change until the New Testament period, with the so-called prosbul of Hillel [designed to protect the rights of creditors]. According to the Mishna (nShevi 10:2–4),[133] the people had to lend to stave off dire poverty in the Roman province, it was necessary to cancel the remission of debts during the sabbath year.[134] Juridically, the pro-missory note was depersonalized, that is, it was transferred to a court. From then on, probably the most significant business law in the Bible no longer had a chance to be practiced either in Judaism or Christianity.

Moreover, there is a central New Testament text showing a new transposition of the same basic idea. In the Lord's Prayer petition, "Forgive us our debts as we have forgiven our debtors" (Mt 6:12), we see a concept in the Greek as well as the Aramaic original behind it, with which the English translation covers both moral/ethical and economic debts.[135] The significance of Torah for Matthew (especially Mt 5:17; 23:2), the inclusion of themes as terminology in Mt 18, but also elsewhere in the Gospel, show that this is not a spiritualization. For those people who are anxious about their daily bread, as a previous petition shows, debts are not a purely spiritual matter.[136] It is already a widely attested tradition within Judaism that every prayer to God for forgiveness must be coupled with a readiness to forgive.[137] We can see in the context of the tradition in which it stands what this petition (using the language of Deut 15:1ff.)[138] achieves theologically in the heart of Christian theology.

We are no longer dealing with a regular forgiveness of debts every seven years, nor with an impetus provided by a state, which cannot be demonstrated from the evidence, nor of a renunciation of Torah practice, as in the prosbul, nor a spiritualization of the concept of debt, and thus a separating of faith and reality as in the usual Christian interpretation, rather, this is a coupling of forgiveness, which we seek from God and need for life, with the remission of debts owed to us, which include all financial debts. We cannot expect forgiveness for our debts unless we are prepared to renounce claim to outstanding debts owed to us. Perhaps it is easier for wealthy Christians[139] to return to a forgiveness of debts of Deut 15 than, with the radicality of Jesus to deprive themselves of all forgiveness.

---

132 See 1 Macc 6:49, 53; Josephus, Ant. 11.338, 13.234, 14.475; in addition to the Muraba't texts (DJD II no. 18.24) and others. For the sources and the re-constructible seven-year rhythm, see Wacholder, *Sabbatical Cycles*; see also Jeremias, *Sabbatjahr*; Noth, *Sabbath Years*; Blosser, *Sabbath Year*; for this, see Wacholder, *Respone*; Safrai, *Implementation* (Hebr.).
133 See Rothkoff, article on Prosbul.
134 For the surmised economic background, see Oakman, *Jesus* 73ff.
135 See Dalman, *Worte Jesu* 334ff.; also now Black, *Muttersprache* 140ff.; Schwarz, *Urgestalt* 226; for the terminology also, e.g. Wolter, article on Schuldner.
136 See Oakman, *Jesus* 153ff. as well as the suggestions in Kippenberg, *Entlassung* 102; Theissen, *Schatten* 207 note 8.
137 JesSir 28:2; for this see especially Rüger, *Mass*.
138 Thus especially Fensham, *Background*.
139 For the understanding of this formulation in Latin America, see Hinkelammert, *Schuldenautomatismus* 141ff.; Cardenal, *Evangelium* I 102.

C. THE SYSTEM OF SOCIAL SECURITY

The laws regarding tithing and the regular forgiveness of debts are the most innovative and radical prescription, but they should be understood as a part of a broader legislation whose structure must be examined. All of the laws are intended to provide materially and socially for the problem groups of the society of the period. The laws seek to prevent or at least to make it more difficult for the free, landowning Israelites, the stratum distinguished by the exodus and the gift of (the) land, from falling into the whirlpool of social decline. The context of these laws demonstrates a well-thought social safety net.[140] It reveals itself best when viewed from the perspective of an Israelite farmer.

Regarding the traditional challenges the farmer faced, we would first mention the fact that he was freed from the burden of two-thirds of the previous tithe-tax (Deut 14:22ff.). This was of great significance, especially for the smaller and already heavily indebted farmers. Other requirements from the state were likewise removed, above all compulsory labor and other payments of tribute. If such an Israelite were forced to borrow because of sickness in the family, poor harvest, drought, warfare, legal problems or other factors, thus making him dependent upon a stronger and wealthier neighbor, he no longer needed to pay interest upon the loan.

The prohibition against interest in the Book of the Covenant is adopted and repeated (Deut 23:20f.). There is a whole group of regulations applying to the usual securities made by pledges for debt in such situations. The widow's (only) garment is excepted (Deut 24:17f.). It is not permitted to keep overnight a pledge necessary for survival from a "poor man" ('*iš ʿānī*) (24:12). Generally, immediate or forcible pledges were not permitted. If it was forbidden in 24:10f. for the faithful to go into the house of a debtor and take a pledge that seemed appropriate or was due to him, it becomes apparent what the usual practice might have been. Deuteronomy, however, formulates the first form of the inviolability of the home, even in cases – justified! – of receiving a pledge. Furthermore, no necessities of life are permitted to be used for a pledge. This is formulated in 24:6:

> 24:6 *No one shall take both millstones or (even only) the upper millstone, for he that (does that) for a pledge takes life (itself).*

140 Lohfink even considers a "society without marginal groups" (*Entwurf einer Gesellschaft*). In many respects his observations and views correspond to my own opinion (see already Crüsemann, *Produktionsverhältnisse*; the discussions of Deuteronomy have barely noticed this study). This applies especially to the analysis of the "welfare system" (Lohfink 35). He is also completely correct in distinguishing the various groups from Deuteronomy itself. But, because aliens remain aliens, that is, they have no real share in the land, they also remain a marginal group and their problems remain as well. And whether in 15:4, 11 the land can be played against the social powers of Israel, in my opinion remains doubtful. There would have been more poverty even in Israel when this was not necessary, nor should it have been. For the system of social laws, see also Levenson, *Poverty and the State*; Epsztein, *Justice Sociale* 177ff.; Kaufman, *Reconstruction*.

Pledges that affect life (*néfeš*) are prohibited.[141] And last but not least: in every indebtedness, there is the prospect that one might be freed of the obligation at the latest in the seventh, that is the Shmitta year.

In spite of all of these limitations regulating the process of receiving a loan, we should not exclude the possibility a person might be enslaved through a personal pledge arising from massive debts. A consequence of bad harvest, sickness or other calamities might make it unavoidable that a person sell himself – thus the formulation of Deut 15:12 – or other persons of his family into slavery. In this case the slave law of Deut 15:12–18 comes into effect. Slaves (male and female) should be released after six years of service. New to this law in comparison to the Book of the Covenant is not only the inclusion of women, but also the claim to a kind of money for "temporary assistance" (verses 13f.) that might enable the person to start independent existence anew.

Another law is even stronger than these regulations against the form of slavery resisted in Deuteronomy:

> Deut 23:16 Slaves who have escaped from their owners shall not be given back to them. 16 They shall reside with you in your midst, in any place they choose in any of your towns, wherever they please; you shall not oppress them.

Nothing exceeds this regulation for the forgiveness of debts (15:1ff.) for its change-provoking radicality. Unlike other ancient Near Eastern laws, in which masters are protected from loss by the escape of slaves,[142] also unlike the many laws in the Book of the Covenant, which attempt to protect the residual rights of slaves (male and female),[143] slaves are protected here in another way.

Every slave has the unlimited right to settle anywhere among God's people and begin a new life, unmolested.[144] The whole nation became a place of asylum for runaway slaves. The freedom to choose a place – we think of how controversial the question of analogous situations are today, how little choice we promise to asylum seekers – is expressly guaranteed, with language shaping Deuteronomy most profoundly: the choice or selection (*bḥr*) of a place (*māqōm*) through God.

A slave can choose as freely as God, where he wants to live. The law aims, if we take it seriously as legislation,[145] directly at the social reality of slavery in the nation of Israel. Where the possibility to escape and live is

---

141 Rabbinic tradition correspondingly expanded the understanding to all double items necessary for existence, Sifre §272; bBM 115a; jBM 9.13.14b.

142 The Code of Hammurabi sets the death penalty for a similar act (§15–20); see also the Code of Urnammu §12f.; for this, see Szlechter, *Affranchissement*; ibid., *Statut*; see also Cardellini, "*Sklaven*"-*Gesetze* 64ff. and elsewhere.

143 See above pp. 151ff.

144 Most commentaries (see Dillmann, Steuernagel, Bertholet, Rad, Mayes, etc.) and partly also rabbinic tradition (see Hoffmann, *Deuteronomium* II 40f.) assume that this refers to flight from foreign territory into Israel. Nevertheless, the "in your midst" upon which the interpretation rests, is overtaxed, see also Weinfeld, *Deuteronomy* 272f. According to Cardellini, "*Sklaven*"-*Gesetze* 278f., these words would be an addition. For the history of the prescription, especially in the New Testament, see Piatelli, *Enfranchissement*.

145 And not only as a prudent admonition – as, for example, referring to Prov 30:10 – Weinfeld, *Deuteronomy* 272f.

guaranteed without limitation, the home of such flight must change the treatment of slaves (male and female) so that it anticipates social ties and economic opportunities. The concept of the "good" (*ṭōb*), which is decisive in the choice of a place of asylum, also appears in the slave law itself. Deut 15:16 opens the possibility of transition into permanent slavery by personal declaration of the slave that he loves his master and things go "well" (*ṭōb*) for him there. The intent here is to influence the right and custom of severe physical punishment of male slaves and sexual exploitation of female slaves[146] in the Book of the Covenant. Since social interrelations appear to make escape advisable only when there is a concern for physical safety or something similar, it appears that it was first among the people of God that such laws paved the social-historical transition from slavery to labor for hire.

Corresponding to this, we find a group, appearing in Deuteronomy for the first time in the history of Israel, wage-laborers. The group includes those who are landless but free and depend on having employment.

> 24:14 *You shall not withhold the wages of poor and needy laborers, whether Israelites or aliens who reside in your land in one of your towns. 15 You shall pay them their wages daily before sunset, because they are poor and their livelihood depends on them; otherwise they would cry to YHWH against you, and you would incur guilt.*

From the outset, we see that wage-laborers apparently were included among the poor ('*ānī w*' '*ebyōn*). The term poor is no longer, as it was in the eighth century, associated with people who were insignificant or in debt – those who were dependent but still technically free landowners.[147] They remain "poor," even if they are working for others after having lost their own land. These people are included here in the laws for social protection, no matter whether they are brothers (that is, fellow Israelites) or aliens (*gēr*). In verse 15 the description of the situation of such a person is precise: his whole life (*néfeš*), his soul, is dependent upon those wages.

As before, traditional landless groups (aliens, widows and orphans) are included along with the wage-laborer, to whose number Deuteronomy adds landless Levites. These socially powerless groups are assigned to the free landowners as clients in several places in the law book, and they are to be included in sacrifice meals and festivals (16:11, 14; cf 12:12, 18). Every third year the tithe gave them something on which to rely. A remnant of each harvest from vineyards and olive groves was to remain in the fields for their benefit (24:19ff.). Furthermore, like all Israelites, they had the right to eat as much as they wanted everywhere in grain fields or vineyards, however, they could not use a sickle or fill a vessel to transport produce from the field (23:25f.). All of the riches of the land were available to them. There need not be any hunger. Even if we presume a long tradition of need, it is only within the late monarchic period that we see something resembling begging.[148] That is, these people are cut off from all means of livelihood. They ought to be able to eat.

---

146 See above pp. 153ff.
147 See above pp. 185ff.
148 See Kessler, *Juda* 107, 124 with reference to Ez 18:7, 16.

This whole inter-coordinated system of laws for social security springs from a fundamental deuteronomic idea: the freedom that has been experienced, which exodus and land represent and which is manifest in the freedom of the agricultural population, includes freedom from requirements of payment of tribute or compulsory labor (to the state). It is limited only by the double connection to the giver of freedom and to those who do not participate in freedom to the same degree. Guarantees of social security and survival are established for all problem groups and those might be threatened. Furthermore, this relationship is not portrayed as a moral appeal for charity, but as law. Only by passing on this freedom and wealth can the continuance of these gifts be secured.

Mosaic Authority and the People's Sovereignty: The Political Constitution

Deuteronomy's regulations related to institutions are its most radical innovations with respect to the Book of the Covenant. Scholars speak of a "constitution" or a "model constitution."[149] This modern concept is as unavoidable as it is appropriate, since there are no analogies in ancient Near Eastern law; fundamentally, the analogies are just in recent constitutions.[150] The state itself becomes the object of regulation.

For subjects like the institution and authorization of royal power, the organization of law, the support of priests and prophets and supervision, the Moses who speaks in Deuteronomy places all decision-making authority in the hands of those addressed as "you." Only on this basis of these texts are we able to conjecture what this fictive dress in speech from the distant past might have meant for its time. The present day understanding of these themes is more strongly influenced by the historical background against which we read them than with other themes. Are they realistic constitutional provisions, through which the questions of power in the state are posed, or are they a utopian model for an unspecified and never realized future?

The State under Torah: The Kingship Law

In the ancient Near East the monarchy was a mediator between the earthly and heavenly realms. As the royal psalms show, Israel generally participated in this view. Especially in Jerusalem, the Davidic king was celebrated as son of God (Ps 2:7), ruler of the world (Ps 2:8f.) and protector of divine justice (Ps 72). He was established and vested by YHWH himself. This is the foil against which deuteronomic king law is to be read.

> Deut 17:14 *When you have come into the land that YHWH your God is giving you, and have taken possession of it and settled in it, and you say, "I will set a king over me, like all the nations that are*

---

149 Especially Lohfink, *Sicherung*, who regards Deuteronomy as a prototype of the modern principle of separation of powers after Montesquieu; Rüterswörden, *Gemeinschaft* makes a comparison with ancient Greek democracy. For older positions, see Preuss, *Deuteronomium*.

150 Or in the area of ancient democracy, for this, see below pp. 245ff.

around me," 15 you may indeed set over you a king whom YHWH
your God will choose. One of your own community you may set as
king over you; you are not permitted to put a foreigner over you,
who is not of your own community. 16 Even so, he must not
acquire many horses for himself, or return the people to Egypt in
order to acquire more horses, since YHWH has said to you, "You
must never return that way again." 17 And he must not acquire
many wives for himself, or else his heart will turn away; also
silver and gold he must not acquire in great quantity for himself. 18
When he has taken the throne of his kingdom, he shall have a copy of
this law written for him in the presence of the levitical priests. 19 It
shall remain with him and he shall read in it all the days of his life,
so that he may learn to fear YHWH his God, diligently observing
all the words of his law and these statutes, 20 neither exalting
himself above other members of the community nor turning aside
from the commandment, either to the right or to the left, so that
he and his descendants may reign long over his kingdom in
Israel.

In this law, the power of the king is doubly limited, by the people
being addressed and by Torah. Initially, the establishment of a king
derives only from the desire of the people, since the protasis comprises
all of verse 14. The desire for a king is also included under the
introductory "When": when the people want a king, one should be set
up. This act of placing one person over others is done by the people, for
the people. We would, at very least, have to ask whether the intent here is
a one-time act, since the establishment of a king implies dynastic
successors. This is not at all convincing, since the intention might be that
the people had possibility for election each time there was to be a new
king, as they would for example, among the descendants of the king who
are mentioned in verse 20.

Thus, the state in general and the one in particular who holds power
would respond to the people's desire for a king. There is still, however,
the other side: the people should only crown someone whom YHWH has
chosen. God and Israel work together, neither can act alone. They are
not permitted to divide or play them off against each other. There is
neither a literary[151] nor historical basis for this. The chain of events after
the death of Amon including the installation of Josiah as well as his
successors (2 Kg 21:24; 23:30) corresponds so closely to what is described
here that we could hardly regard it as accidental. The people decide that
they want a king, and they install him; his power comes from the people,
but the people remain with the traditional Davidic dynasty, the family
selected by YHWH. After the death of Josiah, the people selected from
that family a person who was politically suitable.

151 E.g. Alt, *Heimat* 265 note 3; Boecker, *Beurteilung* 49 note 1; Mayers, commentary
271; García Lopez, *Roi* 284 suggest that the relative clause in verse 15, which
speaks of choosing by God, disturbs the context. How often has not a perception
that something might have been disturbing at the time, basically been reached in
advance, and thus renounces enlightenment from a different idea in its
assessment.

Other formulations in the law are better understood as having come from the late monarchic period than the exilic; what affects possession of the land has already been alluded to.[152] It is not known whether there was a real danger that a foreigner might sit on the throne in Jerusalem, for example, in conjunction with the coup against Amon (2 Kg 21:23), where in any case the intention was to eliminate the Davidic dynasty. Still, as indeed in other situations, it was possible.

The kingship law is one part of Deuteronomy about which scholars agree on the stratification. There is much to suggest, for example, that the three parallel prohibitions against acquiring in verses 16f. (especially the first) were added after the fact. It is even more clear that the most explicit reference in verses 18ff. back to deuteronomic law itself could not have belonged to the oldest conception of this book.[153] The reflexivity could only belong to a later phase. Of course, all of these emendations are much more comprehensible as originating in a late preexilic than an exilic context. Except for these references, there are no others that give us convincing reasons for an absolute dating.

In verses 16f. the political possibilities of the monarchy are extremely limited. The king is not supposed to have too many horses, wives or money. These three are intended to bring together the three traditional fields of activity. The first, and probably most important, deals with military forces. Horses and the chariots that belong with them were the most powerful weapon of the period and in prophecy of the eighth-century symbolize military strength.[154] We must add here that according to the war law of Deut 20, the militia no longer served the absolute rule of the king. We are dealing with a professional army and the types of weapons appropriate to it. Of course, chariots and horses are no longer mentioned in the historic texts of the last preexilic period, so we must also question their existence in Judah.[155] Did the law – perhaps in connection with other circumstances, for example, restrictions from the major powers – affect this?

An examination of the possible purpose (*l*ma 'an*) as well as the consequence of this kind of armament is extremely instructive. These could have been the tools to lead the nation back to Egypt (verse 16). Of course, the expression is an exaggeration,[156] but there are at least two ways to interpret it. Is it dealing with a subjugation of the people by compulsory labor, as once happened in Egypt? Or is it about dependence on Egypt in foreign policy and military affairs?[157] Egypt was always an alternative to reliance upon the eastern powers (either Assyria or Babylon), which is demonstrated by the see-saw politics, which determined so many phases of Jewish history.

152 See above pp. 210ff.
153 See Rüterswörden, *Gemeinschaft* 60ff., who regards 17:14f., 16a, 17*, 20 as a base stratum. Similarly, e.g. Steuernagel, commentary; Seitz, *Studien* 231ff. Anyone who regards the entire king-law as deuteronomic, rejects such differentiations, e.g. Preuss, *Deuteronomium* 54.
154 Isa 2:7ff.; 30:16; 31:1; Hos 14:3; Mi 5:9; cf Ps 20:8 and elsewhere.
155 Thus especially, Junge, *Wiederaufbau*; now also Kessler, *Juda* 144f.
156 This concerns the nation as a whole, not, e.g. the sale of a single slave (thus Steuernagel, commentary 118) to Egypt.
157 Thus Horst, *Privilegrecht* 139.

God does forbid the people to return to Egypt.[158] The formulation, "You must never return that way again . . ." (verse 16) at least presumes an attempt in this direction. There is, however, a way to combine the two interpretations: Jehoiakim, who was made king by Pharaoh Neco II, and against the will of the Jewish *'am hā 'āreṣ* (2 Kg 23:34), had forced his people into unpaid, compulsory labor (Jer 22:13ff.). Furthermore, he imposed high tribute for Egypt (2 Kg 23:35). In any case, the text of Deut 17:16b is much more difficult to understand as having come out of the exilic period, than if Israel were at the moment in a situation that the exodus had previously eliminated.

The fact that the king was forbidden to have "many wives" in verse 17, is connected with the foreign policy relationships and marriages entered into by Solomon (1 Kg 3:1, 11:1ff.). The "turning away of the heart" can best be understood, if it is interpreted as dealing with the religious dangers connected with affairs of the heart. We need not comment upon the acquiring of gold and silver, the piling up of treasures at the expense of the people.

We might regard all of Deuteronomy, especially the tax system, as a commentary upon this. The three-fold prohibition against "acquiring" (or "making much") is aimed at limiting these activities and it includes appropriate controls. Nevertheless, in this way there is notification that even these areas of the king's activity are under the control of law. The professional army, foreign policy relationships, administration of the state treasury were all part of his duties. On the other hand, he was denied control of cultic activity, the militia, which was certainly quite important at this time, the administration of justice, and taxation, a previously important source of revenue.

Deuteronomy represents itself as a speech by Moses, later written down (Deut 31:9). There are only a few places where the speech anticipates the book in written form (e.g. 17:18f.). The idea that the king should carry a copy of the Torah with him and that he should have it constantly, wherever he goes, makes the constitutional status of the document apparent. The law is over the king. As king, he is to be a model Israelite.[159] Again, there is no reason to regard this as exilic.[160] According to Jer 8:8, there was a written Torah in preexilic Jerusalem that was known by that name. At latest, Josiah as king possessed the book in written form when it was "discovered" as described in 2 Kg 22, and both he and the people were obligated from that point on (2 Kg 23:1–3). It is

---

158 Lohfink, *Bezugstext*, sees an allusion to Hos 11:5; Reimer, *Return to Egypt*, to Deut 28:68 and Ex 14:13.

159 Thus Lohfink, *Sicherung* 316.

160 The verse is unanimously regarded as deuteronomic, see Wellhausen, *Composition* 192; Steuernagel, commentary 118f. Rad, commentary 85; Mayes, commentary 273; Galling, *Königsgesetz* 138; Seita, *Studien* 233; Garcia Lopez, *Roi*; Rüterswörden, *Gemeinschaft* 63; otherwise, e.g. Dillmann, commentary 323f. As support, Rüterswörden refers to the late character of all references to a Torah book in Deuteronomy, which settles nothing for an absolute dating (see Jer 8:8). Verses 14ff. use the deuteronomic "you" while verses 18f. formulate rules specifically for the king. It should be mentioned that the situation that verse 18 presupposes – that the king gets the Torah book from the levitical priests – corresponds precisely with what is said in 2 Kg 22. For this, see below p. 272.

not the question *whether* there should and will be a monarchy again, which underlies this formulation, but the concern that the king might elevate himself above his brothers (again), from whose number he first came (verse 15). The concern is with what is needed to continue to live in Israel (verse 20), which neither Jehoahaz (2 Kg 23:31ff.) nor Jehoiachin (2 Kg 24:8f.) were granted. There is nothing to point to the problems of the exilic period; even the clearly later strata of the kingship law are much more easily understood as continuations and realizations from the time between 640 and 586 BCE.

Completely depriving the king of power, something so astonishing in the ancient Near East, raises the inescapable question, "Who had the power and authority to do that?" The kingship law authorized the people to set up kings, and the authority speaking in this law must be over both king and people. We will see what this is all about in the provisions for the legal system and in prophetic material.

Legal Autonomy and the Word of Moses: The Organization of the Court

Alongside the establishment of the king and concern for right worship, the sovereignty of the people is expressed in the law with particular clarity.

> Deut 16:18 *You shall appoint judges and officials throughout your tribes, in all your towns that YHWH your God is giving, and they shall render just decisions for the people. 19 You must not distort justice; you must not show partiality . . . 20 Justice, and only justice you shall pursue, so that you may live and occupy the land that YHWH your God is giving you.*

This law is at the pinnacle of all institutional laws; it is also their foundation. Compositionally, the fact that the theme of chapter 12 is taken up again in verses 21f. with the prohibition of asherah and pillars, and again in 17:2ff. with the problem of falling away from YHWH, is an important expression of the significance of this law. The question of the unity of cultic sites and the exclusive veneration of YHWH is most closely connected with the deuteronomic regulation of the courts. Everything is involved. The rule of two witnesses formulated in 17:6f. is expressly connected with a harsh reaction to blasphemy against the first commandment.

Above all, however, Deut 16:18 formulates the basic tenet underlying the judicial organization of Deuteronomy: the people set up judges. The authority which is being addressed performs the act itself.[161] It was not, for example, as normally practiced during the monarchic period, when the king installed judges but did not set up the court, (e.g. in 17:8ff.). The tension between the sovereign people and the central legal authority is of special significance here.

161 See especially Macholz, *Justizorganisation* 335. Suzuki, *Reformation* 34 regards "you" as "an organization of the administration, since this body of authority can appoint an official judge and an officer to each local community." Methodologically, this is a circular argument that would make a case for a stratification in deuteronomic law (for this, Walkenhorst, *Deuteronomiumsforschung*).

"Scribal leaders" (*šoṭ⁽ᵉ⁾rîm*) are mentioned in addition to judges in 16:18. We would probably expect the usual kind of official (*śar* or *sōfēr*) here, but Deuteronomy avoids this term entirely, using a word referring to the activity of writing that does not come with great connotative baggage.[162] We are dealing with a function, which simply designates the activity that they are to perform on behalf of the people. These are administrators, who, like the judges, are set up by the people, and who play a role, for example, in the army (20ff.).

In Deut 16:19f., following immediately, we find the formulation of the basic rules for the way a person should act in a trial. In so doing, the parallel rules of the Book of the Covenant are varied (Ex 23:1ff.) and amplified by the important formulations of verse 19. The double "justice . . . justice" (*ṣédeq ṣédeq*, verse 20) designates the ultimate goal for all provisions of the law.

Correspondingly, the reference to the goal of justice in 6:25 and 24:13[163] structures nearly all of deuteronomic law. The juxtaposition of the establishment of judges and the admonition for all to justice shows that the responsibility for justice, and therefore the practice of Torah itself, is not transferred to the judges with this judicial organization. It remained with the people as a whole. The fact that we find elders with judiciary function parallel to the judges throughout Deuteronomy fits with this law. Both together form the two pillars of the administration of justice, and there is no reason based on biblical or extra-biblical parallels for separating them (e.g. by literary criticism).[164]

The continuing responsibility that "you" bear for everything having to do with law determines also the other relevant provisions for a legal organization, which can only be discussed here in general terms. In Deut 19:1–13 there is a command to establish asylum cities to which people who have involuntarily committed murder might be able to escape. The most likely interpretation is that they became necessary because Deut 12 had abolished all the holy places and altars except Jerusalem.[165]

When the Book of the Covenant made the distinction between murder and other acts of homicide,[166] it referred to the proximity of such places of refuge. Responsibility for the establishment of these places (Deut 9:1ff.) and the carrying out of the activity connected with them (verses 12f.) was given to the people without restriction. Other provisions, such as the repeated two-witness rule (17:6f.; 19:15ff.), the application of the talion law in case of false testimony punishing only the false witness for the crime with which the defendant was charged, or the limitation of

---

162 For the verb *šṭr* see KBL³ 1368. It is highly unlikely we might be permitted to conclude a pre-state office on the basis of the few pre-deuteronomic references. For this, see Rütersworden, *Beamte* 109–111.

163 Here we have *ṣᵉdāqāh*.

164 It might be that, like Rofé, *Organization of Justice*, that one could make a literary-critical argument out of precisely that and ascribe the mention of the elders to a pre-deuteronomic tradition. The juxtaposition of elders and judges is practically the norm both in Israel and the rest of the ancient Near East, see above pp. 78ff. This demonstrates beautifully the methodological untenability of a procedure that makes its own contents into a principle for literary-critical operations.

165 See especially Rofé, *Cities of Refuge*; for this, see above p. 177.

166 See above pp. 174ff.

corporal punishment to forty lashes (25:1–3), are all entrusted to the judge.

The central court described in 17:8–13 is clearly not within the jurisdiction of the people and the judges whom they have established, but, of course, neither is it within the jurisdiction of the king. It is in contrast to these authorities. What was said previously about the structure and significance of this court, need not be repeated.[167] It had responsibility for rendering decisions only in difficult cases which had been referred to it by the other courts in the land, and it gave legal advice that the courts might use in future proceedings. It was first and foremost an organ for the development of law. It spoke with the authority of Moses himself. People were not permitted to depart from its decisions either to the right or to the left,[168] and in this way evil was purged from Israel.[169] Its dicta had the same dignity as Moses or the Mosaic law book itself.

Authority that can be Scrutinized: The Law about Prophecy
In Deut 18:15 it was announced to Israel:

> 18:15 YHWH your God will raise up for you a prophet like me from among your own people; you shall heed such a prophet.

This type of prophecy, which also speaks with the authority of Moses, is "as he is." It is only on the basis of the totality of all of the provisions of 18:9–22 that we can identify what is intended by the constitution here conceived for the people of God.

The law begins in verses 9–14[170] with a detailed prohibition against the religious practices of the non-Israelite residents of the land.

> 18:9 When you come into the land that YHWH your God is giving you, you must not learn to imitate the practices of those nations. 10 No one shall be found among you who makes a son or daughter pass through fire . . .

Here we see with clarity nowhere else so apparent that the fiction of the acquisition of the land (that is about to take place) could only be understood as coming out of a time which presumes this possession of the land to exist without restriction, even though it might have been endangered. In the view of the authors, the prohibition against all known mantic practices[171] in verses 10–13 must have applied to any situation and could not have been lifted because of loss of the land (during the exile).

All of the customary means of foretelling the future (and consequently influencing that future) are prohibited for Israel. Many of these were being practiced in and around Palestine. In the uncertain times of the late monarchic period, with the rapidly changing geo-political constellations, the question, "What is going to happen?" was heard more frequently

---

167 See above pp. 96f.
168 Deut 5:32; 17:20; 28:14.
169 Deut 13:6; 17:7; 19:19; 21:21; 22:21f.; 24:7.
170 Verses 9–15 give no impetus, as Rütersworden correctly shows, to literary-critical activity. For the whole, see also Habel, *Prophet*; Chiesa, *Promessa*.
171 See especially Rütersworden, *Gemeinschaft* 78ff. (Lit.).

than before. What is stated in Deut 29:29 applies for deuteronomic thinking in general: "The secret things belong to YHWH our God, but the revealed things belong to us and our children for ever to observe the words of this Torah." Torah itself, together with the formulae of blessing and cursing, includes a function that avails itself of other possibilities of influence.

There is, however, one great exception, the promised prophet. Scholars agree that this should be analyzed as an iterative. There will *repeatedly* be such a prophet. His word is to be regarded as that of Moses. It certainly means that he cannot contradict what Moses said elsewhere, namely in his Torah book. This deals with an open future. Alongside the "word" of the central court, there is this prophet, the figure in whom Israel is able to participate in the future, and thus in whom Israel can also hear God's word.

There is obvious literary stratification in the statements that follow in 18:16ff. In verse 16 Moses reaches back to the situation at Horeb, to the "day of assembly" (*yōm haqqāhāl*), when Israel was no longer able to bear the voice of God, in other words, the situation described in Deut 5. Unlike elsewhere in deuteronomic law, there is a long passage of divine speech quoted in verses 17–20. It is not until verse 20 that we return to Moses speaking. It has often been said that Deut 5, with its connection of Decalogue-proclamation on Horeb and Moses' speech on the east bank of the Jordan, certainly does not belong among the older deuteronomic strata.[172] Here also in 18:16–20 we are dealing with more recent material.[173]

Of course, the relationship to Deut 5 is not a simple one, for in Deut 5 it is Moses himself who gets to hear the entire law in the place of the people and then he repeats it to the people in Moab. Deut 5 is concerned with the relationship of the Decalogue to the remainder of the law. But here in Deut 18:16ff. a future prophet "like Moses" is announced, who will function as a mediator, transmitting the unbearable Word of God with the authority of Horeb. Deut 18:16ff. is not entirely equivalent to Deut 5. We must rather understand them as independent parallels, meaning also that we cannot rely on a dating in the exilic period for Deut 5. Furthermore, we note that the idea that there might be a more recent growth phase with the return to Moses speaking in verse 21 over against verses 16–20 is not at all convincing. It is much more likely that verses 21f. (perhaps originally formulated slightly differently) connect to verse 15.[174]

As always, the problem treated in verse 21 was shaped in a special way by the last preexilic period. Frequently, diametrically contradictory prophetic statements about the same situation appear in opposition to each other. We find these especially in the material from the Jeremiah tradition (23:27f. and elsewhere), and Jeremiah was shaped, especially in the deuteronomistic strata (e.g. Jer 1:4ff.), in the pattern of Deut 18, as the

172 See above pp. 44f. and elsewhere.
173 See (largely including verses 21f.) Preuss, *Deuteronomium* 55; Seitz, *Studien* 243; Mayes, commentary 282f.; Hossfeld/Meyer, *Prophet* 150ff.
174 Thus Garcia Lopez, *Profeta* 302f.; Suzuki in Walkenhorst, *Deuteronomium-forschung*.

one in whose mouth God himself places his Word.[175] The situation foreseen in verse 21 is extremely unprophetic.

> *18:21 You may say to yourself, "How can we recognize a word that YHWH has not spoken?" 22 If a prophet speaks in the name of YHWH but the thing does not take place or prove true, it is a word that YHWH has not spoken. The prophet has spoken it presumptuously; do not be frightened by it.*

In view of what is said in verse 18, could someone faced with important problems really hold out and recommend such waiting for the verification of a prophetic statement until sometime in the future? Is any historical verification simply a supplemental legitimization of a prophetic statement as the word of God? Jeremiah's reference to the penetrating power of the true word (Jer 23:29) is speaking a different language. But even to ask such a question is to question what is prophetic. The wisdom of the law-giver is a different kind.

As with other legislation, in order to understand this law, we probably must regard it as a procedural rule.[176] It is certainly not formulated from the perspective of a true prophet or even one who is persecuted and embattled, but it is even less representative of the perspectives of those who have persecuted and eliminated unpopular prophets. We see how it happens with, for example, the king's destruction of the written form of Jeremiah's proclamation described in Jer 36, the killing of other YHWH prophets also recorded there (26:20ff.), or the threat of arrest and trial described in Jer 26. The law should be read against the background of such conflicts, and then it appears to be an extremely liberal law. Where one word contradicts another, and it is difficult to tell which is the Word of God, then people are to wait, in accord with the rule. They are not to persecute, prohibit, accuse or even condemn to death. No law can assist the decision where the purported "word of God" is put on a level above Moses (see Deut 13). The resolution can and must remain open, and that is precisely what happens here.

The group of officials who listen to Jeremiah in Jer 26 and 36[177] bring him to a hearing before the king, saving him from the clutches of the state and bringing him to a safe place (Jer 36:19), did exactly as they were supposed to do, according to Deut 18. They did not necessarily identify with the prophet and his message, but they did allow the possibility that what he was saying and not the others was the true Word of God.

Their behavior corresponds precisely with the good will and critically reserved neutrality of Deut 18:21f. These are even members of the same families who were involved with the discovery and implementation of the Torah book in the temple.[178] Of course, we can ask which came first, the law or the action; it is a question of the chicken or the egg. Could we really imagine that this text with the criterion of verse 21 could come from the exilic period? Naturally this basic principle proved correct,

---

175 Thus now, Herrmann, *Jeremia* especially 50.
176 Thus not as a simple promise, as Preuss, *Deuteronomium* 138. Also Hossfeld/ Meyer, *Prophet* speak of the shattering of legal regulations.
177 For this, see Kessler, *Prophetisches Reden*; Hardmeier, *Micha un Jesia*.
178 For this, see below pp. 266ff.

contributing increasing significance to prophetic writings and traditions. Still, this is the beginning of a prophetic message, proclaiming something radically new of an eschatological type. The declarations of a new covenant with Torah written in the heart (Jer 31:31ff.), or those declarations of the ways of all people to the God of Israel (Isa 45:8ff.) – viewed from the perspective of Deut 18 remains open today, whether this is true prophecy. Eschatological prophecy in a real sense is not within the purview of deuteronomic prophetic law.

Justice in War: The Law of Warfare

Scholars generally regard deuteronomic war law in Deut 20 as an especially utopian text. With its unrealistic demands, it could only have come from a time when the people did not have responsibility for their own state and their own policies.[179] If we compare them with eschatological images of peace and the pacifist ethic based upon them (at that time as well as today) the same text appears less critical toward a fatalistic reality. The same law presumes the existence of war with the subjugation of opponents. Could this contrast lead to an appropriate prescription?

We must first address a special problem. In verses 15–18 there is mention of the cities of the nations that Israel will shortly encounter west of the Jordan and which they are to destroy. The procedure described in verses 10–14 cannot apply here. In verses 15–18 there is thus a clearer comparison with the land conquest tradition in Ex 34 and 23, as it is formulated in Deut 7.[180] We ought to remember that the nations listed in Deut 20:17 had no parallels in late monarchic period Israel.[181] The command was valid for a one-time historical activity that, by the time of the development of the text, was a time long past. Deut 20:15–18 is an admonition, not instruction. If we want to know why Deuteronomy needed a war-law for that particular time, we will need to examine the remainder of the chapter. One result of this comparison with the theory of the conquest is that all of the other places mentioned would have to be regarded as "far away" (verse 17). We would not, however, be permitted to use this as a key to an interpretation, as if it were dealing with military operations far from home.

What wars are being referred to here?[182] There are no references to them. There is never any reflection upon the conditions under which war would be possible, permitted or commanded. It is exclusively a list of rules for any imaginable war. Viewed historically, the wars waged by

---

179 See Wellhausen, *Composition* 192; Höscher, *Komposition* 253 and elsewhere; Rad, commentary 130ff; Preuss, *Deuteronomium* 140; see also Rofé, *Laws of Warfare* 36f. who, among others, refers to the fact that even the felling of fruit trees is permitted (bBQ 91b; Sifre §204).

180 See Rofé, *Laws of Warfare* 28f.

181 See above p. 130.

182 Here also there are clearly recognizable indications of stratification. Thus verses 2f. in formulated in the second person plural (instead of second singular) and then 5ff. uses its own language, see Rofé, *Rules of Warfare* 33f. The parallels to Deut 24:5 show that chapter 20 as a whole, or at least 20:5–7 belong to a later stratum. But this says nothing about the absolute dating. During this entire period, there were only wars that originated with Israel, as is presumed here, under Josiah.

Josiah under the circumstances of the collapsing Assyrian empire were the only ones to be carried out independent of the great influence of the superpower.

It is generally theorized that the revival of national potential also had consequences for military planning.[183] Many features of the chapter, like the concentration on the question of the conquest of the cities from verse 10 on, might be connected with this. The reference to the exodus in verse 1 is also important Israel is seen in the same theological coordinates as elsewhere in Deuteronomy. It is determined by the exodus (and the gift of the land, which is not explicated here). Whatever is being talked about here with the wars in Deut 20, it is not about the establishment of an Israelite empire.

We may list the following as rules for waging war:

– *Autonomy of the people.* This is as important here as it is in other fundamental questions of state and law. "When you go out to war . . ." is the way the first verse begins. As in the following verses, there is no other subject here who might share the command with "you." War must begin with the people and they wage it. War-law is entrusted to them alone. Besides the priests only the "scribal leaders" (*šoṭ⁾rîm*) are mention in verses 2–4. According to verses 5–9, these people are to muster and organize the people. Otherwise, as it says in verse 9, they are to put commanders (*śārē ṣ⁽bā⁾ōt*) over the people. This is not the vague "someone" that we find in many translation, but even these scribal leaders are responsible for setting up military leadership. It is extremely important that these "scribal leaders" themselves – according to Deut 16:18 – are installed by the people, and according to the term that is used, they have limited functional assignments. Even military leadership is subordinate, if indirectly, to the self-determination of the people.

– *The other side of fear.* Preparation for war begins with deciding who should not and need not fight. In verses 5–7, we read that everyone who had built a new house, or planted a vineyard, or not yet married the person to whom he was engaged, was to be sent home. No one else should be able to "consecrate" what these men had begun; that would be a curse (cf 28:30). The theory that this is an old pre-deuteronomic taboo law is probably correct, because these people would probably endanger a military venture.[184] Of course, these three conditions were not exactly uncommon among young men, so that a significant number of people were eliminated from the potential fighting force.

The regulation in verse 8, is clearly emphasized above the others. "Is anyone afraid or disheartened?" (*hayyārē⁾ w⁽rak hallēbāb*) that person is freed from military service. Thus, any person who is himself afraid and could himself spread fear among the others, would remain at home. Fear, a reason for evading military service – such wisdom in Torah![185] As with

---

183 See especially Junge, *Wiederaufbau.*
184 See e.g. Rad, commentary 131ff.; also Rofé, *Laws of Warfare* 34, who regards this as an exegesis of 24:5.
185 For evaluation in rabbinic tradition, see Gurewicz, *Deuteronomic Provisions.*

other laws, we would have to ask what exactly the law-giver intended. In spite of the divine admonitions announced at the beginning, such fear is not criticized or repressed here. If we think through the problem in light of a real war, the degree of actual threat is highlighted. Where the concern was for physical survival, where the presence of the enemy seems more dangerous than a possible war, the warriors lose their fear. This rule makes wars of aggression, entirely outside of Israel's own territory, possible only under circumstances of great ideological significance (e.g. a so-called holy war). Deuteronomy, with its emphasis on exodus and the gift of the land, makes such a situation extremely rare, the more so if we disregard wars for acquisition of land.

– *Respect for the civilian population.* The heart of the law is verses 10–14. The cities should be offered peace (verse 10). The theory is that subjugation implies forced labor (*mas*) and slavery (*'bd*). If the offer of peace is rejected, only adult males (the defense forces) should be killed. Women and children should be spared. There is much evidence for atrocities of war, including, for example, the cutting open of pregnant women[186] or the murder of infants.[187] The parallel to the conduct in war of the great powers[188] is clear. The concern here is to limit these atrocities. No one would argue that part of the intent of war was to pillage and subjugate. We are not justified in drawing further conclusions regarding the historical context than these. We are unable to draw a further parallel between the treatment of those who have been conquered and what Deuteronomy says elsewhere about the treatment of minorities and aliens.

– *Protection for the necessities of life.* According to verses 19f., the enemy's fruit trees should not be destroyed.

> 20:19b *Are trees in the field human beings that they should come under siege from you?*

War is waged against a particular people, not against their trees as providers of support for the present and future. This kind of activity was practiced in Israel (2 Kg 3:19, 25), and there are numerous Assyrian portrayals in text and picture of this military strategy, especially cutting down fruit trees.[189]

The deuteronomic war law does not deal with questions of impetus and motives for war. It does not develop a doctrine of the just war. It *does* presume the reality of war, even for Israel. It presents regulations for behavior when war occurs. In modern terms, Deut 20 follows along the line of the Geneva Convention.[190] Thus, a path was begun to bridge the gap between reality and unrealistic utopia. This path contained the first few steps toward a taming of war.

186 2 Kg 8:12; 15:16; Hos 14:1; Am 1:13.
187 2 Kg 8:12; Isa 13:16; Hos 10:14; 14:1; Nah 3:10; Ps 137:8f.
188 For atrocities committed by the Assyrian army, see Meissner, *Babylonien* I 107ff.
189 Meissner *Babylonien* I 111.
190 After the second Gulf war there was likewise a demand for the expansion of the Geneva Convention to cover harm to the environment.

Theocracy as Democracy: The Model Constitution

The use of a term like "constitution" as a designation for the political demand of deuteronomic law cannot be avoided.[191] All of the groups, strata, organizations, institutions of the period are covered by it in such a way that their rights together with limitations are listed. In spite of the serious limitation of the monarchy, there is nothing like a return to pre-state conditions or organizational forms.[192] It is not just the roles of the monarchy and the officials that demonstrate this, but above all, even the power of the planned judicial system, which here for the first time intervenes in the area of the otherwise completely independent families and clans.[193] This is a civil society, but one in which power is widely distributed, and where significant amounts of authority resides with those whom the law addresses. For this reason, the use of this concept "constitution" seems plausible. Deuteronomy omits the detailed regulation of individual areas that we see in the Mishpatim of the Book of the Covenant.[194] What is designated as a principle to regulate law in the Book of the Covenant,[195] to an even greater degree dominates in Deuteronomy.

Of course a concept like constitution is imposed from without. The Old Testament itself had not developed any terminology of its own for the political aspects of Torah. The important new conceptual language[196] in Deuteronomy was for essential phenomena, which already could be observed in the Book of the Covenant and described, but without being named.[197] The unique innovations of deuteronomic thinking are not yet formulated in clear terms.[198] We see rooted here the difficulty that, to this very day, theological conceptual language has problems dealing with political dimensions. Methodologically, this lack necessitates careful description, in which comprehension of contents and structure must take precedence over any conceptual arrangement. Nevertheless, contemporary understanding cannot reject appropriate conceptualization, even if it can only be used with reservation.

For the political sphere, Greek terminology offers itself as a supplement to the general, modern notion of a constitution. If we want to understand the specifics of this, the thought-provoking juxtaposition *theocracy as democracy* presents an interesting image. Simultaneously, we see what is specifically Israelite, and not in the Greek term. The concept of theocracy was coined by the hellenistic Jew, Flavius Josephus, for the characteristic constitution of his people.[199] He did this in order to supplement and counteract the classic Greek concepts of constitutional

---

191 See above p. 234.
192 Unlike the opinion of Preuss, *Deuteronomium* 140, postexilic Israel, about whom this is written, was conceived as "predominantly an apolitical power" and consequently oriented toward the period of the judges. As long as we can hear an echo or even a new version of older amphictionic circumstances in Deuteronomy (as e.g. G. v. Rad) an orientation toward pre-state conditions would be obvious.
193 See below pp. 252ff.
194 Of course the family laws offer a kind of analogy, see below p. 257.
195 See above pp. 194f.
196 See above pp. 203f.
197 We might think, e.g. of Torah, chosen, love, etc.
198 This also applies, e.g. to the demand for cultic unity.
199 Josephus, *Contra Apionem* II 165; for this, see above p. 62.

thinking. Josephus hit the central point of difference dead center: the concept of divine law-giver and ruler. Of course, even with Josephus – thus, from its very beginning – the term was equated with the ruling priesthood. With this wording Josephus determined the discussion until this very day.

Whether or not the concept, understood this way, might fit for Josephus' Roman period, it certainly did not apply to the biblical period, especially for the thinking of Deuteronomy. God's rule was not conducted by the priests. They had a relatively slight role in Deuteronomy. Looming much larger was the group to whom Moses handed over the law, the ones addressed as "you," the representatives of the people as a whole. The sovereignty of the people underlying the law compels us to speak of something like a democracy.

The complete transfer of all power to the free people of the land means a tremendous break with the great authorities of ancient Near Eastern and also Israelite–Judean society. The form in which the law appeared, a speech from the long distant past, is directly and centrally connected to this claim. If the reconstruction of pre-deuteronomic legal history presented here is correct, there was at most a fragment, which was older, found in a slender supplemental stratum of the Book of the Covenant. Only the immense claim of deuteronomic law makes this speech inescapable, producing the first and oldest example of pseudepigraphy in the Bible.

The form of direct, divine speech, as the Book of the Covenant, Ex 34:11ff. or the Decalogue presented it, was apparently no longer adequate. For cultic and religious questions, God's words were conveyed by priests and prophets. Of course, priests were fundamentally subordinate to the sacral claim of the monarchy, as also most of the prophets of the period. The conflicts of a few critical prophets with certain kings are well-known. But, what authority could, as Deuteronomy does, outrank prophets, priests, kings and officials and the entire nation, binding them with their regulations? What institution or authority at that time, under the call of direct, divine revelation, could eliminate the power of powerful institutions like the Davidic divine monarchy together with the temple he established and its priests?

Since the authority speaking in the law is located in the distant past, the emphasis given to tradition[200] in societies of this kind is taken at face value and the law is shifted to an entirely new legal and political plane. The Judean *'am hā'āreṣ*, having been freed from all of the powers of their own society, portrayed their freedom as having been established by God alone and extracted the political shape of this freedom and its expression in a written constitution by the fiction of a speech by Moses. The present freedom was in the form of a connection to a canonical past. Deuteronony was shaped as the comprehensive will of God in written form, and it was around this that the biblical canon was formed. Freedom in this form was developed with it, irrevocably shaping biblical faith down to modern times.

200 The stimulating analysis of the structure of authority in Deuteronomy by Schäfer-Lichtenberger (Autorität), unfortunately fails to take full account of the temporal dimension in their reflections.

The uniqueness of Deuteronomy's political thinking can be grasped more clearly with a comparison to relationships in the Greek polis. Rüterswörden began such a comparison,[201] referring to close parallels in the limiting of citizens rights to free, landowning males, the common presumption of a personal instead of territorial union, the analogous role of family and familial terminology, but we should also mention the structure of the judiciary, the dominant role of justice for human coexistence and the historically early limiting of the power of the monarchy. Rüterswörden sees differences in the roles of priests and prophets as well as the fact that in Israel there was a law deprived of human ability to shape and change.[202]

On what are such commonalities based? Ultimately we may not need to ascribe them to a very distant past. Christian Meier has referred to the fact that what is really noteworthy for Greece, was not that at some time in the distant past there were features of an original equality, but that in the course of development of Greek culture, equality was preserved, strengthened and extended.[203] The perception of equality, norms for justice, the transfer of familiar concepts into the areas of law and politics, and not least "the beginning of a 'concept of collective responsibility'",[204] all of this might, like the parallel manifestation in Israel, be rooted in the periods. It was preserved by much significant and radical historical change and consequently reshaped. We are dealing with an astonishingly new manifestation of civil society in the form of a broadly placed authority for decision making and responsibility.

In view of the many significant parallels in the pre-history as well as political form of something like democracy, the differences are all the more important: the decisive development of political thinking in Israel as it is expressed in Deuteronomy took place under the domination of Assyria and came about in response to it. Generally, the great prophetic material, especially the Book of the Covenant, is regarded as a reaction to the catastrophe of the northern kingdom in 722 BCE. The characteristic combination of juridical and religious-cultic laws with provisions for social protection of aliens and poor, widows and orphans was developed against this background. If the concern in Greece, as in Israel, was for the political shape of freedom, despite all of their close kinship we can attempt to grasp profound differences in the following points:

– Freedom from oppression and foreign domination was not simply assumed in Israel. For broad sections of the population, it was already undeniably lost, and for the remainder it was in grave danger. In view of the superiority of the great powers around them, this freedom could not be guaranteed by military strength. It was described theologically in Deuteronomy by the themes of exodus and the gift of the land. It is upon these not obvious gifts of God that everything is based. Everything is due to the power of God. Practically speaking, freedom is the foremost gift.

---

201 Rüterswörden, *Gemeinschaft* 95ff. For Greek democracy, see especially Meier, *Entstehung.*
202 Rüterswörden, *Gemeinschaft* 103.
203 Meier, *Enstehung* 54.
204 Raaflaub, *Anfänge* 16f.

– The basic difference is that a law not submitted to the people became the foundation of their freedom, democracy even appears to be just theocracy. We should note what is regulated in this law and what is not. The laws never treat procedure. *How* judges and officials are to be chosen, *who* participated in the installation of a king and *how* they did it, *whether* or not there were assemblies of the people, *how* the ʻam hāʼāreṣ was organized – to the great regret of historians, all of these remain undiscussed or barely mentioned. The omission of all formal characteristics of democracy is directly connected to the central difference.

– On the other hand, it seems to me that there is nothing arguing against the concept of "democracy," not even the foundation in the form of a Mosaic law which exceeds the authority of the people. At the time in Israel for which Deuteronomy was conceived and written, there was no institutionalized power above the people who were addressed as "you." Prophecy and the central court were not yet subject to the people, but they had only limited possibility to effect change and no power to carry it out. Deuteronomic law is not only supreme over the nation to whom it applies, above all, it is over the king and the Assyrian occupation force.

– Since the political regulations are concerned with basic questions, a modern analogy from everyday business and its principles may be helpful.[205] Human rights, basic rights, constitutional principles, etc. are above shifting majorities and constellations. They are comparable to principles in deuteronomic law, given by God through Moses to his people. They are the basic rules for the preservation of the freedom given to the people. Within their framework, all political power lies with the people.

Patriarchy and Public Power: Family Law

In addition to the area of state and public authorities Deuteronomy includes a second great area of human life within the law-giving of Torah: the family. There is only one single law dealing with it in the Book of the Covenant – the law against sleeping with an unbetrothed girl (Ex 22:15f.).[206] The concern there was with the question of bride price, which fits within the area of personal property, with the result that this perspective dominates the discussion. On the other hand, deuteronomic law operates on a broad front, dealing with themes of marriage, sexuality, marriage regulations, inheritance and thus also the legal status of women in society. Few Torah themes have had as significant an effect upon the history of Christendom as this, nevertheless, there is extremely dubious continuity.

The Legal Status of Women: The Problem of Inclusive Language
The great number of feminist theological studies on the subject of the significance and realities of life of women in the Old Testament and in

205 See above pp. 194f.
206 See above pp. 163f.

ancient Israel have left the legal texts of the Old Testament virtually untouched.[207] The classic view is still observed:[208] there is an unshakeable basis in these texts for the inferior position of women in a patriarchal society. We would need to consult other texts to find positive points of view.

In fact, we do encounter a masculine world in the legal texts. The judiciary is almost exclusively in the hands of males. The texts address men and make them the subjects of their laws. Women only appear where the specific roles of wife and mother cannot be avoided. If we limit ourselves to the perspectives from the explicit mention of women in the legal texts,[209] we see that women were dependent for their entire lives, first upon their fathers, then husbands. Only in a few cases (e.g. as widow or mother) are they generally in the situation of legal independence. This applies especially to the area of cult. If we are to judge from the times they are mentioned in the cultic portions of the legal texts, they must have been almost entirely excluded.[210]

We can doubt neither the patriachal structure of ancient Israelite society, nor the fact that this is reflected in their law. The reason that it is nevertheless inappropriate to reconstruct not only the actual role of women in society but also their legal status exclusively on the basis of explicit references to women, lies in that "mysterious ability of masculine designations to include women,"[211] in other words, the inclusivity of language.

"By marriage, the husband and wife are one person in law: That is, the very being, or existence of the woman is suspended during the marriage, or at least is *incorporated* . . . into that of the husband."[212] This statement makes clear that even in modern times, especially in law, masculine terms and formulations read literally exclude women, but in fact they do include women, The significance of this for law (and not just English law) in modern times[213] (and, e.g. also for many regulations of our faculties today), applies also to the Torah text of the ninth or fourth centuries BCE.

The main methodological problem for the understanding of the legal position of women is the way women are hidden within masculine terminology. Where it seems that only men are being discussed, it does not mean immediately that they were the only ones to have a particular right. Rather, it indicates that the rights of women are not being discussed. This is an important example from the difficult field of "what

---

207 An overview in Wacker, *Gefährliche Erinnerungen*; as examples we would mention: Trible, *Rhetoric of Sexuality*; ibid., *Texts of Terror*; Meyers, *Discovering Eve*; Brenner, *Israelite Women*; Bal (included in) *Anti-Covenant*; Ljung, *Silence or Suppression*; see also Gerstenberger/Schrage, *Frau und Mann*. Engelken, *Frauen* does not discuss the most important group, the free, adult women.

208 See de Vaux, *Lebensordnungen* I 75ff.; also e.g. Heister, *Frauen* 55ff.

209 See, e.g. Crüsemann, *Mann und Frau* 25ff.

210 Heister, *Frau* speaks expressly of the "exclusion of women from cultic activity" (96, cf 89). We see clearly different accents in Bird, *Place of Woman*; indeed, according to Bird, women were excluded from sacrifice (415f. note 34).

211 Pusch, *Alle Menschen* 43. She correctly emphasizes that this is not just about a linguistic phenomenon, but also a matter of societal power.

212 Blackstone, *Commentaries* 503; see Pusch, *Alle Menschen* 41 note 9.

213 For this, generally, especially, E. Koch, *Versuch*.

is taken for granted in the history of law."[214] The critical point, hidden within what is obviously a masculine perspective, can make the difference: Where does masculine terminology include women and where not? Since, as far as we can tell, studies thus far have not raised this issue,[215] we will raise a few central points here.

– Numerous pieces of legislation apply also to women. In many areas of law, this cannot be doubted. If the law in Ex 21:12 is phrased purely as masculine, "A man who kills a man . . ." (*makke 'îš*), women are also included as both potential victims as well as perpetrators. The case of an injury to a pregnant woman 21:22 culminating in her death, is a part of the section 21:12, 18–37 (German), with which it is connected, which treats the topic of physical injuries with and without mortal consequence in conjunction with the overarching statement in 21:12.[216] The rule "a life for a life" also applies to the death of a woman. What 21:22f. makes explicit for the understanding of 21:12, according to the intention of the law giver, would also have applied elsewhere. The same rules apply for women who kill others or are themselves killed as for men. This could not be otherwise for questions in the area of rights, as well as property.

The omission of wives from the list of men being addressed is interesting. Are they not to participate in the festivals? We must categorically exclude that possibility. It is inconceivable that they had less right to participation in the intimate celebrations than, for example, slave or refugee women. This could only mean that wives are also included in the word "you" as part of Israel, the people of God.[217]

– There are only a few cases in which a statement applies to both sexes, and both women and men are mentioned. In Deut 17:2, for example, women and men are accused of breaking the covenant. It seems to be the importance of the subject that compels the author to such an unusual embellishment of the obvious. This is also illustrated by the parallel (13:7), where first males then females who lead people astray are listed: brother, son, friend, daughter and wife.

The inclusion of wife along with husband in the priestly guilt offering laws in Num 5:6 is especially important,[218] "When a man or woman wrongs another. . . ." The text explicitly regulates how property offenses are to be handled (restitution plus a fifth of the value as punitive damage), in addition to which a ram is to be offered to God for atonement (verse 8). There can be no doubt that in parallel offenses women were also to bring such a sacrifice. For this reason, we can be sure that women might also be included in the broad range of priestly sacrificial texts where only men are mentioned as making sacrifice. Num 5:6, 8 proves

214 Daube, *Das Selbstverständliche.*
215 See, however, Bird, *Translating Sexist Language*, as well as now Braulik, *Haben Frauen . . . geopfert?*
216 See above pp. 159ff.
217 According to Braulik, *Haben . . . Frauen geopfert?* this especially includes offering sacrifice.
218 See below pp. 316f.

that according to priestly sacrificial theology, women were capable of sacrificing.

- Finally, in addition to the Old Testament legal texts, there is archaeological evidence referring to women's legal rights. There are about thirteen extremely important seals with the names of women. This is, of course, less than 5 percent of all of the name seals,[219] but they prove that women were treated as fully valid under law.[220] They, for example, made contracts and served as witnesses.[221] The fact that women appear on the seals as daughter (*bat*) or wife (*'ēšet*) of a man does not exclude legal independence. Prov 31:16 gives evidence regarding the purchase and ownership of property.

In my opinion, we can make the following working hypothesis: We should reverse our way of thinking – where men are discussed, women are not necessarily excluded. They ought to be included in legal and cultic texts where they are not expressly excluded, or where other issues are not raised.[222] The weighty language of Deuteronomy which addresses free, landowning males as representatives of the entire nation – "you" – does not consider women to be part of the groups excluded from this (like Levites, priests, aliens, slaves), but rather includes them in "you." Exodus and the gift of the land (and thus the wide range of deuteronomic Torah) also applied to them.

Families in Court: Examples

On one hand, deuteronomic family law reflects the incontrovertible reality of marriage and family, especially the role of women in the patriarchal society of iron age Israel.[223] Existing social structures were legally fixed. On the other hand, this fixing and the form in which it appeared represented a clearly perceivable break with Israel's older legal-historical culture. We can only understand the theological significance of Torah properly here if we pay attention to what is intended within the social context. A theologically legitimate relation in this area cannot look different than it does in matters of slavery, social justice or the state. It is just that the accents must change in view of the different history of reception.

Deuteronomy's laws accomplish something most noteworthy when they require intra-familial conflicts be submitted to a public court of

---

219 Avigad, *Contribution* 206 gives this number. It correlates with the total number of 385 published seals and seal impressions (*Contribution* 195). The most important examples: Vattioni, Sigilli no. 59–64, 116, 152, 215, 226, 324, 412.

220 Especially the discovery of a seal impression (Avigad, *A Note*) shows that these seals were really used and not simply worn as jewelry.

221 Avigad 205 asserts an obvious contradiction between these seals and the legal texts; similarly, e.g. Winter, *Frau und Göttin* 75f. Isn't it more likely that we are reading the legal texts incorrectly? Do they present women as the "personal property of their husbands" (Winter 75)?

222 See, especially Schüssler Fiorenza, *Brot* 52.

223 As the ethnological comparison material shows, they are quite similar to many societies and are ultimately connected with the family as a producing, consuming community, see Crüsemann, *Mann und Frau*; Albertz, *Überleben*; Meyers, *Eve*; ibid. *Procreation*. For an overview of all the source material, see Mace, *Marriage*; Terrien, *Heart*; most recently, Emerson, *Woman*.

elders in session at the gate.[224] This profound curtailment of the rights of the *pater familias* is a significant turning point in the history of law, similar to the distinction made between murder and homicide. There is here a securing of rights for all, especially for women and children, that was previously unknown, and which toppled the patriarchal power structure.

Let us look first at the law of the "stubborn son" (Deut 21:18–21).

> 21:18 *If someone has a stubborn and rebellious son who will not obey his father and mother, who does not heed them when they discipline him, 19 then his father and mother shall take hold of him and bring him out to the elders of his town at the gate of that place. 20 They shall say to the elders of that place, "This son of ours is stubborn and rebellious. He will not obey us. He is a glutton and a drunkard." 21 Then all the men of the town shall stone him to death. So you shall purge the evil from your midst; and all Israel will hear, and be afraid.*

Intra-familial, inter-generational conflict was supposed to be resolved publicly, before the court of elders at the gate. A death sentence is to be carried out by all the men of the city. The background of this law is familiar, because of the many Old Testament texts reporting sons grossly mistreating aged parents: robbing (Prov 28:24), mocking (Prov 30:17), and eviction (Prov 19:26) are all mentioned.

Similar to the capital offense formulations of Ex 21:15, 17, the "parent" commandment of the Decalogue[225] addresses the subject of striking or cursing elders. It is obvious that when the threat of selling of children or other family members into debt slavery arose, this could lead to serious family conflict. Furthermore, there was no longer the great religious security offered by the ancestor cult.[226] On the other hand, the father of a family had nearly unlimited power over his children. In pre-deuteronomic times there was no public control. We see how much this right was taken for granted in Gen 42:37, when Reuben gave his father Jacob the power to kill his children – Jacob's grandchildren – in the event his efforts failed. Even in Zech 13:3, in the case of turning away from the God of Israel (Deut 13) parents were given the right to kill their children. Of course, the whole matter of child sacrifice should be seen in the context of this question.[227]

To be sure, the question of what exactly the son in Deut 21:18ff. said is not answered. The description is "stubborn and rebellious" (*sōrēr ūmōrē*) probably means a more long-term disobedience and questioning of the fundamental relationship.[228] The complaint that he is a "glutton and a drunkard" makes it clear there is long-term offense against principles of behavior;[229] perhaps there is also a squandering of the family's resources,

---

224 For this, see Daube, *Landmarks*.
225 See Albertz, *Hintergrund*; Crüsemann, *Freiheit* 58ff.
226 See Lorenz, *Totenkult*.
227 See Westermann, *Genesis* II 437f.; Green, *Sacrifice*; Kaiser, *Kinderopfer*.
228 Thus with Bellefontaine, *Rebellious Son* 16–19.
229 Thus with Bellefontaine, *Rebellious Son* 21ff. For this thesis, there might be a supplemental connection with a second very different legal case. If the argument presented here seems inadequate, the second case would augment it.

which the parents had pointed out. With all of this, however, his activity is something less than the offenses of striking and cursing of parents described in Ex 21:15, 17.

Not only unusual offenses are to be resolved outside the family, the habitual questioning of parental authority is also to go to court. If offenses suggest stronger measures, they are to be made public. Parents should bring evidence of long-term admonition. Furthermore, the complaint is only valid if brought by both parents. This is one of the cases where the appearance of a woman is explicitly required. All of this comes together to support the claims of the parents against the son. The new element is that, where matters of life and death are concerned, they are subject to public control.[230]

The second example is that of the levirate marriage, with its consequent problem of the right of inheritance in the death of a childless, but married man.[231] The custom that the brother of a deceased man should beget children with the dead man's childless wife, is connected with patrilineal right of inheritance, patrilineal family structure and the great significance of name. In the narrative of Gen 38, it is the father who compels his adult sons to fulfill the levirate function (verses 8ff.). The story of Onan shows that this is not necessarily enforceable. Ultimately, Tamar was able to secure her rights only by deceitful action. All mention of levirate in the Old Testament deals with the problem of the refusal of the affected men, or the difficulties which the women encounter carrying out the law. It is only the trickery of Tamar and the combining of nocturnal deception and the kindness of Boaz that help matters along. For the affected men, this is a completely altruistic act. They are concerned about inheritance, which is not their own, and an heir who will get property that would otherwise fall to them.

In Deut 25:5–10, there is first a description of the levirate rule and its purpose (verses 5f.), and from verse 7 the concomitant problems are discussed.

> 5:7 *But if the man has no desire to marry his brother's widow, then his brother's widow shall go up to the elders at the gate and say, "My husband's brother refuses to perpetuate his brother's name in Israel; he will not perform the duty of a husband's brother to me." 8 Then the elders of his town shall summon him and speak to him. If he persists, saying, "I have no desire to marry her," 9 then his brother's wife shall go up to him in the presence of the elders, pull his sandal off his foot, spit in his face, and declare, "This is what is done to the man who does not build up his brother's house." 10 Throughout Israel his family shall be known as "the house of him whose sandal was pulled off."*

A woman who is left in the lurch has the right to bring a case before the elders of the city. The pressure of public opinion, the fear of exposure and shame that the law-giver places in this situation are obvious.[232] The

---

230 See below pp. 259f.
231 See Mittelmann, *Levirat*; Legget, *Levirat*; Westbrook, *Levirate*; Davies, *Inheritance Rights* among others.
232 The observation of Daube, *Culture* that there is clearly present a culture of shame, is important.

court does not possess the means to compel: how could they? Public complaint, public action with admonition and the disclosure of the problem, public dishonor in a symbolic act are all means at the woman's disposal. And the woman is not just the complainant here, she executes the verdict with all publicity. To the skills of a person like Tamar or Ruth in defending their rights, the court adds the possibility of a public trial.

The third example comes from the narrow area of sexual law. In Deut 22:13–21 a young wife is defamed. ". . . a man marries a woman, but after going in to her, he dislikes her and makes up charges against her . . . 'I did not find evidence of her virginity.'"[233] The details of this case are extremely complex; we refer to the very thorough study made by Locher.[234] Contrary to ancient Near Eastern parallels, such activity here is not simply grounds for divorce, it is regarded as the equivalent of adultery, a capital offense,[235] and can also lead to the death penalty for the guilty woman (verse 21). The girl's parents go before the elders of the city and say that the man had falsely accused their daughter. The parents are then to offer public proof of her virginity (verses 15–17). If the proof is sufficient, the man who made the charge, which was proven false, should be whipped and made to pay a fine of 100 shekels. According to verse 29, this is double the bride price. Furthermore, he may not divorce her.[236] If the charge cannot be disproved, the girl is to be taken to the door of her father's house where she will be stoned (verses 20f.). Of course, a slanderous husband is not condemned to death, as talion law (Deut 19:18) requires false testimony.[237]

Undoubtedly, the law presupposes the traditionally high value placed upon virginity, and its intent is to ensure virginity by these provisions.[238] Nevertheless, what is remarkable is the public forum in which all of these activities are resolved. The parents of the young woman have the right and the duty to protect their daughter and her reputation in front of her husband. The death sentence can only be passed in the public forum. This breaks the matter-of-factness with which Jacob could condemn a daughter-in-law who was suspected of "playing a whore" (Gen 38:24). There is no longer mention of taking a matter into one's own hands, as in the rape of Dinah (Gen 34).[239] What is important is that the patriarchal power of the husband over his wife has been broken by the rights of her original family. It is not just the sexual offense that belongs in public court, but also slander about such an offense.

233 See the conclusive summary of the problems, Locher, *Ehre* 385.
234 Locher, *Ehre*.
235 Locher, *Ehre* 385.
236 Cf Deut 22:28f.
237 See Locher, *Ehre* 380. He refers to the special role of the husband seeing this as a possible reason for this difference in value of a husband and a wife. In my opinion we should rather consider it to be a consequence of the two witness rule (19:15). In the case of verses 20f. an additional man would have to be able to be brought in as a witness, in contrast to the false testimony of the husband, for which no eye-witness would be imaginable.
238 See however, Frymer-Kensky *Law* 93 on this. According to this study, one could not count on being able to fulfill this law, since in doubtful cases the parents would have adequate time to find blood for the bedding.
239 See above pp. 68f.

In the remaining sexual provisions of deuteronomic law, there are no longer any technical rules. Especially in the laws given in 22:13–21, we could not imagine another responsible jurisdiction than the one in the preceding laws. The usual rules of codification, as well as the spirit of Deuteronomy, make this quite clear. It is not conceivable that, in adultery (22:22) or rape (22:25ff.), for example, the intent is that there be a kind of self-enforced justice or lynch law. Here also conflicts, especially when they concern matters of life and death, ought to be taken care of in front of the publicly meeting courts of elders at the gates of the towns.

> 22:22 *If a man is caught lying with the wife of another man, both of them shall die, the man who lay with the woman as well as the woman. So you shall purge the evil from Israel.*

This formulation shows clearly that for a legal description of the act of adultery, only the woman, not the man, need be described as married. He can only disrupt other people's marriages, not his own. The structure of patriarchal marriage, with its great emphasis upon the securing of the legitimacy of heirs, etc. is clearly recognizable. The law-giver, in any case, exclude a possibility, to which Prov 6:32–35 alludes. If the husband agrees, the court can levy an expiatory fine (6:35). The "also" or "as well as" (*gam*) in Deut 22:22 which make both man and woman equal, mark a legal-historical turning point.[240] The other possibility, which this aphorism asserts, is excluded: The jealous, betrayed husband no longer has the right to kill if the couple are caught in the act.[241] Even in intra-familial and sexual conflicts, the life of the woman is not at the mercy of her husband, likewise the children. Only the public court has jurisdiction.

Finally, in two other laws we find limitations placed on traditional patriarchal rights. According to Deut 21:15–17, the father does not have the right to give preference to the son of his favorite wife over his actual firstborn. We would have to surmise similar opportunities to complain for those who are passed over, the wife or son. We must assume that 24:1–4, dealing with divorce, we must assume the normal case would not, as such, have involved a public trial and decision.[242] Nonetheless, Deut 24:1–4 denies the right of remarrying the woman, if in the meantime she has remarried. This is an unusual provision[243] for which we might think there to be little discernible need,[244] the law-giver here certainly makes a significant change in patriarchal power.

Doubtless, in many of these laws traditional rights and structures are established, which means, simultaneously, that they lose the great

---

240 See Daube, *Landmarks* 179.
241 For this, see the discussion of this point in the relationship of law and reality between Phillips, *Family Law*; McKeating, *Sanctions*; Phillips, *Another Look*.
242 In addition to Phillips, *Family Law*; see also Yaron, *Divorce*; Nembach, *Ehescheidung*; Zakuvitch, *Divorce*.
243 Especially Yaron, *Restoration* emphasizes the special position of this biblical law. The Koran recognizes a contradictory law, which permits a third remarriage, if the wife had meanwhile married someone else (*Sura* 2.231).
244 For a discussion, see Yaron, *Restoration*; Wenham, *Restoration*; Toeg, *General Law*; Westbrook, *Prohibition*. Does this not rather concern an analogy to incest law (Yaron, Wenham), or are financial reasons involved, namely the unrepaid dowry because of the woman's debt (*'erwat dabar*) (Westbrook)?

flexibility of oral, freely asserted rights.[245] Family law was an area where non-state structures held on the longest, which meant it was to the advantage of generally unlimited patriarchal power. The beginnings of written law, as presented in the Mishpatim, had as little effect here as did the Book of the Covenant as a whole. It was Deuteronomy that finally made the breakthrough.

The Social-Historical Background

In order to examine the reason and impetus for such change, together with its correlation with other themes in deuteronomic law, we should probably begin with the linguistic structure of the law. In form, it is very close to the Mishpatim, so we will describe it in those terms.[246] It is exclusively casuistic legislation. In a whole series of cases, the impetus for individual cases and the precedent cases connected with them are clearly apparent. This applies to the complex case in 22:13ff. as well as the prohibition against remarriage in 24:1ff. Extremely unusual cases, not everyday ones, form the ground floor of written law. The transition from trial protocol to law[247] was a hands-on process. For that reason we must assume that they had the same institutional background, that is, it is difficult to doubt that they both originated in the activities of the Jerusalem central court.[248]

Of course these sexual and family laws are not all in a single block, like the Mishpatim of the Book of the Covenant. Rather, they are divided into four passages (21:10–21; 22:13–29; 24:1–4; 25:5–12). They are a part of the variegated and thematically mixed chapters 21–25. Because of their similarity, we might guess that within them there are fragments of a collection that at one time belonged together.[249] This would also mean that they are certainly older than deuteronomic law itself. Method-ologically, this would be hard to support, because it relies ultimately upon *form-critical* observations alone, that is, the formal relationship of the laws together with their thematic relatedness. These, however, are not legitimate literary-critical reasons. There is no real evidence for such a discrete collection.

Still, the subjects form an important theme in Deuteronomy, and we should investigate their significance for the deuteronomic movement. It can be demonstrated for the Mishpatim of the Book of the Covenant, that the questions in it, which led to comprehensive legal regulation, represented central problems in norms for society of the ninth and eighth centuries. This applies to the question of slavery but also for the problem of the death penalty, physical force, matters of personal property and aliens.

For this reason we might surmise that the urgent need for regulation in the area of family law was an entirely new impetus toward codifi-cation. Even if individual and consequently perhaps older judgments found use, it must be questioned why Deuteronomy found it necessary

245 See above p. 75.
246 See Preuss, *Deuteronomium* 130.
247 Thus, especially Locher, *Ehre* 83ff.; ibid., *Prozessprotokoll*.
248 See above pp. 90ff., 166f.
249 See especially, Rofé, *Sex Laws*.

to take this area up in such detail. Or, to put it more precisely: no other area of life is so thoroughly illuminated by the assistance of casuistic sample decisions, together with juridical analysis, as this one. The political, constitutional provisions are clearly on an entirely different plane than those of the provisions for social protection.

In fact, now we see that questions of marriage and adultery received special significance in the texts approximately contemporary with Deuteronomy. There is a frequent generalization of Israel in the book of Jeremiah that, "they are all adulterers" (9:2) and "the land is full of adulterers" (23:10, cf also 5:7; 7:9; 13:27). Jeremiah especially accuses the false prophets of adultery – in general (23:14) as well as by name (29:23). This appears to have been an important criterion for him in questions of false prophecy.[250]

Here adultery as a threat to the social order[251] gains special significance as an expression of a particular constellation. Scholars have reckoned that "adultery" (n'f) includes a relationship to other gods, that is, it is not meant to refer to just a breach of the marital relationship.[252] Nevertheless, it is difficult to find direct evidence for this or even to assume it is probable. In any case, it is far more likely that for Jeremiah adultery was a concrete form of what he complained about in the entire late preexilic period. There is "deception" ($šéqer$) in everything, according to the theme of the entire book:[253] deceit and deception, self-deceit and self-deception, which also includes the family. The questioning of traditional norms of relationships appears to have had deep and far-reaching influence. Where Hosea laments sexual behavior in connection with religious ritual, Jeremiah is apparently concerned about sexual misbehavior, which, as such has religious significance.

Assyrian policy contributed to the dissolution of traditional social forms and customs, but especially the flow of refugees after the fall of the northern kingdom contributed to the development of a large slum section of Jerusalem, spreading social misery.[254] As in the eighth century, critical prophecy complained mightily regarding the enslavement of free Israelites, the theft of land and the physical power of the powerful (and the relevant passages in the Book of the Covenant subjected these problems to legal regulation),[255] so also now in the seventh/sixth centuries, Jeremiah and Ezekiel complained that the land is full of deceit and adultery.

There is a falling away from the God of Israel displayed in this social injustice, and contemporary law books attack these problems with a wealth of detailed legislation. This happened in the style of ancient Near Eastern legislation (or the Mishpatim), and for that reason, it occurred almost without explicit foundation. Related figures of speech simply appeared, referring to the need to remove evil. There was lacking, however, an elaborate connection of this theme with

250 See also Ez 18:6,15; 22:10f.
251 Thus especially Williams, *Examination*.
252 See e.g. Freedman/Willoughby, article on *nā'ap* 124ff.
253 See Overholt, *Falsehood*.
254 Thus in conjunction with the corresponding, brief references in Meyers, *Eve* 192ff.
255 See above pp. 151ff., 159ff.

the central theological motifs and thought structure of deuteronomic law.

The death penalty in cases of adultery and lost virginity – there is hardly anything else so typical of the harshness of Old Testament law, or so far removed from the liberality of New Testament (and modern) thinking. Little attention has been paid to the legal–historical process itself or the history of its varying reception in Judaism and Christianity. In any case, what is new is that when family law was written down, there was public judicial control of patriarchal power. Simultaneously, family conflicts were included in the regulations of Deuteronomy. This applies, for example, to the strict application of the rule of two witnesses in all cases involving capital offense (Deut 19:15ff.).

What had to be said explicitly about apostasy and sacral blasphemy (17:6) is only presupposed here. Only father and mother together can bring a charge against their son or the husband of their daughter (21:18ff.; 22:13ff.). Insofar as the charge is a matter of the life or death of his wife, a husband cannot accuse his wife without corroboration. In my opinion, when we view them against the background of conditions in a patriarchal society of this kind, deuteronomic legislation brought about an astonishingly general, new equality between men and women. It is no accident that Deuteronomy 4:16 contains the broadest statement of this, or that the God of Israel is neither male nor female, or that the first commandment only makes sense in connection with the second and its relationship to the sexuality of God.

Overview: Radicalization and Non-observance

Already the chapter of curses (Deut 27) shows how little the norms of deuteronomic law dealing with sexual relationships (in their entirety or even just the most important ones) have been correctly understood. Relationships with a person's father's wife (verse 20),[256] with a half-sister (verse 22) or with a mother-in-law (verse 23) are all placed under a curse. They are behavior for which alone a divine – not a human – judiciary is responsible (see Ex 22:18).[257]

The subject of prohibited sexual relationships[258] occurs frequently in the Holiness Code.[259] Two closely related chapters, Lev 18 and 20, demonstrate priestly thinking's great interest in the subject. Above all, there is a catalog of prohibited degrees of relationship employed in Lev 18:6ff. which itemizes details of the daily life of a woman in her husband's house in a patrilocal society.[260] In addition, we find listed, relationships with a menstruating woman (Lev 18:19), adultery (verse 20), homosexuality (verse 22) and sodomy (verse 33). These are the horrors which those who used to live in the land committed (verses 3, 27) and through which Israel becomes unclean, so that it "vomits" the people out (verses 28ff.). The prohibitions in Lev 18 correspond to the

---

256 There is a parallel to this only in 22:30, which of course is connected with marriage (*lqh*), while 27:20 intends sexual relationship.
257 For the special position of Deut 27, see e.g. Fabry, *Dekalog*. He theorizes a late addition, aiming at the Holiness Code, which shows a certain correspondence with the Decalog.
258 For the evidence in the ancient Near Eastern world, see Hoffner, *Incest*.
259 For the literary evidence, see below pp. 277ff., cf p. 296.
260 See Elliger, *Gesetz*; Bigger, *Family Laws*; Halbe, *Inzestverbote*.

capital offense provisions in chapter 20, where, at the heart of the Molech cult, there is a form of child sacrifice (20:2ff.).

It is there that the whole area of sexual relation is integrated into Torah. In order for this to become clear, we must make reference to two things. First, clearly the background against which this is said is the basic conception of the Holiness Code of sacred and profane, clean and unclean,[261] which exclude an immediate and direct transfer to judicial practice. Lev 20:4f. shows this especially clearly, where it discusses the fact that Molech sacrifice should remain uncharged because God will carry out the punishment. Second, above all, there is a fundamental distinction made in priestly law between acts committed intentionally (*beyād rāmāh*) and those that are done simply out of inattentiveness (*bišegāgā*)[262] (see especially Num 15:22–21. In the latter case simple atonement sacrifice is prescribed. This means that the rigidity of the law is not loosened by atonement and forgiveness.[263]

While these texts safeguard the whole area of sexual relationships by means of significant provisions for capital punishment, it is apparent that at the same time a course has been followed in the community which has led in practice to non-observance of these rigid laws. In addition to already known biblical rules for conduct (e.g. the requirement for at least two eye-witnesses in cases of capital offense), we now find the requirement that there be previous warning.[264] Only then is the commandment considered to have been broken *consciously*, but such a combination of circumstances hardly ever happens. As in other areas of criminal law, this provision can only be considered rigid when it is taken out of its context in the totality of Torah with its practice. Separate provisions, such as the law of the rebellious son, have been interpreted within rabbinic tradition in such a way that this situation could never actually have arisen.[265]

Finally, it is not accidental that the protection of life (verse 5) as well as the defense against the people of God accommodating themselves to the practices of the surrounding nations (verse 3, cf 20:23) is specified in Lev 18 as well as being the goal of all instruction in Torah.[266] Both are to be observed in creative interaction with these traditions.

Desacralization and Security of Rights: The Protection of Nature and Animals

"As the housewife who has cleaned a room takes care that the door is closed so that the dog doesn't come in and track up the house with his dirty paws, so European thinkers take care that no animals run around in the field of ethics." Albert Schweitzer's characterization of European ethics,[267] particularly Christian ethics, does not apply to Torah. Further-

---

261 See Goddman, *Diet and Sex*; see also below pp. 305ff.
262 See e.g. Rendtorff, *Leviticus* 150ff.; as well as below pp. 318ff.
263 See below pp. 310ff.
264 See mSan 5.1, tSan 11.1, bSan 40b, and others.
265 Thus Kraus, *Sanhedrin* 240 on the basis of mSan 8.1, jSan 26a, Sifra §218–220, bSan 68b/69a; according to the last citation only a period of three months in the life of the boy are in question.
266 See Petuchowski, *Bräuche*.
267 A. Schweitzer, *Kultur und Ethik* 362f.; cf Landmann, *Tier* 41.

more, in Deuteronomy as elsewhere, we find laws for the protection of animals, plants and the purity of nature. The idea, current from Schopenhauer[268] to Drewermann,[269] that the roots of "forgottenness of nature"[270] and especially Christian lack of sympathy for animals lie in Old Testament Judaism is based on faulty knowledge of the texts[271] and Jewish tradition.[272]

Contrary to what Paul presumes in his rhetorical question in 1 Cor 9:9f., God does indeed care about the oxen. Of course we do not recognize the correlation of this theme with the central theological tenets of deuteronomic thinking on first glance, but only this correlation will be able to free such laws from the character of historical accident and be able to show their theological necessity.

In order to be able to recognize more clearly what is special, let us look first at the Torah history that precedes Deuteronomy. The exclusive veneration of the God of Israel took the form of a praxis that from the very beginning included what we call nature. This is a basic theme of the oldest documents containing rules for exclusive veneration; Ex 34:11ff.[273] and Deuteronomy incorporate all of the essential features. The seasonal rhythm of the annual festivals and the completely independent week participate in this, as well as the offering of the firstborn of animals (Deut 15:19ff.) and firstfruits (especially 26:1ff.), or the relations to animals in customs of sacrifice and food (Deut 14:21. An animal is not a thing for the Mishpatim but a subject of law,[274] for whom the death penalty applies as it does to guilty people (Ex 21:18ff. cf Gen 9:5), which as we know has been practiced in the west until modern times. The Book of the Covenant, which integrates all of this, adopts sacral traditions like those saying that "holy men," or more precisely, "men of the shrine", eat no carcass, implying that they also eat no blood (Ex 22:30). Above all, animals were included in the regulations regarding relationships with the poor and social enemies; people ought to help them (23:4f.).[275]

Deuteronomy takes up this subject by itself, separating it from the others. According to Deut 22:1–4, help is to be given for strays and animals who have been entrusted to the care of people (verse 4). Thus, from the very beginning, Torah presumes an agricultural ethic, which proceeds from the assumption of a deep inter-connectedness with

---

268 Schopenhauer, *Grundlagen* §8, §19.7; *Parerga* II §177.
269 Drewermann, *Fortschritt* 71ff. with direct, anti-semitic invectives and the key sentence, "The Bible itself contains a single, wretched passage that the righteous person has pity on his animals, and the command not to muzzle the ox while threshing, but it does not contain a single sentence speaking of the right of animals to protection from the brutality and greed of people, or even to sympathy and protection in need" (100) was based exclusively on the reference to Schopenhauer. He adopts Schopenhauer's reference to "Judaized animal haters and worshipers of reason" (Schopernhauer, *Grundlagen* §19.7).
270 See Altner, *Naturvergesssenheit*.
271 See the overview of the discussion in Liedke, *Tier-Ethik*; see especially Pangritz, *Tier*; Henry, *Tier*; Westermann, *Mensch*; Bartelmus, *Tierwelt*.
272 See Landmann, *Tier*; Stein, *Tier*; see also Löw, *Thierschutz*; Unna, *Thierschutz*; in summary Marcus, *Prolegomena zu einer jüdischen Umweltethik*.
273 See above pp. 131ff.
274 See Fernsham, *Liability of Animals*.
275 See above pp. 187ff.

animals and formulates such traditions as newly binding instructions
from God.

In addition to these already traditional provisions, in many places
Deuteronomy makes explicit provision for protection of birds (22:6f.) and
working domestic animals. Furthermore (to remain with the theme of
animals), there is a whole long catalog of edible and non-edible animals.
The significance and theological function of such texts is only revealed
when we examine them in correlation with the basic rules regarding the
unity of cultic sites, taken in the deuteronomic form of the cultic practice
oriented in the unity of God.

Since legitimate sacrifices were only to be offered at the sites selected
by God, there was, as we know, a "decontrol" of so-called secular
butchering.[276] According to Deut 12, animals in the towns could have
been eaten at will, without direct connection to cultic activity. Several
times there is comparison made to game animals – gazelle and deer
(verses 15, 20). These could be eaten by clean or unclean men (that is,
those who do or do not have access to the cult). The killing of animals is
thus separated from the context of worship; ritual ties are removed.
Viewed over the long haul, this process is one (of many) roots from which
animals grew into valuable material for people. The religious significance
of animals, the coupling of the killing of animals and sacrifice was
noticeably weakened. Animals are restored to people in a new way. Thus,
it is clear that in relation to the God of the Bible, the realm of the sacred
has been reduced and the world became secular.

Of course, the Old Testament, particularly Deuteronomy, took this
step in close association with another. First, the separation of these,
which belong together, made Christian indifference toward animals
possible, and enabled Christians to have an anti-semitic view of
European history on this subject right into modern times. Deut 12 even
places immediate restrictions on the use of wild game as food animals.
Their blood may not be consumed (15f., 22f.). Unlike the priestly texts
(Lev 17:13), Deut 12 does not simply presume this limitation on wild
game. The theological significance of the prohibition against consuming
blood is formulated in Deuteronomy: "for the blood is life (néfeš), and
you shall not eat the life (néfeš) with the meat" (Deut 12:23; cf. Lev 17:11).
The decontrol of butchering did not imply an unrestricted attack on "life"
itself. If nothing else in Jewish ethics, the required removal of blood
prevented killing animals for pure pleasure.[277]

Deuteronomic law created significant additional counter-weight to
deal with consequences of the decontrol of secular butchering. It is not
accidental that we find the first list of animals that should not be eaten

---

276 The opinion of McConville, Law 44ff.; cf Seebass, Vorschlag zur Verinfachung 96,
    that there might have been secular butchering long before Deuteronomy could be
    supported on 1 Sam 14:32–35 alone. Nevertheless, the concern there was not
    simply the consumption of blood (thus, e.g. without detailed discussion, Long,
    King Saul 121) which was not affected by Saul's construction of an altar, but rather
    eating "on" ('al) the blood. Cf Lev 10:26 as well as Grintz, Do Not Eat who with
    Maimonides considers the possibility of a chthonic blood ritual. In any case, "The
    wrong lies in the fact that this area [the sacral-F.C.] was not adequately
    protected," thus Stoebe, 1 Samuel 268 note 3, see also Donner, Verwerfung 33.
277 See Milgrom, Dietary Laws; ibid., Ethics.

precisely where the killing of animals is separated from the cult, Deut 14:3–21.[278]

We can surmise with some certainty that there are older cultural rules typical of many groups at work here. Dietary customs are a part of every culture.[279] It is just that some pre-deuteronomic texts indicate such rules do not possess great significance or theological meaning, and they certainly did not receive religious sanction.[280]

The separation of cult and everyday life occurring in deuteronomic cultic unity necessitated reflection upon which part of creation had been given to people to eat. As the list of Deut 14 indicates, there is only a small proportion which may be eaten. The edible include cattle, sheep and goats as well as a series of animals that can be hunted (verses 3ff.), clean birds (verse 11), as well as the rather marginal number of aquatic animals with fins and scales (verse 9).

Deuteronomic law does not limit itself to such food regulations. Apart from the aquatic animals, it takes up dietary laws again in the form of provisions for protection. They amplify what was given in the introductory chapters (12 and 14) of the law and ensure them against potential misuse. They deal first with birds (ṣippōr).

> 22:6 *If you come upon a bird's nest, in any tree or on the ground, with fledglings or eggs, with the mother sitting on the fledglings or the eggs, you shall not take the mother with the young. 7 Let the mother go, taking only the young for yourself, in order that it may go well with you and you may live long.*

"It is interesting that there is such an emphatic promise in a command dealing with so much detail: the protection of a mother bird is placed on the same level as honoring a human mother (5:16)."[281] Conversely, perhaps the emphasis of the final clause, which elsewhere is connected with the observation of divine instructions in their entirety,[282] would lead to a questioning of one's own values. Still, Christianity uncoupled itself from Torah so profoundly that a new, extremely threatening experience was required to cause it to re-evaluate the relationship between people and birds. It also demonstrates that connecting people with nature does not require an opposition between "humanity" and utilitarianism.[283]

In any case, deuteronomic law applies the simple but important maxim that the reproductive capability of birds is part of God's plan, which here as elsewhere is intended to preserve life. In the context of the entire deuteronomic law, the question poses itself: to what degree are birds representative of all non-domestic animals suitable for hunting.

---

278 See the overview in Chang, *Abominable Things*. In addition to the commentaries, see especially Wigand, *Vorstellung*; Döller, *Reinheitsgesetze*; Yerkes, *Unclean Animals*; Kornfeld, *Tiere*; Goodman, *Laws*; Milgrom, *Ethics*; ibid. *System*; Soler, *Dietary Prohibitions*; critical of this Alter, *New Theory*; most recently especially Firmage, *Dietary Laws*. For cultic purity in general, see below pp. 307f.
279 See Douglas, *Reinheit*; for a critique, see especially Milgrom, *Ethics* 176ff.
280 E.g. Gen 43:32.
281 Bertholet, commentary 68.
282 See 4:40, 5:33, only "long life" 4:26; 6:2; 11:9; 17:20; 26:15.
283 Thus e.g. Bertholet and Steuernagel, commentaries.

In 25:4, the cow, the most important of the domestic animals is discussed after having been mentioned in 12; 14:4, 24; 15:19ff.; 18:3; 22:1ff.

25:4 You shall not muzzle an ox[284] while it is treading out the grain.

This law is frequently interpreted as symbolic or figurative, not least by Paul (1 Cor 9:9). And theories have been rendered out of its context in the framework of deuteronomic law.[285] Nevertheless, it could hardly be doubted that this is, first and foremost, a rule for the treatment of a domestic animal.[286] This is shown by wide-ranging rabbinic discussions of particulars of the treatment of animals.[287] Thus, the prohibition against tormenting an animal illustrates the purpose of the law – to care for animals.[288] The ox, which is a work and food animal for people, here gains rights similar to those of human beings (see Deut 23:25). Every conscious addition to the suffering of animals is prohibited.

What applies to other areas of law, for example, in the Mishpatim or deuteronomic marriage laws, also applies here. The way this was codified suggests that only especially important matters are regulated by the law – or at least specifically regulated. Simultaneously, however, they are so selected and arranged in the composition that an astonishingly broad area is addressed and thoroughly covered.

Correspondingly, if we read all of the provisions in deuteronomic law regarding behavior toward animals as an entity, we see that in addition to the uncoupling of meat eating from sacrifice there is a comprehensive regulation that is indeed theologically necessary taking seriously the fact that animals are subjects of law and that human power over them is limited to precisely circumscribed situations. In biblical thinking secularity means legally secured protection for the animal world and not a lack of rights. The lack of concern for nature in Europe is also grounded in lack of attention in Torah, but creation is still the subject of law there.[289]

There are two other provisions affecting areas of creation beyond the animal world. We find a prohibition against planting two different things in a vineyard in Deut 22:9–11. In Lev 19:19 this is turned into a fundamental prohibition against planting two different things together. Furthermore, two different kinds of animals are not to work together, nor should flax and wool be mixed together in clothing. This strict priestly tradition of keeping separate things apart, not mixing different things, is connected with attention to differences between species. "What God has divided, let no one put together."[290]

In one of the deuteronomic war laws in Deut 23:10–15, we find provisions that serve to keep a military encampment clean, but which

---

284 *Sor* is not the same as our "ox," see KBL³ 1346ff.
285 See Carmichael, *Ceremonial Crux*; Noonan, *Muzzled Ox*; Eslinger, *Drafting Techniques*.
286 See also Nielsen, *Ox*, who reconstructs an old "taboo calendar" (104) on the basis of isolated statements in Deuteronomy. He compares this calendar with the Gezer calendar.
287 See the important study, Lisowsky, *Deut 25:4*.
288 bBM 90a; see Lisowski, *Deut 25:4* 150f.
289 For the formulation and contemporary problems, see e.g. Evers (ed.), *Schöpfung*.
290 For a discussion and theological interpretation, see below pp. 325f.

could serve as a model for the maintenance of the cleanliness of the environment.

> 23:13 With your utensils you shall have a peg,[291] when you relieve yourself outside, you shall dig a hole with it and then cover up your excrement. 14 Because YHWH your God travels along with your camp, to save you and to hand over your enemies to you, therefore your camp must be holy, so that he may not see anything indecent among you and turn away from you.

Undoubtedly, "Holiness begins with cleanliness, and this cleanliness is roughly the beginning of all purity."[292] From this we derive a principle, according to which everyone is responsible for getting rid of their own waste. Failure to apply this calls to mind the befouled condition of our modern world. Above all, this atavistic concept of God might be significant for our future; the protecting and saving presence of God among his people will not endure stench and filth – and how clean the desert might have been then. That God has a nose is a case where Gospel appears as Law.

Political Freedom and Canonical Commitment: The Step toward "Scripture"

The importance of its contents alone does not make it possible to explain the binding power which deuteronomic law attained and caused it to become the heart of the biblical canon. This is shown by a comparison with great texts, rich in tradition from the surrounding ancient Near Eastern world or of classical antiquity. As great as the significance of the code of Hammurabi or the Homeric epics might have been, we are unable to demonstrate that they had the power to influence generations by means of an expanded canon[293] nor did they have a power to claim the authority of the will of God upon his people.

Even this authority together with its mediator, Moses who is speaking out of a distant past, are not an adequate explanation. We see this in the report of the "discovery" of a law book in the Jerusalem temple in the eighteenth year of King Josiah in 2 Kg 22f. Neither the dignity of the place where it is discovered, nor its transmission through highest priests, nor the claim of God (or Moses) who is speaking in the texts, nor the simple content of the texts (especially 2 Kg 22:11) are sufficient. We ought also to examine what the prophetess Huldah had to say (22:13ff.), but even this is not enough to give power to the law.

That only happens in the festive covenant ceremony (bᵉrit) in which the king obligated himself to this law in front of the elders and all of the people, and the people joined in (2 Kg 23:1–3). bᵉrit is an even more important act of obligation. Everything is necessary to "establish" (qūm hiph) the words of this book, thus to give it power (verse 3). Only in this way does its validity become something that cannot be evaded in practice (verses 4ff.). This is the view of the report in the exilic books of the Kings.

291 *Yātēd* is a tent peg, which can be made of metal. See Steuernagel, commentary.
292 Th. Mann, *Gesetz* 651.
293 For this, see Colpe, *Sakralisierung* as well as A. and J. Assman (ed.), *Kanon*.

Thus, we must presume this report talks about nothing less than the heart of deuteronomic law, separating the report from the event producing the profound historical changes by at least a generation. What can we recognize about this process with which the change in normative tradition is marked for canonic development?

The Presupposition: The Deuteronomic Movement

In order to understand, it would be wise to look first at Deuteronomy's writer groups and their supporters. At the same time we can summarize what has already been discussed.

Deuteronomy is one of the few Old Testament writings for which we can lift the mask of anonymity, which covers the faces of those who wrote it, if only a little. A series of recent studies have identified and described the aristocratic Jerusalem families we encounter in conjunction with the discovery of the law book. They were part of the conflicts of the Jeremiah period and can be traced for about three generations, up to the beginning of the exilic period.[294] The great interest the texts have in certain names and functions of Jerusalem officials shows a little more about groups which produced literature during the exilic period. A series of seals or seal impressions from the end of the monarchic period, in part giving evidence of the same names, proves that these families actually existed.[295] It is inconceivable that Deuteronomy itself, which bears so many marks of a multi-generation development, or the comprehensive literary collections, which scholars describe as deuteronomistic, could have developed independent of these groups. Nevertheless, exactly how these correlations are to be conceived must remain open.

According to 2 Kg 22:4ff., in 622 BCE Hilkiah, the high priest of the Jerusalem shrine, handed over the law book to the Shaphan, the "scribe" (one of the most important of the officers of the king at this time).[296] These two people are representatives of two families who had for decades been involved with Judah's destiny. Hilkiah's grandson was in all probability that Seraiah (see 1 Chr 6:13; Ezr 7:1) the last functioning high priest in Jerusalem before the exile, who was killed by Nebuchadnezzar (2 Kg 25:18ff.).[297] Hilkaiah's son Azariah, to whom a seal impression can be traced back, probably held office in the interim.[298] There is another son of Hilkiah mentioned in Jer 29:3, Gemariah. There, together with a son of Shaphan, he functioned from 598 BCE as an emissary between Jerusalem and the first Captivity.

We have no certain knowledge, but there are certain possibilities with other appearances of this name. Thus, also the prophet Jeremiah was the

---

294 Yeivin, *Families*; Weinfeld, *Deuteronomy* 158ff.; Lohfink, *Historische Kurzgeschichte* 73ff.; Hardmeier, *Prophetie* 443ff.; Kessler, *Staat* 200f. and others.

295 See especially Avigad, *Hebrew Bullae*; Shiloh, *Hebrew Bullae*. For the problem of identifying seals of historical personages, see Avigad, *Identification*.

296 See Mettinger, *State Officials* 25ff.; Rüterswörden, *Beamte* 85ff.

297 See Hardmeier, *Prophetie* 443, who wonders whether he is also identical with the Seraiah of Jer 36:26, despite the different father's names (Ezriel - Azariah).

298 Shiloh, *Hebrew Bullae* 29 (no. 27, see Fig. 2, no. 6) as well as Schneider, *Azariahu* for identification.

son of a priest Hilkiah (Jer 1:1). Another interesting thesis in this context suggests that Eliakim might be the son of Hilkiah in Isa 22:20–23.[299] According to this post-Isaianic "investiture oracle,"[300] Eliakim was assigned a position of unique character. He is not a king, but he is "father" to the residents of Jerusalem and the House of Judah, he alone held the rightful key to the House of David, and the "key" role in which he functioned was controlled by no one, not even the king.

There is a very interesting theory, even if it cannot be proven, that he was the governor, who functioned as temporary ruler during the minority of King Josiah. If this is correct, it would be evidence for a connection between the members of the high priestly family with the events around the accession to the throne of Josiah and in general with "secular" political duties.[301] Shaphan, the central political figure of the Josian period (2 Kg 22:3, 8–10, 11, 12, 14), had four sons who are known to us: Ahikam (2 Kg 22:12, 14; Jer 26:24), Gemariah (Jer 36:10, 12, 25),[302] Elasah (Jer 29:3) and Jaazaniah (Ez 8:11). The son of Gemariah was named Micah (Jer 36:11, 13). Ahikam's son is that Gedaliah, who after the fall of the temple and the city safeguarded the last remainder of political autonomy (2 Kg 25:22–25; Jer 39:14; 40:5–9, 11–16; 41:1f. among others).[303]

We see in these figures and their families, as well as others from this period whose names are known,[304] the political exponents of the Judean *'am hā'āres* who held decisive power in their hands. Their behavior toward Jeremiah with his critical prophecy matches precisely what the prophet law in Deut 18 demanded.[305]

In order to understand the background of Deuteronomy, it is especially important that analysis, as Weinfeld has done it,[306] of the linguistic and content traditions points in the same direction. The many connections to wisdom can best be explained by a provenance in wisdom and scribal groups. The same thing is true for contemporary contractual literature. It can be regarded as additional support when Jer 8:8 views Torah in the late monarchic period together with the activity of wisdom and scribal groups.[307]

---

299 Thus, Hardmeier, *Prophetie* 440f.
300 Wildberger, *Jesaia* 844; for the problem of the text, see pp. 842ff.
301 The famous and much discussed seal of Eliakim with the title *na'ar ywkn* from which several impressions have been known for some time, has in the meantime been clearly dated in the eighth century (not the seventh/sixth). See TUAT II 567f.; for the history of the research, see especially Garfinkel, *Eliakim, Na'ar Yokan Seal*.
302 A seal impression with the same name and the same paternal name in Shiloh, *Bullae* 29 (no. 2, compare Fig. 8, no. 6. See, however, the thoughts against this identification in Avigad, *Hebrew Bullae* 129 note 164.
303 Possibly, the seals of a Gedaliah, the manager of the palace (*'šr 'l hbyt*) from Lachish (Vattioni, *Sigilli* no. 149; Semlik, *Dokumente* 127) or of a Gedaliah, servant of the king (*'bd hmlk*; Avigad, *Hebrew Bullae* 24f.; TUAT II 567) are connected with him.
304 See especially Kessler, *Staat* 200.
305 See above pp. 240ff.
306 Weinfeld, *Deuteronomy*.
307 See above pp. 23ff.

This milieu replaces the long-held theory that Deuteronomy originated in Levitical groups.[308] Certainly, the theory that Deuteronomy's special rhetoric came out of Levitical preaching[309] is hardly tenable in view of the fact that there is attestation for this activity only centuries later in chronistic texts. We must also hesitate to connect this too closely with cultic groups in the narrower sense, considering the clear differences between deuteronomic and actual priestly texts. Because we know next to nothing about Levites of the later monarchic period, even the most important statements of Deuteronomy itself are debated,[310] this theory has little value for historical explanation.

The great role which the Levites had in Deuteronomy is remarkable and requires explanation. According to Deuteronomy, it is an important feature that all priests are Levites and all Levites are potential priests (especially 18:1ff.). In spite of all the difference from priestly concepts, there remains a strong layer of cultic perspective, as evidenced by Deuteronomy's interest in a central shrine.

Already here in Deuteronomy, for example, 14:2 and especially 7:6, Israel is called a "holy people," chosen to serve their God. Of course, holiness is not yet the legally decisive key concept,[311] but without the participation of priestly-Levitical groups we could hardly imagine the development and practice of deuteronomic law.[312] It is no accident that the book was found in the temple and that it was intimately connected with the Levitical priests (Deut 17:18; 31:9).

Every comparison of Deuteronomy with other traditions of the same period (e.g. that of the priests, but also that of the so-called deuteronomistic texts) shows the uncommon breadth of traditions, subjects, aspects and interests which it unites. The deuteronomistic history of Joshua through 2 Kings records history, following the standards set by Deuteronomy, nevertheless, it only enlists the law for this in sections. Only the question of cultic unity is adopted here, not the social justice connected with it. What became an inner unity in deuteronomic law, presuming a rather broad cooperation of different groups, after the death of Josiah broke apart into quickly dissolving political constellations.

A resistance movement had developed under the pressure of Assyrian domination and was further thought through at the urging of the eighth-century prophets, being processed in the Book of the Covenant. Now it was considered further. The *'am hā'āreṣ*, who after the murder of Amon seized power as a farmers' liberation movement and

---

308 See e.g. Bentzen, *Josianische Reform*; Lindblom, *Herkunft*; Eissfeldt, *Einleitung* 297. Especially influential were Rad, *Deuteronomium-Studien* 148. See the overview of variants of this thesis in Hoppe, *Levitical Origins* 27ff. For critique, in addition to Weinfeld, *Deuteronomy* 54ff. and elsewhere; see Hoppe, *Levitical Origins*; Bettenzoli, *Leviti* and others.

309 Thus especially Rad, *Predigt des Deuteronomiums*; for a critique, in addition to Weinfeld, *Deuteronomy* 10ff. especially 54ff.; see Matthias, *Levitische Predigt*.

310 For this, see Gunneweg, *Levite* 69ff.; furthermore, Wright, *Levites*; Emerton, *Priests*; Abba, *Priests*; Bettenzoli, *Leviti* and others.

311 See below pp. 301ff., especially 305ff.

312 Similarly already Rad, who considered a cooperation between Levitical groups and the Judean *'am hā'āreṣ*, e.g. *Deuteronomium Studien* 147f.

maintained it during the childhood of Josiah, apparently became a kind of catchment area for varying traditions and groups. Nevertheless, it is also clear that the traditionally aristocratic groups in Jerusalem – as they are expressed in royal and Jerusalem theology, and the priestly groups (in the narrower sense) – as the priestly texts and Ezekiel characterize them, played no part in this movement.

The Founding of Freedom as the Origin of the Canon

The first biblical pseudepigraph came about in the late monarchic period with Deuteronomy's claim to be a speech by Moses, given before the people entered the land.[313] It was not chosen for inclusion in an extant canon because of its prestige, as later writings were. The phenomenon of a written canon came more from this book and the power that it had. In order to gain a better understanding of this process, summarize a few aspects.

- The historical background is the time when the Judean ʿam hāʾāreṣ seized power after the court coup against Amon. As we have seen, this movement, which had put a child upon the throne, held the actual power for several decades. Several stories give us the names of their representatives. The event had the characteristic of an agricultural liberation movement, which is especially reflected in the corresponding social laws of Deuteronomy.

- The development and structure of deuteronomic law cannot be separated from the institution of the Jerusalem central court. What applies to the Jerusalem central court, also applies here. Only here could we imagine the knowledge of ancient Near Eastern legal culture and juridical authority, which, for example, stands behind the marriage and family laws but also behind the well-thought inner unity of this corpus. According to Deut 17:8f. this court speaks with the same authority as Deuteronomy itself – the authority of Moses.

- If Deuteronomy is formulated as a creative interpretation of older traditions like that of the exodus, the self-understanding as freedom of the deuteronomic movement with its center in the constitutional provisions, it can only do so in the name of an authority who is above the king who was himself established by God on Zion, as well as above everyone else in the present who speak in the name of God. This was achieved by making the book speak through the words of a speech by Moses, through which an old tradition of legitimation of the Jerusalem court achieves a new shape (Ex 18).

- We are unable to say how the actual freedom of the ʿam hāʾāreṣ and the authorization of the people formulated in Deuteronomy relate toward each other temporally and substantively with the protection of the entire divine will. Each is at the root of the other. Probably the many traces of growth in the law, which was so closed with respect to its content, reflect this relationship and its unfolding.

If these observations and the theses are at least basically correct, then the following inevitable questions result:

313 See Perlitt, *Deuteronomium* 3.

- Can and should this temporary situation shift into a permanent condition, and how could that happen? This question was raised at latest with the approaching manhood of the child-King Josiah.[314]
- Can and will the king return Judah to the normalcy which formerly had prevailed in the ancient Near East?
- Will justice and the military be subordinate to royal power?
- Will the tithe be reintroduced?
- Will compulsory labor, etc. be reintroduced?

We should no more doubt that groups were interested in these things than that the corresponding traditions continued to have an effect. The increasing power vacuum that came into existence with the collapse of the Assyrian empire could only have intensified this problem.

Such thoughts would be pure speculation, were there not two texts from entirely different perspectives that deal with the transfer of deuteronomic law into permanent status: Deut 26:16 and 2 Kg 22f. Both texts are aimed at a particular act of obligation to the law by all of Israel.

(a) According to the narrative in 2 Kg 22f., everything started with the "discovery" of a Torah book in the temple (22:8ff.). Reading this text caused the king to be profoundly shaken (22:11), following which he ordered a prophetic verification (22:12ff.). None of this, however, put the law into effect. Before there could be a report of the application of reform measures and the celebration of Passover (23:4ff.), there was a ceremonial act of obligation:

> 23:1 *Then the king directed that all the elders of Judah and Jerusalem should be gathered to him. 2 The king went up to the house of YHWH, and with him went all the males of Judah, all the inhabitants of Jerusalem, the priests, the prophets and all the people, both small and great; he read in their hearing all the words of the book of the covenant that had been found in the house of YHWH. 3 The king stood by the pillar and made a covenant before YHWH to follow YHWH, keeping his commandments, his decrees and his statutes with all his heart and all his soul, to perform the words of this covenant that were written in this book. All the people joined in the covenant.*

This act was carried out in as public a manner as possible. First the elders were gathered as representatives of the people, then the entire male population of Judah (*kol-'iš yᵉhūdā*), all of the citizenry including all free men and the citizens of Jerusalem.[315] After this came the entire remaining population from small to great, led by the priests and prophets.[316] The book was made known by a public reading. Then the king "cut" (*krt*) the

---

314 Could the fact that the events of 622 BCE occurred in the twenty-fifth year of the life of Josiah be significant? According to Num 8:24 this is the age at which Levites began their service (but according to Num 4:2ff. the age was 30).
315 See Isa 5:3, see also Zeph 1:4.
316 This enumeration is so carefully worked out that it hardly gives occasion for literary-criticism (contrary, e.g. Würthwein, *Könige* II 452ff.; Spieckermann, *Juda* 71ff.).

"covenant" (b'rīt), that is, the obligation[317] to keep the law and practice all of its provisions. It is difficult to identify anything concrete in this procedure. For the covenant ceremony the king stands on a particular place that appears to be a podium or a pillar ('ammūd, see 2 Kg 11:14).[318] We are unable to tell whether the ceremony of the "cutting of the covenant" here, as other examples from a comparable period involved the ritual cutting of animals, thus symbolizing the ceremonial oath of allegiance (see Jer 34:18f.; Gen 15:10, 17). We can tell however that the king entered an obligation that bound him alone. Only then did the rest of the people join in, assuming the same bond for themselves.[319]

There is disagreement over where these texts belong literarily, how close they are to the events of 622 BCE and to what degree they contain historical material.[320] There is much in favor of the theory that 23:1–3 is part of a narrative by one of the authors of the deuteronomic history or the Books of Kings.[321] Nevertheless, a strong stylization and typification[322] is unmistakable. Of course, the text speaks from a certain distance, and it is aimed at the practices which are reported in connection with it, dealing simply with certain religious aspects of the law, not the whole thing. Thus, we may not infer the historic self-understanding for the participants of 622 BCE directly. Rather, it ought to be read as the aetiology of the value of deuteronomic law.[323] As always in such cases, it is not the explanation that is offered which is to be regarded as historical, but only the fact of explaining. This is even the value of the law: that the king as well as the people are subject to the law and are bound by it.

Since historians have studied the process of the development of the law back almost to the point of its discovery, we begin to suspect conscious deception. Was there pious or perhaps less than honorable deception at the beginning of the history of the biblical canon?[324] The deception continues, whether we know who was deceived – the king himself, Shaphan, the people or only later readers?

317 For the translation of b'rīt as "obligation" instead of the usual "covenant," see Kutsch, *Verheissung*; ibid., article on b'rīt; for critique, see Weinfeld, article on b'rīt; for the relationship of the two concepts, see Crüsemann, *Recht und Theologie* 31.
318 See Fabry, article on 'ammūd 207.
319 For the structure of the procedure, see Kutsch, *Verheissung* 17, 165ff.; see also the critique of other theories, e.g. a covenant between God and people with the king as mediator, or a covenant between king and people.
320 For the history of the research, see Lohfink, *Diskussion*; lit. also above, p. 209.
321 Thus especially Lohfink, *Cult Reform*; ibid., Gattung. The thesis that 22:3–12, 13,* 15–20 contains an "historical short story" allegedly from the deuteronomic history, is by far, in my opinion the best supported theory. However, even Spieckermann, *Juda* arrives at a thesis of an alleged deuteronomic history foundation in his thorough analysis (30–159), which includes portions of the reform report. For a critique, see Lohfink, *Diskussion* 42ff. For an assessment of 23:3 (ibid. 44), also Müller, 2 *Kön* 23:3 *deuteronomistisch?* Hoffmann, *Reformen* 200ff., as well as Würthwein, *Könige* II 454f., regards the verse as part of a later deuteronomic stratum. Nevertheless, they do not consider the differences from usual deuteronomic language.
322 Hoffmann, *Reform* 201, speaks of an "ideal scene".
323 Thus, with Würthwein, *Josianische Reform* 407. The close relationship of verse 3 to Deuteronomy 6 (especially 6:17) underscores particularly the close connection with deuteronomic law; with Lohfink, 2 *Kön* 23:3.
324 For what follows, see the thoughts and references in Spieckermann, *Juda* 156ff.

If the statement is correct that the narrator of 2 Kg 22f. really believed in the existence of an old book from the time of Moses, then the same thing must be true of his sources. It would also be correct that for those directly involved, it must have been a new version of what they regarded as ancient tradition. How often revolutions believe they are restoring old law, and in the process produce whole new societal forms.

Still, unfortunately, this very self-awareness withholds access to the participants; we cannot get behind the aetiology. Moreover, there is an amazing parallel, which might shed some light on this process. According to the text of Deuteronomy itself, the law book was placed in the hands of the Levitical priests; it was also in the temple (thus in 17:18; 31:9) and also in the hands of the elders (31:9). These priests were supposed to make the people aware of the text by reading it to them (31:10ff.).

What is commmanded in 17:18 is especially remarkable. The king sits on his throne – thus he is officially in office – and he is supposed to have a second copy made of the text found in the temple. He is then supposed to judge according to it. The parallel is remarkable and certainly could not be an accident: the law book came from the hands of the priests to the reigning king, who is then (also) supposed to function on the basis of that book. We can imagine without difficulty that what 2 Kg 22f. reports follows the model of a process described in Deut 17:18 (with the ceremonial obligation to this book) from the distance of at least a few generations.

(b) Deut 26:16–19 also speaks of a comparable commitment:

> 16 *This very day YHWH your God is commanding you to observe these statutes and ordinances; so observe them diligently with all your heart and with all your soul.*

> 17 *Today you have obtained YHWH's agreement; to be your God; (and) for you to walk in his ways, to keep his statutes, his commandments and his ordinances, and to obey him.*

> 18 *Today YHWH lets you declare yourselves: to be his treasured people, as he promised you, and to keep his commandments;*

> 19 *for him to set you high above all nations that he has made, in praise and in fame and in honor; and for you to be a people holy to YHWH your God, as he promised.*

This passage stands between the law Deut 12:2–26:15 and the beginning of the blessing and cursing chapter 27f., thus a central position in the overall construction. It is clearly focussed on the present.[325] This is illustrated by the "today" (*hayyōm*), which is dramatically emphasized by three-fold repetition. In the beginning of verse 16 it is even intensified, "This very day" (*hayyōm hazzē*). The verb forms underscore the claim made for the present. In verse 16 there is a participle: God is present, he is about to instruct you. And the two clauses in verses 17 and 18, constructed exactly parallel, have the same performatory character,

---

325 See Perlitt, *Bundestheologie* 102f.

especially in conjunction with the "today:"[326] "whom YHWH lets you declare herewith . . ." Of course, within the framework of the entirety of Deuteronomy and its invented history, "today" appears to refer to the assembly gathered in Moab. Nevertheless, the formulations seem to burst any fixed narrative. There is a great bracketing of distant past with the present.[327]

The frequent change of subjects in verses 17–19, paralleling the precisely similarly constructed introductory statements in verses 17 and 18, has prompted frequent attempts at literary stratification and working out an original form.[328] In principle this is hard to dispute, however, there are no grammatical breaks, nor is the present text so garbled that it requires cleaning up in order to enable an appropriate interpretation.[329] Even if the text were developed in several steps, what we have is extremely concise and well thought out. It is a typical example of so much material in Deuteronomy. It is not a hypothetically reconstructed, purely contradictory explanation, taking this as referring to God and people. Only the connection made by indications of purpose which are formulated with an infinitive, makes the theological intent clear. Both partners speak for each other.[330]

Verse 16 is primarily connected to the preceding law. It is supposed to be put into effect on that day and to determine practice from that day onward. Unlike the remainder of Deuteronomy, it is not talking about a distance put between the proclamation itself in east Jordan and the completion of the conquest of the land as the event that puts the substance of the proclamation into action. The proclamation is in force immediately. The verse has clear connections to preceding passages, especially Deut 12:1 and 6:4.

We find an extremely unusual, contradictory explanation of the agreement between God and Israel given in verses 17–19. Both parties seem to have initiated the agreement. This understanding of the text is largely connected with the way the fundamental structure is understood. Since scholars generally regard the idea that this is a real causative as untenable,[331] it is not entirely out of the question that the hiph. of '*mr* (otherwise not attested anywhere) is interpreted in a rather improbable and artificial way either as an intensification in the sense of "proclaim,"[332] whereby Israel would be the speaker in verse 17,[333] (or in the sense of "supporting" or "agreeing").[334] Nevertheless, a simple causative is more likely.[335]

326 For this function of the purely affirmative conjunction, see Bergsträsser, *Grammatik* II (Verbum) §6e; Brockelmann, *Syntax* §41d; there are examples in Deut 4:26; Jer 1:10; 40:4; Ps 2:7; for the last as well as the entire matter, see Blum, *Ps 2:7c*.
327 Ps 95:7 is comparable. There also "today" refers directly to the events in the distant past . We are also reminded of Ps 81. See also above pp. 82ff.
328 Smend, *Bundesformel* 14; Perlitt, *Bundestheologie* 104f.; Rose, *Ausschliesslich-keitsanspruch* 103ff.
329 See especially, Lohfink, *Bundesformel* 228ff.
330 Thus especially Lohfink, *Bundesformel* 231ff.
331 Especially clearly Vriezen, *Hiphil* 208f.
332 Thus Smend, *Bundesformel* 14f.
333 See especially Lohfink, *Bundesformel* 231 with a convincing critique of Smend.
334 Thus in conjunction with Vriezen, *Hiphil*, especially Lohfink, *Bundesformel* 234f.
335 Thus now also Gesenius 18th ed. 77.

The following interpretation suggests itself on the basis of the context: Verse 17 is most likely a brief summary of what has preceded in Deuteronomy. In it YHWH – through Moses – above all in the introductory speeches of Deut 6ff. about liberation, selection, and the gift of the land, has spoken about what this Godhood means. The infinitives that follow summarize the observance of Torah by Israel as the intent of divine activity. Conversely, verses 18f. formulates the promise of Israel to be his and his alone. This includes the observance of the law, but it aims at raising the people, who are downtrodden and humiliated, for the glory of God.[336]

The conflicting nature of the declaration, so often regarded as objectionable, can most easily be understood if we relate it to the law which precedes it. While Israel, "today" hears and obeys Torah, from that point on the Godhood of God causes this to be declared for Israel and their successors. While Israel – as God desires – affirms the content of the law, especially the unique position that God assigns it. We would even have to understand the two-fold promise in verses 18f. first as a reference to the promise formulated in Deuteronomy itself.[337] This interpretation is close to that of Smend, according to which Deut 26:17–19 associates itself with the covenant obligation scene under Josiah, as it is described in 2 Kg 23:1–3.[338] Naturally, we are unable to prove this, and the precise connection in each case must remain unresolved, but the opposing reasons are even less convincing.[339] The basic structure stands in tension with both Deuteronomy and its historic vesture and deuteronomic ideas.[340]

It is not a matter of course that a law should end with this kind of ceremonial formula of obligation. Neither the Book of the Covenant nor the Pentateuch as a whole does so. This alone argues in favor of the idea that there is a relationship between the two obligation texts connected

---

336 With Jer 13:11, 33:9 we would have to think of the praise of God rather than of Israel, see Mayes, *Deuteronomy* 339.

337 See Lohfink, *Bundestheologie* 351; otherwise, especially, Skweres, *Rückverweise* 176f. who notes Ex 19:5f. He does not think that Deut 7:6 and 14:2, 21 are linked because they might not be promises. But what if Israel consciously accepted *that* which comes about through God's action, should we really expect that the promise is only realized through the acceptance? How would we then explain Deut 7:14?

338 Smend, *Bundesformel* 16f. along with the adoption and concretization of earlier opinions – e.g. Bertholet, *Deuteronomium* 82f.; Hempel, *Schichten* 86; Rad, *Gottesvolk*.

339 The main argument to the contrary is the deuteronomic language, see Perlitt, *Bundestheologie* 104ff.; Lohfink, *Bundesformel*; ibid. *Bundestheologie*; Preuss, *Deuteronomium* 148; see also below note 340.

340 The reference to deuteronomic language and corresponding parallels leads at least to a relative classification, the immediate realization in an evaluation of the historical distance, is problematic here as elsewhere. Above all, important questions are not analyzed. How does such an obligation formulated in a performative way fit in the context of deuteronomic history? Would it not be more likely to *narrate* the obligation to the law instead of having it appear in a formula like this? The presumed direct, divine speech is less likely in deuteronomic thinking than in Deuteronomy itself. It is perhaps best understood out of a time during which the historic dress was still immediately lucid in its authoritative power for legal and political problems.

with Deuteronomy. We must be clear that such an express, public act of self-commitment, including king and people – like the one that these two texts presume – is extremely unusual. The commandments formulated with divine authority expect to be followed, since a voluntary obligation is not necessarily unconditional. We remember the mission of Ezra, where the law was instituted without popular election or choice. There are actually only parallels in Ex 24, a text that cannot be dated before the events under Josiah,[341] as well as Josh 24, where the decision is not connected with a written text that came into existence at a later time (verse 26). This text also cannot be assigned to an earlier period.[342]

Scholars have largely interpreted the two acts of obligation in definitely religious categories. We hear again and again about the "faithful king." Naturally the deuteronomic language that determines both texts is concerned with central religious questions. Nevertheless, the infinitives of Deut 26:17ff. are more burdened with pietistic categories than the contents warrant with such an understanding.

If we relate them to the entire deuteronomic law, including its social and political provisions, we find that we are not dealing with an "almost disagreeably rhetorical enforced compliance of Israel."[343] Rather, it is nothing less than the coming into action of a comprehensive constitution for the people and the king. Only the political dimension of the activity, which naturally ought never to be separated from the theological and religious speech,[344] makes clear the actual sense of the scene, and probably also why it occurs here and not some place else.

If the king recognizes the deuteronomic constitutional provisions, this permits him to function in his traditional role most extensively. Only through this act do the people become sovereign, as they ought to be according to deuteronomic law, and, in political reality, as it was since the insurrection against Amon was crushed. What was accomplished was the conscious act of the "establishment of freedom."[345] Precisely there the heart of the biblical canon was developed.

341 See above p. 45.
342 See above pp. 32, 39.
343 Perlitt, *Bundestheologie* 104.
344 We should remember here especially the public character of Torah in Judaism which is rooted here. For this, see Baumgarten, *Public Document*.
345 Thus in conjunction with Hannah Arendt, *Revolution* 35, 281 and elsewhere, who describes especially the American revolution with its establishment of a free constitution.

7

The Priestly Writing:
The Necessary Transformation

With my demise I bear witness to a new shrine
for the land of the old law.

C. Busta[1]

Literary Structure and Historical Locale

The Holiness Code as a Part of the Priestly Writing

When reconstructing Israelite legal history, the so-called Holiness Code (H)[2] in Lev 17–26 is usually viewed as a further codification, coming after Deuteronomy.[3] In the same way that deuteronomic law extended, corrected and amplified the Book of the Covenant, the Holiness Code continues the Book of Deuteronomy. Nevertheless, recent scholarship has regarded the Holiness Code as a part of the priestly writings, no longer seeing it as having been at one time an independent law book.[4] If this is true, not only the Holiness Code, but also the priestly writings as a whole must be regarded as having been intended to be an appendage to Deuteronomy. In what follows we will examine very briefly the reasons for such a view and the most important literary decisions.

Probably the strongest argument for viewing the Holiness Code as having been an independent law book at one time is that the structure as well as much of its content show parallels to deuteronomic law and the Book of the Covenant.[5] At the beginning of each, there are fundamental provisions regarding the altar and the sacrifices to be offered there (Lev 17; cf Deut 12; Ex 20:24ff.) at the end there are blessings and curses (Lev 26; cf Deut 27f.; Ex 23:20ff.) and a concluding subscript (26:46). Themes like the sabbatical year (Lev 25; cf Deut 15:1ff.; Ex 23:10f.), festival calendar (Lev 23; cf Deut 16; Ex 23:14ff.), slave law (Lev 25:39ff.; cf Deut

---

1 *Cordelia* (Jentzsch, ed. *Dunkel* 96).
2 The name originated with Klostermann, *Ezechiel*, and is based on formulations like Lev 19:2.
3 E.g. Boecker, *Recht* 162ff.; Patrick, *Law* 145ff.; Martin-Achard, *Lois* 43ff.; in addition to the "introductions" and many others.
4 Thus the otherwise systematic assessment as well as the concrete results of extraordinarily divergent studies by Elliger, *Leviticus*, e.g. pp. 14ff.; Wagner, *Existence*; Cholewinski, *Heiligkeitsgesetz* especially pp. 334ff.; Cortesi, L'esegesi; Preuss, *Heiligkeitsgesetz*; Knohl, *Priestly Torah*; Blum, *Pentateuch* 318ff. Otherwise, most recently, Mathys, *Liebe* 82ff.; however, without serious discussion of the problem.
5 See e.g. Eissfeldt, *Einleitung* 310ff.

15:12ff.; Ex 21:2ff.), prohibition of usury (Lev 23:35ff.; cf Deut 23:20ff.; Ex 22:26), sexual and family law (Lev 18, 20; cf Deut 21ff.) show thematic continuity in conjunction with numerous corrections in detail, as especially Cholewinski has demonstrated.[6] On the basis of this it follows that what we have is "a legal corpus, similar to Deuteronomy and filling in the gaps of that book.... Many of its [Deuteronomy's] prescripts [seemed to the redactors] to be incomplete, archaic, too radical or theologically inadequately supported."[7]

Fundamentally, such connections – even the individual serious arguments that can be adduced for the previous independent existence of the Holiness Code – are by no means adequate to support the theory. Attempts to demonstrate a special position for Lev 17–26 within the great mass of priestly laws by means of contradictions with other portions must be regarded as failures.[8] This complex is no foreign body in the context. All of the important features of the section have parallels in other priestly material, and there are no real contradictions. There is no repetition in Lev 17 of the rules from Gen 9 regarding the handling of blood, as some maintain there to be.[9] The first text deals with rules for all of post-Noah humanity, and the second contains refined regulations for Israel with its special relation to God, which the resumption as well as the differences explain.

In form and content, the Holiness Code is most closely connected to the priestly stratum of the entire Sinai law. The typical superscripts of the individual sections (17:1; 18:1; 19:1, etc.) are not at all unusual; they have appeared before (cf Lev 11:1; 12:1; 15:1; 16:1) as well as after (cf 27:1, Num 1:1; 2:1; 4:1; 5:1, etc.). If we try to lift these elements which clearly belong to the totality of the priestly writings, we will find an essential unity of the texts as well as their subdivision into laws directed toward Israel (18:1; 19:1; 20:1; 22:26; 23:1; 23:33; 24:1; 25:1), toward the Aaronic priests (Lev 21:1, 16; 22:1) as well as toward both together (17:1; 22:17). There is no tension between this system of superscripts and the text itself. Furthermore, Lev 17–26 fits best in the compositional structure of the priestly legislation from Sinai, which unfolds itself with an inner logical consistency.[10] After the setting up of the tent shrine with all its appoint-

---

6 Cholewinski, *Heiligkeitsgesetz* 339, cf 327 and elsewhere.
7 Cholewinski, *Heiligkeitsgesetz* 338.
8 The repeatedly mentioned contradictions (see Kuenen, *Einleitung* 84ff., 26ff.; Baentsch, *Leviticus* 388, 404f., 412f.; Bertholet, *Leviticus XV*) deal with smaller linguistic differences as well as content nuances, which are better explained by the theory of the use of older material, following Blum, *Pentateuch* 322 note 133. In his summary, Cholewinski, *Heiligkeitsgesetz* 334 speaks of "small observations" which affect the differences between his main redaction of H (HG) and Pg. The small number of these, which he regards as important, are supposed to be a critique of the theological "innovations of the Pg writings," thus the omission of a Sinai covenant and the omission of the significance of human activity (339f.). The second is clearly a circular argument (because H contributes the missing material), the first makes the (here disputed) assumption that there was a Sinai pericope with covenant before P (see above pp. 46ff.).
9 See Bertholet, *Leviticus* 57, against, e.g. Milgrom, *Prolegomenon*; for the subject, see below pp. 291ff.
10 For what follows, see most recently Blum, *Pentateuch* 300ff. (Lit.), also Wagner, *Existence*.

ments (Ex 25–40), we have the dwelling of the divine presence (Ex 40:34ff.). Then follows the ordering of worship which is to be held in this shrine (Lev 1–10), together with rules for sacrifice (1–7) and the instituting of priests (8f.), at the end of which there is a description of the first sacrifice (Lev 9:22ff.). Following this we have the great complex of rules for purity and sanctification (Lev 11–26) all gathered around Lev 16, the ritual for the Day of Atonement, which functions as the center of 11–26. The last great block of regulations, the ordering of the camp, attaches to this.

We cannot separate the Holiness Code out of this.[11] It also explains why only here do the parenetic elements specific to it[12] appear intensified. Lev 17–26, just like other parts (e.g. the sacrifice laws in Lev 1–7), is a relatively independent part of the priestly writings. Within the priestly Sinai legislation, it represents the part in which "the variety of life and the everyday could be held accountable outside of worship."[13] Only here are we dealing with law in the narrower sense, and thus with subjects as they are treated in other law books, for example, marriage, bodily injury, slaves, business, etc. For that reason the parallels in structure and subject-matter to other law books are, of course, no accident. It was intentional, but it was also intended that this subject-matter find its traditional structure all bound in a much broader, more comprehensive priestly view.

If we read the Holiness Code as an integral part of the priestly writings, we see immediately that the usual comparisons with deuteronomic law or the Book of the Covenant are inadequate. Many of the themes treated in the older law books have parallels outside of Lev 17–26 in other portions of the priestly composition. There is, for example, the weekly day of rest, which appears in Ex 34:21 as well as the Book of the Covenant, and it is already based in creation in the priestly writings (Gen 1f.) and then it is discovered before Sinai in Ex 16 and in 31:12ff. it is simply made obligatory.

The prohibition against murder (Ex 21:12 and elsewhere) with its legal consequences, and the consumption of blood (Ex 22:30; Deut 12) are classified as commands given to Noah in Gen 9. The subject of mixed marriage appears in Gen 27:46–28:9, passover in Ex 12. The list of animals which may and which may not be eaten (Deut 14) has a parallel in Lev 11. Sacrifice regulations which correspond to the older laws are found not just in Lev 22, but already even in Lev 1–7. The Holiness Code is completely lacking in rules for judicial procedure, but we do find them, for example, in Num 5, Lev 27 and Num 18 treat the tithe and other cultic offerings. Lev 17 represents a certain general parallel to Deut 12 and Ex 20:24ff., but we would also have to include the entire priestly shrine together with its appointments (Ex 25–31; 35–40).

It is the priestly writing as a whole that stands in sequence of law books with the Book of the Covenant and Deuteronomy. The Holiness

---

11 Blum, *Pentateuch* 321f. correctly refers to the fact that this clear compositional structure also makes the thesis that H might have been conceived as an amplification of an older P foundation (Elliger, Cholewinski) improbable.

12 See Blum, *Pentateuch* 319.

13 Köckert, *Leben* 31.

Code is only a portion of it, indeed the one in which the debate with the previous legal tradition has a special place.[14] It is obvious that a turning-point is marked by the literary insertion of the laws into a narrative framework beginning with the creation of the world. This uncovers problems which far exceed the scope of what we can discuss here. Even more than before, there is necessary a concentration upon the innovative impulse, the most important contribution to Torah. We will have to allow the following brief references to recent research to suffice, concerning the literary foundation of the entire priestly writing.

- The basic literary investigation of the priestly writings is into its character. Are we dealing with a dissectable, formerly independent writing[15] or an interpretation-stratum that simply amplified and explicated the older texts[16] (or the larger document which lay before it), or was Blum[17] successful in his attempt to prove that such an alternative is basically invalid? For what follows, we can temporarily ignore this basic question. The question of what the priestly material looked like is not germane to the line of reasoning to be followed here. The few aetiological arguments for Israelite legal customs, usually regarded as pre-priestly narrative material,[18] hardly touch the basic questions. The important legislation of the priestly material, in the context of its historical representation, gives us a very good idea of what is intended.[19]

- The one great exception is, of course, the question of the Sinai pericope and the pre-priestly legal texts which are situated there. It is quite improbable that the priestly texts presuppose a Sinai pericope with Decalogue, Book of the Covenant, or even a concluding of the covenant.[20] The priestly writings have in mind only Ex 32–34 in connecting Sinai with the giving of the law (if we omit the problem of Ex 18 for the moment).[21] The construction of the priestly shrine laws of Ex 25–31; 35–40 cause us to expect a literary composition around this block. The continuity of contents is obvious. At Sinai there was concern about correct worship, together with God's accompanying presence among his people despite sin and falling away. On the other hand we can rule out the idea that the

---

14 The scholarly work on H has been so strongly affected by literary-critical studies (in addition to Elliger, commentary, see especially Küchler, *Heiligkeitsgesetz*; Kilian, *Untersuchungen*) and tradition-historical studies (especially Reventlow, *Heiligkeitsgesetz*), that thus far there is hardly an analysis of the compositional structure – besides Blum, *Pentateuch* 319ff., see also below pp. 326f.

15 Thus the classic source theory; especially Wellhausen, *Composition* and most of the introductions; most recently the disputing of P as a redaction stratum, Lohfink, *Priesterschrift* 221ff.; Zenger, *Bogen* 32ff.; Koch, *Kein Redaktor*; Emerton, *Priestly Writer*.

16 Thus Cross, *Myth* 293ff.; Seters, *Abraham* 279ff.; Rendtorff, *Pentateuch* 112ff.; Utzschneider, *Heiligtum*; Vervenne, *'P' Tradition*; additional literature in Blum, *Pentateuch* 229 note 2.

17 Blum, *Pentateuch* 229.

18 We think, e.g. of Gen 32:33, Ex 4:24, possibly also Gen 22.

19 See below pp. 290ff.

20 See above pp. 46ff.

21 See above pp. 50ff.

priestly writings include Deuteronomy in their overall composition even as regards literature.[22] The few allegedly priestly passages in Deuteronomy (especially at the end) could never prove it.[23]

– The priestly texts are indisputably *the* stratum of the Pentateuch that scholars are able to identify with great security and with very few exceptions in the broad consensus.[24] But in addition to its character, there is a great deal of dispute over its inner literary stratification.[25] There can be no doubt that in many places there is evidence of a great deal of work on the texts; we can establish the existence of older material and multiple emendations. For interpretation and understanding, of course, the following three methodological aspects are extremely important.

– The question of the inner unity of the text should be of equal importance to that of potential stratification. Careless preference for literary-critical operations over structural analysis and exegesis of content is methodological stupidity. Above all, we have seen from the debate over Gen 1 that literary dismemberment has overlooked and distorted the intended unity of the text.[26]

– Just as in deuteronomic law, emendations, new aspects, amplifying nuances do not necessarily contradict each other. Obvious literary extrapolation on the one hand, and intentional inner unity of a complex of laws on the other are not *a priori* mutually contradictory. If the priestly texts, like the deuteronomic, are a *developing unity* formed by a school over the course of a long period of time, emendations can clarify the meaning. For that reason, traces of literary development are not to be viewed in isolation as contradictory, but they must be taken in the context of their relationship to the whole work.[27]

– Of course the most important thesis for literary stratification within the priestly material is that of a narrative base stratum to which laws

22 Deuteronomy itself, in any case, contains a narrative structure in relatively late strata, which goes back to Horeb (Deut 1–3; 4, see also 5; 9f.). This demonstrates, however, that thus far there is no literary connection with the parallels in the Tetrateuch.

23 For these texts (Deut 1:3; 32:48–52; 34:1a, 7–9) see Perlitt, *Priesterschrift*, who feels these are *not* actual priestly texts.

24 Text lists in Eissfeldt, *Einleitung* 265; Smend, *Entstehung* 47ff.; Noth, *Überlieferungsgeschichte* 17ff.; Elliger, *Geschichtserzählung* 174f.

25 While Rad, *Priesterschrift* theorizes a complete double stratification, which has found practically no adherents, the thesis of a narrative base stratum, which was later filled out with legal material, has gained acceptance. See Wellhausen, *Prolegomena* 384; ibid., *Composition* 184; Noth, *Pentateuch* 7ff.; Elliger, *Geschichtserzählung*; Lohfink, *Priesterschrift*; and most recently (especially radical) Weimar, *Struktur*; ibid., Sinai.

26 Steck, *Schöpfungsbericht* has, by pointing out the inner unity and logic, convincingly refuted the widely held thesis of literary stratification (especially Schmidt, *Schöpfungsgeschichte*).

27 For an example, we refer to Köckert (*Leben* 41ff.) who finds emendations to the older P text. This is supposed to portray the demand for the circumcision of slaves as an "empty ritual" (43), because any relation of the person circumcised to God's promise is lost (42f.). We are unable to conclude whether or not this is true with the use of P's statements regarding aliens and non-Israelites (for this, see also below pp. 295f.).

were added.[28] On the basis of this, we can say that the priestly writing is connected with the theme of Torah from Gen 2:1, i.e. from the very beginning. It is inseparably woven into the fabric of the narrative.[29] What happened on Sinai is only the high point of what had begun a long time before and does not end with Num 10.[30] This means that it is rather unlikely that we might be able to make a contrast between the narrative and the laws into some kind of literary principle. Practically, however, this is probably what usually happens.[31] In so doing, important, even necessary features of the material regarded as secondary to the basic document are overlooked.[32] There has been as little success in reconstructing the Ur- or base forms of the priestly writings convincingly as with Deutoronomy. Even methodologically, smooth processes should be treated separately from clear stratification.

– *The overall shape of the Pentateuch with its combining of narrative and law* – or to use later language, of Haggadah and Halakah – *developed with the priestly writings*. Attempts to play one off against the other in form and content, both historically and theologically, sidestep both the clear literary evidence as well as the task itself, to understand this correlation – the unity of both. It is, of course, obvious that the deuteronomic concept of Torah which indicates this unity to be at latest deuteronomistic (especially Deut 1:5), was not used in the priestly writings.[33] The priestly writings still do not have their own term for what was intended by the entire Pentateuch. Until this very day there is no other way to describe this unity of historical remembrance and present instruction, of historical representation and historical anchoring of norms than by the concept of Torah.[34]

Exilic Plans for the Future and Priestly Archetypes

Scholars are surprizingly unified on the time of the development of the priestly writings and the author groups. It may be intrinsic to the subject-matter that this unity includes a considerable amount of vagueness.

As we know, we are indebted to J. Wellhausen for the insight that the priestly writings, with all of the texts that are part and parcel, could not have developed before the period of the exile.[35] The attempts by

28 See the literature above in note 25.
29 See especially Köckert, *Leben* and also below pp. 290ff.
30 See below, pp. 361ff.
31 A typical statement would be: "But also the portion of the instructional elements in Gen 1–Ex 16 need further qualification" (Weimar, *Struktur* 83 note 14), which, of course, always presupposes what it is that is to be proven.
32 Thus, after Gen 1, 9 the subject of the consumption of meat is not taken up again until Lev 17 (see below pp. 292ff.). The omission of the subject of mixed mariage in H is connected with Gen 27:46–28:9.
33 The dominance of the priestly technical term (Jer 18:18; Hag 2:10ff.) for lay training (see Lev 6:2, 7, 18; 7:1, 11, 37, etc.) is decisive here. Even in collective expressions (especially Lev 26:46) only the plural occurs.
34 With, e.g. Blum, *Pentateuch* 288.
35 Wellhausen, *Prolegomena*; for the history of the research, see e.g. Perlitt, *Vatke*; Thompson, *Mose*; Lohfink, *Priesterschrift* especially 226 note 33.

Kaufmann and a few others[36] to question this are not convincing.[37] Quite independent of the question of to what degree older material was included within it, there can be no doubt that the priestly writings generally presuppose the exile and are reacting to it. Along with deuteronomism and a new eschatological character of salvation the most important new assessment is the theological treatment of the catastrophe. There is an intensive reshaping and new version precisely where older traditions and predecessors are no longer demonstrable; this is even the case to a great degree in the area of law. There is no impetus for the supposition that it might be otherwise in areas where we do not have the possibility of control. For that reason conclusions regarding the age of the priestly tradition are only admissible in places where comparison with other texts permit them.

It is more difficult to answer the question in the actual sense, whether this is an exilic work written before 539 or 520 BCE. The few references to actual historical circumstances[38] most likely presume the continuance of the exile, and quite apparently there are close relationships with exilic prophetic texts.[39] Above all, important fundamental theological issues are most likely to be understood out of the context of this period.[40] On the other hand, there are important reasons for a rather early postexilic dating.[41] Thus, for example, there is much to argue that the shrine texts have a connection with the circumstances under which the Jerusalem temple and its cult were newly founded during the Persian period.[42] There are also many texts which argue for an origin in a time without a temple, while others still rather presuppose a functioning cult.

We can clarify the problem with an example. In Lev 25, the seventh or sabbatical year (verses 2–7) was separated from all of the social connections ascribed to it, especially in Deut 15. Such activity would more likely be tied to the "super" seventh year, the year of jubilee, held in the 49th or 50th year (verses 8ff.). Deut 15 demands an extremely radical, complete return to the starting point. In so doing, the entire first part of the chapter (verses 14–34) deals with the possession of the land. All changes in ownership of the land are to be identified and made returnable. Now, as we have seen frequently, this time span is hard to distinguish from a half century, so that we count from 587/6 on to 538/7, then to a time during which, according to the edict of Cyrus, all the questions raised in Lev 25 must be answered. To whom does the land

---

36 Kaufmann, *Religion* especially 175ff.; Haran, *Temples* 132ff.; Hurvitz, *Study*; ibid., *Dating*; Zevit, *Converging Lines*.

37 For a discussion, see especially Utzschneider, *Heiligtum* 60ff., who refers to the fact that reference is made to the founding and construction of a temple. See also the discussion of the temporal sequence of the corresponding slave provisions in Kaufmann, *Deuteronomy* 15 or Japhet, *Relationship*.

38 Especially Lev 26, for this, see Wellhausen, *Composition* 170f.

39 In addition to Ezekiel we would especially mention Deutero–Isaiah; for this, see Eitz, *Studien*.

40 As examples we cite the question of the presence of God (Janowski, *Schekina-Theologie*), the portable temple (Fritz, *Temple*), or the omitted significance of the land for matters of law (see below pp. 308f.).

41 See especially Blum, *Vätergeschichte* 452ff.; ibid., *Pentateuch*.

42 Utzschneider, *Heiligtum*.

belong now and in the future? To whom does property, houses, etc. in Judah and Jerusalem belong?[43] As we know, this problem is one of the most difficult for the postexilic period, approximately during the phase of the initial temple construction.[44] This means that Lev 25 had a very clear connection with the period of the end of the exile and the beginning of the postexilic period.

The priestly writings originated in the period that was no longer dominated by the cry over guilt and what was lost, but rather consequences and new beginnings. The proximity to Deutero–Isaiah on the one hand, to the questions of the period of Haggai and Zechariah on the other, is the historical background against which the texts speak most clearly. The literary character makes a sharp distinction between exilic and postexilic rather problematic. In contrast, the priestly texts seems to presuppose the period of Ezra and Nehemiah.[45]

The unanimous use of the term "priestly writings" or something similar (e.g. "priestly code") shows how certain scholars are with regard to the group of authors. There is not doubt that it is an exilic/postexilic group of priests to whom we are indebted for these texts. The priestly point of view, priestly language, interests and modes of thinking are apparent throughout the work. Correspondingly, we often find theories among scholars, which attempt to interpret the priestly writings (or the holiness-laws) "as a program for the exiles, who had begun to make plans for postexilic life, to understand."[46] Nevertheless, we need to be careful. As much as we are able to connect some of the features of the priestly shrine-texts with concrete questions regarding the rebuilding of the Jerusalem temple, [47] there are an equal number of elements within the texts to which this event does not apply.[48] One aspect of the problem is the very obvious relationship between shrine and creation.[49] The archetypal/ideal and practical/blueprint categories cannot always be clearly differentiated, but neither may they be played off against each other. Thus, the distinction is rather important here, that the shrine-texts

---

43 Thus especially Wallis, *Jobel-Jahr-Gesetz*; Robinson, *Jobel Jahr* 476.; ibid., *New Economic Order*. According to the sabbath year calendar of Wachholder, *Calendar* 33 the year 537–6 would be a sabbath year, but not 587/6 – rather 586/5. Might we be permitted to connect lack of clarity of the text in Lev 25 with the question of whether the jubilee year was held every forty-nine or fifty years?

44 See Donner, *Geschichte* II 411.

45 When Blum, *Pentateuch* connects his P composition directly with the questions of the authorization of the Persian empire, thus with the time of Ezra, in my opinion this is contradicted by the evidence of the legal texts, and these are hardly marginal for these questions. Deuteronomy, in any case, is certainly not part of the P composition. And we would dispute that also for the Book of the Covenant (as well as the Decalogue). That would require a considerable step beyond P (which always integrated them into narrative material), see below pp. 329ff.

46 Thus Mathys, *Liebe* 18.

47 With Utzschneider, *Heiligtum*.

48 For this as well as for what follows, see especiually Blum, *Pentateuch* 301ff., who discusses several possibilities mentioned by other scholars and comes to rather precisely considered formulations; from the older literature, see especially Fritz, *Tempel* 153, "realization . . . in word."

49 See Blum, *Pentateuch* 306ff. (ibid. 307 note 75, literature); now also Janowski, *Tempel*.

are intended for a one-time procedure,[50] but other instructions, from the dietary regulations beginning in Gen 9 up to those of the holiness-laws, claim permanent applicability, and they also lasted into and shaped the postexilic period for Israel.

In order to be able to study the groups of priests who are behind the priestly texts, a study of the parallels in Deuteronomy can be helpful. First, this reduces the level of interest in things political (which might be historically conditioned) but above all, Deuteronomy's social laws. Lev 25 again serves as an example. There, the regular forgiveness of debts in the seventh year (Deut 15:1ff.) and the manumission of slaves, which had happened every seven years ever since the Mishpatim (Ex 21:2ff.; Deut 15:12ff.), were both set aside. There was a legally sanctioned manumission only in the year of jubilee (Lev 25:39ff.). Considering the length of the life of the average slave, this shifted freedom into "never-neverland." Of course, the free relatives of persons enslaved had the right to purchase the freedom of their family at any time (verses 48ff.).

There was no prototype for this right to redemption – $g^{e}ull\hat{a}$ – (which also applied to the ownership of land – verses 24ff.) in the preexilic law books and it never appears elsewhere until the very end of the monarchic period (Jer 32:6).[51] According to Lev 25, this was not really a purchase of freedom. It never says that slaves were, as it is most often phrased, actually "freed." More often, they went from the hands of foreigners into those of relatives.

The reversion of legal matters to families, of course, had something to do with the circumstance of the exilic period; but it is also true that the priestly groups did not continue the radicality of deuteronomic legislation, or even of the Book of the Covenant. We are even compelled to speak of an attempt to withdraw deuteronomic social legislation. Certainly texts like those of the time of Nehemiah (especially Neh 10:32) show how the entirety of Torah was not enforced.[52]

In spite of this difference, we must be careful with concepts like "anti-deuteronomic priestly school."[53] Of course, neither the political nor the social decisions of Deuteronomy were taken away. Nevertheless, we must be equally emphatic that essential concepts of deuteronomic law were lifted entirely. This did not, as commonly viewed, affect just the question of cultic unity; and though it is almost universally denied, it also was felt in the question of secular butchering.[54] Israel was already designated as a holy people (thus also, to a special degree, subject to ritual laws of purity of holiness) even in Deuteronomy (Deut 7:6; 14:2; 21; 26:19; 28:9), and that had roots even in the Book of the Covenant (Ex 22:30).[55]

Provisions regarding sacrifice, cult calendar, etc. dominated an astonishing continuity between deuteronomic law and the priestly

---

50 Thus with emphasis Blum, *Pentateuch* 301 note 52, against the thesis that we are dealing with something like ritual here (Koch, *Priesterschaft*).
51 See Kessler, *Erlöser*.
52 See below pp. 340ff.
53 Cholewinski, *Heiligkeitsgesetz* 343.
54 For one such interpretation of Lev 17 in the framework of P, see below pp. 292ff.
55 For the interpretation of Ex 19:6 in this context, see below p. 360.

writings in all questions of cultic-priestly origin, and this existed basically since the text of Ex 34:11ff., which may have mediated the continuity. Naturally, there were innovations in the priestly area, among which we would include all of the questions of atonement and the forgiveness of sins,[56] but there was something else as well: Not only were cultic-ritual provisions from the preexilic legal tradition not taken back, they were not even corrected.

Insofar as they concern questions of priestly/ritual matters, the priestly writings stand within the tradition of preexilic legislation, and where their interest is concentrated, there is no break in the tradition. There was also continuity within the support groups. If there was priestly opposition to the cult policy of Deuteronomy (even though we know little about it, it was historically probable), it is possible that we would find the people who compiled the priestly writings among the "fathers" of the priests.

It is much more likely that the priestly writings came about because of a breakdown in the unity of priestly and non-priestly groups noted since the Book of the Covenant. They are not in opposition to the cultic decisions of Deuteronomy. There was, however, a shift in accent allowing almost complete dominance of such themes, noticeably reducing areas such as politics and social relationships.

In a negative way, this argues in favor of the thesis that the priestly writings were the verbal expression of the priestly groups who had worked together in and around the Jerusalem high court up until the exile. Now freed of this (compulsory?) coalition, they began to unfold their own tradition. Put positively, we can conclude from this that they (and probably only they) were in the position to react appropriately to the demands of the exile. They subjected the tradition to a transformation which alone could make a future possible.

The Legal-Historical Challenge of the Exile

The priestly writings are the answer of Israel's legal history to the investigation of all of the previous basic teachings upon which Torah tradition was built. The overall design is present with the inclusion of broad legislative sections. Thus there was a new foundation, and it was only upon this base that the final shape of Torah could be achieved. Its achievement, and therefore probably actually its theology, can only be comprehended if we keep the legal-historical challenge, which brought the exile along with it, sharply in focus.

It is noteworthy that scholars have rather ignored the specifically legal aspects of this epoch (in contrast to the religious and theological, political and social).[57] Really, all of the previous foundations upon which law was based, insofar as they are represented in the written legal corpora, fell away, or serious doubts were raised about them.

---

56 See below pp. 310ff.
57 See especially the references in Janssen, *Juda* 48f., 80ff.; Niehr, *Rechtsprechung* 101f. For the situation during the exile, see also Ackroyd, *Exile*; ibid., *Israel*; Oded, *Judah* 476ff.; Donner, *Geschichte* II 381ff.

Naturally, the well-known religious aspects of the exile[58] had direct relevance for law. All preexilic legal texts were connected with the exclusive veneration of Israel's God. This is the nucleus around which this unity collected the breadth of legal and cultic traditions, but the power of this God had been fundamentally called into question. Even more, the whole issue was raised anew, whether precisely this concentration upon the one God had not led to neglect of duties to other gods and goddesses (Jer 44!), making the catastrophe possible.

We ought to mention a whole series of questions which raise themselves in the area of law beyond these and other general questions that go along with the exile, touching upon Torah tradition.

> – The legal organizations of the preexilic period did not continue. With the loss of national independence, the royal legal organizations tied to the government also fell away. The officials who functioned in the judicial system with and alongside the elders no longer existed,[59] independent of whether they were set up by the king or (according to Deut 16:18) the people. Thus the overall shape of the typical law court of the monarchic period collapsed. We should by no means expect the elders alone to carry out judicial functions. According to Lam 5:14, the elders kept themselves far away from the gate, the place of gathering and judicial functions. They sit, as Lam 2:10 tells us, in silence on the ground. Thus, like prisoners, they were despotically beaten and walked upon (Lam 3:34). Furthermore – and in the sight of God! – justice was perverted and unrighteous action gained the upper hand (3:35f.). It must also be assumed that so important an institution as the Jerusalem high court, with its connections to court and temple, disappeared.

If Lam 5:8f. says that "slaves rule over us," this also profoundly affects the question of the judicial organization. We probably should associate these slaves with Babylonian officials.[60] Judah was now part of a Babylonian province in which the entire government was directly or indirectly subject to the occupation forces. The statement, "Of course, there were Babylonian commissars, and the Babylonian judiciary was functioning in the towns,"[61] cannot be attested from the sources, but in all probability it is true. It does not argue against this that according to the Ezekiel texts, even in the Captivity itself, we recognize a kind of self-government, with the elders as the decision-making authority (Ez 8:1; 14:1; 20:1; cf Jer 29:1). It is rather doubtful whether they could safeguard legal functions in a real sense.

> – Deuteronomy, especially in its constitutional provisions, placed Torah over king and state.[62] Even if that had been questioned since the reign of Jehoiakim, it was a demand of their own God and thus a part of the identity of the group connected with deuteronomism. Still, this was not meant for nor could it apply to the foreign power,

---

58 In addition to the material in Janssen, *Juda*, see e.g. Perlitt, *Anklage*.
59 See above pp. 80ff.
60 See the commentaries of Kraus, Kaiser, Boecker.
61 Fohrer, *Geschichte* 192; see also Niehr, *Rechtsprechung* 101f.
62 See above pp. 234ff.

the New Babylonian empire. Even if one did not believe in the superiority of the foreign gods these were the only ones to whom this could apply, insofar as they were inseparable from a certain legal and social praxis. Could people remain with their own God when the constitutive Torah tradition connected with the God could no longer be practiced?

What this generally meant becomes clear in the question of the ownership of land. Deuteronomy tied the validity of God's instructions to the accession of the land and living in it.[63] Nevertheless, it was also true that "the land of our inheritance has fallen to foreigners" (Lam 5:2). Many were exiled and lived far away in the Captivity, but even in Judah the land ownership relationships were overturned.[64] Large sections of the land had fallen to others, to the lowest part (*dallet*) of the *'am hā'āreṣ* (2 Kg 24:14; cf 25:12; Jer 39:10; 40:7; 52:15f.). Here we must remember the fundamental, legal-historical fact, that the subject of all legislation of all of the preexilic corpora – the party addressed by God, to whom all law was entrusted – was exclusively the free, and, above all, land-owning Israelite. Independent of all of the detailed regulations from the Babylonians, this presupposition no longer applied. Israel had lost its land. For this reason alone, the continued application of previous legal corpora was impossible.

– Before and during the time when they held the land, the status of freedom which was the presupposition of legislation was referred to by the code word "exodus." The people who were addressed in the laws were those who had been freed by the "leading out," and the laws and regulations of the liberator God fundamentally applied to the guarantee of this freedom. Especially in Deuteronomy and the Decalogue related to it, this is the basic structure of thought for the self-concept of the laws,[65] and this began already in the Book of the Covenant. Nevertheless, this foundation had now fallen away.

Israel was back again to where it was before the exodus, under foreign domination, and together with the élite of its society, back in a house of slavery. This applied to the nation and to the people as individuals. There is a sentence at the end of the deuteronomic history, saying that all, great and small, departed for Egypt (2 Kg 25:26), thus, for all practical purposes, an erasure of the event of liberation that stood at the beginning of the history of this nation.

– There is an altar law at the beginning of the preexilic legal corpora (Ex 20:24ff.; Deut 12). The presence of God at a holy place, the communication enabled by this, is – in spite of all of the differences between the Book of the Covenant and Deuteronomy – common to both. A functioning and existing cult is undoubtedly already a presupposition of the very oldest written legal texts.[66] The pivotal position of the altar law is by no means accidental. It only renders

63 See above pp. 210f.
64 See Janssen, *Juda* 49ff.
65 See above pp. 219f. and elsewhere.
66 See above pp. 131ff., 165f., 171ff.

explicit what had previously been implied. The entire literary composition and legal conception of the law texts presume this foundation is constitutive. This affects the many provisions regarding sacrifice, festivals, cultic offerings or sacral-legal procedure. But it is more than that. The presence of the God who is experienced in the cult holds the whole thing together. With the loss of the only legitimate shrine (according to Deuteronomy), the bottom falls out of the entire conception of preexilic law books.

– Last but not least, we should remember the catastrophe of the exile came as it was supposed to. For the groups who continued the Torah tradition, this meant that Israel had not kept Torah. It came from their own God, from the one who had given them Torah. All of the curses and frightful things formulated in Ex 23:23ff. and especially in Deut 27f. came to pass. The previous legal tradition was not just no longer applicable; Israel was also shattered upon it. The freedom and the possession of the land that Israel was instructed to guard in these texts was lost because they did not even practice this law.

When all is said and done, the crisis must have had a profound effect upon the area of Torah tradition. We should have no doubt that in Judah as in the Captivity, the remnants of old earlier common law continued to be practiced, while operating under and alongside Babylonian authorities, especially where they did not impinge upon things political; rather they had the status of custom or habitual behavior. Nevertheless, all substantive detail which had been adopted since the ninth century formative for the exclusive veneration of YHWH was not in force or under critical re-examination.

So far as we can tell, the majority of exilic theologians dealt with the problem of their time by detailing of legal tradition, leaving out the question of the authority of the divine will, which required thorough study. Deuteronomic history develops the failure of Israel regarding Torah especially with respect to the unity of cultic sites; eschatological prophecy awaits a new revelation of divine justice at some time in the future. According to Jer 31:31f. the shift of Torah into the human heart is a part of this. Especially in the Jeremiah tradition, there is a general distillation to essential points, for example, the first commandment.[67]

As far as we can tell, only the priestly writings created the opportunity to connect a person's entire life with the unity of God, holding fast to the breadth of Torah tradition, which cannot be surrendered, and to the combination of cultic and legal, theological and ethical demands. It did this by a profound transformation of all previous law. A foundation developed here into which, at a later time, preexilic legal texts were also integrated and thus could be given a new appearance. The most important innovation that this legal-historical mutation produced will be discussed shortly. We will find the following accents.

– The priestly writings detached the will of God, as expressed in laws, from exodus, the cult and possession of the land, thus creating the foundation for life in the diaspora (pp. 290–301 below).

67 See the texts referred to above pp. 40ff., for example.

– The priestly writings interpreted the exodus in a radically new way, thus enabling a basis for law that is not born (exclusively) by landowning, free citizens (pp. 301–310 below).

– The priestly writings make atonement and forgiveness central for the cult and thus integrate Israel's failure with regard to Torah into Torah itself (pp. 310–322 below).

Rituals of the Diaspora

The overall plan of the priestly writings is exceedingly clear. It places the comprehensive Sinai legislation, with the establishment of shrine and cult, at the forefront of a narrative which contained the most important stations of their early history: patriarchs, sojourn in Egypt, exodus and desert journey. What had been begun in Deuteronomy with the reorientation of the law into a speech by Moses before the conquest of the land, and then was amplified in later deuteronomistic strata by a retrospective of the events since the sojourn at the mountain of God (Deut 1–5; 9f.) is here carried forward resolutely. The law, above all the constituting of the cult, became a part of a wide-ranging narrative.

In spite of the long and continuous debate regarding the sense and purpose of the priestly writings, their design, their goal, their theology,[68] I find the obvious and basic sense in this design is hardly ever clearly expressed. What is occasionally noted regarding individual texts, like Gen 17 or Ex 12,[69] can be applied more broadly. It is perhaps precisely because the priestly writings have the establishment of the shrine, together with all of the forms of conduct that are associated with it as the heart and center of their theology (in other words, the center is at Sinai), that they intend to create a picture of a life before and with God, which is thus similar to the situation *before* this event, *before* God's indwelling in the place of his creation. That picture does *not* presuppose the cult.

A life before God and with God's will, but without a functioning cult together with everything upon which the priestly writings depend – this must have been directly relevant not only for the exilic period without a temple,[70] it must be important for every Jewish diaspora. Scholars who draw parallels between creation and the establishment of the cult are correct.[71]

It is almost as though on Sinai a second, new world came into being. Nevertheless, neither the world nor Israel can be reduced to this second creation. The world without such a cult and without such a presence of the creator in it is not really Godless. Sinai is centered around the

---

68 See Lohfink, *Priesterschrift*; Brueggemann, *Kerygma*; Blenkinsopp, *Structure*; Boorer, *Intention*; Sæbø, *Priestertheologie*; Klein, *Message*; Zenger, *Bogen*; Fritz, *Geschichtsverständnis*; most recently, especially Blum, *Pentateuch* 287ff. In spite of the many differences in accent, much could be adopted from his work on the wide-ranging analysis of the discussion thus far.

69 See e.g. Schmitt, *Exodus* 82ff.; Köckert, *Leben* 48 regarding passover in each.

70 The texts referred to in the following section relate frequently to this period as the background for the picture in P.

71 See the literature above in note 49 as well as Blenkinsopp, *Structure*.

establishment of the shrine, so all of the commandments given there, including the great mass of priestly laws, demonstrate the existence of such a holy place. They are rules whose purpose is to protect the holiness of this center and guide people to it, rules corresponding to the holy thing residing there.[72]

When the presuppositions no longer exist, as in the exilic period without a temple, and – even more important – where they did no exist permanently, as in the worldwide diaspora, the commandments related to them could claim no validity. They lose their meaning, which endures only in relation to God's continuing presence. Furthermore, this corresponds precisely to that which the preexilic legal texts were saying with their positioning of the altar laws in first place.

Still, we cannot reduce the priestly writings to the Sinai law. They unfolded in a long series of laws what was in force before and without such presence of God. They do not all presume the existence of the cult, nor do they indicate awareness of a holy place or regulations which relate to it. Perhaps it is with God's word to Abraham in Gen 17:1 (see also 6:9) that we can see summarized what they are aiming at, "Walk before me, and be blameless." An existence face to face with God, in wholeness (*tāmîm*), this means without fault, without any deficiency. Thus, we must say with reservation that this is possible without a cult. In what follows, we will discuss the most important of these rules.

Capital Punishment and the Consumption of Blood

The first block of divine instructions is in *Gen 9:2–7* in conjunction with the covenant with Noah after the flood.[73] The covenant God established here (verses 8–17) with the sign of the bow in the clouds (verses 12ff.)[74] contained God's unconditional and unbreakable promise that never again would a catastrophe like the flood come upon the created world. It was a covenant, extending far beyond humanity, which included all life (verses 9f., 12f., 17f.). According to the way the priests portrayed it, the flood came because creation had become corrupted by the power that was growing within it (especially Gen 6:11–13).

Originally, people, like animals, were only given plants for food (1:29). In spite of the harsh terms used,[75] humanity's "dominion" included no

---

72 See below pp. 301ff.
73 For the significance of Gen 9:1–17 in the overall context of the original P history, see especially Ebach, *Bild Gottes*; Zenger, *Bogen*; see also Stachowiak, *Sinn*; de Boer, *Remarques*; Dequeker, *Noah*. While the literary integrity of 9:1–17 was unchallenged for a long time (see e.g. Noth, *Überlieferungsgeschichte* 17; Elliger, *Sinn* 174; Westermann, *Genesis* I 461ff. and many others), McEvenue, *Narrative Style* 67ff. regards verses 4–6, thus the important commandment formulation, as secondary. Zenger, *Bogen* 105, supports this argument with additional information; see also Lohfink, *Priesterschaft* 222 note 29; Weimar, *Struktur* 85 note 18. See also the detailed critique of this, including the central criticism of arguing in a circle – which is convincing, in Ebach, *Bild Gottes* 40f.
74 In addition to Keel, *Bogen*; see especially Zenger, *Bogen*.
75 Both of the words used, "have dominion" (*rdh*) and "subdue" (*kbš*) in other places refer exclusively to a domination against the will of those who are subordinate, including the use of force. It never refers to the relation of a king to his own people. The harshness extends to the rape of a woman (Esth 7:8). The attempts now in

killing of any kind. The violence that entered creation destroyed defense-
less creation. There was a new order after the flood. Since force could
not be eliminated, it had to be tamed and controlled. Animals were
made subject to humanity in a new way: people ruled over them (9:2).
As verse 3 says, they were all given to humans for food. If fear and killing
had become a part of creation, which was a separation from the original
condition of creation, "very good" (1:31), and which threatened total
annihilation, there had to be rules now so that this terror could be
controlled.

One of these rules was the protection of human life (verses 5–7). The
penalty against murder, whether by human or by animal, was set by God
– death, in order to protect life.[76] The basic rule of Ex 21:12, placed at the
beginning of the Book of the Covenant section on physical injury, is here
formulated for all of humanity. It is thus separated from any connection
with the cult or associated exclusively with Israel; it applies to all. Next to
it stands the statement regarding the killing of animals in Gen 9:4, "Only
you shall not eat flesh with its life, that is, its blood."[77] While human
blood should not be shed, animal blood is not supposed to be eaten. The
definition of the correlation of life (*néfeš*) and blood (*dām*), centering
around formulations like Deut 12:23 and Lev 17:11, 14, also applies here
(see also verse 5).[78] The dietary law, probably ancient Israelite, which
underlies Ex 22:30 and receives new emphasis with the decontrol of
secular butchering, is here connected with all of humanity and made into
the ethical equivalent of the commandment against murder. Power over
and fear of animals do not mean control over life itself.

What is here formulated for humanity after Noah and from which
Judaism's later Noachic rules for humanity came,[79] is naturally also
intended (and practically speaking, is especially intended) for Israel. As
for other aspects of priestly thinking, the priestly dietary regulations are
to be conceived in concentric circles around the shrine.[80] While only the
abstention from blood applied to humanity in general, the rules for Israel
were more restrictive. The prescriptions given to Israel at Sinai severely
limited the wide latitude in food animals permitted by Gen 9:3.[81] Besides
oxen, sheep and goats, there were only a few mammals left that could be
hunted. The group of animals intended for sacrifice at the shrine was
even more limited. Only three kinds of domestic animal could be used,
and among them – only animals without blemish (Lev 22:17ff.). In
general scholars have seen a contradiction between the regulations in Lev
17 and the decontrol of secular butchering in the observance of the

---

fashion to dilute this harshness (see e.g. Koch, *Gestaltet die Erde*), are exegetically
untenable and they miss the intended sense. They change into an idyll the
severity observed here, which characterized human culture regarding animals
and the earth since the neolithic, and which has played a role in many societies
since.

76 For the details, see e.g. Diebner/Schult, *Todesstrafe*; Ernst, *Menschenblut*.
77 For the problem of this sentence, see Westermann, *Genesis* I 462ff.
78 See Seebass, article on *néfeš* 549.
79 See above p. 3.
80 See especially Milgrom, *Ethics* 167ff., 177ff..
81 For these dietary laws, see above pp. 261ff.

prohibition against blood in Deut 12 (see 15f., 23f.).[82] Lev 17:3f. is seen as a cancellation of the possibilities that Deut 12 had opened.[83]

> 17:3 *If anyone of the house of Israel slaughters an ox, or a lamb or a goat in the camp, or slaughters it outside the camp,*
>
> 4 *and does not bring it to the entrance of the tent of meeting, to present it as an offering to YHWH before the tabernacle of YHWH, he shall be held guilty of bloodshed; he has shed blood.*

The only difference between the killing of animals and the killing of people is that an animal is offered according to the regulations regarding sacrifice (that is, it is brought to the sanctuary). Otherwise, exactly as in homicide, the death penalty applies (17:4).

But does Lev 17 really contradict Deut 12? Like the entire Sinai law of the priestly writings, including the Holiness Code, Lev 17 should only be interpreted in the context of its overall design. Lev 17 presumes the existence of the tent of meeting (thus the presence of God and also a functioning cult). Certainly, butchering "outside the camp" was supposed to be prohibited (17:3b).[84] Elsewhere in the priestly writings, however, the expression "outside the camp" (*mihūs lamah°nē*) refers exclusively to concrete opposition to the camp itself. Outside of the camp is where people who are unclean live,[85] where executions take place,[86] it is where the sin offering is brought[87] and other unclean things.[88] Someone who is "outside the camp" belongs – even negatively – to the camp.

"Outside" is constituted by the cult. Being outside the camp does not mean "somewhere in the world," but rather somewhere near where the camp is placed. As often in the priestly writings, we are unable to ascertain a clear transfer of the ideal relationships during the archetypal period of the desert and Sinai to the reality of the narrative present.[89] Nevertheless, we certainly cannot regard all of creation as existing "outside the camp." We might disagree whether the prohibition of secular butchering implied in Lev 17 was practiced historically only within Jerusalem or in the entire Persian province of Judah. It was small enough that it would not have been impossible to do this.[90] We may certainly not, however, transfer and associate Lev 17 with the entire Captivity. That which applied to all of humanity according to Gen 9 – the consumption of blood – also applied to Israel and the Israelites in Babylon. Neither the restrictions of Lev 11 nor the regulations regarding

82 See e.g. Milgrom, *Prolegomenon*; ibid., *Ethics* and many others.
83 Thus especially Cholewinski, *Heiligkeitsgesetz* 149ff. Lev 17 is "a direct revocation of the permission for secular butchering guaranteed by Deut 12:15, 20–22" (165).
84 For the idea of the camp in the priestly writings, see Kuschke, *Lagervorstellung*; most recently especially Wright, *Disposal* 232ff. (especially the two illustrations 224 and 247).
85 Lev 13:46; 14:3; Num 5:3f.; 12:14f.; 31:19.
86 Lev 24:14, 23; Num 15:35f.
87 Ex 29:14; Lev 4:12, 21; 8:17; 9:11; 16:27; Num 19:3.
88 Lev 6:4; 14:40, 41, 45, 53; Num 19:9, see also Lev 10:4, 5.
89 See Blum, *Pentateuch* 305f. His thoughts on the P shrine are, with the proverbial pinch of salt, also true for the "camp."
90 The fact that Lev 14:40, 41, 45, 53 (see above note 88) has "outside the city" (*mihūs hā'ir*) instead of "outside the camp" may point in this direction.

sacrifice could by intention apply to the diaspora. On the other hand, we should see that Gen 9 ought also to apply to Israel.

For the relationship of the priestly writings to Deuteronomy, this means that the most we can say is that there was a dispute over proper behavior within the precincts of the temple, and how much territory this area should include. Furthermore, it means that we may not retroject the regulations of a later diaspora Judaism directly to the earliest beginning of a theological mastery of such a situation. That the Levitical purity regulations, and with them the dietary laws of Lev 11/Deut 14 could find application in diaspora groups (and therefore also on the time after the destruction of the temple) should not be seen as before or independent of their pharisaic interpretation.[91]

Covenant and Circumcision

As we know, in addition to the covenant formulated in Gen 9 between God and humanity there is only one other, the covenant with Abraham in Gen 17. In both texts we find some of the most interesting covenant theology in the Old Testament. Neither example deals with reciprocal activity, or even with the possibility of revocation or breaking. Rather, both cases deal with an obligating and unbreakable promise from God.[92] Nothing, even the failure of the human partner, can call this into question. The independence of both is placed in the center.

It is expressly formulated several times in Gen 17 that this is an eternal covenant (verses 7, 13, 19) valid for Abraham and all of his descendants, through the chain of generations (verses 7, 9). This sworn promise of God includes increased numbers of descendants and nationhood (5f.), the possession of the land (forever! verse 8), even the development of a state, the return of their own kings (verses 6, 16) and above all, that he would be their God.

The circumcision of Abraham and his male descendants served as a "sign" of this covenant (verse 10). For this reason the term "covenant" (*b*rit*) is really used reciprocally. Of course, it does not imply mutual dependence. The failure to carry out circumcision does not call God's promise into question. It only leads to that person being shut out of their family (verse 14): For an exilic situation this is basically something self-evident.

Efforts to reconstruct (as much as possible) a purely narrative priestly base stratum also in Gen 17, have led to a perception that formulations containing concrete instructions or even the consequences of human failure to carry something out, are secondary (especially verses 12–14).[93] Nevertheless, there is no impetus for this from the structure of the text or

---

91 See Neusner, *Rabbinic Traditions* III especially 288ff.; most recently Maier, *Zwischen den Testamenten* 269ff.

92 Kutsch, *"Ich will euer Gott sein"* correctly emphasized this, but with almost exclusive concentration on the meaning of words. His literary-critical activity in the line of his *b*rit* interpretation are less convincing. For this, see Westermann, *Genesis* 17 (cf ibid. 78, note especially for Kutsch). See also *Genesis* II 251ff. (Lit).

93 While Kutsch, *"Ich will euer Gott sein"* 378 suggests the adoption of older material (which therefore doesn't quite fit), Zenger, *Bogen* 150 note 43; Weimar, *Abrahamsgeschichte*; Köckert, *Leben* 41ff. (verses 12a, 13b/12b, 13a, 14) consider multi-step redaction; see already Steuernagel, *Genesis* 17.

the linguistic usage.[94] One must already have come to some kind of a "pure" theology, holding fixed notions about a narrative work or ritual particularities, in order to regard such significant literary critical activity as necessary.

The fact that, apart from the covenant with Abraham, there are no covenant formulations in priestly language that have led to continuing discussions among scholars.[95] If we are correct in out presentation of the genesis of the Sinai pericope in Ex 34:10, the priestly writings would have integrated within themselves a text with a covenant formulation. It, however, does not have the weight that is due to a text like Gen 17. Of course, apart from any decision in this question, we can say that the priestly writings are all basic promises from God to his people: the connection with God, existence as a nation, possession of the land, even political independence coming before and separate from any functioning cult. They are not tied to it. The connection to God and all of his promises is also in force during the exile and diaspora, and circumcision is the sign. Thus an old folk custom, which probably received a new and important significance during the exile, was filled with new meaning.

It is probably appropriate to say about the connection of Gen 17 to the events at Sinai, that it represents the fulfillment of the Abrahamic covenant, but that is hardly enough.[96] What happened on Sinai is not generally grasped by the somewhat legal category of covenant. The priestly writings use it to describe extra-cultic activity around the world and without connection to the sanctuary. At Sinai we are not dealing with the promise and obligation of God, but with his presence and what followed from that presence. It is not because God promises and Israel responds, but because God in his tremendously ominous holiness is present that Israel – but not just Israel! – must respond. Every deviant act is not disobedience that will be punished, but a danger to which people expose themselves.

This difference becomes clear in the question of the non-Israelites. While the regulations applicable in the vicinity of the holy God must apply to all people who come there, the situation in the profanity of exile is quite different. Only someone who belongs can participate in the activities between God and Abraham (and his descendants). For this reason, according to Gen 17:13 slaves also were to be circumcised.[97]

94 See especially McEvenue, *Narrative Style* 149ff., who works out the text structure; Lohfink, *Priesterschrift* 222 note 29; especially Blum, *Komposition* 420ff.
95 Zimmerli, *Sinaibund* is particularly effective; he has undertaken a deliberate critique of the Sinai covenant. Cross, *Myth* 320; Blum, *Komposition* 430f., and others suggest that P presupposes older covenant texts. Most recently, see especially Blum, *Pentateuch* 294.
96 With a somewhat different accent, see Blum, *Pentateuch* 294.
97 See also below p. 298. Köckert, *Leben* 43 would see the inclusion of slaves here as "empty ritualism," since there exists no relationship to God and his promise. He also criticizes the threat of punishment in verse 14. Apart from the fact that the intent of this verse in the context of P has not been investigated, we also should state that we already presume (old) information about what is theologically right and proper. In spite of Köckert's attempt in this essay to dignify the concept of law in P (to be sure, the understanding of the law, not its contents), there is clearly still the old notion current from Wellhausen through Noth that a good law is turned into dead ritualism by later accretion.

Endogamy

In Gen 27:46–28:9, the priestly stratum says that Rebecca is disturbed about Esau's marriage with Hittite women (26:34f.). For that reason Isaac issues a prohibition, "You shall not marry one of the Canaanite women" (28:1). This prompts Jacob to travel to relatives in Mesopotamia in order to find a wife there. When Esau learned of this prohibition (28:6ff.), he also married a relative, a daughter of Ishmael (verse 9).

This motivation for Jacob leaving Laban corresponds to what the priestly writings express narratively in Gen 27 with Jacob's deception and its consequences. The subject of endogamy was, of course, extremely important during the exilic period. The solidarity of the groups in exile could not be imagined without it. "Actually, after the Israelite–Judean state ceased to exist, the family became the community form that protected the continuity of Israel and its religion."[98] During the postexilic period, the mixed marriage conflicts of the Ezra–Nehemiah period show how very old rules regarding endogamy here gained new and central significance. Old prohibitions against intermixing in the Torah tradition (Ex 34:16; Deut 7:3) were brought back into play in a new, radical form. If this was about divine prohibitions, the priestly writings place new accents. The prohibition of marriage relations with Canaanite women was ultimately a prohibition issued by Jacob in reaction to Rebecca's fears. There is no divine authority behind it. This is only patriarchal tradition.

Despite all the rigors of the priestly sexual laws in Lev 18 and 20, Deuteronomy seems unaware of this limitation. The fact that during the postexilic period there were special priestly groups who supported close familial connections with the neighboring nations, to the irritation of Nehemiah (especially Neh 13:28f.) may not be separated from this. Endogamy was not essential for them so they did not enforce it rigorously. This may be directly connected with what they regarded as central: nearness to the sanctuary makes people, even outside of Israel, ultimately equal.

Passover

Of all the commandments and rituals introduced by the priestly writings before the Sinai event (as a result, they were independent of the temple cult and could be practiced away from it) passover is closest to the actual cult. Nevertheless, all characteristics of real cultic activity are absent. Correspondingly, scholars have correctly theorized that it was specially conceived for the situation as a sign of hope for those in exile,[99] but this also applied to other future generations of the diaspora.

There is, however, even more dispute over the textual foundation here than in Gen 9 or 17. It is certain that of the extensive passover regulations in chapters 11–13 of Exodus, 12:1–20, 28, 40ff. belong in the broadest sense to the priestly writings.[100] We can also see quite clearly

98 Westermann, *Genesis* II 547.
99 Thus especially, Schmitt, *Exodus* 82ff.
100 See e.g. Noth, *Überlieferungsgeschichte* 18, Eissfeldt, *Einleitung* 250f. and others (see above note 24).

that there are addenda to the priestly writings in verses 15–20 and 43ff.[101] But in the remaining text also, which generally seems unified, there is a whole series of strata.

With very few exceptions,[102] of course, the essential portions of these verses, including the actual killing of the passover, are part of the basic document.[103] We can entirely disregard here the questions, whether the priestly writings thus adopted earlier ritual texts and to what degree they can be reconstructed.[104] In contrast, the fading away of all provisions that formulate ritual particulars, such as, for example, the date (verses 2, 6a), the advance selection (verse 4), the unblemished state of the animal (verse 5) or the instructions regarding preparation and eating verses 9f.)[105] can be seen as arguing in a circle. How could this be supported without a preliminary grasp of the passover tradition, which is attributed to the priestly document? If, however, this document is aware of a ritual before Sinai, similar to a sacrifice, we must reckon with the details. Even if such details seem to have been added gradually (nothing argues for this), only essentials would have been added.

The instruction to keep the passover before the crucial evening in Egypt and leaving on the exodus is given as speech from God. If the ritual language already from verse 2 on, implied that the once for all event was to become a permanently effective ritual instruction, this is made explicit in verse 14: this is to become an eternal law (*huqqat 'ōlām*) which is to be carried out by all future generations as a remembrance (*zikkārōn*). It is classified as a remembrance of the first exodus, but it can be taken as a transparent reference to new departures. They were to celebrate with readiness to depart and prepared for the journey (verse 11), with appropriate haste and urgency (*bᵉhippasōn*).[106] Like any sacrament, with which passover has repeatedly been compared,[107] there are connections to the past as well as to the present and the future. People celebrate it in remembrance of the departure and also at the brink of a new departure. The "next year in Jerusalem" of the later Haggadah is already substantively present in Ex 12.

The diaspora situation is already clearly recognizable in the ritual provisions. The passover is to be celebrated in families (verse 3); where there are insufficient people to warrant an entire lamb, it is to be celebrated with neighbors (verse 4). While it is to be done in families, it nevertheless affects the entire congregation (*'ēdā, qāhāl*, verses 3, 6). It is through and through a community event.[108]

---

101 See Ellliger, *Sinn* 174, who reduces Pg to verses 1, 3–14, 28, 40f.
102 Thus especially Ska, *Les Plaies* 23ff. (for a critique, see Köckert, *Leben* 45 note 69) and Lohfink, *Priesterschrift* 222 note 29, who only finds Pg in verses 37a, 40–42.
103 Thus in differing ways Laaf, *Paschafeier* 10ff.; Weimar, *Struktur* 85 note 18; Kohata, *Jahwist* 261ff.
104 See the extensive discussion in Rendtorff, *Gesetz* 56ff.
105 Thus the studies referred to above in note 103; see also Köckert, *Leben* 49ff.
106 For a comparison with Deutero-Isaiah, see Eitz, *Studien*.
107 Thus especially Füglister, *Heilsbedeutung*; Haag, *Pascha* especially 115ff.; Schmitt, *Exodus* 84.
108 With Rofé, *Introduction* I 48f., Blum, *Pentateuch* 335f. note would see here a hidden reference to a killing in the sanctuary, thus corresponding to Lev 17 and other texts. This would remove the place of the founding of passover to before Sinai.

There is no question of a sacrifice. The priestly writings are clear on this: sacrifices are part of the cult, which does not exist here. The prescriptions formulated in verse 9 separate the passover lamb from a sacrifice. I think that it would not contradict this if, nevertheless, the animals must fulfill the requirements of ritual provision for sacrifice. In the moment of departure, which leads to nothing else than the place of God,[109] Israel already acts in anticipation of the rules that will apply there.

This goes even further. Even the blood, to which priestly thinking attributes great significance in connection with atonement rituals[110] – "the life of the flesh is in the blood" (Lev 17:11) – appears almost in its own role. Door posts and lintels were to be marked with it according to verse 7. The protection against annihilation, which is guaranteed by the cultic act of atonement, prefigures protection from being struck by God (verse 13). Ultimately – as shown by the dimension – this also applies to all of the gods of alien powers. In this context the concept of the "sign," which is a part of all pre-Sinai rituals of the priestly document, reappears in verse 13. As it is so remarkably phrased, it is a sign for "you" – that is, for Israel, that God will not harm you.

A few other statements are obviously additions; they are not in substantive disagreement with the remaining text of the priestly writings, but offer important and helpful supplementary information. In verses 43ff. we are dealing with the participation of non-Israelites in the passover meal. It is frequently emphasized that this applies exclusively to those who are circumcised, and it is true for both slave and free.

The statement in verse 49 that one and the same Torah applies to Israelites and aliens, has a different consequence here than in other passages of the priestly document (cf Lev 24:22; Num 15:15f.). Thus, according to the passover provisions in Num 9, such limitation is not necessary (verse 14). We should not regard this as a contradiction. Num 9 is clearly concerned with the circumstances in the "camp," that is, in the context of the sanctuary and cult.

The prohibition here concerns something not discussed in Ex 12: uncleanness on the part of those who are participants (Num 9:6ff., 13) for whom a *post facto* celebration is prescribed. This also applied to those who were traveling (verse 10). Prescriptions regarding purity have nothing to be gained in foreign, unclean lands like Egypt; their validity presupposes proximity to the holy. Conversely, God's constant law applies to citizen or foreigner alike in this proximity, indeed, in every respect, even in the cultic provisions (Lev 24:22; Num 15:15f.). Just as with the slaves in Gen 17:12f., this applies in the secular, in that only those who are counted among Israel by circumcision are permitted to join at the table with its promises. Conversely, in the presence of the holy,

---

Since that passover would also have been celebrated somewhere in the vicinity of the sanctuary, as texts like Lev 23, Num 9 and others attest, there might be an adaptation. We should not, however, undervalue the archetypal function of customs not located at the sanctuary. There could also be gatherings in the exile and in the diaspora.

109 See below pp. 301ff.
110 See below p. 311 and elsewhere.

appropriate ritual behavior is absolutely commanded of whatever nation or faith.

Finally, in Ex 12:15–20 there are provisions for the feast of unleavened bread. Already in Deut 16 passover was connected with this annual, agricultural festival. This connection was continued, even the attested Ex 12:15ff., in the diaspora.[111] Here also a week-long festival with unleavened bread was celebrated. Like the speech about the holiness of the assembly, which was entirely against the usual concepts of the priestly document, the fact that the seven-day week with sabbath was presupposed here shows that the strict priestly conception was no longer entirely observed. At least, the text attests how gradually even the three annual festivals, which in Deuteronomy as in the priestly document were connected with the sanctuary and its functions, were accepted in the non-cultic diaspora.

Sabbath

In the overall structure of the priestly document, the subject of the sabbath has an especially remarkable function. It brackets the entire pre-Sinai portion and then leads directly into the center of the Sinai law. By means of the seven days of creation the structure of Gen 1 rests upon the sabbath structure of the week. At the end, God himself rests, thus sanctifying the seventh day (Gen 2:2f.). The priestly document's central concept of the "holy" (*qdš*) appears here for the first time. What this implies is first apparent only in the Sinai pericope. The theme of sabbath thus shapes the last priestly narrative before Sinai in Ex 16.

The literary structure of this chapter has been largely clarified by the work of Ruprecht.[112] Unlike earlier attempts, which tried to find several Pentateuch sources at work here,[113] he finds a clearly discernible priestly narrative (verses 1–3, 6–7, 9–27, 30, 35a), which was expanded and interpreted by later deuteronomistic additions (verses 4f., 28f., 31, 34). Only here is there something like a real sabbath *commandment*, indeed it refers back to something previously issued. This probably connects back to Ex 15:25f.

This example of deuteronomistic redaction of a priestly text is of considerable significance for the entire work. It demonstrates that there is not a clear, one-track sequence in the (later) strata. The analysis is generally accepted.[114] It makes the structure of the priestly text essentially clearer than attempts to derive the theme of sabbath out of an original narrative,[115] which incorporates the event into the premise.

---

111 Laaf, *Pascha-Feier* 137 would conclude on the basis of the terminology that the feast of unleavened bread was here observed at the temple. It is equally possible that temple language would have been employed at the celebrations in the remote diaspora.

112 Ruprecht, *Stellung*.

113 See the overview of the critique of the earlier studies in Fritz, *Wüste* 9 note 1 and especially Maiberger, *Manna* 809ff.

114 See e.g. Blum, *Pentateuch* 146ff.; Köckert, *Leben* 46f.; Rose, *Deuteronomist* 51f.; Fritz, *Tempel* 2 note 10.

115 Thus especially Maiberger, *Manna*; Scharbert, *Exodus*; Weimar, *Struktur*; Lohfink, *Priesterschrift*.

If we follow this reconstruction, Israel discovers the sabbath structure of creation on its journey in the desert. The feeding of the people between departure and Sinai, even between departure and the accession of the land (verse 35) follows in sabbath rhythm. On the day before the sabbath twice as much is gathered, thus enough for two days (verse 22), but on the sabbath there is nothing to be found (verse 27). This difference from the sabbath commandment that first appeared in Ex 31:12ff. does not argue that we find the beginning of the Sinai activity in Ex 16.[116] Israel is not yet at the mountain of God, even though it is near.

Here for the first time God appears to Israel in the form in which he comes at Sinai and is also encountered in the sanctuary (Ex 24:16f.; 40:34f.). According to Ex 16:10, Israel sees the glory turned toward the desert and the *kabod* of its God in the midst of the desert.[117] If God, as we are told with the same root, glorified himself when he saved Israel at the sea in Ex 14 (verses 4, 10, 17),[118] this *kabod* is clearly recognizable, even if still veiled in the cloud. After the revelation to Abraham under the name of 'ēl-šadday (Gen 17:1) and to Moses under his own name YHWH (Ex 6:2f.), here he becomes gradually visible. It is clear that in this way the priestly document develops a dense network of increasing and expanding statements about God. Ex 16 plays a special role in this.

For Israel, as for all groups in the Captivity, its own characteristic rhythm became perceptible before the events on Sinai, even before the presence of the holy itself that required special regulation. With the sabbath rhythm, connected to feeding in foreign and desert lands, Israel is as close to the actual form of God as it is possible to be without the shrine. By participating in the sabbath rhythm, Israel, which does not live in the presence of God, can catch sight of God himself. Nevertheless, (nearly) everything is potentially present without the obligating commandment. The connection with the shrine emerges especially through interaction with the concept of the "holy." As God sanctifies the sabbath by his inactivity (Gen 2:3), he sanctifies Israel itself in conjunction with the sabbath commandment (Ex 31:13). Hidden, without the "electrical field" of the holy with its positive and negative possibilities, Israel, even in the desert, participates in this holiness when it ventures into the sabbath rhythm.

Summary

The priestly document, with all of its laws apparently focussed entirely on the cult, opened a world theologically which enabled a "profane" participation in God. By the fact that it has strictly divided between the holy and the profane – precisely in accord with the assignment of the priest (Lev 10:10) – it portrays a world of the profane alongside that of the holy. The rules, which are constituted by the presence of the holy, do not (yet) apply here.

That does not mean, however, that it is a world without God. In this world it is possible to live, as Abraham was commanded in promise (Gen 17:1), to live before God and therefore completely. It is impossible to live

116 Against Zenger, *Bogen* 157; see also Beuken, *A Rule*.
117 See especially Westermann, *Herrlichkeit*; Struppe, *Herrlichkeit*.
118 For these relationships, see Blum, *Pentateuch* 296.

a way of life according to Israel's own law while in the exile and diaspora, but it is here that the basic commandment against murder applies without restriction. It is not possible here to have their own cult, and with it a life in the direct presence of God, but it is here that the covenant – the only one with Israel – is concluded and its promises are permanently valid.

A picture of life in the diaspora was created by means of ritual activity like the abstention from eating blood, circumcision, passover as a celebration of the beginning of freedom, and participation in the sabbath, which of course was expanded in later periods, but which at the very first enabled and inaugurated theologically. God's law and God's promise are thus experienced as a sign, and the concept of sign appears with variation in all of these texts. Such a life is possible not *with* but *before* God, and then without blemish or restriction (*tamim* Gen 17:1).

Holiness as the Shape of Freedom[119]

Exodus as Sanctification

The coded language in which the exodus narrative speaks of freedom, which in deuteronomic law, as in the Decalogue, had supplied the theological validation of the commandments of God, was interpreted anew in the priestly texts. It retained its significance, even increasing, but in a new form.

In the proclamation to Moses of the coming activity in Ex 6:2–12,[120] in which God introduced himself by name (verse 3), referring to the covenant with Abraham (verse 4) and the groaning of the people in slavery in Egypt (verse 5), we read:

> *Ex 6:6 I am YHWH, and I will free you from the burdens of the Egyptians and deliver you from slavery to them. I will redeem you with an outstretched arm and with mighty acts of judgment. 7 I will take you as my people, and I will be your God. You shall know that I am YHWH your God, who has freed you from the burdens of the Egyptians.*

The goal of the liberating exodus, even prior to the gift of the land (verse 8), is the bringing together of God and people. What was announced in the covenant with Abraham (Gen 17:7) was given shape in the exodus. In the same way, the activity in the central text of Ex 29:43ff. is described in terms of the so-called covenant formula,[121] where the concern is with the intent of all that happened on Sinai.[122]

> *Ex 29:45 I will dwell among the Israelites, and I will be their God. 46 And they shall know that I am YHWH their God, who brought them out of the land of Egypt that I might dwell among them.*

This act of leading out had God's living in the midst of Israel as its goal.

119 For what follows , see also Crüsemann, *Exodus*.
120 For this text, see Schmidt, *Exodus* I 266ff.
121 See Smend, *Bundesformel*; Schmid, *Ich will euer Gott sein*.
122 For the significance and function of this text, see Koch, *Eigenart* 48ff.; Walkenhorst, *Hochwertung* 15ff.; Janowski, *Sühne* 317ff.; Blum, *Pentateuch* 297.

A series of priestly passages from the Holiness Code in the category of "holiness" helps explain more precisely what these formulations mean.[123] Thus, it says in Lev 22 in connection with provisions regarding sacrifice (verses 17–30) and the admonition to observe the laws regarding keeping God's name holy (verses 31b, 33), "I am YHWH; I sanctify you, I who brought you out of the land of Egypt to be your God: I am YHWH" (verses 32b, 33). There are four participial expressions here side by side designating sanctification (*mᵉqaddiškēm*) and leading out (*hammōṣi*) by God. Both may not be connected as temporally separate. Both describe the same process: the leading out into community with God is the process of sanctification.

Matters are formulated quite similarly in Lev 11:44f. We read in connection with the prescriptions regarding clean and unclean animals: "For I am YHWH your God; sanctify yourselves therefore and be holy, for I am holy. You shall not defile yourselves with any swarming creature that swarms upon the earth. For I am YHWH who brought you up from the land of Egypt, to be your God; you shall be holy, for I am holy."

The action of God described in the indicative is the exodus alone. This act placed Israel into a relationship with God, which resulted in the behavior consequent to the condition of holiness – making oneself holy. The exodus had the function of sanctification by God.

Passages in Lev 20 and 18 speak especially clearly. Reference is made to the former residents of the land that Israel is supposed to inherit in Lev 20:24ff., in conjunction with capital offense provisions for sexual misconduct, and therefore their practices (*huqqōt*, verse 23) are discussed.

"I am YHWH your God; I have separated you from the peoples. You shall therefore make a distinction between the clean animal and the unclean ... You shall be holy to me; for I YHWH am holy, and I have separated you from the other peoples to be mine" (Lev 20:24b, 25a, 26).

Here "separation," or "contrast" (*bdl*, hiph.),[124] is a priestly technical term, which describes the most important duties of a priest (Lev 10:10f.) This priestly dividing of things that do not belong together is employed to characterize the separation of Israel from other nations. The isolation finds parallels in behavior; it is thus the enforcement of the proper distinction.

The process of sanctification and of separation from other nations is identical. Both were completed in the exodus. This is especially clear in Lev 18:3, with the legal and ethical passages of the Holiness Code following the introductory altar provisions in Lev 17.

"You shall not do as they do (*maᵃsé*) in the land of Egypt, where you lived, and you shall not do as they do (*maᵃsé*) in the land of Canaan, to which I am bringing you. You shall not follow their statutes (*huqqōt*). My statutes and ordinances shall you keep, following them: I am YHWH your God" (Lev 18:3f.).

The leading out of Egypt was made concrete in the customs and forms of life practiced there. The leading into the land of Canaan means that Israel will not conform to the customs and usages there. Through the

123 See Lubscyk, *Auszug* 169f., and especially Zimmerli, *Heiligkeit*.
124 See Otzen, article on *bādal*.

exodus, Israel was in a special status, separated from other nations, and they alone were obligated to observe God's commandments.

The reference to the exodus in the Holiness Code generally presumes its understanding as separation from the nations and sanctification; only in this way does its function make sense. This applies, for example, to 19:36. Immediately before, in verse 34, the exodus is mentioned as support for love of aliens, in exactly the same way as happened already in the Book of the Covenant (Ex 22:20; 23:9) and Deuteronomy (Deut 10:19; 24:17f., 22).

If the substantive correlation is directly apparent here, it is not clear in what follows. What is the substantive connection between the exodus and the requirement to have "honest balances, honest weights, an honest ephah and an honest hin" in 19:36? Similarly, in Lev 25, the special prohibition against charging interest is connected with the leading out from Egypt, together with the only purpose for that action: "to be your God." Only when we grasp the exodus as a separating out for God, a sanctification by and for him, is the correlation clear.[125]

Zimmerli has given a precise description of what happens in the texts to which we have just referred, "After all is said and done, 'holiness' is a characteristic that is not first acquired from the nation or the priests, but rather something from the previous leading out of his people by Yahweh, which is simultaneously an act of separation, the self-same quality of Israel and its priests. The declaration of ownership is the foundation for the demand for holiness."[126] All ethical and legal statements of the priestly collection of laws rest upon this, and this applies generally. "The aspect of holiness determines the Code even in the places where the term *qdš* itself is missing."[127] The text of the Holiness Code is pervaded by the repeated phrase "I am YHWH." As a *ceterum censeo* it refers to fundamental connection between God and people.

The exodus is understood differently in this priestly theology than it is in the preexilic literature. It is not the social, legal or political status of Israel that is thus designated, but just Israel's closeness to God. Of course, the concept of holiness had already been used in the earlier legal texts, but there it had exclusive connection to cultic themes, like dietary prohibitions or mourning rituals.[128] In the Holiness Code this is extended much farther and made into a key for all legal questions. It is not the existence of free, landowning groups or the political freedom of the nation that is connected with the exodus, but the separation from other nations and their customs, and the association with and closeness to God himself. This closeness is the shape of freedom for which the concept of exodus is responsible.

The significance of this must show itself immediately in the texts in which the problem of the loss of freedom and the possession of the land

---

125 For the further connections to the exodus in H (Lev 25:42, 55; 26:13, 45) see below pp. 304ff.
126 Zimmerli, *Heiligkeit* 503.
127 Mathys, *Nächstenliebe* 108.
128 See Ex 22:30 (dietary customs); Deut 7:6 (context: inter-marriage and alien shrines); Deut 14:2, 21 (context: mourning rituals and dietary customs), in addition to Deut 26:19; 28:9.

is treated. That had happened even for large groups of the population, indeed, the people as a whole. It had become the background against which the priestly texts first begin to speak. The Holiness Code treated the loss of freedom and land for individual Israelites in Lev 25 and for the entire nation in Lev 26. The fact that both chapters are brought together as a unity by a system of headings in 25:1f. may be connected with the common subject-matter.[129]

As he is described in detail in Lev 25:39ff., the impoverished Israelite is not to be treated as a slave, but as a wage earner. He may be allowed to return to freedom in the year of jubilee. This means that we are dealing with the institution of debt slavery here, and the extension of the period of service from seven years (Ex 21:2ff.; Deut. 15:14ff.) to forty-nine was a significant diminishing of the rights of a slave. It shows how the priestly document reduced the social position of slaves compared with deuteronomic assessments.

Nevertheless, something important in the history of law happens here. This is the first step in the process of the elimination of slavery altogether and its change into paid labor. Verse 42 bases the requirement to treat fellow Israelites as wage earners, not as slaves, on the fact that "they are my servants, whom I brought out of the land of Egypt, I am YHWH your God." Thus all Israelites became slaves of God through the exodus and the distinction between slave and free has been lost with respect to their relation with God. God's demands upon his people apply to all, independent of their social and legal status. Even those who are in reality slaves remain a part of the group that God has taken to himself in an inalienable relationship by means of the exodus. The Holiness Code and the entire priestly law addresses them as well. God's will with respect to cult, ethics and law applies to those who have lost their freedom, as it does for others.

What applies to the situation of the slave also applies for those who have lost their property. This is shown by the two important parallels in Lev 25:23 just cited: "The land shall not be sold in perpetuity, for the land is mine; with me you are but aliens and tenants." The relationship of an individual and his family with God does not depend upon possession of land and the rights connected to it. The relationship with God established by the exodus is independent of the possession of land and cannot be placed in doubt by the loss of that land.

Throughout the entire composition of the priestly document there is compelling expression of the idea that the constituting of the entire cult – thus the indwelling of God in Israel with its consequent nearness to God – happens on Sinai, outside of the land and before Israel took up residence in it. Loss of land and freedom by individual Israelites and their families does not affect the relationship to God.

Lev 26, with which the Holiness Code concludes (especially verse 46) and which assumes an important place in the entire priestly law,[130] shows that the priestly interpretation of the exodus remains the basis for the relationship to God even in the deeply encumbered crisis of the exile. In

129 A comment by Matthias Millard.
130 See most recently especially Blum, *Pentateuch* 300f. and even more so 325f.

the blessings and cursings, both positive (verses 3–13) and – in all their breadth – negative (verses 14–43), consequences of conduct toward God and his demands are handled. The subject of the exodus appears at the end of each of the two strongly contrasting, long portions of the chapter, forming conclusions to the respective passages (verses 13, 45).

Scholars disagree over the interpretation of Lev 26, whether the "If" placed at the beginning, in verse 3, represents a placement of condition upon the promises that appear otherwise in the priestly document unconditionally.[131] Doubtless, the formulations in Lev 26:9, 11 are reminiscent of those in Gen 17; Ex 6 and Ex 29.[132] Is the eternal covenant, which nothing jeopardizes, not even human guilt and refusal, now made dependent upon the condition of obedience? I think that the very appearance of the exodus theme at the end of both parts of the chapter shows the opposite. The exodus as a concrete form in which the promise of God became a reality, that is, the connecting of God and people by what is described as sanctification, is the foundation that nothing can place in doubt, upon which the alternative played out in Lev 26 is first constructed.

Thus we read at the end of the promises of blessing and salvation in Lev 26:13: "I am YHWH your God, who brought you out of the land of Egypt, to be their slaves no more; I have broken the bars of your yoke and made you walk erect." The image of the breaking of the yoke[133] and walking upright shows that concrete social and political liberation is intended much more than the passages cited here, which interpret the exodus in a priestly manner. We should not remove this too far from exodus liberation code language. The priestly document, as it told the story, referred repeatedly to the groaning and slave labor of Egypt.[134] Observing God's instructions brings this very side into prominence again.

Naturally, in spite of the unconditional promise of God, Israel's conduct is not without consequence.[135] The proximity to God is dangerous, and the land can become so unclean, as is so frequently stated (Lev 18:25, 28; 20:22) that it practically vomits its residents out for defiling it. All this is the background for the many threats in Lev 26:14–39. As bad as it might get, however, at the end we find the reference to God's foundation laying act, which remains untouched.

From Lev 26:40 on, the discussion is about confession of sins. This opens the possibility for a change. Exile means punishment of Israel, but not repudiation (44a): ". . . for I am YHWH their God; but I will

---

131 See Lohfink, *Abänderung* 160; Blum, *Pentateuch* 325f.

132 Particulars in Lohfink, *Abänderung* 160; Blum, *Pentateuch* 325f.

133 We note especially the role this image played in conjunction with the Babylonians and the exile in the Jeremiah tradition (Jer 27:2; 28:10, 12, 13), see also Isa 58:6, 9.

134 Ex 6:6; see also 1:11; 2:11; 5:4f.

135 Blum, *Pentateuch* 327, "To chop off these statements in one or another way would mean, in other words, to condemn the tradents to muteness, either with respect to the past and the present or the future. It may be that for a priestly 'covenant theology,' as it is presented in Gen 9, 17, and elsewhere, and in view of the experience of the exile, there is no reasonable alternative to the conceptual juxtaposition of Lev 26:3, 9, 13f. and 26:41ff."

remember in their favor the covenant with their ancestors whom I brought out of the land of Egypt in the sight of the nations, to be their God. I am YHWH" (44b, 45).

This means that the act of the exodus, which happened in the sight of the nations, forms the enduring foundation upon which God can and would build, even in the troubles of the period of exile. He led Israel out of Egypt with the single purpose of being Israel's God. Israel should and must respond to this status through its behavior. God's action, however, remains and continues even if Israel does not respond. The arrangement of God and people accomplished in the exodus represents the keeping of the covenant with Abraham, and it is independent of failure on Israel's part. It allows punishment to be understood as a consequence of guilt, but the special status remains unaffected.

Holiness as a Legal Principle

At the center of priestly thinking we find the concept of holiness.[136] All of the laws dispensed on Sinai apply to conduct in the presence of God. Therefore it treats largely cultic themes. In addition to the construction and furnishing of the shrine itself, the bulk of the laws are made up by those applying to priests, sacrifice, and purity. Nevertheless, nearly all the subjects treated in the preexilic legal tradition are included here. Of course, balance and proportion are shifted to a dominance of cultic regulations, still, the combination of such cultic and religious instruction with legal, ethical and social themes that developed with the Book of the Covenant also determines the priestly law. Slavery, physical injury, family and sexuality, interest and indebtedness, even issues which are strictly speaking political – practically no subject is omitted in order to establish freedom by means of a constitution based on deuteronomic law. What does this mean for justice, that these are in a context shaped by cultic concerns?

In order to understand this, we must look farther afield than priestly theology. The central concept of holiness is not something that is specific to Israel. Israel shared it with many religions[137] and probably adopted it from other Canaanite religions. The gods themselves and everything in close proximity to them in nature or among people[138] are classified as "holy," using the same term. Here[139] as elsewhere, the holy is the special place delimited from the profane – thus the holy area, the temple, is separated from the profane by a wall, a (*haram*) – or by the special time. For the contemporary world, which has virtually no acquaintance with the holy, Rudolph Otto's classic definition – the holy is an overwhelming and fascinating mystery (*mysterium tremendum et fascinans*) – remains

---

136 See especially Koch, *Eigenart* 41ff.
137 For the religio-historic material, see Otto, *The Idea of the Holy*; Éliade, *Religions*; ibid., *The Holy*; Callois, *Mensch*; Wunnenberger, *Le Sacré*; as well as the overview in Kippenberg, article on Heilig.
138 Kornfeld/Ringgren, article on *qdš* 1182. For the Canaanite and special Ugaritic evidence, see Schmidt, *Aussage*; Cazelles, *Impur*; ibid., *Pur*; Xella, *QDS*.
139 For the Old Testament in addition to the overviews in Gilbert, *Sacre*; Terrien, *The Numinous* as well as the literature in note 145f. For the archaeological evidence, see Crüsemann, *Ritualbad*.

helpful.[140] If we want a comparison (with all of the limitations and problems that such parallels have), the image of an electrical field or radioactivity – the concepts are especially helpful in English.

For the theology of the priestly document, the personal presence of God himself in the form of his glory (*kābōd*) is decisive. In conjunction with the instructions (Ex 25–31) for the erecting of the sanctuary in which God would live, we read in a passage[141] central for the entire priestly document regarding the tent (Ex 29:42b–46):

> *I will meet with you to speak to you there. I will meet with the Israelites there and it shall be sanctified by my presence. I will consecrate the tent of meeting and the altar; Aaron also and his sons I will consecrate to serve me as priests. I will dwell among the Israelites and I will be their God. And they shall know that I am YHWH their God, who brought them out of Egypt that I might dwell among them. I am YHWH their God.*

Here the concern is with the presence of God, the opportunities, but also the dangers that God's proximity to his people offers. The priestly document articulates the basic theological problem of closeness to and distance from God in a special way. The creator God is not (only) in heaven or in some kind of transcendental state, but he is known and experienced in the immediate present. What is described in Lev 10:10 as the most important duty of the priests: to distinguish (*bdl*) between holy and profane, clean and unclean, is exactly what the priestly document does both overall and in dealing with particulars. Scholars have correctly employed the image of concentric circles to illustrate the priestly gradation of the degree of proximity to God.[142] The positions closest to God himself, as servers at the home and altar of God, are reserved for priests who have been set apart and consecrated, the sons of Aaron. There is access to the holy of holies in the temple, the space of God himself, only for the high priest once each year for the purpose of the ritual purification (Lev 16:2). The people selected by God for this purpose (and whose God he would be), lived in the circle outside that of the priests, as the priestly camp structure in Num 1ff. describes it. Between the priests and the people, almost like a protective divider, were found the Levites. Israel is separated from all of the other nations by this nearness to God.

It is not necessary to go into the plethora of ritual laws in the priestly document here.[143] They all have the intention that this community, desired by God with Israel, become righteous. Along with the central procedure of cultic expiation,[144] it is appropriate at least to mention the great area of cultic purity laws (Lev 11–15).[145] Here also broad religio-

---

140 Otto, *The Idea of the Holy*, especially chapters 4 and 6. For Otto, see e.g. Colpe, ed. *Discussion.*

141 Cf pp. 278ff.

142 Most recently especially Milgrom, *Ethics.*

143 See especially Haran, *Temples*; Milgrom, *Cult*; ibid., *Studies* and many others.

144 See below pp. 310ff.

145 See especially, Frymer-Kensky, *Pollution*; Milgrom, *System*; ibid., *Rationale*; in addtion to Paschen, *Rein*; Darling, *Levitical Code*; as well as the literature above in notes 136–140 for the dietary laws. There is an overview of the history of the research in Budd, *Holiness.*

historic and ethnological parallels have proven helpful.[146] In priestly language the pair of concepts clean/unclean have nothing to do with ethics or law.[147]

In many respects, unclean situations are not only unavoidable, but they are also commanded by God. Anything that has to do with genital discharge – ejaculation, blood, menstruation, birth – renders unclean, but even more so the touching of a corpse. Dead bodies and blood are the things that contaminate most, but they are in no way forbidden or discriminated against.[148] Finally, in its understanding of itself it is generally concerned with rules that are intended to enable the entirety of life without hindrance.[149] Ritual uncleanness only becomes "dangerous" when it comes in contact with holy things. The rules for the elimination of uncleanness (Lev 11–15) go out of effect at evening, with or without washing, and in even more cases through rituals of purification.

Israel, however, was not only to keep cultic-ritual rules in the presence of God, but also ethical-legal. The priestly writings are thus in line with older traditions.[150] Texts like Isa 6:5f. or the ethical conditions for access to the shrine in Ps 15 and 24 show that parallel requirements existed already in the preexilic shrine.[151] We can even discern earlier forms and traditions in the texts of the Holiness Code.[152] Preexilic legal texts are likewise positioned in God's cultic presence by the altar laws appearing at their outset. The notion that priestly thinking, once one component of many and now standing at the center is a new element in the priestly document. Basic differences in details are not as significant as they might be,[153] but are only variety in the way thought is expressed. Even justice, which is what this is about, is shaped by the "radioactivity" emanating from the God who is present.

The most important legal-historical innovation coming from this priestly assessment deals with the question of the applicability of the laws. Preexilic laws were always directed toward the free property owners.[154] Now the situation is quite different. The system of titles in the Holiness Code[155] recognizes only two classifications: The law applies either to the Israelites or to the priests, or both together. Israel is designated by the term "sons of Israel" (*bᵉnē yisrāʾēl*). This is a genealogical description. Especially in deuteronomic law, the groups of Israelites described by familial relations and whose God YHWH would be, are different. In priestly law all social distinctions based on ownership

---

146 See Henninger, article on Pureté; Toorn, *Pureté Rituelle*, and especially Douglas, *Reinheit*; for analysis in view of the Old Testament material, see Milgrom, *Ethics*.
147 See especially Hermisson, *Sprache* 84ff.
148 See especially Wright, *Two Types*.
149 See especially Milgrom, *Rationale*.
150 See e.g. Otto, *Kultus*; see also Ringgren, *Prophetical Conception*; Schilling, *Das Heilige*; Dommershausen, *Heiligkeit*; Kornfeld, *QDS*.
151 See Koch, *Tempeleinlassliturgien*; Steingrinsson, *Tor*; Beyerlin, *Heilsordnung*; Otto, *Kultus*; Hossfeld, *Nachlese* and others.
152 The literature listed above on p. 279 note 14 tried intensively to reconstruct earlier patterns and traditions.
153 See especially Cholwenski, *Heiligkeitsgesetz*.
154 See above pp. 167., 196., 219ff.
155 See above pp. 278f.

of land or legal freedom are gone. Nearness to God does not depend upon these things, so these things are equal under law for God.

Another distinction is strengthened by this point of view: between men and women. In the preexilic legal tradition, in accord with the patriarchal social structure and system of ownership of the time, men are addressed explicitly.[156] Of course the subjugation of the familiar power structures under public control effected by deuteronomic legislation had some consequences here.[157] Priestly thinking, however, strengthened patriarchal structures and reestablished them. Women did not have an especially good place in its systematic presentation of the nearness of God.[158] The court of women in the Jerusalem temple, placed between the court of the Israelite men and that of the gentiles, is an expression of this priestly point of view.

The legal norms found here are still thought-provoking today, "There shall be for you and the resident alien a single statute" (Num 15:15). This basic principle is emphatically formulated in the priestly texts more than once (Ex 12:49; Lev 24:22). Thus, considering the inclusion of all rights and all obligations, what applies to the alien – even the non-Israelite – is nothing less than what applies to Israel itself.[159] We cannot speak of proselytes in the later sense, as has often been done.[160] It is not so much conversion, not even a question of faith that is decisive for the priestly document, as elsewhere in postexilic literature.[161]

What is important is what is always central for priestly thinking: closeness to God. Within his "power field" rules are observed, they apply "objectively" like a high voltage power source. For that reason they could be no different for Israel than they are for anyone else. The question of circumcision cannot be of importance in any place where this power field of the "holy" is not in force.[162] It is no accident that with the priest–prophet Ezekiel, aliens receive a share in the land just as the Israelites themselves (Ez 47:22f.).

Here also theological thinking is not in complete unanimity with genealogical. It is always the people of Israel for whom the electing purpose of God applies. In preexilic Israelite law, it was not the Israel that could be understood geneaologically to whom Torah was entrusted, but the free land-owner, and it was these people that were subject to the law. In priestly thinking, God made Israel, the descendants of Abraham, into a nation, and he wanted to dwell in their midst. This presence of God, however, is described in a theology, in which, ultimately, the problem of the nearness of God broke apart all distinctions, not only between free and slave, but also between Israelite and non-Israelite.

156 For the problems, see above pp. 167., 219ff.
157 See above pp. 249ff.
158 In complete contrast to the other Old Testament texts and traditions, see Bird, *Place and Women*.
159 E.g. sacrifice (Lev 17:8; 22:18), passover (Num 9:14), sexual laws (Lev 18:26), prohibitions against Moloch (20:2). See Crüsemann, *Fremdenliebe* 22ff. as well as above pp. 184f.
160 E.g. Kellermann, article on *gūr* 988; especially Bertholet, *Stellung*. For proselytism, see above, the literature on p. 185 note 393.
161 We think especially of the Mishnah problem (Ezra 9f.; Neh 10:31; 13:23ff.; Mal 2:10ff.) which apparently is not soluble with religious adaptation.
162 See above p. 298 for the difference between Ex 12:43ff. and Num 9:14.

Max Weber observed an "increasing *theologization* of law" in the sequence of the collections of Israelite law from Book of the Covenant through Deuteronomy to the Holiness Code,[163] and many have accepted this view. Of course, we note something in this theologization quite significant for the history of law: a concept of equality before God and his law was developed within the process. Independent of their status, the law applied for land owner and wage earner, slave and free, rich and poor, even Israelite and non-Israelite. This was one of the presuppositions: people could hold fast to the will of God, even those who are exiled and have lost their rights.

Life with Guilt: Expiation and Forgiveness

It is possible to have a life in the presence of the holy God, as the priestly texts outline it in their Sinai pericope, only if sin and denial are immediately atoned for and forgiven. For that reason the removal of guilt guaranteed by God stands in the center of priestly cultic law. This is already observable in the spacial arrangement: It determines the furnishings of the holy of holies in the Sinai sanctuary. The holy of holies is not empty, as in fact it was in the postexilic temple, but there is a thing whose name comes from the word for cultic atonement (*kp*, pi.).[164] Because of this association, its name (*kappōret*) should be translated "monument of atonement"[165] or "atonement device."[166] God communicated with his people from this place. It, as nothing else, symbolized God's readiness to forgive and the fellowship between humanity and God.

This is a new accent in the history of legal texts. It represents a necessary consequence of the process of working through the exile and the guilt that led to it. Preexilic laws were theologically directed toward the protection of the gifts of God, freedom and residence in the land. To these great gifts of God, presumed by Torah tradition, the forgiveness which was institutionalized in the tradition is now added. There are clear indications that the priestly texts could reach back to more ancient, preexilic roots and traditions.[167] Of course it is impossible to reconstruct the preexilic theology of atonement, and it only achieved its postexilic state after significant changes.

In the face of a tremendous devaluation of even this feature of priestly theology in the wake of Wellhausen – as "human self-atonement"[168] – its new theological accessibility was an important step and a significant

---

163 Weber, *Judentum*.
164 See Lang, article on *kipper* and especially Janowski, *Sühne*.
165 Thus Janowski, *Sühne* 272; there 271ff. references to the tradition of translation (Luther: *Gnadenstuhl* "seat of grace").
166 Thus Utzschneider, *Heiligtum* 121; for the problem, see also de Tarragon, *Kapporet*.
167 Clearest is the ritual of Isa 6:6f. See now Hurovitz, *Isaiah's Impure Lips*. In contrast, sacrifices with an atoning function (Janowski, *Sühne* 177ff.) or "sin offerings" (Rendtorff, *Opfer* 62f.) are not demonstrable. We are left with literary-critical and tradition-historical analyses of the priestly texts (which at best provides hypothetical results) and religio-historical analogies. Still the most probable is an old tradition behind the ritual of the scapegoat in Lev 16, see below note 186. See the overview of the local surrounding traditions in Moraldi, *Espiazione*.
168 Thus Köhler, *Theologie* §52, for the entire Israelite cult.

achievement for Christian reception of the Old Testament.[169] Nevertheless, an intentionally narrow correlation with New Testament atonement theology has led to a partially problematic perception of the texts. This applies especially to the theory which identifies the sacrificial animal with the guilty person; the animal is supposed to die in the human's place, enabling a release of the life that is owed.[170] Everyone who tries to understand this must come to grips with the basic difference between atonement for the community and nation, and atonement for a guilty individual.

Sin Offering and the Day of Atonement: The Pardoned People

From the priestly perspective, it seems there was above all a long-time accumulation of guilt which finally unleashed the catastrophe of the exile. From this arise formulae such as those referring to the idea that the land, which has been made unclean, will vomit its residents out, as it had already done to the former residents (Lev 18:25, 28: 20:22). The notion is similar that "the land shall enjoy its sabbath years as long as it lies desolate, while you are in the land of your enemies; then shall the land rest, and enjoy its sabbath years. As long as it lies desolate . . ." (26:34f.).

In order to avoid this kind of heaping up of sin and impurity in the future, God himself prepares means of atonement. The most important is the blood of the sacrificial animal, and the correlation is formulated most precisely in Lev 17:11.

> *17:11 For the life [or, the soul] of the flesh is in the blood; and I have given it to you for making atonement for your lives [your souls] on the altar; for, as life [the soul], it is the blood that makes atonement.*

The renewed prohibition against any consumption of blood is based on this.[171] We are unable to discuss the details of priestly thinking here, exactly how the atoning power of blood is formulated, for example.[172] In all probability the concern is with a purification of the unclean shrine[173] and not of a person.[174] All notions of substitution by a sacrificial animal, dying in place of the person, are also inappropriate. Above all, the ritual of laying hands on the animal, upon which theories of transfer are based,

169 First, especially Koch, *Sühnanschauung*; ibid., *Sühne und Sündenvergebung*; then Rad, *Theology* I 276ff.; then Gese, *Sühne* and the expansion of his thesis in Janowski, *Sühne* especially pp. 350ff.; ibid., *Auflösung*.

170 Thus in conjunction with Gese, *Sühne*, especially Janowski, *Sühne* 220f. This thesis is connected with an interpretation (hardly tenable) of the hand gesture of laying hands on the head as an identification with the animal. For critique, see already Matthes, *Sühnegedanke*; see also Füglister, *Sühne durch Blut* 145f., as well as, especially Rendtorff, *Leviticus* 32ff. (excursus). In individual cases the sacrifice does not atone for crimes punishable by death, see below pp. 314ff.

171 For this text, see especially, Milgrom, *Prolegomenon*; Füglister, *Sühne durch Blut*; Schenker, *Zeichen des Blutes*; Janowski, *Sühne* 242ff.

172 In addition to the literature referred to in notes 169 and 171, see especially the relevant studies by Milgrom (*Cult and Conscience; Studies*), as well as Brichto, *Slaughter*; Levine, *Presence*; Kiuchi, *Purification Offering*. See the overview of the most important types of interpretation in Lang, article on *kipper* 308ff.

173 Thus especially Milgrom, *Israel's Sanctuary*.

174 Thus especially Zohar, *Repentance*. For a critique, see Milgrom, *Modus Operandi*.

cannot be interpreted in this way.[175] As deeply as atonement is connected with blood, this does not prevent the priestly author from connecting atonement, (e.g. when someone cannot afford the cost) with the flour offering (Lev 5:11–13).[176]

Above all, the "sin offering" (*ḥaṭṭāʾt*) described in Lev 4f. – or (for individuals) the "guilt offering" (*ʾāšām*) – had the function of atonement.[177] While for individual Israelites the provisions regarding procedure in sacrifices of this kind are extremely complex (Lev 4:27–5:26, compare for "rulers" in 4:22–26), the provisions for "anointed priests" (4:3–12), the "cultic representative(s) of the whole people"[178] (4:13–21) are not shaped by motives, circumstances and exceptions to the same degree. The special significance of these two sections of the law has already appeared; the so-called "major blood ritual" is practiced only with them.[179] In this ritual the blood of the sacrificial animal is sprinkled inside the tent shrine seven times against the curtain that hid the holy of holies (4:6, 17), while in the ritual for the individual Israelite the blood was only smeared on the horns of the altar of burnt offerings at the entrance of the tent of meeting (4:7, 18, 25, 30, 34; 5:9). Furthermore, the flesh of an atonement sacrifice may not be eaten, as it could be in other sacrifices (6:23), rather it should be burned outside the camp (6:30, cf 4:11f., 21). At the end of the law regarding the sin offering for the congregation,[180] we read: "The priest completes the atonement action for them and they shall be forgiven" (4:20).[181]

The goal of all priestly activity is formulated here: forgiveness. The passive voice shows a "passive of deity" quite clearly.[182] It is God himself who forgives and binds himself with the opportunity that he opened. This is human self-atonement in the same sense as it is in the "comfortable words" of forgiveness in Christian worship.

Sin offerings are made for particular occasions. They apply, as the superscription says, fundamentally for those who sin "unintentionally in any of YHWH's commandments, about things not to be done, and does any one of them" (Lev 4:2). The basic concern is that the act is commited unintentionally (*bišᵉgāgā*).[183] This automatically presumes that awareness of the sin occurs after the fact. We may associate the repeatedly used verb

---

175 See above note 170.
176 In contrast, Milgrom, *Graduated Hattāʾt*, would find here a special kind of sacrifice with its own impetus.
177 In what follows we will attempt with Milgrom, Kiuchi, Rendtorff and others to interpret the text presented in the framework of P, and thus not take it apart diachronically at the outset.
178 Rendtorff, *Leviticus* 152.
179 This terminology is used in conjunction with Gese, *Sühne*; Janowski, *Sühne* 222ff.; Rendtorff, *Leviticus* 159f.
180 The kind of conclusion is absent in the sin offering for the anointed priests. From this there is an important correlation with the ritual of the Day of Atonement in Lev 16 and its significance for the priests. See Kiuchi, *Purification Offering* 128, 156ff.; Rendtorff, *Leviticus* 159f.
181 Translation after Rendtorff, *Leviticus* 138.
182 See the overview of the formulations in Janowski, *Sühne* 250ff. For the figure of speech and its origin, see Machholz, *Passivum Divinum*, see the overview of *slḥ* in Göbel, *Vergebung*.
183 See below pp. 319ff.

'*āšēm* with this.[184] This probably also applies to the substantive regarding the priest's sin in verse 3 (cf 6:7), "So that the whole congregation is surely aware of his guilt."[185] Verses 13f. then speaks clearly: "If the whole congregation of Israel errs unintentionally and the matter escapes the notice of the assembly," this paraphrases the unintentionality, "and they become aware of their guilt, since the sins with which they have sinned have become known." We are dealing here, first, with transgressions of the commandments of God, of which the sinners themselves are unaware. We must remember the totality of cultic regulations formulated in the priestly writings. Unintentional infractions are, of course, not necessarily to be regarded as petty mistakes. On the contrary, since we are concerned with objective violations of sacral law, things that cannot be at all avoided, represent an especially significant danger.

Nevertheless, the remission of sin of which the sinner is at first unaware, becoming conscious of them, is not enough to guarantee a permanent existence near God. There is something at the center of priestly atonement theology, expressly dedicated to this subject: the Day of Atonement (*yōm hakkippūrim*). Only in the ritual of the Day of Atonement does the *central element*, the "atonement device" in the holy of holies, begin to function. Lev 16, a chapter whose significance is already indicated by its central position between the two complexes – the priestly purity laws (Lev 11–15) and the Holiness Code (Lev 17–26) deals with this.

In the center of the ritual (we are unable to give a detailed analysis of the ritual here),[186] we find the well-known ritual, in which two goats were a sin offering for the community. From verse 5 the subject is a sin offering (*ḥaṭṭā᾽t*), but one having an unusual character. It was a sin offering both for the officiating priest (3:11ff.) and also for the community. One of the goats was killed and its blood then sprinkled on the "mercy seat" (verses 14f.) in the Most Holy Place, the place of God's presence. In this way the sanctuary, which had been defiled through the people's uncleanness and transgression, was purified (verses 16ff.). It is clear that in this way the customary ritual of the sin offering, according to Lev 4, was enhanced and so virtually brought to a conclusion. Atonement having been made for the sanctuary and its equipment, all the sins of the people were confessed over the second goat and placed on his head, after which he

---

184 Thus Kiuchi, *Purification Offering* 31ff.; Rendtorff, *Leviticus* 152f., in addition to below p. 320.
185 Translation here and in the following in conjunction with Rendtorff, *Leviticus* 138.
186 Scholars have worked almost exclusively with reconstructed pre-forms of the text. See the analyses in Elliger, *Leviticus* 200ff.; Wefing, *Entsühnungsritual*; Aartun, *Versöhnungstag*; Janowski, *Sühne* 266ff.; Otto, *Fest* 70ff. and others. Certainly, we are dealing with traditions older than P. The ritual of of the goat for Azazel is in a certain tension with other theological concepts in P. There have been many attempts to trace the religio-historic lineage of the ritual and/or the name (considering a Canaanite background, see Tawil, '*Azazel*; Wyatt, *Atonement Theology*; Loretz, *Leberschau*; for an Egyptian background, see Görg, *Azazel*; for female deities, see Deiana, *Azazel*; for Hurrian or Hittite background, see Janowski, *Azazel* [literature], see already Landersdorfer, *Parallelen*). Nevertheless, the text should first be interpreted, even in its details, in conjunction with the entire P system, see especially Kiuchi, *Purification Offering* 143ff.

was driven into the wilderness. We are probably to interpret this as follows: the guilt of the nation that has been transferred to the priest is shifted from him on to the goat,[187] and is thus eliminated.

Several times it is stated emphatically in Lev 16 that with these rituals *all* sins of the nation are atoned for and eliminated. We read in verse 16 that the shrine should be atoned for, "because of the uncleanessess of the people of Israel, and because of their transgressions, all their sins." In verse 17 the action applies to "all the assembly of Israel," and according to verse 21 "all the iniquities of the people of Israel, and all their transgressions, all their sins" are confessed over the goat, and then the goat carries "all their iniquities to a barren region."[188] Yet again, verse 30 mentions that the Israelites are purified of all their sins. The same thing is repeated as a conclusion in verse 34. The statements use all the important terms for sin and blasphemy used in the Old Testament.

Of course, the restrictions of Lev 4:2 or 4:13 have been overcome. We are no longer dealing exclusively with sins committed unintentionally, this means all sin. There can be no doubt, on the basis of the overall view of priestly theology, that an annual, complete cleansing of the entire nation is what is intended. This is the only way that life can be led, in spite of a variety of sins, without threat from the righteous anger of God. This is the only way there can be a permanent coexistence of God and people, grounded in God's choice of Israel and the exodus.

Between Eradication and Forgiveness: The Guilty Individual

In so far as priestly atonement theology is connected with the pardoning of the entire nation, it speaks clearly. It is much more complicated, even partially self-contradictory regarding the guilt of the individual in Israel, nor have scholars resolved the issues.

Difficulties are already apparent in the structure of Lev 4f. Of course, first in 4:27–35 there is clear parallel to the previous sections regarding atonement for unintentional actions (verse 27). In chapter 5, however, there are apparently several competing structural principles.[189] There is the question of the object to be offered, including the possibility of a goat (4:28–31) or a sheep (4:32–35), for which, in cases of poverty, a bird or a flour offering may be substituted (5:7–10, 11–13). If we are, dealing here again with the "sin offering" (compare the same blood ritual, 4:25, 30, 34; 5:9), then 5:15f., 17–19, 20–26 is about a "guilt offering" (*'āšām*). In spite of remaining unclarity, this is probably also intended in 5:1–6.[190] This kind of sacrifice is not a blood rite, and its relation to the sin offering is loaded with many difficulties. We need only refer to the fact that there is practically no difference between the problems treated in 5:17 and those in 4:27ff.[191] Since ultimately Lev 5:16, 26 deals only with

187 For local factors and traditions, see Strobel, *Sündenbock-Ritual*.
188 After Kiuchi, *Purification Offering*.
189 See most recently, Rendtorff, *Leviticus* 143ff.
190 Thus e.g. Rendtorff, *Opfer* 209 and *passim*; otherwise Kiuchu, *Purification and Offering* 21.
191 It is unlikely that the latter is simply a continuation of the former as Milgrom, *Cult and Conscience* 74ff. suggests.

forgiveness obtained from God, we can avoid attempting to distinguish these.[192]

The sin offering of Lev 4:27ff. applies first to unintentional acts committed by individual Israelites. This does not continue what the superscription in 4:2 began, but rather it underscores what was stated in Num 15:22–31.[193] What applies for the congregation as a whole applies also to individuals: forgiveness for acts committed unwittingly can be gained by a sin offering (Num 15:28). Aliens are fully included (verse 29). What, however, Lev 4 only presumes, Num 15:30f. makes explicit: whoever acts "high-handedly" (*bᵉyād rāmā*) – in other words, "intentionally" – is "cut off" (*krt*, niph., verses 30f.)[194] from the nation.

Against this background, how are we to understand the cases described in Lev 5? Clearly, 5:2, 3 is dealing with unintentional sin (the handling of unclean people, animals or things remains "hidden" or "unwitting" – *neˤlam*); 5:4 (the rash oath),[195] in 5:15 (unintentional sin in holy things) and 5:17 (yet again a general formula for unwitting acts). Nevertheless, the problem in verse 1 is already a borderline case. It is fundamentally not a case of unwitting action, if someone listens to perjured testimony that is obviously harmful to someone else and does nothing about it, keeping what he or she knows to themselves.[196] The cases discussed in 5:20ff. dealing with perjury in cases of property crimes in sacral law, are quite clear.[197] As we know, especially from the Book of the Covenant, when there are no witnesses, competing property claims are decided by a sacral oath (Ex 22:7ff.).[198] Perjury of this kind, to one's own benefit, could hardly be unintentional.

Sin and guilt offerings deal generally with atonement for acts committed against God himself. Only in a few of the cases discussed (Lev 5:1, 4, 17, 21ff.; 19:20, 22) are other human beings sinned against. Property gained through perjury must be returned. The injured party should receive an additional 20 percent of the value of the goods involved. That fact that this is certainly less than the amount as given in the relevant passages of the Book of the Covenant,[199] shows that according to the priestly writings the legal settlement of the case achieved by the return of

---

192 See Schötz, *Schuld- und Sühneopfer*; Moraldi, *Espiazione* 138ff., 170ff.; see especially Rendtorff, *Opfer* 207ff, who reaches a diachronic explanation; otherwise, Snaith, *Sin and Offering*, and especially, Milgrom, *Cult and Conscience* 127f., according to whom *hattāᵓt* deals with cultic impurity, and *ᵓāšām* with profanation, most recently Schenker, *Unterschied* containing an attempt at a comprehensive system (121ff.).

193 For the relationship of these two texts, see Milgrom, *Two Pericopes*; see also Kellermann, *Sündopfergesetz*.

194 See below pp. 317f.

195 Spiro, *Law*, would connect verses 2–5 with the situation in verse 1.

196 Lev 19:20–22 may also be a borderline case, dealing with an act atoned for by guilt offering in which a person has intercourse with a slave woman who is already betrothed. In any case, it is not said whether or not her legal status was known to the perpetrator. For this, see Milgrom, *Betrothed Slave-Girl*; Schwarts, *Slave-Girl Pericope*.

197 Milgrom, *Cult and Conscience* 94ff. has shown that these are not in themselves just property offenses, but the problem lies with the oath (for that reason, simple theft is not mentioned); cf ibid., *Missing Thief*.

198 See above pp. 164.

199 For a detailed comparison, see Marx, *Sacrifice de Réparation*.

the goods and compensatory payment for atonement (and thus divine forgiveness) must take precedence.

The formulations of Num 5:6f. go an important step farther than the previously mentioned Num 5:6f. This likewise deals with atonement gained through a sacrifice.[200]

> *Num 5:6 When a man or a woman wrongs another,[201] and thus is unfaithful to YHWH, and the person is aware of the sin, 7 they shall confess the sin that they have committed and the person shall pay back what he owes to its full value and add to it one fifth, giving it to the person he wronged.*

After this, there are provisions for a situation in which the injured party might not have relatives. In that case payment is made to God "for the priest" (5:8). Most scholars regard this text as a close parallel to Lev 5:20ff.; it was simply amplified. The different formulation of the beginning is of special importance. The reference to a woman in addition to a man shows clearly that in all cases that deal with sin and/or guilt offerings, women are included. In these cases, they have complete capability of functioning in the cult.[202] Furthermore, it is incontrovertible that we are dealing with sins against people that as such are directed against God.

In my opinion, however, this does not particularly mean that the cases are the same as in Lev 5:20ff.[203] Num 5:6 says nothing about an oath that directly affects the relation with God, nor can we conclude this from the concept of "infidelity" (*ma'al*) to YHWH.[204] We are dealing rather with all property offenses settled by the return of goods plus additional damages. It is theologically important that they are all regarded as offenses against God. Unfortunately, under the regulations of Num 5:6ff., it is only hypothetically possible to classify, for example, also cases of physical injury (for which Lev 24:19f. applies the talion formula), since we have no explicit references.

To try to summarize this evidence: the individual Israelite finds atonement and forgiveness in cases of sacral offense committed unintentionally, as well as property offenses that are generally not unintentional, if return of the goods as well as payment of compensation to the victim has taken place.[205]

200 This is clearly shown by the reference to the atonement ram in verse 8.
201 Literally: The sins of/against people (*hattā't hā'ādām*). The interpretation as a subject genitive is generally accepted (see commentaries, Keil, Gray, Dillmann, Baentsch, Holzinger, Noth) and has the usual usage. Arguing for an objective genitive are (emphatically) Milgrom, *Cult and Conscience* 105 note 388, cf ibid., *Repentance* 53 note 18; as well as Ehrlich, *Randglossen* 123f.; cf Sturdy, *Numbers* 42. This would mean that *all* sins against people would simultaneously be sins against God.
202 See above pp. 250ff.
203 Thus almost all the commentaries, Keil, Baentsch, Dillmann, Holzinger and others, Noth, *Numbers* 43ff. supports it with a close connection to Lev 5:20ff.
204 As Milgrom, *Cult and Conscience* 106 does. See his understanding of the concept of the term ibid., 16ff. Nevertheless, the word or the priestly concept hardly allows itself to be interpreted so narrowly.
205 In saying this, we ignore many of the other occasions for sacrifice for atonement . See e.g. Ex 29, 30; Lev 8, 12, 14, 15; Num 6, 8.

For an overall picture of the priestly approach to the sins of individuals, we look now especially at the long list of cultic offenses, which include the penalty of being "cut off" (*krt*, niph.) from nation and family.[206] This applies to the cultic taboos of Lev 18, verse 29 indicates the penalty; Lev 20 prescribes the death penalty for these offenses. "Cutting off" is prescribed for the sacrifice to Molech (20:2–5), consultation of the dead (20:6), violation of passover (Num 9:13; Ex 12:15, 19, sabbath (Ex 31:14), Day of Atonement (Lev 23:29f.) and circumcision (Gen 17:14), for consumption of blood (Lev 7:27; 17:10, 24) or illegitimate sacrifice (Lev 17:4, 9), plus other violations of cultic regulations (Ex 30:33, 38; Lev 7:18, 20f., 25; 19:8; 22:3, 9; Num 4:18; 19:13, 20 as well as 15:30f.).

The formulations themselves speak of an activity of God, thus it is not possible to tell whether the intention is that the death penalty itself be carried out by the people.[207] The formulations of Lev 20:4f. may also be especially important for this. If the '*am hā'āreṣ* is not supposed to carry out the death penalty in a case of sacrifice to Molech, God himself will take care of the punishment. This may also apply at least for the cases that follow immediately: inquiry of the dead (20:6), sexual misconduct with the death penalty. How such "cutting off" is to happen is illustrated by the specimen narratives regarding offense against the divine name (Lev 24:1ff.) or the sabbath (Num 15:32ff.).

Num 16:22 describes what the priestly writings are dealing with in such "distancing" of the guilty from the community of the people: "O God, the God of the spirits of all flesh, shall one person sin and you become angry with the whole congregation?" Korah and his followers, who were the ones to whom this petition refers, were consequently "swallowed up" by the earth, and even before that, the congregation was supposed to keep away from them (verse 24). Separation from everyone who consciously or intentionally offends against the presence of God and his commandments is just as necessary for life in the presence of the holy as God's readiness to forgive. Since the sins of individuals affect the congregation as a whole (because their guilt and impurity consists of the sum of those individual sins), divine punishment for conscious offenses as well as atonement for the nation on the day of atonement is not directly self-contradictory.

It is, of course, remarkable that the basic principle in Num 15:30f., according to which atonement is assured only for unintentional sins, at least in the cases described in Lev 5:20ff., probably also appears in 5:1; 19:20ff. and Num 5:6f. For this reason, Milgrom would propose that even sins committed intentionally may be atoned for and forgiven.[208] The interpretation of later Judaism[209] is based on the priestly texts' self-understanding. Milgrom also refers to the significance of an acknowledgment of sin in cases where the transgression was intentional (Lev 5:1–4; 16:21; 26:40; Num 5:6f.).[210] For repentance and confession of sins, the persons who have committed the acts must first "feel themselves to

---

206 See Wold, *Kareth*.
207 See also the thoughts of Hasel, article on *kārat* 326.
208 See especially Milgrom, *Cult and Conscience* 104ff.
209 See below pp. 321f.
210 Milgrom, *Cult and Conscience* 108ff.

be guilty." This is how Milgrom would interpret the important verb
'*šm*.[211] The "high-handed" sins of Num 15:30f might for that reason
be those that are unrepented. All other acts, even wittingly committed
but later repented, would be included in the comprehensive formulation of Lev 16. The Day of Atonement also applies to sins of the individual.

It is unlikely, however, that this interpretation really fits the self-
understanding of the priestly texts. The disputed verb '*šm* cannot really
bear the weight. Milgrom also makes Lev 5:20ff. and Num 5:6, where we
are dealing with intentional infractions, into model situations for many
other cases. Breaking the basic rule of Num 15:30f., according to which
only unintentional sins can be atoned for, Lev 5:20ff. and Num 5:6f. have
discernible grounds. Once the door is open, however, it is possible to
annul cases of perjury in a sacral oath that are otherwise difficult.[212]
Above all, however, the possibility in these cases of a complete restitution
and compensation for the injured party must play a role. The fact that
these cases are treated in such detail means that we may not simply
generalize them. We find no example by which serious infractions of the
fundamental cultic order – especially for cases for which "cutting off" is
prescribed – can by confession and repentance be included among the
offenses covered by the comprehensive forgiveness of the Day of Atonement.

It is thus most likely, exegetically speaking, that the priestly writings
were aware of atonement for individuals only in cases of unintentional
sin (plus a few other offenses), for the sake of the preservation of the
nation. These include, above all, property offenses in which it is possible
to make restitution. In situations of conscious and/or intentional mis-
deeds, there was the expectation of a judgment, which would ultimately
be carried out by God himself.

Awareness of Guilt: The Revelation of Subjectivity
There is no formulation in the priestly writings indicating that God is
ready to forgive, as formulated in Ez 18:21, which permits the individual
to change at any time, even in serious, intentional offenses and even
enjoining such change. Since this is the case, is it then appropriate to say
that "forgiveness as justification of the godless . . . was unknown, even in
the postexilic period,"[213] and thus Torah required substantive
emendation by the witness of Christ? In view of texts like Ez 18 and Ps
103 this assertion, of course, cannot even be discussed in so generalized a
fashion. We can only deal with the questions of whether and how, in the
concrete cultic and legal statements of Torah, a guilty individual can have
access to God's readiness to forgive.

In order to gain a proper understanding, we must first have a clear
comprehension of the significance of the priestly distinction between
intentional and unintentional sins. It obviously appears in the thinking
of the priestly writings in the place where two fundamental ideas collide.

---

211 Milgrom, *Cult and Conscience* 3ff.
212 Thus Phillips, *Undetectable Offender*. He must, however, presume that Num 5:6f. is
     likewise dealing with a false sacral oath.
213 Thus Koch, *Sühne und Sündenvergebung* 232.

The one is, as it were, the objective side of the presence of the holy and the consequent necessity to observe regulations in order to avoid significant danger. The other is the understanding of this God as one who lives in Israel to atone and forgive, whose immediate presence is represented by the "monument of atonement" in the holy of holies. From this tension, the legal and theological historical significance of which cannot be overlooked, the classification and distinction between intentional-planned and unintentional-accidental acts grew outward from homicide to other areas of conduct. It grew out of the always objective, but also threatening character of the presence of God. A permanent closeness to God is possible only because at least unintentional – thus mainly unavoidable – offenses could find unlimited atonement and forgiveness.

What exactly does the priestly document mean by this distinction? How does it, unlike earlier attempts, establish clear conceptuality? The basic difference between intentional and unintentional acts[214] was first developed regarding homicide, and though the first attempts were tentative, as we have seen, there was not a fixed conceptuality and particular examples dominated.[215] Furthermore, we find summary and explanatory formulations in the priestly writings along with the examples or in their place.[216]

Above all, the fact that Num 35:11, 15 and Jos 20:3, 9 uses the term *šᵉgāgā* about the priesthood in cases of homicide, thus having a new conceptual understanding of the old difference, shows that we are dealing mainly with a corresponding formulation. The important word *šᵉgāgā* is connected with the verb *šgh*, the basic meaning of which is well-known.[217] It refers to something like the "going astray" of a herd (Ez 34:6), the "misleading" of a blind person (hiph. Deut 27:18, cf Job 12:16, Prov 28:10), but it is also used for sexual/erotic wandering (Prov 5:19f., 23). Thus, sins committed out of error or uncertainty are intended.

The opposite, according to Num 15:30f., is an action that is done with "high arm or high hand" (*bᵉyād rāmā*). This term is otherwise only attested in Ex 14:8 (P) and – probably dependent upon it – Num 33:3. Israel leaves Egypt with a raised arm. This is probably a gesture of spite, perhaps even threat. We are reminded of statues of gods represented with a raised hand.[218]

Attempts to get away from this kind of interpretation and to understand the concept more precisely, run into difficulties. We could hardly suggest that the offender was simply unaware of the *consequences* of the act. He quite probably knew very well what he had done.[219] The expression apparently is not directly related to the subjective frame of mind of the perpetrator, rather, the intent is to assert completely

214 For the large amount of biblical material, see Daube, *Error and Accident*; ibid., *Sin, Ignorance and forgiveness*. Unfortunately, Daube barely goes into specific priestly concepts.
215 See above pp. 174ff.
216 Lev 4:13; 5:2, 3, 4; especially 5:5, 17f.; Num 15:24.; 35:16ff.
217 See Knierim, article on *šgh*.
218 Thus Labuschagne, *bᵉyād rāmā*; Firmage and others, article on *rum* 427f.
219 Thus Milgrom, *Cultic šᵉgāgā* .

objective, legally ascertainable facts, as it did in the parallel regulations regarding homicide.[220]

Attempts to comprehend as precisely as possible what is intended are limited by a fundamental methodological problem. Here, as in other cases, we must investigate what is behind a refinement familiar to us but formulated historically much later. This means grasping a not yet completely refined (thus – in retrospect – not quite clear) conceptualization. This refinement in the priestly writings, of course, enabled later refinements; it even prompted them. It should not, however, be judged on the basis of them. Obvious cases such as entirely unavoidable situations causing someone to become unclean,[221] mistakes regarding prohibitions, lack of knowledge regarding rules, lack of self-control,[222] etc. are not distinguished. Perhaps typical statements like, "I didn't mean that," or "There was no intention . . ." in our daily life offer a certain parallel. Other central concepts remain essentially in dispute. Thus so important a verb as 'šm can be reproduced with "be/become guilty or culpable,"[223] or "feel oneself to be guilty,"[224] or "become aware of one's guilt."[225]

It is both clear and important that the priestly writings did not adopt other developments, though comparable in many respects, from their own period. We remember here the role of the "heart" in deuteronomic/ deuteronomistic theology. God's commandments, especially the first, are to be observed, "with all your heart, and with all your soul, and with all your might" (Deut 6:5; 30:14); they demand that Israel "circumcise your heart" (Deut 10:16; 30:6). According to Jeremiah, there was a promise to write the Torah "on their hearts" (31:33).

All these and similar phrases[226] are related to the problem of internalizing the norms of Torah; they are to be practiced from within. There is a reflection of the applicability of norms underlying this, which were certainly radicalized by the experience of failure in the exile. In response to this, the priestly writings formulated something more objective. They were dealing with a statement of the problem, developed in the area of law, with a view toward the objective presence of the holy. With it the subject is not involved with questions of applicability and obligation, but only with the experience of the inevitability of failure. This assessment of the process of becoming guilty itself, even if it is only dealing with objectively ascertainable facts, makes reflection on the subjective circumstances unavoidable.

---

220 Thus Knierim, article on *sgg* 871 as an emphatic critique of Milgrom; also Rendtorff, *Leviticus* 149f.

221 We think of the uncleanness involved with birth, Lev 12.

222 See e.g. Lev 5:4.

223 Thus e.g. Elliger, *Leviticus* 77f.; Kellermann, article on *'āšām*; Janowski, *Sühne* 256f.; Gesenius.

224 Milgrom, *Cult and Conscience* 7ff.

225 Kiuchi, *Purification Offering* 31ff.; Rendtorff, *Leviticus* 152f.

226 We are reminded, e.g. of the key concept of return (*šûb*) and its significance for the individual in Ez 18. On the basis of the fact that P, e.g. in Lev 5:20ff. does not mention return, Milgrom would conclude that P is older than the corresponding prophetic texts. Nevertheless, P is concerned with other aspects. Acknowledging an error is not the same thing as returning.

Quite obviously, the priestly writings did not only not formulate the far-reaching consequences of this step themselves – which is why it would be exegetically incorrect to ascribe the formulation to them – they were not able to penetrate them themselves. The priestly distinction between intentional and unintentional sins laid the foundation for the wide-ranging reflection on the problem of the awareness of guilt and on the question of what guilt actually is, which remains to this day unconcluded. With all reticence we would outline a few of the aspects:

– Within the context of the priestly writings, subjective aspects (for example, questions of the perpetrator's awareness) almost must necessarily be involved. The problem of whether and when an act is committed *biš^egāgā* must have led to the discovery and emergence of many intervening degrees of awareness. We should remember that the regulation is connected with commandments given by God (Lev 4:2 and elsewhere). Does ignorance or imprecise knowledge make an act unintentional? Or, when is an act "high-handed?" Does a person ever intend something after its consequences are apparent?

Milgrom's interpretation, that guilt and repentance for intentionally committed acts makes them unintentional,[227] may not be quite what the priestly authors wanted to express, but the tension between mistake and the mortal danger of being "cut off" is so great that it slants everything in one direction.

– This distinction necessarily reached a whole new dimension, at latest when the priestly law was joined with other Old Testament legal texts. Whatever was originally intended by YHWH's commands in Lev 4:2, this formulation certainly includes all of Torah, including the Book of the Covenant and Deuteronomy. In addition to the demand for obedience with "all your heart and all your soul," we find legal provisions which include the death penalty. If, according to later rabbinic tradition, the death penalty required evidence of a consciously intended act (requiring prior warning including reference to the consequences),[228] this view was an inescapable consequence of the entirety of Torah. In practical terms this meant that the death penalty was rarely possible, if ever.

– Rabbinic Judaism's interpretation of the texts, perhaps not Torah alone but the juxtaposition of Torah with prophetic writings in the larger canon (e.g. Ez 18), makes this conclusion unavoidable. According to this interpretation, there is a four-step path:[229] If a person transgresses against a commandment and then repents, that contrition suspends punishment, and the Day of Atonement brings expiation. If a person has committed sin meriting banishment or death, and that person repents, that contrition and the Day of

227 Milgrom, *Cult and Conscience* 123.
228 In mSan 5.1, tSan 11.1; bSan 40b and elsewhere.
229 See tYom 4(5), 6–8; jYom 8.1.45b; jSan 10.1.27c; jShevu 1.9(6)33b; bYom 86a; Mekh. Jithro. The following summary in close conjunction with Safrai, *Versöhnungstag* 43ff. (texts also in, e.g. Billerbeck I 636), see also Petuchowski, *Dialektik*; Magonet, *Versöhnungstag*.

Atonement set the punishment aside, and repentance ends the
wrong. Finally, in cases of intentional profanation of the divine name,
penitence and the Day of Atonement complete one-third of the
expiation, grief a second third, and grief with death the final third.

– There are problems of an awareness of guilt rooted here, including
modern problems of juridical culpability and the entire tradition of
Christian theological reflection upon guilt and repentance. For
example, when Paul says in Rom 7 that a person does not do the
good that he wants but does evil, this is not primarily dealing with a
break between God's commands in Torah and the power of sin as it
becomes apparent in human beings, rather it presents a meditation
on the relationship of conscious and unconscious activity with
respect to the commandments entirely within the context of Torah.
The evil that people do not intend, but which they do, according to
Torah is precisely that for which God guarantees expiation and
forgiveness.

Love of Neighbor and Its Context: A Summary

The Narrower Context: Love as Sum and Goal

It is the priestly law, which in Lev 19:18 formulates the command to
"love your neighbor." Of course, Christian exegetes have expended
much effort to play down its significance in the New Testament, and to
show that it is "restricted."[230] For the New Testament, however, love of
one's neighbor together with love of God is the essence of the whole
law. In general, the goal and fulfillment of the law is love (Matt 12:28ff.;
Rom 13:8ff.). We find complete support for such an understanding of
love as the sum of the ethical demands in Lev 19:18,[231] for in 19:11–18
there is a well-proportioned unity at the end of which stands the
command to love our neighbor, summarizing and surpassing all that has
come before.

> 11   You shall not steal;
>   you shall not deal falsely;
>   and you shall not deceive, a man his fellow man.[232]
>
> 12   You shall not swear falsely by my name,
>   profaning the name of your God:
>   I am YHWH.
>
> 13   You shall not defraud your neighbor;
>   you shall not steal;
>   and you shall not keep for yourselves the wages of a laborer until
>   morning.

230 See e.g. Stade, *Geschichte* 510 note 3; Bertholet, *Leviticus* 67f.; Elliger, *Leviticus*
     s259; in his own way also Maass, *Selbstliebe*. These judgments by "scholarship"
     adopt one of the banners of anti-semiticism (see Lehr, *Anti-semitismus* 29f.).
     Cohen, *Nächstenliebe*, for example, has disputed this attitude. For a Jewish
     apology, see also Kohler, *Nächstenliebe*; Maybaum, *Erklärung*; Jacob, *Auge um Auge*
     133ff.
231 For the following, see Mathys, *Liebe* 58ff.
232 This translation of ʿāmit in conjunction with Buber, *Weisung* 326.

14 *You shall not revile the deaf*
    or put a stumbling block before the blind;
    you shall fear your God:
    I am YHWH.

15 *You shall not render an unjust judgment;*
    you shall not be partial to the poor
    or defer to the great;
    with justice you shall judge your neighbor.

16 *You shall not go around as a slanderer among your people,*
    and you shall not profit by the blood of your neighbor:
    I am YHWH.

17 *You shall not hate in your heart any one of your kin;*
    you shall reprove your neighbor
    or you will incur guilt yourself.

18 *You shall not take vengeance or bear a grudge against any of your*
    people,
    but you shall love your neighbor as yourself.
    I am YHWH.

The passage is divided by the four-fold "I am YHWH" (*ᵃnī yhwh*) thus producing four strophes, the first containing five lines and the remainder six each. Most of the statements are commands, but the simple statements play a special role. There are no positive statements in the first strophe, only the last line of verse 12, "profaning the name of your God," lacks a "not" (*lᵓo*).[233] In contrast the second and third strophes each have a positive statement, which they emphasize in this special way.[234] The last contains two such statements.

The contents of the strophes are clearly graduated. Verse 11 deals with significant, obvious property offenses: theft, false dealings and deception. The prohibition against perjury (verse 12), by which God's name is dishonored, is connected to this theme (but not exclusively), because oaths had a special role in sacral judicial proceedings regarding property conflicts (Ex 22:7ff.; Lev 5:20ff.). The second half of verse 13 deals with provisions for the protection of the physically handicapped, those blind and deaf,[235] and for the wages of the day laborer. The phrases used at the beginning apply to those who are less able in business, people whom it is possible to oppress and/or rob (Mi 2:1f.; Jer 21:12; 22:3 and others). The third strophe, beginning with verses 15f., deals with behavior in court, where all[236] find justice. In this institution everyone

233 Mathys would also interpret this statement as a "generalizing" of verses 12 12a (*Liebe* 59).
234 Mathys, *Liebe* 70 regards these as emendations which make comprehensive, generalized statements about what preceded them. Is there, however, really compelling reason for them to be added to a previously existing structural unity from an earlier tradition? Of course, they do rework what is itself a combination of earlier traditions, but it is doubtful whether the earlier forms can be reconstructed.
235 See Gewalt, *Taube und Blinde*.
236 With Schwarz, *"Begünstige nicht"* the "lifting up of the countenance" of the weak could be a prohibition of discrimination against (not initially preference for).

had legal (or seemingly legal) means to cause the death of another person by slander.

The last strophe, verses 17f., deals with conflicts between "you" and other people. The perspective is probably not so much that of dealings with a guilty neighbor,[237] but, as the first line tells us, things that take place "in your heart" – we would probably say "in your head (or soul)." Concealed hatred ought to be replaced by reproof (Prov 28:23 and others).[238] There is a possibility that a person might harm another[239] through long harbored resentment or vengeance.[240] If what is commanded is ultimate love, what we have in reality was originally a command to love your enemies.[241] The positive formulation, however, is not just connected with themes that immediately precede it; conduct in business or social relationships is also included.

Thus, what the context causes to be emphasized, supports what we can tell about the meaning of "love."[242] This word, just as in English, can be understood in a variety of ways: *eros* and *agape*. It never means exclusively inner feelings, but always includes activity. It is important that the word appears in Assyrian official documents. We read in a contract from Assarhaddon (680–669 BCE), who admonishes his vassals, "If you do not love Assarhaddon . . . just as you love your (own) soul."[243]

The fact that this appears in the context of a treaty text, shows how little this has to do with feelings. Conduct that can be checked and tested is what Assarhaddon had in mind: loyalty of the kind that people generally want for themselves. Furthermore, in the unusual Hebrew construction where there is a dative (l^e) not an accusative – as we have in 1 Kg 5:15; 2 Chr 19:2 – we are not dealing with simply "loving." This is never used for relationships to God, to women (or men) or children; it refers to "loving assistance."[244] The intention is that we do all the good for our neighbor we would do for ourselves.[245]

Some find ostensible limitation of the Old Testament commandment especially in conjunction with the "neighbor,"[246] who is to be regarded as a "fellow citizen."[247] In fact, the word "neighbor" ($r\bar{e}^{a\varsigma}$) is parallel to

---

237 Thus Mathys, *Liebe* 63–77.
238 For the history of the intra-biblical reception, see Kugel, *Hidden Ground*.
239 In Lev 22:9 and Num 18:32 the expression should be understood in accord with this translation. See also Mathys, *Liebe* 65, against, e.g. Noth, *Leviticus* 160f.
240 The expression *ntr* is only otherwise employed in Jer 3:5, 12; Nah 1:2; Ps 103:9 and there is used of God. It apparently refers to a long held animosity.
241 Mathys, *Liebe* 81. He regards the expansion to love of aliens in Lev 19:34 as the development of a general command to love our neighbors. Nevertheless, in my opinion, the overall structure of verses 11–18 is conceived too much as a unity to be able to limit this "love" to the problems in the last strophe.
242 Mathys, *Liebe* 12f.
243 TUAT I.166, Matthys, *Liebe* 26. Further evidence for this kind of political custom in and outside the Old Testament in Matthys, *Liebe* 20ff.
244 See especially Malamat, *"You Shall Love Your Neighbor,"* see also Rücher, *Warum*; for similar theses in older literature, see Mathys, *Liebe* 4ff.
245 Buber's well-known interpretation and translation, "He is like you" (*Weisung* 326; see ibid., *Zwei Glaubensverweisen* 701; for the precedecessors Liebe 6f.) is philologically improbable. See Vriezen, *Bubers Auslegung*.
246 See above note 230.
247 Thus in reality, Elliger, *Leviticus* 259.

brother (*'āḥ*, verse 17), "fellow citizen" (*'āmīt*, verses 11, 15, 17) and the "sons of your people" (*b'nē 'ammekā*, verse 18). The entire section (Lev 19:11–18) is aimed at everyday life – relationships with the people with whom one lives. Special rules are also formulated for those whom one hates or against whom one has a grudge. Is this so different from the love of enemies in the New Testament?

There is still verses 33f. It seems the priestly writers anticipated nit-pickers by deliberately stretching the concept to include aliens (*gēr*). In order to protect the distance from the Christian interpretation, some say[248] that the people of God have been divided in the meantime. The complete legal equality of all aliens with Israelites as the priestly texts know it, however, is not at all dissolved, it is rather an important consequence of equal nearness to God.[249]

The Wider Context: Love as Portion and Aspect

If Lev 19:11–18 has much to do with the commandment of love, and it appears as the sum of our relationship to our neighbor, a glance at the larger context shows both the fact that when we concentrate upon God's will in the double command of love, something irreplaceable is lost, and has been lost for Christian ethics; and also why this happens.

If the traditional assessment of the commandment of love supports the connection, viewed from one side, yet when viewed from the other there appears to be no correlation in contents.

> 19:18 You shall love your neighbor as yourself:
> I am YHWH.
> 19 You shall keep my statutes!
> You shall not let your animals breed with a different kind;
> you shall not sow your field with two kinds of seed
> nor shall you put on a garment made of two different materials.

The break could hardly be greater with respect to feelings. On one side, a high point of biblical ethics and theological concentration, thus far unsurpassed: on the other, an unusual, incomprehensible[250] custom, which must at any rate be regarded as Jewish (if it did not come from profoundest heathendom).[251] At least it seems that verse 19 is of absolutely no relevance for Christian theology or modern ethics.

---

248 Elliger, *Leviticus* 259.
249 See above p. 309.
250 Unfortunately, neither here nor in the parallel Deut 22:9 are there references to the reasons or the concepts associated with this. One of the critical terms is probably an Egyptian loan-word (*ša'aṭnētz*, see Görg, *Textilbezeichnung*; KBL³ 1487). Naturally, such a distinction or creating-of-a-distinction is suggestive of priestly thinking and connections to the created orders of Gen 1 suggest themselves, see especially Houtman, *Forbidden Mixtures*. Is that, however, an adequate explanation? The connection drawn by Carmichael, *Forbidden Mixtures* to Gen 49:8ff. is rather imaginative. With Milgrom, *Consecration*, we should note that the fabric prohibited here is used in the holy of holies (Ex 23:1; 31), the high priest's clothing (28:6) and in the priest's "sash" (39:29). Thus, it was apparently something holy which the regular Israelites were only allowed to approximate (Num 5:38).
251 Thus Elliger, *Leviticus* 259.

The transition from verses 18 to 19 is the crudest in this chapter. Its themes seem to be a disordered jumble.[252] Scholars often note that they are unable to find a unified theme, or that they must force the material to achieve order.[253] Perhaps we can get the sense by reconstructing earlier documents.[254] Attempts to find the Decalogue underlying the text,[255] which are then classified as theologically important, are the high-point of a methodologically questionable activity in which form-critical observation is turned into a literary-critical principle, in fact, practically the only principle. It is a complete, methodologically systematized offense against the sense of the text. What in heaven's name do redactors think they are doing? They have made a total mess out of a beautifully constructed pattern. Did this happen all at once or in stages? What holds this text together is obviously a concept of holiness to which belongs such an interconnection of themes by subject-matter. For that reason, we can never grasp the sense by going behind the text.[256]

There is a clearly recognizable subdivision and classification of the material.[257] We refer first to the overall structure of the Holiness Code. The specifications in the superscriptions distinguish three groups of laws. One group is for the Israelites (Lev 18:1f.; 19:1f.; 20:1f.; 23:1f., 9f., 33f.; 24:1f.; 25:1f.) – thus the entire nation. Another group is for Aaron and his sons (21:1, 16f.; 22:1f.) – thus the priests. And finally, the third block is directed toward both groups together (17:1f.; 22:17f.). The last two texts frame three groups directed toward the people (18, 19, 20) or the priests (21:1–15, 16–24; 22:1–16). In this framework 17 is concerned with the offering of sacrifice and its location, and 22:17–33 with the condition of the sacrificial animals. The chapters directed toward Israel (18–20) are also framed. Chapter 18 deals with forbidden sexual relations, especially with female relatives, and chapter 20 contains provisions for capital offense wherein a larger part of the themes of chapter 18 are taken up again.

There is an essentially concentric arrangement of the many themes in Lev 19. We see clear chiastic parallels: conduct toward parents and elders (including the question of (ancestral) spirits in verses 3a, 31f.; sabbath (verses 3b, 30); relations with foreign deities (verses 4, 26b–29); animal sacrifice (5–8, 26a); and finally, regulations for planting and harvest (verses 9f., 23–25). The whole is framed by reference to the holy God and his action in the exodus, and the demand follows from these that Israel must act accordingly (verses 1f., 36b., 37). Now that we are aware that the

---

252 Noth, *Leviticus* 162f.
253 Thus Hoffmann, *Leviticus* II 27. Mathys, e.g. speaks of Lev 19 as one of the murkiest part(s) of the Old Testament (*Liebe* 71) using words like "irrationality" and "jumble" (72).
254 Research model in Mathys, *Liebe* 73ff.
255 See especially Elliger, *Leviticus* 245ff.; already Morgenstern, *Decalogue*; Mowinckel, *Geschichte*. Thus predecessors already in rabbinic exegesis, see Hoffmann, *Leviticus* II 28.
256 See, however, Jagersma, *Leviticus* 19 (and Mathys, *Liebe* who relies upon him) with the expressed warning about playing the themes off against each other or dividing them.
257 The material that follows incorporates material from Andrea Ruwe which he will support in detail in a planned dissertation on the Holiness Code.

subject of verse 19, made the center by the weighty introduction, "You shall keep my statutes,"[258] already has connections to the statements on planting and harvest in verses 9f., 13–15 (but because of the reference to animals, it is also related to verses 5–8, 26a where the discussion is about animal sacrifice), the chapter proves to be a well-ordered whole.

Verses 11–18, with their ethical instructions grouped around love for neighbors and the legislation in verses 20–22, should be regarded as interconnected. In the latter we have a quite complicated situation[259] where a slave woman (thus subordinate to her master), was already betrothed (thus legally a wife belonging to another man). If she were free, both parties would receive the death penalty (Lev 20:10). Of course, the case is viewed exclusively from the priestly (i.e. sacral-legal) perspective. This is a sin, which is to be expiated with a guilt offering. The death penalty is prevented for the woman who finds herself caught between two claims. The case shows that the process of developing new law on the basis of individual precedent cases (already noted in the Book of the Covenant and Deuteronomy) is continued. In its own way, the connection of verses 11–18 to 20–22 reflects the juxtaposition of casuistic legislation which at least touches upon judgments in precedent cases and ethical pronouncements unrelated to particular cases, which even in this connection retain the character of basic legal principles.[260]

Lev 19 contains the same breadth that the Old Testament law books had had since the development of the Book of the Covenant. It includes the relationship to the land, to its plants and animals, to other gods as well as love for neighbors and aliens, but the statutory regulations are of an extremely complex nature. All of this taken together constitutes behavior appropriate to the holiness of God. The reduction of biblical ethics to the double command of love goes back to the relationship with the world in all its breadth, formulated in the genesis of Torah. Finally, now as modern bio- and genetic technology approach what seemed like a harmless activity – mixing kinds (forbidden by Lev 19:19) – we see its terrifying dimensions, and Christian theology starts to see how absolutely necessary it is that we love our neighbors.

---

258 Thus with Elliger, *Leviticus* 244, who, however, draws no conclusions.
259 See Milgrom, *Slave Girl*; Schwartz, *Slave-Girl Pericope*.
260 See above pp. 194f.

8

❧

The Pentateuch as Torah:
The Way as Part of the Goal

There came a voice of revelation saying,
"These and those are words of the living God.".
Babylonian Talmud, *Erubin* 13b[1]

The Pentateuch as a Product of the Persian Period

Literary Presuppositions and Conceptual Self-Designation

The historical juxtaposition of the legal corpora in the Pentateuch are parts of one law of Moses. Codes criticizing previous laws, which they sought to replace, were combined with those laws into a single entity. The sequence of laws became a cooperation, and contradiction became cooperation. The path to the goal became part of the goal, in fact it basically became the goal, for little that was substantially new was added.

Frequently, portrayals of Israelite legal history ignore this, culminating with strata the authors believed to be latest.[2] It was, however, only by means of this step that Torah was developed, which then became the basis of the entirety of later Jewish legal history. It is only when we understand this process that we appreciate the text, which is the only starting point for a reconstruction of the history that precedes it.

Nevertheless, the process by which the Pentateuch as a whole was developed was apparently subordinate to other laws, which were in effect when the earlier legal texts came into existence. They all adopted and expanded the contents and important decisions of their predecessors, incorporating and editing more or less clearly identifiable documents. As in other legal corpora, however, the conception is, by and large, consistent, and its solution lay within the historical challenge presented. For the moment, however, repetitions and contradictions of the most egregious kind remain unresolved. That sort of thing seems almost a compositional principle of the Pentateuch.

---

1 See also jBer 1.7.3b.72–74. We are dealing with the conflict between the schools of Hillel and Shammai. Both interpretations are God's Word. Nevertheless, the halakha, i.e. the teaching to be followed, will be decided in accordance with Hillel's word. For the phenomenon of the voice of revelation (*bat qol*), see Kuhn, *Offenbarungsstimme.*

2 See e.g. Noth, *Gesetze*; Boecker, *Recht*: Patrick, *Law*; Martin-Achard, *Loi.* It is not atypical that Noth does not base his understanding of the law as "an absolute authority of the late period" in the Pentateuch, in which all of the texts and theological values exist which Noth emphasizes. Instead, he employs a rather vague authority.

In what follows we will investigate the historical circumstances, theological conception and legal meaning of this process and its consequences. As an introduction, here are the most important literary presuppositions on which this examination is based:

It is critical that we distinguish the overall form of the Pentateuch and its final redaction(s) from the priestly writings, which would contradict theories suggesting that we regard the development of the main priestly document (followed by a few less significant redactions) as the critical formative step for canonical Torah.[3] The following reasons are especially important:

- However we want to deal with the literary structure and scope of priestly writings (or of a priestly document), they do not include Deuteronomy. Why this great corpus was included, and in some way integrated into the priestly writings, is beyond the purview of this discussion. The juxtaposition of the two legal corpora, most significant in scope and influence, makes up the actual inner tension and thus also something of the "essence" of the Pentateuch. Its shape developed as they were brought together.

- On the other hand, the Pentateuch presumes that the books of Moses were separate from the Book of Joshua and the books associated with Joshua: Judges, Samuel and Kings. Some "finger prints," however, lead from the Pentateuch at least to Josh 24, which suggests earlier correlations.[4] Furthermore, we probably cannot deny the presence of part of the priestly texts or priestly redaction in Joshua.[5] It is, however, only the separation of the Book of Joshua that makes the Pentateuch an independent authority, the book of Torah.[6]

What is certainly true for Deuteronomy is also probably true for the Book of the Covenant and the Decalogue. For our purposes we need not deal with whether the priestly stratum incorporated and reshaped earlier narrative texts, and which these were. It is extremely unlikely that it presumed a comprehensive Sinai pericope including a theophany and the concluding of a covenant.[7] Because of the priestly conception Sinai became the central place of the proclamation of God's will. The markedly deuteronomistic construction of the Sinai pericope in Ex 19–24 incorporated the pre-priestly legal corpora. As a whole, however, it represented a post-priestly textual area that approximates or is part of the final redaction.

---

3 Thus Blum, *Pentateuch* 361. This affects his entire assessment. See also, e.g. Lohfink, *Priesterschrift*, who suggests that the investigation of the self-understanding of the Pentateuch is the same as for P.
4 See e.g. the correlation of Gen 33:19; 50:25f.; Ex 13:19; Josh 24:32ff. There are also connections between Gen 35:1ff. and Josh 24, among others. See Blum, *Vätergeschichte* 40f.; ibid., *Pentateuch* 363.
5 Against the generally accepted opinion of Noth, *Studien* 182ff. (see already Wellhausen, *Prolegomena* 356f.), most recently especially Lohfink, *Priesterschrift* 222ff. (especially note 30) and Blum, *Pentateuch* 224ff. emphatically referred to the correlations. See also Mowinckel, *Tetrateuch*; Peterson, *Priestly Material*; Blenkinsopp, *Structure*; Cortese, *Joshua* 13–21 among others. For an overview of the research, see Auld, *Joshua*.
6 See Freedman, *Formation of the Canon*.
7 See above pp. 46ff.

Thus the final form of the Pentateuch deals especially with a new way of combining older materials. Apart from the narratives, new legal materials amplifying the already extant corpora are only found in the Book of Numbers. Surprisingly, there were additional laws having a post-priestly character, which were given on the way through the desert. The innovations in content resemble what the previously described new codification had intended, but on another level.[8] We will not reconstruct the literary growth either here or for the non-priestly Sinai pericope, the problems are well-known. It is clear, however, that we must reckon on a longer coexistence of priestly and deuteronomistic strata (or their corresponding groups).

Let us begin with the question of the designation and therefore the self-understanding of this creation.[9] Thus far I have used the term "Torah" to describe the overall structure. To what degree is this justified? The question gets us directly into the old debate, whether the Pentateuch, as a whole, is narrative or law. There are great differences of opinion on this question, especially between Christianity and Judaism.[10] There are about equal amounts of both, weighed quantitatively,[11] and since neither term was used at that time, perhaps such an alternative is already misleading for our effort to comprehend how the Pentateuch understands itself. *Tora* means something different than history or law. Did, however, "the" or "a" concept of Torah, already present from the start, become the name of the whole once it had come into existence? For this there are more aspects to note.

As nearly as I can tell, there is only clear evidence for the use of the term Torah to describe the Pentateuch as a whole, including narrative portions, from the second century BCE. Thus, in Job 30:12 the narrative of Gen 34 is regarded as part of the "law." The law is introduced as the first part of the canon in the prolog to Jesus Sirach. For the period before this, including the late strata of the Old Testament itself, including the evidence in the books of Chronicles, Ezra and Nehemiah,[12] O. Eissfeldt's statement applies: "We cannot tell for sure whether this comprehensive use of this term already appears in the Old Testament, since the places under consideration can all be understood in such a way as to include only the legal parts (Ezr 10:3; 2 Chr 30:16; Neh 8:3; 2 Kg 14:6)."[13] The same is true of related expressions, such as "Book of Moses."

Against the background of earlier interpretations and especially the use as a technical term for priestly instruction, *tora* as we know became the most important concept for Deuteronomy and the will of God formulated in it (Deut 4:8, 44, etc.).[14] Of course, in many places this "book of Torah" contained references to history (especially the exodus) which

---

8 See below pp. 351ff., especially pp. 358ff.
9 For what follows, see Crüsemann, *Pentateuch als Tora.*
10 See Lohfink, *Priesterschrift* 213, cf de Pury/Römer, *Pentateuque* 67ff., Amsler, *Les Documents* 235ff.; for the overall problem, see also Cazelles, *Pentateuque.*
11 If we count the chapters (a very approximate assessment!), there are about 97 that are generally narrative and 90 chapters of laws. The decision is really arbitrary especially in Numbers (see Num 1–3 and the like).
12 See below p. 334.
13 Eissfeldt, *Einleitung* 206.
14 For the term, see Liedke/Peters, article on *tora* and see above pp. 1f.

appear in the context of the founding of many laws. Torah is later the most important concept for the law of Ezra, where we are unable to tell what shape it had.[15] Were we to ask whether the word *tōrā* might also designate narrative complexes, two texts might bear on the question, both originating in deuteronomic/deuteronomistic theology.

One text is Ps 78. In verse 1 the poet, employing wisdom language, describes what is to follow as "my Torah" (*tōrāti*). This includes, from verse 12, a generous historical narrative. Israel's history is an important part of wisdom instruction. Interestingly, the same thing is true of YHWH's Torah, mentioned in verses 5 and 10. "Witness and instruction" (*tōrā, 'ēdūt*), which God instituted in Israel (verse 5), are supposed to be handed down from fathers to sons (verses 5f.) with the intent that they would put their trust (*késel*) in God. Thus, the remembrance of historical acts (*ma'al*ᵉ*lē-'ēl*) and keeping the commandments (*miṣwōt*) are parallel (verse 7). In verse 10, the combination "covenant" (*b*ᵉ*rît*) and "*tōrā*" parallels verse 11 "deeds and marvels." If the narrative beginning in verse 12 (in which, as in nearly all historical summaries, the giving of the law is omitted) is understood as a concretization and demonstration of what was said in verses 5 and 10, the proclaiming of Torah will include history. Thus narrative and Torah should not be separated.[16]

Obviously, *tōrā* became a designation for history in Deut 1:5, "Beyond the Jordan in the land of Moab, Moses undertook to expound this law as follows." By means of the last word (*lēmōr*), the speech starting at verse 6 is designated as the beginning of Torah. Therefore, the first three chapters of Deuteronomy, a historical review, are clearly a part of Torah itself. This applies to the present text, independent of how we might explain its current state, or whether or not we regard it as a late emendation,[17] as most do, and independent of the meaning of the verb (*b'r*).[18]

From the evidence, we cannot tell for sure whether the word *tora* was the chief concept of the Pentateuch from the beginning, or whether the designation of the earlier Deuteronomy, the deuteronomistic, was expanded to the narrative portions, and only later became the name for the whole thing. The word *tōrā* clearly can designate the narrative portions and, what is even more important, there is no other term for the self-understanding of this gigantic work.[19] In summary, the evidence suggests that the redaction and canonization of the Pentateuch may have taken place without a name and a label for the whole concept, but it is improbable.

The Temporal and Historical Framework

When did the Pentateuch as we have it come into being? Of course, we must presume long literary processes. Such procedures have already been accepted regarding the growth within the priestly texts, and they

15 See above pp. 105f., and below pp. 337ff.
16 See Kraus, *Psalms* II 127f.
17 Thus Noth, *Studien* 28 note 1; Mittmann, *Deuteronomium* 13ff.; Preuss, *Deuteronomium* 84.
18 Mittmann, *Deuteronomium* 14f. would, on the basis of Deut 27:8, Hab 2:2, confer the meaning "to write, reduce to writing" on the verb *b'r*; nevertheless, see also Amsler, *Loi orale* 52 note 4; Perlitt, *Deuteronomium* 22f.
19 For *dat* see below pp. 337ff.

are also probable for the juxtaposition of priestly and deuteronomistic strata.[20] We are talking about the time when the great legal texts (Book of the Covenant, Deuteronomy, and the priestly writings) were brought together in a single document. Furthermore, this is the time at which the literary productive work on the Pentateuch came to an end. On the basis of the sources the two questions are inseparable.

The Pentateuch must have come into existence between the exile and the beginning of the hellenistic period – in other words, during the Persian period. This *terminus post quem* can be determined with certainty. In general scholars agree that such a work could not have existed during the exilic period. There are clear historical references, especially in the execration chapters of Deuteronomy and the priestly Holiness Code.[21] It is unanimously agreed that the deuteronomistic history was developed at that time, in which Deuteronomy formed a literary unity with Joshua through 2 Kings.[22] Even the priestly writings in their present form originated in the postexilic period.[23]

The end of productive literary work is much harder to fix and it is highly disputed. We can no longer refer to the separation from the Samaritans (who regarded only the Pentateuch as canonical scripture), which for a long time was regarded as important.[24] Of course, there was the building of the Samaritan temple on Mount Gerizim at the beginning of the hellenistic period,[25] but that still did not mean a definitive separation from Judaism.

The separation occurred at the time of the destruction of the temple by John Hyrcanus 129–128 BCE.[26] In spite of the long, common textual history and other arguments,[27] the question remains, whether it is likely, in view of the cultic schism that came about because of the construction of their own temple, that a canonical book would be adopted, which was developed after the split. It would be easier to imagine additional common textual history and other forms of mutual influence than the later adoption of a document originating after the separation.[28]

Other aspects, however, are more important. Today it is assumed that the Greek translation of the Pentateuch was made in the middle of the third century BCE.[29] Thus, in any case, it agrees with Pseudo-Aristeas. Such a translation, however, presupposes the conclusion and canonic validity.[30] This is supported by the fact that there is no evidence of hellenism or the disputes that came about with it in the

20 See above pp. 47ff., 280f., and below pp. 349ff. and elsewhere.
21 E.g. Deut 28:36, 68; Lev 26:33ff., 41ff.
22 For the discussions, see Kaiser, *Einleitung* 172ff.
23 See above pp. 282ff.
24 See especially, Purvis, *Samaritan Pentateuch*; Coggins, *Samaritans*.
25 See Kippenberg, *Garizim* 48ff.; Mor, *Samaritan History* 5ff.
26 See Kippenberg, *Garizim* 87ff.; Mor, *Samaritan History* 16.
27 Especially Purvis, *Samaritan Pentateuch* 98ff.; see also Tov, *Proto-Samaritan Texts* 398f.
28 With due caution, see also Tov, *Proto-Samaritan Texts* 3948f.
29 See Jellicoe, *Septuagint* 55; Brock, article on Bible translations 163; Hanhart, *Septuagintforschung* 4f.; ibid., *Bedeutung* 67; Dorival, *Septante* 56ff.; Tov, *Bibelübersetzungen* 134f.
30 See, e.g. Hanhart, *Bedeutung* 71ff.

Pentateuch.[31] All of this suggests that it is quite likely the Pentateuch was completed at the beginning of the hellenistic period, that is, the last third of the fourth century. It may have been the wide-ranging changes in the geo-political situation, with its unforeseen consequences for Judea and Judaism as a whole that – at latest – brought the redactional work to an end.

The Law of Ezra and the Authorization of the Kingdom

Rabbinical tradition regarded Ezra as a second Moses,[32] and since the beginnings of historical-critical research with Spinoza,[33] the relation of Pentateuch and the law of Ezra has been a key question for the development of Torah. We will now try to work out, in spite of gross unclarities, what can be regarded as reliable material about the historical Ezra.

For a long time scholars have been deeply divided over everything about Ezra.[34] Beginning with his dates, there is practically nothing over which there is consensus. The only available reference speaks of the seventh year of the reign of Artaxerxes (Ezr 7:7f.), nevertheless, this is neither clear nor uncontroverted.[35] If we associate this reference with Artaxerxes II, we arrive at the year 458, and if the third king of this name is intended, 398 BCE is the date. The important connection to the person and work of Nehemiah (who came to Jerusalem in 445 BCE) is questionable.[36] It is especially doubtful whether Ezr 7–10 or Neh 8–10 represent reliable sources. Furthermore, since it has been demonstrated that the order of the present form of the books of Ezra and Nehemiah is by no means secondary or accidental, but in every respect they have been consciously shaped, especially theologically,[37] the theory of a pre-chronistic[38] Ezra source is even less likely.[39]

31　For a possible exception in Num 24:24, see below pp. 347f.
32　See Kraft, *"Ezra" Materials*; for the rabbinical picture, see Munk, *Esra* as well as above pp. 105f.
33　Spinoza, *Traktat* 149ff. and elsewhere; for this, see Kraus, *Geschichte* 61ff.
34　There is an overview of the history of the research and the positions in Lebran, *Esragestalt*; there is a brief outline of the problems in Williamson, *Ezra*. See Widengren, *Persian Period*; Donner, *Geschichte* II 416ff.; Meier, *Zwischen den Testamenten*; Stern, *Persian Empire* for the period of the restoration; see also Koch, *Ezra*; Cross, *Reconstruction*. For the methodological problems raised by the sources, see Ackroyd, *Problems*. He draws an analogy from chess: "the movements of a limited number of pieces, themselves restricted as to mobility, are not unlike the moving to and fro the pieces in the Achameid period for Judah. But checkmate eludes us" (54).
35　See the overview in Kellermann, *Esradatierung*. Methodologically, all attempts to improve the number in Ezr 7:7 by emendation are fundamentally questionable; see Emerton, *Did Ezra Go* 1ff.; Williamson, *Ezra* 56. Gunneweg, *Esra* 126ff., e.g. regards the number as a purely theological construct and thus historically useless.
36　See the overview of the discussion of the relationship of both in Yamauchi, *Reverse Order*; Clines, *Ezra* 15ff. Doubt regarding the traditional dating of Nehemiah in Saley, *Date*.
37　Thus especially Gunneweg, *Interpretation*; ibid., *Esra* 28ff.; Eskenazi, *Age of Prose*; ibid., *Structure*; see also the discussion between Eskenazi, *Ezra-Nehemia* and Clines, *Force of the Text*.
38　We need not attempt to resolve here the much discussed question, whether Ezr/Neh were conceived with 1/2 Chr as a single literary work, or as two different authorities (Japhet, *Common Authorship*; Williamson, *Israel*; Thronveit, *Linguistic Analysis*; Tashir, *Reinvestigation*; Ackroyd, *Concept of Unity* among others). Of course we are dealing with chronicles by closely connected author (groups), but there are clear differences (most recently see especially Talmon, *Esra-Nehemia*).
39　See already the earlier critiques of Torrey, *Ezra Studies*; Hölscher, *Esra und Nehemia*; see especially Kapelrud, *Question of Authorship*; see also Noth, *Studien* 145ff.,

As with Meyer and Schaeder, we are still concerned with evaluating the Aramaic letter of Artaxerxes in Ezr 7:11–26.[40] According to the letter Ezra was assigned by the king to go with a group of exiles to Jerusalem, and there "to make inquiries about Judah and Jerusalem according to the law of your God, which is in your hand" (verse 14). In addition to being given a significant contribution from the court and the diaspora to the temple, they are granted the right to demand support from the state tax system in the trans-Euphrates satrapy (verses 21ff.); temple employees are declared free of taxes (verse 24). The important statements (in addition to verse 14) are in verses 25f.:

> Ezr 7:25 *"And you, Ezra, according to the God-given wisdom you possess, appoint magistrates and judges who may judge all the people in the province Beyond the River who know the laws of your God; and you shall teach those who do not know them. 26 All who will not obey the law of your God and of the king, let judgment be strictly executed on them, whether for death or for banishment or for imprisonment.*[41]

Is there a genuine Persian decree which underlies the entire Ezra story,[42] or is this decree an invention of the chronicler?[43] There really is not much unity in the text[44] and it is clearly written from a Jewish perspective.[45] The subordination of the entire satrapy of Trans-Euphrates[46] to the law of Israel is neither historically probable nor does the narrative, as it follows the decree, rely on its existence. The theory that Ezra or the Jewish people themselves wrote the document, having it approved at a later time,[47] is hardly tenable. All in all, arguments against genuineness seem to prevail today, but certainty is hard to achieve.

Of course, there are important references suggesting the text presumes historical reality and it aspires to the origin of that reality. That said, even critics who would regard the letter as a product of judaistic invention, the work, e.g. of someone like the chronicler, must simultaneously

---

Smitten, *Esra*. The thesis of a pre-chronist Ezra source (e.g. Ahlemann, *Esra-Quelle*; Mowinckel, *Studien III*; Rudolph, *Esra und Nehemia* XXIV; most recently – with care – Williamson, *Ezra-Nehemiah* XXVIIIff., as well as Daniels, *Composition*) is difficult to support.

40 Lebram, *Esragestalt* 117, with reference to Meyer, *Entstehung* and Schaeder, *Esra*, both of whom assess the genuineness of the Aramean document.

41 Translation in conjunction with Gunneweg, *Esra* 128.

42 Thus Meyer, *Entstehung* 60ff.; Noth, *Studien* 145ff.; Galling, *Bagoas* 165ff.; Cazelles, *Mission*; Kellermann, *Nehemia* 60ff.; Smitten, *Esra* 11ff.; Clines, *Ezra* 102ff.; Williamson, *Ezra/Nehemiah* 98ff.; Donner, *Geschichte* II 426ff.; Blenkinsopp, *Ezra* 146f. There are only allusions to the questions: which parts are genuine or where was emendation done?

43 See most recently Gunneweg, *Esra* 129ff.; Lebram, *Esragestalt* 117ff.; Becker, *Esra/Nehemia* 43ff.

44 See especially the other addresses in verses 21–24. Here as elsewhere scholars presume literary work.

45 Especially Gunneweg, *Esra* 129ff.; Lebram, *Esragestalt* 117ff.

46 For this great fifth satrapy, see e.g. Donner, *Geschichte* II 297ff.; Dandamaev/Lukonin, *Ancient Iran* 948ff.; and especially Rainey, *Satrapy*.

47 Already Meyer, *Entstehung* 65.

acknowledge that it asserts a kernel of historical reality.[48] Thus, on the
one hand, Kaiser says, "We must acknowledge that we have an edifying
story in the Book of Ezra,"[49] regarding which, "we are better off avoiding
a historical evaluation of this text."[50] On the other hand, the same author
says: "We might now regard the historical value of the Ezra narrative as
more or less believable, and as a result, regard Ezra to be the man who
brought the Pentateuch from Babylon to Jerusalem ... but we must
assume that the Pentateuch, *at latest at the turn of the 5th/4th centuries*, was
essentially *complete*, and in the course of the next century achieved its
unequalled place of honor. This is the only way the origin of the Ezra
narrative is comprehensible."[51] Even an unhistorical aetiology can
describe what is real!

Gunneweg is of a similar opinion in his commentary of the Book of
Ezra. After thorough testing of the arguments, he too comes to the
opinion that Ezr 7:12–26 does not represent an original document of
the Persian government, but rather "a Jewish text and a component
of the chronicler's narrative." Nevertheless, according to Gunneweg,
we should not doubt the core of the material is historical. "Historically –
that is, in the sense of the harsh reality – ... the legal position of the
postexilic Jewish community was centered in Judah and Jerusalem but
also outside the narrower homeland. It was characteristic that the
Persians recognized traditional law, but they also declared it to be legally
binding."[52]

The conception of the decree of Artaxerxes, which at first seems purely
theological, "proves to be an aetiology of the autonomous Jewish community around the temple and synagogue based in law and synagogal
jurisdiction.[53] Thus, it can also be said: "If the chronicler associates
Persian recognition of Torah with the person of Ezra, it may indeed be
that Ezra was involved in this area."[54]

While skeptical about the Artaxerxes decree, we must accept the
important statement in Ezr 7:25, which equates the laws of God and of
the Persian king as both legally applicable and juridically binding. There
was a policy of the Persian empire, known today from a whole series of

---

48 Lebram, especially, represents an exception. He regards the entire Ezra stratum of
    the books of Ezra and Nehemiah to be the product of the period after 180 BCE
    (*Esragestalt* 126ff.). It is a "critique of a radical group, faithful to the law, against
    the temple theocracy of the Hasmoneans" (131); behind it is "the pharisee's
    demand to recognize the law of Moses as the constitution of Jerusalem" (132). The
    historical Ezra is perhaps, according to Neh 12:1, 13 and Ezr 4 a figure of the exilic
    period. A late dating of this kind for clearly chronistic texts is improbable; the
    usual placement between 400 and 200 might be hard to dispute. Lebram supports
    his position exclusively on the fact that in Jesus Sirach, in contrast to Nehemiah
    (49:13), is passed over in silence, presuming that such a figure was unknown. The
    remark-able situation can be explained in other ways – e.g. that Jesus Sirach was
    interested in construction (thus Begg, *Non-mention*; see also, e.g. Höffken, *Warum
    schweigt*).
49 Kaiser, *Einleitung* 181.
50 Kaiser, 181f.; The statement is made in relation to the lists in the Book of Ezra.
51 Kaiser, 407 where the arguments of pp. 179–183 are summarized.
52 Gunneweg, *Esra* 140.
53 Gunneweg, *Esra* 139.
54 Gunneweg, *Esra* 141.

examples, which sanctioned local law through the empire, recognizing it as binding.[55] The best known example of these is the collecting and codifying of Egyptian law which remained in effect under Darius I.[56] Another important example is what is fixed in the trilingual stele from the Letoön at Xanthos, bearing resolutions of the congregation of Xanthos affecting the cult of Carian gods.[57] After studying the relevant texts, P. Frei categorized "the process of recognition of local norms by authorities of the empire "as state authorization."[58]

The same thing is also largely true for Israel: Israelite law, thus the traditional law of the God of Israel, simultaneously became the law of the Persian empire for Jews: according to Ezr 7:25, for all who live in the satrapy of Syria.[59] This situation, wherein the Persian government recognized the existing written law, is presumed to have been the case on the basis of what we know about the features of Persian policy, according to all of the Old Testament sources and especially according to the further history of the hellenistic period.[60] The Ezra story with the edict of Artaxerxes at its center is the aetiology of this policy. Historical particulars are not especially enlightening but it is historically probable that this event was connected with a person named Ezra.

The main question remains: how did a law, coming into force in this way, relate to the Pentateuch? Scholars have investigated every conceivable possibility to identify the law of Ezra. It may, e.g. have been the Pentateuch, the priestly writings, the Holiness Code or even Deuteronomy.[61] Convincing support for a particular answer is, however, hard to find.

It is, of course, expressly said that this is a new law, but in principle the inhabitants already knew the contents (Ezr 7:25). The nature of empire authorization makes this seem plausible. Furthermore, the chroniclers were probably already thinking of the Pentateuch,[62] but were writing at a much later time. If we cannot identify the law of Ezra according to the evidence we have, we ought not to speculate.

---

55 See especially Frei, *Zentralgewalt*. For the so-called Persian policy of tolerance and the great religious and legal variety there, see e.g. Donner, *Geschichte* II 392ff.; Dandamaev/Lukonin, *Ancient Iran* 116ff.; Briant, *Pouvoir central* 3ff.; ibid., *Polytheismes*. Koch, *Weltordnung*, has attempted to describe the religio-historic background for this openness.

56 Spiegelberg, *Chronik*; for this, see Reich, *Codification*; Dandamaev/Lukonin, *Ancient Iran* 125.

57 Metzger, among others, *Fouilles de Xanthos*; see Frei, *Zentralgewalt* 12ff.

58 Frei, *Zentralgewalt* 13. See Kippenberg, *Erlösungsreligionen* 181f., who would rather speak of "sanctioning by the empire."

59 See Blum, *Pentateuch* 345ff.

60 See especially *Kippenberg*, Erlösungsreligionen 183ff.

61 See the overview in Kellermann, *Esragesetz*. Presuming an early dating of Ezra, before Nehemiah, he comes to the conclusion that this was Deuteronomy (381ff.); he furthermore thinks that the document could have contained exclusively the legal texts. This thesis has now been adopted by Kippenber, *Erlösungsreligionen* 127ff. This raises the significant question how the entire Pentateuch might have come out of this. That would presuppose a great change in the relationships.

62 See below, pp. 341ff.

Is there a correlation of the law of Ezra with the Pentateuch? This is especially disputed by Rendtorff.[63] He refers to fundamental differences between the law in Ezr 7, designated with a Persian loan word (*dāt*), and what is called *tōrā* in Neh 8, saying that these must be kept separate. In Ezr 7 we are concerned with a law that "has a purely legal meaning."[64] On the other hand, Neh 8 describes Ezra's activity entirely as reading Torah in worship.[65] He was "the first of whom it could be said that he studied and taught *tora*."[66]

Both activities were brought together in later redactional processes, especially in Ezr 7:6. Rendtorff is surely correct to note that Ezr 7:12ff. and Neh 8 present different perspectives, different languages, and probably also different literary documents, which were brought together at a later time. Nevertheless, even for Rendtorff they are bracketed together in the picture presented for example in Ezr 7:6, if I understand correctly.[67]

Still, the exposition of the word *dāt* is not entirely convincing.[68] To be sure, *dāt* is probably really "not a specific designation for Jewish religion or Jewish 'law'."[69] We would not argue, however, that it becomes a designation even for those in important places. If we read in Esth 3:8 regarding Israel, "their laws (*dātēhem*) are different from those of every other people, and they do not keep the king's laws (*dātē hammélek*)," *dātēhem* can only refer to the law of Israel, in other words *tora*, which raises questions about the meaning of the law of God and the law of the king in Ezr 7. In Dan 6:6 the "law of God" (*dāt ᵉlālēh*) can only refer to Torah. What Aramaic word would be a better equivalent to *tōrā* than *dāt*? The only other candidate might be *dīn*.[70] In later legal language *dāt* as well as *dīn* is used in aramaic phrases like "the law of Moses and Israel" in marriage contracts.[71] Thus, there is nothing to dispute the idea that *dāt* in Ezr 7:12ff. can also refer to Torah.

Analogous situations of authorization by the Persian empire are not limited to legal procedures in the narrow sense. Clearly, at least cultic (thus religious) questions are a part of this. No matter what we want to call the law of Ezra, since it deals with older, already traditional Israelite law (this is one of the few points over which there is no controversy), it *could not* have involved legal matters only. Already in the Book of the Covenant alongside legal requirements in the strictest sense there are

---

63 Houtman, *Ezra* also contests any correlation between the law of Ezra and the Pentateuch because a few laws in Ezra/Nehemiah have no parallel in the Pentateuch. For a critique, see Williamson, *Ezra* 93, who points out the exegetical methods which underlie the the variants. For the central text, see below, Neh 10; see below 395ff.

64 Rendtorff, *Esra* 183, where the arguments of 169–173 are summarized.

65 See also Wahl, *Grundelemente*.

66 Rendtorff, *Esra* 183.

67 Rendtorff, *Esra* 183.

68 For the following critique, see also Williamson, *Ezra* 92f.; Kratz, *Translatio Imperii* 228ff.

69 Rendtorff, *Esra* 168.

70 The usual word in Targum *'ōrāyetā* (see Jastrow, *Dictionary* 34) is only attested much later.

71 For *dāt* see tKet 4.9; see Beyer, *Die aramäischen Texte* 325; for *dīn* see the marriage contract from Wadi Murabba'at, *Beyer* 309.

cultic, religious, theological and ethical demands together with their justification. This is true for later Israelite law books up through the Pentateuch. To posit a legal document, similar to ancient Near Eastern law books, underlying the law of Ezra would contradict the entire history of Israelite law. It is in the decree of Artaxerxes of Ezra 7, in the midst of dealing with the Jerusalem temple and cult, that we find a subject dealing with the contents of *dāt*.

Thus it follows that we are unable to conclude even the shape of the law of Ezra, the date of Ezra's investiture or his activity from the sources. How ever this law might have looked, how much it was like the finished Pentateuch; it was out of this law that what we know as the Pentateuch developed somewhere near the end of the Persian period. This and already its pre-forms, as the law of the God of Israel, were simultaneously established as law by the Persian king. "What was in legal substance . . . the law of God, was in legal form the law of the state."[72]

In my opinion, we can come to irrefutable conclusions regarding our understanding of Torah without giving fundamentally unsupportable answers to the many controverted questions about Ezra and his law. From this understanding we can draw conclusions for the following interpretation of the Pentateuch as a whole.

The Pentateuch in the Social-Political Field: Supporting Groups and Tendencies

In what follows we will attempt to grasp the social context in which the Pentateuch achieved its final form. Indeed, on the basis of our limited knowledge of the historical context, it is a question of dealing with the elementary observations and reflections made about the social-political role and function of the Pentateuch during the Persian period, which ought to supplement what has been said about Moses and his significance.[73] Methodologically, we will connect the final form of the Pentateuch with the most important, clearly discernible political and social powers. Unlike the issue of historical sequence, we have a clearly reliable source: the memoir of Nehemiah. In Neh 1:1–7:5abα, 12*, 13* (over which scholars are almost entirely in agreement), we have an authentic report of Nehemiah.[74] Certainly, the text reproduces only a

---

72 Gunneweg, *Esra* 138. For this first step in the development of the canon, see also Kratz, *Translatio Imperii* 233ff.; Steck, *Kanon* 236ff.; ibid., *Abschluss der Prophetie* 13ff.

73 See above pp. 102ff.

74 See especially Kellermann, *Nehemia*, who considers 1:1–7:5abα: 12:27aα, 31f., 37–40; 13:4, 5aα, 6a, 7abα, 6a, 7abα, 8–10bα, 11–21, 22b, 23a, 24a, 25–31 part of the original Nehemiah document (in summary, p. 55f.). The further discussion has been based upon this, frequently only criticizing in details, see e.g. Williamson, *Ezra/Nehemiah* XXIVff.; Blenkinsopp, *Ezra* 46 among others; see also Kaiser, *Einleitung* 182 note 15 (with a "fine analysis" that is methodologically hardly tenable). Gunneweg also speaks of an "incontrovertible, authentic, draft by Nehemiah" (*Nehemia* 176), the basic elements of which can no longer be ascertained in detail (178f.) because of chronistic redaction. In view of this discussion, the general thesis that the document goes back to the chronicler and is in no place authentic (Becker, *Esra/Nehemia* 8), is hardly tenable.

brief glimpse from the end of the second third of the fifth century, and this from a subjective point of view.[75] Nevertheless, we can see the basic historical pattern, it had not altered dramatically before the change to hellenism.

Those in Debt and the Priests: The Social Coalition

According to Nehemiah's memoir and other contemporary sources, e.g. the Book of Malachi, there were two observable, fundamental conflicts within the population of the small province of Judah, which was a sub-unit of the Trans-Euphrates satrapy.[76] The one was the common, ancient antagonism, already so important during the preexilic period) between the indebted small farmers and their richer creditors. In Neh 5 the opposition came to a head, because of the compulsory construction of the wall.[77] Nehemiah was able to enact an initially "one-off" remission of debts. It is clear that special circumstances like the political necessity to complete the work on the wall, the pressure of the population and their strike, as well as his influence as the Persian governor (*peḥā*) permitted him to prompt the aristocrats to take such a step.

On the other hand, there were the very different interests of the laity, especially the less consequential, agricultural population, and the cult personnel consisting of priests and Levites in the Jerusalem temple. Their material support, which relied especially upon the offering of the tithe, was always in danger (Neh 3:10ff.; Mal 3:8). This was also true for permanent support for the entire temple cult. The lack of wood for the permanent sacrificial fire (Lev 6:12) indicates the obvious difficulties (Neh 10:35; 13:31). The extremely poor province with its enormous economic problems stood at the limits of survival.

In view of these two basic conflicts, the Pentateuch and its laws have a very clear purpose. There were the large number of priestly laws imposing the regular tithe on priests and laity (Num 18), which also obligate the offering of firstfruits (firstborn, etc.) for all Israelites. On the other hand there were the social laws in the Book of the Covenant and Deuteronomy, such as the prohibition against charging interest (Ex 22:24; Deut 23:20; cf Lev 25:36ff.); regular remission of debts (Deut 15:1ff.); manumission of slaves (Ex 21:2ff.; Deut 15:12ff.); slave asylum (Deut 23:16f.); and general protection for the weak in society. It was especially the connection of older, preexilic laws with the priestly, which enabled a clear connection to the social nexus in the province of Judah during the Persian period. It was not just the priestly laws that dominated during this period, as was presumed to be the case for a long time after Wellhausen. The significance of the coexistence of differing traditions is recognizable right here.

One document clearly underscores this trend: the agreement in Neh 10 to observe a series of actually important laws from Torah. According to the covenant, the people entered a written obligation agreeing to observe the following ten requirements:

75 This is emphasized by Clines, *Nehemiah Memoir*. "Nehemiah is a liar" (125).
76 For the borders and the history, see below pp. 348f.
77 See especially Kippenberg, *Religion und Klassenbildung* 55f.

1. No mixed marriages (v. 31);
2. Sabbath (v. 32a);
4. The offering of a third of a shekel, as a yearly temple tax for the bread of the Presence, as well as for regular public sacrifice, including sin offering (*haṭṭāʾōt*) for the people (vv. 33–34);
5. The regular contribution of wood for the temple (v. 35);
6. Firstfruits (v. 36);
7. Firstborn (v. 37);
8. A regular contribution of dough, fruit, wine and oil (v. 38a);
9. Tithe (vv. 38b–40);
10. Regular care for the temple (v. 40b).

This is the earliest extant document of a detailed explication of Torah. There is much to suggest that it originates from a time when the text of the Pentateuch was not yet in its final canonic form. Thus, the requirement of a regular temple tax in the form of a third of a shekel is only attested here. On the other hand, in Ex 30:11ff.; 38:25f. reference is made to a half shekel tax, and the later Jewish temple tax supports it on this mention of an, initially "one-off", levy.[78] General considerations argue that the higher offering represents the later version.[79] Scholars are divided whether Neh 10 is a pre-Chronicler document, of about the time of Nehemiah[80] or not.[81] Since the text has clear connections to the problems of the Nehemiah memoir, especially Neh 13, but other themes also appear,[82] it is frequently regarded as a later document.[83] Reference to a remission of debt in the seventh year (10:32b) is only connected to Neh 5, but rather than being unique, this is to be a regular payment. The solemn form of the written personal obligation, which parallels the "we" style of the text, is especially noteworthy (10:1, 13).[84] This is noteworthy because it is not just the authority of God but also that of the Persian king behind the law. Does this, as Gunneweg suggests,[85] reflect the transition to the hellenistic period? Still, all questions of dating can and should remain open.

78 See Liver, *Ransom*; for the later Jewish practice, see e.g. also Safria, *Wallfahrt* 70f. and elsewhere.
79 Thus Blenkinsopp, *Ezra/Nehemiah* 76; Rudolph, *Esra* 178; considers a possible change in the system of measurement Williamson, *Ezra/Nehemiah* 325f. (with Clines, *Nehemiah* 10) theorizes a dependency upon the exodus passages.
80 Thus e.g. Bertholet, *Esra* 76; Rudolph, *Esra* 172ff.; Galling, *Chronik* 242; Jepsen, *Neh 10* 98ff. (see also 100ff.) who allows the question whether this is a literary fiction or a document of post-Nehemiah origin, to remain open.
81 Thus e.g. Hölscher, *Esra* 545; Gunneweg, *Nehemiah* 131ff., 135ff.
82 Indeed six themes are attested in Neh 13 (tithe 13:10ff., temple care 13:11, sabbath 13:15ff., marriage 13:23, wood 13:31, firstfruits 13:31), regarding forgiveness of debts it is comparable to Neh 5. The temple tax firstborn and priestly offering are entirely absent.
83 See the thoughts of Kellermann, *Nehemia* 39ff., however, see also Williamson, *Ezra/ Nehemiah* 330f.
84 The long list of names interrupts the complete sentence verses 1, 30b and for that reason has been regarded as an insertion (with many others, Williamson, *Ezra* 27). The question of its origin (e.g. Jepsen, *Nehemia* 10) can remain entirely unresolved here.
85 Gunneweg, *Nehemia* 131f.

Quite apart from how old we regard this text as being, it is the oldest outside the Pentateuch to identify divine law as a *combination* of all the great law texts. The incorporation of important priestly texts such as the law of the tithe in Num 18 and the priestly conception of offering (sin offering) is incontrovertible. The obligation to guarantee remission of debts in the seventh year, as we find it in Neh 10:32b, clearly contradicts the ideas of Lev 25 and adopts Deut 15:1ff. The renunciation of profit from harvest, also occurring in that year, is not found in Deut 15, coming, as shown by the term "renounce, hand over" (*nṭš*), not from Lev 25:1–7, but from Ex 23:11, the Book of the Covenant. In the Ezra–Nehemiah period, the much disputed question of mixed marriage, which verse 30 places at the head of the provisions, is an activation, necessitated by the exile, of Ex 34:16, Deut 7:3; [86] and in this radicality it has no basis in the priestly texts.[87] The Book of the Covenant, Deuteronomy and the priestly law, all three great law codes form the basis of Neh 10; the legal aspect of the entire Pentateuch is fully present.

At the same time, Neh 10 is powerful evidence for the beginning of the interpretation of law. Clines's demonstration of this is impressive.[88] The way in which biblical texts are taken up and used parallels the basic principles of later rabbinic interpretation. Thus, in part, the actual legal norm is replaced by the procedure of its practice, e.g. when the demand for a permanent sacrificial fire (Lev 6:5) is made possible by the obligation to supply wood, which is regulated in detail. Or, when the tithe offering (Neh 13:10ff., Mal 3:8), which is frequently not observed, is secured by the process in which those who are profiting (the Levites) receive the tithe under the supervision of a priest (verses 38bf.). This is what the Mishnah tractate Abot calls a "fence around Torah" (Abot 1.1),[89] and is connected with the men of the great assembly (thus the time after Ezra).

Neh 10 attests what is also apparent in other places: with the development of the Pentateuch there came a need for its interpretation. Which laws should apply and how the different formulations fit together, all of this requires continuing interpretation in and through practice. The fact that the Pentateuch contains differing corpora that have not been adjusted makes interpretation more than usually necessary.

The gathering of laws from completely different levels of social concern and the way they have been arranged, already by Nehemiah himself, especially in Neh 10, permits us to come to solid conclusions regarding the authorities behind the development, at least in its use in the province of Judah. Combining the interests of the free farmers with those of the cult personnel is very important.[90] The great emphasis upon the subject of debt in all comparable ancient societies gives the enforcement of Deut 15:1ff. a weight, which generally balances the scales

---

86 See above pp. 128ff.
87 See above pp. 296f.
88 Clines, *Nehemiah* 10.
89 See Zeitlin, *Halaka* 17; Patte, *Early Jewish Hermeneutics* 107ff.
90 Blum, *Pentateuch* 359 criticizes my earlier (*Perserzeit* 214f.) descriptions "compromise" and "coalition." The former may be confusing (even though the priestly tradition did not, as Blum suggests, require forgiveness of debts and manumission of slaves to the same degree as the deuteronomic tradition) since it does not cover the process of extensive addition. He is further correct that Neh 5

from the perspective of the participants for the many cultic offerings.[91] This "coalition" is clearly distinguished from other contemporary social groups in Judea, e.g. the aristocratic-wisdom and eschatological-prophetic groups. Socially as well as literally, they clearly stand along-side Torah.[92] Simultaneously, it is precisely these two great theological groups or schools that stand out from among the material interests investigated here, which with a variety of other reasons underlie the overall composition of the Pentateuch.[93] On a new level, the new arrangement of (deuteronomic) social law and (priestly) cultic law in the Pentateuch doubled the basic principle of Torah, which was established in the Book of the Covenant, and which, if in a different way, shaped all of the pre-canonical legal corpora.

Judea and the Diaspora: The Unity of the Nation

Israel's existence was scattered since, at the very latest, the beginning of the Babylonian exile. Even the postexilic reestablishment of the temple cult and the development of a separate province of Judea did not lead to a self-contained association of settlements.[94] A basic document of Judaism, recognized as the law of the Persian empire, would also be required to secure the relationship of Judah with the rest of the diaspora. The Pentateuch succeeded as being canonically valid only because it fulfilled this function. Its basic structure responds to this assignment precisely. By adopting and developing the relevant foundational material secured by the priestly writings,[95] especially in the stories of the patriarchs, they sketched a picture of life with the God of Israel. This was immediately relevant and applicable for the diaspora. We must, of course, make a distinction between the eastern and the Egyptian diaspora.

Historically, the influence of the eastern diaspora[96] during the Persian period was tremendous. It is, in fact, difficult to overstate its importance. The figures who gave decisive stimulus to the reshaping came from here. At first it was Sheshbazzar and Zerubbabel and then Ezra and Nehemiah. They came directly from the king and their actions were obviously very closely coordinated with the king's intentions. We may surmise that the

---

does not present *"direct* evidence" for a coalition of priests and free farmers (thus also Schmitt, *Plagenerzählung* 200f., especially note 28). Historically, *how* they cooperated remains unclear. Even Nehemiah's memoir only gives us a vague impression of the milieu. Since, however, the interests of other groups recognizable at this time, especially the aristocracy, did not have an opportunity, it is probably still justified, perhaps even necessary, to speak of something like a social coalition.

91 See now especially Kippenberg, *Erlösungsreligionen*, stakes his reconstruction of religious history on activities around the problem of indebtedness.

92 See Crüsemann, *Perserzeit* 218ff.

93 See above pp. 47f. and below pp. 356ff.

94 We need only make reference here to the conflict of returnees and old-Judeans, which especially at the beginning, overlapped the fundamental social conflicts. It had a decisive affect on the history of the province. See Schulz, *Political Tensions*.

95 See above pp. 290ff. Since there was not much that was fundamentally new to the conception of the overall composition in the priestly writings, the following description can be rather brief.

96 See Bickermann, *Captivity*, for the problem of the diaspora during the Persian period, see Coggins, *Origins*.

law of Ezra, or the Pentateuch, was shaped and edited there. Nevertheless, lacking the necessary sources, we must allow this question to
remain completely unresolved. In any case, before Ezra's mission, his
law, as it is emphasized in Ezr 7:25, was well-known to those for whom it
mattered: those for whom the law gained new significance because of his
mission.

Business documents give us rather a good picture[97] of day-to-day life
in the eastern diaspora, but we know next to nothing about their religious
life.[98]

We should not, however, conceive of this life in analogy to later
diaspora Judaism, e.g. of the Roman period. None of the elements is here
yet, because they only begin to develop at this time. This applies above
all to the synagogue,[99] which we may not yet presume to exist. It was
probably pharisaism, with its new interpretation of Torah independent
of the cult site, that penetrated the everyday life of the laity with its Torah
commandments. Apart from basic priestly regulations for any diaspora[100]
– circumcision, passover, sabbath, endogamy as well as the prohibition
against blood – there is no evidence of a religious life.

The stories of the patriarchs do offer us an extremely graphic portrayal
of life in the interaction between the eastern diaspora and Judea. This is
also true for the final form of Genesis, quite independent of questions
regarding the age of relevant passages or the literary-redactional processes. The patriarchs had their homeland in Babylon proper. Abraham
left Ur-Kasdim (Gen 11:28, 31) and went by stages to Palestine. There are
repeated references to connections to his place of origin, especially
through marriages.[101]

It was from that homeland, according to Gen 24, that Isaac received a
wife, and it was there that Jacob fled from Esau, gaining his wives and
wealth from Laban. Quite in contrast to Egypt, there were no conflicts
with rulers. If there were problems, they were with relatives, as e.g.
between Jacob and Laban. To be sure, Abraham was supposed to leave
Mesopotamia and go to the Promised Land in order to be blessed there
(Gen 12:1–3), and this probably also applied to all of his descendants.
Other relatives, however, remained behind and established the foundations for the wealth of the nation.

If the center of the empire was in the east, during the Persian period
Egypt was a country that was frequently shaken by insurrection
(especially 486–484, 460–454, 405 BCE) since the conquest of Cambyses
(525 BCE), until it finally became independent again (401 BCE). Finally, it

---

97 See especially Zadoq, *Jews in Babylonia*; ibid., *Some Jews* among others; in addition
    to Wallis, *Sozial Situation*; Coogan, *Life in the Diaspora*; in general also Eph'al,
    Western Minorities.
98 With Eph'al, *Western Minorities* 88.
99 The description in Neh 8 has features of the later synagogue service, see especially
    Rendtorff, *Esra* 178ff.; see also Wahl, *Grundelemente*. For the development of the
    synagogue, see Levine, *Formative Years*. Further, Hruby, *Synagogue*; Safrai,
    Synagogue; Gutmann, *Origins* (as well as other contributions in this volume);
    Griffiths, *Egypt*.
100 See above pp. 290ff.
101 For what follows, see Diebner/Schult, *Ehen der Erzväter*. The conclusions
    regarding the age of the text are not convincing. For an articulated anaylsis, see
    Blum, *Vätergeschichte*.

was conquered again in 342 BCE.[102] This history must have played a significant role for Egypt's neighbor, the province of Judah,[103] but it also must have affected the fate of the Jewish diaspora in Egypt. Unfortunately, we know little about it.[104] Actually, we only have the documents about the Jewish military colony in Elephantine to shed light on the events here.[105] There are some things, such as the fact that apparently there were gods (including Anat) venerated alongside the God of Israel in the temple there, that correspond to the historically uncertain reports of the beginning (especially Jer 44) of the diaspora there.

The portrait that the Pentateuch paints of Egypt and its relationships with Israel is marked by deep ambivalence. On one hand it is a country where a person can especially find escape from hunger. This was already true of Abraham (Gen 12:16ff.), and it is illustrated by the events around Joseph and his brothers. There is an abrupt change from one pharaoh to the next (Ex 1:8), and the picture is affected by the exodus tradition. When dealing with the eastern powers, who were more important and more powerful at the time of the final redaction, there is no parallel to the idea that all the powers of God must be mobilized to defeat Egypt's pharaoh and his forces (Ex 5–14). If prophetic language and concepts played a part in this in addition to ancient tradition, it is important that Egypt, which is here attacked and from whom Israel escapes, was a dangerous and aggressive power for the Persian king.[106]

Persian Rule: The Difference it made for Prophecy

As the texts tell us, both Ezra and Nehemiah came with a direct, personal assignment from the Persian king. The relative autonomy of the province of Judah, which was completed during the time of their activity,[107] was part of Persian policy. Shortly after the Megabyzus insurrection,[108] the period of activity of Nehemiah and Ezra,[109] is closely connected with the great Persian interest in the pacification of this region of the empire. The tolerance that was guaranteed ended where Persian interests were

102 See Dandamaev, *Political History* (see pp. 351ff. for a chronological overview); see especially Salmon, *Les Relations*; Ray, *Egypt*.
103 See e.g. Kaiser, *Zwischen den Fronten*.
104 See Porten, *Jews in Egypt*.
105 See e.g. Porten, *Archives*.
106 When Schmitt, *Plagenerzählung* correctly finds prophetic traditions at work in these texts then we must note in these contexts what prophecy means in the Pentateuch in order to be able to make a proper evaluation. See below, p. 347.
107 A whole series of new, pertinent sources has been revealed (among others: seals, coins, etc.), since Alt, *Rolle Samarias* advanced the thesis that it was only through the mission of Nehemiah that Judah achieved the rank of independent province. Previously, it had been part of Samaria. Of course, the question, at what date did the independent province come into existence, cannot be answered with complete surety even today. Nevertheless, the comprehensive and intensive discussions of all the questions connected with this in Williamson, *Governors* have made it extremely likely that already Sheshbazzar and Zerubbabel (who both have the same title as Nehemiah – *peha*) were presiding over an independent province.
108 See Dandamaev, *Political History* 244ff.; see also, e.g. Ackroyd, *Jewish Community* 154.
109 See e.g. Margalith, *Political Role* for an early dating. There would have been a correlation with the renewed political independence around 401 BCE for a late dating of Ezra at 398 BCE.

affected – that is, in what concerned the support of authority and payment of the required taxes.[110] For that reason we may assume that there was nothing in the legal documents recognized by the empire's authorization that could contradict these interests.

Already in the Aramaic chronicle of the Book of Ezra there was warning about the revival of old Israelite and especially Jerusalem traditions of independence (Ezr 4:12f.; 15:19f.). Danger threatened Nehemiah's work, when he was libeled about wanting to set up an independent monarchy (Neh 6:6, cf already 2:19). Interestingly, prophets also played a role in this. They are alleged to have been bought by Nehemiah in order to proclaim him king (6:7). Thus, we are probably to understand Nehemiah's difficulties with the prophetess Noadiah and other prophets as being behind this (6:14).

The correlation of monarchy and prophecy suggests messianic proclamation. The prophecy of this period known to us is generally dominated by eschatological and early apocalyptic ideas. The end of all foreign domination is a continuing theme in all of this. Beginning with what Haggai has to say about Zerubbabel, it is clear that we are also dealing concretely with freedom from Persian domination. It was no more than of secondary importance for the Persians whether the report concerned an annihilating judgement (e.g. Isa 63:3ff.; Joel 3–4), or a peaceful pilgrimage by the people to Zion to bring their wealth there (Isa 60) or instruction to be received (Isa 2:2ff./Mi 4:1ff.).

Against such a background, we can hardly over-estimate the importance of the description of Moses at the end of the Pentateuch (Deut 34). Contrary to deuteronomic prophetic law with its promise of a constant flow of prophets like Moses (Deut 18:15ff.), Moses is here elevated above all other prophets, which is critical for an understanding of the whole work. "Never since has there arisen a prophet in Israel like Moses, whom the Lord knew face to face. He was unequaled for all the signs and wonders . . ." (Deut 34:10f.). Moses and his Torah supersede all other prophecy in a fundamental way.[111]

If we choose to reject the Pentateuch on this basis and are aware of the great role of eschatology and early apocalytic at this time, the enormous work must be regarded as extremely unprophetic and uneschatological, even anti-eschatological. This characterization in no way implies that it did not adopt prophetic traditions and continue the functions. This is not only clear for the early traditions, but also for many narrative contexts and formulations.[112]

---

110 See e.g. Donner, *Geschichte* II 393f. For the Persian tax system, see especially Tuplin, *Administration* 137ff.

111 With Blenkinsopp, *Prophecy and Canon* 80ff. It is too indiscriminating to say that the Pentateuch redactors were entirely positive toward prophecy as Schmitt, *Plagenerzählung* 200 note 24 suggests (see also Blum, *Pentateuch* 88, 359). The ranking of Moses above all other prophets is clearly a criticism of other prophets. A "complementary" relation of law and prophecy, as Schmitt formulates in conjuction with Perlitt, *Mose* 591f. is, of course, possible. That would mean, however, that the Pentateuch itself is not prophetic, nor would it subordinate itself to any prophecy; the history of the canon supports this.

112 See e.g. W. H. Schmidt, *Nachwirkungen*; Smend, *Ende*; H.-C. Schmitt, *Redaktion* and others.

In any case, the question is still whether this origin gives the text something like prophetic features,[113] or whether – more likely – the opposite is the case.[114] If prophetic characteristics are adopted in the plague narratives when pharaoh was hardened, it does not tell us whether and how such things worked prophetically at the time of the final redaction.[115] In any case, it never achieved the critical power of contemporary prophecy. This was significantly affected by eschatological–pre-apocalyptic expectation, according to which Israel's domination by foreign powers was to be brought to an end. We cannot, however, find such expectation anywhere in the Pentateuch. To be sure, we find great promises made repeatedly to the patriarchs, but they are restricted to a limited area. Alongside these there are a very few places in which very broad exegesis might produce an eschatological sense. In some of these, like the protoevangelium (Gen 3:15) or the Shiloh statement of Gen 49:10f., such an interpretation contradicts the clear sense of the text.

There are probably only two places in all the many chapters that speak of a divinely instituted, world-wide shift in power, the fourth song of Balaam and the conclusion of the song of Moses. Both passages are rather unclear and their exegesis is controverted. We cannot tell about whom is Num 24:24 speaking, or who is meant by the ships from Kittim.[116] It might be a cryptic reference to Alexander the Great and the end of the Persian empire. In Deut 32:43 there are significant textual differences between LXX and MT, so that it is nearly impossible to determine the original text with certainty.[117] Apart from these two marginal places, there is nothing that might be interpreted as endangering the power of Persia.

---

113 This is apparently the opinion of Schmitt, *Plagenerzählung* 199f. in his critique of my thesis (*Perserzeit*). He finds a "cooperation of prophetic groups in the development of the Pentateuch" (201). Nevertheless, neither the reception of prophetic traditions, which is undisputed, nor the reference to the "imposing opus of the prophetic books" originated at this time (201) disputes the fact that the decisive feature of contemporary prophecy as well as of the prophetic redactors, that is to say, a thoroughly eschatological outlook, is absent from the Pentateuch. We do not find hope for an earth-shaking action of God, but rather the contemporary practice of Torah together with the political space necessary to follow it, which shapes figures like Ezra and Nehemiah and the central figures of the Pentateuch. At the time of the development this was a contrast (and it still was for the Sadducees, for example). It is true that it was not an absolute, but rather a complementary opposite. In the history of canon Torah remained dominant. For the relationship, see for example also W. H. Schmidt, *Pentateuch und Prophetie*. Regarding Plöger's critique (*Theokratie* 129ff. for the dialog Schmitt, *Plagenerzählung* 202), there are clearly at least three groups in postexilic Judaism (the evidence hardly justifies the idea of "mediating forms" – against Schmitt 202 note 35). Many confusions in the discussion go back to attempts to reduce them to two groups.
114 For the ambivalent role of the Egyptians in this context, see above p. 345.
115 Against Schmitt, *Plagenerzählung*. Only this can resolve the issue, not, however, the tradition–historical provenance of language, motives, etc.
116 The interpretation of these statements extend from the sea people (Vetter, *Seherspruch* 55f.) to the Seleucids (Noth, *Numbers* 169).
117 See e.g. Bogaert, *Trois Rédactions*; Luyten, *Overtones*.

The Neighboring Provinces: The Open Promise

Nehemiah, and perhaps also Ezra,[118] functioned as governors (*pehā*) of the province of Judah, which was a separate part of the satrapy and independent of Samaria.[119] Judah[120] is a small area; there is only a distance (north–south) of about 50 km between Beth-Zur and Bethel. We can tell quite clearly from Nehemiah that at all costs the neighboring regions wanted to prevent the construct of the wall (Neh 2:19f.; 3:33ff. among others), which the Aramaic chronicle had already recognized (Ezr 4:8ff.). The disagreements went as far as verging on military conflicts (Neh 4:1ff., especially verse 10).

We only need to look at a map of the province of Judah, together with the neighboring regions of Samaria, Ashdod, Idumea, Moab and Ammon,[121] comparing them with the places and areas promised to the patriarchs in order to discover an essential message of the Pentateuch at the time in which it received its final form. It was first called the Promised Land in Gen 12, in conjunction with the journey of Abraham. He came first to Shechem, where he received the promise, "To your offspring I will give this land," and built an altar there (Gen 12:6f.). Then he camped between Bethel and Ai where he built an altar, and finally he went into the Negev (verses 8f.). From here the story continues through all the many promise texts up to the climax in Deut 34. Before Moses' death, God showed the whole land to him from Mount Nebo, and there is a precise description: "the whole land: Gilead as far as Dan, all of Naphtali, the land of Ephraim and Manasseh, all of the land of Judah as far as the Western Sea, the Negev and the plain – that is, the valley of Jericho, the city of palm trees – as far as Zoar" (34:1–3). All of it "is the land of which I swore to Abraham, Isaac and Jacob, saying, 'I will give it to your descendants'" (verse 4).

Moses was not permitted to enter the land, and the Jews of the Persian period possessed only a small fraction of it. From the long list of places in Deut 34, this is Judah, but not to the sea, and the district of Jericho. Everything else that has been promised and sworn lies in hostile neighboring provinces. The important places of the promises and patriarchal traditions, like Beersheba, Hebron, Mamre, Shechem, Mahanaim and others lie outside. Bethel and Ai were disputed border localities.[122] This means that only a portion of the promises have been fulfilled, and they would have to wait for the rest. So, as the conflicts between the provinces of the region under Persian rule were apparently possible, it was also possible in this way to sustain a claim to the great districts of the neighboring provinces as having been promised by their God.

They must, however, remain promises. The same thing was not true for the conquest of the land through Joshua's military campaigns and the consequent division among the tribes of Israel. Torah ends in Deut 34

118 Thus e.g. Margalith, *Political Role*.
119 For the question of the period in which this independency began, see above note 107.
120 For the question of the province of Judah, see Stern, *Province*; McEvenue, *Political Structure*; see also Betlyon, *Provincial Government*.
121 See e.g. Alt, *Judas Nachbarn*, and now especially Lemaire, *Population et Territoires* (map, p. 74).
122 Welten, *Geschichte* 123ff., especially 128.

with the death of Moses and the renewal of the promise. Scholars have found or theorized literary threads in many places connecting the Pentateuch with the Book of Joshua or even beyond. There is even the theory of an original Hexateuch, there are theories of connections between Deuteronomy and the deuteronomic history, and other ideas abound.

The much discussed question, why the Pentateuch, as an independent authority, was separated from all of the other documents with which it (or parts of it) might correlate, belongs among the literary problems that cannot be resolved by literary-historical methods alone. The key to the understanding lies in the validity of the Pentateuch as Israel's Torah, the legitimation experienced as the law of the Persian empire. There is no way that a report of the conquest of the most powerful of the neighboring provinces by force and their apportionment to Israel could find a place among legal documents valid in this way. That only applies to the traditions of the Books of Samuel, which aim toward an independent nation-state. It was only in another time, and then with a little less pomp, that this early document could, together with the later prophets, become part of the canon.[123]

Composition Components and their Theology

A Persian Legal Principle as Background

The following attempt to examine the inner theological sense of the Pentateuch composition must be limited to a very few, exceptionally remarkable and important characteristics. It is not just its size and complexity that make the study of its historical sense so difficult in every case. Some of its structural characteristics do not permit us to anticipate a clear result, rather they cause it to appear incomplete. This includes the juxtaposition of narrative and law,[124] but also probably the peculiarity of combining together several, different, older, contradictory laws. In legal–historical terms this is quite remarkable. It probably also made a significant contribution to the potency of Torah, that it constantly withdrew fresh material from itself.

A certain need to have a single law, a single document as the divine law of their own God must have continued to exist from the beginning of the process of the empire's authorization of their law. This would be a law to which all Israel would submit, and it would be valid as the law of the king. A juxtaposition of different, mutually contradictory laws would diverge from the intent. Why, then, were Israel's various older legal codes not adjusted? In principle it would have been easy to arrange them as a single, consistent picture of the will of God as we find it in the tradition. That is precisely what any exegesis must achieve from the outset. Correspondingly, this is to be observed in any of the older legal documents, in the priestly documents and into the postexilic period. Each of them, if our literary analysis is correct, have incorporated older material – previous collections of legislation – creating a relatively

123 For the prophetic canon, see Steck, *Kanon*; ibid., *Abschluss der Prophetie*.
124 See, for example, Nasuti, *Identity*.

homogenous, new entity. Why was this not handled in this way? Instead of this approach, why was an additive principle selected, which led to so many repetitions and so many obvious contradictions?

It is not a sufficient explanation to fall back on the inviolable dignity of the older texts. It is even a question of how and why, in the relatively short period since the exile and the development of the priestly writings, attitudes toward their own tradition had so completely changed. Why was the wording of these texts still regarded as more or less sacrosanct, so that something that is obviously no longer practicable could not be deleted but something new could or had to be placed alongside of it?

There is an Old Testament parallel for the idea of the unalterability of written law, and I suggest that we attempt to use it by way of explanation. In Esth 8, Esther asked the king to revoke the written decree he had previously sent, decreeing the extermination of the Jews in all the provinces (verse 5). The king, who had meanwhile changed his mind, answered: "You may write as you please with regard to the Jews, in the name of the king, and seal it with the king's ring.[125] Still an edict written in the name of the king and sealed with the king's ring cannot be made retroactive" (8:8). The new edict has the purpose of preventing what the old decree had commanded. Practically speaking, it cancelled the results of the first decree by enabling the Jews to defend themselves and take revenge (verse 11). Such a complicated route is necessary because, as it says in verse 8, "an edict written in the name of the king and sealed with the king's ring cannot be revoked." New law can be placed alongside older law without formally canceling the first, even when the second contradicts the first.

Scholars are divided over whether there was really a Persian legal principle at work here.[126] There is, in any case, no further direct evidence for such a custom.[127] Still, as the Book of Esther shows, Israel thought this was a Persian legal principle. This too is a fact, even if it does not correspond to historical reality. Nevertheless, there are a few other places that regard the written laws of the Medes and the Persians as permanently valid (Esth 1:19; Dan 6:9, 13, 16). Taken on their own, these formulations only mean that the decrees currently in force were permanently valid. In conjunction with Esth 8:8 they could also be understood in the sense of applying to the decree under discussion.

For Frei, the applicability of the decrees well into the future was closely connected with the fact that the instructions were written.[128] Once something is written, it becomes permanent. He mentions the fact that the process of authorization of the Trilingue of Letoon was written and

---

125 The word *kī* probably retains its basic, deictic meaning in a concessive sense. See Meyer, *Hebräische Grammatik III* 104f.
126 See most recently, e.g. Dandamaev/Lukonin, *Institutions* 117, where such a principle is called "primitive law" for Persia. Unfortunately, there is no evidence. For Old Testament evidence, see Dandamaev/Lukonin, *Institutions* 118.
127 The occasional reference (e.g. Porteous, *Daniel* 72f.) to Diodorus Siculus XVII 30 does not fit. There we have the irrevocability of the preceding murder (see Frei, *Zentralgewalt* 36 note 64).
128 Frei, *Zentralgewalt* 23ff.

thus its character as "document" and its validity are connected.[129] Frei even suggests that we might be able to see the origin of the authorization of the empire in this practice.[130] When certain norms (of local institutions, for example) are transferred to the authority of the empire, and this authority writes them down, they receive permanent legal applicability.

Can we, should we see a correlation between this principle of Persian law and the characteristics of Torah?[131] When Ezra or others before or after him in the Persian empire refer back to their own ancient, written law to gain the authorization of the empire, it is likely and perhaps inevitable that they regard their own tradition – thus YHWH's action – as analogous to that of the king. What was presented in ancient written law in Israel and happened in the name of God, was permanently established and could not be revoked. Because it was written, it had permanent validity. Things that were different, even contradictory, must be placed alongside without making compensatory adjustment. Israel transferred to scribes and legal authorities responsibility for decisions regarding needs for adjustment in the substance and decisions regarding actual proceedings.

There is something fundamental to the biblical canon that developed with this process, whose inner logic cannot be derived from the legal history of Israel. There is a kind of "tolerance" produced by this juxtaposition and interplay of texts, which, as parts of one canonic document, contradict each other directly in significant points. God's will is not a more or less closed system, nor is it a principle for the integration of many truths into a single entity. It comprises things mutually exclusive. This does not just apply to the present, but is also true for the things that have come from various times and eras. The canon, which came into existence with Torah, functioned throughout the various periods as an enduring foundation, because it helped to illuminate and explain widely differing situations and demands. This characteristic, however, is closely connected with and corresponds to the inner structure of the canonical text. It is this feature of the Pentateuch composition that really contributes something new to the previous corpora. Its power is, of course, only apparent as we view the overall history of reception. We can only deal with drawing attention to a few features of Torah here.

"Do not let God speak to us" (Ex 20:19): The Role of the Decalogue
The Decalogue (Ex 20; Deut 5) plays a role in the composition of the Pentateuch that cannot be overemphasized. As the introduction to the

---

129 We read in line 19 of the inscription, "This law has he written" (*dth dk ktb*), which refers to the decree of the people of Xanthos (line 6); see Dupont-Sommer in Metzger, *Xanthos* VI 136f. Unfortunately, what follows, which is critical for an exact understanding, is faulty. We should probably interpret the text, which is nearly impossible to understand (*mhṣsn*) as Dupont-Sommer does (*mhḥsn*). Frei, in conjunction with a suggestion by Dupont-Sommer, interprets the text , "so that people take note" (*Zentralgewalt* 24f., especially note 73), so that legal validity is specially dependent upon the written nature of the law.

130 Frei, *Zentralgewalt* 25.

131 See, with a different accent, Bardke, *Esther* 368 note 3, who compares this "horror of rigid and irrevocable human law" with the presumed parallel qualities of Jewish law.

central Sinai law in Ex 20 it rises above the rest of the laws because it alone was given as God's direct word to the nation. The mediating role of Moses only comes about because of the fearful reaction of the people who were unable to bear God speaking to them directly (20:19). The function of Ex 20 as literary connection becomes very clear in the way that, unlike its parallel (Deut 5), it establishes the foundation of the sabbath commandment (Ex 20:11) in Gen 2:1–3, therefore the beginning of the enormous work. On the other hand, the Decalogue and its proclamation is repeated in Deut 5, thus representing one of the means by which Deuteronomy is connected to the very different Tetrateuch. The tradition–historical position of the Decalogue is in accord with this literary-reference function. As a whole, it is quite close to Deuteronomy and its theology, but the version in Ex 20 clearly shows signs of priestly amplification and redaction. The unity of the Sinai pericope, which is composed of differing materials, is achieved through its shape.

This special position of the Decalogue in the compositional unity of Old Testament law must be examined.[132] Of course, it only came about in its current form in the later phases of the redaction. Ex 20 had the more self-contained Deut 5 as its immediate model.[133] What does the elevated status of the text over against the rest of Torah mean?

Theologically, this question deals with nothing less than the position of the Decalogue in Christian theology, its ethics and especially its catechesis. The Decalogue has played a very special role, beyond that of the rest of Torah, since the days of the early church.[134] It has been regarded as a summary of the divine will that transcends time, as the essence of natural law and biblical ethics. While only a few of the remaining contents of the rest of Torah have been adopted and applied to Christianity in an incidental and eclectic manner, the Decalogue is regarded differently. Jewish exegesis and tradition has been critical of this special role, and have sought to prevent this appropriation.[135] Closer inspection quickly shows that the contents of Torah do not support such a special position for the Decalogue. It cannot be regarded as a kind of

---

132 For the Decalogue itself, see Crüsemann, *Dekalog*. Everything suggests that the Decalogue belongs in or near Deuteronomy, thus it is already dependent upon the critical Torah structures which developed with the Book of the Covenant. Its contribution to Old Testament legal history, along with its function in the law, lies more in its precision, clarity and ability to teach, rather than in its contents as such. It would be different if it belonged *before* the Book of the Covenant. Even Lohfink, *Unterschied* 77ff., who thinks that it might possibly be quite old, must agree that there are no discernible reasons for this. If Vincent, *Dekalogforschung* would place the norms formulated within the Decalogue before the crises of the eighth century, where they appear in prophecy (and the Book of the Covenant), then precisely that is improbable. The explication and formulation require reasons, and we find late, mature phrasing of these norms in the Decalogue.

133 Since the studies of Perlitt, *Bundestheologie* 77ff., Hossfeld, *Dekalog*; Nicholson, *Decalogue*; this is no longer in dispute; see now also Lohfink, *Unterschied* 76f. Nothing, however, is decided regarding the relationship of the versions of the texts themselves; see most recently Graupner, *Dekalogfassungen*; Hossfeld, *Dekalogfassungen*; Lohfink, *Unterschied* 75. It remains unresolved here.

134 See Borgeault, *Décalogue*; Rothlisberger, *Kirche am Sinai*.

135 Most recently, Stemberger, *Dekalog* 99ff.; also Vermes, *Decalogue*; Vokes, *Ten Commandments*; Schreiner, *Dekalog*.

summary, or the essence of Torah, nor was it ever intended to be such. Too many central themes are absent entirely and, as the history of interpretation shows, when interpreted into the Decalogue, they have rather little power.[136]

When we examine the meaning, role and function of the "elevated" Decalogue in the canonic shape of the Pentateuch and the Sinai pericope, we are asking whether this traditionally special role can be legitimized. Can or should it be regarded in some way, as the sum and summary of God's will, to dominate the rest of Torah? Is the disregard of Torah in Christian ethics and tradition in some way justified?

After various other attempts, Norbert Lohfink most recently has worked out the canonical special role.[137] He did it in a new way, after convincingly rejecting older attempts, e.g. that of Claus Westermann.[138] Westermann believed that there is a basic difference between commandment and law, which was valid up into the Pauline theology of law, and he supported this in Hebrew legal terminology as well as the age and provenance of the traditions in accord with the assessment of Albrecht Alt. In view of the textual evidence as well as recent scholarly discussion, none of this is tenable. Lohfink emphasizes that the Decalogue is divine speech in no way different from the rest of Torah, consequently it may not be extracted from Torah.

About this special position of the Decalogue, Westermann and Christian theology in general are largely in agreement.[139] It comes, according to Lofink, solely from the function that the canonic text ascribes to this text. To the degree that the portrayals in Deut 5 as well as Ex 20 permit us to recognize a "difference" in the basic significance between the Decalogue and the rest of Torah, which is quite pertinent for the entire Old Testament, and behind which we cannot go.[140] The Decalogue receives a higher position in the canonical composition with respect to the rest of the law, which is only supposed to be interpreted as an unfolding of what had been established in the Decalogue.[141] It somehow anticipates the rest of the will of God[142] and would have a "key position" for interpretation.[143] Lohfink thinks that already in Deut 5 there is a conception of parts of the law hidden in this formal elevation of the Decalogue above the rest of Torah.[144] This, of course, involves the "historical relativity of all other legal traditions in Israel."[145] The distinction between temporally conditioned or changing norms and those that are permanent and unalterable is critical. For the redactors, the elevation of the Decalogue was part of the "distinction developed in the Old Testament between what changes and what endures in the will of God."[146] The

136 See Crüsemann, *Dekalog* 3ff.
137 Lohfink, *Unterschied*.
138 Lohfink, *Unterschied* 65–74.
139 Thus at the end of Lohfink, *Unterschied* 89.
140 Lohfink, *Unterschied* 80ff.
141 Lohfink, *Unterschied* 80.
142 Lohfink, *Unterschied* 84.
143 Lohfink, *Unterschied* 64.
144 Lohfink, *Unterschied* 80.
145 Lohfink, *Unterschied* 81.
146 Lohfink, *Unterschied* 89.

immutable heart, the Decalogue, was placed before, and thus ultimately above, the remaining alterable law.

The traditional matrix of Christian Torah reception – that is, the special position of the Decalogue – is newly established here. The following critique is not intended to attack what Lohfink has done. It does not detract from the ever present need to be concrete, which the individual laws demonstrate, but which simultaneously renders them subject to changing conditions, nor does it intend to make the Decalogue the sum of all the laws. It is neither intended to remove the authority of the Decalogue as God's word to Moses, nor to withhold from it the Pauline criticism of the law. Nevertheless, of course, with all of these refinements, the essential, traditional role of the Decalogue as an expression of moral and natural law, which transcends time, is newly established. Exegetically, this happens in a remarkable way. The critical notion, which the special position of the Decalogue illustrates – its ability to transcend the bounds of time, meaning that it is not subject to historical and societal change – is not supported anywhere by exegesis of contents. On the contrary, quite astonishingly, it appears as an unproven presupposition by Lohfink.[147] Even the notion that special position of the Decalogue is a "theory" dealing "somehow" with their contents is not supported exegetically.

In both places (Ex 20 and Deut 5), the statements of the biblical text itself lead in an entirely different direction. The difference between the Decalogue and everything that follows lies completely and exclusively in the fact that it is *direct speech by God*. The difference is in the mode not the content. It is never indicated that what is said in this way is special or different from the rest of Torah. As we know, for each of the commandments in the Decalogue, there are more or less precise parallels in the other parts of Torah. Of course, the formulations included in the Decalogue are much more general, covering many more possible offenses,[148] but none of this has anything to do with timelessness.

We cannot dispute that the introduction of a collection of laws states something especially important for the document. This is shown by the introductions to all of the biblical collections of laws, but it is illustrated especially well by the Decalogue itself. Nevertheless, this should not cause us to think that this introduction of a speech is able to summarize everything else, or that it is more important, or that everything else is just an unfolding. The redactors nowhere assume that the very concrete individual collections of laws – the Book of the Covenant, Deuteronomy and the priestly law – are temporally bound in their concreteness and their detail, thus the will of God formulated in them might change with the circumstances, or be lost altogether. Ultimately, is this idea not a product of modern historical consciousness? It is precisely the process of the integration of entirely different, older laws, with very different regulations, into a single Torah that permits us to recognize something completely different. The remaining history of Jewish law accomplishes the same thing. Practically speaking, of course, new situations could

147 Lohfink, *Unterschied* 81.
148 See especially Schmidt, *Erwägungen*.

render old laws partially or entirely unusable; this is particularly true of the kingship law, legislation regarding sacrifice, and many social laws. Nevertheless, the will of God formulated in them endures and is never rendered historically relative. On the other hand, it hardly needs to be mentioned that for modern historical consciousness, naturally even the Decalogue is included in the mutability of all things human.

Of course, Ex 20, like Deut 5, says something very different about the special position of the Decalogue than Lohfink wants, and we will discuss this next. It is not something in the contents that gives it a special position, but only the mode of direct speech by God. What we have here is a problem in communication. The break from direct speech by God, desired by the people after this introduction, is the aetiology for the position of Moses as mediator for the transmission of all other commands.

Now, of course, there is attestation elsewhere for a critique of Mosaic authority. In Num 12:2 Miriam and Aaron ask, "Has YHWH spoken only through Moses? Has he not spoken through us also?" (Cf also Num 16f.) In Ex 20/Deut 5, however, we are not dealing with this kind of questioning of Moses' authority. There is no alternative to him, and furthermore, Deut 5 presents the whole as a recapitulation, formulated in Moses' own words. Thus, we find here no questioning of Moses' authority.

In order to begin to grasp the significance of this break, we assume that Deut 5 is a model for Ex 20. "Because it is in Deut 5, Pentateuch redaction must also have introduced it at a later time into the Sinai pericope of the Book of Exodus" – I am in agreement with Lohfink's observation.[149] Literary combination of Tetrateuch and Deuteronomy was only possible in this way. We should remember the following:[150]

- Deut 5 involves a new version of the tablet tradition of Ex 34, wherein the deuteronomically influenced Decalogue is inserted in place of the cultic text Ex 34:11ff.

- This was probably already a reaction to the inclusion of Ex 32–34 in the priestly writing, and

- Thus deuteronomic law is likewise connected to Sinai, the place that is becoming increasingly important as the place of the giving of the law (Deut 5:31).

In short, amplifying older deuteronomic law with Deut 5 and the Decalogue cited there, had the function, above all, of connecting the law proclaimed in Moab with the new place of the giving of the law. What was first intended to contrast with the priestly conception, verified itself and increased in significance with the development of the canonical Pentateuch. If Ex 20 is modelled after the example of Deut 5, and at the same time is an expression of what deuteronomic and priestly strata have in common, then it is here that we can begin to understand the significance of the special position of the Decalogue.

149 Lohfink, *Unterschied* 76; see above note 133.
150 See above pp. 46ff., 55ff.

God's revelation on Sinai begins with the concentrated, striking formulation of the Decalogue. It is an introduction, but it should not at all be taken as the summary of all that follows. Because the people could not endure the voice of God, Moses was made a mediator. All other laws were handed down from God to Moses, and only later were they shared with the people. In importance they were all equal, no one ranked above the other. The priestly document is presented as God's word to Moses on the mountain. Stereotypically, the laws are introduced with variations of the sentence, "YHWH spoke to Moses: Say to the Israelites ..." The carrying out of the commands themselves, together with their consequences are only described in a few places.[151] Conversely, deuteronomic law was transmitted orally to the people in Moab before Jericho. We never learn where and how this happened; we only have the summary phrase in Deut 5:31. Like the Book of the Covenant, both come from the two-party conversation of God and Moses. Deuteronomy is thus not a "second law," and the priestly document is unable to claim superiority because of its origin on Sinai.

Herein lies the special achievement of the Decalogue; more precisely, the interruption of the transmission of the law, which was desired by the people, and the introduction of Moses as mediator: In this way we have the theological and substantive equality of all of the laws that taken together form the Pentateuch. I am in complete agreement with Lohfink's observation, that with the Decalogue and its position, there was achieved "a historical relativity of all other legal traditions in Israel,"[152] but I would understand it differently. The Decalogue does not claim a higher rank than the other laws, nor is this suggested anywhere. Everything is God's word and enduring will. Because, however, everything else was transmitted only to Moses, the distinctions between the laws become relative. It makes no difference whether the laws were given on Sinai through God's words or on Moab through Moses.

Exegetically, the special position currently granted to the Decalogue in Christian ethics must be regarded as misleading. Neither the exegesis of the Decalogue nor that of the other laws, nor of the difference in the way they were transmitted, is able to support this position. According to the canonical text of the Old Testament, the Decalogue is not the will of God in any sense that is not also true of the rest of Torah. It is neither the summary, nor the timeless principles of Torah. The many attempts to gain a single comprehensive will of God from the Decalogue alone result in problematic abbreviation of that will, and they are connected with the serious aberrations in church history and Christian policy. The difference from the rest of Torah lies exclusively in the mode of transmission, and the significance of this is revealed in the history of the composition. The Decalogue, or more precisely, the change in the manner of transmission that occurs after it, functions as a rectifier for the various corpora, which are present in the canonic Sinai pericope or Deuteronomy. They are all

---

151 Thus, the instructions in Ex 25ff. are carried out in 35ff. Aaron is consecrated as a
     priest, etc. but especially the commands from Lev 11 on are the words of God
     alone, except that they are transmitted to the people.
152 Lohfink, *Unterschied* 81.

equally God's Word. Aggressive attempts to lift the Decalogue out of everything else, making it alone the basis for Christian ethics, have cut Christianity off from Israel's Torah. They are exegetically untenable and theologically, they ought not be continued.

"All the congregation are holy" (Num 16:3): The Open Conflict

For eyes schooled in two hundred years of Pentateuch criticism, nearly every passage of this gigantic work dissolves into a variety of disparate material, strata and blocks. Still, many generations of perceptive Bible readers hardly notice most of the alleged contradictions and tensions. When viewed in a "scholarly" fashion, many of these fissures resemble the hair-line cracks in old pictures, and we can't see the picture for the cracks. Many, perhaps even most passages are formed out of completely different traditions and texts into amazingly concise (certainly not accidental or awkward), rational entities.

On the whole, this also applies to the Sinai pericope and the texts anchored within it. The text as we have it represents itself as being completely logical and expressive, if we take it seriously as literature and theology. Even the obvious contradictions between the legal corpora were no great problem for the history of interpretation that began with canonization. Many of them were settled by the practice of adding rival provisions, as the tithe laws show.[153]

Against this background, the cases become all the more important in which not only is no attempt made to balance the problematic redactions, but where the contradictions are frequently allowed to remain with harsh obviousness. In this respect probably the most important subject area may be the one where we find the most insurmountable contradictions between the two theological camps which together shaped the Pentateuch. This is the disagreement over the holiness of the people (or the privilege of the priesthood). There is no consensus here or, more precisely, the consensus consists of not trying to conceal contradictions.

To work our way through this conflict, it is probably best to begin with the priestly narrative of Num 16, which is entirely wrapped up in this question. The text takes material which is clearly older, giving indication of multiple stratification (even intra-priestly).[154] Nevertheless, it is not only possible, but it is methodologically and substantively appropriate to read it as having been intended to be a single entity.[155] The chapter

153 See above p. 222.
154 There is only inconsequential disagreement among scholars that the Dathan-Abiram episode in verses 12–15, 25–34 represents a pre-priestly text (wherein glosses, etc. are not considered here), see e.g. Noth, *Pentateuch* 32; ibid., *Numeri* 108; Fritz, *Wüste* 24ff.; Coats, *Rebellion* 158ff.; Ahuis, *Authorität* (who otherwise works with a broad deuteronomic stratum), most recently Schart, *Konflikt* 220; see even Milgrom, *Rebellion* 135f. This older core finds itself imbedded in a P center, which however is not generally regarded as a part of the P base stratum (Noth, *Pentateuch* 19 note 59; as well as – unsupported – e.g. Elliger, *Sinn* 175; Lohfin, *Priesterschrift* 222f. note 29; Schart, *Konflikt*, 137 note 1). Nevertheless, the model sketched of the priestly wilderness narrative by Westermann, *Herrlichkeit Gottes* 128ff. fits Num 16 exactly (see Blum, *Pentateuch* 267). Blum, *Pentateuch* 265f. shows that even the priestly stratum in this chapter is not unified, but represents many claims.
155 See Magonet, *Korah Rebellion*, as well as Blum, *Pentateuch* 263ff.

begins with Korah, Dathan, Abiram and 250 élite representatives of the people bringing serious charges against Moses and Aaron: "You have gone too far! All the congregation are holy, every one of them, and YHWH is among them. So why then do you exalt yourselves above the assembly of YHWH?" (verse 3).

The ensuing extremely complex narrative permits us to see different claims (or charges) raised among the among the various groups, and they are also concluded differently. There are Dathan and Abiram who basically challenge Moses' rule. Raising serious charges, they declare that they will not follow him (verses 12–14). They were swallowed by the earth (verses 31–34). Korah, who appears as a leader of a group of Levites, was swallowed up with them. His charges involved the priestly position that had been allotted to them (especially verses 8–11). They appear to question the difference between priests and Levites, which was so important for priestly theology. Finally, there are the 250 lay people designated as the élite leaders of the people (verse 2). Because the whole congregation is holy, they demand that the privileges reserved for Moses and Aaron (thus the priesthood) be revoked. As a punishment, they were killed by a fire that came out of the sanctuary (verse 35). The priestly answer to this mutiny was an ordeal which Moses initiated (verses 5, 7, 16–18). God used the incense offering reserved for the priests but offered by a person not authorized to show whom he regarded to be holy.

For the priestly narrator this was obviously an evil common to a variety of groups, but one with a common root. It lay in the claim of the ringleaders in verse 3, at the beginning of the story. The holiness of the entire congregation obviates any need for Moses and Aaron's special status. God's nearness to all Israelites – "YHWH is among them" (verse 3) – ought not to be connected with the privileges and groups to special holiness. For the priestly authors the claims of the Levites to the priesthood and of the laity to holiness are essentially identical. Basically, this raises questions about the concept of graduated holiness running throughout the entire priestly work. As necessary and salutary as this priestly status is to the special closeness of God, according to verses 20ff., it was only the prayer of those who were privileged for the whole people that saved them from destruction. The narrative that follows in Num 17 expressly underscores the role of the élite yet again.

What is behind this attack, the destruction of which Num 16 describes so impressively, is precisely the understanding of holiness that Deuteronomy and the texts around the narrative demonstrate. Scholars have seen this quite clearly.[156] The rebels' complaint in Num 16:3 parallels what is said with very similar language in Deut 7:6 and 14:2 (see also Ex 19:7). Of course, for the priestly text the whole people was made holy by the exodus and therefore could be in the presence of God.[157] This was expressly stated again in Num 15:40, immediately before the conflict in

---

156 See already Bentzen, *Priesterschaft* 281., as well as especially, Weinfeld, *Deuteronomy* 228ff.; Friedmann, *Exile* 69; Kraus, *Heiliges Volk* 41f.; Blum, *Pentateuch* 270f., 334f.
157 See above pp. 301ff.

Num 16.[158] There are suggestions of important statements, especially those we find in the Holiness Code, "You shall be holy for I YHWH your God am holy" (see Lev 19:2 among others).

The holiness of the people is not in dispute, only its consequences. According to the priestly understanding, the holiness of the people does not exclude the special holiness of the Levites and priests but presumes that it is a possibility. Only because Aaron and his priestly descendants as Israel's representatives are aware of the special problems of close proximity to God, can they exist as God's holy people. The atonement rites are the greatest example of this.

Deuteronomy, however, expressly makes Levites and priests equal in 18:6ff. It grants full priestly rights to each Levite, clearly guaranteeing to them fewer material shares in sacrifices and tithes, and it subordinates them to the people and their representatives. Correspondingly, they are only responsible for a marginal share of the judicial process. In contrast to priestly hierarchical thinking, the holiness of the people is realized with rather democratic institutions.

Num 16, part of the priestly writings not included in Deuteronomy, is a sharp rebuke of deuteronomic thinking and theology. It is a part of a broad "debate about Israel's identity as YHWH people and the tangible conflicts of interest woven into it,"[159] which existed between priestly and deuteronomic, but also priestly and Levitical groups. While Deuteronomy is part of the same Torah, to which also Num 16 and the basic priestly texts belong – where the structures defended here are unfolded (Num 3 and 18 among others) – here we find clearly antithetical concepts coming together to form a single entity.

We find the same contrast in the narrative passages of the Sinai pericope. We only need recall that there is little in the texts themselves, especially in the heavily deuteronomically influenced texts of Ex 19 and 24, where there are contradictions and repeated breaks of the narrative thread, to help understand the sense of these breaks.[160] What is important is the question of what actually holds these texts together, not unraveling them into various literary threads, which has been notoriously unsuccessful here. Along with this, we have the problem of priestly privilege or the right of access to the presence of God, not the only, but certainly an especially clear and open conflict.

The promise in Ex 19:3ff. is placed before the entire Sinai narrative as we have it.[161] It is a preliminary sign, an advance explanation of what follows.[162] As we find in God's first words to Moses from the mountain, God brought the people to himself (verse 4). If they heed his voice and keep the covenant, they will be his possession (*segullā*, verse 5) and will become a kingdom of priests (*mamlēket kōhᵃnîm*) and a holy people (*gōy qādōš*, verse 6). The closeness to God achieved

158 Blum, *Pentateuch* 335 note 5 refers to this.
159 Blum, *Pentateuch* 335.
160 See above pp. 28ff.
161 For the position in context, see Blum, *Pentateuch* 47ff. as well as Rendtorff, *Text in seiner Endgestalt.*
162 See Dozeman, *Spatial Form.*

through the exodus is demonstrated by the holiness and priestly status of the whole nation.[163] This is certainly a deuteronomistic text,[164] and the deuteronomistic reception of the priestly concept of holiness is of special importance. If the concept of holiness became a key legal term in the priestly writings, with which the legal tradition could be reshaped in the situation of the exile,[165] this fundamental idea could be used deuteronomistically here and be placed at the head of all the Sinai laws as an indication for interpretation.

Along with the reception, the formulation contains a critique of the priestly conception. The nation becomes a "priestly kingdom" (*mamléket kōhᵃnim*, verse 6). The expression is aimed at a political community or a state[166] consisting of priests. We find a related notion from the post-exilic period in Isa 61:6. The expression is apparently intended to mean that all Israelites will become priests or will exercize priestly function. There is some question about the existence of degrees within the divine–human relationship in Israel, with the kind of basic legal consequence that the priestly texts seem to recognize. The fact that they serve as an introduction to the events at Sinai shows the importance attaching to this question. The material dealt with in Ex 19:6 is taken up again in Ex 24, this time in a narrative form: the ritual which the young men of the people perform as a covenant ceremony corresponds to the priestly consecration (Ex 29:20; Lev 8:24, 30). The people, as a whole, are consecrated as priests, and actual priests do not take part.[167]

The same basic questions – to what degree are the people as a whole permitted to draw near to God, and whether (if so, which) mediators exist (or ought to exist) – run through the stories in Ex 19 and 24. According to Ex 19:10, the people are to prepare for God's arrival on the mountain by acts of ritual cleansing. Verses 12, 13a make that concrete: boundaries are established for the people. The mountain, sanctified by the presence of God, in many respects corresponds to a sanctuary with God present. It may not be touched, under penalty of death (verse 13a). This, however, is hardly an absolute boundary, because verse 13b tells us exactly the opposite: "When the trumpet sounds a long blast, they may go up the mountain."

How close the people may come to God is clearly an unresolved issue. When God descends upon the mountain, amid all of the signs appropriate to a theophany (verse 20), the people are warned to step back (verse 21). There would be mortal danger for anyone looking upon God. Even the priests, whose duties bring them in close proximity to God, are

163 From the wide-ranging discussion about the meaning of the terms used, see Dillmann, *Exodus* 214; Scott, *Kingdom*; Martin-Achard, *Israël*; Coppens, *Royaume*; Schüssler-Fiorenza, *Priester* 131ff. Blum, *Pentateuch* 51 note 22 correctly criticizes the variety of interpretations which make the sense less concrete, but more metaphoric and generalized, most recently, e.g. Fuhs, *Heiliges Volk* 158; Mosis, *Aufbau*.

164 See Perlitt, *Bundestheologie* 167ff.

165 See above pp. 306ff.

166 *mamléket* means monarchy, government, to be sure, as an institution (Sybold, article on *melek* 941).

167 Thus convincingly, Ruprecht, *Exodus 24* 167; cf Blum, *Pentateuch* 51f.

only able to do so because of the ritual purification which they have received (verse 22). On the other hand, according to verse 24 priests are specifically excluded from this nearness to God; only Moses and Aaron are allowed to come.

This conflict is carried on in chapter 24. In verse 1 there is a command to Moses, Aaron, Nadab and Abihu as well as the seventy elders to go up the mountain. One group was to represent the priests and the other stood for the entire nation. They are then to pray from a distance (verse 1b), only Moses was permitted to come closer. The representatives, like the people themselves, were to observe the distance (verse 2). After the covenant ceremony is described in verses 3–8 (in which the priests do not play a role, and in which there is a kind of priestly consecration for the people), they all (Moses, Aaron, Nadab, Abihu and also the seventy elders) go up the mountain. They see the God of Israel and they eat a meal in the immediate presence of God.

Such an overt juxtaposition of directly contradictory material is found almost nowhere else. Here, if anywhere, we need literary criticism, but it has not given us a convincing explanation. We are unable to isolate clear strata, nor do we have an explanation why no redactional attempts have made to explain what is happening here. The evidence suggests an intentional commemoration of a disagreement between two completely different conceptions.

Nothing here is smoothed over, because apparently there was nothing to smooth over. A compromise would be inconceivable. This feature may be especially important for an appropriate understanding of the development as well as the theological significance of the Pentateuch. There are so many things in common between groups or schools at the time of development as we see them on the one hand in prophetic-eschatological circles, and on the other in wisdom-aristocratic groups,[168] that even such significant differences did not force them apart.

A holy text containing such an obvious, profound contradiction may be affected by that contradiction in a special way. Ever since, communities who connect themselves to the heart of the canon developed here have lived with similar contradictions and continue to do so: Sadducees and Pharisees, the Eastern and Western churches, Protestantism and Catholicism – and perhaps all others. The same larger context establishes the common priesthood of all the faithful and the dignity of the priesthood. We will allow the question whether other parts of the canon have altered this (especially the prophets) to remain unresolved here.

"And thereafter, throughout your generations" (Num 15:23):
Instructions for the Journey into the Future

After staying at Sinai for almost two years, Israel left in order to go to the Promised Land (Num 10:11ff.). At Sinai they heard the Decalogue and turned away in fear. It was there that Moses received the Book of the Covenant, and Israel pledged itself to it. It was at Sinai that they received instructions for the construction of the shrine, and it was built. The priests

---

168 See Crüsemann, *Perserzeit*.

were consecrated and the cult begun. The calf was made at Sinai, and ultimately God's promise was renewed. Israel received the stone tablets, and it was there that Moses heard the remainder of the laws, which were only announced to the people at the end of the journey through the desert. As the final version of Torah has it, Israel received all of its law from this mountain.

Nevertheless, when the people left, they fell into deep conflicts rather quickly (Num 11–14). Very shortly they hear the direct, unmediated words of God, "YHWH spoke to Moses and said: Speak to the Israelites and say to them . . ." (Num 15:1f.). A stream of laws followed as if Israel were still at Sinai. After Korah's rebellion and the consequent crushing of that activity and his followers (chapter 16f.), God spoke to Aaron (chapter 18) and then to Moses and Aaron together with commandments for the people (chapter 19). This is continued, especially, in the last part of the Book of Numbers. There, the daughters of Zelophehad request the right to inherit from their father and receive it upon instruction from God (chapter 27). It is here that we find the most comprehensive cultic calendar in the Old Testament (chapter 28f.), the rules for making vows (chapter 30), regulations for the establishment of places of asylum (chapter 35), and finally, once again, the right of women to inherit (chapter 36). These are laws like those received on Sinai, but they are given on the way through the desert. Nowhere is it indicated, as it is in Deut 5, that these actually came from Sinai.[169]

Scholars agree that these texts are among the latest passages in the Pentateuch[170] – this is essential for their understanding – outside of the actual priestly writings.[171] The content as well as the language of many of theses texts are alien to priestly thinking. Thus, Num 18 gives the most important material foundation for the entire cult personnel with the instructions for the tithe to support Levites and priests.

Other texts are also clear continuations or amplifications of the priestly system; for example, the provisions for making sacrifice in Num 15 extend the otherwise unknown drink offering or they supplement parts of the law of sin offering. Num 19, with the instructions for the production of a special water of purification from the ashes of the red heifer, belong here.

Still, there are also clear tensions with the priestly text. It is especially important that these laws are hard to combine with basic priestly concepts. The priestly document contains a variety of laws situated *before* Sinai, and thus gives a priestly-theological foundation for the situation in the diaspora.[172] This, however, does not mean that it becomes a kind of appendage within the Book of Numbers.

This is especially shown by the fact that the institution for which the priestly writings expressly provides, plays no part in the transmission of

---

169 For the rabbinic interpretation, see Bamberger, *Torah after Sinai.*
170 See Noth, *Studien* 190ff. with an outline of the results 217; ibid., Numbers. Finally, especially Schart, *Konflikt* 55ff. places this text outside the composition he calls the "final text" of Num 10–21.
171 This applies in each case for the researchers who attempt to work out a base document (e.g. Elliger, *Sinn* 174f.; Lohfink, *Priesterschrift* 222ff. and elsewhere).
172 See above pp. 290ff.

the law. In establishing the atonement device (*kappōret*) in the holy of holies they created a place of which it is said – the very first time it is mentioned: "There I will meet with you, and from above the mercy seat, from between the two cherubim that are on the ark of the covenant, I will deliver to you all my commands for the Israelites" (Ex 25:22). Shortly before they left Sinai, this was repeated (Num 7:89). The presence of God among his people, which is given when the splendor of God (*kābōd*) enters the holy of holies, becomes a kind of moveable Sinai.

According to Lev 1:1, God speaks the entire sacrificial law from this tent (compare Ex 40:34–38).[173] This, however, never takes place in Num 10–36. Of course, we find important priestly traditions in which the "splendor" appears and God acts from the shrine all over in this section. There are, e.g. Num 14:10; 16:19; 17:7 as well as 20:6. Always the decisive resolution of the conflict portrayed is achieved by the intervention of God who is present in the tent shrine.[174]

Nowhere, however, do we have the pronouncement of laws from this place. They do not dovetail the priestly conception with the critical question of the source and authority of the additional laws. The sample narratives (Num 15:32ff.; 27:1ff.; 36:1ff.) are not accidental, but are connected with wide-ranging questions about the difference between "Moses," Aaron and other cultic representatives.[175]

We are dealing here with texts that together shaped the final redaction(s). Some are similar to priestly writings, but closer examination shows them to have features which are probably also typical of deuteronomism. The final texts, from Num 25:1 on, are in any case explicitly situated in that place about which Moses addressed the deuteronomic law in Moab across from Jericho (especially Num 35:1). They are already influenced by the combining of Tetrateuch and Deuteronomy, as well as the separation of the Pentateuch from Joshua.

In order to understand the sense of these post-Sinai laws, we should begin by taking a look at the overall composition of Num 10–36.[176] Immediately after their departure, Israel was enmeshed in conflicts that had mortal consequences. In Num 11 we find the desire for meat and for a return to slavery in Egypt, in Num 12 the insurrection of Miriam and even Aaron against Moses, and finally in Num 13f. the questioning of the purpose of the entire journey through the desert, in the spy narrative. These end with the divine decree that no one of the old Sinai generation would live to see the promised land (14:28ff.).

It is only immediately after the announcement of this generation break in Num 15 that we have the first block of post-Sinai laws. The next big turning point gives the second census of the nation in Num 26. At the end of this we have the statement that the generation of the first census in Num 1 is no longer alive (26:64f.). In other words, we have an entirely new generation. At the center of this generation we have the question of

173 For the – also syntactical – correlation, see Rendtorff, *Leviticus* 22f.
174 See Westermann, *Herrlichkeit Gottes* 128ff.; also Rendtorff, *Offenbarungs-vorstellungen* 48.
175 See above pp. 102ff.
176 For what follows, see Olson, *Death of the Old* especially 83ff., 165ff.

the right of women to inherit. It is certainly significant that this subject is again taken up in the last chapter (Num 36), which deals with the new generation and its wandering in the desert.

The context permits us to see the theological intent. These texts are not about the orientation of the subjects of the commandments to the record of the exodus – as in the variety of deuteronomic traditions of the various places where the law was given.[177] Rather, the question addressed is how God's new instructions ought to be heeded under changed circumstances among entirely new generations.

The conclusion of the revelatory event at Sinai cannot be the end of God's revelation. Israel received new instructions on its journey between Sinai and the promised land when they needed them. In content, these were extrapolations, realizations, supplements and amplifications of subjects and questions that had already been regulated in the revelation at Sinai – such as sacrifice, sabbath, priests, purity, festivals, places of asylum.

However, it also deals with subjects which had not appeared before, e.g. manner of dress (15:37ff.), vows (30) and the basic subject of inheritance, and thus the legal position of women (27, 36). Especially the illustrative narratives, which begin at Sinai (Lev 24:10ff.; Num 9:6ff.) and continue in the desert (Num 15:32ff., and chapters 27 and 36), show to what degree we have the necessary reaction to problems that have newly arisen and were not already treated in Sinai Torah. The renewed treatment of the theme of Num 27 in chapter 36 shows how in the course of events problems continue to develop and continually require new legal regulation.

Fixing God's will in written form, in the shape of a book, requires amendment by means of continuously innovative, divine speech; it ought not lead to rigidity. The canon and the living voice belong together. The history of the development of the canon shows[178] step by step how the two condition and supplement each other. At the very center, in Deuteronomy, there was the establishment of the central court as well as a prophet like Moses; both speak permanently with the authority of Moses, and both institutions are of great importance: the sanhedrin invoked the one, and the other ultimately produced the second part of the canon – the prophets. In the priestly writings the place from which God will speak in the future establishes itself in the center of the sanctuary, around which everything else revolved. The final redaction, with its revelations of the law on the journey through the desert, in the midst of mortal dangers both from within and without, created another model.

At only one place is there an opening into the world of the narrator and the reader. In Num 15:22f., as part of the introduction to the expanded sin offering law, we are told that God speaks through Moses "from the day YHWH gave the commandment and there-after through-out your generations" (verse 23b). Linguistically, it is not clear whether this sentence is connected with the divine

177 See above pp. 38ff.
178 Crüsemann, *Vaterland*.

declaration[179] – God speaks through Moses throughout all generations – or rather with Israel's offenses.[180] The latter sense, however, in which we are at least able to listen along – in the same way that later rabbinic interpretation does – corresponds precisely with what complements the written Sinai revela-tion as a conception of an oral Torah (*tōrā šel pē*).[181]

It also understands itself as having come from Sinai and Moses. This concept is expressed quite clearly in the Talmudic legend, according to which Moses himself entered the school of Rabbi Akiba and sat in the eighth row – and was unable to understand anything. Even that was a "halakha of Moses from Sinai" (bMenahot 29b). This concept of a continuing revelation that is and remains fundamentally connected with Sinai, is probably already based in the reports of new commandments on the march through the desert as described in Numbers.

The written principle and the living voice belong inseparably together. They are part of the development of the first part of the canon and a part of the tension contained in it. The one informs the other. Alongside Torah comes the prophetic canon and the expectation of an eschatological revelation of Torah.[182] Without this living voice there would be a danger of rigidity. What the Christian church generally does in connection with the foundation of the biblical canon is no less problematic. It has forgotten the indispensable base – Israel's Torah – in favor of the new revelation. The problems with which we live are not least a result of this process, which has distorted God's living voice; God's Word remains tied to his Torah.

The Unity of God and the Unity of Torah: A Starting Point for a Christian Reception of Torah

As we said at the outset,[183] Christian theology has also made a distinction between what is still valid and what no longer applies. Both historical distance, and the attendant changed historical reality alike compel such activity. This practice is also employed by the most orthodox Judaism. It always requires a creative hermeneutic and disavows any blind fundamentalism. Theologically such a separation seems unavoidable in a very basic sense: Christians are not supposed to become Jews. Nevertheless, what is the heart and center of Torah eliminates all such divisions, whether between the Decalogue and the rest of the law,

---

179 Thus especially Brin, *Numbers XV* citing Sifre §111 as well as Rashi; see also Toeg, *Halachic Midrash*.

180 Olson, *Death of the Old Man* 168 note 13. He rejects Brin's thesis, referring to the syntactical structure and its parallels in 1 Sam 18:9; Ez 39:22. He himself, however, points out the emphasis in the five-fold repetition of "throughout your (coming) generations" (*lᵉdōrōtēkēm*) in verses 14, 15, 21, 23, 38. Furthermore, the case of the person gathering wood on the sabbath we are dealing with the sample "application of a law to a new situation which requires a divine judgment" (172). The accent that Olson himself places upon the individual laws scattered throughout the composition of the Book of Numbers, corresponds exactly with that of the rabbinic tradition of understanding 15:23.

181 Cf Schäfer, *Dogma*.

182 Isa 42:1ff., 2:1ff. and others. See Davies, *Torah*; Jervell, *Tora*; Schäfer, *Torah*.

183 See above p. 4.

between the first commandment and that of circumcision, between ritual and moral law, between the traditions of social justice and patriarchal animosity toward women.

Here at the end of our discussion of the genesis of Torah, we can describe more precisely what both entail. We can summarize many observations with the thesis that the steps toward the development of Torah are an inseparable part of the way in which Israel formulated the unity of God ever more clearly. We need remind ourselves of only a few points.

At the beginning of the history of written law in Israel, somewhere in the ninth century BCE, there were probably two documents. The one (Ex 34:11f.) formulated regulations for a strict veneration of the one God in the context of an iron age, agricultural world. The other (Ex 21f.) is a collection of laws in the ancient Near Eastern tradition in which important societal conflicts of the era were given regulations intended to introduce justice (that is, compensation). The coming together of these two legal documents with principles for the protection of the economically as well as legally most vulnerable in society in the Book of the Covenant, can be called the actual birth of Torah structure. Thus, a part of exclusive veneration is law together with the justice that is a part of that law.

Deuteronomic law expanded the purview significantly. Above all, it now included wide-ranging political and other public institutions, the family as well as the treatment of animals and the rest of the environment. In scope all area of life were thus included in God's instructions. Still, out of experiences during the exile, the priestly writings expanded the purview once again. They had to move beyond the foundations of previous law-functioning cult, ownership of land, effective freedom. Independent of all social presuppositions, Israel was here subordinated to the divine command in the overall area of creation. We see the change in the fact that first position is given to the creation of the world instead of an altar law. Furthermore, the inclusion of guilt and forgiveness means that an entirely new area of experience has been added. The entire composition of Torah ultimately binds all of these steps together into a single document.

What was achieved in this history, sketched in a cursory manner here, is nothing less than a process in which the entire reality of a period, all areas of human life and experience are exposed to the light of Israel's God. The path from exclusive veneration to something resembling basic monotheism could only be traversed if all of the realities saturated and dominated by the many deities of polytheism were disclosed in a new way. The unity of God had to achieve a new form by a reworking of all of reality together with a redefinition of that reality. Otherwise there would only have been isolated (e.g. prophetic) initiatives. On the basis of experiences with the God of Israel, those areas must be included in which previously only other gods acted. The genesis of Torah, with its stepwise inclusion of new areas of reality, illustrates this process. Torah became the medium in the process, which the unity of God and the variety of areas of experience and reality were brought together. For that reason the identity of the biblical God is dependent upon the connection with his Torah.

All of this can only mean that – quite apart from the historical distance – Torah alone can be the foundation of a biblically oriented Christian ethic. It is, however, formulated for Israel, not for all of humanity. The one will of the only God has Israel as an inseparable human partner. It is not possible to remove Israel from Torah, nor can we replace Israel with Christianity. The dilemma contained in that statement can only be resolved by a Christian reception of Torah which enters into Torah as formulated for Israel, not for the Church. Thus it makes the unity of God, Torah and Israel as its foundation from which all concrete interpretation proceeds. Historical foundatiöns ought to be prepared for this kind of reception; it is much more than an exegetical task.

In conclusion, the starting point for such a hermeneutic, is formulated nowhere more clearly than Deut 4:5–8.[184] A reception of Torah that does not divide its unity, and does not seek to replace Israel will always be amazed that we are told about "the peoples" (*'ammīm*) here (verse 6). There are two reasons for this surprise: the uniqueness of God's nearness to Israel (verse 7) and even the content of Torah itself: in other words, that which this book is supposed to be talking about in verse 8: "What other great nation has statutes and ordinances as just as this entire law that I am setting before you today?"

184 See Braulik, *Weisheit, Gottesnähe und Gesetz*; besides Levenson, *Theologies of Commandment* 25ff.

Bibliography

(Abbreviations are from S. Schwertner, *Theologische Realenzyklopädie, Abkürzungsverzeichnis*, Berlin/New York 1976.[1] Multiple titles by the same author are in alphabetical order.)

Aartun, K, "Studien zum Gesetz über den großen Versöhnungstag Lv 16 mit Varianten," StTh 34, 1980, 73–109

Abba, R., "Priests and Levites in Deuteronomy," VT 27, 1977, 257–267

Abel, R. L., "Theories of Litigation in Society – »Modern« Dispute Institutions in »Tribal« Society and »Tribal« Dispute Institutions in »Modern« Society as Alternative Legal Forms," in: *Alternative Rechtsformen und Alternativen zum Recht*, Jahrbuch für Rechtssoziologie und Rechtstheorie 6, Opladen 1980, 165–191

Abramsky, S., "The House of Rechab – Genealogy and Military League," ErIs 8, 1967, 255–26

Achenbach, R., *Israel zwischen Verheißung und Gebot. Literarkritische Untersuchungen zu Deuteronomium 5–11*, EHS.T 422, 1991

Ackroyd, P. R., *Chronicles – Ezra – Nehemia: The Concept of Unity*, ZAW.S 100, 1988, 189–201

—, *Exile and Restoration. A Study of Hebrew Thought of the Sixth Century B.C.*, Philadelphia 1968

—, *I & II Chronicles, Ezra, Nehemiah*, TBC, 1973

—, *Israel under Babylon and Persia*, NCB.OT 4, London 1970

—, "Problems in the Handling of Biblical and Related Sources in the Achaemenid Period," in: A. Kuhrt/H. Sancisi-Weerdenburg (ed.), *Achaemenid History* III. *Method and Theory*, Leiden 1988, 33–54

—, "The Jewish Community in Palestine in the Persian period," in: *The Cambridge History of Judaism*, vol. 1. *Introduction; The Persian Period*, Cambridge 1984, 130–161

---

1 Additional abbreviations: BN = *Biblische Notizen*; JBTh = *Jahrbuch für Biblische Theologie*; JSOT = *Journal for the Study of the Old Testament*; NBL = Neues Bibel-Lexikon; NEB = Die Neue Echter Bibel; SBAB = Stuttgarter Biblische Aufsatzbände; TUAT = O. Kaiser Hg., Texte aus der Umwelt des Alten Testaments, 1982ff.

Aharoni, Y., Arad Inscriptions, Engl. trans. Jerusalem 1981
—, "The Horned Altar of Beer-Sheba," BA 37, 1974, 2–6
Ahlemann, F., "Zur Esraquelle," ZAW 59, 1942/43, 77–98
Ahuis, F., *Autorität im Umbruch. Ein formgeschichtlicher Beitrag zur Klärung der literarischen Schichtung und der zeitgeschichtlichen Bezüge von Num 16 und 17. Mit einem Ausblick auf die Diskussion um die Ämter der Kirche*, CThM 13, 1983
Aistleitner, J., *Die mythologischen und die kultischen Texte aus Ras Shamra*, Bibliotheca Orientalis Hungarica VII, Budapest 1964
Albertz, R., "Das Überleben der Familie sichern. Die Aussagen über Ehe und Sexualität sind zeitbedingt," LM 25, 1986, 401–405
—, "Die Religionsgeschichte Israels in vorexilischer Zeit," in: *Die Bibel. Das Alte Testament in Bildern erzählt von E. Lessing*, München 1987, 285–360
—, "Hintergrund und Bedeutung des Elterngebots im Dekalog," ZAW 90, 1978, 348–374
—, "»Ihr seid Fremdlinge in Ägyptenland gewesen« – Fremde im Alten Testament," in: idem., *Der Mensch als Hüter seiner Welt. Alttestamentliche Bibelarbeiten zu den Themen des konziliaren Prozesses*, Calwer Taschenbibliothek 16, Stuttgart 1990, 61–72
Albright, W. F., "The Judicial Reform of Jehoshaphat," in: *Alexander Marx Volume*, ed. S. Lieberman, New York 1950, 61–82
Alexy, R., Theorie der Grundrechte (1985), 1986
Allegro, J. M., "Uses of the Semitic Demonstrative Element in Hebrew," VT 5, 1955, 309–312
Alonso Schökel, L., "David y la mujer de Tecua: 2 Sm 14 como modelo hermenéutico," Bib. 57, 1976, 192–205
Alt, A., "Die Heimat des Deuteronomiums" (1953), in: idem., *Kleine Schriften* II, 1953, 250–275
—, "Die Rolle Samarias bei der Entstehung des Judentums" (1934), in: ibid., *Kleine Schriften* II, ³1964, 316–337
—, "Die territorialgeschichtliche Bedeutung von Sanheribs Eingriff in Palästina" (1930), in: ibid., *Kleine Schriften* II, 1953, 242–249
—, "Die Ursprünge des israelitischen Rechts" (1934), in: ibid., *Kleine Schriften* I, 1953, 278–332
—, "Judas Nachbarn zur Zeit Nehemias" (1931), in: ibid., *Kleine Schriften* II, ³1964, 338–345
—, "Zur Talionsformel" (1934), in: ibid., *Kleine Schriften* I, 1953, 341–344
Alter, R., "A New Theory of Kashrut," *Commentary* 68, 1979, 46–52
Altner, G., *Naturvergessenheit. Grundfragen einer umfassenden Bioethik*, Darmstadt 1991
Amit Y., "Hidden polemic in the conquest of Dan: Judges xvii–xviii," VT 40, 1990, 4–20
Amram, J. W., "Retaliation and Compensation," JQR 2, 1911/12, 191–211

Amsler, S., "Les documents de la loi et la formation du Pentateuque," in: A. de Pury (ed.), *Le Pentateuque en Question*, Genf ²1991, 235–257

—, "Loi oracle et loi écrite dans le Deutéronome," in: N. Lohfink (ed.), *Das Deuteronomium*, BEThL LXVIII, Leuven 1985, 51–54

Andersen, F. I./Freedman, D. N., *Hosea. A New Translation with Introduction and Commentary*, AncB 24, 1980

Andreades, A. M., *Geschichte der griechischen Staatswirtschaft. Von der Heroenzeit bis zur Schlacht bei Claironeia*, Germ. trans. München 1931, reprint Hildesheim 1965

Archi, A., "La formazione del diritto nell« Anatolia ittita," in: A. Theodorides et al., *La formazione del diritto nel Vicino Oriente Antico*, Naples and Rome 1988, 61–75

Asmussen, J. P./Laessø, J. (ed.), *Handbuch der Religionsgeschichte*, 3 vols., Göttingen 1971ff.

Assmann, J., *Ma'at. Gerechtigkeit und Unsterblichkeit im Alten Ägypten*, München 1990

Assmann, A.u. J. (ed.), *Kanon und Zensur. Archäologie der literarischen Kommunikation* II, München 1987

Assmann, A.u. J./Hardmeier, C. (eds.), *Schrift und Gedächtnis. Archäologie der literarischen Kommunikation* I, München 1983

Assyrian Dictionary of the Oriental Institute of the University of Chicago, ed. J. J. Gelb et al., Chicago 1965ff.

Auerbach, E., "Die Feste im alten Israel," VT 8, 1958, 1–18

Auld, A. G., "Cities of Refuge in Israelite Tradition," JSOT 10, 1978, 26–40

—, *Joshua, Moses and the Land. Tetrateuch – Pentateuch – Hexateuch in a Generation since 1938*, Edinburgh 1980

Aurelius, E., *Der Fürbitter Israels. Eine Studie zum Mosebild im Alten Testament*, CB 27, 1988

Avigad, N., "A Note on an Impression from a Woman's Seal," IEJ 37, 1987, 18f.

—, *Discovering Jerusalem*, Nashville 1980

—, *Hebrew Bullae from the Time of Jeremiah. Remnants of a Burnt Archive*, Jerusalem 1986

—, "The Chief of the Corvée," IEJ 30, 1980, 170–173

—, "The Contribution of Hebrew Seals to an Understanding of Israelite Religion and Society," in: *Ancient Israelite Religion*, FS F. M. Cross, Philadelphia 1987, 195–208

—, "On the Identification of Persons Mentioned in Hebrew Epigraphic sources" (Hebr.), ErIs 19, 1987, 233f.

Axelsson, L. E., *The Lord Rose up from Seir. Studies in the History and Traditions of the Negeb and Southern Judah*, CB.OT 25, 1987

Baentsch, B., *Das Bundesbuch Ex. XX 22 – XXIII 33. Seine ursprüngliche Gestalt, sein Verhältnis zu den es umgebenden Quellenschriften und seine Stellung in der alttestamentlichen Gesetzgebung*, Halle 1892

Baentsch, B., *Exodus – Leviticus – Numeri*, HK I/2, 1903

Bal, M. (ed.), *Anti-Covenant. Counter-Reading Women's Lives in the Hebrew Bible*, Bible and Literature Series 22, Sheffield 1989

Bamberger, B. J., "Revelations of Torah after Sinai," HUCA 14, 1941, 97–113

Barag, D., "A Silver Coin of Yohanan the High Priest" (hebr.), Qad. 17, 1984, 59–61

Barbiero, G., *L'asino del nemico: Non violenza e amore del nemico nella legislazone dell'Antico Testamento (Es 23,4–5; Dt 22,1–14; Lv 19,18)*, AnBib 128, 1991

Bardtke, H., *Das Buch Esther*, KAT XVII,5, Gütersloh 1963

Barkun, M., *Law without Sanctions. Order in Primitive Societies and the World Community*, New Haven and London 1968

Barr, J., "Biblical Law and the Question of Natural Theology," in: T. Veijola (ed.), *The Law in the Bible and in its Environment*, Publications of the Finnish Exegetical Society 51, Helsinki and Göttingen 1990, 1–22

Bartelmus, R., "Die Tierwelt in der Bibel. Exegetische Beobachtungen zu einem Teilaspekt der Diskussion um eine Theologie der Natur," BN 37, 1987, 11–37

—, "Mk 2,27 und die ältesten Fassungen des Arbeitsruhegebotes im AT. Biblisch-theologische Beobachtungen zur Sabbatfrage," BN 41, 1988, 41–64

Barth, H., *Die Jesaja-Worte in der Josiazeit. Israel und Assur als Thema einer produktiven Neuinterpretation der Jesajaüberlieferung*, WMANT 48, 1977

Barth, H.-M., "Gesetz und Evangelium I. Systematisch-theologisch," TRE XIII, 1984, 126–142

Barth, K., *Evangelium und Gesetz*, TEH 32, 1935 (= TEH 50, ³1961)

Bartlett, J. R., "The Use of the Word רֹאשׁ as a Title in the Old Testament," VT 19, 1969, 1–10

Baskin, D. R., *Pharaoh's Counsellors. Job, Jethro, and Balaam in Rabbinic and Patristic Tradition*, Program in Judaic Studies 47, 1983

Baumgarten, A., "The Torah as a public document in Judaism," SR 14, 1985, 17–24

Baumgarten, J. M., "On the Non-Literal Use of *ma 'ăśēr/dekatē*," JBL 103, 1984, 245–251

Baumgartner, W., "Zum Problem des »Jahweengels«," SThU 14, 1944, 97–102 = idem., *Zum Alten Testament und seiner Umwelt. Ausgewählte Aufsätze*, Leiden 1959, 240–246

Bechmann, U., *Das Deboralied zwischen Geschichte und Fiktion. Eine exegetische Untersuchung zu Richter 5*, St. Ottilien 1989

Becker, J., *2 Chronik*, NEB Liefg. 20, Würzburg 1988

—, *Esra/Nehemia*, NEB Liefg. 25, Würzburg 1990

Becker, U., *Richterzeit und Königtum. Redaktionsgeschichtliche Studien zum Richterbuch*, BZAW 192, 1990

Beer, G./(Galling, K.), *Exodus*, HAT I/3, 1939

Begg, C., "Ben Sirach's Non-mention of Ezra," BN 42, 1988, 14–18

Bellefontaine, E., "Customary Law and Chieftainship: Judicial Aspects of 2 Samuel 14.4–21," JSOT 38, 1987, 47–72

—, Deuteronomy 21,18–21: "Reviewing the Case of the Rebellious Son," JSOT 13, 1979, 13–31

Ben-Barak, Z., "The Appeal to the Kings as the Highest Authority for Justice," in: »*Wünschet Jerusalem Frieden*«, hg. v. M. Augustin/ K.-D. Schunck, Frankfurt/M. 1988, 169–177

Ben-Dov, M., "A Fragment of a Hebrew Inscription from First Temple Times Found on the Ophel," Qad. 17, 1984, 109–111

Benoit, P./Milik, J. T./de Vaux, R. (ed.): *Discoveries in the Judaean Desert II. Les Grottes de Murabbaʿât*, Oxford 1961

Bentzen, A., *Die Josianische Reform und ihre Voraussetzungen*, Copenhagen 1926

—, "Priesterschaft und Laien in der jüdischen Geschichte des 5. Jahrhunderts," AfO 6, 1930/31, 280–286

Bergren, R. V., *The Prophets and the Law*, MHUC 4, 1974

Bergsträsser, G., *Hebräische Grammatik* (1918), reprint Hildesheim 1962

Bernhardt, K.-H., Art. אָז, ThWAT I, 1973, 151–159

Bertholet, A., *Deuteronomium*, KHC V, 1899

—, *Die Bücher Esra und Nehemia*, KHC XIX, 1902

—, *Die Stellung der Israeliten und der Juden zu den Fremden*, Freiburg and Leipzig 1896

—, *Leviticus*, KHC III, 1901

Betlyon, J. W., "The Provincial Government of Persian Period Judea and the Yehud Coins," JBL 105, 1986, 633–642

Bettenzoli, G., "I Leviti e la riforma deuteronomica," RSLR 22, 1986, 3–25

Beuken, W. A. M., "Exodus 16.5,23: A Rule Regarding the Keeping of the Sabbath?" JSOT 32, 1985, 3–14

Beyer, K., *Die aramäischen Texte vom Toten Meer*, Göttingen 1984

Beyerlin, W., "Die Paränese im Bundesbuch und ihre Herkunft," in: *Gottes Wort und Gottes Land*, FS W. Hertzberg, Göttingen 1965, 2–29

—, *Die Rettung der Bedrängten in den Feindpsalmen der Einzelnen auf institutionelle Zusammenhänge untersucht*, FRLANT 99, 1970

—, "Gattung und Herkunft des Rahmens im Richterbuch," in: *Tradition und Situation*, FS A. Weiser, Göttingen 1963, 1–29

—, *Weisheitlich-kultische Heilsordnung. Studien zum 15. Psalm*, Biblisch-Theologische Studien 9, Neukirchen-Vluyn 1985

Beyerlin, W. (ed.), *Religionsgeschichtliches Textbuch zum Alten Testament*, GAT 1, 1975

Bialoblocki, S., *Die Beziehungen des Judentums zu Proselyten und Proselytentum*, Berlin 1930

Bianchi, H., *Alternativen zur Strafjustiz. Biblische Gerechtigkeit. Freistätten. Täter-Opfer-Ausgleich*, München and Mainz 1988

—, "Das Tsedeka-Modell als Alternative zum konventionellen Strafrecht," ZEE 18, 1974, 89–110

Bickerman, E. J., "The Babylonian Captivity," in: *The Cambridge History of Judaism*, vol. I. *Introduction; The Persian Period*, Cambridge 1984, 342–357

Bickert, R., *Die List Joabs und der Sinneswandel Davids. Eine dtr bearbeitete Einschaltung in die Thronfolgeerzählung: 2 Sam xiv 2–22*, VT.S 30, 1979, 30–51

Bietenhard, H. (ed.), *Der tannaitische Midrasch Sifre Deuteronomium*, *Judaica et Christiana* 8, Bern 1984

Bigger, S. F., "The Family Laws of Leviticus 18 in their Setting," JBL 98, 1979, 187–203

Billerbeck, P./Strack, H. L., *Kommentar zum Neuen Testament aus Talmud und Midrasch* I-V, München 1922ff, Nachdr. [7]1978

Bird, Ph. A., "The Place of Women in the Israelite Cultus," in: *Ancient Israelite Religion*, FS F. M. Cross, ed. P. D. Miller et al., Philadelphia 1987, 397–419

—, "Translating Sexist Language as a Theological and Cultural Problem," *Union Theological Seminary Quarterly Review* 42, 1988, 89–95

Birkeland, H., "Hebrew zǣand Arabic *ḏū*," StTh 2, 1949/50, 201f

Black, M., *Die Muttersprache Jesu*, BWANT 115, 1982

Blackstone, W., *Commentaries on the Laws of England*, Vol. 1, London [18]1821

Blau, J., "Short Philological Notes on the Inscription of Meša'," *Maarav* 2, 1979/80, 143–153

—, "Über homonyme und angeblich homonyme Wurzeln," VT 6, 1956, 242–248

Blenkinsopp, J., *Ezra – Nehemia. A Commentary*, London 1989

—, *Prophecy and Canon. A Contribution to the Study of Jewish Origin*, Notre Dame/Ind. 1977

—, "The Structure of P," CBQ 38, 1976, 275–292

Bloch, E., *Naturrecht und menschliche Würde*, Gesamtausgabe Vol. 6, Frankfurt/M. 1961

Blome, F., *Die Opfermaterie in Babylonien und Israel*, SSAOI 4, 1934

Blosser, D., *The Sabbath Year Cycle in Josephus*, HUCA 52, 1981, 129–139

Blum, E., *Die Komposition der Vätergeschichte*, WMANT 57, 1984

—, "Psalm 2,7c – eine performative Aussage, in ספר רנדטורף," FS R. Rendtorff, DBAT Beih.1, Dielheim 1975, 4–8

—, "Studien zur Kompositon des Pentateuch," BZAW 189, 1990

Blumenfeld, D. L., "The Terminology of Imprisonment and Forced Detention in the Bible," Ph.D. Diss. New York 1977

Blumenthal, E., *Altägyptische Reiseerzählungen: Die Lebensgeschichte des Sinuhe. Der Reisebericht des Wen-Amun*, Leipzig 1982

Boecker, H. J., *Die Beurteilung der Anfänge de Königtums in den deuteronomistischen Abschnitten des 1. Samuelbuches. Ein Beitrag zum Problem des »Deuteronomistischen Geschichtswerks«*, WMANT 31, 1969

—, *Klagelieder*, ZBK 21, 1985

—, *Recht und Gesetz im Alten Testament und im Alten Orient*, Neukirchen-Vluyn ²1984

—, *Redeformen des Rechtslebens im Alten Testament*, WMANT 14, 1964

Boer, P. A. H. de, "Quelques remarques sur l'arc dans la Nuée (Gen 9,8–17)," in: C. Brekelmans (ed.), *Questions disputées d'Ancient Testament*, BEThL 33, ²1989, 105–114

—, "Some Remarks on Exodus xxi 7–11. The Hebrew Female Slave," *Orientalia Neerlandica*, Leiden 1948, 162–166 = idem., "Selected Studies in Old Testament Exegesis," OTS 27,1991, 33–37

Bogaert, P.-M., "Les trois Rédactions conservées et la forme originale de l'envoi du Cantique de Moïse (Dt 32,43)," in: N. Lohfink (ed.), *Das Deuteronomium*, BEThL 68, 1985, 329–340

Bohannan, P., *Justice and Judgement among the Tiv*, London ²1968

Booij, Th., "Mountain and Theophany in the Sinai Narrative," Bib. 65, 1984, 1–26

—, "The Background of the Oracle in Psalm 81," Bib. 65, 1984, 465–475

Boorer, S., "The Kerygmatic Intention of the Priestly Document," ABR 25, 1976, 12–20

Borger, R., "Akkadische Rechtsbücher," TUAT I/1, 1982, 32–95

Bornkamm, G., Art. πρέσβυς κτλ., ThWNT VI, 1959, 651–683

Bornkamm, H., *Luther und das Alte Testament*, Tübingen 1948

Borowski, O., *Agriculture in Iron Age Israel*, Winona Lake, Ind. 1987

Bottero, J., "Le »Code« de Ḫammu-rabi," Scuola Normale Superiore (Pisa), Annali della Scuola Superiore di Pisa, 3. Ser., 12, Firenze 1982, 409–444

Bourgeault, G., *Décalogue et morale chrétienne. Enquête patristique sur l'utilisation et l'interprétation chrétienne du décalogue de ca. 60 à ca. 220*, Paris 1971

Bovati, P., *Ristabilire la guistizia*, AnBib 110, Rom 1986

Braulik, G., "Das Deuteronomium und die Geburt de.s Monotheismus," in: *Gott der einzige. Zur Entstehung des Monotheismus in Israel*, ed. E. Haag, QD 104, 1985, 115–159 = idem., *Studien zur Theologie des Deuteronomiums*, SBAB 2, 1988, 257–300

—, *Deuteronomium 1 – 16,7*, NEB Liefg. 15, Würzburg 1986

—, "Die Abfolge der Gesetze in Dtn 12–26 und der Dekalog," in: *Das Deuteronomium. Entstehung, Gestalt und Botschaft*, ed. N. Lohfink, BEThL 68, 1988, 252–272 = idem., *Studien zur Theologie des Deuteronomiums*, SBAB 2, 1988, 231–255

Braulik, G. "Die Ausdrücke für »Gesetz« im Buch Deuteronomium," Biblica 51, 1970, 39–66 = idem., *Studien zur Theologie des Deuteronomiums*, SBAB 2, 1988, 11–38

—, *Die deuteronomischen Gesetze und der Dekalog. Studien zum Aufbau von Deuteronomium* 12–26, SBS 145, 1991

—, "Die Freude des Festes. Das Kultverständnis des Deuteronomiums – die älteste biblische Festtheorie," in: *Theologisches Jahrbuch* 1983, 13–54 = idem. *Studien zur Theologie des Deuteronomiums*, SBAB 2, 1988, 161–218

—, "Die Funktion von Siebenergruppierungen im Endtext des Deuteronomiums," in: *Ein Gotteine Offenbarung*, FS N. Füglister, ed. F. V. Reiterer, Würzburg 1991, 37–50

—, "Gesetz als Evangelium. Rechtfertigung und Begnadigung nach der deuteronomischen Tora," ZThK 79, 1982, 127–160 = idem., *Studien zur Theologie des Deuteronomiums*, SBAB 2, 1988, 123–16

—, "Haben in Israel auch Frauen geopfert? Beobachtungen am Deuteronomium," in: *Zur Aktualität des Alten Testaments*, FS G. Sauer, Frankfurt/M. 1991, 19–28

—, "Weisheit, Gottesnähe und Gesetz. Zum Kerygma von Deuteronomium 4,5–8," in: *Studien zum Pentateuch*, FS W. Kornfeld, Wien 1977, 165–195 = idem., *Studien zur Theologie des Deuteronomiums*, SBAB 2, 1988, 53–93

—, "Zur Abfolge der Gesetze in Deuteronomium 16,18 – 21,23. Weitere Beobachtungen," Bib. 69, 1988, 63–92

Brekelmans, C., "Deuteronomy 5, Its Place and Function," in: *Das Deuteronomium. Entstehung, Gestalt und Botschaft*, ed. N. Lohfink, BEThL 68, 1985, 164–173

Brenner, A., *The Israelite Woman. Social Role and Literary Type in Biblical Narrative*, Sheffield 1985

Briant, P., "Polythéismes et empire unitaire. (Remarques sur la politique religieuse des Achémenides)," in: *Les grandes figures religieuses. Fonctionnement, pratique et symbolique dans l'Antiquité*, Centre de Recherches d'Histoire Ancienne 68, Paris 1986, 425–438

—, "Pouvoir central et polycentrisme culturel dans l'empire Achéménide. Quelques réflections et suggestions," in: H. Sancisi-Weerdenburg (ed.), *Achaemenid History I, Sources, Structures and Synthesis*, Leiden 1987, 1–31

Brichto, H. C., "On Slaughter and Sacrifice, Blood and Atonement," HUCA 47, 1976, 19–55

—, "The Worship of the Golden Calf: A Literary Analysis of a Fable on Idolatry," HUCA 54 1983, 1–44

Bright, J., *Jeremiah*, AncB 21, [2]1984

Brin, G., "Numbers xv 22–23 and the Question of the Composition of the Pentateuch," VT 30, 1980, 351–354

Brock, S. P., "Bibelübersetzungen I,2. Die Übersetzungen des Alten Testaments im Griechischen," TRE VI, 1980, 163–172

Brockelmann, C., *Hebräische Syntax*, Neukirchen 1956

Brongers, H. A., "Der Eifer des Herrn Zebaoth," VT 13, 1963, 269–284

Broshi, M., "La population de l'ancienne Jérusalem," RB 82, 1975, 5–14

—, "The Expansion of Jerusalem in the Reigns of Hezekiah and Manasseh," IEJ 24, 1974, 21–26

Brueggemann, W., "The Kerygma of the Priestly Writers," ZAW 84, 1972, 397–414

Brunner, R. (ed.), *Gesetz und Gnade im Alten Testament und im jüdischen Denken*, Zürich 1969

Buber, M., *Zwei Glaubensweisen* (1950), Werke I. *Schriften zur Philosophie*, Heidelberg 1962, 651–782

Buber, M./Rosenzweig, F., *Bücher der Geschichte, verdeutscht von . . .* , Cologne and Olten 1966

—, *Die fünf Bücher der Weisung verdeutscht von . . .* , Cologne and Olten 1954

Buchholz, J., *Die Ältesten Israels im Deuteronomium*, GTA 36, 1988

Budd, P. J., "Holiness and Cult," in: *The World of Ancient Israel. Sociological, Anthropological and Political Perspectives*, ed. R. E. Clements, Cambridge 1989, 275–298

—, "Priestly Instruction in Pre-Exilic Israel," VT 23, 1973, 1–14

Budde, K., *Der Segen Moses'. Dt. 33*, Tübingen 1922

Burrows, M., "The Complaint of Laban's Daughters," JAOS 57, 1937, 259–276

Caillois, R., *Der Mensch und das Heilige*, Germ. trans. München 1988

Campbell jr., E. F., *Ruth*, AncB 7, 1975

Caquot, A., "Les bénédictions de Moïse (Deutéronome 33,6–25). I Ruben, Juda, Levi, Benjamin," Sem. 32, 1982, 67–81

Cardascia, G., "La formazione del diritto in Assiria," in: A. Theodorides et al., *La formazione del diritto nel Vicino Oriente Antico*, Naples and Rome 1988, 51–60

—, "La Place du talion dans l'histoire du droit pénal à la lumière des droits du Proche-Orient ancien," in: *Mélanges Jean Dauvillier*, Toulouse 1979, 169–183

—, "Le Statut de l'Étranger dans la Mésopotamie Ancienne," in: *L'Étranger, Recueil de la Societé Jean Bodin* 9, 1958, 105–117

Cardellini, I., *Die biblischen »Sklaven«-Gesetze im Lichte des keilschriftlichen Sklavenrechts. Ein Beitrag zur Tradition und Redaktion der alttestamentlichen Rechtstexte*, BBB 55, Bonn 1981

Cardenal, E., *Das Evangelium der Bauern von Solentiname. Gespräche über das Leben Jesu in Lateinamerika*, 4 vols. Gütersloh [3]1980

Carlson, R. A., "Élie à l'Horeb," VT 19, 1969, 416–439

Carmichael, C. M., "A Ceremonial Crux: Removing a Man's Sandal as a Female Gesture of Contempt," JBL 96, 1977, 321–336

—, "Forbidden Mixtures," VT 32, 1982, 394–415

Carmichael, C. M., *Law and Narrative in the Bible. The Evidence of the Deuteronomic Laws and the Decalogue,* Ithaca, N.Y. and London 1985
—, "On Separating Life and Death. An Explanation of Some Biblical Laws," HThR 69, 1976, 1–7
Carroll, R. P., *Jeremiah. A Commentary,* London 1986
Cassuto, U., *A Commentary on the Book of Exodus* (Hebr. 1951), Engl. trans. Jerusalem ³1983
Cavaletti, S., "In significato di mashsheh yad in Deut. 15,2," *Antonianum* 31, 1956, 301–304
Cazelles, H., "Études sur le Code de L'Alliance," Paris 1946
—, "Impur et sacré à Ugarit," in: *Al-Bahit,* FS J. Henninger, 1976, 37–47
—, *Institution et Terminologie en Deut I 6–17,* VT.S XV, 1966, 97–112
—, "Jérémie et le Deutéronome," RSR 38, 1951, 5–36, Engl.: "Jeremiah and Deuteronomy," in: *A Prophet to the Nations. Essays in Jeremiah Studies,* ed. L. G. Perdue/B. W. Kovacs, Winona Lake 1984, 89–111
—, "L'Alliance du Sinai en Ex 34,10–27," in: *Mélanges bibliques et orientaux en l'honneur de M. M. Delcor,* ed. A. Caquot et al., AOAT 215, 1985, 57–68 = idem., *Autour de l'Exode* (Études), Paris 1987, 175–185
—, "L'auteur du code de l'alliance," RB 52, 1945, 173–191
—, "La mission d'Esdras," VT 4, 1954, 113–140
—, "Le Pentateuque comme Torah," in: idem., *Autour de L'Exode* (Études), Paris 1987, 9–52
—, "Pur et impur aux origines de l'Hébreu et à Ugarit," MUSJ 49, 1975/76, 443–449
—, "Torah et Loi, préalables à l'étude historique d'une notion juive," in: idem., *Autour de L'Éxode* (Études), Paris 1987, 131–141
Celan, P., *Zeitgehöft. Späte Gedichte aus dem Nachlaß,* Frankfurt/M. 1976
Chamberlain, G. A., "Ex 21–23 and Dt 12–26: A Form-Critical Study," Diss. Boston Univ. Graduate School 1977
Chan, K.-K., "You Shall Not Eat These Abominable Things: An Examination Of Different Interpretations Of Deuteronomy 14, 3–20," *East Asia Journal of Theology* 3, 1985, 88–106
Chiesa, B., "La promessa di un profeta (Deut., 18,15–20)," BeO 15, 1973, 17–26
Childs, B. S., *Introduction to the Old Testament as Scripture,* Philadelphia 1979
—, *The Book of Exodus. A Critical Theological Commentary,* OTL, 1974
Cholewinski, A., *Heiligkeitsgesetz und Deuteronomium. Eine vergleichende Studie,* AnBib 66, 1976
Christensen, D. L., "Prose and Poetry in the Bible. The Narrative Poetics of Deuteronomy 1,9–18," ZAW 97, 1985, 179–189
Claburn, W. E., "The Fiscal Basis of Josiah's Reforms," JBL 92, 1973, 11–22

Clements, R. E., *Deuteronomy*, Sheffield 1989

Clines, D. J. A., *Ezra, Nehemia, Esther*, New Century Bible Commentary, Grand Rapids 1984

—, "Nehemiah 10 as an Example of Early Jewish Biblical Exegesis," JSOT 21, 1981, 111–117

—, "The Force of the Text. A Response to Tamara C. Eskenazi's »Ezra-Nehemia: From Text to Actuality«," in: J. C. Exum (ed.), *Signs and Wonders. Biblical Texts in Literary Focus*, Atlanta 1989, 199–215

—, "The Nehemiah Memoir: The Perils of Autobiography," in: *What Does Eve Do to Help? and Other Readerly Questions to the Old Testament*, JSOT.S 94, 1990, 124–164

Coats, G. W., *Rebellion in the Wilderness. The Murmuring Motif in the Wilderness Traditions of the Old Testament*, Nashville/New York 1968

—, "The King's Loyal Opposition: Obedience and Authority in Exodus 32–24," in: *Canon and Authority*, FS W. Zimmerli, Philadelphia 1977, 91–109

Cody, A., *A History of O.T. Priesthood*, AnBib 35, 1969

Cogan, M./Tadmor, H., *II Kings. A New Translation with Introduction and Commentary*, AncB 11, 1988

Coggins, R. J., *Samaritans and Jews. The Origin of Samaritanism Reconsidered*, Atlanta 1975

—, *The First and Second Books of the Chronicles*, CBC O.T. 11, 1976

—, "The origins of the Jewish diaspora," in: R. E. Clements (ed.), *The World of Ancient Israel. Sociological, Anthropological and Political Perspectives*, Cambridge 1989, 163–181

Cohen, B., *Jewish and Roman Law. A Comparative Study*. 2 vols., New York 1966

Cohen, D., "Greek Law: Problems and Methods," ZSRG.R 106, 1989, 81–105

Cohen, H., "Die Nächstenliebe im Talmud. Als ein Gutachten dem königlichen Landgerichte zu Marburg erstattet (1888)", in: idem., *Der Nächste. Vier Abhandlungen über das Verhalten von Mensch zu Mensch und der Lehre des Judentums*, Berlin 1935, 29–52

—, *Religion der Vernunft aus den Quellen des Judentums. Eine jüdische Religionsphilosophie*, reprint Wiesbaden 1978

Cohen, M., "Le »Ger« biblique et son statut socio-religieux," RHR 207, 1990, 131–158

Cohen, M. L., "Backgrounds of the Biblical Law against Usury," CSSH 6, 1964, 250–267

Colpe, C., "Sakralisierung von Texten und Filiationen von Kanons," in: A. u. J. Assmann (ed.), *Kanon und Zensur. Archäologie der literarischen Kommunikation* II, München 1987, 80–92

Colpe, C., (ed.), *Die Diskussion um das* »*Heilige*«, WdF 305, 1977

Conrad, D., "Einige (archäologische) Miszellen zur Kultgeschichte Judas in der Königszeit," in: *Textgemäß*, FS E. Würthwein, ed. A. Gunneweg/O. Kaiser, Göttingen 1979, 28–32

—, "Studien zum Altargesetz. Ex 20, 24–26," Diss. Marburg 1968

Conrad, J., Art. זָקֵן *zāqen* κτλ., ThWAT II, 1977, 639–650

Conroy, C., "Reflections on the Exegetical Task. Apropos of Recent Studies on 2 Kg 22–23," in: *Pentateuchal and Deuteronomistic Studies. Papers read at the XIIIth IOSOT Congress Leuven 1989*, ed. C. Brekelmans u. J. Lust, BEThL 94, 1990, 255–268

Coogan, M. D., "Life in the Diaspora. Jews at Nippur in the Fifth Century B.C.," BA 37, 1974, 6–12

Cooper, A., "The Plain Sense of Exodus 23:5," HUCA 59, 1988, 1–22

Coote, R. B., "Yahwe Recalls Elijah," in: *Traditions in Transformation*, FS F. M. Cross, ed. B. Halpern/J. D. Levenson, Winona Lake/Ind. 1981, 115–120

Coppens, J., "Exode XIX6: Un royaume ou une royauté des prêtres?" EThL 53, 1977, 185f.

Cornill, C. H., *Das Buch Jeremia*, Leipzig 1905

Cortese, E., *Josua 13–21. Ein priesterschriftlicher Abschnitt im deuteronomistischen Geschichtswerk*, OBO 94, 1990

—, "L'esegesi di H (Lev. 17–26)," RivBib 29, 1981, 129–146

Cowley, A. (ed.), *Aramaic Papyri of the Fifth Century B.C.*, Oxford 1923, reprint Osnabrück 1967

Cross, F. M., "A Reconstruction of the Judaean Restoration," JBL 94, 1975, 4–18

—, *Canaanite Myth and Hebrew Epic. Essays in the History of the Religion of Israel*, Cambridge/Mass. 1973

Cross, F. M./Freedman, D. N., *Studies in Ancient Yahwistic Poetry*, SBLDS 21, Missoula 1975

—, "The Blessing of Moses," JBL 67, 1948, 190–210

Crüsemann, F., "»Auge um Auge . . .« (Ex 21,24f). Zum sozialgeschichtlichen Sinn des Talionsgesetzes im Bundesbuch," EvTh 47, 1987, 411–426

—, "». . . damit er dich segne in allem Tun deiner Hand. . .« (Dtn 14,29). Die Produktionsverhältnisse der späten Königszeit, dargestellt am Ostrakon von Meṣad Ḥashavjahu, und die Sozialgesetzgebung des Deuteronomiums," in: *Mitarbeiter der Schöpfung*. Bibel und Arbeitswelt, ed. L. u. W. Schottroff, München 1983, 72–103

—, "». . . er aber soll dein Herr sein« (Gen 3,16). Die Frau in der patriarchalischen Welt des Alten Testaments," in: idem.,/H. Thyen, *Als Mann und Frau geschaffen. Exegetische Studien zur Rolle der Frau*, Kennzeichen 2, Gelnhausen 1978, 13–106

Crüsemann, F., "». . . wie wir vergeben unseren Schuldigern«. Schulden und Schuld in der biblischen Tradition," in: *Impulse*. FS A. Jäger, Bielefeld 1991 (Privatdruck), 131–141 = M. Crüsemann/ W. Schottroff (eds.), *Schuld und Schulden. Biblische Traditionen in gegenwärtigen Konflikten*, München 1992

—, "5. Mose 6,4–6," JK 51, 1990, 303–307

—, *Bewahrung der Freiheit. Das Thema des Dekalogs in sozialgeschichtlicher Perspektive*, KT 78, 1983

—, "Das »portative Vaterland«. Struktur und Genese des alttestament-lichen Kanons," in: A. u. J. Assmann (ed.), *Kanon und Zensur. Archäologie der literarischen Kommunikation* II, München 1987, 63–79

—, *Das Bundesbuch – Historischer Ort und institutioneller Hintergrund*, VT.S 40, 1988, 27–41

—, "Der Exodus als Heiligung," in: *Die Hebräische Bibel und ihre zweifache Nachgeschichte*. FS R. Rendtorff, ed. E. Blum et al., Neukirchen 1990, 117–129

—, "Der Pentateuch als Tora. Prolegomena zur Interpretation seiner Endgestalt," EvTh 49, 1989, 250–267

—, *Der Widerstand gegen das Königtum. Die antiköniglichen Texte des Alten Testamentes und der Kampf um den frühen israelitischen Staat*, WMANT 49, 1978

—, "Der Zehnte der israelitischen Königszeit," WuD 18, 1985, 21–47

—, "Die Eigenständigkeit der Urgeschichte. Ein Beitrag zur Diskussion um den »Jahwisten«," in: *Die Botschaft und die Boten*, FS H. W. Wolff, ed. J. Jeremias/L. Perlitt, Neukirchen-Vluyn 1981, 11–29

—, "Ein israelitisches Ritualbad aus vorexilischer Zeit," ZDPV 94, 1978, 68–75

—, "Fremdenliebe und Identitätssicherung. Zum Verständnis der »Fremden«-Gesetze im Alten Testament," WuD 19, 1987, 11–24

—, "Israel in der Perserzeit. Eine Skizze in Auseinandersetzung mit Max Weber," in: W. Schluchter (ed.), *Max Webers Sicht des antiken Christentums. Interpretation und Kritik*, 548, 1985, 205–232

—, "Recht und Theologie im Alten Testament," in: *Studien zu Kirchenrecht und Theologie* I, ed. K. Schlaich, Texte u. Materialien der FEST A 26, Heidelberg 1987, 11–81

—, "Tendenzen der alttestamentlichen Wissenschaft zwischen 1933 und 1945," WuD 20, 1989, 79–103

—, "Tora und christliche Ethik," in: R. Rendtorff/E. Stegemann (eds.), *Auschwitz – Krise der christlichen Theologie*, München 1980, 59–177

Curtis, E. L., *The Books of Chronicles*, ICC, Edinburgh (1910) ²1952

Dalman, G., *Arbeit und Sitte in Palästina*, I – VII, Gütersloh 1928ff., reprint 1964

—, *Die Worte Jesu*, Leipzig ²1930

Dandamaev, M. A., *A Political History of the Achaemenid Empire*, Engl. transl. Leiden 1989

—, "Der Tempelzehnte in Babylonien während des 6.-4. Jh.v.u.Z.," in: *Beiträge zur Alten Geschichte und deren Nachleben* I, FS F. Altheim, Berlin 1969, 82–90

—, "Politische und wirtschaftliche Geschichte," in: *Beiträge zur Achämenidengeschichte, Historia*, Einzelschrift 18, ed. G. Walser, Wiesbaden 1972, 15–58

Dandamaev, M. A./Lukonin, V. G., *The Culture and Social Institutions of Ancient Iran*, Cambridge 1989

Daniels, D. R., *Hosea and Salvation History*, BZAW 191, 1990

—, "The Composition of the Ezra-Nehemiah Narrative," in: *Ernten, was man sät*, FS K. Koch, ed. D. R. Daniels et al., Neukirchen 1991, 311–328

—, "The Creed of Deuteronomy xxvi Revisited," in: J. A. Emerton (ed.), *Studies in the Pentateuch*, VT.S 41, 1990, 231–242

Darling, A. S., "The Levitical Code: Hygiene or Holiness," in: *Medicine and the Bible*, ed. B. Palmer, Exeter 1986, 85–99

Daube, D., "Biblical Landmarks in the Struggle for Women's Rights," *Juridicial Review* 90, 1978, 177–197

—, "Das Selbstverständliche in der Rechtsgeschichte," ZSRG.R 90, 1973, 1–13

—, "Direct and Indirect Causation in Biblical Law," VT 11, 1961, 246–269

—, "Error and Accident in the Bible," RIDA 2, 1949, 189–213

—, "Law in the Narratives," in: idem., *Studies in Biblical Law*, 1947, 1–73

—, "Lex Talionis," in: idem., *Studies in Biblical Law*, Cambridge 1947, 102–153

—, "Rechtsgedanken in den Erzählungen des Pentateuchs," in: *Von Ugarit nach Qumran*, BZAW 77, 1958, 38–41

—, *Sin, Ignorance and Forgiveness in the Bible*, London 1960

—, *Studies in Biblical Law*, Cambridge 1947

—, "The Culture of Deuteronomy," *Orita* 3, 1969, 27–52

—, "Witnesses in Bible and Talmud," in: idem./C. Carmichael, *Biblical Laws of Talion*, Oxford 1986, 3–20

Davies, D. R., "Rebellion, Presence, and Covenant: A Study in Exodus 32–34," WThJ 44, 1982, 71–87

Davies, E. W., "Inheritance Rights and the Hebrew Levirate Marriage," VT 31, 1981, 138–144.257–268

Davies, W. D., *Torah in the Messianic Age and/or the Age to Come*, Philadelphia 1952

Deiana, G., "Azazel in Lv. 16," Lat. 54, 1988, 16–33

Deissler, A., *Zwölf Propheten: Hosea, Joël, Amos*, NEB Liefg. 4, Würzburg ²1985

Delcor, M., "Astarté et la fécondité des troupeaux en Deut. 7,13 et parallèles," UF 6, 1974, 7–14

Delekat, L., *Asylie und Schutzorakel am Zionsheiligtum*, Leiden 1967

Demare, S., "La valeur de la loi dans les droits cunéiformes," APD 32, 1987, 335–346

Demosthenes, *Oratio XXIV. Against Timocrates*, in: Werke III, ed. J. H. Vince, The Loeb Classical Literary, ³1964, 372–511

Dequeker, L., "Noah and Israel. The everlasting divine covenant with mankind," in: C. Brekelmans (ed.), *Questions disputées dAncien Testament*, BEThL 33, 1974, 115–129

Diamond, A. S., *Primitive Law, Past and Present*, London 1971

Diebner, B. J., "Exodus 15,22–27 und der Beginn der Wüstenzeit »Israels«," DBAT 2O, 1984, 122–159

—, "Gen 34 und Dinas Rolle bei der Definition »Israels«," DBAT 19, 1984, 59–75

Diebner, B. J./Schult, H., "Das Problem der Todesstrafe an Tier und Mensch in Genesis 9,5–6," DBAT 6, 1974, 2–5

—, "Die Ehen der Erzväter," DBAT 8, 1975, 2–10

Diestel, L., *Geschichte des Alten Testamentes in der christlichen Kirche*, Jena 1869

Dietrich, M./Loret, O., "'DB und 'DB im Ugaritischen," UF 17, 1986, 105–116

—, "Ug. *bṣqlʻrgz* und he. *b ṣqlnw* (2 Reg 4,42), *ʻgwz*," UF 18, 1986, 115–120

—, "Ugaritische Rituale und Beschwörungen," TUAT II, 1988, 300–357

Dietrich, M./Loretz, O./Sanmartin, J. (ed.), *Die keilalphabetischen Texte aus Ugarit*, AOAT 24, 1976

Dietrich, W., *Jesaja und die Politik*, BEvTh 74, 1976

Dijk, J. v., "Neusumerische Gerichtsurkunden in Baghdad," ZA 55, 1963, 70–90

Dillmann, A., *Die Bücher Exodus und Leviticus* (ed. V. Ryssel), KEH 12, Leipzig ³1897

—, *Numeri, Deuteronomium und Josua*, KEH 3, ²1886

Dion, P.-E., "»Tu feras disparaître le Mal du Milieu de toi«," RB 87, 1980, 321–349

—, "Deutéronome 21,1–9: Miroir du dévelopement légal et religieux d'Israël," SR 11, 1982, 13–22

Dohmen, C., Art. מַסֵּכָה *massekāh*, ThWAT IV, 1984, 1009–1015

—, *Das Bilderverbot. Seine Entstehung und seine Entwicklung im Alten Testament*, BBB 62, ²1987

—, "Dekalogexegese und kanonische Literatur. Zu einem fragwürdigen Beitrag C. Levins," VT 37, 1987, 81–85

—, "»Eifersüchtiger ist sein Name« (Ex 34,14). Ursprung und Bedeutung der alttestamentlichen Rede von Gottes Eifersucht," ThZ 46, 1990, 289–304

—, "Was stand auf den Tafeln vom Sinai und was auf denen vom Horeb? Geschichte und Theologie eines Offenbarungsrequisits," in: F.-L. Hossfeld (ed.), *Vom Sinai zum Horeb. Stationen alttestamentlicher Glaubensgeschichte*, Würzburg 1989, 9–50

Dohmen, D., "Ein kanaanäischer Schmiedeterminus *(NSK)*," UF 15, 1983, 39–42

Döller, J., *Die Reinheits- und Speisegesetze des Alten Testaments in religionsgeschichtlicher Beleuchtung*, Münster 1917

Domar, E. D., "The Causes of Slavery or Serfdom: A Hypothesis," JEconHist 30, 1970, 18–32

Dommershausen, W., "Heiligkeit, ein alttestamentliches Sozialprinzip?" ThQ 148, 1968, 153–166

Donner, H., *Die Verwerfung des Königs Saul*, SbWGF XIX/5, 1983

—, *Geschichte des Volkes Israel und seiner Nachbarn in Grundzügen*, GAT 4, 2 vols., 1984 and 1986

Donner, H./Röllig, W., *Kanaanäische und aramäische Inschriften*, 3 vols. (1964), Wiesbaden ³1979

Dorival, G., "Les origines de la Septante: la traduction en grec des cinq livres de la Torah," in: idem./M. Harl/O. Munnich, *La Bible grecque des Septante*, Paris 1988, 39–82

Doron, P., "A New Look at an Old Lex," *Journal of the Ancient Near Eastern Society of the Columbia University* I/2," 1969, 21–27

Douglas, M., *Reinheit und Gefährdung. Eine Studie zu Vorstellungen von Verunreinigung und Tabu*, Germ. trans. 712, 1985

Dozeman, T., "Spatial Form in Exod. 19: 1–8a and the Larger Sinai Narrative," Semeia 46, 1989, 87–101

Draffkorn, A. E., "Iläni/Elohim," JBL 76, 1957, 216–224

Dreier, R., "Der Begriff des Rechts," *Neue Juristische Wochenzeitschrift* 39, 1986, 890–896 = in: idem., *Recht – Staat – Vernunft. Studien zur Rechtstheorie* 2, 954, 1991, 95–119

—, "Göttliches und menschliches Recht," ZEvKR 32, 1987, 289–316

Drewermann, E., *Der tödliche Fortschritt. Von der Zerstörung der Erde und des Menschen im Erbe des Christentums*, Regensburg ³1981

Driver, G. R./Miles, J. C., *The Assyrian Laws*, Oxford 1935, reprint 1975

—, *The Babylonian Laws*, 2 vols., Oxford (1955) ⁴/³1968

Duhm, B., *Das Buch Jeremia*, KHC XI, 1901

—, *Das Buch Jesaja*, HK 3/1, ⁴1922, reprint 1968

Düll, R., *Das Zwölftafelgesetz*, München ⁵1976

Dumbrell, W. J., "In those days there was no king in Israel; every man did what was right in his own eyes," JSOT 25, 1983, 23–33

Dux, G., *Rechtssoziologie. Eine Einführung*, UTB 241, 1978

Dworkin, R., *Bürgerrechte ernstgenommen*, Germ. trans. Frankfurt/M. 1990

Ebach, J., "Bild Gottes und Schrecken der Tiere. Zur Anthropologie der priesterlichen Urgeschichte," in: idem., *Ursprung und Ziel. Erinnerte Zukunft und erhoffte Vergangenheit*, Neukirchen 1986, 16–47

Eder, W., "The Political Significance of the Codification of Law in Archaic Societies," in: K. Raaflaub (ed.), *Social Struggles in Archaic Rome. New Perspectives on the Conflict of the Orders*, Berkeley 1986, 262–300

Ehrlich, E. L., "Tora im Judentum," EvTh 37, 1977, 536–549

Eising, H., Art. זָכַר *zākar*, ThWAT II, 1977, 571–593

—, *Formgeschichtliche Untersuchung zur Jakobserzählung der Genesis*, Emsdetten 1940

Eißfeldt, O., *Einleitung in das Alte Testament*, Tübingen ³1964

—, *Erstlinge und Zehnten im Alten Testament*, BWANT 22, 1917

—, "Goethes Beurteilung des kultischen Dekalogs von Ex 34 im Lichte der Pentateuchkritik," ZThK 63, 1966, 135–144 = idem., *Kl. Schr.* IV, Tübingen 1968, 221–230

—, "Zum Zehnten bei den Babyloniern" (1918), in: idem., *Kl. Schr.* I, 1962, 13–22

Eitz, A., "Studien zum Verhältnis von Priesterschrift und Deutero-jesaja," Diss. Heidelberg 1969

Elbogen, I., *Der jüdische Gottesdienst in seiner geschichtlichen Entwicklung*, Frankfurt/M. 1931, reprint 1962

Elhorst, H. J., "Eine verkannte Zauberhandlung (Dtn 21₁₉)," ZAW 39, 1921, 58–67

Éliade, M., *Das Heilige und das Profane*, Hamburg 1984

—, *Die Religionen und das Heilige*, Salzburg 1954

Elliger, K., "Das Gesetz Leviticus 18*," ZAW 67, 1955, 1–25 = idem., *Kleine Schriften zum Alten Testament*, ThB 32, 1966, 232–259

—, *Leviticus*, HAT I/4, 1966

—, "Sinn und Ursprung der priesterlichen Geschichtserzählung," ZThK 49, 1952, 121 – 143 = idem., *Kleine Schriften zum Alten Testament*, ThB 32, 1966, 174–198

—, "Zur Analyse des Sündopfergesetzes," in: *Verbannung und Heimkehr*, FS W. Rudolph, Tübingen 1961, 39–50

Emerton, J. A., "Did Ezra Go to Jerusalem 428 B.C.?" JThS NS 17, 1966, 1–19

—, "Priests and Levites in Deuteronomy," VT 12, 1962, 129–138

—, "The Priestly Writer in Genesis," JThS NS 39, 1988, 381–400

Emmerson, G. I., *Hosea. An Israelite Prophet in Judean Perspective*, JSOT.S 28, 1984

—, "Women in Ancient Israel," in: *The World of Ancient Israel. Socio-logical, Anthropological and Political Perspectives*, ed. R. E. Clements, Cambridge 1989, 371–394

Engelken, K., *Frauen im Alten Israel. Eine begriffsgeschichtliche Studie zur Stellung der Frau im Alten Testament*, BWANT 7/10 (130), 1990

Eph 'al, I, "The Western Minorities in Babylonia in the 6th – 5th Centuries B.C., Maintenance and Cohesion," *Orientalia* 47, 1978, 74–90

Epsztein, L., *La justice sociale dans le Proche-Orient Ancien et le peuple de la Bible*, Paris 1983

Ernst, A., "»Wer Menschenblut vergießt . . .«. Zur Übersetzung von באדם in Gen 9,6," ZAW 102, 1990, 252–253

Eskenazi, T. C., "Ezra-Nehemia: From Text to Actuality," in: J. C. Exum (ed.), *Signs and Wonders. Biblical Texts and Literary Focus*, Atlanta 1989, 165–197

—, *In an Age of Prose. A Literary Approach to Ezra-Nehemia*, SBLMS 36, 1988

—, "The Structure of Ezra-Nehemiah and the Integrity of the Book," JBL 107, 1988, 641–656

Eslinger, L., "More Drafting Techniques in Deuteronomic Laws," VT 34, 1984, 221–226

Evans, C. D., "Judah's Foreign Policy from Hezekiah zu Josiah," in: idem. (ed.), *Scripture in Context. Essays on the Comparative Method*, Pittsburgh Theol. Monogr. Ser. 34, 1980, 157–178

Evers, T. (ed.), *Schöpfung als Rechtssubjekt?* 8. Theologen-Juristen-Gespräch, Hofgeismarer Protokolle 269, 1990

Ewil, H., "'Azazel The Prince of the Steepe. A Comparative Study," ZAW 92, 1980, 43–59

Fabry, H.-J., Art. עַמּוּד *'ammûḏ*, ThWAT VI, 1989, 204–209

—, "Art. דַּל dal κτλ., ThWAT II, 1977, 221–244

—, "Noch ein Dekalog! Die Thora des lebendigen Gottes in ihrer Wirkungsgeschichte. Ein Versuch zu Deuteronomium 27," in: *Im Gespräch mit dem dreieinigen Gott*, FS W. Breunig, ed. M. Böhnke/ H. Heinz, Düsseldorf 1985, 75–96

Falk, Z. W., "Exodus 21,6," VT 9, 1959, 86–88

—, *Hebrew Law in Biblical Times*, Jerusalem 1964

—, "Hebrew Legal Terms" (I), JSS 5, 1960, 350–354; (II), JSS 12, 1967, 241–244; (III), JSS 14, 1969, 39–44

Fantar, M. H., "A propos d'Ashtart en Méditerranée Occidentale," RSFen 1, 1973, 19–29

Feldman, D. M., *Birth Control in Jewish Law. Marital Relations, Contraception, and Abortion as set Forth in the Classic Texts of Jewish Law*, New York 1968

Fendler, M., "Zur Sozialkritik des Amos. Versuch einer wirtschafts- und sozialgeschichtlichen Interpretation alttestamentlicher Texte," EvTh 33, 1973, 32–53

Fensham, F. C., "Das Nicht-Haftbar-Sein im Bundesbuch im Lichte der altorientalischen Rechtstexte," JNWSL 8, 1980, 17–34

—, "Liability of Animals in Biblical and Ancient Near Eastern Law," JNWSL 14, 1988, 85–90

—, "New Light on Ex 21₆ and 22₇ from the Laws of Eshnunna," JBL 78, 1959, 160–161

—, "The Legal Background of Mt vi 12," NT 4, 1960, 1f.

—, "The Role of the Lord in the Legal Sections of the Covenant Code," VT 26, 1976, 262–274

Fensham, F. C., "Widow, Orphan and the Poor in Ancient Near Eastern Legal and Wisdom Literature," JNES 21, 1962, 129–139

Feucht, C., *Untersuchungen zum Heiligkeitsgesetz*, ThA 20, 1964

Finkelstein, I., *The Archaeology of the Israelite Settlement*, Jerusalem 1988

Finkelstein, J. J., "Ammi-Ṣaduqa's Edict and Babylonian »Law Codes«," JCS 15, 1961, 91–104

—, "The Ox That Gored," TAPhS 71/72, 1981, 1–89

Finkelstein, L., "An Eye for an Eye," *The Menorah Journal* 24, 1936, 207–218

—, "The Men of the Great Synagogue (circa 400–170 B.C.E.)," in: *The Cambridge History of Judaism*. II *The Hellenistic Age*, Cambridge 1989, 229–244

—, (ed.), *Siphre ad Deuteronomium* (1939), New York ²1969

Finley, M. I., *Antike und moderne Demokratie* (1973), Germ. trans. Stuttgart 1987

—, *Die antike Wirtschaft* (1973), Germ. trans. Vienna 1977

—, "Die Schuldknechtschaft," (1965), in: H. G. Kippenberg (ed.), Seminar, Die Entstehung der antiken Klassengesellschaft, stw 130, 1977, 173–204

Firmage, E., "The Biblical Dietary Laws and the Concept of Holiness," in: J. A. Emerton (ed.), *Studies in the Pentateuch*, VT.S 41, 1990, 177–208

Firmage, E. B./Milgrom J./Dahmen, U., Art. רום *rûm*, ThWAT VII, 1990, 425–434

Fisch, H., "»Eldad and Medad are Prophesying in the Camp« – Structuralist Analysis of Numbers XI (Hebr.)," in: *Studies in Bible and Exegesis* II. FS Y. Elitzur, Ramat-Gan 1986, 45–55

Fischer, G., *Jahwe unser Gott. Sprache, Aufbau und Erzähltechnik in der Berufung des Mose* (Ex. 3–4), OBO 91, 1989

Fishbane, M., *Biblical Interpretation in Ancient Israel*, Oxford 1985

Flanagan, J., "Chiefs in Israel," JSOT 20, 1981, 47–73

Fleischer, G., *Von Menschenverkäufern, Baschankühen und Rechtsverkehrern. Die Sozialkritik des Amosbuches in historisch-kritischer, sozialgeschichtlicher und archäologischer Perspektive*, BBB 74, 1989

Flusser, D./Safrai, S., "Das Aposteldekret und die Noachitischen Gebote," in: FS H. Kremers, Neukirchen 1986, 173–192

Fohrer, G., *Einleitung in das Alte Testament*, Heidelberg ¹²1979

—, *Geschichte Israels. Von den Anfängen bis zur Gegenwart*, UTB 708, ³1982

Fontala, C. Alonso, "La esclavitud a través de la Biblia," EstB 43, 1985, 89–124

Foresti, F., "Storia della redazione di Dtn. 16,18 – 18,22 e le sue connessioni con l'opera storica deuteronomistica," *Teresianum* 39, 1988, 1–199

Foucault, M., Überwachen und Strafen. Die Geburt des Gefängnisses, dt. Übers. stw 184, 1977

Freedman, D. N., "The Formation of the Canon of the Old Testament. The Selection and the Identification of the Torah as the Supreme Authority of the Postexilic Community," in: E. B. Firmage et al., *Religion and Law. Biblical-Judaic and Islamic Perspectives*, Winona Lake 1990, 315–331

Freedman, D. N./Willoughby, B. E., Art. עִבְרִי *'ibrî*, ThWAT V, 1986, 1039–1056

—, Art. מַלְאָךְ *mal 'āk*, ThWAT IV, 1984, 887–904

—, Art. נָאַף *nā'ap*, ThWAT V, 1986, 123–129

Freehof, S. B., *The Book of Jeremiah*, The Jewish Commentary for Bible Readers, New York 1977

Frei, P., "Zentralgewalt und Lokalautonomie im Achämenidenreich," in: idem.,/K. Koch, *Reichsidee und Reichsorganisation im Perserreich*, OBO 55, 1984, 7–43

Frick, F. S., "The Rechabites Reconsidered," JBL 90, 1971, 279–287

Friedman, R. E., *The Exile and Biblical Narrative. The Formation of the Deuteronomistic and Priestly Works*, HSM 22, 1981

Fritz, V., "Das Geschichtsverständnis der Priesterschrift," ZThK 84, 1987, 426–439

—, *Einführung in die Archäologie*, Darmstadt 1985

—, *Israel in der Wüste. Traditionsgeschichtliche Untersuchung der Wüstenüberlieferung des Jahwisten*, MThSt 7, 1970

—, *Tempel und Zelt. Studien zu dem Tempelbau in Israel und zu dem Zeltheiligtum der Priesterschrift*, WMANT 47, 1977

Frymer-Kensky, T. S., Law and Philosophy: "The Case of Sex in the Bible," Semeia 45, 1989, 89–102

—, "Pollution, Purification, and Purgation in Biblical Israel," in: *The Word of the Lord Shall Go Forth*, FS D. N. Freedman, ed. C. L. Meyers/M. O'Connor, Winona Lake 1983, 399–414

—, "The Judicial Ordeal in the Ancient Near East," 2 vols., Diss. Yale 1977

—, "Tit for Tat. The Principle of Equal Retribution in Near Eastern and Biblical Law," BA 43, 1980, 230–234

Fuchs, E., "»For I Have the Way of Women«: Deception, Gender, and Ideology in Biblical Narrative," *Semeia* 42, 1988, 68–83

Füglister, N., *Die Heilsbedeutung des Pascha*, StANT 8, 1963

—, "Sühne durch Blut – Zur Bedeutung von Leviticus 17,11," in: *Studien zum Pentateuch*, FS W. Kornfeld, ed. G. Braulik, Vienna 1977, 143–164

Fuhs, H. F., "Heiliges Volk Gottes," in: J. Schreiner (ed.), *Unterwegs zur Kirche. Alttestamentliche Konzeptionen*, QD 110, 1987, 143–167

Gabel, J. B./Wheeler, C. B., "The Redactor's Hand in the Blasphemy Pericope of Leviticus XXIV," VT 30, 1980, 227–229

Gadegaard, N. H., "On the So-Called Burnt Offering Altar in the Old Testament," PEQ 110, 1978, 35–45

Gagarin, M., *Drakon and the Early Athenian Homicide Law*, New Haven and London 1981

—, *Early Greek Law*, Berkeley 1986

Galling, K., "Bagoas und Esra," in: idem., *Studien zur Geschichte Israels im persischen Zeitalter*, Tübingen 1964, 149–184

—, "Das Königsgesetz im Deuteronomium," ThLZ 76, 1951, 133–138

Galling, K., *Die Bücher der Chronik, Esra, Nehemia*, ATD 12, 1954

—, "Goethe als theologischer Schriftsteller," EvTh 8, 1948/49, 529–545

—, (ed.), *Textbuch Zur Geschichte Israels*, Tübingen ³1979

Gamberoni, J., Art. מָקוֹם *māqôm*, ThWAT IV, 1984, 1113–1124

—, "». . . O, wenn doch das ganze Volk Jahwes Propheten wären . . .!« (Num 11,29b)," ThGl 67, 1977, 113–126

Gamoran, H., "Talmudic Usury Laws and Business Loans," JSJ 7, 1976, 129–142

—, "The Biblical Law against Loans on Interest," JNES 30, 1971, 127–134

—, "The Talmudic Law of Mortgages in View of the Prohibition Against Lending on Interest," HUCA 52, 1981, 153–162

Gandz, S., "The Calendar of Ancient Israel," in: FS M. Vallicrosa, vol. I, Barcelona 1954, 623–646

Garbini, G., "Il cantico di Debora," ParPass 33, 978, 5–31

García López, F., "Analyse littéraire de Deutéronome, V-XI," RB 84, 1977, 481–522; 85, 1978, 5–49

—, "Le Roi D'Israel: Dtn 17,14–20," in: N. Lohfink (ed.), *Das Deuteronomium. Entstehung, Gestalt und Botschaft*, Leuven 1985, BEThL 68, 277–297

—, "Una profeta como Moisés. Estudio crítico de Dt 18,9–22," *Simposio Bíblico Español*, Madrid 1984, 289–308

Garfinkel, Y., "The Eliakim Na'ar Yokan Seal Impressions. Sixty Years of Confusion in Biblical Archaeological Research," BA 53, 1990, 74–79

Geiger, Th., *Vorstudien zu einer Soziologie des Rechts*, Neuwied u. Berlin, ²1970

Gemser, B., *The Importance of the Motive Clause in Old Testament Law*, VT.S 1, 1953, 50–66

Gerleman, G., *Ruth. Das Hohe Lied*, BK VIII, ²1981

Gerstenberger, E., Art. עָזַב *'āzab* κτλ., ThWAT V, 1986, 1200–1208

—, *Wesen und Herkunft des »apodiktischen Rechts«*, WMANT 20, 1965

Gerstenberger, E./Schrage, W., *Frau und Mann, Biblische Konfrontationen*, Stuttgart 1980

Gese, H., "Bemerkungen zur Sinaitradition," ZAW 79, 1967, 137–154 = idem., Vom Sinai zum Zion. Alttestamentliche Beiträge zur biblischen Theologie, BEvTh 64, 1974, 31–48

—, "Das Gesetz," in: idem., *Zur biblischen Theologie. Alttestamentliche Vorträge* (1977), Tübingen 1989, 55–84

Gese, H., "Die Religionen Altsyriens," in: idem./Maria Höfner/ K. Rudolph (ed.), *Die Religionen Altsyriens, Altarabiens und der Mandäer*, Die Religionen der Menschheit 10,2, Stuttgart 1970, 3–232

—, "Die Sühne," in: idem., *Zur biblischen Theologie. Alttestamentliche Vorträge* (1977), Tübingen ³1989, 85–106

Gesenius, W./Buhl, F., *Hebräisches und aramäisches Handwörterbuch über das Alte Testament*, Berlin ¹⁷1915, reprint 1962

Gesenius, W./Kautzsch, E., *Hebräische Grammatik*, Hildesheim 1962 (reprint of 28th ed. of 1909)

Gesenius, W./Meyer, R./Donner, H., *Hebräisches und aramäisches Wörterbuch über das Alte Testament*, Berlin ¹⁸1987

Gewalt, D., "Taube und Blinde nach Leviticus 19,14," DBAT 22, 1985/86, 119–139

Giblin, C. H., "Structural Patterns in Jos 24,1–15," CBQ 26, 1964, 50–69

Gilbert, M., "Jérémie en conflit avec les sages?" in: P.-M. Bogaert (ed.), *Le livre de Jérémie. Le Prophète et son milieu, les oracles et leurs transmission*, BEThL 54, 1981, 105–118

—, "Le sacré dans l'Ancien Testament," in: L. Ries et al. (ed.), *L'expression du sacré dans les grandes religions*, Louvain – la Neuve 1978, 205–289

Gilula, M., "An Offering of »First Fruits« in Ancient Egypt," *Tel Aviv* 1, 1974, 43f.

Ginsberg, "H. L., "Notes on »The Birth of the Gracious and Beautiful God«," JRAS 67, 1935, 45–72

Glassner, J. J., "L'hospitalité en Mésopotamie ancienne: aspect de la question de l'étranger," ZA 80, 1990, 60–75

Globe, A., "The Text and Literary Structure of Judges 5,4–5," Bib. 55, 1974, 168–178

Gluckman, M., *Politics, Law and Ritual in Tribe Society*, Oxford 1965

—, "Reasonableness and Responsibility in the Law of Segmentary Societies," in: H. Kuper/L. Kuper (ed.), *African Law: Adaption and Development*, Berkeley 1965, 120–146

Gnuse, R., "Calf, Cult, and King, The Unity of Hosea 8,1–13," BZ NF 26, 1982, 83–92

Göbel, Ch., "»Denn bei dir ist die Vergebung . . .«. slḥ im Alten Testament," *Theologische Versuche* 8, 1977, 21–33

Goethe, J. W. v., *Weissagungen des Bakis* (1798–1800). *Vorspruch* (1814), *Poetische Werke*. Vollständige Ausgabe vol. 1, Stuttgart o.J., 241–248

—, "Zwo wichtige bisher unerörterte biblische Fragen zum erstenmal gründlich beantwortet von einem Landgeistlichen in Schwaben, Lindau a. Bodensee 1773," *Schriften zu Literatur und Theater*, Gesamtausgabe vol. 15, Stuttgart o.J., 46–55

Goldschmidt, L. (ed.), *Der Babylonische Talmud mit Einschluß der vollständigen Mišnah*, bilingual ed., 9 vols., reprint Haag 1933–35

Goldstein, A. S., "Conversion to Judaism in Bible Times,' in: D. M. Eichhorn (ed.), *Conversion to Judaism*, 1965, 9–32

Goodman, L. E., "The Biblical Laws of Diet and Sex," *Jewish Law Association Studies* II, Atlanta 1986, 17–57

Gordon, C. H., "An Akkadian Parallel to Deuteronomy 21,1ff," RA 33, 1936, 1–6

Görg, M., Art. זהר *zāhar* κτλ. ThWAT II, 1977, 544–550

—, "Beobachtungen zum sogenannten Azazel-Ritus," BN 33, 1986, 10–16

—, "Der Altar – Theologische Dimensionen im Alten Testament," in: *Freude am Gottesdienst*. FS J. G. Plöger, (ed.) J. Schreiner, Stuttgart 1983, 291–306

—, "Der »Fremde« (gēr), ein Fremdwort im Alten Testament?" BN 25, 1984, 10–13

—, "Eine rätselhafte Textilbezeichnung im Alten Testament," BN 12, 1980, 13–17

—, "Zur Identität der »Seir-Länder«," BN 46, 1989, 7–12

Gottwald, N. K., *The Tribes of Yahweh. A Sociology of the Religion of Liberated Israel 1250–1050 B.C.E.*, New York 1979

Graf, K. H., *Der Prophet Jeremia*, Leipzig 1862

Graupner, A., "Zum Verhältnis der beiden Dekalogfassungen Ex 20 und Dtn 5. Ein Gespräch mit Frank-Lothar Hossfeld," ZAW 99, 1987, 308–329

Gray, G. B., *A Critical and Exegetical Commentary on Numbers*, ICC 4, 1903, ³1956

Gray, J., *I & II Kings. A Commentary*, London ²1970

—, *The Legacy of Canaan*, VT.S 5, 1957

Green, A. R. W., *The Role of Human Sacrifice in the Ancient Near East*, American School of Oriental Research, Diss.Ser.1, Ann Arbor 1975

Greenberg, M., "Another Look at Rachel's Theft of the Teraphim," JBL 81, 1962, 239–248

—, *Ezekiel, 1–20. A New Translation with Introduction and Commentary*, AncB 22, 1983

—, "More Reflections on Biblical Law," in: S. Japhet (ed.), *Studies in Bible*, Jerusalem 1986, 1–17

—, "Some Postulates of Biblical Criminal Law," in: *Jehezkel Kaufmann Jubilee Volume*, Jerusalem 1960, 5–27 = in: J. Goldin (ed.), *The Jewish Expression*, New Haven and London ²1976, 18–37

—, "The Biblical Conception of Asylum," JBL 78, 1959, 125–132

Greidanus, S., "The Universal Dimension of Law in the Hebrew Scriptures," SR 14, 1985, 39–51

Gressmann, H. (ed.), *Altorientalische Bilder zum Alten Testament*, Berlin/Leipzig ²1927

Griffiths, J. G., "Egypt and the Rise of the Synagogue," JThS N.S. 38, 1987, 1–15

Grimme, H., *Das israelitische Pfingstfest und der Plejadenkult*, Paderborn 1907

Grintz, J. M., "»Do not eat of the Blood«. Reconsiderations in setting and Dating of the Priestly Code," ASTI 8, 1970/71, 78–105

Groß, H., *Klagelieder – Schreiner*, J., Baruch, NEB, Würzburg 1986

—, "Tora und Gnade im Alten Testament," *Kairos* 14, 1972, 220–231

Gruber, M., "The Source of the Biblical Sabbath," *Journal of the Ancient Near Eastern Society of the Columbia University* I/2, 1969, 14–20

Guggisberg, F., "Die Gestalt des Mal'ak Jahwe im Alten Testament," Diss. Neuenburg 1979

Guilding, A. E., "Notes on the Hebrew Law Codes," JThS 49, 1948, 43–52

Gunkel, H., "Elia, Jahve und Baal," RV II/8, 1906, 1–76

—, *Genesis*, HK I,1, ⁶1964

Gunneweg, A. H. J., "Das Gesetz und die Propheten. Eine Auslegung von Ex 33,7–11; Num 11,4 – 12,8; Dtn 31,14f; 34,10," ZAW 102, 1990, 169–180

—, *Esra*, KAT XIX1, 1985

—, A. H. J., *Leviten und Priester. Hauptlinien der Traditionsbildung und Geschichte des israelitisch-jüdischen Kultpersonals*, FRLANT 89, 1965

—, "Mose in Midian" (1964), in: idem., *Sola Scriptura. Beiträge zu Exegese und Hermeneutik des Alten Testaments*, Göttingen 1983, 36–44

—, *Nehemia*, KAT XIX,2, 1987

—, "Zur Interpretation der Bücher Esra-Nehemia. Zugleich ein Beitrag zur Methode der Exegese," in: *Congress Volume*, Vienna 1980, VT.S 32, 1981, 146–161

—, " עם הארץ – A Semantic Revolution," ZAW 95, 1983, 437–440

Gurewicz, S. B., "The Deuteronomic Provisions for Exemption from Military Service," ABR 6, 1958, 111–121

Gutmann, J., "The Origin of the Synagogue, The Current State of Research," in: idem. (ed.), *The Synagogue. Studies in Origins, Archaeology and Architecture*, New York 1975, 72–76

Haag, E. (ed.), *Gott, der einzige*, QD 104, 1985

—, Art. כִּי, ThWAT I, 1973, 668–682

—, *Vom alten zum neuen Pascha. Geschichte und Theologie des Oster-festes*, SBS 49, 1971

Haas, P., "»Die He Shall Surely Die«, The Structure of Homicide in Biblical Law," *Semeia* 45, 1989, 67–87

Haase, R., *Die keilschriftlichen Rechtssammlungen in deutscher Übersetzung*, Wiesbaden ²1979

Haase, R., *Einführung in das Studium keilschriftlicher Rechtsquellen*, Wiesbaden 1965

Habel, N. C., "Deuteronomy 18 – God's Chosen Prophet," CTM 35, 1964, 575–582

Hacklett, J./Huehnergard, J., "On Breaking Teeth," HThR 77, 1984, 259–275

Hahn, J., *Das »Goldene Kalb«. Die Jahwe-Verehrung bei Stierbildern in der Geschichte Israels*, EHS.T 154, Frankfurt/M. u. Bern 1981

Halbe, J., *Das Privilegrecht Jahwes Ex 34,10–28*, FRLANT 114, 1975

—, "Die Reihe der Inzestverbote Lev 18,7–18. Entstehung und Gestaltstufen," ZAW 92, 1980, 60–88

—, "Erwägungen zu Ursprung und Wesen des Massotfestes," ZAW 87, 1975, 324–346

—, "»Gemeinschaft, die Welt unterbricht«. Grundfragen und -inhalte deuteronomischer Theologie und Überlieferungsbildung im Lichte der Ursprungsbedingungen alttestamentlichen Rechts," in: N. Lohfink (ed.), *Das Deuteronomium*, BEThL 68, 1985, 55–75

Hallo, W. W., "New Moons and Sabbaths: A Casestudy in the Contrastive Approach," HUCA 48, 1977, 1–18

Hamner, R. (ed.), *Sifre. A Tannaitic Commentary of the Book of Deuteronomy*, Yale Judaica Ser.24, New Haven and London 1986

Hamp, V./Botterweck, G. J., Art. רִין *dîn*, Th II, 1977, 200–207

Hanhart, R., *Die Bedeutung der Septuaginta für die Definition des »Hellenistischen Judentums«*, VT.S 40, 1988, 67–80

—, "Zum gegenwärtigen Stand der Septuagintaforschung," in: *De Septuaginta*, FS J. W. Wevers. ed. A. Pietersma/C. Cox, Missisauga, Ont. 1984, 3–18

Haran, M., "Das Böcklein in der Milch seiner Mutter und das säugende Muttertier," ThZ 41, 1985, 135–159

—, *Temples and Temple-Services in Ancient Israel. An Inquiry into the Character of Cult Phenomena and the Historical Setting of the Priestly School*, Oxford 1978

Hardmeier, C., "Die Propheten Micha und Jesaja im Spiegel von Jereremia XXVI und 2 Regum XVIII-XX. Zur Prophetie-Rezeption in der nach-joschijanischen Zeit," in: *Congress Volume*, Leiden 1989, VT.S 43, 1991, 172–189

—, "Jer 29,24–32 – »eine geradezu unüberbietbare Konfusion«? Vorurteil und Methode in der exegetischen Forschung," in: *Die hebräische Bibel und ihre zweifache Nachgeschichte*, FS R. Rendtorff, ed. E. Blum et al., Neukirchen 1990, 301–317

—, "Jesajaforschung im Umbruch," VuF 31, 1986 3–31

—, *Prophetie im Streit vor dem Untergang Judas. Erzählkommunikative Studien zur Entstehungssituation der Jesaja- und Jeremiaerzählungen in II Reg 18–20 und Jer 37–40*, BZAW 187, 1989

—, *Texttheorie und biblische Exegese. Zur rhetorischen Funktion der Trauermetaphorik in der Prophetie*, BEvTh 79, 1978

Hasel, G. F., Art. נָגִיד *nāgîd*, ThWAT V, 1986, 203–219

—, Art. כָּרַת *kārat*, ThWAT IV, 1984, 355–367

—, "»New Moon and Sabbath« in Eighth Century Israelite Prophetic Writings (Isa 1, 13; Hos 2, 13; Amos 8, 5)," in: »*Wünschet Jerusalem Frieden*«, ed. M. Augustin/K.-D. Schunck, Frankfurt/M., 1988. 37–64

Häusler, E., "Sklaven und Personen minderen Rechts im Alten Testament, masch." Diss. Cologne 1956

Hehn, J., *Siebenzahl und Sabbath bei den Babyloniern und im Alten Testament*, Leipzig 1907

Heichelheim, F. M., *Wirtschaftsgeschichte des Altertums* (1938) reprint Leiden 1969

Heinen, K., "Die Last gemeinsam tragen. Mitverantwortung in Num 11," in: *Mitverantwortung aller in der Kirche*, ed. F. Courth/A. Weiser, Limburg 1985, 106–117

Heinisch, P., "Das Sklavenrecht in Israel und im Alten Orient," StC 11, 1934/35, 201–219.276–290

Heister, M.-S., *Frauen in der biblischen Glaubensgeschichte*, Göttingen ²1986

Hejcl, *Das alttestamentliche Zinsverbot im Lichte der ethnologischen Jurisprudenz sowie des altorientalischen Zinswesens*, BSt XII/4, Freiburg 1907

Helck, W., "Die Ägypter und die Fremden," *Saeculum* 15, 1964, 103–114

—, "Maat – Ideologie und Machtwerkzeug," in: *Ernten, was man sät*, FS K. Koch, ed. D. R. Daniels et al., Neukirchen 1991, 11–19

Heller, J., "Sjema 'als fundament van »monotheïsme«?" *Amsterdamse cahiers voor exegese en Bijbelse theologie 10*, 1989, 37–44

Hellwig, A., *Das Asylrecht der Naturvölker*, Berliner Juristische Beiträge I, 1903

Heltzer, M., "On the Tithe Paid in Grain in Ugarit," IEJ 25, 1975, 124–128

—, *The Internal Organization of the Kingdom of Ugarit (Royal service-system, taxes, royal economy, army and administration)*, Wiesbaden 1982

—, *The Rural Community of Ancient Ugarit*, Wiesbaden 1976

Hempel, J., *Die Schichten des Deuteronomiums*, Leipzig 1914

Hendel, R. S., "Images of God in Ancient Israel," *Bulletin of the Anglo-Israel Archaeological Society* 8, 1988/89, 81–82

Hengel, M., *Judentum und Hellenismus*, Tübingen 1969, ³1988

Hengel, M./Neusner, J. et al. (eds.), *Übersetzung des Talmud Yerushalmi*, Tübingen 1975ff.

Henninger, I., "Pureté et impureté. L'histoire des religions," DBS 9, 1979, 339–430

Henry, M.-L., *Das Tier im religiösen Bewußtsein des alttestamentlichen Menschen*, Tübingen 1958

Hentig, H. v., *Die Strafe*, 2 vols., Berlin 1954.1955

Hentschel, G., *2 Könige*, NEB 11, Würzburg 1985

—, *Die Elijaerzählungen. Zum Verhältnis von historischem Geschehen und geschichtlicher Erfahrung*, EThSt 33, 1977

Hentschke, R., *Satzung und Setzender. Ein Beitrag zur israelitischen Rechtsterminologie*, BWANT 5,3, 1963

Hermisson, H.-J., *Sprache und Ritus im altisraelitischen Kult. Zur »Spiritualisierung« der Kultbegriffe im Alten Testament*, WMANT 19, 1965

Herrmann, S., "Die konstruktive Restauration. Das Deuteronomium als Mitte biblischer Theologie," in: *Probleme biblischer Theologie*, FS G. v. Rad, München 1971, 155–170 = idem., *Gesammelte Studien zu Geschichte und Theologie des AT*, ThB 75, 1986, 163–178

—, *Jeremia*, BK XII, Liefg. 1ff. 1986ff.

Herzog, Z., *Das Stadttor in Israel und in den Nachbarländern*, Mainz 1986

—, (ed.), *Beer-Sheba II. The Early Iron Age Settlements*, Tel Aviv 1984

Heschel, A. J., *Der Sabbat. Seine Bedeutung für den heutigen Menschen*, Germ. trans. Neukirchen 1990

Hinkelammert, F., "Der Schuldenautomatismus. Wirtschaftspolitische und wirtschaftstheoretische Zugänge zur Verschuldung Lateinamerikas" (Span. 1988), in: K. Füssel et al. (eds.), »... in euren Häusern liegt das geraubte Gut der Armen«. Ökonomisch-theologische Beiträge zur Verschuldungskrise*, Fribourg 1989, 79–190

Hirth, V., *Gottes Boten im Alten Testament. Die alttestamentliche Mal 'ak-Vorstellung unter besonderer Berücksichtigung des Mal 'ak-Jahwe-Problems*, ThA 32, 1975

Hitzig, F., *Der Prophet Jeremia*, Leipzig 1841

Hoebel, E. A., *Das Recht der Naturvölker. Eine vergleichende Untersuchung rechtlicher Abläufe* (1954), Germ. trans. Olten and Freiburg 1968

Hoegenhaven, J., *Gott und Volk bei Jesaja. Eine Untersuchung zur biblischen Theologie*, AThD 24, 1988

Höffken, P., "Eine Bemerkung zum religionsgeschichtlichen Hintergrund von Dtn 6,4," BZ NF 28, 1984, 88–93

—, "Warum schweigt Jesus sirach über Esra?" ZAW 87, 1975, 184–202

Hoffner, H. A., "Incest, Sodomy, and Bestiality in the Ancient Near East," in: *Orient and Occident*, FS C. H. Gordon, AOAT 22, 1973, 81–90

Hoffmann, D., *Das Buch Levitivus*, 2 vols., Berlin 1905/06

—, *Das Buch Deuteronomium*, 2 vols., Berlin 1913, 1922

Hoffmann, H.-D., *Reform und Reformen. Untersuchungen zu einem Grundthema der deuteronomistischen Geschichtsschreibung*, AThANT 66, 1980

Hoftijzer, J., "David and the Tekoite Woman," VT 20, 1970, 419–444

—, "Ex. xxi 8," VT 7, 1957, 388–391

Hoheisel, K., *Das antike Judentum in christlicher Sicht*, Studies in Oriental Religion 2, Wiesbaden 1978

Holladay, W. L., *Jeremiah 1. A Commentary on the Book of the Prophet Jeremiah. Chapters 1–25*, Philadelphia 1986

—, *The Architecture of Jeremiah 1–20*, London 1976

Hölscher, G., *Die Bücher Esra und Nehemia*, HSAT II, ⁴1923, 491–562

—, "Komposition und Ursprung des Deuteronomiums," ZAW 40, 1922, 161–255

Holzinger, H., *Exodus*, KHC II, 1900

—, *Numeri*, KHC IV, 1903

Hoppe, L., "Elders and Deuteronomy. A Proposal," EeT(O) 14, 1983, 259–272

—, "The Levitical Origins of Deuteronomy Reconsidered," BR 28, 1983, 27–36

Hornung, E., Maat "Gerechtigkeit für alle? Zur altägyptischen Ethik," ErJb 56, 1987, 385–427

Horovitz, J., "Auge um Auge, Zahn um Zahn," in: FS H. Cohen, Berlin 1912, 609–658

Horst, F., "Das Privilegrecht Jahwes" (1930) = idem., *Gottes Recht. Studien zum Alten Testament*, ThB 12, 1961, 17–154

—, "Der Eid im Alten Testament," EvTh 17,1957, 366– 384 = idem., *Gottes Recht. Studien zum Recht im Alten Testament*, ThB 12, 1961, 292–314

—, "Recht und Religion im Bereich des Alten Testaments" (1956), in: idem., *Gottes Recht. Studien zum Alten Testament*, ThB 12, 1961, 260–291

Hossfeld, F.-L., *Der Dekalog. Seine späten Fassungen, die originale Komposition und seine Vorstufen*, OBO 45, 1982

—, "Du sollst dir kein Bild machen! Die Funktion des alttestamentlichen Bilderverbots," TThZ 98, 1989, 81–94

—, "Einheit und Einzigkeit Gottes im frühen Jahwismus," in: *Im Gespräch mit dem dreieinen Gott. FS W. Breunig*, ed. M. Böhnke/H. Heinz, Düsseldorf 1985, 57–74

—, "Nachlese zu neueren Studien der Einsetzungsliturgie von Ps 15," in: *Die alttestamentliche Botschaft als Wegweisung*, FS H. Reinelt, ed. J. Zmijewski, Stuttgart 1990, 135–156

—, "Zum synoptischen Vergleich der Dekalogfassungen. Eine Fortführung des begonnenen Gesprächs," in: idem (ed.), *Vom Sinai zum Horeb*, FS E. Zenger, Würzburg 1989, 73–117

Hossfeld, F.-L./Kalthoff, B., Art. נצל *nṣl*, ThWAT V., 1986, 570–577

Hossfeld, F.-L./Meyer, J., *Prophet gegen Prophet. Eine Analyse der alttestamentlichen Texte zum Thema: Wahre und falsche Propheten*, BiBe 9, 1973

Hossfeld, F.-L./Reuter, E., Art. נשׂא *nāśā'* II, ThWAT V, 1986, 658–663

Houtman, C., "Another Look at Forbidden Mixtures," VT 34, 1984, 226–228

Houtman, C., "Ezra and the Law, in: Remembering all the Way . . . ," OTS XXI, 1981, 91–115

Hruby, K., *Die Synagoge. Geschichtliche Entwicklung einer Institution,* Zürich 1971

Huber, W./Tödt, H.-E., *Menschenrechte. Perspektiven einer menschlichen Welt,* Stuttgart 1977

Huffmon, H. B., "Ex 23,4–5. A Comparative Study," in: *Old Testament Studies,* FS J. M. Myers, ed. H. N. Bream et al., Philadelphia 1974, 271–278

—, "Priestly Divination in Israel," in: *The Word of the Lord Shall Go Forth.* FS D. N. Freedman, ed. C. L. Meyers/M. O'Connor, Winona Lake 1983, 355–359

Hurovitz, V., "Isaiah's Impure Lips and Their Purification in Light of Akkadian Sources," HUCA 60, 1989, 39–89

Hurvitz, A., *A Linguistic Study of the Relationship between the Priestly Source and the Book of Ezekiel. A New Approach to an Old Problem,* Cahiers de la RB 20, Paris 1982

—, "Dating the Priestly Source in Light of the Historical Study of Biblical Hebrew a Century after Wellhausen," ZAW.S 100, 1988, 88–100

Hüttenmeister, F./Reeg, G., *Die antiken Synagogen in Israel,* 2 vols., supp Tübinger Atlas d. Vorderen Orients, Wiesbaden 1977

Hutter, M., "Das Werden des Monotheismus im alten Israel. Bemerkungen zur neueren Diskussion," in: *Anfänge der Theologie,* FS J. B. Bauer, ed. N. Brox et al., Graz 1987, 25–39

—, Hiskija. *König von Juda. Ein Beitrag zur judäischen Geschichte in assyrischer Zeit,* Grazer Theologische Studien 6, Graz 1982

Hyatt, J. P., "Jeremiah and Deuteronomy," JNES 1, 1942, 156–173 (= *A Prophet to the Nations. Essays in Jeremiah Studies,* ed. L. G. Perdue/B. W. Kovacs, Winona Lake 1984, 113–127)

Inscriptions Revealed. Documents from the Time of the Bible, the Mishna and the Talmud, Israel Museum Cat. No. 100, Jerusalem 1973

Ishida, T., "»The People of the Land« and the Political Crises in Judah," AJBI 1, 1975, 23–38

—, "The Structure and Historical Implications of the Lists of Pre-Israelite Nations," Bib. 60, 1979, 461–490

Isser, S., "Two Traditions: The Law of Exodus 21, 22– 23 Revisited," CBQ 52, 1990, 30–45

Jackson, B. S., "Biblical laws of Slavery: A Comparative Approach," in: L. J. Archer (ed.), *Slavery and Other Forms of Unfree Labour,* London 1988, 86–101

—, *Essays in Jewish and Comparative Legal History,* SJLA 10, 1975

—, "History, Dogmatics and Halakhah," in: *The Jewish Law Annual.* Suppl. 2: *Jewish Law in Legal History and the Modern World,* Leiden 1980, 1–25

Jackson, B. S., "Ideas of law and legal administration. A semiotic approach," in: R. E. Clements (ed.), *The World of Ancient Israel. Sociological, Anthropological and Political Perspectives*, Cambridge 1989, 185–202

—, "Legalism and Spirituality: Historical, Philosophical, and Semiotic Notes on Legislators, Adjuctors, and Subjects," in: E. B. Firmage et al. (ed.), *Religion and Law, Biblical-Judaic and Islamic Perspectives*, Winona I.ake 1990, 243–261

—, "Reflections on Biblical Criminal Law" (1973), in: idem., *Essays*, 1975, 25–63

—, "Some Literary Features of the Mishpatim," in: »*Wünschet Jerusalem Frieden*«, ed. M. Augustin/K.-D. Schunck, Frankfurt/M. 1988, 235–242

—, "Some Semiotic Questions for Biblical Law," in: *The Oxford Conference Volume*, ed. A. M. Fuss, Jewish Law Association Studies III, Atlanta 1987, 1–25

—, *Theft in Early Jewish Law*, Oxford 1972

—, "The Goring Ox" (1974), in: idem., *Essays*, 1975, 108–152

—, "The Problem of Exod. XXI, 22–5 (Ius Talionis)" (1973) in: idem. *Essays*, 75–107

Jacob, B., *Auge um Auge. Eine Untersuchung zum Alten und Neuen Testament*, Berlin 1929

Jacob, E., *Esaïe 1–12*, Commentaire de l'Ancien Testament VIIIa, Geneva 1987

—, "Variations et constantes dans la figure de l'Ange de YHWH," RHPhR 68, 1988, 405–414

Jagersma, H., *Leviticus 19. Identiteit -Bevrijding – Gemeenschap*, SSN 14, 1972

—, "The Tithes in the Old Testament," in: *Remembering all the way . . .* , OTS XXI, 1981, 116–128

Janowski, B., "Auslösung des verwirkten Lebens. Zur Geschichte und Struktur der biblischen Lösegeldvorstellung," ZThK 79, 1982, 25–59

—, "Azazel – biblisches Gegenstück zum ägyptischen Seth? Zur Religions-geschichte von Lev 16,10.21f.," in: *Die Hebräische Bibel und ihre zweifache Nachgeschichte*, FS R. Rendtorff, ed. E. Blum et al., Neukirchen 1990, 97–110

—, "Erwägungen zur Vorgeschichte des israelitischen šᵉlamîm-Opfers," UF 12, 1980, 231–259

—, "»Ich will in eurer Mitte wohnen«. Struktur und Genese der exilischen Schekina-Theologie," JBTh 2, 1987, 165– 193

—, "Tempel und Schöpfung. Schöpfungstheologische Aspekte der priesterschriftlichen Heiligtumskonzeption," JBTh 5, 1990, 37–69

—, *Sühne als Heilsgeschehen. Studien zur Sühnetheologie der Priesterschrift und zur Wurzel KPR im Alten Orient und im Alten Testament*, WMANT 55, 1982

Janssen, E., *Juda in der Exilszeit. Ein Beitrag zur Frage der Entstehung des Judentums*, FRLANT 51, 1956

Janzen, J. G., "On the Most Important Word in the Schema (Deuteronomy VI 4–5)," VT 37, 1987, 280–300

Japhet, S., "Historical Reliability of Chronicles," JSOT 33, 1985, 83–107

—, "The Relationship between the Legal Corpora in the Pentateuch in Light of Manumission Laws," in: idem. (ed.), *Studies in Bible*, Jerusalem 1986, 63–89

—, "The Supposed Common Authorship of Chronicles and Ezra-Nehemia Investigated Anew," VT 18, 1968, 330–371

Jastrow, M., *A Dictionary of the Targumim, the Talmud Babli and Yerushalmi, and the Midrashic Literature*, New York 1950

Jellicoe, S., *The Septuagint and Modern Study*, Oxford 1968

Jenni, E., *Das hebräische Pi'el. Systematisch-semasiologische Untersuchung einer Verbalform im Alten Testament*, Zürich 1968

Jentzsch, B. (ed.), *Ich sah das Dunkel schon von Ferne kommen. Erniedrigung und Vertreibung in poetischen Zeugnissen*, München 1979

Jepsen, A., "Nehemia 10," ZAW 66, 1954, 87–106

—, *Untersuchungen zum Bundesbuch*, BWANT III/5, 1927

Jeremias, Joachim, "Sabbatjahr und neutestamentliche Chronologie," ZNW 27, 1928, 98–103 = idem., *Abba. Studien zur neutestamentlichen Theologie und Zeitgeschichte*, Göttingen 1966, 233–238

Jeremias, Jörg, Art. נביא *nābi'* Prophet, THAT II, 1976, 7–26

—, *Das Königtum Gottes in den Psalmen. Israels Begegnung mit dem kanaanäischen Mythos in den Jahwe-König-Psalmen*, FRLANT 141, 1987

—, *Der Prophet Hosea*, ATD 24/1, 1983

—, *Kultprophetie und Gerichtsverkündigung in der späten Königszeit*, WMANT 35, 1970

—, *Theophanie. Die Geschichte einer alttestamentlichen Gottes-vorstellung*, WMANT 10, ²1977

Jervell, J., "Die offenbarte und die verborgene Tora. Zur Vorstellung über die neue Tora im Rabbinismus," StTh 25, 1971, 90–108

Jobling, D., *The Sense of Biblical Narrative. Three Structural Analyses in the Old Testament (I Samuel 13–31, Numbers 11–12, I Kings 17–18)*, JSOT.S 7, Sheffield ²1986

Johnson, B., Art. מִשְׁפָּט *mišpāṭ* κτλ., ThWAT V, 1986, 93–107

Johnstone, W., "The Decalogue and the Redaction of the Sinai Pericope in Exodus," ZAW 100, 1988, 361–385

Josephus, Fl., *Antiquitates Judaicae*, with Engl. trans. 6 vols., ed. H. S. J. Thackeray et al., The Loeb Classical Library (1930–62), London 1967–69

—, *Contra Apionem*, with Engl. trans., ed. H. S. J. Thackeray, The Loeb Classical Library (1926), London 1976

Joüon, P., *Grammaire de l'Hébreu Biblique*, Rom 1923, reprint 1965

Junge, E., *Der Wiederaufbau des Heerwesens des Reiches Juda unter-Josia*, BWANT IV/23(75), 1937

Jüngling, H.-W., "»Auge für Auge, Zahn für Zahn«. Bemerkungen zu Sinn und Geltung der alttestamentlichen Talionsformeln," ThPh 59, 1984, 1–38

—, Richter 19 – *Ein Plädoyer für das Königtum. Stilistische Analyse der Tendenzerzählung Ri 19,1– 30a; 21,25*, AnBib 84, 1981

Kaatz, S., "Maimonides und das Talionsprinzip," Jesch. 13, 1926, 43–50

Kahana, Y./Munk, N./Slae, M., "Estimating Bodily Damages according to Jewish Law, A Comparative Study," in: *Jewish Law Association Studies* II, *The Jerusalem Conference Volume*, ed. B. S. Jackson, Atlanta 1986, 103–142

Kahle, P. E., *Die Kairoer Genisa*, Germ. trans. Berlin 1962

Kaiser, O., "Beobachtungen zur sogenannten Thronnachfolgeerzählung Davids," EThL 64, 1988, 5–20

—, *Das Buch des Propheten Jesaja. Kapitel 1–12*, ATD 17, ⁵1981

—., "Den Erstgeborenen deiner Söhne sollst du mir geben. Erwägungen zum Kinderopfer im Alten Testament" (1976), in: idem., *Von der Gegenwartsbedeutung des Alten Testaments. Gesammelte Studien zur Hermeneutik und zur Redaktionsgeschichte*, ed. V. Fritz et al., Göttingen 1984, 142–166

—, *Einleitung in das Alte Testament*, Gütersloh ⁵1984

—, *Klagelieder*, ATD 16/2, ³1981

—, "Zwischen den Fronten. Palästina in den Auseinandersetzungen zwischen dem Perserreich und Ägypten in der ersten Hälfte des 4. Jahrhunderts" (1972), = in: idem., *Von der Gegenwartsbedeutung des Alten Testaments. Gesammelte Studien*, ed. V. Fritz et al., Göttingen 1984, 189–198

—, (ed.), *Texte aus der Umwelt des Alten Testaments*, vol. I, *Rechts- und Wirtschaftsurkunden. Historisch-chronologische Texte*, Gütersloh (1982–)1985; vol. II: *Orakel; Rituale, Bann- und Votivschriften, Lieder und Gebete*, Gütersloh (1986–)1991

Kapelrud, A. S., *The Question of Authority in the Ezra- Narratives. A Lexical Investigation*, SNVAO.HF 1944/1, 1944

—, "A Reconstruction of the Social Welfare System of Ancient Israel," in: *In the Shelter of Elyon*, FS G. W. Ahlström, ed. W. B. Barrick/ J. R. Spencer, JSOT.S 31, 1984, 277–286

—, "Deuteronomy 15 and Recent Research on the Dating of P," in: *Das Deuteronomium*, ed. N. Lohfink, BEThL 68, 1985, 273–276

—, "The Structure of the Deuteronomic Law," *Maarav* 1, 1978/9, 105–158

Kaufmann, Y., *The Religion of Israel*, New York ²1972

Kedar-Kopfstein, B./Botterweck, G. J., Art. חַג *ḥaḡ* κτλ ThWAT II, 1977, 730–744

Keel, O., *Das Böcklein in der Milch seiner Mutter und Verwandtes. Im Lichte eines altorientalischen Bildmotivs*, OBO 33, 1980

—, "Der Bogen als Herrschaftssymbol," ZDPV 93, 1977, 141–177

—, (ed.), *Monotheismus im alten Israel und seiner Umwelt*, BiBe 14, 1980

Kegler, J., "Prophetisches Reden und politische Praxis Jeremias. Beobachtungen zu Jer 26 und 36," in: W. Schottroff/W. Stegemann (ed.), *Der Gott der kleinen Leute. Sozialgeschichtliche Auslegungen*, vol. 1, München/Gelnhausen 1979, 67–79

Keil, C. F., *Biblischer Commentar über den Propheten Jeremia und die Klagelieder*, BC III/2, 1872

—, *Biblischer Commentar über die Bücher Mose's*, vol. II, *Leviticus, Numeri und Deuteronomium*, Leipzig ²1870, reprint Gießen and Basel 1987

Kellermann, D., Art. מַצָּה *maṣṣāh* u.a., ThWAT IV, 1984, 1074–1081

—, Art. אָשָׁם κτλ. *'āšam*, ThWAT I, 1973, 463–472

—, Art. חָמֵץ *ḥmṣ*, ThWAT II, 1977, 1061–1068

—, Art. גּוּר *gūr* u.a., ThWAT I, 1973, 979–991

—, "Bemerkungen Zum Sündopfergesetz in Num 15,22ff," in: *Wort und Geschichte*, FS K. Elliger, ed. H. Gese and H. P. Rüger, AOAT 18, 1973, 107–113

Kellermann, U., "Anmerkungen zum Verständnis der Tora in den chronistischen Schriften," BN 42, 1988, 49–92

—, "Erwägungen zum Esragesetz," ZAW 80, 1968, 373–385

—, "Erwägungen zum Problem der Esradatierung," ZAW 80, 1968, 55–87

—, *Nehemia. Quellen, Überlieferung und Geschichte*, BZAW 102, 1967

Kennedy, J., "The Social Background of Early Israel's Rejection of Cultic Images," BTB 17, 1987, 138–144

Kertelge, K. (ed.), *Das Gesetz im Neuen Testament*, QD 108, Freiburg 1986

Kessler, R., "Das hebräische Schuldenwesen. Terminologie und Metaphorik," WuD NF 20,1989, 181–195

—, "Die Querverweise im Pentateuch. Überlieferungsgeschichtliche Untersuchung der expliziten Querverbindungen innerhalb des vorpriesterlichen Pentateuchs," Diss. theol. Heidelberg 1972 (manu-script)

—, "Die Rolle des Armen für Gerechtigkeit und Sünde des Reichen. Hintergrund und Bedeutung von Dtn 15,9; 24,13.15," in: *Was ist der Mensch . . .? Beiträge zur Anthropologie des Alten Testaments*, FS H. W. Wolff, ed. F. Crüsemann et al., München 1992, 153–163

—, "»Ich weiß, daß mein Erlöser lebet«. Sozialgeschichtlicher Hintergrund und theologische Bedeutung der Löser-Vorstellung in Hiob 19,25," ZThK 89, 1992, 13–158

—, "Staat und Gesellschaft im vorexilischen Juda," Diss., Bethel 1990

Kevers, P., "Étude littéraire de Genèse XXXIV," RB 87, 1980, 38–86

Kevers, P., "Les »fils de Jacob« à Sichem," in: *Pentateuchal and Deuteronomistic Studies. Papers read at the XIIIth IOSOT Congress Leuven 1989*, ed. C. Brekelmans/J. Lust, 1990, 41–46

Kilian, R., *Jesaja 1–12*, NEB, Würzburg 1986

—, *Literarkritische und formgeschichtliche Untersuchungen des Heiligkeits-gesetzes*, BBB 19, 1963

Kinder, E./Haendler, K. (ed.), *Gesetz und Evangelium. Beiträge zur gegenwärtigen theologischen Diskussion*, WdF CXLII, 1968

Kippenberg, H. G., "Heilig und profan, 1. Religionswissenschaflich/ biblisch," EKL II, [3]1989, 432–436

—, "Die Entlassung aus Schuldknechtschaft im antiken Judäa: Eine Legitimitätsvorstellung von Verwandtschaftsgruppen," in: G. Kehrer (ed.), *»Vor Gott sind alle gleich«. Soziale Gleichheit, soziale Ungleichheit und die Religion*, Düsseldorf 1983, 74–104

—, "Die Typik antiker Entwicklung," in: idem. (ed.), *Seminar, Die Entstehung der antiken Klassengesellschaft*, 130, 1977, 9–62

—, *Die vorderasiatischen Erlösungsreligionen in ihrem Zusammenhang mit der antiken Stadtherrschaft*, Heidelberger Max-Weber-Vorlesungen 1988, 917, 1991

—, *Garizim und Synagoge*, RW 30, 1971

—, *Religion und Klassenbildung im antiken Judäa. Eine religionssoziologische Studie zum Verhältnis von Tradition und gesellschaftlicher Entwicklung*, StUNT 14, [2]1982

Kippenberg, H. G./Wewers, G. A. (ed.), *Textbuch zur neutestamentlichen Zeitgeschichte*, GNT 8, 1979

Kirchenamt der EKD (ed.), *Strafe: Tor zur Versöhnung? Eine Denkschrift der Evangelischen Kirche in Deutschland zum Strafvollzug*, Gütersloh 1990

Kittel, H.-J., "Die Stammessprüche Israels. Genesis 49 und Deuteronomium 33 traditionsgeschichtlich untersucht," Diss. Berlin (Kirchl. Hochsch.) 1959

Kittel, P., *Die Bücher der Chronik*, HK I/6, 1902

Kiuchi, N., *The Purification Offering in the Priestly Literature. Its Meaning and Function*, JSOT Suppl. Ser. 56, 1987

Klein, R. W., "The Message of P," in: *Die Botschaft und die Boten*, FS H. W. Wolff, ed. J. Jeremias/L. Perlitt, Neukirchen 1981, 57–66

Klengel, H., "Die Rolle der »Ältesten« (LÚ[MEŠ]ŠU.GI) im Kleinasien der Hethiterzeit," ZA 23, 1965, 223–236

Klíma, J., "Die juristischen Gegebenheiten in den Prologen und Epilogen der mesopotamischen Gesetzeswerke," in: *Travels in the World of the Old Testament*, FS M. A. Beek, Assen 1974, 146–169

—, "L'apport des scribes mésopotamiens à la formation de la jurisprudence," FolOr 21, 1980, 211–220

—, "La perspective historique des lois Hammourabiennes," CRAI, 1972, 297–317

Kline, M. G., "Lex Talionis and the Human Fetus," JETS 20, 1977, 193–201

Klingenberg, E., *Das israelitische Zinsverbot in Torah, Mišnah und Talmud*, Mainz and Wiesbaden 1977

Klopfenstein, M. A., Art. שׁקר *šqr*, THAT II, 1976, 1010–1019

—, "Das Gesetz bei den Propheten," in: *Mitte der Schrift? Ein jüdisch-christliches Gespräch*, Judaica et Christiana 11, Bern 1987, 283–297

Klostermann, A., "Ezechiel und das Heiligkeitsgesetz," ZLThK 38, 1877, 401–445 = idem., *Der Pentateuch. Beiträge zu seinem Verständnis und seiner Entstehungsgeschichte*, Leipzig 1893, 368–418

Knapp, D., *Deuteronomium 4. Literarische Analyse und theologische Interpretation*, GTA 35, 1987

Knauf, E. A., "Zur Herkunft und Sozialgeschichte Israels. »Das Böcklein in der Milch seiner Mutter«," Bib. 69, 1988, 153–169

Knierim, R., Art. אָוֶן *'āwæn*, THAT I, 1971, 81–84

—, Art. שׁגג *šgg*, THAT II, 1976, 869–872

—, Art. מעל *m'l*, THAT I, 1971, 920–922

—, "Exodus 18 und die Neuordnung der mosaischen Gerichtsbarkeit," ZAW 73, 1961, 146–171

—, "Customs, Judges and Legislators in Ancient Israel," in: *Early Jewish and Christian Exegesis. Studies in memory of W. H. Brownlee*, ed. C. A. Evans/W. F. Stinespring, Atlanta 1987, 3–15

—, "The Problem of Ancient Israel's Prescriptive Legal Traditions," *Semeia* 45, 1989, 7–25

Knobel, A., *Der Prophet Jesaja*, KEH, ²1854

Knohl, I., "The Priestly Torah Versus the Holiness School, Sabbath and the Festivals," HUCA 58, 1987, 65–117

Koch, E., "Vom Versuch, die Frage »ob die Weiber Menschen seien, oder nicht«," aus den Digesten zu beantworten, *Rechtshistorisches Journal* 1, 1982, 171–179

Koch, H., *Jenseits der Strafe. Überlegungen zur Kriminalitäts-bewältigung*, Tübingen 1988

Koch, K., Art. מוֹעֵד *mô 'ed*, ThWAT IV, 1984, 744–750

—, Art. כּוּן *kûn*, ThWAT IV, 1984, 95–107

—, "Die Eigenart der priesterlichen Sinaigesetzgebung," ZThK 55, 1958, 36–51

—, "Die Hebräer vom Auszug aus Ägypten bis zum Großreich Davids," VT 19, 1969, 37–81

—, "Die israelitische Sühneanschauung und ihre historischen Wandlungen," (manuscript) Diss., Erlangen 1956

—, *Die Priesterschrift von Ex 25 – Lev 16. Eine überlieferungsgeschichtliche und literarkritische Untersuchung*, FRLANT 71, 1959

—, "Ezra and the Origin of Judaism," JSS 19, 1974, 173–197

Koch, K., "Gestaltet die Erde, doch heget das Leben! Einige Klarstellungen zum dominium terrae in Genesis 1," in: *Wenn nicht jetzt, wann dann? FS H.-J.* Kraus, ed. H.-G. Geyer et al., Neukirchen 1983, 23–36 = idem., *Spuren des hebräischen Denkens*, 223–237

—, "P – kein Redaktor! Erinnerung an zwei Eckdaten der Quellenscheidung," VT 37, 1987, 446–467

—, "Sühne und Sündenvergebung um die Wende von der exilischen zur vorexilischen Zeit," EvTh 26, 1966, 217–239 = idem., *Spuren hebräischen Denkens*, 184–205

—, *Spuren hebräischen Denkens. Gesammelte Aufsätze*, vol. 1, ed. B. Janowski and M. Krause, Neukirchen 1991

—, "Tempeleinlaßliturgien und Dekaloge. Studien zur Theologie der alttestamentlichen Überlieferungen," in: FS G. v. Rad, ed. idem. R. Rendtorff, 1971, 45–60 = idem., *Spuren hebräischen Denkens*, 169–183

—, "Weltordnung und Reichsidee im alten Iran," in: P. Frei/idem., *Reichsidee und Reichsorganisation im Perserreich*, OBO 55, 1984, 45–116

Köckert, M., "Das nahe Wort. Zum entscheidenden Wandel des Gesetzesverständnisses im Alten Testament," ThPh 60, 1985, 496–519

—, "Leben in Gottes Gegenwart. Zum Verständnis des Gesetzes in der priesterlichen Literatur," JBTh 4, 1989, 29–61

—, *Vätergott und Väterverheißungen. Eine Auseinandersetzung mit Albrecht Alt und seinen Erben*, FRLANT 142, 1988

Koffmahn, E., "Sind die altisraelitischen Monatsbezeichnungen mit den kanaanäisch-phönikischen identisch?" BZ 10, 1966, 197–219

Kohata, F., *Jahwist und Priesterschrift in Exodus 3–14*, BZAW 166, 1986

Kohler, K., "Die Nächstenliebe im Judentum," in: *FS H. Cohen*, Berlin 1912, 469–480

Köhler, L., "Die hebräische Rechtsgemeinde" (1931), in: idem., *Der hebräische Mensch*, Tübingen 1953, 143–171

—, *Theologie des Alten Testaments*, Tübingen ⁴1966

Köhler, L./Baumgartner, W., *Lexicon in Veteris Testamenti Libros*, Leiden 1958 (KBL)

Köhler, L./Baumgartner, W./Stamm, J. J., *Hebräisches und aramäisches Lexikon zum Alten Testament*, Leiden 1967–90 (HAL)

Koopmans, W. T., *Joshua 24 as Poetic Narrative*, JSOT.S 93, 1990

Kornfeld, W., "QDŠ und Gottesrecht im Alten Testament," in: *Congress Volume Vienna 1980*, VT.S 32, 1981, 1–9

—, "Reine und unreine Tiere im Alten Testament," *Kairos* 7, 1965, 134–147

Kornfeld, W./Ringgren, H., Art. קדשׁ *qdš*, ThWAT VI, 1989, 1179–1204

Korosqqe, V., "Keilschriftrecht," in: HO I.Abt., Erg.Bd.3, Orientalisches Recht, 1964, 49–219

Koschaker, P., *Neue keilschriftliche Rechtsurkunden aus der El-Amarna-Zeit*, Leipzig 1928

Kottje, R., *Studien zum Einfluß des Alten Testamentes auf Recht und Liturgie des frühen Mittelalters (6.-8. Jahrhundert)*, BHF 23, 1964

Kraft, R. A., "»Ezra« Materials in Judaism and Christianity," in: ANRW II, 19/1, 1979, 119–136

Kratz, R. G., *Translatio imperii. Untersuchungen zu den aramäischen Danielerzählungen und ihrem theologiegeschichtlichen Umfeld*, WMANT 63, 1991

Kraus, F. R., "Ein zentrales Problem des altmesopotamischen Rechts: Was ist der Codex Ḫammurabi?" *Genava* NS 8, 1960, 283–296

—, *Königliche Verfügungen in altbabylonischer Zeit*, Leiden 1984

Kraus, H.-J., "Das Alte Testament in der »Bekennenden Kirche«," *Kirche und Israel* 1, 1986, 26–46 = idem., *Rückkehr zu Israel. Beiträge zum christlich-jüdischen Dialog*, Neukirchen 1991, 237–258

—, "Das heilige Volk," in: *Freude am Evangelium. FS A. de Quervain*, München 1966, 50–61 = idem., *Biblisch-theologische Aufsätze*, Neukirchen 1972, 37–49

—, "Das Telos der Tora. Biblisch-theologische Meditiationen," JBTh 3, 1988, 55–82 = idem., *Rückkehr zu Israel. Beiträge zum christlich-jüdischen Dialog*, Neukirchen 1991, 93–120

—, *Die prophetische Verkündigung des Rechts in Israel*, ThSt 51, 1957

—, *Geschichte der historisch-kritischen Erforschung des Alten Testaments*, Neukirchen ⁴1988

—, *Gottesdienst in Israel. Grundriß einer alttestamentlichen Kultgeschichte*, München ²1962

—, *Klagelieder (Threni)*, BK XX, ³1968

—, *Psalmen*, BK XV, 3 vols., ⁷1989

—, *Psalms*, trans. Hilton C. Oswald. 2 vols. Minneapolis: Augsburg 1987

—, *Reich Gottes: Reich der Freiheit. Grundriß systematischer Theologie*, Neukirchen 1975

—, *Systematische Theologie im Kontext biblischer Geschichte und Eschatologie*, Neukirchen 1983

—, "Tora und »Volksnomos«," in: *Die Hebräische Bibel und ihre zweifache Nachgeschichte, FS R. Rendtorff*, ed. E. Blum et al., Neukirchen 1990, 641–655 = idem., *Rückkehr zu Israel. Beiträge zum christlich-jüdischen Dialog*, Neukirchen 1991, 223–236

—, *Worship in Israel*. Trans. Geoffrey Buswell. Richmond 1966

Krauß, S., "Sanhedrin-Makkot," in: *Die Mischna. Text, Übersetzung und ausführliche Einleitung*, ed. G. Beer et al., vol. IV/4.5, Gießen 1933

Krecher, "Das Rechtsleben und die Auffassung vom Recht in Babylonien," in: W. Fikentscher et al. (eds.), *Entstehung und Wandel rechtlicher Traditionen*, Freiburg and München 1980, 325–354

Kreuzer, S., *Die Frühgeschichte Israels in Bekenntnis und Verkündigung des Alten Testaments*, BZAW 178, 1989

Krückmann, O., "Beamter. b) Die Beamten zur Teit der ersten Dynastie von Babylon," RLA I (1932=) 1981, 449–451

Krüger, T., *Geschichtskonzepte im Ezechielbuch*, BZAW 180, 1989

Küchler, F., *Das Heiligkeitsgesetz Lev 17–26. Eine literarkritische Untersuchung*, Königsberg 1929

Kuenen, A., *Historisch-kritische Einleitung in die Bücher des Alten Testamentes hinsichtlich ihrer Entstehung und Sammlung*, I,1, Leipzig 1887

Kugel, J, "On Hidden Hatred and Open Reproach: Early Exegesis of Leviticus 19: 17," HThR 80, 1987, 43–61

Kugelmass, H. I., "Lex Elionis in the Old Testament," Ph.D. Diss. University of Montreal 1981

Kuhn, P., *Bat Qol. Die Offenbarungsstimme in der rabbinischen Literatur. Sammlung, Übersetzung und Kurzkommentierung der Texte*, Eichstätter Materialien 13, 6. Philosophie und Theologie 5, Regensburg 1989

—, *Die Offenbarungsstimme im Antiken Judentum*, Texte und Studien zum antiken Judentum 20, Tübingen 1989

Kümmel, H. M., "Bestechung im Alten Orient," in: W. Schuller (ed.), *Korruption im Altertum*, Munich and Vienna 1982, 55– 64

Kuschke, A., "Die Lagervorstellung der priesterschriftlichen Erzählung," ZAW 63, 1951, 74–105

Kutsch, E., Art. בְּרִית *bᵉrît*, THAT I, 1971, 339–352

—, "Der Sabbat – ursprünglich Vollmondtag?" (1984), in: idem., *Kleine Schriften zum Alten Testament*, BZAW 168, 1986, 71–77

—, "»Ich will euer Gott sein«. *bᵉrît* in der Priesterschrift," ZThK 71, 1974, 361–388

—, "Menschliche Weisung – Gesetz Gottes. Beobachtungen zu einem aktuellen Thema," in: *Gott ohne Eigenschaften?* ed. S. Heine / E. Heintel, Vienna 1983, 77–106 = idem., *Kleine Schriften zum Alten Testament*, BZAW 168, 1986, 247–273

—, *Verheißung und Gesetz. Untersuchungen zum sogenannten »Bund« im Alten Testament*, BZAW 131, 1973

L'Heureux, C. E., "The Redactional History of Isaiah 5.1 – 10.4," in: *In The Shelter of Elyon*, FS G. W. Ahlström, ed. W. B. Barrick / J. Spencer, JSOT.S 31, 1984, 99–119

Laaf, P., *Die Pascha-Feier Israels. Eine literarkritische und überlieferungs-geschichtliche Studie*, BBB 36, 1970

—, "חג שבעות, das Wochenfest," in: *Bausteine biblischer Theologie*, FS G. J. Botterweck, BBB 50, 1970, 169–183

Labuschagne, C. J., "The Meaning of *bᵉyād rāmā* in the Old Testament," in: *FS J. P. M. van der Ploeg*, ed. W. C. Delsman et al., AOAT 211, 1982, 143–148

Landersdorfer, S., "Keilschriftliche Parallelen zum biblischen Sündenbock (Lev 16)," BZ 19, 1931, 20–28

Landmann, M., *Das Tier in der jüdischen Weisung*, Heidelberg 1959

Lang, B., Art. נכר *nkr*, ThWAT V, 1986, 454–462

Lang, B., Art. כִּפֶּר *kippær*, ThWAT IV, 1984, 303–318

—, "Die Jahwe-allein-Bewegung," in: idem. (ed.), *Der einzige Gott*, München 1981, 47–83

—, (ed.), *Der einzige Gott. Die Geburt des biblischen Monotheismus*, München 1981

Langlamet, F., "Israel et »l'habitant du pays«. Vocabulaire et formules d'Ex., xxxiv,11–16," RB 76, 1969, 321–350.481–507

Latte, K., "Mord" (griechisch), PRE 31, 1933, 278–289

Lauterbach, J. Z. (ed.), *Mekilta des Rabbi Ishmael*, with Engl. trans., 2 vols. (1933), Philadelphia ³1976

Lebram, J. C. H., "Die Traditionsgeschichte der Esragestalt und die Frage nach dem historischen Esra," in: H. Sancisi-Weerdenburg (ed.), *Achae-menid History* I. *Sources, Structures and Synthesis*, Leiden 1987, 103–138

Leemans, W. F., "*kidinnu*, un symbole de droit divin babylonien," in: *Symbolae ad ius et historiam antiquitatis pertinentes*, FS J. C. van Oven, Leiden 1946, 36–61

Leggett, D. A., *The Levirate and Goel Institutions in the Old Testament. With Special Attention to the Book of Ruth*, Cherry Hill 1974

Lehming, S., "Versuch zu Ex 32," VT 10, 1960, 16–50

—, "Zur Überlieferungsgeschichte von Gen 34," ZAW 70, 1958, 228–250

Lehr, S., *Antisemitismus – religiöse Motive im sozialen Vorurteil*, Abhandlungen zum christlich-jüdischen Dialog 5, 1974

Lemaire, A., "Le Sabbat à l'Époque Royale Israélite," RB 80, 1973, 111–185

—, "Les ostraca paleo-hebreux des fouilles de l'Ophel," Levant 10, 1978, 156–161

—, "Populations et territoires de la Palestine à l'époque perse," *Transeuphratene* 3, 1990, 31–74

—, "Vengeance et justice dans l'Ancien Israël," in: *La vengeance*, vol. 3, *Vengeance, pouvoirs et idéologies dans quelques civilisations de l'Antiquité*, ed. R. Verdiers/J.-P. Poly, Paris 1984, 13–33

Lemche, N. P., "Andurārum and Mišarum: Comments on the Problems of Social Edicts and their Application in the Ancient Near East," JNES 38, 1979, 11–22

—, "The »Hebrew Slave«. Comments on the Slave Law Ex. xxi 2–11," VT 25, 1975, 129–144

—, "The Manumission of Slaves – the Fallow Year – the Sabbatical Year – the Jobel Year," VT 26, 1976, 38–59

Levenson, J. D., "Poverty and the State in Biblical Thought," *Judaism* 25, 1976, 230–241

—, "The Theologies of Commandment in Biblical Israel," HThR 73, 1980, 17–33

Levin, C., "Der Dekalog am Sinai," VT 35, 1985, 165–191

Levin, C., *Die Verheißung des neuen Bundes in ihrem theologie-geschichtlichen Zusammenhang ausgelegt*, FRLANT 137, 1985

Levinas, E., "Namenlos," in: idem., *Eigennamen. Meditationen über Sprache und Literatur*, Germ. trans. Munich and Vienna 1988, 101–106

Levine, B. A., *In the Presence of the Lord. A Study of Cult and some Cultic Terms in Ancient Israel*, SJLA 5, 1974

Levine, L. J., "The Second Temple Synagogue: The Formative Years," in: *The Synagogue in Late Antiquity*, ed. idem., Philadelphia 1987, 7–31

Levy, Y./Milgrom, J./Ringgren, H./Fabry, H.-J., Art. עֵדָה *'edāh*, ThWAT V, 1986, 1079–1093

Liebeschütz, *Das Judentum im deutschen Geschichtsbild von Hegel bis Max Weber*, Tübingen 1967

Liedke, G., "»Tier-Ethik« – Biblische Perspektiven," ZEE 29, 1985, 160–173

—, Art. דִּין *dîn*, THAT I, 1971, 445–448

—, Art. יכח *ykḥ* hi., TH I, 1971, 730–732

—, Art. שפט *šp̄ṭ*, THAT II, 1973, 999–1009

—, Art. רִיב *rîb*, THAT II, 1976, 771–777

—, Art. תקק *ḥqq*, THAT I, 1971, 626–633

—, *Gestalt und Bezeichnung alttestamentlicher Rechtssätze. Eine formgeschichtlich-terminologische Studie*, WMANT 39, 1971

Liedke, G./Petersen, C., Art.; תּוֹרָה *tōrā*, THAT II, 1976, 1032–1043

Lienemann, W. (ed.), *Die Finanzen der Kirche. Studien zu Struktur, Geschichte und Legitimation kirchlicher Ökonomie*, München 1989

Liermann, H., "Abgaben," TRE I, 1977, 329–347

Lindars, B., "Torah in Deuteronomy," in: *Words and Meanings*, FS D. W. Thomas, Cambridge 1968, 117–130

Lindblom, J., *Erwägungen zur Herkunft der josianischen Tempelur-kunde*, SMHVL 1970–1971, 3, Lund 1971

—, "Theophanies in Holy Places in Hebrew Religion," HUCA 22, 1961, 91–106

Lipiński, E., Art. נָקַם, ThWAT V, 1986, 602–612

—, Art. מכר *mkr*, ThWAT IV, 1983, 869– 875

—, "Juges 5,4–5 et Psaume 68,1–11," *Biblica* 48, 1967, 185–206

—, "L'«esclave hébreu«," VT 26, 1976, 120–124

—, "Nešek and *tarbît* in the Light of Epigraphic Evidence," OLoP 10, 1979, 133–141

—, "Sale, Transfer and Delivery in Ancient Semitic Terminology," SGKAO 15, 1982, 173–185

—, (ed.), *State and Temple Economy in the Ancient Near East*, 2 vols. OLA 5.6, 1979

Lisowsky, G., "Dtn 25,4 לֹא־תַחְסֹם שׁוֹר בְּדִישׁוֹ Du sollst dem Rinde bei seinem Dreschen nicht das Maul verbinden," in: *Das ferne und das nahe Wort*, FS L. Rost, BZAW 105, 1967, 144–152

Liver, J., "The Half-Shekel Offering in Biblical and Post-Biblical Literature," HThR 56, 1963, 173–198

Liverani, M., "Communautés de village et palais royal dans la Syrie de IIème millénaire," JESHO 18, 1975, 146–164

—, "La Royauté syrienne de l'âge du bronze récent," in: P. Garelli (ed.), *Le Palais et L Royauté*, CRAI xix, Paris 1974, 329–356

Livingston, D. H., "The Crime of Leviticus xxiv 11," VT 36, 1986, 352–354

Liwak, R., "Überlieferungsgeschichtliche Probleme des Ezechielbuches. Eine Studie zu postezechielischen Interpretationen und Komposi-tionen," Diss. Bochum 1976

Ljung, I., *Silence or Suppression. Attitudes towards Women in the Old Testament*, Uppsala 1989

Locher, C., *Die Ehre einer Frau in Israel. Exegetische und rechtsvergleichende Studien zu Deuteronomium 22, 13–21*, OBO 70, 1986

—, "Dtn 22,13–21. Vom Prozeßprotokoll zum kasuistischen Gesetz," in: *Das Deuteronomium*, ed. N. Lohfink, BEThL 68, 1985, 298–303

Loersch, S., *Das Deuteronomium und seine Deutungen*, SBS 22, 1967

Löw, A., *Thierschutz im Judenthume nach Bibel und Talmud*, Brünn ²1891

Loewenstamm, S. E., "Exodus xxi 22–25," VT 27, 1977, 352–360 = idem., *Comparative Studies in Biblical and Ancient Oriental Literatures*, AOAT 204, 1980, 517–525

—, "The Seven-Day-Unit in Ugaritic Epic Literature," in: idem., *Comparative Studies in Biblical and Ancient Oriental Literatures*, AOAT 204, 1980, 192–209

—, "נשך and מתרבית," JBL 88, 1969, 78–80

Lohfink, N., "»Gewalt« als Thema alttestamentlicher Forschung," in., idem. (ed.), *Gewalt und Gewaltlosigkeit im Alten Testament*, QD 96, 1983, 15–50

—, "»Ich bin Jahwe, dein Arzt« (Ex 15,26). Gott, Gesellschaft und menschliche Gesundheit in der Theologie einer nachexilischen Pentateuchbearbeitung (Ex 15,25b.26)," in: *»Ich will euer Gott werden«. Beispiele biblischen Redens von Gott*, SBS 100, ²1982, 11–73 = idem., *Studien zum Pentateuch*, SBAB 4, 1988, 91–155

—, "2 Kön 23,3 und Dtn 6,17," Bib. 71, 1990, 34–42

—, "Deuteronomium," NBL Liefg. 3, 1990, 414–418

—, "חָרַם ḥāram, ThWAT III, 1982, 192–213

—, "יָרַשׁ jāraš, ThWAT III, 1982, 953–985

—, "Besprechung von Knapp, Dtn 4," ThR 84, 1988, 279–281

—, "Bundestheologie im Alten Testament. Zum gleichnamigen Buch von Lothar Perlitt," in: idem., *Studien zum Deuteronomium und zur deuteronomistischen Literatur* I, SBAB 8,1990, 325– 361

—, "Darstellungskunst und Theologie in Dtn 1,6 – 3,29," *Biblica* 41, 1960, 105–134 = idem., *Studien zum Deuteronomium und zur deuteronomistischen Literatur* I, SBAB 8, 1990, 15–44

Lohfink, N., "Das deuteronomische Gesetz in der Endgestalt – Entwurf einer Gesellschaftohne marginale Gruppen," BN 51, 1990, 25–40

—, "Das Deuteronomium: Jahwegesetz oder Mosegesetz? Die Subjekt-zuordnung bei Wörtern wie »Gesetz« im Deuteronomium und der deuteronomistischen Literatur," ThPh 65, 1990, 387–391

—, "Das Hauptgebot. Eine Untersuchung literarischer Einleitungsfragen zu Dtn 5–11," AnBib 20, 1963

—, "Der Begriff »Bund« in der biblischen Theologie," ThPh 66, 1991, 161–176

—, "Die Abänderung der Theologie des priesterlichen Geschichtswerks im Segen des Heiligkeitsgesetzes. Zu Lev 26,9.11–13," in: *Wort und Geschichte*, FS K. Elliger, ed. H. Gese and H. P. Rüger, AOAT 18, 1973, 129–136 = idem., *Studien zum Pentateuch*, SBAB 4, 1988, 157–168

—, "Die Bedeutung von hebr. *jrš* qal und hif.," BZ 27, 1981, 14–33

—, "Die Gattung der »Historischen Kurzgeschichte« in den letzten Jahren von Juda und in der Zeit des babylonischen Exils," ZAW 90, 1978, 319–347 = idem., Studien zum Deuteronomium und zur deuteronomistischen Literatur II, SBAB 12, 1991, 55–86

—, "Die *huqqîm ûmišpāṭîm* im Buch Deuteronomium und ihre Neubegrenzung durch Dtn 12,1," *Bibl.* 70, 1989, 1–29 = idem., *Studien zum Deuteronomium und zur deuteronomistischen Literatur* II, SBAB 12, 1991, 229–256

—, "Die Priesterschrift und die Geschichte," in: *Congress Volume Göttingen 1977*, VT.S 29, 1978, 169–225 = idem., *Studien zum Pentateuch*, SBAB 4, 1988, 213–254

—, "Die Schichten des Pentateuch und der Krieg," in: idem. (ed.), *Gewalt und Gewaltlosigkeit im Alten Testament*, QD 96, 1983, 51–110 = idem., *Studien zum Pentateuch*, SBAB 4, 1988, 255–315

—, "Die Sicherung der Wirksamkeit des Gotteswortes durch das Prinzip der Schriftlichkeit der Tora und durch das Prinzip der Gewalt-enteilung nach den Ämtergesetzen des Buches Deuteronomium (Dtn 16,18 – 18,21)," in: *Testimonium Veritati*. FS W. Kempf, FTS 7, 1971, 143–155 = idem., *Studien Zum Deuteronomium und zur deuteronomistischen Literatur* I, SBAB 8, 1990, 305–223

—, "Dt 26,17–19 und die »Bundesformel«," ZKTh 91, 1969, 517–553 = idem., *Studien zum Deuteronomium und zur deuteronomistischen Literatur* I, SBAB 8, 1990, 211–261

—, "Gibt es eine deuteronomistische Bearbeitung im Bundesbuch?" in: *Pentateuchal and Deuteronomistic Studies. Papers read at the XIIIth IOSOT Congress Leuven 1989*, ed. C. Brekelmans/J. Lust, BEThL 94, 1990, 91–113

Lohfink, N., "Gott auf der Seite der Armen. Zur »Option für die Armen« im Alten Orient und in der Bibel," in: idem., *Das Jüdische am Christentum*, Freiburg 1987, 122–143

—, "Hos. XI 5 als Bezugstext von Dtn. XVII 16," VT 31, 1981, 226–228 = idem., *Studien zum Deuteronomium und zur deuteronomistischen Literatur* II, SBAB 12, 1991, 143–156

—, "Kennt das Alte Testament einen Unterschied von »Gebot« und »Gesetz«? Zur bibeltheologischen Einstufung des Dekalogs," JBTh 4, 1989, 63–89

—, "Kerygmata des Deuteronomistischen Geschichtswerks," in: *Die Botschaft und die Boten*, FS H. W. Wolff, eds. J. Jeremias / L. Perlitt, Neukirchen-Vl. 1981, 87–100 = idem., *Studien zum Deuteronomium und zur deuteronomistischen Literatur* II, SBAB 12, 1991, 125–142

—, Rez. U. Rüterswörden, "Von der politischen Gemeinschaft zur Gemeinde. Studien zu Dt 16,18 – 18,22" (BBB 65, 1987), ThLZ 113, 1988, 425–430

—, "The Cult Reform of Josiah of Judah: II Kings 22–23 as a Source for the History of Israelite Religion," in: *Ancient Israelite Religion*, FS F. M. Cross, ed. P. D. Hanson et al., Philadelphia 1987, 459–475 = idem., "Die Kultreform Joschijas von Juda. 2 Kön 22–23 als religions-geschichtliche Quelle," *Studien zum Deuteronomium und zur deuteronomistischen Literatur* II, SBAB 12, 1991, 209–256

—, "Zum rabbinischen Verständnis von Dtn 12,1," in: *Die alttestamentliche Botschaft als Wegweisung*, FS H. Reinelt, ed. J. Zmijewski, Stuttgart 1990, 157–162 = idem., *Studien zum Deuteronomium und zur deuteronomistischen Literatur* II, SBAB 12, 1991, 287–292

—, "Zur deuteronomischen Zentralisationsformel," *Bib.* 65, 1984, 297–329 = idem., *Studien zum Deuteronomium und zur deuteronomistischen Literatur* II, SBAB 12, 1991, 147–178

—, "Zur Geschichte der Diskussion über den Monotheismus im Alten Israel," in: *Gott, der einzige*, ed. E. Haag, QD 104, 1985, 9–25

—, "Zur neueren Diskussion über 2 Kön 22–23," in: idem., (ed.), *Das Deuteronomium*, BEThL 68, 1985, 24–48 = idem., *Studien zum Deuteronomium und zur deuteronomistischen Literatur* II, SBAB 12, 1991, 179–208

Löhr, M., *Das Asylwesen im Alten Testament*, SKG.G 7/3, 1930

Lohse, E., συνέδριον, ThWNT VII, 1964, 858–869

Long, V.P., *The Reign and Rejection of King Saul. A Case for Literary and Theological Coherence*, SBLDS 118, Atlanta 1989

Loretz, O., "Die steinernen Gesetzestafeln in der Lade. Probleme der Deuteronomium-Forschung zwischen Geschichte und Utopie," UF 9, 1977, 159–161

—, "Ex 21,6; 22,8 und angebliche Nuzi-Parallelen," *Bibl.* 41, 1960, 167–175

Loretz, O., *Habiru – Hebräer. Eine sozio-linguistische Studie über die Herkunft des Gentiliziums 'ibrî vom Appellativum ḫabiru*, BZAW 160, 1984

—, *Leberschau, Sündenbock, Asasel in Ugarit und Israel*, Ugar.-Bibl. Literatur 3, Altenberge 1985

—, "Vom kanaanäischen Totenkult zur jüdischen Patriarchen- und Elternehrung," JARG 3, 1978, 149–204

Lubsczyk, H., *Der Auszug Israels aus Ägypten*, EThSt 11, 1963

—, "Die Bundesurkunde. Ursprung und Wirkungsgeschichte des Deuteronomiums," in: *Pentateuchal and Deuteronomistic Studies. Papers read at the XIIIth IOSOT Congress Leuven 1989*, ed. C. Brekelmans/J. Lust, BEThL 94, 1990, 161–177

Luckenbill, D. D., *The Annals of Sennacherib*, Chicago 1924

Luhmann, N., *Rechtssoziologie*, 2 vols. Hamburg 1972

Lust, J., Ez., XX,4–26. "Une parodie de l'histoire religieuse d'Israel," in: *De Mari à Qumran*, FS J. Coppens, vol. I, 1969, 127–166

Luxemburg, R., "Die russische Revolution." *Politische Schriften* III, ed. O. K. Flechtheim, Frankfurt/M. [3]1971, 106–141

Luyten, J., "Primeval and Eschatological Overtones in the Song of Mose (Dt 32,1–43)," in: N. Lohfink (ed.), *Das Deuteronomium*, BEThL LXVIII, 1985, 341–347

Maaß, F., "Selbstliebe nach Leviticus 19,18," in: *FS F. Baumgärtel*, Erlangen 1959, 109–113

Mabee, C., "Jacob and Laban. The Structure of Judicial Proceedings (Genesis xxxi 25–42)," VT 30, 1980, 192–207

—, "The Problem of Setting in Hebrew Royal Judicial Narratives," Diss. Claremont 1977

Mace, D. R., *Hebrew Marriage. A Sociological Study*, London 1953

Macholz, G. Ch., "Das »Passivum Divinum«, seine Anfänge im Alten Testament und der »Hofstil«," ZNW 81, 1990, 247–253

—, "Die Stellung des Königs in der israelitischen Gerichtsverfassung," ZAW 84, 1972, 157–182

Macholz, G. Ch., "Psalm 29 und 1 Könige 19," in: *Werden und Wirken des Alten Testaments*, FS C. Westermann, ed. R. Albertz et al., Göttingen and Neukirchen 1980, 325–333

—, "Zur Geschichte der Justizorganisation in Juda," ZAW 84, 1972, 314–340

Magonet, J., "Der Versöhnungstag in der jüdischen Liturgie," in: H. Heinz et al. (ed.), *Versöhnung in der jüdischen und christlichen Liturgie*, QD 124, 1990, 133–154

—, "The Korah Rebellion," JSOT 24, 1982, 3–25

Maiberger, P., *Das Manna. Eine literarische, etymologische und naturkundliche Untersuchung*, Ägypten und Altes Testament 6, Wiesbaden 1983

Maier, J., "Torah und Pentateuch, Gesetz und Moral. Beobachtungen zum jüdisch und christlichtheologischen Befund," in: A. Vivian (ed.), *Biblische und Judaistische Studien*, FS P. Sacchi, Judentum und Umwelt 29, Frankfurt/M. 1990, 1–54

—, "Urim und Tummim," *Kairos* 11, 1969, 22–38

—, *Zwischen den Testamenten. Geschichte und Religion in der Zeit des zweiten Tempels*, NEB vol. 3, Würzburg 1990

Malamat, A., "The Historical Background of the Assassination of Amon, King of Judah," IEJ 3, 1953, 26–29

—, "»You Shall Love Your Neighbor As Yourself«. A Case of Misinterpretation?" in: *Die Hebräische Bibel und ihre zweifache Nachgeschichte*, FS R. Rendtorff, ed. E. Blum et al., Neukirchen 1990, 111–115

Maloney, R. P., "Usury and Restriction on Interest-Taking in the Ancient Near East," CBQ 36, 1974, 1–20

—, "Usury in Greek, Roman and Rabbinic Thought," *Traditio* 27, 1971, 79–109

Malul, M., *The Comparative Method in Ancient Near Eastern and Biblical Legal Studies*, AOAT 227, 1990

Mann, Th., "Das Gesetz, in: idem., *Die Erzählungen*. vol. 2, Frankfurt/M. 1975, 621–672

Mantel, H., *Studies in the History of the Sanhedrin*, Cambridge 1961

—, "The Nature of the Great Synagogue," HThR 60, 1967, 69–91

Marböck, J., נבל *nāḇāl*, ThWAT V, 1986, 171–185

Marcus, M., "Prolegomena zu einer jüdischen Umweltethik," in: *Israel und Kirche heute. Beiträge zum christlich-jüdischen Dialog*, FS E. L. Ehrlich, Freiburg 1991, 376–385

Margaliot, M., "Marah (Exod. 15, 22–27) and Its Position between Exodus and the Sinai Covenant," *Shnaton* 4, 1980, 129–150

Margalith, O., "The Political Role of Ezra as Persian Governor," ZAW 98, 1986, 110–112

Marquardt, F.-W., "Zur Reintegration der Tora in eine Evangelische Theologie," in: *Die Hebräische Bibel und ihre zweifache Nachgeschichte*, FS R. Rendtorff, ed. E. Blum et al., Neukirchen 1990, 657–676

Martin-Achard, R., נֵכָר *nēkār*, THAT II, 1976, 66–68

—, גּוּר *gūr*, THAT I, 1971, 409–412

—, "Israël, peuple sacerdotal," VC 18, 1964, 11–28 = idem., *Permanence de l'Ancien Testament. Recherches d'Exégèse et de Theologie*, Cahiers de la RThPh 11, 1984, 129–146

Martin-Achard, R., *La Loi, don de Dieu. Aux sources de l'Ancien Testament*, Aubonne 1987

—, "Récents travaux sur la loi du talion selon l'Ancien Testament," RHPhR 69, 1989, 173–188

Marx, A., "Sacrifice de Réparation et Rites de Levée de Sanction," ZAW 100, 1988, 183–198

Mathias, D., "»Levitische Predigt« und Deuteronomismus," ZAW 96, 1984, 23–49

Mathys, H.-P., *Liebe deinen Nächsten wie dich selbst. Untersuchungen zum alttestamentlichen Gebot der Nächstenliebe (Lev 19,18)*, OBO 71, 1986

Matthes, J. C., "Der Sühnegedanke bei den Sündopfern," ZAW 23, 1903, 97–119

Mauer, G., "Die »Gesetze« von Ešnunna – eine Schreiberübung," BN 42, 1988, 36–43

Maybaum, S., "Erklärung einiger biblischer Stellen," in: *FS H. Cohen*, Berlin 1912, 405–410

Mayer, G., יכה *ykḥ*, ThWAT III, 1982, 620–628

Mayes, A. D. H., *Deuteronomy*, NCeB, London 1979

Mays, J. L., *Hosea. A Commentary*, London 1969

Mazar, A., "Giloh, An Early Israelite Settlement Site Near Jerusalem," IEJ 31, 1981, 1–36

McBride, S. D., "Deuteronomium," TRE VIII, 1981, 530–543

McConville, J. G., *Law and Theology in Deuteronomy*, JSOT.S 33, 1984

McDaniel, Th. F., *Deborah Never Sang. A Philological Study of Deborah (Judges Chapter V)*, Jerusalem 1983

McEvenue, S. E., *The Narrative Style of the Priestly Writer*, AnBib 50, 1971

—, "The Political Structure in Judah from Cyrus to Nehemiah," CBQ 43, 1981, 353–364

McKane, W., *A Critical and Exegetical Commentary on Jeremiah. Vol. I: Introduction and Commentary on Jeremiah I-XXV*, Edinburgh 1986

—, *Prophets and Wise Men*, SBT 44, 1965

McKay, J. W., "Exodus XXIII 1–3.6–8: A Decalogue for the Administration of Justice in the City Gate," VT 21, 1971, 311– 325

McKeating, H., "Sanctions against Adultery in Ancient Israelite Society, with some Reflections on Methodology in the Study of Old Testament Ethics," JSOT 11, 1979, 57–72

—, "The Development of the Law of Homicide in Ancient Israel," VT 25, 1975, 46–68

McKenzie, D. A., "Judicial Procedure at the Town Gate," VT 14, 1964, 100–104

McKenzie, J. L., "The »People of the Land« in the Old Testament," *Akten des 24. internationalen Orientalisten-Kongresses München 1957*, Wiesbaden 1959, 206–208

—, "The Elders in the Old Testament," *Bib.* 40, 1959, 522–540

—, "The Historical Prologue of Deuteronomy," *Fourth World Congress of Jewish Studies* I, 1967, 95–101

Meier, C., *Die Entstehung des Politischen bei den Griechen*, 427, 1983

Meier, W., "».. . Fremdlinge, die aus Israel gekommen waren . . .« Eine Notiz zu 2 Chronik 30,25f. aus der Sicht der Ausgrabungen im Jüdischen Viertel der Altstadt von Jerusalem," BN 15, 1981, 40–43

Meinhold, J., *Sabbat und Woche im Alten Testament*, FRLANT 5, 1905

Meissner, B., *Babylonien und Assyrien*, vols. I + II, Heidelberg 1920

Mendelsohn, I., *Slavery in the Ancient Near East*, New York 1949

—, "The Conditional Sale into Slavery of Free-Born Daughters in Nuzi and the Law of Ex 21,7–11," JAOS 55, 1935, 190–195

—, "The Family in the Ancient Near East," BA XI, 1948/2, 24–40

Menes, A., *Die vorexilischen Gesetze Israels im Zusammenhang seiner kulturgeschichtlichen Entwicklung*, BZAW 50, 1928

Merendino, R. P., *Das deuteronomische Gesetz*; BBB 31, 1969

Merz, E., *Die Blutrache bei den Israeliten*, BWANT 20, 1916

Meshel, Z., "Kuntillet 'Ajrud. A Religious Centre from the Time of the Judaean Monarchy on the Border of Sinai," *Israel Museum Catalogue* 175, Jerusalem 1978

Mettinger, T. N. D., *Solomonic State Officials. A Study of the Civil Government Officials of the Israelite Monarchy*, CB.OT 5, 1971

Metzger, H. et al., *Feuilles de Xanthos. Tome VI. La stèle trilingue du Létôon*, Paris 1979

Meyer, E., *Die Entstehung des Judentums*, Halle 1896, reprint Hildesheim 1987

—, *Geschichte des Altertums* II/2, ⁴1965

Meyer, R., *Hebräische Grammatik*, I-IV, 3rd ed. Berlin 1966–72

Meyers, C., *Discovering Eve. Ancient Israelite Women in Context*, Oxford and New York 1988

—, "Procreation, Production, and Protection: Male–Female Balance in Early Israel," JAAR 51, 1983, 569–593

Michaeli, F., *Les livres des Chroniques, d'Esdras et Nehemie*, CAT 16, 1967

Michaelis, W., χράτος χτλ., ThWNT III, 1938, 905–914

Michel, D., *Grundlegung einer hebräischen Syntax* 1, Neukirchen 1977

Mikliszanski, J. K., "The Law of Retaliation and the Pentateuch," JBL 66, 1947, 295–303

Mildenberg, L., "Yəhud-Münzen," in: H. Weippert, *Palästina in vorhellenistischer Zeit. Handbuch der Archäologie in Vorderasien* II/l, München 1988, 719–728

Milgrom, J., "A Prolegomenon to Leviticus 17,11," JBL 90, 1971, 149–156 = idem., *Studies in Cultic Theology and Terminology*, SJLA 36, 1983, 96–103

—, "First-born," IDB Suppl., Nashville (1962), ⁸1988, 337f.

—, *Cult and Conscience. The Asham and the Priestly Doctrine of Repentance*, SJLA 18, 1976

—, "Ethics and Ritual: The Foundations of the Biblical Dietary Laws," in: *Religion and Law. Biblical-Judaic and Islamic Perspectives*, ed. E. B. Firmage et al., Winona Lake 1990, 159–191

Milgrom, J., "Israel's Sanctuary: The Priestly »Picture of Dorian Gray«" (1976), in: idem., *Studies in Cultic Theology and Terminology*, 75–84

—, "Korah's rebellion: A Study in Redaction," in: *De la Tôrah au Messie*, Mélanges H. Cazelles, ed. M. Carrez et al., Paris 1981, 135–146

—, "Rationale for Cultic Law: The Case of Impurity," *Semeia* 45, 1989, 103–109

—, *Sancta Contagion and Altar/City Asylum*, VT.S 32, 1981, 278–310

—, *Studies in Cultic Theology and Terminology*, SJLA 36, 1983

—, "The Betrothed Slave-girl, Lev 19₂₀₋₂₂," ZAW 89, 1977, 43–50

—, "The Biblical Diet Laws as an Ethical System," in: idem., *Studies in Cultic Theology and Terminology*, 104–118

—, "The Consecration of the Priests. A Literary Comparison of Leviticus 8 and Exodus 29," in: *Ernten, was man sät*, FS K. Koch, ed. D. R. Daniels et al, Neukirchen 1991, 273–286

—, "The Cultic Šᵉgāgah and Its Influence in Psalms and Job," JQR 58, 1967, 115–125 = idem., *Studies in Cultic Theology and Terminology*, SJLA 36, 1983, 122–132

—, "The Graduated Ḥaṭṭā't of Leviticus 5, 1–13," JAOS 103, 1983, 249–254

—, "The Modus Operandi of the Ḥaṭṭā't. A Rejoinder," JBL 109, 1990, 111–113

—, "The Priestly Doctrine of Repentance," RB 82, 1975, 186–205 = idem., *Studies in Cultic Theology and Terminology*, SJLA 36, 1983, 47–66

—, "The Priestly Impurity System," in: *Proceedings of the Ninth World Congress of Jewish Studies*, Jerusalem 1986, 121–127 (sic!)

—, "The Two Pericopes on the Purification Offering," in: *The Word of the Lord Shall Go Forth*, FS D. N. Freedman, ed. C. L. Meyers/ M. O'Connor, Winona Lake 1983, 211–215

—, "You Shall Not Boil a Kid in Its Mother's Milk. An Archaeological Myth Destroyed," *Bible Review* 1/3, 1985, 48–55

Millard, M., *Die noachidischen Gebote. Zur Endgestalt der Bibel, ihrer inner- und nachbiblischen Auslegung*, Magisterarbeit Hochschule für Jüdische Studien, Heidelberg 1989

Minette de Tillesse, C., "A reforma de Josias," *Revista biblica brasileira* 6, 1989, 41–61

Minokami, Y., *Die Revolution des Jehu*, GThA 38, 1989

Mittelmann, J. M., *Das altisraelitische Levirat. Eine rechtshistorische Studie*, Leipzig 1934

Mittmann, S., *Deuteronomium 1₁-63 literarkritisch und traditionsgeschichtlich untersucht*, BZAW 139, 1975

Moberly, R. W. L., *At the Mountain of God. Story and Theology in Exodus 32–34*, JSOT.S 22, 1983

Moberly, R. W. L., "»Yahweh is one«: The Translation of the Shema," in: *Studies in the Pentateuch*, VT.S 41, 1990, 209–215

Mölle, H., *Der sogenannte Landtag zu Sichem*, 42, 1980

Mommer, P., *Samuel. Geschichte und Überlieferung*, WMANT 65, 1991

Moor, J. C. de, *The Rise of Yahwism. The Roots of Israelite Monotheism*, BEThL 101, 1990

Mor, M., "I. Samaritan History. 1. The Persian, Hellenistic and Hasmonaean Period," in: A. D. Crown (ed.), *The Samaritans*, Tübingen 1989, 1–18

Moraldi, L., *Espiazone sacrificale e riti espiatori nell'ambiente biblico e nell'Antico Testamento*, AnBib 5, 1956

Morgan, D. F., "The So-Called Cultic Calendars in the Pentateuch: A Morphological and Typological Study," Diss. Claremont 1974

Morgenstern, J., "The Decalogue of the Holiness Code," HUCA 26, 1955, 1–27

Mosis, R., "Ex 19,5b.6a: Syntaktischer Aufbau und lexikalische Semantik," BZ NF 22, 1978, 1–25

—, *Untersuchungen zur Theologie des chronistischen Geschichtswerks*, Freiburg 1973

Mowinckel, S., *Studien zu dem Buche Ezra-Nehemia, III. Die Esrageschichte und das Gesetz Moses*, SNVAO HF, NS 7, 1965

—, *Tetrateuch-Pentateuch-Hexateuch*, BZAW 90, 1964,

—, "Zur Geschichte der Dekaloge," ZAW 55, 1937, 218–235

—, *Zur Komposition des Buches Jeremia*, Oslo 1914

Mühl, M., *Die Gesetze des Zaleukos und Charondas*, Leipzig 1929 (= *Klio* 22, 1929, 105–124.432–463)

—, *Untersuchungen zur altorientalischen und althellenischen Gesetzgebung*, *Klio*. Beiheft 29 (N.F. 16), 1933

Müller, A. R., "Der Text als russische Puppe? Zu P. Weimars »Die Berufung des Mose«," BN 17, 1982, 56–72

—, "2 Kön 23,3 deuteronomistisch?" BN 35, 1986, 26–29

Müller, H.-P., נָבִיא *nābî'*, THAT V, 1986, 140–163

—, עשתרת *'štrt*, ThWAT VI, 1989, 453–463

Müller, K., "Tora für die Völker. Die noachidischen Gebote im Beziehungsfeld zwischen Judentum und Christentum," Diss. theol. Heidelberg 1991

Munk, M., "Esra Hasofer nach Talmud und Midrasch," JJLG 21, 1930, 129–198 (reprint 1975)

Murray, R., "New Wine in Old Wineskins." XII Firstfruits, ET 86, 1974/5, 164–168

Myers, J. M., *II Chronicles. Introduction, Translation and Notes*, AncB 13, 1965

Na'aman, N., "Canaanites and Perizzites," BN 45, 1988, 42–47

Nasuti, H., "Identity, Identification, and Imitation: The Narrative Hermeneutics of Biblical Law," *Journal of Law and Religion* 4, 1986, 9–23

Naveh, J., "A Fragment of an Ancient Hebrew Inscription from the Ophel," IEJ 32, 1982, 195–198

Neef, H.-D., "Der Sieg Deboras und Baraks über Sisera. Exegetische Beobachtungen zum Aufbau und Werden von Jdc 4,1– 24," ZAW 101, 1989, 28–49

—, *Die Heilstraditionen Israels in der Verkündigung des Propheten Hosea*, BZAW 169, 1987

Nelson, B., *The Idea of Usury*, (1950) Chicago ²1969

Nembach, U., "Ehescheidung nach alttestamentlichem und jüdischem Recht," ThZ 26, 1970, 161–171

Neu, R., *Von der Anarchie zum Staat. Entwicklungsgeschichte Israels vom Nomadentum zur Monarchie im Spiegel der Ethnosoziologie*, Neukirchen 1992

Neufeld, E., "The Prohibitions against Loans at Interest in Ancient Hebrew Laws," HUCA 26, 1955, 355–412

Neusner, J., *Rabbinic Traditions about the Pharisees before 70*, 3 vols. Leiden 1971

Newman, K. S., *Law and Economic Organization. A Comparative Study of Preindustrial Societies*, Cambridge 1988

Nicholson, E. W., *The Book of the Prophet Jeremiah, Chapters 1–25*, CBC, 1973

—, "The Decalogue as the Direct Address of God," VT 27, 1977, 422–433

—, "The Meaning of the Expression עם הארץ in the OT," JSS 10, 1965, 59–66

Nicolaisen, C., "Die Auseinandersetzung um das Alte Testament im Kirchenkampf," Diss. Hamburg 1966

Nicolsky, N. M., "Das Asylrecht in Israel," ZAW 48, 1930, 146–175

Niehr, H., *Der höchste Gott. Alttestamentlicher JHWH- Glaube im Kontext syrisch-kanaanäischer Religion des 1. Jahrtausends v.Chr.*, BZAW 190, 1990

—, "Grundzüge der Forschung zur Gerichtsorganisation Israels," BZ NF 31, 1987, 206–227

—, "Herrschen und Richten. Die Wurzel špṭ im Alten Orient und im Alten Testament," 1986

—, *Rechtsprechung in Israel. Untersuchungen zur Geschichte der Gerichtsorganisation im Alten Testament*, SBS 130, 1987

Nielsen, E., *Die Zehn Gebote. Eine traditionsgeschichtliche Skizze*, AThD 8, 1965

—, "Moses and the Law," VT 32, 1982, 87–98 = idem., *Law, History and Tradition. Selected Essays*, Copenhagen 1983, 119–128

—, *Shechem. A Traditio-Historical Investigation*, Copenhagen ²1959

—, "»Weil Jahwe unser Gott ein Jahwe ist« (Dtn 6,4f.)" (1977), in: *Beiträge zur alttestamentlichen Theologie*, FS W. Zimmerli, Göttingen 1977, 288–301 = idem., *Law, History and Tradition*, Copenhagen 1983, 106–118

Nielsen, E., »You Shall Not Muzzle an Ox While it is Treading Out the Corn«, Dt. 25,4 (1975), in: idem., *Law, History and Tradition*, Copenhagen 1983, 94–105

Niemann, H. M., *Die Daniten. Studien zur Geschichte eines altisraelitischen Stammes*, FRLANT 135, 1985

Nietzsche, F., "Jenseits von Gut und Böse," in: *Werke* II, ed. K. Schlechta, München 1966, 563–759

Noll, P., *Diktate über Sterben & Tod*, Zürich 1984

Noonan, J. T., "The Muzzled Ox," JQR 70, 1979/80, 172–175

Norden J., *Auge um Auge – Zahn um Zahn*, Berlin 1926

Nordheim, E. v., "Ein Prophet kündigt sein Amt auf (Elia am Horeb)," *Bib.* 59, 1978, 153–173

North, R., "Flesh, Covering, and Response Ex. xxi 10," VT 5, 1955, 204–206

—, "Maccabean Sabbath Years," *Bibl.* 34, 1953, 501–515

Noth, M., "Das Amt des »Richters Israel«," in: *FS Bertholet*, Tübingen 1950, 414–417 = idem., *Gesammelte Studien zum Alten Testament* II, ThB 39, 1969, 71–85

—, *Das Buch Josua*, HAT I/7, ²1953

—, *Das dritte Buch Mose. Leviticus*, ATD 6, 1962

—, *Das zweite Buch Mose. Exodus*, ATD 5, 1959

—, *Das vierte Buch Mose. Numeri*, ATD 7, 1966

—, Die Gesetze im Pentateuch, SKG.G 17,2, 1940 = idem. Gesammelte

—, *Exodus: a commentary*. Trans. J. S. Bowden. London: SCM, 1962 Philadelphia. Westminster, 1962

—, *History of Pentateuchal Tradition*. Trans. Bernhard W. Anderson. Englewood Cliffs: Prentice Hall, 1972

—, *Leviticus: a commentary*. Trans. J. E. Anderson. London: SCM, 1965 Philadelphia: Westminster, 1971

—, *Studien zum Alten Testament*, ThB 6, ²1960, 9–141

—, *Überlieferungsgeschichte des Pentateuch* (1948), Darmstadt ²1964

—, *Überlieferungsgeschichtliche Studien. Die sammelnden und bearbeitenden Geschichtswerke im Alten Testament* (1943), Darmstadt ³1967

Novak, D., *The Image of the Non-Jew in Judaism. A Historical and Constructive Study of the Noachide Laws*, Toronto Studies in Theology 14, 1983

Nowack, N., "Das Bundesbuch," in: *Beiträge zur alttestamentlichen Wissenschaft*, FS K. Budde, BZAW 34, 1920, 132–140

Nyberg, H. S., "Das textkritische Problem des Alten Testaments am Hoseabuche demonstriert," ZAW 52, 1934, 241–254

—, *Studien zum Hoseabuche. Zugleich ein Beitrag zur Klärung des Problems der alttestamentlichen Textkritik*, UUA 1935, 6, 1935

Oakman, D. E., *Jesus and the Economic Questions of His Day*, Studies in the Bible and Early Christianity 8, Lewiston/Queenston 1986

Oded, B., "Judah and the Exile," in: *Israelite and Judaean History*, ed. J. H. Hayes/J. M. Miller, London 1977, 435–488

Oden, R., "Taxation in Biblical Israel," JRE 12, 1984, 162–181

Olivier, H., "The Effectiveness of the Old Babylonian Mēšarum Decree," JNSL 12, 1984, 107–113

—, "The Periodicity of the MĒŠARUM again," in: *Text and Context*, FS F. C. Fensham, Sheffield 1988, 227–235

Olson, D. T., *The Death of the Old and the Birth of the New: The Framework of the Book of Numbers and the Pentateuch*, Brown Judaic Studies 71, 1985

Olyan, S., "*Hăšālôm*: Some Literary Considerations of 2 Kings 9," CBQ 46, 1984, 652–668

Oppenheimer, A., *The 'Am Ha-Aretz. A Study in the Social History of Jewish People in the Hellenistic-Roman Period*, ALGHL 8, 1977

Orlinsky, H. M. (ed.), *Notes on the New Translation of the Torah*, Philadelphia 1969

Osten-Sacken, P. v.d., "Befreiung durch das Gesetz," in: *Richte unsere Füße auf den Weg des Friedens*, FS H. Gollwitzer, ed. A. Baudis et al., München 1979, 349–360 = idem., *Evangelium und Tora. Aufsätze zu Paulus*, ThB 77, 1987, 197–209

—, *Die Heiligkeit der Tora. Studien zum Gesetz bei Paulus*, Neukirchen 1989

—, *Evangelium und Tora. Aufsätze zu Paulus*, ThB 77, 1987

Osumi, Y., *Die Kompositionsgeschichte des Bundesbuches Ex 20,22b – 23,33*, OBO 105, 1991

Oßwald, E., *Das Bild des Mose in der alttestamentlichen Wissenschaft seit J. Wellhausen*, ThA 18, 1962

Otto, E., פָּסַח *pāsah*, ThWAT VI, 1989, 659–682

—, "Feste und Feiertage. II. Altes Testament," TRE XI, 1983, 96–106

—, *Das Mazzotfest in Gilgal*, BWANT VI,7 (107), 1975

—, "Die Geschichte der Talion im Alten Orient und Israel," in: *Ernten, was man sät*, FS K. Koch, ed. D. R. Daniels et al., Neukirchen 1991, 101–130

—, "Die rechthistorische Entwicklung des Depositenrechts in altorientalischen und altiraelitischen Rechtskorpora," *Zeitschrift der Savigny-Stiftung für Rechtsgeschichte* 105, 1988, 1–31

—, "Interdependenzen zwischen Geschichte und Rechtsgeschichte des antiken Israel," *Rechtshistorisches Journal* 7, 1988, 347–368

—, *Jakob in Sichem. Überlieferungsgeschichtliche, archäologische und territorialgeschichtliche Studien zur Entstehungsgeschichte Israels*, BWANT VI/10, 1979

—, *Jerusalem. Die Geschichte der Heiligen Stadt. Von den Anfängen bis zur Kreuzfahrerzeit*, Stuttgart 1980

—, *Körperverletzungen in den Keilschriftrechten und im Alten Testament. Studien zum Rechtstransfer im Alten Testament*, AOAT 226, 1991

Otto, E., "Kultus und Ethos in Jerusalemer Theologie. Ein Beitrag zur theologischen Begründung der Ethik im Alten Testament," ZAW 98, 1986, 161–179

—, *Rechtsgeschichte der Redaktionen im Kodex Ešnunna und im »Bundesbuch«. Eine redaktionsgeschichtliche und rechtsver-gleichende Studie zu altbabylonischen und altisraelitischen Rechtsüberlieferungen*, OBO 85, 1989

—, "Rechtssystematik im altbabylonischen »Codex Ešnunna« und im altisraelitischen »Bundesbuch«. Eine redaktionsgeschichtliche und rechtsvergleichende Analyse von CE §§ 17; 18; 22–28 und Ex 21,18–32; 22,6–14; 23,1–3.6–8," UF 19, 1987, 175–197

—, "Sozial- und rechtshistorische Aspekte in der Ausdifferenzierung eines altisraelitischen Ethos aus dem Recht," Osnabrücker Hochschulschr., Schriftenreihe d. FB III, 9, 1987, 135–161

—, *Wandel der Rechtsbegründungen in der Gesellschaftsgeschichte des antiken Israel. Eine Rechtsgeschichte des »Bundesbuchs« Ex XX 22 – XXIII 13*, Studia Biblica III, Leiden 1988

Otto, R., *Das Heilige* (1917), Breslau [8]1922

—, *The Idea of the Holy: an inquiry into the irrational factor in the idea of the divine*. Trans. John W. Harvey. Second edition. London: OUP 1950

Otzen, B., עָמָל ʻāmāl, ThWAT VI, 1987, 213–220

—, בדל, ThWAT I, 1973, 518–523

Ouaknin, M.-A., *Das verbrannte Buch. Den Talmud lesen*, Germ. trans. Weinheim and Berlin 1990

Overholt, Th.W., *The Threat of Falsehood. A Study in the Theology of the Book of Jeremiah*, SBT 2/16, London 1970

Pangritz, W., *Das Tier in der Bibel*, München and Basel 1963

Paschen, W., *Rein und unrein. Untersuchungen zur biblischen Wortgeschichte*, StANT 24, 1970

Patrick, D., *Old Testament Law*, Atlanta 1985

Patte, D., *Early Jewish Hermeneutics in Palestine*, Missoula 1975

Patterson, R. B., "The Widow, the Orphan and the Poor in the OT and the Extra-Biblical Literature," BS 139, 1973, 223–234

Paul, M. J., *Het Achimedisch punt van de Pentateuchkritiek: Een historisch en exegetisch onderzoek naar de verhouding van Deuteronomium en de reformatie von koning Josia (2 Kon 22–23)*, 'S-Gravenhage 1988

—, "King Josiah's Renewal of the Covenant (2 Kings 22–23)," in: *Pentateuchal and Deuteronomistic Studies. Papers read at the XIIIth IOSOT Congress Leuven 1989*, ed. C. Brekelmans and J. Lust, BEThL 94, 1990, 269–276

Paul, S. M., "Biblical Analogues to Middle Assyrian Law," in: *Religion and Law. Biblical-Judaic and Islamic perspectives*, ed. E. B. Firmage et al., Winona Lake 1990, 333–350

—, "Studies in the Book of the Covenant in the Light of Cuneiform and Biblical Law," VT.S 18, 1970

Peckham, B., "The Composition of Deuteronomy 5–11," in: *The Word of the Lord Shall Go Forth*, FS D. N. Freedman, ed. C. L. Meyers/ M. O'Connor, Winona Lake 1983, 217–240

Perlitt, L., Anklage und Freispruch Gottes. "Theologische Motive in der Zeit des Exils," ZThK 69, 1972, 290–303

—, *Bundestheologie im Alten Testament*, WMANT 36, 1969

—, "Dtn 1–3 im Streit der exegetischen Methoden," in: *Das Deuteronomium. Entstehung, Gestalt und Botschaft*, ed. N. Lohfink, BEThL 68, 1985, 149–163

—, *Deuteronomium*, BK 5, 1990/91

—, "Deuteronomium 6,20–25: Eine Ermutigung zu Bekenntnis und Lehre," in: *Glaube – Bekenntnis – Kirchenrecht*, FS Ph. Meyer, 1989, 222–234

—, "»Ein einzig Volk von Brüdern«. Zur deuteronomischen Herkunft der biblischen Bezeichnung »Brudera," in: *Kirche*, FS G. Bornkamm, ed. D. Lührmann and G. Strecker, 1980, 27–52

—, "»Evangelium und Gesetz im Deuteronomium," in: T. Veijola (ed.), *The Law in the Bible and in its Environment*, Publications of the Finnish Exegetical Society 51, Helsinki and Göttingen 1990, 23–38

—, "Mose als Prophet," EvTh 31, 1971, 588–608

—, "Priesterschrift im Deuteronomium?," ZAW.S 100, 1988, 65–88

—, *Vatke und Wellhausen*, BZAW 94, 1965

Perlman, A. L., "Asherah and Astarte in the Old Testament and Ugaritic Literatures," Ph.D. Diss Graduate Theol. Union 1978

Pesch, O. H., "Begriff und Bedeutung des Gesetzes in der katholischen Theologie," JBTh 4, 1989, 171–213

Pesch, R., *Die Apostelgeschichte. 2. Teilband. Apg 13–28*, EKK V/2, 1986

Petersen, J. E., "Priestly Material in Joshua 13–22, A Return to the Hexateuch?," *Hebrew Annual Review* 4, 1980, 131–146

Petschow, H., "Zur »Systematik« in den Gesetzen von Eschnunna," in: *Symbolae iuridicae et historicae M. David dedicatae* II, Leiden 1968, 131–143

—, "Zur Systematik und Gesetzestechnik im Codex Hammurabi," ZA 57, 1965, 146–172

—, "Beiträge zu Codex Ḥammurapi," ZA 76, 1986, 17–75

—, "Die §§ 45 und 46 des Codex Ḥammurapi. Ein Beitrag zum altbabylonischen Bodenrecht und zum Problem: Was ist der Codex Ḥammurapi?," ZA 74, 1984, 181–212

Petuchowski, J. J., "Die »Bräuche der Völker«," *Judaica* 38, 1982, 141–149

—, "Zur Dialektik der Kappara. Einführung in das jüdische Verständnis von Umkehr und Ver söhnung," in: H. Heinz et al., (ed.), *Versöhnung in der jüdischen und christlichen Liturgie*, QD 124, 1990, 184–196

Pfeiffer, R. H., "The Transmission of the Book of the Covenant," HThR 24, 1931, 99–109

Phillips, A., "A Fresh Look at the Sinai Pericope," VT 34, 1984, 39–52.282–294

—, *Ancient Israel's Criminal Law. A New Approach to the Decalogue*, Oxford 1970

—, "Another Look at Adultery," JSOT 20, 1981, 3–25

—, "Another Look at Murder," JJS 28, 1977, 105–126

—, "NEBALAH – A Term for Serious Disorderly and Unruly Conduct," VT 25, 1975, 237–242

—, "Some Aspects of Family Law in Pre-exilic Israel," VT 23, 1973, 349–361

—, "The Case of the Wood-gatherer Reconsidered," VT 19, 1969, 125–128

—, "The Law of Slavery: Exodus 21,2–11," JSOT 30, 1984, 51–66

—, "The Undetectable Offender and the Priestly Legislators," JThSt N.S. 36, 1985, 146–150

Philo, *De Decalogo*, in: *Opera quae supersunt*, vol. IV, Berlin 1902, 269–307

—, "Ueber die zehn Worte, die der Hauptbegriff der Gesetze sind," in: L. Cohn (ed.), *Die Werke in deutscher Übersetzung*, vol. 1, Breslau ²1912, 371–409

Piattelli, D., "The Enfranchisement Document on Behalf of the Fugitive Slave," Jewish Law Association Studies III, Atlanta 1987, 59–85

Pirenne, J., "Le Statut de l'Étranger dans l'Ancienne Egypte, in: L'Étranger." *Recueils de la Societé Jean Bodin* 9, 1958, 93–103

Ploeg, J. M. v.d., "Les anciens dans l'Ancien Testament," in: *Lex tua Veritas*, FS H. Junker, Trier 1961, 175–191

—, "Slavery in the OT," VT.S 22, 1972, 72–87

Plöger, J. G., *Literarkritische, formgeschichtliche und stilkritische Untersuchungen zum Deuteronomium*, BBB 26, 1967

Pons, J., "Le vocabulaire d'Ézéchiel 20: Le prophète s'oppose à la vision deutéronomiste de l'histoire," in: J. Lust (ed.), *Ezekiel and His Book*, BEThL 74, 1986, 214–233

Porath, R., "Die Sozialkritik im Jesajabuch. Redaktionsgeschichtliche Analyse," Diss. theol. München 1986

Porten, B., *Archives from Elephantine. The Life of an Ancient Jewish Military Colony*, Berkeley 1968

—, "The Jews in Egypt," in: *The Cambridge History of Judaism. I. Introduction; The Persian Period*, Cambridge 1984, 372–400

Porteous, N. W., *Das Buch Daniel*, ATD 23, ²²1968

Porter, P. A., *Moses and Monarchy. A Study in the Biblical Tradition of Moses*, Oxford 1963

Pospišil, L., *Anthropologie des Rechts. Recht und Gesellschaft in archaischen und modernen Kulturen*, Germ. trans. München 1982

Preiser, W., "Zur rechtlichen Natur der altorientalischen »Gesetze«," in: *FS Karl Engisch*, Frankfurt/M. 1969, 17–36

Preß, R., "Das Ordal im alten Israel," ZAW 51, 1933, 121–140.227–255

Preuß, H. D., "Heiligkeitsgesetz," TRE XIV, 1985, 713– 718

—, *Deuteronomium*, EdF 164, 1982

Pritchard, J. B. (ed.), *Ancient Near Eastern Texts Relating to the Old Testament*, Princeton [3]1969

Procksch, O., *Die Genesis*, KAT I, [2/3]ed. 1924

—, *Jesaia I (Jaes 1–39)*, KAT IX, 1930

Purvis, J. D., *The Samaritan Pentateuch and the Origin of the Samaritan Sect*, HSM 2, 1968

Pury, A. de (ed.), *Le Pentateuque en Question. Les origines et la compositon des cinq premiers livres de la Bible à la lumière des recherches récentes*, La Monde de la Bible, Genf [2]1991

Pury, A. de/Römer, Th., "Le Pentateuque en Question: Position du Problème et brève Histoire de la Recherche," in: A. de Pury (ed.), *Le Pentateuque en Question*, Geneva [2]1991, 9–80

Pusch, L. F., *Alle Menschen werden Schwestern. Feministische Sprachkritik*, edition suhrkamp 1165, 1990

Raaflaub, K., "Die Anfänge des politischen Denkens bei den Griechen," HZ 248, 1989, 1–32

—, *Die Entdeckung der Freiheit*, München 1975

Rad, G. v., "Beobachtungen an der Moseerzählung Exodus 1–14" (1971), in: idem., *Gesammelte Studien* II, ThB 48, 1973, 189–198

—, *Das erste Buch Mose*, ATD 2–4, [9]1972

—, *Das fünfte Buch Mose, Deuteronomium*, ATD 8, 1964

—, "Das formgeschichtliche Problem des Hexateuch" (1938), in: idem., *Gesammelte Studien zum Alten Testament* (I), ThB 8, [4]1971, 9–86

—, "Das Gottesvolk im Deuteronomium" (1929), in: idem., *Gesammelte Studien zum Alten Testament* II, ThB 48, 1973, 9–108

—, "Deuteronomium Studien" (1947), in: idem., *Gesammelte Studien* II, ThB 48, 1973, 109–153

—, *Deutoronomy: a commentary*. Trans Dorothea Barton. London: SCM, 1966; Philadelphia: Westminster, 1966

—, "Die Predigt des Deuteronomiums und unsere Predigt" (1961), in: *Gesammelte Studien* II, ThB 48, 1973, 154–164

—, *Die Priesterschrift im Hexateuch. Literarisch untersucht und theologisch gewertet*, BWANT 65, 1934

—, *Genesis: a commentary*. Trans. John H. Marks. London: SCM, 1961, 1963, 1972; Philadelphia: Westminster, 1961

—, *Theologie des Alten Testaments*, vol. I [9]1987, vol. II [9]1987

—, *Theology*. Trans D. M. G. Stalker. 2 vols. Edinburgh: Oliver & Boyd, 1965; New York: Harper & Row, 1965

Radjawaneh, A. N., "Israel zwischen Wüste und Land. Studien zur Theologie von Deuteronomium 1–3," Diss. theol. Mainz 1972

Rainey, A. F., "The Satrapy »Beyond the River«," AJBA 1, 1969, 51–79

Ratner, R./Zuckermann, B., "»A Kid in Milk«?: New Photographs of KTU 1.23, Line 14," HUCA 57, 1986, 15–60

Ray, J. D., Egypt: "Dependence and Independence (425–343 B.C.)," in: H. Sancisi-Weerdenburg (ed.), *Achaemenid History I, Sources, Structures and Synthesis*, Leiden 1987, 79–95

Reich, N. I., "The Codification of the Egyptian Laws by Darius and the origin of the »Demotic Chronicle«," in: *Mizraim* I, 1933, 178–185

Reichert, A., "Altar," BRL², 1977, 5–10

Reimer, D. J., "Concerning Return to Egypt: Deuteronomy XVII 16 and XXVIII 68 Reconsidered," in: *Studies in the Pentateuch*, VT.S 41, 1990, 217–229

Reimer, H., "Ein »totales Ende«? Studien zum Inhalt der Anklagen und zur sozialen Identität der vom Unheil Bedrohten in der radikalen Prophetie des Amos anhand der »frühesten Kompositionen« im Amosbuch," Diss. Kirchl. Hochschule Bethel 1990 = *Richtet auf das Recht! Studien zur Botschaft des Amos*, SBS 149, 1992

Renaud, B., *Je suis un Dieu jaloux*, Paris 1963

—, "La théophanie du Sinaï Ex 19–24. Exégèse et théologie," *Cahiers de la Revue Biblique*, Paris 1991

Rendtorff, R., *Das überlieferungsgeschichtliche Problem des Pentateuch*, BZAW 147, 1977

—, "Der Text in seiner Endgestalt. Überlegungen zu Exodus 19," in: *Ernten, was man sät*, FS K. Koch, ed. D. R. Daniels et al., Neukirchen 1991, 459–470

—, "Die Bedeutung der Tora für die Christen," in: B. Rübenach (ed.), *Begegnungen mit dem Judentum*, Stuttgart 1981, 213–221

—, "Die Erwählung Israels als Thema der deuteronomischen Theologie," in: *Die Botschaft und die Boten*, FS H. W. Wolff, ed. J. Jeremias/L. Perlitt, Neukirchen 1981, 75–86

—, *Die Gesetze der Priesterschrift. Eine gattungsgeschichtliche Untersuchung*, FRLANT 44, 1954

—, "Die Offenbarungsvorstellungen im Alten Israel," in: W. Pannenberg (ed.), *Offenbarung als Geschichte*, KuD Beih.1, 1961, 21–44 = idem., *Gesammelte Studien zum Alten Testament*, ThB 57, 1975, 39–59

—, "Esra und das »Gesetz«," ZAW 96, 1984, 165–184

—, *Leviticus*, BK III Liefg.1/2, 1985/90

—, *Studien zur Geschichte des Opfers im Alten Israel*, WMANT 24, 1967

Rendtorff, R./Henrix, H. H. (ed.), *Die Kirchen und das Judentum. Dokumente 1945 bis 1985*, Paderborn and München 1988

Renger, I., "Hammurapis Stele »König der Gerechtigkeit«. Zur Frage von Recht und Gesetz in der altbabylonischen Zeit," WO 8, 1976, 228–235

Renov, I., "The Seat of Moses," IEJ 5, 1955, 262–267

Reuss, E., *Die Geschichte der Heiligen Schrift des Alten Testaments*, Braunschweig ²1890

Reuter, E., קנא *qn'*, ThWAT VII, 1990, 51– 62

Reventlow, H. Graf, *Das Heiligkeitsgesetz formgeschichtlich untersucht*, WMANT 6, 1961

Reviv, H., *The Elders in Ancient Israel. A Study of a Biblical Institution* (Hebr.), Jerusalem 1983

—, "The Traditions Concerning the Inception of the Legal System in Israel: Significance and Dating," ZAW 94, 1982, 566–575

Richter, W., *Die Bearbeitungen des »Retterbuches« in der deuteronomischen Epoche*, BBB 21, 1964

—, "Zu den »Richtern Israel«," ZAW 77, 1965, 40– 72

Ries, G., *Prolog und Epilog in Gesetzen des Altertums*, MBPF 76, 1983

Riesener, I., *Der Stamm עבד im Alten Testament. Eine Wortuntersuchung unter Berücksichtigung neuerer sprachwissenschaftlicher Methoden*, BZAW 149, 1979

Ringgren, H., עוד *'wd*, ThWAT V, 1986, 1107–1130

—, Art. מעל *mā'al*, ThWAT IV, 1984, 1038–1042

—, Art. חקק *ḥāqaq*, ThWAT III, 1982, 149–157

—, Art. יקש *yāqaš*, ThWAT III, 1982, 866–868

—, Art. גרש *gāraš*, ThWAT II, 1977, 72–74

—, "Israelite Prophecy: Fact or Fiction?" *Congress Volume Jerusalem 1986*, VT.S XL, 1988, 204–210

—, *The Prophetical Conception of Holiness*, UUA 12, 1948

Roberts, S., *Ordnung und Konflikt. Eine Einführung in die Rechtsethnologie*, Stuttgart 1981

Robinson, B. P., "Symbolism in Exod. 15: 22–27,' RB 94, 1987, 376–388

Robinson, G., "A New Economic Order: The Challenge of the Biblical Jubilee," in: S. Amirthan (ed.), *A Vision for Man*, FS J. R. Chandran, Madras o.J., 363–379

—, "Das Jobel-Jahr. Die Lösung einer sozialökonomischen Krise des Volkes Gottes," in: *Ernten, was man sät*, FS K. Koch, ed. D. R. Daniels et al., Neukirchen 1991, 471–494

—, *The Origin and Development of the Old Testament Sabbath. A Comprehensive Exegetical Approach*, Beiträge zur biblischen Exegese und Theologie 21, 1988

—, "The Prohibition of Strange Fire in Ancient Israel," VT 28, 1978, 301–317

Robinson, Th. H./Horst, F., *Die Zwölf Kleinen Propheten*, HAT I/14, Tübingen ³³1964

Roeroe, W. A., "Das Ältestenamt im Alten Testament," Diss. theol. Mainz 1976

Rofé, A., "Family and Sex Laws in Deuteronomy and the Book of Covenant," *Henoch* 9, 1987, 131–159

Rofé, A., *Introduction to Deuteronomy*. Part I. (Hebr.), Jerusalem ²1977

—, "Joshua 20: Historico-Literary Criticism Illustrated," in: *Empirical Model for the Development of the Hebrew Bible*, ed. J. H. Tigay, Philadelphia 1985, 131–147

—, "Methodological Aspects of the Study of Biblical Law," in: *The Jerusalem Conference Volume*, ed. B. S. Jackson, Jewish Law Association Studies II; Atlanta 1986, 1–16

—, "The Arrangement of the Laws in Deuteronomy," EThL 64, 1988, 265–287

—, "The History of the Cities of Refuge in Biblical Law," in: *Studies in Bible*. ed. S. Japhet, Jerusalem 1986, 205–239

—, The Law about the Organisation of Justice in Dt (16,18–20; 17,8–13) [Hebr.], Beth Miqra 21, 1975/76, 199–210.318

—, "The Laws of Warfare in the Book of Deuteronomy: Their Origins, Intent and Positivity," JSOT 32, 1985, 23–44

Rose, M., *Der Ausschließlichkeitsanspruch Jahwes. Deuteronomische Schultheologie und die Volksfrömmigkeit in der späten Königszeit*, BWANT 106, 1975

—, *Deuteronomist und Jahwist. Untersuchungen zu den Berührungspunkten beider Literaturwerke*, AThANT 67, 1981

Rosenbloom, J. R., *Conversion to Judaism. From the Biblical Period to the Present*, Cincinnati 1978

Rost, L., "Das kleine geschichtliche Credo," in: idem., *Das kleine Credo und andere Studien zum Alten Testament*, Heidelberg 1965, 11–25

Rost, L., "Die Gerichtshoheit am Heiligtum," in: *Archäologie und Altes Testament*, FS K. Galling, ed. A. Kuschke and L. Rost, Tübingen 1970, 225–231

—, *Die Überlieferung von der Thronnachfolge Davids*, BWANT 3/6 (42), 1926 = in: idem., *Das kleine Credo und andere Studien zum Alten Testament*, Heidelberg 1965, 119–253

—, *Die Vorstufen von Kirche und Synagoge im Alten Testament. Eine wortgeschichtliche Untersuchung*, BWANT 4/24, 1938, reprint Darmstadt 1967

Roth, M. T., "Scholastic Tradition and Mesopotamian Law: A Study of FLP 1287. A Prism in the Collection of the Free Library of Philadelphia," Ph.D. Diss. University of Pennsylvania 1979

Rothkoff, A., "Prosbul," EJ 13, 1971, 1181f.

Röthlisberger, H., *Kirche am Sinai. Die Zehn Gebote der christlichen Unterweisung*, SDGSTh 19, 1965

Röttger, H., *Mal'ak Jahwe – Bote von Gott. Die Vorstellung von Gottes Boten im hebräischen Alten Testament*, Frankfurt/M. 1978

Rowley, H. H., "The Prophet Jeremiah and the Book of Deuteronomy," in: *Studies in Old Testament Prophecy*, FS Th. H. Robinson, Edinburgh 1950, 157–174

Rubin, S., "Der »nasciturus« als Rechtssubjekt im talmudischen und römischen Rechte," *Zeitschr. für vergleichende Rechtswissenschaft* XX, 1907, 119–156

Rücker, H., *Die Begründungen der Weisungen Jahwes im Pentateuch*, EThSt 30, 1973

—, "Warum wird '*āhab* (lieben) im Alten Testament selten zur Bezeichnung für Nächstenliebe gebraucht?," in: I. Reindl (ed.), *Dein Wort beachten*, Leipzig 1981, 9–15

Rudolph, W., *Chronikbücher*, HAT I/21, 1955

—, *Das Buch Ruth. Das Hohe Lied. Die Klagelieder*, KAT XVII, 1–3, 1962

—, *Esra und Nehemia, samt 3. Esra*, HAT I/20, 1949

—, *Hosea*, KAT XIII/1, 1966

—, *Jeremiah*, HAT I/12, ³1968

Rüger, H.-P., »Mit welchem Maß ihr meßt, wird euch gemessen werden«, ZNW 60, 1969, 174–182

Ruppert, L., "Der Umgang mit dem Volksangehörigen und mit dem Fremden im alttestamentlichen Gottesvolk," in: *Und wer ist mein Nächster? Reflexionen über Nächsten-, Bruder- und Feindesliebe*, ed. J. Horstmann, Kath. Akad. Dokumentationen 5, Schwerte 1982, 1–36

Ruprecht, E., "Exodus 24,9–11 als Beispiel lebendiger Erzähltradition aus der Zeit des babylonischen Exils," in: *Werden und Wirken des Alten Testaments. FS C. Westermann*, ed. R. Albertz et al., Göttingen and Neukirchen 1980, 138–173

—, "Stellung und Bedeutung der Erzählung vom Mannawunder (Ex 16) im Aufbau der Priesterschrift," ZAW 86, 1974, 269–307

Ruschenbusch, E., ΣΟΛΩΝΟΣ ΝΟΜΟΙ, Historia Einzelschriften Heft 9, Wiesbaden (1966) 1983

—, "ΦΟΝΟΣ. Zum Recht Drakons und seiner Bedeutung für das Werden des Athenischen Staates," *Hist* 9, 1960, 129–154

Rüterswörden, U., *Die Beamten der israelitischen Königszeit. Eine Studie zu śr und vergleichbaren Begriffen*, BWANT VI/17 = 117, 1985

—, *Von der politischen Gemeinschaft zur Gemeinde. Studien zu Dt 16,18 – 18,22*, BBB 65,1987

Sæbø, M., "Priestertheologie und Priesterschrift. Zur Eigenart der priesterlichen Schicht im Pentateuch," in: *Congress Volume Vienna 1980*, VT.S 32, 1981, 357–374

Safrai, S., *Das jüdische Volk im Zeitalter des Zweiten Tempels*, Neukirchen-Vluyn 1978

—, "Der Versöhnungstag in Tempel und Synagoge," in: H. Heinz et al., (ed.), *Versöhnung in der jüdischen und christlichen Liturgie*, QD 124, 1990, 32–55

—, *Die Wallfahrt im Zeitalter des zweiten Tempels*, Forschungen zum jüdisch-christlichen Dialog 3, Neukirchen 1981

—, "Jewish Self-Government," in: S. Safrai/M. Stern (eds.), *The Jewish People in the First Century*, vol. I, Assen 1974, 377–419

Safrai, S., "The Practical Implementation of the Sabbatical Year after the Destruction of the Second Temple" (Hebr.), *Tarbiz* 95, 1965/66, 304–328; 96, 1966/67, 1–21

—, "The Synagogue," in: idem.,/M. Stern (eds.), *The Jewish People in the First Century*, vol. II, Assen 1976, 908–944

Saley, R. J., "The Date of Nehemiah Reconsidered," in: G. A. Tuttle (ed.), *Biblical and Near Eastern Studies*, FS La Sor, Grand Rapids 1978, 151–165

Salmon, P., "Les relations entre la Perse et l'Égypte de VIe au IVe siècle av. J.-C.," in: *The Land of Israel: Cross-Roads of Civilizations*, ed. E. Lipiński, Orientalia Lovaniensa Analecta 19, 1985, 147–168

Salomon, R., *Le prêt à intérêt en législation juive*, Paris 1932

Salonen, E., *Über den Zehnten im alten Mesopotamien. Ein Beitrag zur Geschichte der Besteuerung*, StOr XLIII 4, 1972

Sauer, G., קִנְאָה *qin 'ā*, ThHAT II, 1976, 647–650

Sauren, H., "Aufbau und Anordnung der babylonischen Kodizes," ZSRG.R 106, 1989, 1–55

—, "Sennachérib, les Arabes, les déportés Juifs," WO 16, 1985, 80–99

Schaeder, H. H., *Esra der Schreiber*, BHTh 5, 1930

Schäfer, P., "Das »Dogma« von der mündlichen Tora im rabbinischen Judentum," in: idem., *Studien zu Geschichte und Theologie des rabbinischen Judentums*, AGJU 15, 1978, 153–97

—, "Die Torah der messianischen Zeit," ZNW 65,1974, 27–42 = idem., *Studien zur Geschichte und Theologie des rabbinischen Judentums*, AGJU 15, 1978, 198–213

Schäfer-Lichtenberger, C., "Exodus 18 – Zur Begründung königlicher Gerichtsbarkeit in IsraelJuda," DBAT 21, 1985, 61–85

—, "Göttliche und menschliche Autorität im Deuteronomium," in: *Pentateuchal and Deuteronomistic Studies. Papers read at the XIIIth IOSOT Congress Leuven 1989*, ed. C. Brekelmans/J. Lust, BEThL 94, 1990, 125–142

—, *Stadt und Eidgenossenschaft im Alten Testament. Eine Auseinandersetzung mit Max Vebers Studie »Das antike Judentum«*, BZAW 156, 1983

Scharbert, J., דוז * *zûd*, ThWAT II, 1977, 550–556

—, *Exodus*, NEB 42, Würzburg 1989

—, *Genesis 12–50*, NEB Liefg. 16, Würzburg 1986, 121–307

—, "Jeremia und die Reform des Joschija," in: P.-M. Bogaert (ed.), *Le livre de Jérémie*, BEThL LIV, 1981, 40– 57

Schart, A., *Mose und Israel im Konflikt. Eine redaktionsgeschichtliche Studie zu den Wüstenerzählungen*, OBO 98, 1990

Schedl, C., "Prosa und Dichtung in der Bibel. Logotechnische Analyse von Dtn 1,9–18," ZAW 98, 1986, 271–275

Schenker, A., "Affranchissement d'un esclave selon Ex 21,7– 11," *Bib.* 69, 1988, 547–556 = idem., *Text und Sinn im Alten Testament. Textgeschichtliche und bibeltheologische Studien*, OBO 103, 1991, 207–216

Schenker, A., "Das Zeichen des Blutes und die Gewißheit der Vergebung im Alten Testament. Die sühnende Funktion des Blutes auf dem Altar nach Lev 17.10–12," MThZ 34, 1983, 195–213 = idem., *Text und Sinn im Alten Testament. Textgeschichtliche und bibeltheologische Studien*, OBO 103, 1991, 167–185

—, "Der Unterschied zwischen Sündopfer Chaṭṭat und Schuldopfer Ascham im Licht von Lv 5,17–19 und 5,1–6," in: *Pentateuchal and Deuteronomistic Studies. Papers read at the XIIIth IOSOT Congress Leuven 1989*, ed. C. Brekelmans/J. Lust, BEThI 94, 1990, 115–123

—, *Versöhnung und Widerstand. Bibeltheologische Untersuchung zum Strafen Gottes und der Menschen, besonders im Lichte von Exodus 21– 22*, SBS 139, 1990

—, "Zeuge, Bürge, Garant des Rechts. Die drei Funktionen des »Zeugen« im Alten Testament," BZ BF 34, 1990, 87–90

Schilling, O., *Das Heilige und das Gute im Alten Testament*, Mainz 1957

Schlesinger, A. C., "Draco in the Hearts of His Countrymen," CP 19, 1924, 370–373

Schlesinger, E., *Die griechische Asylie*, Gießen 1933 (reprint. New York 1979)

Schmid, H., *Die Gestalt des Mose. Probleme alttestamentlicher Forschung unter Berücksichtigung der rentateuchkrise*, EdF 237, 1986

Schmid, H. H., *Der sogenannte Jahwist. Beobachtungen und Fragen zur Pentateuchforschung*, Zürich 1976

—, "Ich will euer Gott sein, und ihr sollt mein Volk sein. Die sogenannte Bundesformel und die Frage nach der Mitte des Alten Testaments," in: *Kirche*, FS G. Bornkamm, Tübingen 1980, 1–25

Schmidt, H., *Das Gebet der Angeklagten im AT*, BZAW 49, 1928, reprinted in: P. Neumann (ed.), *Zur neueren Psalmenforschung*, WdF 192, 1976, 156–167

Schmidt, K. L., "Israels Stellung zu den Fremdlingen und Beisassen und Israels Wissen um seine Fremdlings- und Beisassenschaft," *Judaica* I, 1945, 269–296

Schmidt, W. H., *Alttestamentlicher Glaube in seiner Geschichte*, Neukirchen ⁶1987

—, *Die Schöpfungsgeschichte der Priesterschrift. Zur Überlieferungsgeschichte von Genesis 1,1 – 2,4a*, WMANT 17, 1964

— *Exodus*, BK AT II/1, 1988

—, *Exodus, Sinai und Mose*, EdF 191, 1983

—, "»Jahwe und . . .«. Anmerkungen zur sog. Monotheismusdebatte," in: *Die Hebräische Bibel und ihre zweifache Nachgeschichte. FS R. Rendtorff*, ed. Blum et al., Neukirchen 1990, 435–447

—, "Nachwirkungen prophetischer Botschaft in der Priesterschrift," in: *Mélanges bibliques et orientaux*, FS M. M. Delcor, ed. A. Caquot et al., AOAT 215, 1985, 369–377

Schmidt, W. H., "Pentateuch und Prophetie. Eine Skizze zu Verschiedenartigkeit und Einheit alttestamentlicher Theologie," in: *Prophet und Prophetenbuch*, FS O. Kaiser, BZAW 185, 1989, 181–195

—, "Überlieferungsgeschichtliche Erwägungen zur Komposition des Dekalogs," VT.S 22, 1972, 201–220

—, "Wo hat die Aussage: Jahwe »der Heilige« ihren Ursprung?" ZAW 74, 1962, 62–66

Schmitt, G., *Der Landtag von Sichem*, AzTh I/15, 1964

—, *Du sollst keinen Frieden schließen mit den Bewohnern des Landes. Die Weisungen gegen die Kanaanäer in Israels Geschichte und Geschichtsschreibung*, BWANT 91, 1970

—, "Ex 21,18f und das rabbinische Recht," in: FS K. H. Rengstorf, Theokratia II, Leiden 1973, 7–15

Schmitt, H.-C., Elisa. *Traditionsgeschichtliche Untersuchungen zur vorklassischen nordisraelitischen Prophetie*, Gütersloh 1972

—, "Redaktion des Pentateuch im Geiste der Prophetie," VT 32, 1982, 170–189

—, "Tradition der Prophetenbücher in den Schichten der Plagenerzählung Ex 7,1–11,10," in: *Prophet und Prophetenbuch*, FS O. Kaiser, BZAW 185, 1989, 196–216

Schmitt, R., *Exodus und Passa. Ihr Zusammenhang im Alten Testament*, OBO 7, ²1982

Schmoldt, H., "Elijahs Begegnung mit Jahwä (1 Kön 19,9–14)," BN 43, 1988, 19–26

Schneider, T., "Azariahu Son of Hilkiahu (High Priest?) on a City of David Bulla," IEJ 38, 1988, 139–141

Schötz, D., *Schuld- und Sündopfer im Alten Testament*, BSHT 18, 1930

Schopenhauer, A., *Parerga und Paralipomena. Kleine philosophische Schriften* II, Sämtliche Werke, ed. W. Frhr. v.Löhneysen, vol. V, Darmstadt ²1968

—, *Preisschrift über die Grundlagen der Moral*, Sämtliche Werke, ed. W. Frhr. v.Löhneysen, vol.III, Darmstadt ²1962, 629–813

Schottroff, W., "Die Armut der Witwen," in: M. Crüsemann/ W. Schottroff (eds.), *Schuld und Schulden. Biblische Traditionen in gegenwärtigen Konflikten*, München 1992

—, *»Gedenken« im Alten Orient und im Alten Testament. Die Wurzel zākar im semitischen Sprachkreis*, WMANT 15, 1964

—, "Goethe als Bibelwissenschaftler," EvTh 44, 1984, 463–485

—, "Kirche als unantastbarer Raum für Flüchtlinge. Biblische und aktuelle theologische Aspekte des Asylrechts," in: L. u. W. Schottroff, *Die Macht der Auferstehung. Sozialgeschichtliche Bibelauslegungen*, München 1988, 89–109

—, "Psalm 23. Zur Methode sozialgeschichtlicher Bibelaus-legung," in: *Traditionen der Befreiung I. Methodische Zugänge*, München 1980, 78–113

Schreiner, J., "Gastfreundschaft im Zeugnis der Bibel," ThZ 89, 1980, 50–60

—, *Jeremia I 1–25,14*; NEB 3, Würzburg ²1985

Schreiner, S., "Der Dekalog in der jüdischen Tradition und im Koran," *Kairos* NF 23, 1981,17–30

Schroer, S., *In Israel gab es Bilder. Nachrichten von darstellender Kunst im Alten Testament*, OBO 74, 1987

Schultz, C., "The Political Tensions Reflected in Ezra-Nehemiah," in: C. D. Evans et al., (ed.), *Scripture in Context. Essays on the Comparative Method*, Pittsburgh Theol. Monogr. Ser. 34, 1980, 221–244

Schultz, F. W., *Das Deuteronomium*, Berlin 1895

Schulz, H., *Das Todesrecht im Alten Testament. Studien zur Rechtsform der Mot-Jumat-Sätze*, BZAW 114, 1969

—, *Leviten im vorstaatlichen Israel und im Mittleren Osten*, München 1987

Schürer, E., *The History of the Jewish People in the Age of Jesus Christ (175 B.C.-A.D. 135)*, A New English Version revised and edited by G. Vermes et al., vol. II, Edinburgh 1979

Schüssler Fiorenza, E., *Brot statt Steine. Die Herausforderung einer feministischen Interpretation der Bibel*, Freiburg/Schweiz 1988

—, *Priester für Gott. Studien zum Herrschafts- und Priestermotiv in der Apokalypse*, NTA 7, 1972

Schwantes, M., *Das Recht der Armen*, Beiträge zur biblischen Exegese und Theologie 4, Frankfurt 1977

Schwartz, B. J., "A Literary Study of the Slave-girl Pericope – Leviticus 19,20–22," in: S. Japhet (ed.), *Studies in Bible*, Jerusalem 1986, 241–255

Schwarz, G., "»Begünstige nicht . . .«? (Leviticus 19,15b)," BZ NF 19, 1975, 100

—, *»Und Jesus sprach«. Untersuchungen zur aramäischen Urgestalt der Worte Jesu*, BWANT 118, 1985

Schweitzer, A., "Kultur und Ethik" (1923), in: idem., *Gesammelte Werke in fünf Bänden*, vol.2, München 1974, 95–420

Schwertner, S., עָמָל *ʿāmāl*, THAT II, 1973, 332–335

Schwienhorst-Schönberger, L., "»Auge um Auge, Zahn um Zahn«. Zu einem antijüdischen Klischee," BiLi 63, 1990, 163–175

—, *Das Bundesbuch (Ex 20,22 – 23,33). Studien zu seiner Entstehung und Theologie*, BZAW 188, 1990

—, "». . . denn Fremde seid ihr gewesen im Lande Ägypten«. Zur sozialen und rechtlichen Stellung von Fremden und Ausländern im alten Israel," BiLi 63, 1990, 108–117

—, "»Dies sind die Rechtsvorschriften, die du ihnen vorlegen sollst«. Zur Struktur und Entstehung des Bundesbuches," in: F.-L. Hossfeld (ed.), *Vom Sinai zum Horeb. Stationen alttestamentlicher Glaubensgeschichte*, Würzburg 1989, 119–143

Scott, R. B. Y., "A Kingdom of Priests (Exodus xix 6)," OTS 8, 1950, 213–219

Sedlmeier, F., *Studien zu Komposition und Theologie von Ezechiel 20*, SBB 21, 1990

Seebass, H., נֶפֶשׁ *nephesh*, ThWAT V, 1986, 531–555

—, Art. "Elia I. Altes Testament," TRE IX, 1982, 498–502

—, "Num. XI, XII und die Hypothese des Jahwisten," VT 28, 1978, 214–223

—, "Vorschlag zur Vereinfachung literarischer Analysen im dtn Gesetz," BN 58, 1991, 83–98

Seeligmann, I. L., "A Psalm from Pre-regal Times," VT 14, 1964, 75–92

—, "Zur Terminologie für das Gerichtsverfahren im Wortschatz des biblischen Hebräisch," VT.S 16, 1967, 251–278

Seitz, G., *Redaktionsgeschichtliche Studien zum Deuteronomium*, BWANT 93, 1971

Sekine, M., "Elias Verzweiflung. Erwägungen in 1 Kön XIX," AJBI 3, 1977, 52–68

Selms, A. v., "The Goring Ox in Babylonian and Biblical Law," ArOr 18, 1950, 321–330

Seters, J. v., *Abraham in History and Tradition*, New Haven and London 1975

—, *In Search of History. Historiography in the Ancient World and the Origins of Biblical History*, New Haven and London 1983

—, "Joshua 24 and the Problem of Tradition in the Old Testament," in: *In the Shelter of Elyon*, FS G. W. Ahlström ed. W. B. Barrick and J. Spencer, JSOT.S 31, 1984, 139–158

Seybold, K., "Elia am Gottesberg. Vorstellungen prophetischen Wirkens nach 1. Könige 19," EvTh 33, 1973, 3–18

Seybold, K./Ringgren, H./Fabry, K.-J., מֶלֶךְ *melek*, ThWAT IV, 1984, 926–957

Shaver, J., "Torah and the Chronicler's History Work: An Inquiry into Chronicler's References to Laws, Festivals and Cultic Institutions in Relation to Pentateuchal Legislation," Ph.D. Diss. Notre Dame 1983

Sherwood, S. K., »*Had God Not Been on My Side*«. *An Examination of the Narrative Technique of the Story of Jacob and Laban Genesis 29,1–32,2*, EHS.T 400, 1990

Shiloh, Y., "A Group of Hebrew Bullae from the City of David," IEJ 36, 1986, 16–38

—, "Elements in the Development of Town Planning in the Israelite City," IEJ 28, 1978, 36–51

Sick, U., "Die Tötung eines Menschen und ihre Ahndung in den keilschriftlichen Rechtssammlungen unter Berücksichtigung rechtsvergleichender Aspekte," 2 vols., Diss. Tübingen 1984

Sieckmann, J.-R., *Regelmodelle und Prinzipienmodelle des Rechtssystems*, Studien zur Rechtsphilosophie und Rechtstheorie 1, Baden-Baden 1990

Siegwalt, G., *La loi, chemin du salut. Étude sur la signification de la loi de L'Ancien Testament*, Bibliothèque Theologique, Neuchâtel 1971

Sigal, Ph., *Judentum*, Germ. trans. Stuttgart 1986

Sigrist, C./Neu, R. (ed.), *Ethnologische Texte zum Alten Testament. Bd.1 Vor- und Frühgeschichte Israels*, Neukirchen 1989

Simon, M., "Sur les débuts du prosélytisme juif," in: *FS A. Dupont-Sommer* 1971, 509–520

—, "The Apostolic Decree and Its Setting in the Ancient Church," in: idem., *Le Christianisme antique et son context religieux*, Scripta Varia II, WUNT 23, 1981, 414–437

Ska, J.-L., "Les plaies d'Égypte dans le récit sacerdotal (Pg)," Biblica 60, 1979, 23–35

Sklba, R. J., *The Teaching Function of the Pre-exilic Israelite Priesthood*, Rome 1965

Skweres, D. E., *Die Rückverweise im Buch Deuteronomium*, AnBib 79, 1979

Smelik, K. A. D., *Historische Dokumente aus dem alten Israel*, Göttingen 1987

Smend, R., "»Das Ende ist gekommen«. Ein Amoswort in der Priesterschrift" (1981), in: idem., *Die Mitte des Alten Testaments*. Gesammelte Studien I, BEvTh 99, 1986, 154–159

—, *Das Mosebild von Heinrich Ewald bis Martin Noth*, BGBE 3, 1959

—, "Das Wort Jahwes an Elia. Erwägungen zur Komposition von 1 Kön 17–19" (1975), in: idem., *Die Mitte des Alten Testaments*. Gesammelte Studien I, BEvTh 99, 1986, 138–153

—, *Deutsche Alttestamentler in drei Jahrhunderten*, Göttingen 1989

—, "Die Bundesformel," ThSt 68, 1963 = idem., *Die Mitte des Alten Testaments*. Gesammelte Studien I, BEvTh 99, 1986, 11–39

—, *Die Entstehung des Alten Testaments*, Stuttgart [4]1989

—, "Theologie im Alten Testament," in: *Verifikationen*, FS G. Ebeling, Tübingen 1982, 11–26 = idem., *Die Mitte des Alten Testaments*. Gesammelte Studien Bd.1, München 1986, 104–117

—, *Wilhelm Martin Leberecht de Wettes Arbeit am Alten und Neuen Testament*, Basel 1958

Smith, M., *Palestinian Parties and Politics that Shaped the Old Testament*, New York and London 1971

Smitten, W. Th. in der, *Esra. Quelle, Überlieferung und Geschichte*, Assen 1973

Snaith, N. H., "Ex 23,18 and 34,25," JThS 20, 1969, 533–534

—, "The Daughters of Zelophehad (Num 36)," VT 16, 1966, 124–127

—, "The Sin-Offering and the Guilt-Offering," VT 15, 1965, 73–80

—, "The Verbs ZĀBAḤ and ŠĀḤAṬ," VT 25, 1975, 242–246

Snijiders, L. A., זָר/זוּר *zûr/zār*, ThWAT II, 1977, 556–564

—, "The Meaning of זָר in the Old Testament. An Exegetical Study," OTS 10, 1954, 1–154

Soden, W. v., *Einführung in die Altorientalistik*, Darmstadt 1985

—, "Zum hebräischen Wörterbuch," UF 13, 1981, 157–164 = idem., *Bibel und Alter Orient*, BZAW 162, 1985, 195–20

Soete, A., *Ethos der Rettung – Ethos der Gerechtigkeit, Studien zur Struktur von Normbegründung und Urteilsfindung im Alten Testament und ihre Relevanz für die ethische Diskussion der Gegenwart*, Würzburg 1987

Soggin, J. A., "Ancient Israelite Poetry and Ancient »Codes« of Law, and the Sources »J« and »E of the Pentateuch," VT.S. 28, 1975, 185–195

—, "Bemerkungen zum Deboralied, Richter Kap.5. Versuch einer neuen Übersetzung und eines Vorstoßes in die älteste Geschichte Israels," ThLZ 106, 1981 625–639

—, "Der judäische 'am-ha 'areṣ und das Königtum in Juda. Ein Beitrag zum Studium der deuteronomistischen Geschichtsschreibung," VT 13, 1963, 187–195

—, Judges. *A Commentary*, QTL, London ²1987

Soler, J., "The Dietary Prohibitions of the Hebrews," *The New York Review of Books* 26.10, 14. June 1979, 24–30

Sonsino, R., "Characteristics of Biblical Law," *Judaism* 33, 1984, 202–209

—, *Motive Clauses in Hebrew Law. Biblical Forms and Near Eastern Parallels*, SBLDS 45, 1980

Sperling, S. D., "Joshua 24 Re-examined," HUCA 58, 1987, 119–136

Spieckermann, H., *Juda unter Assur in der Sargonidenzeit*, FRLANT 129, 1982

Spiegelberg, W., *Die sogenannte demotische Chronik des Pap. 215 der Bibliothèque Nationale zu Paris*, Leipzig 1914

Spier, E. *Der Sabbat*, Berlin 1989

Spina, A. F., "Israelites as *gērîm*, »Sojourners«, in Social and Historical Context," in: *The Word of the Lord Shall Go Forth*, FS D. N. Freedman, ed. Meyers/M. O'Connor, Winona Lake 1983, 321–33;

Spinoza, B., *Theologisch-politischer Traktat*, ed. G. Gawlick, PhB 93, 1976

Spiro, A., "A Law on the Sharing of Information," *Proceedings of the American Academy for Jewish Research* 28, 1959, 95–101

Spitteler, G., "Konfliktaustragung in akephalen Gesellschaften, Selbsthilfe und Verhandlung," in: *Alternative Rechtsformen und Alternativen zum Recht*, Jahrbuch für Rechtssoziologie und Rechtstheorie 6, Opladen 1980, 142–164

Stachowiak, L., "Der Sinn der sogenannten Noachitischen Gebote (Genesis IX 1–7)," in: *Congress Volume Vienna 1980*, VT.S 32, 1981, 395–404

Stade, B., *Biblische Theologie des Alten Testaments* I, Tübingen 1905

—, *Geschichte des Volkes Israel*, 2 vols. Berlin 1887 and 1888

Stähli, H.-P., עזב '*zb*, THAT II, 1979, 249–252

—, *Knabe – Jüngling – Knecht. Untersuchungen zum Begriff* נער *im Alten Testament*, Beiträge zur biblischen Exegese und Theologie 7, 1978

Stamm, J. J., "Elia am Horeb," in: *Studia Biblica et Semitica*, FS Th. C. Vriezen, Wageningen 1966, 327–334

—, "Fremde, Flüchtlinge und ihr Schutz im Alten Testament und in seiner Umwelt," in: A. Mercier (ed.), *Der Flüchtling in der Weltgeschichte*, Bern 1974, 31–66

—, "Zum Altargesetz des Bundesbuches," ThZ 1, 1945, 304–306

Steck, O. H., *Der Abschluß der Prophetie im Alten Testament. Ein Versuch zur Frage der Vorgeschichte des Kanon*, Biblisch theologische Studien 17, Neukirchen 1991

—, "Der Kanon des hebräischen Alten Testaments. Historische Materialien für eine ökumenische Perspektive," in: *Vernunft des Glaubens*, FS W. Pannenberg, Göttingen 1988, 231–252

—, *Der Schöpfungsbericht der Priesterschrift. Studien zur literar-kritischen und überlieferungsgeschichtlichen Problematik von Genesis 1,1 – 2,4a*, FRLANT 115, ²1981

—, *Überlieferung und Zeitgeschichte in den Elia- Erzählungen*, WMANT 26, 1968

Stegemann, E., *Der eine Gott und die eine Menschheit. Israels Erwählung und die Erlösung von Juden und Heiden nach dem Römerbrief*, Heidelberg 1981

—, "Die umgekehrte Tora. Zum Gesetzesverständnis des Paulus," *Judaica* 43, 1987, 4–20

Stein, G., "Das Tier in der Bibel. Der jüdische Mensch und sein Verhältnis zum Tier," *Judaica* 36, 1980, 14–26.57–72

Steingrimsson, S. Ö., זמם *zmm*, ThWAT II, 1977, 599–603

—, *Tor der Gerechtigkeit. Eine literatunvissenschaftliche Untersuchung der sogenannten Einzugsliturgien im AT, Ps 15; 24,3–5 und Jes 33,14–16*, Arbeiten zu Text und Sprache im Alten Testament 22, St. Ottilien 1984

Steins, G., "»Sie sollen mir ein Heiligtum macken«. Zur Struktur und Entstehung von Ex 24,12 – 31,18," in: F.-L. Hossfeld (ed.), *Vom Sinai zum Horeb. Stationen alttestamentlicher Glaubensgeschichte*, Würzburg 1988, 145–167

Stemberger, G., "Der Dekalog im frühen Judentum, in: »Gesetz« als Thema Biblischer Theologie," JBTh 4, 1989, 91–103

Stendebach, F. J., "Altarformen im kanaanäisch-israelitischen Raum," BZ NF 20, 1976, 180–196

—, Art. עָנָה '*ānāh*, ThWAT VI, 1989, 233–247

Stern, E., "The Archaeology of Persian Palestine," in: *The Cambridge History of Judaism* I, 1984, 88–114

Stern, E., "The Persian Empire and the political and social history of Palestine in the Persian Period," in: *The Cambridge History of Judaism I. Intro-duction; The Persian Period*, Cambridge 1984, 70–87

—, "The Province of Yehud, the Vision and Reality," *The Jerusalem Cathedra* 1, 1981, 9–21

Stern, M., "Aspects of Jewish Society, The Priesthood and other Classes," in: *The Jewish People in the First Century*, ed. S. Safrai/ M. Stern, vol. II, Assen 1976, 561–630

Steuernagel, C., "Bemerkungen zu Genesis 17," in: *Beiträge zur alttestamentlichen Wissenschaft*, FS K. Budde, hg. v. K. Marti, BZAW 34, 1920, 172–179

—, *Das Deuteronomium*, HK I/3/1, ²1923

Stier, F., *Gott und seine Engel im Alten Testament*, ATA XII,2, 1934

Stoebe, H.-J., *Das erste Buch Samuelis*, KAT VIII,1, 1973

Stohlmann, S., "The Judaean Exile after 701 B.C.E.," in: *Scripture in Context* II, ed. W. W. Hallo et al., Winona Lake 1983, 147–175

Stolz, F., "Exegetische Anmerkungen zum Aufsatz von H. Bianchi, »Das Tsedeka-Modell als Alternative zum konventionellen Strafrecht«" (ZEE 1974, S.89ff), ZEE 18, 1974, 246–247

Strobel, A., "Das jerusalemische Sündenbock-Ritual. Topographische und landeskundliche Erwägungen zur Überlieferungsgeschichte von Lev 16,10.21f," ZDPV 103, 1987, 141–168

Stroud, R. S., *Drakon's Law on Homicide*, Berkeley/Los Angeles 1968

Struppe, U., *Die Herrlichkeit Jahwes in der Priesterschrift. Eine semantische Studie zu kᵉbôd YHWH*, Österreichische Biblische Studien 9, Klosterneuburg 1988

Sturdy, J., *Numbers*, Cambridge 1976

Sukenik, E. L., *Ancient Synagogues in Palestine and Greece*, London 1934

Suzuki, Y., "Deut. 6,4–5. Perspectives as a Statement of Nationalism and of Identity of Confession," AJBI 9, 1983, 65–87

—, "Deuteronomic Reformation in View of the Centralization of the Administration of Justice," AJBI 13, 1987, 22–58

Szegedy-Maszak, A., "Legends of the Greek Lawgivers," in: *Greek, Roman and Byzantine Studies* 19, 1978, 199–209

Szlechter, E., "L'affranchissement en droit suméro-akkadien," AHDO-RIDA 1, 1952, 125–195

—, "Le statut de l'esclave aux époques sumérienne et paléobabylonienne," Studi Biscardi, Milano 1982, 311–326

Tagliacarne, P., "»Keiner war wie er«. Untersuchung zur Struktur von 2 Könige 22–23," Münchener Universitätsschriften. Philosophische Fakultät Altertumskunde und Kulturwissenschaft, Arbeiten zu Text und Sprache im Alten Testament 31, 1989

Talmon, Sh., "Der judäische עם הארץ in historischer Perspektive" (1967), in: idem., *Gesellschaft und Literatur in der Hebräischen Bibel. Gesammelte Aufsätze*, Band 1, Information Judentum 8, 1988, 80–91

Talmon, Sh., "Esra-Nehemia, Historiographie oder Theologie?," in: *Ernten, was man sät*, FS K. Koch, ed. D. R. Daniels et al., Neukirchen 1991, 329–356

—, "The Gezer Calendar and the Seasonal Cycle of Ancient Canaan" (1963), in: idem., *King, Cult and Calendar in Ancient Israel*, Jerusalem 1986, 89–112

Talshir, D., "A Reinvestigation of the Linguistic Relationship Between Chronicles and Ezra-Nehemia," VT 38, 1988, 165–193

Talmud Jeruschalmi, Krotoschin 1866

Tarragon, J.-M. d., "La kapporet est-elle une fiction ou un élément du culte tardif?" RB 88,1981, 5–12

—, "Le Culte à Ugarit d'après les textes de la Pratique en cunéiformes alphabétiques," CRB 19, Paris 1980

Terrien, S.," The Numinous, the Sacred and the Holy in Scripture," BTB 12, 1982, 99–108

—, *Till the Heart Sings, A Biblical Theology of Manhood and Womanhood*, Philadelphia 1985

Theißen, G., *Der Schatten des Galiläers. Historische Jesusforschung in erzählender Form*, München ³1987

Theodorides, A., "La formation du droit dans l'Égyypte pharaonique," in: idem. et al., *La formazione del diritto nel Vicino Oriente Antico*, Naples and Rome 1988, 13–33

Thiel, W., Die deuteronomistische Redaktion von Jeremia 1–25, WMANT 41, 1973

—, *Die deuteronomistische Redaktion von Jeremia 26–45*, WMANT 52, 1981

—, *Die soziale Entwicklung Israels in vorstaatlicher Zeit*, Berlin ²1985

Thompson, R. J., "Mose and the Law in a Century of Criticism since Graf," VT.S 19, 1970

Throntveit, M. A., "Linguistic Analysis and the Question of Authorship in Chronicles, Ezra and Nehemiah," VT 32, 1982, 201–216

Tigay, J. H., "An Empirical Basis for the Documentary Hypothesis," JBL 94, 1975, 329–342

Timm, S., *Die Dynastie Omri. Quellen und Untersuchungen zur Geschichte Israels im 9. Jahrhundert vor Christus*, FRLANT 124, 1982

Timpe, D., "Moses als Gesetzgeber," *Saeculum* 31, 1980, 66–77

Toeg, A., "A Halakhic Midrash in Num XV 22–31," *Tarbiz* 1973/74, 1–20 (hebr.)

—, "Does Deuteronomy XXIV,1–4 Incorporate a General Law on Divorce?" *Dine Israel* II, Tel Aviv 1970, English Section, V-XXIV

—, *Lawgiving at Sinai. The course of development of the traditions bearing on the lawgiving at Sinai within the Pentateuch, with a special emphasis on the emergence of the literary complex in Exodus xix-xxiv*, Jerusalem 1977 (Hebr.)

Toorn, K. v.d., "La pureté rituelle au Proche-Orient Ancien," RHR 206, 1989, 339–356

Torrey, C. C., *Ezra Studies* (1910), New York ²1970

Tov, E., "Die griechischen Bibelübersetzungen," ANRW II, 20/1, 1987, 121–189

—, "Proto-Samaritan Texts and the Samaritan Pentateuch," in: A. D. Crown (ed.), *The Samaritans*, Tübingen 1989, 397–412

Trebolle-Barrera, J. C., *Jehú y Joás. Texto y composición literaria de 2 Reyes 9–11*, Valencia 1984

Trible, Ph., *God and the Rhetoric of Sexuality*, Philadelphia ³1983

—, *Texts of Terror. Literary-Feminist Readings of Biblical Narratives*, Philadelphia 1984, Germ. trans., *Mein Gott, warum hast du mich verlassen? Frauenschicksale im Alten Testament*, Gütersloh ²1990

Tsevat, M., בְּכוֹר (bᵉkōr), ThWAT I, 1973, 643–650

—, "The Prohibition of Divine Images According to the Old Testament," in: »Wünschet Jerusalem Frieden«, ed. M. Augustin/ K.-D. Schunck, Frankfurt/M. 1988, 211–220

Tullock, J. H., "Blood Vengeance among the Israelites in the Light of its New Eastern Background," Diss. Vanderbilt 1966

Tuplin, Ch., "The Administration of the Achaemenid Empire," in: I. Carradice (ed.), *Coinage and Administration in the Athenian and the Persian Empires*, British Archaeological Reports, Intern. Series 343, Oxford 1987, 109–166

Unna, I., *Tierschutz im Judentum*, Frankfurt/M. 1928

Urbach, E. E., *The Laws Regarding Slavery As a Source for Social History of the Period of the Second Temple, the Mishnah and Talmud*, Papers of the Institute of Jewish Studies, vol. l, London and Jerusalem 1964, 1–94

Urquiza, J., "Jahweh und sein Mal'akh," Diss. Viennna 1972

Utzschneider, H., *Das Heiligtum und das Gesetz*, OBO 77, 1988

—, *Hosea – Prophet vor dem Ende. Zum Verhältnis von Geschichte und Institution in der alttestamentlichen Prophetie*, OBO 31, 1980

Valentin, H., *Aaron. Eine Studie zur vor- priesterschriftlichen Aaron-Überlieferung*, OBO 18, 1978

Vannoy, R. J., "The Use of the word *hāᵉlōhîm* in Exodus 21, 6 And 22, 7,8," in: *The Law and the Prophets*, FS O. T. Allis, ed. J. H. Skilton et al., 1974, 225–241

Vattioni, F., "I sigilli ebraici," Bib. 50, 1969, 357–388

—, "I sigilli ebraici TI," *Augustanianum* 11, 1971, 447–454

Vattioni, F., "Sigilli ebraici. III." *AION* 38, 1978, 228–254

Vaulx, J. D., "Refuge (Droit d'asile et villes de refuge dans l'Ancien Testament)" in: DBS 9, 1979, 1480–1510

Vaux, R. D., *Das Alte Testament und seine Lebensordnungen*, 2 vols. Freiburg Germ trans. ²1966

—, "Le sens de L'expression »Peuple de pays« dans L'Ancien Testament et le rôle politique du peuple en Israël," RA 58, 1964, 167–172

Veijola, T., *Das Königtum in der Beurteilung der deuteronomistischen Historiographie*, STAT 198, 1977

—, "Die Propheten und das Alter des Sabbatgebots," in: *Prophet und Prophetenbuch*, FS O. Kaiser, BZAW 185, 1989, 246–264

—, *Verheißung in der Krise. Studien zur Literatur und Theologie der Exilszeit anhand des 89. Psalms*, AASF 220, 1982

Velde, H. T., "Erntezeremonie," LÄ II, 1977, Sp.1–4

Verme, M. Del, "La »Prima decima« nel Giudaismo del secondo tempio," *Henoch* 9, 1987, 5–38

Vermes, G., "The Decalogue and the Minim," in: *In Memoriam Paul Kahle*, BZAW 103, l968, 232–240 = idem., *Post-Biblical Jewish Studies*, SJLA 8, 1975, 169–177

Vermeylen, J., *Du prophete Isaie à l'apocalyptique. Isaie, I-XXXV, miroir d'un demi-millénaire d'expérience religieuse en Israël.* vol. I, Paris 1977

—, "L'affaire du veau d'or (Ex 32–34). Une clé pur la »question deuteronomiste«?" ZAW 97, 1985, 1–23

—, "Les sections narratives de Deut 5–11 et leur relation à Ex 19–34," in: *Das Deuteronomium. Entstehung, Gestalt und Botschaft*, ed. N. Lohfink, BEThL 68, 1985, 174–207

Vervenne, M., "The »P« Tradition in the Pentateuch, Document and/ or Redaction? The »Sea Narrative (Ex 13,17–14,31) as a Test Case," in: *Pentateuchal and Deuteronomistic Studies. Papers read at the XIIIth IOSOT Congress Leuven 1989*, ed. C. Brekelmans/J. Lust, BEThL 94, 1990, 67–90

Vetter, D., *Seherspruch und Segensschilderung. Ausdrucksabsichten und sprachliche Verwirklichungen in den Bileam-Sprüchen von Numeri 23 und 24*, CThM 4, 1974

Vincent, J., "Neuere Aspekte der Dekalogforschung," BN 32, 1986, 83–104

Vischer, L., "Die Zehntforderung in der Alten Kirche," ZKG 70, 1959, 201–217 = in: idem., *Ökumenische Skizzen*, Frankfurt/M. 1972, 88–108

Visaticki, K., "Die Reform des Josija und lie religiöse Heterodoxie in Israel," Diss. Theol. Reihe 21, St. Ottilien 1987

Vokes, F. E., "The Ten Commandments in the New Testament and in First Century Judaism," StEv 5, 1968, 146–154

Vollmer, J., עשׂה *'sh*, THAT II, 1976, 359–370

—, *Geschichtliche Rückblicke und Motive in der Prophetie des Amos, Hosea und Jesaja*, BZAW 119, 1971

Volz, P., *Der Prophet Jeremia*, KAT X, ²1928

Vriezen, T. C., "Bubers Auslegung des Liebesgebots, Lev 19,18b," ThZ 22, 1966, 1–11

—, "Das Hiphil von *'amar* in Deut. 26,17.18," JEOL 17, 1964, 207–210

Wacholder, B. Z., "The Calendar of Sabbath Years During the Second Temple Era. A Response," HUCA 54, 1983, 123–133

Wacholder, B. Z., "The Calendar of Sabbatical Cycles during the Second Temple and the Early Rabbinic Period," HUCA 44, 1973, 153–196 = idem., *Essays on Jewish Chronology and Chronography*, New York 1976, 1–44

Wacker, M.-T., "Gefährliche Erinnerungen. Feministische Blicke auf die hebräische Bibel," in: idem (ed.), *Theologie feministisch. Disziplinen, Schwerpunkte, Richtungen*, Düsseldorf 1988, 14–58

Wagner, V., *Rechtssätze in gebundener Sprache und Rechtssatzreihen im israelitischen Recht*, BZAW 127, 1972

—, "Zur Existen des sogenannten »Heiligkeitsgesetzesa," ZAW 86, 1974, 307–316

—, "Zur Systematik in dem Codex Ex 21_2 – 22_{16}," ZAW 81, 1969, 176–182

Wahl, O., "Grundelemente eines festlichen Wortgottesdienstes nach Neh 8,1–12," in: *Die Freude an Gott – unsere Kraft*, FS O. B. Knoch, Stuttgart 1991, 47–59

Walkenhorst, K.-H., "Hochwertung der Namenserkenntnis und Gottverbundenheit in der Höhenlinie der priesterlichen Geschichtserzählung," AJBI 6, 1980, 3–28

—, "Neueste Deuteronomiumsforschung in Japan," BZ 33, 1989, 81–92

—, "Warum beeilte sich Mose niederzufallen? Zur literarischen Einheit von Ex 34,8f," BZ NF 28, 1984, 185–213

Wallis, G., "Das Jobeljahr-Gesetz, eine Novelle zum Sabbath-Gesetz," MIOF 15, 1969, 337–345

—, "Die soziale Situation der Juden in Babylonien zur Achämenidenzeit auf Grund von fünfzig ausgewählten babylonischen Urkunden," manuscript. Diss. Berlin 1952

Walther, A., *Das altbabylonische Gerichtswesen*, Leipzig 1917, reprint. Leipzig 1968

Wambacq, B. N., "Les Maṣṣôt," Bibl. 61, 1980, 31–54

Wanke, G., "Bundesbuch," TRE VII, 1981, 412–415

Ward, E. F. D.," Superstition and Judgment. Archaic Methods of Finding a Verdict," ZAW 89, 1977, 1–19

Warmuth, G., הָדַר *hāḏār*, ThWAT II, 1977, 357–363

Waterman, L., "Pre-Israelite Laws in the Book of the Covenant," AJSL 38, 1921, 36–54

Weber, M., *Das antike Judentum. Gesammelte Aufsätze zur Religionssoziologie III*, Tübingen 1921

Wefing, S., "Untersuchungen zum Entsühnungsritual am großen Versöhnungstag (Lev. 16)," Diss. Bonn 1979

Weiler, G., *Jewish Theocracy*, Leiden 1988

Weiler, I., "Zum Schicksal der Witwen und Waisen bei den Völkern der Alten Welt," Saec. 31, 1980, 157–193

Weimar, P., "Das Goldene Kalb. Redaktionskritische Erwägungen zu Ex 32," BN 38/39, 1987, 117–160

Weimar, P., *Die Berufung des Mose. Literaturwissenschaftliche Analyse von Exodus 2,23 – 5,5*, OBO 32, 980

—, "Gen 17 und die priesterschriftliche Abrahamsgeschichte," ZAW 100, 1988, 22–60

—, "Sinai und Schöpfung. Komposition und Theologie der priesterlichen Sinaigeschichte," RB 95, 1988, 337–385

—, "Struktur und Komposition der priesterschriftlichen Geschichtsdarstellung" BN 23, 1984, 81–134

Weinfeld, M., "Tithes," EJ 15, 1971, 1156–1162

—, בְּרִית (b^erît), ThWAT 1, 1973, 781–808

—, *Deuteronomy and the Deuteronomic School*, Oxford 1972

—, "Judge and Officer in Ancient Israel and in the Ancient Near East," *Israel Oriental Studies* 7, 1977, 65–88

—, *Justice and Righteousness in Israel and the Nations. Equality and freedom in Ancient Israel in light of social justice in the Ancient Near East*, Jerusalem 1985 (Hebr.)

—, "Sabbatical Year and Jubilee in the Pentateuchal Laws and their ancient Near Eastern Background," in: T. Veijola (ed.), *The Law in the Bible and in Its Environment*. Publications of the Finnish Exegetical Society 51, Helsinki and Göttingen 1990, 39–62

—, "The Ban of the Canaanites and its Development in Israelite Law" (Hebr.), *Zion* 53,1988,135147

—, "The Decalogue, Its Significance, Uniqueness, and Place in Israel's Tradition," in: *Religion and Law. Biblical–Judaic and Islamic Perspectives*, ed. E. B. Firmage et al., Winona Lake 1990, 3–47

—, "The Origin of Humanism in Deuteronomy," JBL 80, 1961, 241–247

—, "The Royal and Sacred Aspects of the Tithe in the O.T." (Hebr.), *Be 'er-Ševa'* 1, Jerusalem 1973, 122–131

—, "The Tribal League at Sinai," in: *Ancient Israelite Religion. Essays in Honour of F. M. Cross*, ed. P. Miller et al., Philadelphia 1987, 303–314

Weingort, A., *Intérêt et crédit dans le droit talmudique*, Paris 1979

Weingort-Boczko, A., "L'interdiction des intérêts en droit français et étranger," RHDF 57, 1979, 235–245

Weingreen, J., "The Case of the Blasphemer (Leviticus XXIV 10ff)" VT 22, 1972, 118–123

—, "The Case of the Daughters of Zelophehad," VT 16, 1966, 518–522

—, "The Case of the Woodgatherer (Num XV 32–36)," VT 16, 1966, 361–364

—, "The Concepts of Retaliation and Compensation in Biblical Law," JSOT 2, 1977, 75

Weippert, H., *Palästina in vorhellenistischer Zeit*. Handbuch der Archäologie. Vorderasien II/1, München 1988

Weippert, M., "Die Petition eines Erntearbeiters aus *Maṣad Ḥăšavyāhū* und die Syntax althebräischer erzählerischer Prosa," in: *Die Hebräische Bibel und ihre zweifache Nachgeschichte*, FS R. Rendtorff, ed. E. Blum et al., Neukirchen 1990, 449–466

Weiser, A., *Das Buch des Propheten Jeremia*, ATD 20/21, ⁶1969

Weisman, Z., "The Personal Spirit as Imparting Authority," ZAW 93, 1981, 225–234

Welker, M., "Erbarmen und soziale Identität," EK 19, 1986, 39–42

—, "Erwartungssicherheit und Freiheit. Zur Neuformulierung der Lehre von Gesetz und Evangelium," EK 18, 1985, 680–683

—, "Gesetz und Geist," JBTh 4, 1989, 215–229

—, "Über Gottes Engel. Systematisch-theologische Überlegungen im Anschluß an Claus Westermann und Hartmut Gese," JBTh 2, 1987, 194–209

Wellhausen, J., *Die Composition des Hexateuchs und der Historischen Bücher des Alten Testaments* (1866), Berlin ⁴1963

—, *Prolegomena zur Geschichte Israels* (1878), Berlin ⁶1927

Welten, P., "Bann I," TRE V, 1980, 159–161

—, "Die Vernichtung des Todes und die Königsherrschaft Gottes. Eine traditionsgeschichtliche Studie zu Jes 25,6–8; 24,21–23 und Ex 24,9–11," ThZ 38, 1982, 129–146

—, *Geschichte und Geschichtsdarstellung in den Chronikbüchern*, WMANT 42, 1973

Wenham, G. J., "The Restoration of Marriage Reconsidered," JJS 30, 1979, 36–40

Werblowsky, R. J. Z., "Tora als Gnade," *Kairos* 15, 1973, 156–163

Westbrook, R., "Biblical and Cuneiform Lawcodes," RB 92, 1985, 247–264

—, "Cuneiform Law Codes and the Origins of Legislation," ZA 79, 1989, 201–222

—, "Lex talionis and Exodus 21,22–25," RB 93, 1986, 52–69

—, *Studies in Biblical and Cuneiform Law*, Paris 1988

—, "The Law of the Biblical Levirate," RIDA 24, 1977, 65–87

—, "The Prohibition on Restoration of Marriage in Deuteronomy 24, 1–4," in: *Studies in Bible*, ed. S. Japhet, Jerusalem 1986, 387–405

Westermann, C., "Die Begriffe für Fragen und Suchen im Alten Testament," KuD 6, 1960, 2–30 = idem., *Forschung am Alten Testament*. Gesammelte Studien II, ThB 55, 1974, 162–190

—, "Die Herrlichkeit Gottes in der Priesterschrift," in: *Wort – Gebot – Glaube*, FS W. Eichrodt, Zürich 1971, 227–249 = idem., *Forschung am Alten Testament*. Gesammelte Studien II, ThB 55, 1974, 115–137

—, *Genesis*, BK I/1 ³1983; I/2 ²1989; I/3 1982

—, *Genesis: a commentary*. 3 vols. trans. John J. Scullion S.J. Minneapolis: Augsburg, 1984, 1985, 1986; London: SPCK, 1984, 1986

Westermann, C., "Genesis 17 und die Bedeutung von berit," ThLZ 101, 1976, 161–170 = idem., *Erträge der Forschung am Alten Testament. Gesammelte Studien III*, ed. R. Albertz, ThB 73, 1984, 66–78

—, "Mensch, Tier und Pflanze in der Bibel," in: *Lese-zeichen für Anneliese Findeiß*, ed. C. Burchard/G. Theißen, DBAT Beih.3, 1984, 89–102

Wette, W. M. L. de, *Dissertatio critico-exegetica qua Deuteronomium a prioribus Pentateuchis libri diversum, alius cuiusdam recentioris auctoris opus esse monstratur*, Jena 1805

Whitelam, K. W., *The Just King. Monarchical Judicial Authority in Ancient Israel*, JSOT.S 12, 1979

Whybray, R. N., *The Intellectual Tradition*, BZAW 135, 1974

—, *The Making of the Pentateuch. A Methodological Study*, JSOT.S 53, 1987

Widengren, G., *Religionsphänomenologie*, Berlin 1969

—, "The Persian Period," in: J. H. Hayes/J. M. Miller (eds.), *Israelite and Judaean History*, London 1977, 489–538

Wiesnet, E., *Die verratene Versöhnung. Zum Verhältnis von Christentum und Strafen*, Düsseldorf 1980

Wigand, K., "Die altisraelitische Vorstellung von unreinen Tieren, "ARW 17, 1914, 413–436

Wildberger, H., *Jesaja*, BK X/1, ²1980; X/2 1978; X/3 1982

Willets, R. F., *The Law Code of Gortyn. Ed. with Introduction, Translation and Commentary*, Kadmos-Suppl.I, Berlin 1967

Willi, T., "Thora in den biblischen Chronikbüchern," *Judaica* 36, 1980, 102–105.148–151

Williams, W. C., "An Examination of the Relationship between Solidarity and Adultery in Ancient Israel," Diss. New York University 1975

Williamson, H. G. M., *1 and 2 Chronicles*, NCeB, 1982

—, "A Reconsideration of עזב II in Biblical Hebrew," ZAW 97, 1985, 74–85

—, *Ezra and Nehemiah*, Sheffield 1987

—, *Ezra, Nehemiah*, Word Biblical Commentary 16, Waco/Texas 1985

—, *Israel in the Books of Chronicles*, Cambridge 1977

—, "The Governors of Judah under the Persians," TynB 39, 1988, 59–82

Willi-Plein, I., *Das Buch vom Auszug. 2. Mose*, Neukirchen 1988

Wilms, F.-E., *Das jahwistische Bundesbuch in Exodus 34*, StANT 32, 1973

Wilson, R. R., "Enforcing the Covenant, The Mechanisms of Judicial Authority in Early Israel," in: *The Quest for the Kingdom of God*, FS G. E. Mendenhall, ed. H. B. Huffmon et al., Winona Lake 1983, 59–75

—, "Israel's Judicial System in the Preexilic Period," JQR 74, 1983/84, 229–248

Winter, J./Wünsche, A., *Mechiltha, ein tannaitischer Midrasch zu Exodus*, Leipzig 1909

Winter, U., *Frau und Göttin. Exegetische und ikonographische Studien zum weiblichen Gottesbild im Alten Israel und in dessen Umwelt*, OBO 53, 1983

Wir und die Juden – Israel und die Kirche. Leitsätze in der Begegnung von Juden und Christen. Text und Dokumentation, ed. Moderamen des Reformierten Bundes, Bad Bentheim o.J. (1990)

Wißmann, H., "Asylrecht I. Religionsgeschichtlich," TRE IV, 1979, 315–318

Woess, F. v., *Das Asylwesen Ägyptens in der Ptolemäerzeit und die spätere Entwicklung*, MBPF 5, 1923

Wold, D. J., "The Kareth Penalty in P, Rationale and Cases," in: P. J. Achtemeier (ed.), *SBL Sem. Papers* 1979, vol. 1, Missoula 1979, 1–46

Wolff, H. W., *Dodekapropheton 1. Hosea*, BK XIV/1, [3]1976

—, *Dodekapropheton 2. Joel und Amos*, BK XIV/2, [2]1975

—, *Dodekapropheton 4. Micha*, BK XIV/4, 1982

—, "Hoseas geistige Heimat," ThLZ 81,1956, 83–94 = idem., Gesammelte Studien, ThB 22, [2]1973, 232–250

—, ""Wissen von Gott« bei Hosea als Urform von Theologie," EvTh 12, 1952/53, 533–554 = idem., *Gesammelte Studien zum Alten Testament*, ThB 22, [2]1973, 182–205

Wolter, M., ὀφειλέτης κτλ. Schuldner/Sünder, EWNT II, Stuttgart 1981, 1344–1347

Wright, D. P., "Deuteronomy 21, 1–9 as a Rite of Elimination," CBQ 49, 1987, 375–386

—, *The Disposal of Impurity. Elimination Rites in the Bible and in Hittite and Mesopotamian Literature*, SBLDS 101, 1987

—, "Two Types of Impurity in the Priestly Writings of the Bible," in: *Proceedings of the Third International Symposium on Medicine in Bible and Talmud*, ed. J. O. Leibowitz, Jerusalem 1988, 180–193

Wright, G. E., "The Levites in Deuteronomy," VT 4, 1954, 325–330

Wünsche, A., "Der Midrasch Kohelet," in: idem., *Bibliotheca Rabbinica. Eine Sammlung alter Midraschim*, vol. I (1880), reprint. Hildesheim 1967

—, *Der Prophet Hosea übersetzt und erklärt mit Benutzung der Ergumim, der jüdischen Ausleger Raschi, Aben Ezra und David Kimchi*, Leipzig 1868

Würthwein, E., *Die Bücher der Könige. 1. Kön 17 – 2. Kön 25*, ATD 11/2, 1984

—, *Der 'amm ha 'arez im Alten Testament*, BWANT 69, 1936

—, *Die Erzählung von der Thronfolge Davids – theologische oder politische Geschichtsschreibung*, ThSt 115, 1974

—," Die Josianische Reform und das Deuteronomium," ZThK 73, 1976, 395–423

Würthwein, E., "Ruth, Das Hohe Lied, Esther," in: idem., *Die Fünf Megilloth*, HAT I,18, 1969

Wunenberger, J. J., *Le sacré*, Paris 1981

Wyatt, N., "Atonement Theology in Ugarit and Israel," UF 8, 1976, 415–430

Xella, P., *I testi rituali di Ugarit I*, Rome 1981

—, "Qdš. Semantica del »sacro« ad Ugarit," in: S. Ribichini (ed.), *Materiali lessicali ed epigrafi I*, Rome 1982, 9– 17

Yamauchi, E. M., "The Reverse Order of Ezra/Nehemiah Reconsidered," *Themelios* 5, 1980, 7–18

Yaron, R., "Biblical Law, Prolegomena," in: B. S. Jackson (ed.), *Jewish Law in Legal History and the Modern World*, Jewish Law Annual Suppl. Leiden 1980, 27–45

—, "On Divorce in Old Testament Times," RIDA 3. Series 4, 1957, 217–228

—, "The Evolution of Biblical Law," in: A. Theodorides et al., *La formazione del diritto nel Vicino Oriente Antico*, Naples and Rome 1988, 77–108

—, *The Laws of Eshnunna* (1969), Jerusalem/Leiden ²1988

—, "The Goring Ox in Near Eastern Laws," in: *Jewish Law in Ancient and Modern Israel*, ed. H. H. Cohn, New York 1971, 50–60

—, "The Restoration of Marriage" JJS 17, 1966, 1–11

Yeivin, S., "Families and Parties in the Kingdom of Judah" (Hebr.), *Tarbiz* 12, 1941/2, 241–267

Yerkes, R. K., "The Unclean Animals of Leviticus 11 and Deuteronomy 14," JQR 14, 1923/24, 1–29

Zaccagnini, C., "La formazione del diritto in mesopotamia. Codificazioni regie e consuetudine nel II millenio a.C.," in: A. Theodorides et al., *La formazione del diritto nel Vicino Oriente Antico*, Naples and Rome 1988, 35–50

Zadok, R., "Some Jews in Babylonian Documents," JQR 74, 1983/4, 294–297

—, *The Jews in Babylonia during the Chaldean and Achaemenian Periods according to the Babylonian Sources*. Studies in the History of the Jewish People and the Land of Israel, Monogr. Ser. III, Haifa 1979

Zakovitch, Y., "The Woman's Rights in the Biblical Law of Divorce," *Jewish Law Annual* 4, 1981, 28–46

Zeitlin, S., "Proselytes and Proselytism during the Second Commonwealth and Early Tannaitic Period," in: FS H. A. Wolfsson Vol. II, Jerusalem 1965, 871–881

—, "The Halaka. Introduction to Tannaitic Jurisprudence," JQR 39, 1948/49, 1–40

Zenger, E., *Das Buch Ruth*, ZBK AT 8, 1986

—, *Die Sinaitheophanie. Untersuchungen zum jahwistischen und elohistischen Geschichtswerk*, 1971

Zenger, E., *Gottes Bogen in den Wolken. Untersuchungen zu Komposition und Theologie der priesterschriftlichen Urgeschichte*, SBS 112, 1983
—, *Israel am Sinai. Analysen und Interpretationen zu Ex 17–34*, Altenberge ²1985
—, "Psalm 87,6 und die Tafeln vom Sinai," in: *Wort, Lied und Gottesspruch. Beiträge zu Psalmen und Propheten*, FS J. Ziegler vol. 2, ed. J. Schreiner, 2, 1972, 97–103
Zevit, Z., "Converging Lines of Evidence Bearing on the Date of P," ZAW 94, 1982, 481–511
—, "The 'Egla Ritual of Deuteronomy 21,1–9," JBL 95, 1976, 377–390
Ziegler, J. (ed.), *Duodezim Prophetae*. Septuaginta vol.XIII, Göttingen ²1967
Zimmerli, W., "Das Gesetz im Alten Testament" (1960), in: idem., *Gottes Offenbarung*. Gesammelte Aufsätze, ThB 19, 1963, 249–276
—, "Das Gottesrecht bei den Propheten Amos, Hosea und Jesaja," in: *Werden und Wirken des Alten Testaments*, FS C. Westermaml, ed. R. Albertz et al., Göttingen and Neukirchen-Vluyn 1980, 216–235
—, *Ezechiel*, BK XIII, 2 Bd., 1969
—, "»Heiligkeit« nach dem sogenannten Heiligkeitsgesetz," VT 30, 1980, 493–512
—, "Sinaibund und Abrahambund," ThZ 16, 1960, 268–280 = idem., *Gottes Offenbarung*, ThB 19, 1963, 205–216
Zimmermann, G., *Die Antwort der Reformatoren auf die Zehntenfrage*, Europäische Hochschulschriften III/164, 1982
Zohar, N., "Repentance and Purification, The Significance and Semantics of חטאת in the Pentateuch," JBL 107, 1988, 609–618
Zucker, H., *Studien zur jüdischen Selbstverwaltung im Altertum*, Berlin 1936
Zuckermandel, M. C. (ed.), *Tosephta. Based on the Erfurt and Vienna Codices, with Parallels and Variants*, rev. ed. Jerusalem 1970

Index of Biblical References

The Old Testament

449

The New Testament